Walking to New Orleans

Walking to New Orleans

*Ethics and the Concept of Participatory Design
in Post-Disaster Reconstruction*

ROBERT R. N. ROSS
AND
DEANNE E. B. ROSS

WIPF & STOCK · Eugene, Oregon

WALKING TO NEW ORLEANS
Ethics and the Concept of Participatory Design in Post-Disaster Reconstruction

Wipf & Stock
A Division of Wipf and Stock Publishers
199 W. 8th Ave., Suite 3
Eugene, OR 97401

www.wipfandstock.com

ISBN 13: 978-1-55635-224-9

Manufactured in the U.S.A.

To all displaced residents
of New Orleans and South Louisiana
who wish to return home.

Contents

Contents

Contents

Contents

Prelude

WALKING TO NEW ORLEANS was born as a joint presentation to the Ethics Section of the American Academy of Religion Annual Meeting held in Washington DC, in November, 2006.[1] Its primary goal was to connect post-disaster reconstruction following Hurricane Katrina to issues of social justice, and to propose an approach to actual rebuilding efforts—the concept of Participatory Design—through a method of collaborative work that intentionally links engineering and ethics. Interest in this idea of cooperative efforts in social rebuilding led to the recommendation to pursue these themes further in a book. The overall purpose of *Walking to New Orleans* remains essentially the same, but adds connections among many more factors—lack of environmental responsibility and inherent problems in the model of 'stewardship' that have increased the fragility of natural protective systems such as coastal marshes and wetlands; the engineering of levees and waterway management systems that work in some respects but create new problems in other areas; the history of New Orleans and South Louisiana that has created a diverse, multi-racial, multi-ethnic society, but also, at various times, unjustly disenfranchised certain groups within that society; the question of whether the series of recovery and reconstruction planning processes have truly engaged existing residents and included the voices of those still-displaced across America; social and environmental issues faced by the American Indian communities who live at the fringes of the Gulf and at the margins of current social structures.

With the inclusion of additional emphasis on environmental concerns, and further examination of the human relationship to the natural world based on the problematic notion of 'stewardship,' it was necessary to slightly rephrase the primary purpose of *Walking to New Orleans*. The book seeks to define an ethical approach to human and environmental

1. "From NOLA to Springfield: Ethics, Race, and Strategies for Urban Reconstruction in a Post-Katrina World."

recovery based on principles of justice and the value of understanding communities as networks of interdependent equals, and link this ethic to practical applications of reconstruction through the discipline of socio-technical engineering and its concept of Participatory Design. Given that central focus, the book also investigates a wide range of complexities that manifest themselves in post-disaster New Orleans and South Louisiana; hopefully all these paths direct the reader back to its central thesis.

Because of the multiplicity of its concerns, the book stylistically combines a variety of modes of expression. It includes technical and philosophical analysis to a level of detail that seems useful; personal experience and anecdotes limited by veracity as well as taste; historical and legal analysis limited by their relevance. Most important, it includes personal accounts from, and dialogues with, many, many individual persons at all levels of society—from a former Mayor of the City of New Orleans to citizens working in neighborhood associations to reconstruct their communities to LUMCON[2] scientists and USACE[3] engineers to the Chiefs and tribal elders of several of the groups of American Indians who live in the Gulf-dependent villages at the marshy edges of land and sea.

Roughly a third of the book deals with identifying and discussing various 'Markers of Complexity' that help understand reasons for the underlying *ambiguity* and intractableness of problematic factors involved with large organizations in disrupted or chaotic states—factors that impacted the level of readiness of South Louisiana both before and after Hurricane Katrina, including the flooding that immediately followed in New Orleans, and the effects of Hurricane Rita in Southwest Louisiana. Numerous issues arise in the course of this discussion. How New Orleans historically came to be the city it was within its geo-physical environment; issues of the use and abuse of the marshes and wetlands of the alluvial delta, and the multiplicity of interests that involve the oil and gas industries, commercial species fishing and shrimping, recent proposals for aquaculture; issues of voting patterns and access to political power; issues throughout the history of engineering projects on levees and waterway management systems by USACE, including their relations with local agencies and boards; issues of the religio-ethical models that have informed attitudes towards nature and use of natural resources.

2. Louisiana Universities Marine Consortium.
3. U.S. Army Corps of Engineers.

Prelude

A second third of the book deals more directly with the philosophical concept of justice, and the social ethics of equality of opportunity—particularly as this relates to the participation of citizens in
multiple, successive recovery and reconstruction planning efforts. We
also examine the needs for, and possibilities of, reshaping social structures to eliminate or reduce pre-existing sources of social injustice. In
terms of reconstruction initiatives, special attention is given to housing
and healthcare needs, not only essential requirements for any functioning society, but a particular necessity for New Orleans and other
communities of South Louisiana to be able to reclaim their former residents—more than 100,000 of whom are still displaced across the United
States. It is here that the concept of Participatory Design and related
principles of socio-technical engineering are introduced as a constructive approach for rebuilding a society. Historically, Participatory Design
came out of new ways of recognizing patterns of behavior in post-WWII
medical treatment of PTSD in England, has been adapted by Critical
Incident Stress Management (CISM) work with firefighters and police,
but also has been incorporated within engineering disciplines where
it has been used in the collaborative development of Expert Systems
such as XCON, an AI-based approach to the configuration of complex
computer networks.

The remainder of the book deals largely with the people of New
Orleans and South Louisiana—families and individuals whose lives were
forever changed—not only by the natural events of two hurricanes and
their aftermath of flooding, but also by the intensification of various forms
of injustice and discrimination in a society, like many others in America,
already experiencing cracks and fragmentation. *Walking to New Orleans*
tries to hear people's voices, and discern their messages. A more detailed
outline to the entire book is provided at the close of Chapter 1.

The Right to Speak

Each of the author's connections with Louisiana is somewhat different,
but hopefully, complementary. Deanne was Special Counsel to the State
Legislature of Louisiana for more than three years, advising the leadership
of both legislative houses on voting issues and redistricting. Prior to that,
she was a civil rights trial attorney for the U.S. Department of Justice,
Voting Section, for ten years, where she argued cases in Louisiana, Selma

Alabama, Texas, Mississippi, and on Indian Reservations in Montana, Arizona, and New Mexico. Currently, she has served as Special Counsel to the City of Springfield (MA), addressing voting redistricting in light of needed urban reconstruction in a racially and ethnically divided city that bears interesting parallels to New Orleans.

My connections, until recently, have largely been with the Cajun and Creole cultures of the southwestern part of the state. As a performing musician[4] I have over the years become friends with other musicians such as Marc and Ann Savoy and Errol Verret;[5] or enjoyed the crawfish at Hawk's (Arceneaux) on Parish Road 2-7 out in the country north of Rayne, past Robert's Cove; or traveled by kayak through portions of the Atchafalaya Basin. My primary background has been as a Professor of both Philosophy and Religious Studies,[6] with a period as a Consulting Engineer for Digital Equipment Corporation, where I became familiar with the concept of Participatory Design, as implemented by Enid Mumford of Manchester University (UK) and the faculty of Computer Science at Carnegie Mellon, then later as Senior Consultant for the National Academy of Public Administration[7] where I adapted aspects of this approach for use with organizations experiencing dysfunction, being restructured, or otherwise forced into transition. Work of this sort has involved federal agencies as diverse as the National Security Agency, the National Science Foundation, the Health Resources and Services Administration, a five-year Department of Justice funded project with juvenile correctional facilities, and the U.S. State Department office responsible for distributing foreign assistance to former Soviet Bloc countries. Other personal connections with Louisiana have been equally diverse: in addition to kayaking through the Atchafalaya around Little Bayou Sorrel, I have experienced Grand Isle during a hurricane, surfed wind waves at Holly Beach, ridden horseback on trail rides, and participated in the *courir* of rural Mardi Gras. Louisiana is a place

4. Leader of the band *les cigognes*, sometimes performing as *mes amis*.

5. And others, including Steve Riley, Geno Delafose, Keith Frank, Step Rideau, Milton Adams, Hadley Castille, Junior Melancon, as well as Marc, Dick Richard, Junior Martin, Randy Falcon, and Charlie Ortego, who have made instruments for me.

6. Earlier as a Teaching Fellow at Harvard and a Philosophy professor at Skidmore College; now, in an attempt to move towards retirement, teaching selected courses at the University of Massachusetts—Boston and Starr King/Graduate Theological Union in Berkeley, California.

7. And as a consultant with the Center for Quality Management, a consortium based in Cambridge, Helsinki, and Stuttgart, in liaison with the Sloan School at MIT.

where joy never ends. But I also have had ties as a minister with the United Houma Nation and the several bands of the Biloxi-Chitimacha communities, and have taught performance-improvement methods at Jetson, the large Juvenile Correctional facility north of Baton Rouge. Beyond that are my family connections with the origins of Riviana Foods in Louisiana[8]—the portrait of my Great Uncle graces a room above the rice processing plant at Abbeville. And then there is the breed of dogs known as *Petit Basset Griffon Vendéen*.

We kept a residence in New Orleans that was largely destroyed by Katrina. Shortly after the storm hit, we returned to salvage what we could, help our friends, and give away what furniture was still usable. It occurred to us that some of the knowledge we had acquired over the years, and the methods by which that knowledge could be applied—whether in the context of legislation and the law or helping to guide complex organizations and communities to redefine themselves—might be of some use to the people trying to rebuild a society after devastating lost. Throughout, a key element in Participatory Design is the ethical notion that those impacted by change (whether from the introduction of new technology or as a consequence of natural disaster) must be ongoing, active participants in the process of (re)design. So, at bottom, *Walking to New Orleans* is about ways to ethically rebuild shattered communities—physically, culturally, racially, economically—and about ways to reknit a physical environment torn asunder not only in the immediate aftermath of Hurricanes Katrina and Rita, but also slowly pulled apart over decades and hundreds of years by the inherent weaknesses in using and misusing the Biblical notion of human 'stewardship' of nature.

A Note about the Title: Walking to New Orleans

As a performing and publishing member of ASCAP (Brattydog Music), I was concerned to make sure there would be no problem using 'Walking to New Orleans' as a title for this book. The song 'Walkin' to New Orleans,' written by Fats Domino in 1960, is under management by BMI and EMI Unart Catalog. Both ASCAP's and BMI's Research Departments said no

---

8. In 1965, Riviana Foods was formed through the merger of River Brand Rice Mills, Inc., founded originally as Southern Rice Sales Co. in 1911 (selling River Brand and Carolina Rice in the 1920s) by my Great Uncle, Julius Ross, and the Louisiana State Rice Milling Company.

permission would be necessary to use a variant of the title for this book, and given its purpose, encouraged me to do so.

Two Images

Louisiana is a place of conflicting images. These two recollections continually played against one another in my mind each time I pulled back from thinking about the complexities *Walking to New Orleans* attempted to address:

Making my way back to Butte La Rose that night, the red ball of the sun dripped slowly but cleanly through the gangling, moss-covered cypress trees into Lake Henderson, at the western edge of the Atchafalaya Basin.[9]

Driving past the stately homes along Lakeshore Drive, on the opposite side of Lake Charles the sun simply faded into the yellow haze behind the smoking stacks and spidery pipes of petrochemical structures that angled against the sky.[10]

le Vendredi saint,
2008

All photographs used in this book
were taken by Robert R. N. Ross

9. The Atchafalaya Basin is America's largest swamp, combining bald cypress lakes and bayous that give way to Spartina grass marshes where it meets the Gulf of Mexico.

10. The structures include the Conoco refinery and Westlake Chemical's low density polyethylene (LDPE), styrene monomer, and linear polyethylene facilities.

Acknowledgments

THERE ARE A GREAT many people—old friends, new friends, and strangers—who so kindly helped along the rather ragged path of where our exploration of the multiple concerns and themes of *Walking to New Orleans* took us. Some helped us uncover an obscure fact or some piece of historical information for which we had been searching; others connected us with the people who were doing the hard work of recovery and reconstruction at various levels, from local neighborhood associations to regional and environmental planning. Many were willing to share their personal stories of hardship and hope. The following are only some of them.

Jeanne and William Dumestre of Broadmoor for their friendship, their gracious hospitality, and for their introduction to their friend and neighbor, Moon Landrieu.

Peirce Lewis, Professor Emeritus of Geography, Penn State University, renown historian of New Orleans, for ongoing conversations and help sorting out details of New Orleans waterway and lock systems. Chris Hallowell, environmental writer and professor of journalism at Baruch College, CUNY, for tracking down dates of meetings he so aptly described, and offering words of encouragement. Bobby Freyou, Records Manager, Louisiana Department of State Lands, Baton Rouge.

Mark Ford, Executive Director, Coalition to Restore Coastal Louisiana. Newman Trowbridge, Jr., General Counsel, Lafayette, Louisiana Landowners Association.

Randy Moertle, Randy Moertle and Associates, Inc., consultant to corporations and organizations with interest in usage of Louisiana coastal marshlands. Clyde P. Martin, Jr., P.E., Director, Hurricane & Flood Protection Programs, Louisiana Department of Transportation and Development. John Wm. Hall (retired), U.S. Army Corps of Engineers, New Orleans District. Carl E. Anderson, Project Management, U.S. Army Corps of Engineers, New Orleans District. Kirby Verret of

Dulac, tribal elder of the United Houma Nation Indians who works hard to keep Indian children in school. Jane Luster of the United Houma Nation. Chief Randy Verdun, Bayou Lafourche Band of the Biloxi-Chitimacha Indians. Chief Albert Naquin, Isle de Jean Charles Band of the Biloxi-Chitimacha Indians, who is trying to save his community from extinction. Marlene Foret, Chairwoman of the Grand Caillou-Dulac Band of the Biloxi-Chitimacha Indians. Robert Love, Louisiana Department of Wildlife and Fisheries. State Senator Reggie Dupré, Jr for District 20 (Lafourche and Terrebonne Parishes) for help on the history of the Pointe-aux-Chenes renaming. Marc Castille, Director of the Pointe-au-Chenes Wildlife Management Area. Lloyd Songe of Houma. Calvin Parfait and Charlie Duthu of *Treater.* Murray Rogers, Harbormaster, Southern Yacht Club, New Orleans. Professor Edward Chesney, Louisiana Universities Marine Consortium (LUMCON) at Cocodrie. David Adams, helicopter pilot who flies to the offshore oil rigs. Karen Hoak, Gulf of Mexico Fishery Management Council.

Tomeka Prioleau, Outreach Specialist, Hazardous Substance Research Centers, EPA Region 6, Louisiana State University. Dr. Danny Reible, Center Co-Director, Hazardous Substance Research Centers and Professor and Chair of the Department of Civil Engineering, University of Texas at Austin. John Moulton, Senior Manager of the Tennessee Valley Authority News Bureau, and Gilbert D. Francis, Jr., of the TVA. Delicia Phillips, P2 Energy Solutions (the oil and gas industry's largest provider of exploration, development, management and productions solutions), San Antonio, Texas.

Larry Miller of Iota, Louisiana, former school administrator and builder of Bon Cajun accordions (retired) and Hadley Castille, Cajun fiddler and songwriter. Along with Zachary Richard and Action Acadian, Hadley helped introduce French immersion classes into St. Landry Parish schools. Zachary Richard for communicating background to one of his songs. Ann and Marc Savoy of Eunice for their friendship and introduction to prairie Cajun culture. Errol Verret for conveying the soul of the Cajun accordion and another reason to visit the Atchafalaya.

Chris Wye, former Director of the Performance Consortium and Program on Improving Government Performance, National Academy of Public Administration. Jeffrey Riddel, Deputy Administrator/ Executive Director of HUD/HANO for helping to explain HUD's reasoning with regard to public housing. Enid Mumford, Emeritus

Acknowledgments

Professor of the University of Manchester, UK, for having introduced me to the concept of Participatory Design. Daniel R. Mandelker, Stemper Professor of Law, Washington University in St. Louis.

Susan Bergson, Program Manager, Urban Health Initiatives, Louisiana Public Health Institute, for enormous help in tracking the state of pre- and post-disaster hospitals and primary healthcare centers in Orleans Parish. Ronnie Goynes and Robert Tessier, Louisiana Dept of Transportation and Development. Kate Moran reporter, who covers mental health for *The Times-Picayune*, for providing a wonderful history of DePaul Hospital and help on matters of post-disaster healthcare. Arnold Hirsch, Ethel and Herman L. Midlo Professor for New Orleans Studies and University Research Professor of Urban History, University of New Orleans. Jordan Hirsch, his son, of Sweet Home New Orleans, a volunteer organization helping the musicians of New Orleans. Allison Plyer of the Greater New Orleans Community Data Center for direction on demographics and census data. Veronica Shindler at ESRI. Juliana Paget, Office of Recovery Management. Patricia V. Dickerson of the U. S. Census Bureau. Sara Mishler of the Geography Division of the U.S. Census Bureau.

Jim Livingston of CityWorks. Keith G.C. Twitchell, President, Committee for a Better New Orleans/Metropolitan Area Committee. Sakura Koné, Common Ground Relief. Alice Craft, Lower Ninth Ward Health Clinic. Shakoor Aljuwani, Episcopal Diocese of New Orleans Homecoming Center. Bill Rousselle of Bright Moments and the Lousiana Disapora Advocacy Project. Jennifer Weishaupt, President, and Doug Joubert, former Treasurer of the Mid-City Neighborhood Organization. Many from the Broadmoor Improvement Association. The library staff of Cameron Parish.

Errors of fact or interpretations based on errors of fact remain entirely the responsibility of the authors.

Madonna on Rubbish
(October, 2005)

High Water Faith
(October, 2005)

1

Introduction

ON BUDDY'S BIRTHDAY

TWELVE HOURS BEFORE A brief—but false—sense of relief that perhaps New Orleans had dodged a bullet *one more time*, major sections of the city were already flooding. As many others, we did not know this. That is, until we saw water pouring in near the Old Hammond Highway bridge that crosses the seventeenth Street Canal on the border of the West End just below the marina, turning Lakeview into islands of red roofs, green tree tops, barely floating above a sea of black liquid. Until we saw massive waves of inundation along the levees of the Inner Harbor Navigational Canal below the Florida Avenue bridge, leaving the pale blue, pink, white, red businesses and houses of the Lower Ninth Ward sinking into olive mud. Until we saw Carrollton Avenue turned into a riverway connecting other riverways that were once cross streets. Until we saw walls of water pouring over helpless 16 foot levee barriers into Chalmette, seat of St. Bernard Parish two miles down river from the border of New Orleans. Until we saw what became perhaps the most disturbing image of all— hundreds of yellow school busses and city vehicles still sitting in their places, unused, in a lake of oil-slicked blue water.

When Hurricane Katrina crossed Florida on Friday August 26, 2005, it was expected to grow from a Category 2 storm into something far larger and more dangerous as it came under the influence of an extension of the North Equatorial Current which is funneled through channels of the Antilles and Caribbean Islands, and through the Yucatan Channel where it gains strength and loops into a giant eddy in the Gulf of Mexico. This current—known as the Loop Current—was warmer by two degrees and stronger than usual during the summer of 2005.

By 4:00 a.m. on Monday August 29, Katrina's center was some 90 miles south-southeast of New Orleans. A Category 4 storm, approaching Category 5, with sustained winds of over 150 mph that covered a diameter of an amazing 200 miles,[1] Katrina was producing 45–50 foot waves off the mouth of the Mississippi, and may already have begun to breach the 17th Street Canal floodwall, as well as produced storm surge that loosed a barge from Nashville's Ingram Barge Company (*ING4727*) to break through the floodwall of the Inner Harbor Navigational Canal (Industrial Canal),[2] and eventually end atop houses in the Lower Ninth Ward.

At 6:10 a.m. Katrina made landfall at Bastian Bay, Plaquemines Parish, near Empire and Buras on the main pass of the Mississippi River about 18 miles north of the terminus of LA 23 at Venice. Just weakened to a Category 3 storm, Katrina had produced a storm surge of 12 feet at Grand Isle to the west, and deposited two giant yellow and blue menhaden[3] vessels, the Sea Falcon and her partner, side by side across LA 23 at Empire. Not quite hidden behind them was a jumble of 30 more smaller vessels, piled on top of one another like the broken toys of a cranky child. In the area of Buras and Triumph, most of the 1100+ households were flattened; masses of livestock and wildlife drowned. The river outlet into the Gulf was shortened by almost 15 miles.

Over the next four hours, Katrina crossed the myriad of islets and marshes of St. Bernard Parish east of Shell Beach and Alluvial City, and at 10:00 a.m. that morning made her final landfall at the Louisiana-Mississippi state line at Pearl River, midway between Bay St. Louis, Mississippi and Slidell, Louisiana. In its wake, the old OST (Old Spanish Trail) bridge over U.S. 90 to Pass Christian was reduced to a row of con-

---

1. At its peak, Hurricane Hunter *Miss Piggy* from Keesler AFB recorded winds approaching 200 mph and a barometric pressure of only 915 mb; Hurricane Camille in 1969 was even lower at 909 mb.

2. The 200 foot 705-ton dry cargo cover-top steel hulled barge, delivered by Zito Fleeting to Lafarge North America, where it had been unloaded and moored at the company's barge terminal, may have been poorly secured when the storm hit, and carried down the Inner Harbor Navigational Canal (INHC); however, storm surge floodwaters may already have overtopped levee walls just below the Florida Avenue bridge near the Jourdan Avenue Wharf at Surekote Road. A series of lawsuits followed; as of January 2008, the case was still afloat before U.S. District Judge Helen G. Berrigan. See Katie Porterfield, "Meet Barge Jetsam," *BusinessTN Magazine,* January 2008, accessible at http://www.businesstn.com/pub/5_1/features/8426-1.html for report on court case status.

3. Menhaden, oily fish used in animal feed, have grown in importance to Louisiana's sea-economy as shrimp production has declined somewhat in recent years.

crete dominoes, all tipped over. After landfall, Katrina was downgraded to a Category 3 storm, and, twelve hours later, to a Tropical Storm.

The islands and marshes at the edges of the Mississippi Delta have long had their ability to function as a buffer to storms on the Gulf seriously compromised. This unique geography that Cajun blues musician Tab Benoit once called a 'magical place where land and water live as one' represents not only a mysterious and beautiful environment, but also a protector of human and animal habitation. Every three miles of such wetlands has the capability of diminishing storm surge by one foot. Following the great Mississippi River flood of 1927, however, levees built along the river to protect farmlands have reduced valuable silt deposits from annual floods that replenish the wetlands, redirecting them far out into the Gulf. Further compromising the coastal wetlands are pipeline canals and navigational shortcuts that allow salt water to enter.[4] This salt water kills marsh grasses and trees and causes further erosion. The Louisiana coastal region once maintained barrier islands over a mile wide, large enough to support an entire plantation. They are now reduced to mere slivers. As Ivor van Heerden, cofounder and deputy directory of the Louisiana State University (LSU) Hurricane Center observed, "We now thoroughly understand the need for coastal restoration as a buffer against the big storms, but land loss continues at an alarming rate."[5] The United States Geological Survey (USGS) puts that at an average of 34 square miles per year. At that rate, by 2050 one-third of coastal Louisiana will have vanished.

Human failures in the presence of the storm have been given great attention in the media; only some will be discussed in the course of this book.[6] But awareness of one unaccepted offer of rescue stuck in our minds. Late in the afternoon of Saturday August 27, New Orleans Mayor Ray Nagin, afraid of liability from forcing the closure of hotels and businesses, had still issued only a voluntary evacuation. Amtrak, after its last regularly scheduled train, offered to run a "dead-head" train later in the

---

4. Coastal Louisiana wetlands contain over 40 percent of the U.S. tidal marshes and support the largest commercial fishery in the lower 48 states. The levees and dams along the mainstream of the Mississippi, started in 1928, and the navigational and pipeline channels of the surrounding marshes, have resulted in a 67 percent decrease in sediment delivered to the Louisiana coast, a necessary process to keep marshlands replenished. See USGS National Wetlands Research Center release, May 21, 2003, accessible at http://www.usgs.gov/releases/pr03_004.htm.

5. van Heerden and Bryan, *The Storm*, 10.

6. Considerably more attention is given to history prior to the storm.

evening to transport equipment out of town to Macombe, Mississippi—a train that had room for hundreds of passengers. The City declined and at 8:30 p.m. this 'ghost train' left New Orleans without a single passenger on board.[7]

August 30 is the birthday of the shortest, hungriest, often the noisiest member of the family—*Fétu de Paille*, aka 'Buddy'—our Petit Basset Griffon Vendéen, then eleven years old. August 30, 2005 was not a day for celebration. Images of a city under watery siege streamed into consciousness. Elderly trapped in attic spaces; dogs and other pets left behind; the fate of cemeteries. In South Louisiana interment often occurs not as burial *in* graveyards, but in tombs *above* ground—the water table is too high for in-ground burial. On *La Toussaint* (All Saints Day), it is the custom of families to go to the cemeteries of their ancestors, paint the tombs white, place flowers on them, decorate with wreaths and family mementos. The connection with ancestors is an important *folk religious* practice of many cultures. But how would families honor their ancestors this coming fall? Would tombs break open, letting loose their sacred contents? Those would be deaths enacted twice over. It felt as if the entire City of New Orleans were slowly dying—yet even in the most secular of lives, the experience of dead places seeks out the possibility of resurrection.

One dead place in my life[8] stands out above others—the death of a Harvard colleague and friend. From Barbados, Romney Moseley had the most musical, liquid voice I ever heard. Despite different origins, our lives paralleled one another's. Each offered ordination in the Episcopal Church; each refused when the Bishop wanted our wives to convert; each with initial marriages that did not last. Shortly before each remarried, we attended a 'Moonie'[9] conference in Tenerife, Canary Islands, but spent considerable time finding gifts for our beautiful brides-to-be. We each had careers in academia—I as a Teaching Fellow at Harvard, then Philosophy professor at Skidmore College; Romney, Dean at Candler School of Theology before going to the University of Toronto. Mostly we lived a good distance apart, but whenever I would call, Romney would always respond with *I was just thinking about you, my friend.*

---

7. See also Dyson, *Come Hell or High Water,* 58.

8 RRNR.

9. An invitation given to professors of Religious Studies to help lend academic legitimacy to scholarly work by followers of Rev. Sun Myung Moon's Unification Church movement.

Introduction

One hot, very stormy June, I was in New Orleans to deliver a paper at an international conference. I had driven all the way from Massachusetts with our dog Mandy, a sweet Yellow Lab.[10] We found a seedy hotel that accepted dogs, but near enough to walk Mandy along the shore of Lake Ponchartrain as the wind whipped waves against the rocks. Periodically I called home to check messages. Late one steamy afternoon, there was a message from Joan, Romney's wife, asking me to call back. When we spoke, her own Barbadian lilt told me quietly how Romney had died conducting Holy Communion at an Episcopal church he occasionally served. The heart attack was sudden; he died before he reached the hospital. The hole felt darker, denser than the thunderstorms that had begun to rage over the city. Romney's young daughter would grow without the guidance of hearing her father's musical voice say *I am thinking about you . . .*

Around 7:00 p.m., still raining, I drove down Esplanade with Mandy by my side, across the railroad tracks, up the ramp onto the wharves that ran along the river; we drove a half-mile downriver across loading platforms, past empty warehouses, until we reached an area south of the sharp bend in the river that made New Orleans the Crescent City. The twin spans of the Crescent City Connection, old cantilever bridges servicing Business U.S. 90, shimmered through the wet mist. On the West Bank across the river was Algiers. In the darkening gloom, one tug with a yellow light plied down river. To the left, huge rusting cranes sat silent in the warm rain, above an oil tanker tied to the riverbank. Even at 85 humid degrees, the leaden sky looked like winter. Tears for my lost friend matched the dark rain streaming down the windshield. Our histories had intertwined like black and white, yin and yang. *You know, I was just thinking about you . . .* I knew it wasn't literally true, yet we picked up the threads of our friendship easily, even if we hadn't spoken in months. I had hoped Romney might return to a position in Cambridge; now he was returning home, to Barbados, to be buried by the sea.

Mandy sat in the front seat as if a beautiful, yellow, fuzzy person, just staring past the wipers at the blurred images of rain and river and city lights. That afternoon I had bought a tape, *Plant Early*, by Jerry Douglas, the world's greatest living Dobro player. The second cut, "La Conversacion," was based on a story Jerry had written about a man celebrating his centennial, recalling the life of a youthful drifter who finds a great love, settles

10. In the pre-Buddy era.

down, then suffers the loss of his beloved. Though he lives many years beyond her passing, his mind always returns to his loss. As the twisting, plaintive, sinewy threads of the music played through the night, Mandy licked my face, nuzzled to be petted, sniffed the scents from the river.

Beyond the waterfront the river flowed south, past the city, past the last outposts of civilization before its silt-laden waters made their final meandering journey through Delta marshes to the Gulf. It passed the Naval embarkation center and Chalmette military cemetery, where the river broadens, spreading into dark mists, lit here and there by points of light; past long tankers tied along the banks, waiting to empty their bellies into the city. The river coiled slowly by more barges, past all the lights, and into the purgatory of the lower coastal plain, eventually to be enveloped by and lost in the sea.

New Orleans is a city that *celebrates* death in its own unique way. It is a city in which death can find meaning, a city that can soothe its pain. It is a city that helped me come to terms with death. But a city that can heal, make death meaningful, *cannot* itself die.

Deanne's thoughts on August 30, 2005 were more ambiguous, recalling the more than three years she had served as Special Counsel to the State Legislature of Louisiana on voting and redistricting issues. Those three years were a blend of successes and frustrations, as is most work with a state government. She knew the Lakeview home of the head of the House of Representatives, along with many others, was now under at least eight feet of water, but she also knew who, in the city, would be likely to suffer the most.

A third recollection was altogether different and one we shared together; it was about New Orleans as a city of joy. Our Petit Griffon Basset Vendéen (PBGV) had been to Louisiana many times, visiting friends everywhere. Buddy had often sampled tasty *boudin* at Marc and Ann Savoy's *boucheries*—an old-time Cajun family music-laced hog-slaughter—at their home in Eunice, Louisiana.[11] Buddy had traveled to the swamp village of Catahoula to participate in *BénéFête* to raise medical funds for Beth Verret, wife of our friend Errol Verret, pirogue-builder and original accordion player in Michael Doucet's Cajun band *Beausoleil*.[12] Buddy's

---

11. Before refrigeration, in Cajun country, families would gather periodically throughout the year for a *boucherie*—a time for preparing meat and sharing it among families for the next months; a time also for social gathering, telling stories, playing music.

12. Later with the Basin Brothers.

most infamous trip was at one Mardi Gras when we visited a friend who had been one of the founders of Tipitina's, the New Orleans club that remains a city musical landmark. Jeanne Dumestre and William were also 'owned' by two large PBGVs, and we thought the dogs would all be happy to socialize while we went to watch one of the krewes parading along St. Charles. After the parade, we stopped to visit other friends at their large Garden District home, then returned to Jeanne's house in Broadmoor only to find *her* two PBGVs nowhere in sight. There was Buddy, in all his glory, prancing around, proudly welcoming us back. Then, from a distance, we heard soft barking and scratching. Buddy had evidently managed to lock Jeanne's two PGBVs in a bedroom in order to have the house all to himself—to rummage around, and search for food treats unimpeded.

Despite its image as a city of self-indulgence, New Orleans is filled with people who attempt to live truly honorable lives—as does Jeanne Dumestre of the PBGVs. Documented in an interview on NPR's *Fresh Air from WHYY* [13] in February, 2006, since 1985 Jeanne has worked as a nurse in the city, helping people with HIV/AIDS but no insurance. The transition from being a founder of Tipitina's, hosting both famous (the Neville Brothers) and not-so-famous—a club which in its early days sometimes included offers of free bananas—to a life of nursing was based on Jeanne's witness of the effects of AIDS in New Orleans. A passion for music transforming into a passion for care-giving was as natural for her as it is to anyone who understands the *healing* power of music. Jeanne has helped thousands of HIV patients at the Louisiana State University Health Science Center. In 2005, she won an HIV Leadership Award for her commitment. Jeanne Dumestre occupies a rare place in New Orleans' music history but even more in changing the lives of patients forced to live at the margins of society. Thus, for both of us, on Buddy's birthday 2005, our hearts ached for Jeanne and for other friends and for all of those whose lives and fortunes were now overwhelmed by a flooded city.

APRÈS LE DELUGE

Our personal losses in the flooding after Katrina were merely material. The contents of an apartment we kept were flooded and drenched, as rains had blown in through broken windows. A new car was submerged and totaled. Several weeks after the storm we secured a rental truck, loaded it

13. The PBS member station in Philadelphia.

with items that could be salvaged, gave furniture to friends and friends-of-friends who needed to refurnish their damaged homes, and began a move to higher ground. In the city we saw an infrastructure and economy only marginally existing. Food markets were closed. Most businesses were closed. Electricity, water, and essential services were largely unavailable. In the evening was the eerie glow of kerosene lamps. At the few fast food places that opened only three or four hours a day, long lines of people awaited the opportunity to buy a hamburger and fries.

As we traversed the city, huge mounds of debris—portions of walls, wire, cables, clothing, personal items, trash and pieces of objects un-known—already grown to more than forty or fifty feet high, glistened in the hot sun, occupied the main intersections of neighborhoods. Horizontal streaks of brown, eight, ten, some twelve feet above ground, marked the high points of flooding on the sides of buildings. Hand-sprayed crosses of codes marked the dates of inspection for bodies—living/dead/human/animals. At 6161 of one street, on 9-16 'SPCA searched no cat'.[14]

In defiance of the brown smears over its placard, the Christian Science Church at 134 Polk Street had posted another sign, redirecting its people to 'Hope & Healing Services' at the functioning First Church of Christ Scientist, 1434 Nashville Avenue. Along every street we passed it was as if those houses that remained intact had regurgitated their insides out onto the sidewalks. Broken limbs adorned with insulation, door panels, pieces of furniture, pictures and family photos. Above one such pile sat a child's doll with long blond hair, a smile painted on her face, arms outstretched, like a Madonna welcoming anyone who might wander by, inviting them to give her a warm embrace. Below her, not so fortunate, was a stuffed red Spiderman, covered with flakes of drying mud.

Trailers and back-hoes had begun to assemble in city parks and the grassy neutral ground between major avenues. Men wearing construc-tion helmets and paper masks wandered about. There was little actual movement. Free-lancers sprayed impromptu signs on convenient vertical

---

14. The FEMA schematic for red or orange X's on houses was generally as follows: A simple slash designated a hasty search, while a large X marked a more thorough primary or secondary search. Date of search was marked at the top; an inscription on the bottom quadrant of the X contained the code for what was found, living or dead—for example, '2 D' indicated two dead bodies inside. The initials of the search squad were sprayed to the left; the right quadrant noted hazards such as unsafe gas lines, downed wires, rats, dead animals, toxic materials.

surfaces offering their services: 'Gutting 352–9003.' Long-term businesses managed more poignant statements:

34 years of business down the drain!
Thanks to the Corp. of Engineers, the state & the levee board.
You can try to fool us, but you can't fool Mother Nature!

The image that perhaps sticks in my mind as much as any was passing the Mid-City Lanes, founded 1941, home of the Rock 'n Bowl and New Orleans' unique combination of bowling lanes with a venue for the best in Zydeco music—from the late Beau Jocque to Keith Frank to Geno Delafose to Nathan and the Zydeco Cha Cha's to Step Rideau. At the time it looked as if this institution would never rise again. It is testimony to New Orleans' persistence that the Rock 'n Bowl was able to reopen in November, two months after Katrina.

Driving eastward out of New Orleans revealed physical devastation only worse. Through the Ninth Ward even what remained was displaced—an entire small bungalow now sat atop a car. Exiting was limited due to bridge destruction. Large portions of the Eastbound I-10 twin spans had collapsed like a child's blocks. The bridge over the Chef Menteur Pass and the bridge over the eight mile Rigolets strait which connects Lake Borgne and Lake Ponchartrain were destroyed. The U.S. 90 Bay St. Louis—Pass Christian Bridge and the Biloxi—Ocean Springs bridges were severely damaged. As we left a city still under water over the remaining I-10 span temporarily made into a two-way passage, the widespread leveling of houses and trees, businesses and large factories. grew worse. Many times in the 'before casinos' past we had walked Mandy, then Buddy, on the white sands of the Gulf beaches around Biloxi. But now, passing highway signs twisted as if in genuflection to an absent god, we had entered an apocalyptic wasteland, slowly drying in the mud and baking in a relentless sun.

VOICES

A variety of books have been written about the impact of Hurricanes Katrina and Rita on the City of New Orleans and on the Gulf Region. Some, such as Jed Horne's *Breach of Faith*, based on interviews with a core of more than three dozen people as metro-editor of *The Times-Picayune*, provide the reporter's ability to chronicle first-hand private experiences and thoughts of storm victims from all walks of life. Others, such as

Michael Eric Dyson's *Come Hell or High Water: Hurricane Katrina and the Color of Disaster*, attempt analysis of the racial, economic, and political dimensions of Katrina that contributed to the inadequacy of government responses to human suffering. Still others, such as Douglas Brinkley's *The Great Deluge* gives the historian's chronicle of five days surrounding the storm based on interviews ranging from Coast Guard officers, survivors, to those in a position to speak for the highest levels of government. Some accounts, such as Ivor van Heerden's *The Storm,* provide a scientist's understanding of engineering failures and the environmental impact of Gulf storms from his perspective as cofounder and deputy director of the LSU Hurricane Center and director of the Center for the Study of Public Health Impacts of Hurricanes. Other journalists, such as Chris Hallowell's *Holding Back the Sea,* written in 2001, examine not only environmental changes to the wetlands of the Gulf of Mexico, but also their human and economic dimensions—changes that in many ways anticipate the eventuality of disasters spawned by Hurricanes Katrina and Rita. Also significant background, and eagerly awaited in its third edition, is Peirce Lewis' *New Orleans: The Making of an Urban Landscape.* Beyond and behind these and other book-length accounts, stand the superb newspaper reporting from *The Times-Picayune,* the *New York Times,* the *Washington Post,* the Baton Rouge *Advocate,* the *Wall Street Journal,* and various journals such as *Indian Country Today,* representing the interests of indigenous tribal groups like the Pointe-au-Chien.

Walking to New Orleans does not attempt to replicate accounts already given. Its purpose is primarily *constructive.* It seeks to define an ethical approach to human and environmental recovery based on principles of justice and the value of understanding communities as networks of interdependent equals, and link this ethic to practical applications of reconstruction through the discipline of socio-technical engineering and its concept of Participatory Design. In order to do that, it is important to give sufficient attention to scientific analyses of environmental use and control factors. This includes the impact of oil and gas interests in the Gulf of Mexico and Coastal Louisiana. It includes results (both intended and otherwise) of the construction of river and waterway control levees by levee boards and the U.S. Army Corps of Engineers (USACE). And it especially includes examination of cases of the human impact of Hurricanes Katrina and Rita on people's lives—not only in the economy of greater New Orleans, but also in the livelihood of residents of the coastal plain of

Southwest Louisiana in areas such as Terrebonne and Cameron Parishes. As is the natural environment, and various economic uses (and misuses) of it, the nature and texture of human lives are not static entities. The lives of many were radically affected by two hurricanes during the summer of 2005. But they were also already undergoing changes set in motion by conditions and events that anteceded the storms.

A fundamental premise of the concept of Participatory Design is that those *affected* by designed changes to their community should be *participants* in the process of their formulation.[15] But if both *environmental* and *human* factors must be given attention in any equation that defines the possibilities for rebuilding and re-knitting shattered communities, the tasks are indeed formidable. Not only is it necessary to consider ethical and legal principles of *fairness* to meaningfully evaluate reconstruction plans, it is also necessary to consider the requirements of the natural environment and to find ways of giving voice to those needs.

Consider first the ethics involved in dealing with *human* factors in reconstruction. The complexities of economic and bureaucratic regulations, political power struggles, structures of racial, ethnic, and social interests have become an inedible gumbo of chaos in the efforts of reconstruction. Sorting out conflicting interests must be guided by determining fundamental human needs and applying principles of fairness. But those needs can only truly be expressed and known through a quite direct and complete participation in the processes of recovery. Whether planning is government-down or neighborhood-up; whether there is a single process or competing processes, New Orleans and Coastal Louisiana must ultimately coordinate plans that can reduce chaos, bad decisions, and misdirection. It has proven difficult enough to ensure that the voices of citizens currently residing in New Orleans are being heard by those making decisions about the city's future. An even greater difficulty is how to incorporate the needs of citizens not geographically present, but dispersed across the country. How can one achieve consensus to make decisions about the needs of communities *as a whole*, when anywhere between 40 to 60 percent of the pre-storm population either remains living in a diaspora away from the region, or, having returned temporarily, has once again left?[16] The dis-

15. Changes resulting directly from design, or from policies that imply design or redesign; 'community' understood in its broadest sense.

16. The Census Bureau puts the loss of population in the greater metropolitan New Orleans area, between August 2005 and January 2006 at 39 percent (from 1,190,615 to

persed population may not even be fully aware of what issues are on the table for decision-making. For example, one of the proposals floated in the current thinking of the Unified New Orleans Plan (UNOP) has been to create "cluster housing." For those wards hardest hit by flooding, and which are likely to remain vulnerable to flooding for the foreseeable future, displaced residents would return not to their old neighborhoods, but would be required to move *elsewhere* in the city where 'clusters' of new housing will eventually be built on higher ground by entrepreneurial developers. This proposal, which has met with little support, is only one of a myriad of ways in which a city remembered may be destined to become only an artifact of its former self. Even quantifying those who have returned to the city is made difficult because a city still in chaos, with crime ever rising, has made relocation in areas outside New Orleans—Baton Rouge, Houston, Dallas, especially—increasingly appealing.

The situation of those forced to move from coastal parishes—St. Bernard, Plaquemines, Terrebonne, Cameron—is somewhat different. Here, some of the population dispersed from the immediate coast has not left the area entirely, but moved inland from towns such as Cameron or Holly Beach that *may never* be rebuilt. In fact, recent census figures have shown that after Hurricane Rita, the population of metropolitan Lake Charles, some 30 miles inland from the Gulf, in fact increased by 15 percent between August 2005 and January 2006 (from 172,890 to 200,732). However, other problems faced by citizens in this region are matters of changing economics and the need for many to find new occupations—from shrimpers or oystermen to mechanics or plumbers—and these factors are resulting in people leaving the region altogether.

Incorporating the voices of *all* existing residents, and especially those still in the diaspora, is a difficult problem faced in applying the principle of Participatory Design. By its nature, *participatory* implies the need for an ongoing presence of citizens. The Community Congress 'town meetings' held in advance of formulating the Unified New Orleans Plan had only a limited degree of success. One of their weaknesses was the unrepresentative selection of participants, especially in the early Congresses.

723,830); for Orleans Parish itself, the loss was 64 percent (from 437,186 to 158,353). Comparable losses in Cameron Parish in Southwest Louisiana, from the 2000 census to a 2006 estimate, were 22 percent. While some residents have returned to the City of New Orleans, others have left, and unofficial best estimates of loss for Orleans Parish as of March 2007 remain at over 41 percent.

Another was the fact that citizen input concerning the material content of particular plans and designs was not used. Far more successful, in that regard, has been the work of various neighborhood associations such as the Broadmoor Improvement Association and grassroots initiatives such as Common Ground Relief. These efforts of resolve and compassion will be discussed in chapters 8 and 9.

When one considers the ethics involved in dealing with factors of the *natural* environment in reconstruction, the planning processes and strategies become even more complex. The human and the natural have historically been caught in what could only be called a 'deadly embrace.' The following brief sketch—while still looking at environmental factors primarily from their human perspective—should make this clear. In many respects, the environmental needs (and dangers) of New Orleans are a consequence of the geographical and meteorological accidents of its history. As an example, from the first tropical storm recorded in the Gulf in September of 1559 to the great Hurricane Camille of 1969, Louisiana has been struck by more than 160 hurricanes in those 410 years—an *average* of close to three per year. In fact, in the very year (1718) when *Nouvelle-Orleans* was founded on rare high ground at a bend of the Mississippi River under the direction of Jean-Baptiste le Moyne, Sieur d'Iberville near a *Chouchoumas* Indian[17] settlement located on a portage to the river from Lake Pontchartrain (probably Bayou St. John but possibly also Bayou Trepagnier), the river flooded and destroyed the tiny collection of thatched huts and gardens. Symbolic of New Orleanian persistence, three hundred more settlers arrived later that year. In its early years, New Orleans was little more than a place of a hundred wretched hovels in a malarious wet thicket of willows and dwarf palmettos, infested by serpents and alligators,[18] with a wild population mixture of trappers, galley slaves, soldiers, gold hunters, and other assorted riffraff. In September of 1722, another storm wiped out much of the settlement, and the rebuilding that followed is what remains in the design of the city's current French Quarter.

Peirce Lewis characterizes the first period (1718–1810) of New Orleans as essentially that of a European city in its physical form and

---

17. The Annochy Indians, a branch of the Sioux, were called this by René-Cavalier, Sieur de la Salle, the Jesuit explorer of the Mississippi River—a derivation of the Indian term for crawfish (*chakchiuma*) that later became Anglicized as 'Houma', the current largest Indian tribal group in Louisiana.

18. As described by priest Pierre François Xavier de Charlevoix.

human orientation.[19] In that period, there was clearly a need for planning and standardization, and ultimately a move toward use of the capabilities of agencies such as the Army Corps of Engineers for levee control. Levees were originally the responsibility of riparian landholders, both to build and maintain; the result, unfortunately, was weak levees that were built to no standard and were poorly maintained. Despite periodic flooding of some five million acres, reliance on this practice continued until the mid-nineteenth century. By 1727, New Orleans had a levee over a mile long, 18 feet wide at its top; outside the city, plantation owners built strings of levees across their own frontage, with occasional cooperation among owners under the supervision of police juries of the parishes.[20]

The Army Corps of Engineers, initially founded in 1775 (formally established in 1802), began its involvement with New Orleans in 1803 when an Army engineer was sent to study its defenses. By 1829, Army engineers turned their attention to the development and maintenance of safe river channels, since the vital transportation link of the Mississippi River was a dangerous waterway, littered with snags, shoals, and wrecked ships.[21] Navigation work has been the Corps' primary role, but the frequent series of floods—the largest in 1927—extended its efforts to effective flood control. Current New Orleans District responsibilities of the Corps includes maintenance of over 2,800 miles of navigable waterways, as well as flood control plans involving levees, floodways (outlets and spillways for excess flood waters), channel improvements to stabilize a waterway's flood carrying capacity, and tributary improvements such as reservoirs, pumping stations, and control structures.

Perhaps the image that best captures the complexity of managing both the Mississippi River and adjacent waterways in the vicinity of New Orleans was one expanded upon by Peirce Lewis in a letter to me of 24 April 2007. Beyond all the many issues pertaining to the Mississippi River–Gulf

19. Lewis, *New Orleans: The Making of an Urban Landscape*, 39 ff.

20. Police juries are forms of parish (comparable to counties in other states) government derived from the old Napoleonic Code. In 1807 Louisiana was divided into 19 parishes based largely on ecclesiastical districts established in 1762 by the Spanish provisional governor. The State Legislative Council created a 12-member jury to serve with the parish judge, charged with the responsibility for executing concerns of the local police and administration of the parish. In 1811, the State adopted an act making members of the police assembly elective and designated this body officially as a "police jury."

21. US Army Corps of Engineers, New Orleans District. Information sheet provided by Kathy Gibbs, CEMVN-PA, Chief, Public Affairs Office, New Orleans.

Outlet (MR–GO),[22] or the location and relocation of port facilities, there is the consequence of the simple fact that, as it passes New Orleans, the Mississippi River is running at about 10 feet above sea level. This means that vessels crossing the Mississippi River, traveling east or west on the Gulf Intracoastal Waterway (GIWW), which is at sea level, must deal with that difference in elevation. In 1909, USACE began construction of locks to permit intracoastal shipping to pass through. The Harvey Lock, where the Harvey Canal meets the Mississippi River, and the Inner Harbor Lock, where the Inner Harbor Navigational Canal (IHNC, also referred to as the Industrial Canal) meets the river, perform the same function—to raise intracoastal ships and barges from sea level waters on the west and east banks to permit crossing the Mississippi. There is also the Algiers Lock, where the Algiers Canal, branching off the Harvey Canal, meets the Mississippi River further downstream.[23]

New Orleans' natural environment has always been one of 'wet streets'—from both river incursions and flooding from heavy rains. In May of 1849, Sauvé's Crevasse, a breach of a levee upriver from the city created the worst flooding in the city's history, leaving over 12,000 people homeless. Some approaches to dealing with river incursions were notably unsuccessful. In 1878, Charles Howell tried using cane mattresses, 200 feet wide by 2,000 to 9,200 feet long, as bank revetments to protect the New Orleans wharves. These proved too fragile after just a few years. Congress created the Mississippi River Commission in 1879. It included USACE, Coast and Geodetic Survey people, and civilians, and made federal money available for national flood protection work. However, the

22. The MR–GO channel, fully completed in 1968, extends from the Inner Harbor Navigational Canal (INHC) in New Orleans to the 38-foot depth contour in the Gulf of Mexico. The stretch with the Gulf Intracoastal Waterway (GIWW) is referred to as the GIWW Reach (mile 66–60). The channel diverts from the GIWW and runs south through wetlands for 37 miles (known as the Inland Reach, mile 60–23). The remaining 23 miles through Breton and Chandeleur Sounds is known as the Sound Reach (mile 23–0). All reaches of the MR–GO navigational channel are authorized as a 36-foot deep, 500-foot bottom width waterway. See U.S. Army Corps of Engineers, New Orleans District, "Draft Integrated Final Report to Congress and Legislative Environmental Impact Statement for the Mississippi River–Gulf Outlet Deep-Draft De-authorization Study," June 2007.

23. See figures 12 and 27 in Lewis, *New Orleans: The Making of an Urban Landscape*. The Inner Harbor Lock, completed in 1921, was built to accommodate the smaller vessels of that time. It has become a bottleneck, preventing large container ships from the Mississippi River from easily gaining access to the Industrial Canal, and forcing the Dock Board to create new container facilities along the River.

primary responsibility for dealing with flooding remained dependent on local efforts. As a result, the Louisiana State Legislature established Levee Districts as subdivisions of state government to try to regulate by law the construction of levees, drainage, and revetments, giving them the power of eminent domain and taxation.

Responsibility for control always seemed to compete with visions of aggrandizement for New Orleans. In 1910, engineer and inventor A. Baldwin Wood developed a plan to drain the swampy land between Lake Pontchartrain and the then-inhabited city. Pumps of his design (still in use by the city) allowed expansion of 'habitable' areas from the higher ground along the crescent of the river (hence the name *Crescent* City) towards the lake. As Peirce Lewis points out, the draining of this backswamp represented a major change for the city. While more levees were built to protect newly drained land, the swamp soil used to build them was at best a watery mixture of organic material, resulting in a drained backswamp, dropped by pumping, to something considerably *below* sea level. Flood protection now became a matter of life and death. Higher parts of New Orleans, such as Gentilly Terrace, became enclaves of wealthy whites, while the lower lying backswamp areas ultimately became black ghettos. Lewis ponders that, in a sense, this engineering marvel itself, the Wood pump, inadvertently became a powerful agent to accelerate racial segregation.[24]

The coastal marshes of Louisiana represent a natural environment that is at once similar to, yet different from urban New Orleans. The human interests involve shipping and creating ways to access the Mississippi River and the Port of New Orleans. By 1822 the Army Corps of Engineers was reporting on snags from bank cave-ins along the Mississippi that were a danger to navigation.[25] Snags included 'planters' (dead trees fixed to the riverbed) and 'sawyers' (trees more loosely anchored that oscillated with the current below the surface). In 1837 the French tried to loosen bars at the mouth of the Mississippi with bucket drags, and Major William Chase explored the possibility of a ship canal to connect the River with the Gulf of Mexico (an early version of the MR–GO idea). By mid-nineteenth century, a survey published in 1851 by civil engineer Charles Ellet, *The Mississippi and Ohio Rivers*,[26] resisted the popular "levees only" thesis,

24. Lewis, *New Orleans: The Making of an Urban Landscape*, 67.

25. Cowdrey, *Land's End*, 5.

26. Cowdrey, *Land's End*, 10.

which saw levees as a sufficient approach to flood control. Instead, Ellet saw river control involving a complex of mutually supporting means— not only levees, but also dredging, reservoirs, artificial outlets and spill-ways. Subsequently, various efforts took place on the Southwest Pass of the Mississippi River's entrance to the Gulf. Harrowing opened a temporary channel in 1852; privately constructed jetties of board and pilings were erected in 1857. In 1870, with the Port of New Orleans deteriorating, in part from silting and sand bars at the mouth of the Mississippi, preventing passage of deeper-draft post-Civil War steamships, James Eads was directed to dredge and construct jetties on the South Pass of the Mississippi outlet to the Gulf. Four years of work began in June of 1875, involving wing dams and 'T-dams' within the pass to scour away the shoal, and sill dams across the Southwest Pass and Pass à Loutre to force more water through the South Pass and keep it open.[27]

The environment of Coastal Louisiana, however, involved far more than issues of access to the Mississippi River and the Port of New Orleans, and saving the shipping hub from being moved to Mobile or Gulfport. Coastal Louisiana is a unique world of its own. Out of the history of a ter-ritory that was once the lair of pirates, the coastal marshlands of Louisiana is the location of many paradoxes. It is an environment where shrimpers, oystermen, nutria hunters, the occasional cattle farmer, Houma Indians and other tribal bands meet oil derrick riggers, pipeline mechanics, mud-men, barge engineers, welders, and warehousemen. Its visual paradox is that while waves of marsh grass stretch east and west, towards Mississippi and Texas, dotted by stands of live oak, USGS records that from 1932 to 2000, Coastal Louisiana has lost some 1,900 square miles of land—roughly an area the size of the state of Delaware. Predicted land loss over the next 50 years more than doubles that amount.

Despite the apparent tranquility of a humid, placid, table-flat landscape that reaches as far as the eye can see, it is a land of great dynamics—from swirls of waterfowl on their mid-North American flyway spiraling against the sky to powerful Gulf currents that sweep along the coast, constantly reconfiguring the narrow barrier islands, and contributing to the influx of saltwater that has moved ever landward. Salty Gulf water inflow has trav-eled as much as 100 miles up the Mississippi River, approaching the water

27. Ibid., 21.

intake pipes of New Orleans,[28] and is disrupting freshwater vegetation of the wide variety of marsh grasses such as fanwort and beggartick. But saltwater intrusion is just one among *many* factors that contribute to a severe loss of these fragile wetlands.

The Louisiana coastal marshes are crisscrossed by more than 20,000 miles[29] of oil and gas pipelines and flowlines. Evidence of former oil derricks can be seen in the keyhole-shaped canals that dead-end into circular pockets where a rig once stood. Perhaps the most astounding image of the vast population of oil and gas wells *inside* the coastal zone is shown on the satellite Map USGS-NWRC 2004-04-0174 of 2 July, 2004.[30] Within the demarcated coastal zone, oil and gas wells are designated by yellow dots; pipelines and flowlines by blue lines. Satellite imagery shows most of the rest of Louisiana north to roughly Natchitoches, north of Alexandria. The picture is reminiscent of the differences between South and North Korea at night. Thousands upon thousands of yellow dots, representing not points of lights from electricity (although it is present at those points), but the locations oil rigs and gas wells; a veritable *mega-city* of yellow dots stretching east and west 250 miles, and north of that zone—*nothing*. A mega-city spawned from the first oil fields of Jennings, Louisiana, dating back to 1904.

Even these brief descriptions should give a sense of the level of *complexity* of issues to be managed by any strategies for post-disaster reconstruction. It is therefore appropriate to discuss a way to identify *types* of complexity—what we will call 'Seven Markers of Complexity'—a set of categories by which to reference some the of different kinds of problems at work in planning for both the revitalization of the City of New Orleans and the restoration of Louisiana's coastal environment. It is possible to understand each of these *markers* of complexity as broadly derivative from a more fundamental concept: the concept of entropy.

28. See Hallowell, *Holding Back the Sea*, 17.

29. Reported in multiple sources, for example by Restore or Retreat (ROR), a non-profit coastal advocacy group based in Thibodaux, Louisiana.

30. Data source from the US Department of the Interior, USGS, National Wetlands Research Center, Coastal Restoration Field Station of the Louisiana Department of Natural Resources Coastal Restoration Division.

Introduction

THE CONCEPT OF ENTROPY

Entropy—as it will be used in *Walking to New Orleans*—is a concept borrowed initially from physics, but also from other sciences, to describe energy that exists but is unavailable for productive use. Energy in such a form can lead to chaos. For the purpose of relating underlying issues in the discussion of 'Seven Markers of Complexity' that follows, this derivative sense of *entropy* can serve as a root metaphor. At the same time, it is worthwhile to briefly point out its historical origins, to make clear certain more specific meanings with which the concept is *not* being used.

From its etymology—the Greek εν (inside) + τρέπω (escape)—the concept of entropy has operated in the second law of thermodynamics, where, given a universe consisting of systems in equilibrium, differences of pressure, density, and temperature tend to equalize over time. This thermodynamic homogeneity limits the ability to extract work. In the classic example of ice melting in a glass described by Rudolf Clausius in 1862, the difference in temperature between a cold glass of ice and the warmer room in which it is situated moves towards equalization, as heat energy from the room spreads to the cooler system of the cold glass and ice. The resulting entropy increases as a function of increase in the magnitude of separation of molecules of the ice.

Entropy accounts for the effects of irreversibility in thermodynamic systems, including its more speculative application to cosmology in which the universe is understood to be doomed to death by increasing entropy—a universe in which all energy has been homogeneously distributed and where no source exists to perform additional work. Roger Penrose, for example, has argued that gravity may contribute to the increase of entropy by a collapsing of dispersed matter into black holes.[31]

Statistical definitions of entropy derive from the work of Austrian physicist Ludwig Boltzmann in 1877. Boltzmann's work, which underwent several stages of development,[32] is popularly remembered for the probabilistic measure of sub-regions as represented in a formula for entropy S engraved above his bust on his tombstone in the Zentralfriedhof (Central Cemetery), Vienna, (but which he never, in fact, wrote down)

---

31. Penrose, *The Road to Reality*, 690 ff.

32. From his early attempt to prove the second law of thermodynamics with a general theorem from mechanics alone to a later recognition that such proof would depend on probability theory.

$$S = k. \log W$$

where k is Boltzmann's constant, 1.38×10^{-23} J K^{-1} (joules per degree Kelvin), and W is *Wahrscheinlickheit*, the number of possible unobservable microstates the observable thermodynamic macroscopic state could realize, based on different positions and momenta of various molecules.

Statistical representations of entropy allow it to be understood as the amount of uncertainty or chaos that remains in a system after observable properties (such as volume, temperature, and density, in the realm of thermodynamics) have been considered. More broadly, entropy may be understood to describe the probability of a system to exist in different possible quantum states. This can be taken as a general approximation of one's degree of lack of knowledge about the system (e.g., von Neumann entropy). The greater the probability of a system to exist in multiple states, the greater the ignorance.

Thus, entropy is more than simply a measure of the randomness of a system. Rather, it is also a description of our inability to see how any given state of a system (in whatever degree of randomness it exists) has come into being and where it may go—particularly in the sense in which we may want to usefully engage or change that system, as in the case of the systems of outflow from freshwater to salt at the Louisiana coastal boundaries of the Gulf of Mexico.

Another sense of entropy derives from information theory that describes the amount of information missing before meaningful reception in a communication loop can take place when the recipient does not know the value of a random variable. Sometimes called *Shannon entropy* after Claude Shannon, who, in 1948, used the concept to examine information in transmitted messages, the 'entropy' of a message system determines the number of queries (yes/no) necessary to ascertain the content of the information of the message. Entropy, in this context, might conceivably be applied to the measure of biodiversity in an ecological system.

Even more broadly construed notions of entropy are definitions that involve economics (the irreversible degradation of natural resources in productive economic activity), psychology (flattening of affect where distinctions of meaning are significant to the functioning of the individual), and sociology (where social equilibrium is measured in terms of both general variables within it and also individual behavior).

The sense of entropy that will be used in *Walking to New Orleans*—and that for which it might serve as a root metaphor for various kinds of intractable complexities that exist in thinking about possible strategies for post-disaster reconstruction—is as a description of what is absent or dysfunctional, either within a single system, or in multiple systems that must interact, in order to allow productive work: that is, the efficient functioning of those systems. It is also used, from a human perspective, to refer to what constitutes barriers to meaningful and productive work—that is, work which is ethically justifiable, particularly in terms of concerns for social justice. Entropy in the latter sense would include those barriers that take the form of inequitable controls over various human activities, conditions of residence, access to political processes, and general freedom in social interactions. What counts as 'work' might consist of the tasks necessary to create a suitable economic base for a city, given its geographical location, population distribution, its sources of economic growth (manufacturing, natural resources, transportation, cultural and leisure activities, etc.); or it might consist of the tasks required to achieve the ecological balance necessary to sustain a natural environment—both as a suitable habitat for natural and human kinds, but also as a protective barrier against unprovoked events such as hurricanes or flooding. What counts as 'controls of the conditions of work' might consist of such things as ensuring suitable and humane living conditions, educational needs, transportation requirements to and from work, fairness in access to opportunities to work, availability of essential services (medical and healthcare, fire and police safety).

Thus, while entropy, as used here, is not *reducible* to the simple measure of randomness in any system, it does focus on the ability to account for those aspects of a system's energy that are unavailable for productive work. Since 'work' presupposes order that is either known (and, generally, quantifiable—for example, the quantitative description of how a manufacturing process is performing in order to achieve Six Sigma, or not more than 3.4 defects per million opportunities), or known in terms of the ability to describe what specific tasks it would take to establish order, entropy may then also be considered to be a measure of the level of disorder or chaos of a system.

SEVEN MARKERS OF COMPLEXITY

1. Instability

An important feature of complex problems is that they are rarely stable over time. Inadequacies or failures of construction materials, changes in the environment or workforce, unanticipated political and economic conditions, and so forth, typically require that problems must be re-thought and redefined. Complex problem solving, therefore, is often a balancing act—with problems being partially solved, then returning in new forms, some of which are more difficult to solve than the original dilemma. Solutions that are politically attractive because they are cheap and acceptable to government can often lead in the wrong direction. Thus, designing any post-disaster problem-solving strategy must involve both ethics and communication. From an ethical standpoint, a strategy pre-supposes establishing and prioritizing a set of values, only then followed by a series of practical operations designed to achieve desired results. In terms of communication, it is critical that communication be framed as an iterative loop—a *cycle* of information passage *from* those designing and implementing a solution program to those benefiting from its re-sults, and *back from* those affected by the program to those designing and implementing it.

There are multiple examples of instability in both the City of New Orleans and the regional coastal environment that will be discussed in more detail in Chapter 4. Perhaps the most obvious in the City of New Orleans is the *literal* instability of base materials used in the construction of the levee barrier walls of the 17th Street Drainage Canal, the Orleans Avenue and London Avenue Canals, and, most likely, levees along the Industrial Canal (Inner Harbor Navigational Canal). Whether or not the materials were suitable from the beginning to be used as a base for insert-ing steel pilings over which concrete retaining walls were built, the high content of organic material within the base clay as well as in the clay and shell embankments made their support function degrade over time, and, ultimately, resulted in rotation of the retaining walls which allowed the disastrous urban flooding.[33]

However, one can point to *instability* in other forms as well. Since Katrina, population flow in and out of New Orleans has not been stable

33. See, for example, van Heerden, *The Storm*, 232.

or predictable. This has been the case not only for workers and residents returning, then leaving again; it has been seen in the particularly painful impact of the many physicians and health care workers who have returned to attempt to resume their practices, but finally decided the absence of medical resources or a place to practice forced them to move elsewhere. In the early period after Katrina, when attempts at reconstruction planning began, there was the instability of competing planning strategies, the lack of consistent leadership, and abortive attempts at solutions that had to be thrown away and restarted. Finally, in the coastal region beyond New Orleans, there has been, in recent years, an environment inherently unstable—both from natural and human-made causes. All of these forms of instability, and others, will be discussed in more detail in subsequent chapters.

2. Unintended Consequences

Unintended consequences—a concept familiar to those involved with user interface design and human–system interaction—refers to unanticipated events resulting from the situation where a local design decision or a solution to problem A causes another problem B to occur (typically at a broader, higher, or more global level). One could regard many of the Army Corps of Engineers' efforts at control of the Mississippi River as producing unintended consequences of various sorts. The dredging of shipping Pass A causes an unintended blockage (or overflow) of Pass B. Or, a commitment to levees that must continually be built up higher and higher places low-lying areas of the city at greater and greater risk. Unintended consequences may occur in other forms as well. Some, discussed in Chapter 6, arise in sociological or legal domains. For example, a piece of poorly-designed state voting legislation, intended to achieve greater opportunities for racial group A (black voters) may inadvertently diminish opportunities for racial group B (Hispanic voters). Others occur in economic domains. The Mississippi River–Gulf Outlet (MR–GO) is an example of unanticipated consequences in both environmental (degradation of surrounding protective marshlands) and economic domains (less shipping usage of the canal than expected, the need to rethink the location of port facilities).

One antidote to eliminating the occurrence of unintended consequences is planning that takes a 'holistic' approach. As a strategy, this differs from traditional scientific methods of dividing large problems into small sections, giving each part to a different group for solution. Commitment to that traditional strategy, in part, may help explain why it has been so difficult for various local and federal agencies—all of whom may have general agreement on goals of protecting the environment and improving economic conditions of those whose livelihoods depend on a viable natural environment—to work successfully together. In terms of solution strategies, a holistic approach, often seen in shared problem-solving tools (whether as simple as the use of an Ishikawa Diagram or as elaborate as Hoshin Planning)[34] enables the causes of the problem and their consequences for different situations and groups to be seen and addressed as an interlinked whole.

Other antidotes to unintended consequences involve the use of controlled experiments or prototyping. Prototyping, ideally, is a form of experimentation using trial designs from which lessons are learned, then applied to new design attempts (rather than simply an early stage of design that proceeds on to finality). In urban planning, especially in the context of post-disaster reconstruction, experimentation is difficult, if not impossible, to the extent that the main focus of government leadership is on reestablishing disrupted lives and rebuilding a damaged economy. One might regard Musician's Village,[35] in the Upper Ninth Ward in New Orleans, as something of a reconstruction experiment. In the domain of the natural environment, however, experimentation and prototyping is more common. As one example, scientists at LUMCON (the Louisiana Universities Marine Consortium),[36] a research and lab facility at the DeFelice Marine Center in Cocodrie at Terrebonne Bay, have examined what the media has termed 'the dead zone,' a region of hypoxia (oxygen starvation) in Louisiana estuaries (and others throughout the world) resulting from nutrient overload, in no small part from the outflow of fertilizers used in farming.[37]

34. An Ishikawa Diagram is the well-known 'fishbone' graphic used to identify a chain of causation and root causes of a problem. Hoshin Planning, derived from *Hoshin Kanri* (lit. "shining metal," and "pointing direction," "target policy"), refers to a structured, systematic process of focused planning that compares an organization's current needs against those five or more years in the future, based on a comprehensive view of both organizational and emerging customer requirements.

35. Discussed in more detail in chapter 7.

36. Discussed in more detail in chapter 10.

37. The effects of hypoxia are debated. According to one theory, as the dead zone enlarges, fish and shrimp flee the diminished oxygen. However, they tend to pile up at the perimeter,

Introduction

A frequent example of the avoidance of unintended consequences occurs every day in medical diagnosis. In differential diagnosis, physicians and surgeons use forms of 'pattern recognition' to connect signs and symptoms presented by the patient with those of their previous encounters. This is a way of ruling out possible, but incorrect, conclusions in the diagnosis, and avoiding early commitments to treatment before comparison of all available data is done.

3. Vicious Cycles and Error Loops

As with unintended consequences, the concept of an error loop is familiar to those involved in the design of human–system interaction, but its forms can occur in many contexts. A fundamental principle of good design requires thinking of a user and the system with which the user must interact as co-routines. A skilled designer must make visible both the system's context and the potential goals of the user to make the user's behavior and the system's response compatible. Often, however, designers do not think of conditions that break user–system interaction as partially completed states of work seeking a goal, but as error states that need to be reported. When this occurs, what the user frequently experiences is an error message (whose meaning is often obscure or unknown) that is repeated over and over again as the user tries to accomplish a task that makes sense to the user but evidently not to the system. The language of such error messages (e.g., the FATAL ERROR + 'some number' that appears on a computer screen) often does little to offer the user alternative strategies of behavior, or the possibility of any intelligent response. The user attempts the same or similar action again, and receives the same or similar error message again. This is a classic error loop. Such loops, unfortunately, can repeat themselves *ad infinitum* or as long as the user has the tolerance to keep trying.

---

creating a high population band that knowledgeable commercial fishermen can exploit. See Hallowell, *Holding Back the Sea*, 100, van Heerden, Colten, and others, as well as CWPPRA and USACE documents for a discussion of this and other examples. LUMCON oversees the Barataria-Terrebonne National Estuary Program (BTNEP), one of 28 National Estuary Programs in the United States, with offices on the campus of Nichols State University in Thibodaux, and participates in the Coastal Restoration and Enhancement through Science and Technology (CREST) program, an alliance of eleven academic institutions in Louisiana and Mississippi, with offices on the campus of LSU, Baton Rouge.

A vicious cycle is a form of error loop in which the same problem keeps returning again and again, often after the problem is thought to have been resolved. Street crime—certainly relevant to current conditions in the City of New Orleans—presents a good example of a vicious cycle. Crime rates rise → funds are expended to put more police on the street → crime rates are initially lowered → funds dry up or crime re-locates → crime rates rise again. Another example, in the immediate aftermath of Hurricane Katrina, involved the need for laborers to perform debris removal and for skilled workers to do re-construction. Despite this need, the City lacked adequate housing for workers, as well as basic human services, for a considerable period after the storm. Therefore, it was difficult to develop anything like a sufficient workforce to do the necessary cleanup and rebuilding.

At a somewhat more complex level are repetitive instances of flooding → levee construction → levee deterioration → repeat flooding → levee repair → levee deterioration → repeat flooding. For example, USACE plans to construct new flood gates (by 2010) at the Seabrook Bridge, the Gulf Intracoastal Waterway, and possibly the Mississippi River–Gulf Outlet (MR–GO) to keep storm surge from entering the Industrial Canal. However, many officials in St. Bernard Parish argue that a floodgate in the Gulf Intracoastal Waterway will actually *increase* the possibility of flooding in both St. Bernard Parish and in New Orleans East.[38]

Vicious cycles occur in many forms in the region of Louisiana's coastal wetlands. In some respects these are the most complex of all, yet some are excruciatingly simple—just intractable and unable to be controlled. Over and above all the various complexities relating to competing interests in using vs. preserving the resource-rich coastal wetlands, is the bare fact that tropical storms and hurricanes return, again and again, year after year, with no expectation that they will all of a sudden *stop* returning. The City of New Orleans and the Gulf region in general simply has a very long history of frequent storms. Efforts to save and rebuild coastal barrier islands (for example, the islands of Chandeleur Sound, Timbalier Island, or the Isles Dernières, which, following a massive hurricane that swept across the island in 1856, fragmented it into five smaller islands: East, Trinity, Whiskey, Raccoon, and Wine), while sometimes Herculean, must be repeated again and again. All too often the end result is ultimately little

---

38. This example shows a common overlap with features of the previous marker, *unintended consequences.*

permanent protection from the constant abuse of storm-driven winds and waves.[39]

4. Problems of Scale

Complexity based on issues pertaining to scale is fairly straightforward. These are problems so enormous that it would appear no resources could ever be available to coordinate efforts to fix them. Historically, the Mississippi River has always presented problems of enormous scale from the standpoint of frequent flooding and navigation. 'Mississippi,' derived from a French rendering of *anishinaabe*, is an expression (probably Ojibwe) meaning 'great river.' It is the second longest river in North America at approximately 2320 miles, by general consensus; in some places, over four miles wide,[40] and the third largest drainage basin in the world (after the Amazon and the Congo Rivers). Dropping from 1475 feet above sea level at its headwaters, the Mississippi is a massive body of moving water that has undergone constant changes in its course, creating vast areas of flooding, as well as bank erosion, snags, ox bows and cul de sacs, and shifting sandbars, making the river a navigational nightmare.

At its southern border, the entire Louisiana coastal wetlands represents a complex environment and ecosystem of both overwhelming scale and enormous national significance. Stretching more than 300 undulating miles from Mississippi, across Louisiana, to eastern Texas, these marshlands, which include the Deltaic and Chenier Plains, were built up from sediment deposited by the Mississippi River since the last major

---

39. The following vicious cycle, far from the shores of Louisiana, is evidence of how repetitive error states exist within the highest domains of government. A consulting team, of which I was a member, produced a set of recommendations to improve the effectiveness and value of the office within the U.S. State Department responsible for overseeing and distributing foreign assistance to former Soviet Bloc countries (EUR/ACE). The report identified endemic problems in the allocation and distribution of foreign assistance that were continually overlooked or ignored, and, therefore, appeared again and again in Southeast Europe and Central Asia. These repetitive failures prevented EUR/ACE from meeting its stated goal of 'coordination'—creation of a *sharable* repository of knowledge so foreign assistance analysis and distribution procedures improved over time, and failures were not repeated in endless loops. A major reason for such repetitive errors was the absence of a formal continuous improvement process or any use of such 'error loop busters' as root cause analysis. Summarized from multiple reports funded by and issued to the U.S. State Department through Management Systems International in 2005.

40. For example, where it is held behind Lock No. 7, near La Crosse, Wisconsin. The Missouri River is slightly longer, at around 2341 miles.

glacial retreat, 15,000 years ago, spawning at least seven major deltas over the last 9,000 years. Around 1400 CE a course change in the river began creating the modern (Balize) delta that reaches the sea.[41] This ecosystem covers approximately 10,700 square miles of Louisiana, and constitutes the largest contiguous wetlands in the lower United States. Immediately inland from Louisiana's coastal marshes, as recently as 100 years ago, existed vast native grasslands, covering portions of twelve parishes, often referred to as the 'Cajun Triangle,' and parts of eastern Texas. The coastal prairie was a flat region, largely consisting of tallgrass, similar to species found in the Midwest, and divided by larger bayous and shallow, intermittent streams, or *coulées*. There was, therefore, not one single prairie, but a series of grassland prairies (the three largest being Calcasieu, Vermillion, and Faquetique, which ran as far north as the town of Ville Platte) broken by gallery forests along the bayous—with intervening isolated settlement areas called *anses* or 'coves.'[42] This territory was once home to a myriad of species that are no longer found in Louisiana, including bison.

To address the current needs of Louisiana's coastal marshes, Congress passed the Coastal Wetlands Planning, Protection and Restoration Act (CWPPRA) in 1990, under the sponsorship of Louisiana Senator John Breaux. Issues of scale can immediately be seen in the CWPPRA-funded 1998 report, "Coast 2050: Toward a Sustainable Coastal Louisiana" that outlined scores of strategies for a multibillion dollar restoration of about 500,000 acres of Louisiana's coast over the next 50 years. Indeed, Louisiana's wetlands, which represent about 40 percent of the wetlands of the continental United States, represent about 80 percent of its marsh losses.[43]

Yet while the idea of coordinating such a vast array of projects seems almost beyond comprehension—and has proven resistant to creation of

41. Lee with Lockwood, "Mississippi Delta. The Land of the River," *National Geographic,* Vol. 164, No. 2, August, 1983, 240.

42. The nautical image of 'cove' perhaps reflects Acadian seafaring origins from Western France and the region of Poitou, and the fact that winds crossing the prairie created billows of waving grass like swells on the sea; the term is retained in areas today such as Robert's Cove, a rural enclave north of Crowley and the location of Hawk's, a tiny restaurant that serves the largest crawfish ever offered for human consumption. For more history of this region, see, for example, Ancelet et al., *Cajun Country* in the Folklife in the South Series.

43. Data from U.S. Geological Survey, Marine and Coastal Geology Program. See also Dr. Bruce E. Fleury of Tulane's Department of Ecology and Evolutionary Biology.

a rational, comprehensive plan[44]—consider the fact that addressing a vast 500,000 acres represents *only seven percent* of the total acreage (6,848,000 acres) of the entire coastal region's 10,7000 square miles. The enormity of the problem of restoration is compounded by the fact that there are multiple reasons for coastal marsh loss. There is no one factor or even a single set of factors. It is not simply fertilizer deposits from inland farming, or toxin deposits from the residue of drilling holes for oil and gas, or the more than 8,200 miles of canals dug for oil and gas exploration and other navigation purposes that contributes to the degradation of the marshlands. There is also continual barrier island degradation from Gulf currents that expose the marshes to increased hurricane storm damage and saltwater intrusion. There is the natural sea level rise, estimated to be approximately one-half foot per century. And if predictions about global warming result in insufficient corrective action within the next forty or fifty years, the question of rebuilding Louisiana's coastal wetlands could well be quite moot. They will no longer exist.

These are problems of scale. Perhaps they are even *beyond* problems of scale. Or perhaps one could look at things as does Prof. Lonnie Thomson, renown glaciologist at Ohio State University, who has conducted more than fifty ice-coring expeditions, many at elevations above 18,000 feet, examining their records that preserve abrupt shifts in climate that have changed the course of human history. Thompson, who once considered a career in coal geology, draws an analogy between glaciers and the canary in the coal mine. Like the bird, glaciers warn humans of the buildup of dangerous gases. In the past, however, "when the canaries stopped singing and died, the miners knew how to get out of the mine. Our problem is, we live in the mine."[45] Or perhaps one can only look at things in the black humor words of country singer Mary Chapin Carpenter: sometimes you're the windshield; sometimes you're the bug.[46] Either way, every day we dis-

---

44. At least until *very* recent efforts at coordination by Governor Bobby Jindal, who signed an executive order on January 23, 2008, to maximize efficiency of state coastal restoration and hurricane protection efforts by requiring all state agencies to comply with the Comprehensive Master Plan for a Sustainable Coast. The plan lays out priorities as recognized by the Coastal Protection and Restoration Authority (CWPPRA), and requires adherence by agencies including the Department of Transportation and Development, the Department of Natural Resources, and the Governor's Office of Coastal Affairs. Its success is still to be proven.

45. Nash, "Chronicling the Ice," *Smithsonian*, July 2007, 74.

46. Original lyrics, Dire Straits.

cover increasing dimensions to how our lives interact with our coastal marshes and wetlands—not only as a rich resource for food, but as fragile protective buffers on which our very survival is dependent.

5. Non-Robust Solutions and Redundancy

Robustness and redundancy are attributes of solutions, which, in their absence, can result in catastrophic failure. The importance of redundancy is most familiar to human functions that must operate under extreme conditions; for example, NASA space flight operations. Transport of human beings beyond the thin, protective envelop of the earth's atmosphere occurs in probably the most hostile environment imaginable—an anoxic, frigid world (approaching 'absolute zero,' Zero Kelvin, or -273 C)[47] without the presence of gravity in which the human body normally functions (except for that induced artificially by spin); an environment also subject to continual bombardment from various particles moving in space at enormous speeds. Any capsule capable of supporting human life in such an environment must, therefore, maintain a high degree of redundancy—two, three, or more levels of backup—simply because the failure of any given system or component could be disastrous.

Redundancy in the New Orleans levee system is present in structures such as the Bonnet Carré Spillway, a flood control mechanism located about 32 miles upstream of downtown in Norco, St. Charles Parish. The spillway was built by the Army Corps of Engineers after the Great Flood of 1927 to lower river stages at New Orleans when the volume of water its levees were designed to handle would be exceeded for a certain period of time. The primary criterion for opening the spillway is based on a river flow or discharge rate exceeding 1.25 million cubic feet/second; not a one-day spike, but a discharge rate expected to continue for some time.[48] When those levels occur, the spillway can be opened to divert floodwaters from the Mississippi River into Lake Pontchartrain and out to the Gulf of Mexico.[49]

Robustness is also an important principle of socio-technical design or any design involving human–system interaction. A robust design is one

47. Actually 2.7 Kelvin because of constant microwave background radiation.

48. The criteria for opening the spillway were given in personal conversation with John Hall, U.S. Army Corps of Engineers, New Orleans District. Levees below the spillway were not designed to be capable of exceeding the level of 1.25 million cu. ft./sec. flow rates.

49. Lake Pontchartrain is actually a large, extended inlet from the Gulf of Mexico through two narrow passages, Chef Menteur Pass and the Rigolets.

that will work as intended regardless of variation in conditions of its use, variations due to deterioration over time, even variation resulting from defects in manufacturing processes. To achieve a design that is 'robust,' the designers must understand where potential sources of variation lie and account for them. One approach to achieving robustness in design can be through 'brute force' techniques—heavier or stronger materials, different tolerances, exceeding specs in areas of potential weakness of function. Robust design can also be achieved by learning more about how the user will actually employ a design under the conditions of their work. This involves the realm of experimentation and user testing to establish feedback loops in order to discover areas of weakness in design or manufacture that can be corrected.

Another aspect of robust design involves the ability to perform with respect to multiple parameters. If a design's operation can be mathematically related to a design parameter, its optimum performance parameters can be calculated; its overall value is typically determined by performance with respect to multiple measures. However, a significant factor determining performance is the design's sensitivity to external or uncontrollable variations. Measures of robustness might typically include a methodology using the Taguchi Method[50] to consider noise factors (environmental variation during a design's usage, component deterioration, etc.) and statistical analysis of variation (ANOVA) concepts to incorporate multiple objectives and constraints in a design to optimize its functionality under diverse conditions.

Dealing with factors such as environmental variation and component degradation applies not only to mechanisms (such as locks, pumping stations, and spillways in the complex levee system) or infrastructure (such as roads, sewerage systems, and building codes) but to groups and individuals themselves. In mass casualty incidents (MCIs) during disaster and post-disaster conditions, the ability to establish a clear chain of command and assignment of areas of responsibility is critical. Moreover, when people have the ability to carry out *multiple* tasks, even if they do not always perform them, the response capability becomes more robust, and, therefore, greater reliability exists in the system. The system as a

50. A robust design method pioneered by engineer and statistician Dr. Genichi Taguchi, who during the late 1950s and 60s at Aoyama Gakuin University in Tokyo, and, in part, while at Bell Labs, developed the application of statistics to improve the quality of manufactured goods.

whole is better able to cope with *unexpected occurrences*—if one function of a system fails, it can be replaced.

Clearly, the question of robustness and redundancy impacts planning for future Katrina events—a necessity, since, while it may not be known when, hurricanes will assuredly happen again, and there is no reason to be confident that the system of levees as it now stands can protect housing or critical services. Redundancy is necessary to provide greater security—multiple evacuation routes, multiple locations for emergency housing, multiple trauma centers, and so forth, coordinated within an overall plan in which communication is robust. Robust in this context particularly includes the ability to communicate in multiple concurrent modes. The *lack* of robustness in communication was a tragic failure in rescue attempts during the 9/11 event. As an EMT and member of the Bristol-Norfolk County Critical Incident Stress Debriefing (CISD) Team, I saw direct evidence of the *inability* of various emergency units—fire, police, EMTs—to communicate with one another during the destruction of the towers at the World Trade Center. The result was over 300 firefighters, EMTs, and police lost. Failures in communication systems to function *across* different emergency services and agencies was also a significant weakness that impacted the level of response in the early days of rescue work after Hurricane Katrina and subsequent flooding.

6. Cross-Domain Interactions

Solving complex problems requires recognition of the importance of interactions (and competitions) among psychological, economic, technical, cultural, and political domains. Solutions, somewhere along the way, must address questions such as: In whose interest is solving this problem? Who will pay the costs of a solution?; What technology can assist? What kinds of solutions will be culturally, socially, politically acceptable? The failure to resolve issues of territoriality, authority, and responsibility frequently result in barriers to achieving a successful, or permanent, solution; such failures can even contribute to making problems worse or more intractable—expressed in the quality management slogan "If you're not part of the solution, you're part of the problem."

One can distinguish several major *types* of interactions (and competitions). The most obvious are those that are *occupation* based. These are the competing interests, for example, among the oil and gas companies vs.

fishermen vs. oystermen vs. trappers vs. shrimpers vs. naturalists vs. levee bureaucrats vs. alligator hunters vs. farmers, etc. A second type is discipline based. These are the various *conceptual* domains and their associated interests: economic vs. political vs. local neighborhood vs. psychological vs. technical vs. industrial vs. ethical, etc. A third type is perhaps the most relevant to achieving consensus about potential solutions to urban and environmental problems (and where differences and competing interests are the most difficult to resolve). These are the competing responsibilities and territorial control issues among various local, regional, and federal *agencies and organizations.* Sometimes the issues are not simply agency vs. agency, or level of government vs. level of government (e.g., city vs. state vs. federal), but an intermingling of legislative acts vs. agency directives vs. court rulings. Thus, one might find, as the source of endless disagreements and the failure to resolve differences among solution strategies, competitions among a seemingly endless list of parties: CWPPRA (the Breaux Act of 1990) vs. USACE's contractual requirements vs. U.S. Fish and Wildlife directives vs. Department of Natural Resources (DNR) goals vs. the Governor's Office of Coastal Activities Science Advisory Panel recommendations vs. the Coalition to Restore Coastal Louisiana (CRCL) principles vs. the Louisiana Advisory Commission on Coastal and Marine Resources reports vs. the Louisiana Wetlands Protective Panel vs. the Wetlands Conservation and Restoration Task Force vs. EPA, and on and on. In fact, the frustrating failure of any process to achieve consensus among some of these agencies and organizations is given in an account by Christopher Hallowell in *Holding Back the Sea.*[51] A meeting of the Technical Committee of the Coastal Wetlands Planning, Protection and Restoration Act (CWPPRA) was called to make final selections among thirty wetlands restoration projects, already cut down during the year from sixty. Various agencies took tables, carving out their turf. USACE officials faced the public. CWPPRA task force representatives took another table and covered it with volumes of papers and charts. The Department of Natural Resources (DNR), the Governor's office, the Natural Resources Conservation Service, EPA, the National Marine Fishers Service (NMFS), and U.S. Fish and Wildlife, in turn, took places they deemed to be of strategic advantage. Called to order by the Corps, as soon as the meeting began

51. Hallowell, *Holding Back the Sea,* 182–90. The exact date and location of the meeting, December 8, 1999, at the Army Corps of Engineers' New Orleans District Headquarters in New Orleans, was provided by Chris in a personal communication.

the thirty candidate projects had been pared down to twenty, apparently by negotiations invisible to the public. Conceptual differences, as well as agency territoriality, were rampant. One agency attacked the shortsightedness of another's cost-benefit analyses; still another complained about the vagueness of attention to long-term outcomes. There were differences of 'meeting style' as well: a representative from DNR authoritatively announced "a big change in philosophy" in the way restoration projects would be chosen under the Breaux Act. There were differences in politics and the analysis of economic data: $300 million spent on CWPPRA projects had thus far accomplished very little against the natural forces eating away at the coast; now the approach would be "designed to fit nature rather than political inclinations." There were differences about the application of technology: DNR proposed costs be segmented into hydrologic basins, then further divided into specific drainage areas and marshes in need of help. That proposal produced resistance, and there was murmuring that DNR's idea was too radical and required deliberation. This provided the opportunity for agencies to *retreat* from deliberation back to their own domains: someone made a motion to table the DNR proposal. It was instantaneously passed, and the meeting dissolved into fragmented reports, with key players, including the primary representative from DNR, packing up and leaving. Chris describes the end result as little more than 'rearranging deck chairs on the *Titanic*.' The different CWPPRA agencies have had a history of never working well together, each having their own cultures and interests—some focusing on barrier islands; others, like U.S. Fish and Wildlife, interested only in marshes.

In a similar vein, but at the local level, a meeting was held to consider twenty-six of *Coast 2050s* [52] strategies earmarked for the Barataria Basin, and decide which CWPPRA projects fit into those strategies. The attendees were given handouts listing projects, and told to rank them 'high,' 'medium,' and 'low,' in terms of efficacy. After initial looks of bafflement, there was murmuring, then squabbles emerged: one landowner didn't want a siphon dumping silt on his land; another was lambasted because he wouldn't let a dredge dig out a canal on his property to let freshwater

52. One of three documents that outlines a jointly developed, federal/state/local, plan to address Louisiana's massive coastal ecosystem by the year 2050, under the leadership of the Louisiana Coastal Wetlands Conservation and Restoration Task Force and the Wetlands Conservation and Restoration Authority. For an account of the Barataria project meeting, see Hallowell, *Holding Back the Sea*, 206–9.

in; an oysterman fussed about freshwater diversions threatening his beds. In this case, the meeting ended without formal adjournment, simply a shuffle of people toward the door.

Between 1970 and 1973 alone, at least eighteen reports were written, summarized in the *Environmental Atlas and Multi-Use Management Plan for South-Central Louisiana*, which made the strong point that wetlands survival was *everybody's* issue, and identified the extent and location of land loss, causation, and recommendations for multiple-use planning for the area's unique ecosystem. But while everything seemed in place for action, there was none, in part because the Louisiana Legislature's string of agencies and multiple task forces, established to *investigate* aspects of coastal environmental deterioration,[53] were unable to produce conclusions sufficiently shared to be acted upon.

It is worth noting that complexities of cross-domain interaction arise not only during the problem-solving phase of dealing with known concerns; they can precipitate future problems from consequences that are *unknown*. They mutate into Unintended Consequences (Marker 2). Perhaps the best example of this is the ironic fact that the *loss* of hurricane protection from the disappearance of wetlands is, in many respects, a direct result of flood-control measures put in place by the Army Corps of Engineers to *protect* the urban infrastructure of New Orleans.[54]

One final example of cross-domain conflict can be located among many others that occurred during rescue efforts after Hurricane Katrina. This was FEMA's failure to accept offers of help from other agencies. The city of West Palm Beach, Florida, had airplanes ready to evacuate stranded Gulf coast residents on Tuesday, August 30, but FEMA refused the offer. Louisiana Wildlife and Fisheries, on Sunday, August 28, pleaded for 300 rubber boats that FEMA ignored. The U.S. Department of Interior offered

53. Hallowell, *Holding Back the Sea*, 193–94. Chris identifies a short list of the large number of organizations that were formed: the Louisiana Advisory Commission on Coastal and Marine Resources; the Louisiana Coastal Zone Management Programs; the Coastal Protection Task Force; the Louisiana Wetland Protection Panel; the Coalition to Restore Coastal Louisiana (CRCL, which was spawned not only from environmental concerns but also those from the state's oil economy); the Wetlands Conservation and Restoration Task Force; the Governor's Office of Coastal Activities Science Advisory Panel, among others.

54. van Heerden, *The Storm*, 161.

FEMA 300 dump trucks and vans, 300 boats, 11 aircraft, and 400 law enforcement officers to help in search and rescue. FEMA turned it down.[55]

7. Progressive Degradation of Human Values and Quality of Life

Complexity associated with the degradation of human values and quality of life is, at times, immediately recognizable—as in the case of those residents of New Orleans who remained in the city, by necessity, during the storm and the aftermath of flooding. These are people, some of whose stories will be told in Chapter 3, who, if lucky, were plucked off their rooftop by a Coast Guard helicopter; if not, who saw their husband die on a wooden door as they tried to float them to Charity Hospital, or who found the remains of a grandmother in the rubble of her house six months later.

The degradation of 'humanness,' however, may often *not* be immediately recognizable. It may be something elusive or masked by what has come to pass as normalcy in a society. It may occur as a result of the loss of livelihood from business restructuring or failure—what euphemistically has been called 'rightsizing.'[56] It may occur as a consequence of demographics and geography. The high pre-Katrina proportion of elderly, poor, and handicapped residents displaced from areas such as the Lower Ninth Ward or Gert Town, for example, creates special uncertainties for reconstruction planning. It may occur in the private recesses of individual awareness, where it is experienced as anxiety and despair about what decision to make about returning—hesitancy based on the lack of medical services and health care, rising crime rates; uncertainties about livelihood and whether one's neighborhood will be secure from future flooding, whether repaired homes will be safe from mold and toxins, whether there will any possibility of recovering a semblance of the life they once knew. These uncertainties spawn still others. Uneven repopulation of neighborhoods—likely to continue into the immediate future—competes with the need to establish neighborhood integrity and stability. Thus, the degradation of factors contributing to 'quality of life' and fundamental human values becomes *progressive*. Each question up for decision seems to fragment into sixteen other questions, equally unanswerable. Coming to a decision about the initial question now becomes almost impossible. Uncertainties

---

55. Brinkley, *The Great Deluge*, 334–36.
56. A sidestep from 'downsizing,' itself a euphemism for 'layoffs.'

about one set of factors precipitate other uncertainties, creating vicious cycles of complexity.

Indeed, the most optimistic repopulation forecasts do not assume anything like a full recovery of severely flood-damaged neighborhoods even by the year 2017. New Orleans, whether it wants to or not, *will be a different city*. The question of *what* one would be returning to, therefore, is itself open to an infinite array of answers. Imagining what 'quality of life' will be like for oneself in a transformed city is not an option; New Orleans *will* be a different city.

In terms of reconstruction planning—such as in the current Unified New Orleans Plan (UNOP), and those that preceded it—one major dilemma is that even if the new city is a *result* of some plan, what will be the level of *ownership* of that new plan. Who will own the city? Whose intentions will it express? Will those who lived in the city prior to Hurricane Katrina have an active and meaningful voice in the reconstruction and reconfiguration of the city they once lived in and loved? To answer these questions is one of the primary tasks of this book.

Even if a *new* New Orleans emerges from a single plan or multiple coordinated plans—*a priori* what most would consider the best possibility for rebuilding the city—one has to recognize that 'planning' may exist only at the conceptual level. The best of plans may never be able to be fully implemented or effected *in reality*. And if the city grows, as have most cities, by an irregular, natural evolution—based on economic necessities (or greed), historical and political contingencies, environmental or demographic changes, and often pure fate—then what will *this city* become, and how different will *that* be from what existed before? Like it or not, one must acknowledge that a good deal of New Orleans' charm has lain in its almost ramshackle, put-together collection of historic homes, shotgun houses, and everything funky in-between. The *charm* results from being able to see—as a resident or a perceptive visitor—that the unique élan vital of *individuals* of enormous ethnic, racial, and cultural diversity has been stamped on this city. Its appeal exists not only in European-planned tourist districts, seen through sub-tropical foliage and bougainvillea and Spanish-inspired wrought iron galleries, but even more in the charm of its diverse neighborhoods—from Tremé to Faubourg Marigny to Holy Cross to the Irish Channel—and ultimately in the magic of individual residences, and home-grown marks of individuality expressed on them, whether some imaginative paint scheme of purple and red, or the large star and the letters 'FD' on the yellow and black 'FD Publishing' house next to the residence of Fats Domino on Caffin and Marais in the Lower Ninth Ward.

New Orleans grew into a city for its residents, but also for out-siders—those who formed the ongoing flow of a 'Second Line'[57] that more and more became part of the economic lifeblood of the city. Over time, in a benign love-hate relation with its observers, New Orleans has become a city of spectacle. Even its tradition of corrupt leadership and ineffective (also corruptible) police have oddly become part of NOLA's appeal for outsiders, who travel there as a quick visit to an American Sodom and Gomorrah—albeit, a considerably tamed one. This is tem-pered by the fact that New Orleanians have always enjoyed being the spectacle of *one another*, as well as a spectacle of others. However, it would be another thing entirely if New Orleans were to become a tourist spectacle *only*—a kind of Disney World version of itself. Unfortunately, belief that such a transformation of New Orleans could, in fact, happen is a serious worry among those who treasure its history of music, art, poetry, and architecture. Thus, at both the macro- and the micro- levels, issues of complexity of 'values' and 'quality of life' in the future identity of New Orleans as a city, as well as in the lives of individuals, abound.

LOOKING FORWARD

What is the path *Walking to New Orleans* will try to follow to emerge with an argument that an understanding of the nature of justice and the ethics of social responsibility strongly leads to adoption of some form of the concept of Participatory Design in post-disaster planning and re-construction for New Orleans and the Gulf coast? In fact, there is not a solitary path, but *multiple paths* that wander through the history of Louisiana as if through the mists of an ancient swamp. Paths of politics and economics, sociology and cultural history, geology and marine bi-

57. The 'second line' is a tradition in brass parades, extended to other musical proces-sions of benevolent societies and social clubs such as Zulu at Mardi Gras, ultimately de-rived from funeral processions that included music as part of the ceremony. The 'first line' would consist of family members and others integral to the ceremony; the 'second line' came to refer to people who followed along behind the 'first line' because they were at-tracted to the music, joining in, often dancing along. In recent times, 'second line' dances have been held independently of funerals, including at such events as convention dinners and inauguration balls.

ology, hydraulics and engineering. Yet common to all these paths is an acknowledgment that the events of Hurricanes Katrina and Rita did not occur in a vacuum. Those horrendous meteorological occurrences, and the human responses to them, were anteceded by histories—of freedoms given and taken away, of government decisions made and not made, of endless competition between attempts at urban planning and the greed of developers, between treating the coastal environment of Louisiana as a natural resource to be treasured or as a field for exploitation. In too many respects, the disaster and chaos that followed these storms were consequences *waiting to happen.*

Chapter 2, "Dark Clouds over the Gulf," discusses a primary underlying conceptual model in Western religious history for understanding the relationship between human and natural environments—the concept of 'stewardship.' Stewardship becomes problematic when it is interpreted as a basis for the exercise of human *privilege* over nature, or as the need to take *dominion* over the natural environment. Along with its inherent weaknesses, stewardship is first considered in its application to the regional environment, as an unspoken model for managing Gulf wetlands as the location of revenue-producing resources against preserving them as a natural habitat and buffer zone. Stewardship is then examined in the urban environment of greater New Orleans, where there is considered some of the history of attempts to control the Mississippi River through levee construction, the creation of levee districts, and issues of interaction with the Army Corps of Engineers. Third, stewardship is considered in its cultural milieu. This includes the changing status of race, class, economics and political power, particularly as seen in the history of voting power in New Orleans; it also includes building patterns in New Orleans, beginning with its expansion towards Lake Pontchartrain and the development of New Orleans East. The importance of neighborhoods in the life of New Orleans is emphasized through a brief characterization of some of their unique cultural qualities and their demographics. Particular attention is given to key dimensions of housing and hospitals. Throughout the chapter are highlighted various instances of social inequities that are born, grow and only fester in anticipation of the forthcoming tragedies of Hurricanes Katrina and Rita –unequal distribution of human tragedies that, in retrospect, should have been anticipated.

Chapter 3, "Katrina's World," gives a graphic and selective account of some of the human events that occurred during, and in the immediate aftermath, of the flooding from Hurricane Katrina, including those connected with Charity Hospital, massive destruction in the Lower Ninth Ward, and a nursing home in Chalmette. This is followed by a somewhat more detailed assessment of the storm's impact from the standpoint of the conjunction of topography, race, and economics. Where one lived and worked turns out to have made an enormous difference in the level of suffering and physical or economic hardship residents of New Orleans experienced. These examples will set the stage for further analyses of underlying issues of race, economics, and political power.

Chapter 4, "Katrina's Legacy: Coming to Terms with the Causes and Effects of Disaster," discusses both proximate and root causes of breaches to the New Orleans levee system, and resulting destruction. Analysis of causation includes not only geological and physical implementation of waterway control mechanisms, but cultural dimension of the problems as well. After a synopsis of proximate causes of levee breaches, east and west, with special attention to flooding resulting from storm surge up the Mississippi River–Gulf Outlet Navigational Channel (MR–GO), and short-term repair work completed and needed, consideration is given to several underlying weaknesses in protecting the City of New Orleans. These include inherent design weaknesses in the protection model of the levee system, bureaucratic impasses in the functioning of federal agencies and the Army Corps of Engineers, issues of subsidence and erosion in levee construction, and naiveté in disaster preparation exercises by local, state, and federal government. Many of these can be understood as broader consequences of the misuse of 'stewardship,' following from belief that the environment is *ours.*

This chapter also gives particular attention to the social dimensions of disaster. Where does causation reflect patterns of ignoring social needs? What complexities in the interrelationships among public leadership, service organizations, and the scientific community exacerbate long-standing environmental concerns? The demographics of post-storm changes in population, available housing, and healthcare resources are discussed in terms of the many complex issues that resulted in abortive attempts to get reconstruction planning going during the first eighteen months after Hurricane Katrina. Some complexities were natural and to be expected, given the enormity of scale of the disaster, but some were distinctly human-originated: in particular, the deflection of attention to real issues during the mayoral election race in the spring of 2006. Competing leadership strategies for at least eighteen months resulted in little or no comprehensive planning for reconstruction.

The primary purpose of *Walking to New Orleans* is not journalistic investigation in order to lay blame on individuals or agencies, but to give *constructive* analyses (and possible alternative solution strategies) of very difficult problems facing post-disaster reconstruction that reflect attributes of the 'Seven Markers of Complexity' outlined earlier. Therefore, to establish suitable boundaries—recognizing there is no way to cover the entire range of post-disaster reconstruction problems, either within New Orleans or in the Gulf coastal region beyond—focus is given to two major areas: housing and healthcare. First, has the city integrated reconstruction planning that addresses the needs of those who have *not yet* returned to New Orleans or other communities with the needs of existing residents of areas most severely damaged by flooding—areas that will likely remain vulnerable to future flooding? Second, has the city reestablished adequate medical care resources for New Orleans, given the loss of Charity Hospital and the exit of many physicians and healthcare professionals from the City?[58] Each of these problems is susceptible to internal vicious cycles, and, in some respects, in competition with one another: for example, a major factor in the decision of displaced residents to return is the question of whether they will be able to find adequate medical care in the area of their old neighborhood—a question of great import to the elderly, or those suffering from chronic conditions such as diabetes or kidney disease that require continuous treatment. At the periphery stand other important concerns as well: finding employment, safety on the streets, rebuilding the public educational system.

Chapter 5, "A Fair Voice: Ethical Principles in Reconstruction Planning," begins with some preliminary considerations of the ethics that underlie concepts critical to post-disaster planning: cooperation, coordination, reciprocity, and design. The overarching goal is to seek a basis for incorporating engineering and ethics within a common conceptual framework. The work of John Rawls is also explored as one way to think about how to incorporate into reconstruction planning a model of justice for citizens who have suffered a history of social and political inequality; who have been marginalized by economics and privilege, and, until recently, limited in access to positions of authority. To address these con-

---

58. The focus on issues of healthcare resources is largely confined to Orleans Parish.

cerns, a four-mode conceptual framework is proposed. The framework (a) outlines several fundamental principles of 'just' democratic processes, (b) identifies ethical relationships among the agents and recipients involved, (c) incorporates facts relating to responsibility to environment and demographic factors, (d) discusses how planning and implementation strategies and tactics emerge from this ethical model.

Chapter 6, "Fairness Under the Law: Legal Issues in Reconstruction Planning," discusses legal principles that derive from the Civil Rights Act of 1964 and the Voting Rights Act of 1965 that are useful in understanding how changes in access to political power come about. The discussion outlines implications of major features of the Voting Rights Act, and several critical concepts: Section 2 protections, Section 5 pre-clearance, single-member districts, and racial bloc voting. The analysis is based directly on Deanne's ten years as a trial attorney in the Voting Section of the U.S. Justice Department and more than three years as Special Counsel to the State Legislature of Louisiana on voting and redistricting issues. In addition to analysis of the relevance of voting issues to reconstruction needs in New Orleans, there is a brief comparison of with a northern minority-majority city: Springfield, Massachusetts. The chapter adds another dimension to concerns about equality of access to political power and reconstruction planning processes, and the ability of minority classes to have an voice in reconstruction decisions.

Chapter 7, "Post-Disaster Planning," reviews the four major reconstruction planning processes for New Orleans that succeeded one another in the months and years after Hurricanes Katrina and Rita: FEMA's ESF-#14, Mayor Nagin's Bring New Orleans Back Commission, the Lambert Planning Process, and the Unified New Orleans Plan (UNOP). Discussion includes their strengths and many weaknesses, the realities of trying to implement their recommendations, and especially the nature and level of citizen participation in those processes. These four processes arose during the first eighteen months after the storms, in which the city often appeared rudderless, filthy, still deeply scarred by the storm, hemorrhaging people it could least afford to lose,[59] with *long-term* planning incoherent or lacking. Economics, bureaucratic regulations, political power struggles, racial and ethnic social structure conspired again and again to create an inedible gumbo of chaos. New Orleans desperately needed a coordinated

---

59. As described by Adam Nossiter.

plan that reduced chaos, bad decisions, and misdirection. The chapter provides examples of how planning process problems are reflected in the 'Seven Markers of Complexity,' and closes with a series of first hand accounts of what various aspects of life in New Orleans are like in its post-Katrina world, in particular, independent work towards reconstruction at the neighborhood level.

Chapter 8, "Participatory Design," begins with a consideration of several writers who deal with questions of ethics and the urban ethos,[60] then discusses the idea of 'conceptual models,' before turning to an elaboration of the concept of Participatory Design itself. The concept of Participatory Design is essentially an *ethics of technology*. It promotes design through dialogue—including interracial and interfaith dialogue—and advocates for social justice and human dignity, based on participation, consensus, and coordination of effort to achieve good living and working conditions for everyone. The chapter traces the historical origins of Participatory Design, provides examples of its use in a variety of contexts, and outlines a particular extension of the concept developed by the author: the Value Analysis process. How the concept of Participatory Design might then be applied to New Orleans' attempts to reconstruct its flood-damaged neighborhoods is considered in terms of such issues as proposals to create 'cluster housing' to avoid what have been called 'jack-o-lantern' neighborhoods,[61] and the re-establishment of adequate medical and healthcare services. Most important, the chapter compares two neighborhoods in more detail: one that has been able to rebuild itself essentially as it was before the storms, one that will end up being considerably transformed. Particular attention is given to the work of local neighborhood associations in each case.

Chapter 9, "Remote Voices," considers the plight of the enormous numbers of former residents of New Orleans still living large distances away from their pre-Katrina homes. The chapter discusses the work of a number of grassroots organizations that have attempted to address vari-

60. For example, in the writings of Gideon Golany, Max Stackhouse, Peirce Lewis, and others.

61. Neighborhoods whose repopulation has been described as resembling scattered teeth among a largely toothless jack-o-lantern because all that has been able to be rebuilt is the occasional house or dwelling unit here, another there, some distance away, with wide spaces of emptiness, weeds growing through concrete slabs, lots still littered with debris in between. The media characterization is only partially accurate, as later discussion will suggest.

ous aspects of the myriad of problems displaced residents face in attempts to return. The organizations include the Louisiana Diaspora Advocacy Project, the Episcopal Diocese of Louisiana Homecoming Center, Common Ground, the Unitarian Universalist Service Committee Gulf Coast Relief program, and various projects to capture the oral histories of displaced residents.

Chapter 10, "Beyond Terrebonne," looks at the particular issues and problems faced by residents of the coastal communities of Louisiana impacted not only by Hurricanes Katrina and Rita, but also by ongoing losses and degradation of the coastal wetlands environment. These issues include changes in the oil and gas, fishing, shrimping, and oyster economies, as well as new concerns arising from the recent prospect to promote Gulf aquaculture—deepwater, offshore, net-enclosed fish farming enterprises. The chapter recounts the author's personal experiences and work with several American Indian tribal communities in the region: the United Houma Nation, the Grand Caillou-Dulac Band of Biloxi-Chitimacha, and the Isle de Jean Charles Band of Biloxi-Chitimacha. While much attention has been given to planning for the rehabilitation of Louisiana's coastal marsh ecology through the Coastal Wetlands Planning, Protection, and Restoration Act (CWPPRA) and the efforts of many non-governmental environmental organizations, the issues faced by these fragile coastal communities, whose bare continued existence is very much at stake, are not well conceptualized and have not been the subject of a great deal of consistent regional planning.

In The Postlude, "Theodicies Reconsidered," some of the problems inherent in various models for understanding the relation between the human and the natural environments, discussed in chapter 2, are revisited. This was prompted by questions of theodicy that a surprising number of ministers and politicians have felt compelled to raise in reflecting on the 'religious' significance of Hurricanes Katrina and Rita from the context of their own particular faith traditions. It is not the intention to reiterate the depths of the long history of questions of the form: How could an omnipotent but also benevolent God permit the destruction of innocent life? Those aspects of the problem of theodicy considered are ones relevant to the constructive purposes of the book. Distinctions are made among punitive and positive theodicies, and between conceptual (logical) and moral atheism. Then, four expressions of how theodicies have actually functioned in the lives and work of individuals are discussed, including one that involves a substantially new understanding of nature; it supports the equality of human and natural environments, and the primacy (before economic considerations) that must be given to the latter in rebuilding losses to Louisiana's coastal marshes and wetlands.

SCYLLA AND CHARYBDIS

In classical Greek mythology, the Argonauts must pass between the sheer rock of Scylla and the whirlpool of Charybdis, where sea spouts hurl waves into the sky—a location later identified with the Strait of Messina. In Ovid's account,[62] a fisherman, Glaucus, amazed by his catch of fish that suddenly stirred and slipped back into the sea, became possessed by an irresistible *longing* for the sea, now seen as more than merely a source of sustenance. Under this spell, the fisherman leapt into the waves, where sea-gods transformed him into a sea creature possessing green hair, sea-blue arms, and a fish's tail. The beautiful nymph Scylla, bathing in the water, saw the transformed Glaucus, and leapt onto a rocky promontory to watch from safety. Glaucus proclaimed his love for Scylla, who ran away into the land. Filled with despair, Glaucus called upon Circe, an enchantress, for a potion to melt Scylla's heart; however, Circe fell in love with Glaucus herself, poured poison into the waters where Scylla bathed, changing her into a monster, from whose body grew serpents and the heads of dogs; there she was transfixed to the rock promontory, devouring everything that came within reach.

The popular expression derived from the myth of Scylla and Charybdis is that of being caught 'between a rock and a hard place.' This simplistic turn of phrase is rendered considerably more interesting by ac-knowledging the passions that run through Ovid's account of its origins. The longings and enchantments of Glaucus, Sylla, and Circe represent the affective dimension of humankind's dual relation to the natural world. We are fearful of its dangers, to be sure, but also enraptured, absorbed by nature—even, like Glaucus, transformed *back into* the natural world, of which, like all other living creatures, we were always a part.

In not dissimilar ways, those who live on the fringes of Coastal Louisiana[63] exist in a dual relation to their complex natural environment.

---

62. *Metamorphoses*, XIII–XIV.

63. New Orleans, despite being some 100 miles upstream from the outlet of the Mississippi River, is also (and increasingly) on the fringe of the Gulf, since nearby Lake

On the one hand, *captured* by this world, continually endangered by it—yet also *captivated* by a wetlands wilderness with its unique flora and fauna, its characteristic marine life and waterfowl.[64] The duality of the relationship of human and natural is a dynamic one. Whether perilous or providential, for those whose lives are dependent on the sea, it is rarely a matter of choice. One lives there because one's family was there. For some, it is inconceivable to live anywhere else—as if the sea were the boundaries of meaning and purpose.

As an environment, the Louisiana coast can be a cruel lover: tropical storms and the hurricanes of summer and fall are ever present, lurking behind the thunderhead clouds that seem to constantly loom at the edges of the horizon of the Gulf. It is an environment of great beauty and power, but also one of foreboding. Many times in its past history, but especially during the late summer of 2005, citizens of this mystical region came to understand just how deadly nature's embrace could be. Whether the future will be one of continued degradation and death, or, in the aftermath of Hurricanes Katrina and Rita, the possibility for a renewed relationship with nature, will be among the questions explored in this book.[65]

Borgne is simply an extension of its waters.

64. It is a wilderness that now bears the many marks of human hands—oil rigs, pipeline canals, navigational channels; exploitation that is as destructive of this natural environment as nature may be of the human presence in it. Yet the forces of nature have never *singled out* human forms of life for destruction.

65. In the *Tao-Te Ching,* Lao Tzu says, "Heaven and Earth are not humane (*jen*). They regard the ten thousand things as straw dogs." *Jen* is also rendered as benevolent, implying nature is *unkind*. Humans are like straw dogs, and if Tao in nature is *unkind*, this has been interpreted to mean Tao is *impersonal*, beyond the reach of prayer. That is incorrect. While Tao is not a person, even a *supreme* person, neither is Tao an impersonal mechanism, the bare patterns of nature unavailable to human discernment. Tao is an invariable *dynamic* in nature of which we are part, and with which we must get in *attunement*. See the translation of the Tao-Te Ching in Wing-Tsit Chan, *A Source Book in Chinese Philosophy,* 141, and further discussion in the Appendix, 788–89. See also R. R. N. Ross, "Non-Being and Being in Taoist and Western Philosophy," *Religious Traditions,* Vol. I, No. 2, 24–38.

Houses Regurgitating Insides
(October, 2005)

Collected Debris
(October, 2005)

2

Dark Clouds Over the Gulf

THE CONCEPT OF STEWARDSHIP

How did people come to form the particular attitudes toward nature by which they lived and guided their economies? In the Western Judeo-Christian world, the conceptual model for understanding the relation between human and natural orders has been largely framed by the Biblical notion of 'stewardship.' However, while this model of the relation between humankind and nature operates very deeply within Western cultural values, as it is depicted in Hebrew Scripture 'stewardship' is inherently an ethically *paradoxical* notion.

'Stewardship' can exist as both a religious, or quasi-religious, framework, but operates in the secular world as well, by supporting various attitudes about how humans feel entitled to use the natural environment as a resource. Moreover, distinctly different models of the relationship between the human and natural orders have existed in other cultures throughout history. Deeply embedded in Chinese culture, for example, the symbol of Yin and Yang presents, in its image of fluid, reciprocating dark and light, yielding and expanding shapes—each containing a seed of the other—a symbol that embodies a whole way of life. The symbol is based on the perception that nature, in its entirety, consists of 'mutually correlated opposites'—opposing but also complementary, and ultimately *harmonious*, forces. These forces make up *all* aspects of life; forces seen in the natural cycles of the seasons, and agriculture based on those cycles—the annual flooding of rivers, the periods of growth and harvest when the floods recede. Yin, conceived of as earth, is female, dark, passive, absorbing. Yang, conceived of as heaven, is male, light, active, penetrating.

Both suggest the interplay and *mutual interdependence* of the human and the natural world.

It remains an open question the extent to which many non-Western cultures maintain a concept of nature as a totality or unified system at all (as opposed to simply interacting with specific natural phenomena, such as mountains, seas, celestial bodies, certain animals). Models that continue to operate among contemporary cultures such as those of Polynesian and Melanesian groups in the South Pacific (or that have existed historically among native American Indian tribes such as the Iroquois, Algonquin, and Wampanoag) seem to function through the notion of a force *within* nature (*mana, orenda, manitou, etc.*) that is imbued with trans-human power. This force is sometimes held is awe or regarded as sacred. It can function in an ethical capacity by regulating human behavior with respect to the natural kingdom (both plant and animal). Most importantly, it places human and natural kind far more on a par with one another than does the intrinsically hierarchical notion of 'stewardship.'

To better understand the historical legacy of the Hebraic concept of stewardship, it is useful to briefly put it in perspective with two other models that, in a sense, represent the extremes of a spectrum of views about nature. Each in its own way raises the question of whether our relationship to nature *is* a religious one, and on what basis we have ethical responsibilities toward nature. One can surmise that, as societies grew more complex, so did the manner of their interaction with the world around them. In their early phases, the attitudes of many ancient cultures toward nature may have been primarily a consequence of the predominant geographical and climatic conditions of the immediate environment. The models with which these early societies operated were correspondingly simplistic. For example, one might expect regularity in the terrain and predictability in weather to elicit feelings of harmony and oneness with nature. Contrariwise, where the land was hostile and the climate unpredictable, one might find a picture of nature identified with demonic powers to be controlled or an enemy to be defeated. Historically, such a contrast appears to be illustrated by the civilizations of ancient Mesopotamia and ancient Egypt.

In ancient Mesopotamia—a region that extended from the Persian Gulf to Armenia, with settlements dating as early as around 5000 BCE— networks of canals were constructed between the Tigris and Euphrates rivers to render the land fertile. The remains of these canals can be seen today in modern Iraq. For the ancient Mesopotamians, the ability of humans to live within the cosmic order was never something *given*. Order had to be *wrested* from nature through warfare with its forces. The dominant feeling in Sumerian[1] and Akkadian[2] myths is one of battle. Nature is chaotic and unpredictable, and must first be overcome for humans to create a hospitable world. In the Akkadian creation epic, *Enuma elis,* for example, nature is portrayed as a primordial chaos—the monster Tiamat, slain by Marduk, who creates the world from parts of her body. After Tiamat is subdued, Marduk then is able to establish a cosmos that is ordered and structured for human life:

> Then the lord paused to view her dead body,
> That he might divide the monster and do artful works.
> He split her like a shellfish into two parts:
> Half of her he set up and ceiled it as sky,
> Pulled down the bar and posted guards.
> He bade them to allow not her waters to escape.
> He crossed the heavens and surveyed the regions . . .
> He constructed stations for the great gods,
> Fixing their astral likenesses as constellations.
> He determined the year by designating the zones:
> He set up three constellations for each of the twelve months.
> After defining the days of the year [by means] of (heavenly) figures,
> He founded the station of Nebiru [the planet Jupiter] to determine their (heavenly) bands,
> That none might transgress or fall short . . .
> In her [Tiamat's] belly he established the zenith.
> The Moon he caused to shine, the night (to him) entrusting.[3]

1. A non-Semitic people of southern Mesopotamia whose earliest settlements date as far back as the Ubaid period, 5300 BCE, and who are credited with inventing the cuneiform system of writing. The term 'Sumerian' may have been given by their Akkadian successors; the Sumerian people referred to themselves simply as 'black-headed people.' Constant wars among Sumerian city-states developed military technology to a high level.

2. A Semitic language, using the cuneiform writing system derived from the Sumerians, dating from ca 2500 BCE, spoken especially by Assyrians and Babylonians, and the empire founded by Sargon of Akkad after his conquest of Sumerian city-states beginning ca 2334 BCE.

3. Speiser, transl., "The Creation Epic" in Pritchard, ed. *The Ancient Near East: An Anthology of Texts and Pictures,* 35–36. See also the translation by Stephanie Dalley in *Myths from Mesopotamia.*

The historical basis for this epic may have been Mesopotamia's own struggle to establish its cities from the ravaging flood plains of the Tigris and Euphrates. In an environment perceived as hostile to order and civilization, people sought to *subdue* the wilderness, rather than work in harmony with it. Unfortunately, this also led to ecological disaster. One of the earliest—the destruction of the Cedars of Lebanon—is depicted in the Gilgamesh epic (the first great heroic epic) by the slaying of Huwawa, the protector of the forests. We can thus see the problems of ecology in the earliest human literature.

Turning to ancient Egypt one finds a quite different model for understanding the relation between human and nature. Un-unified settlements along the Nile in the Chalcolithic or first 'pre-dynastic period' appeared as early as 5500 BCE. However, the unification of Egypt, along with the advent of writing, is traditionally placed at the beginning of the First Dynasty[4] of Menes,[5] who is credited with joining Upper and Lower Egypt into a single, centralized monarchy, ca 2925 BCE, founding the capital at Memphis, as well as various irrigation works. However, Menes is a creation of later record, and other objects dated from this period suggest Aha, probable successor to Narmer, as the actual founder of the First Dynasty, an argument reinforced by the size and grandeur of Aha's tomb at Abydos.[6] The world of ancient Egypt ended with the Thirtieth Dynasty of Nekhtnebef (Nechtanebo I), who ruled from 380–362 BCE, and the conquest of Alexander the Great, 332 BCE. In contrast to Mesopotamia, one finds with Egypt the perception of a natural environment far more hospitable. The regularity of the annual flooding of the Nile was relatively predictable, and supported Egyptian religious attitudes that generally saw

4. Despite the fact that some early pre-dynastic kings left behind stylized symbols and signs that contained information beyond their being simple pictorial images.

5. Called so by 3rd century BCE historian, Manetho; also referred to as Min by Herodotus.

6. The earliest king-list is found on the Palermo Stone, a large basalt stele fragment held in the Palermo Archaeological Museum in Sicily, dated to the Fifth Dynasty (ca 2494–2345 BCE), inscribed with hieroglyphic texts describing reigns of kings of the first five dynasties. The text includes mythological rulers up to Horus who is said to have given the throne to Menes. The Narmer Palette, discovered in 1898 by British Egyptologists James Quibell and Frederick Green in the ruins at Hierakonpolis, dated to a 3100 BCE, prominently displayed in the Egyptian Museum in Cairo, is a greenish stone shaped like a shield. At the top register of the palette, above two serpopards (long-necked lions) held on leashes by two bearded men, there is carved a figure, shown in stride, of an early Egyptian ruler identified as Narmer.

nature as rational and periodic. The natural world was the locus of cycles human life could depend upon. Indeed, the daily birth, journey, and death of the sun, and the annual rebirth of the river became the two central features that dominated much of Egyptian life and religious speculation. Rather than combatants with nature, Egyptian gods were themselves *reflections* of nature, displaying ways in which the natural world was life-supporting and beneficial to human existence. Re, a deity supreme and worshipped above all others, was the Sun God whose daily movements were the paradigm of regularity. Similarly, Osiris, the god of dying and rising vegetation, symbolized cycles within the physical universe from which humans could fined nurture. What is perhaps most striking is the perception that nature itself constitutes a symmetry. For just that reason, order did not need to be *imposed* upon nature. Nature was already compatible with human life and rationality.

This brief comparison shows two *extremes* of human attitudes toward nature: nature as *foreign* to human reason, the enemy of human endeavor vs. nature as *compatible* with human reason. But how do we, in contemporary Western culture, understand and incorporate the natural world into our religious or secular lives? What does 'nature' *mean* to us? If the extremes of ancient Mesopotamia and Egypt represent the *boundaries* of our understanding (nature as friend vs. nature as foe)—pictures that are certainly incomplete but, nevertheless, *simple*—then how do *we* grasp 'nature'?

Contemporary Earth Day prompts many to try to find a spiritual basis for a renewed relationship to the natural world, its study, and to the concerns of ecology. But the attitudes toward nature of Western culture have already been, in large part, informed by the legacy of the ancient Israelites, as expressed in Hebrew Scriptures. The Bible, of course, is a document that has influenced the world far beyond any claims it makes about nature. Nevertheless, Hebrew Scripture does embody a picture of the relations between persons and nature that operates very deeply in our historical consciousness. That Biblical picture is a paradoxical one: humans are raised *above* nature at the same time that they are created as *part* of it.

On the one hand, *both* humans and the natural world alike are the creation of God. "The earth is the Lord's" expresses the fact that everything, for the ancient Israelites, owes its very existence to God—a God, moreover, who wholly transcends his own creation. God created the world, rules it from above, retains ultimate dominion over both humankind and nature. In this way, nature is able to be seen as the *manifestation* of divine power. The natural world is itself the locus of the *revelation* of God, echoed in Psalm 19:1, where it is proclaimed that "The heavens are telling the glory of God; and the firmament proclaims his handiwork."[7] Further, since the cause for any existence is a divine act, all created things—plants, beasts of every kind, even monsters—are essentially good. Contrary to other cultures of the ancient Near East, the Israelites saw *all* animals, clean and unclean, as having their proper place in the order of things. Yet while goodness in the natural order is universal, the goodness of plants and animals and humankind is not something they possess *intrinsically*. All goodness is *derivative* from God. This is a primary theological message of the opening verses of Genesis, and its interpretation as a doctrine of *creatiio ex nihilo*—that the *mere fact that a world exists* is good because God has imbued it with goodness. God's act of creation is an expression of divine goodness. In this sense, all living forms are equally dependent on God, since God is the ultimate source of all being and goodness.

On the other hand, and not necessarily consistent with the former, Hebrew Scriptures establish the relationship of God, nature, and humans as a hierarchical one, governed by the concept of 'stewardship.' As a steward is the one who manages the affairs of an estate on behalf of his lord or employer, the Biblical notion of stewardship entrusts nature to mankind, God's servant, who then has dominion over it. In Genesis 1:26–28:

> Then God said, "Let us make humankind in our image, after our likeness: and let them have dominion over the fish of the sea, and over the birds of the air, and over the cattle, and over all the wild animals of the earth, and over every creeping thing that creeps upon the earth." So God created humankind in his own image, in the image of God he created them: male and female he created them. And God blessed them, and God said to them, "Be fruitful and multiply, and fill the earth and subdue it; . . ."

"Image of God" in this passage entails an important analogy: God : human :: human : nature. The analogy, that is, establishes a hierarchy of authority. As God has authority over humans, humans have dominion over the earth: we have the authority to rule it, to subdue it, to use it for our own purposes. This tradition of seeing the earth as 'ours to be used' is, unfortunately, often extended to the mistaken conclusion that the earth

---

7. This hymn to God links both the creation of the sun within the heavens and the giving of the law that binds humanity to God.

belongs to us. Any number of both historical and contemporary religious thinkers[8] have tried to harmonize the language of Hebrew Scripture with respect for the earth or the concerns of modern ecology. Nevertheless, it is a very radical statement of human authority over the earth that gets expressed in Genesis 9:2–3:

> "The fear and dread of you [humankind] shall be upon every beast of the earth, and upon every bird of the air, upon everything that creeps on the ground, and on all the fish of the sea; into your hand they are delivered. Every moving thing that lives shall be food for you; and as I gave you the green plants, I give you everything."

The picture generated by this passage is not a comfortable one. Indeed, God appears to have revised an earlier command of vegetarianism (Genesis 1:29–30), extending the human dominion over creation.

There is, of course, another side to stewardship: namely, our moral responsibility for the natural order, also established in God's act of creation. We may rule but we must also care for nature. Our relation to the natural order is governed by our moral obligation to God and obedience to God's will. Nature is *entrusted* to us by God. Thus, while we may have the freedom to use it, we are also accountable for that use. Nowhere does our freedom become a warrant for abuse.

The problem is that our use of the natural environment is often not perceived as abuse because of the very complexity of that environment. Oil and gas companies may not have had the *intention* to erode Louisiana's coastal marshes and wetlands; they simply did not foresee—might argue *could not have* foreseen—the damage their drilling or cutting canals through the marshlands would cause. This view, of course, is a best case premise. The borderline between unforeseen—or unforeseeable—and sheer carelessness or indifference is hard to draw. The evidence is strong that oil well drillers were always simply able to get away with dumping all the toxic muck that came up during the drilling process—including radioactive mud—right next to the well as long as it was enclosed by levees.[9] What made the ethical borderline between unforeseen and indifferent

---

8. Both Catholic and Protestant, for example: St. Francis of Assisi and Paul Tillich. See Paul Santmire, *The Travail of Nature: The Ambiguous Ecological Promise of Christian Theology*, which traces both spiritual and ecological motifs in Christian theology, the latter concerned to express the human spirit's rootedness in nature and the biophysical order, emphasizing God's immanence as the power of life.

9. Hallowell, *Holding Back the Sea*, 84.

even harder to see was the fact that re-vegetation in many cases would grow right up to the edges of those toxic pits, making everything, from a distance, look fine and healthy.

The philosophical position of *Walking to New Orleans* is that the concept of 'stewardship' is most likely an inherently flawed notion, because it retains the picture that the natural order is without rights of its own, without *intrinsic* rights of preservation. One sees the flaw of 'stewardship' in arguments that essentially preserve the fundamental *rights* of the human over the natural—arguments that make the case for preserving the natural environment so that natural resources will still be available *for human use* in future generations. That argument, while giving the appearance of ecological concern, does not give up the underlying picture that nature is *ours* to be used and to control.

Within Western thought, there have been alternatives to the Biblical concept of stewardship. In American culture, perhaps the most significant was the view of nature expressed by the New England Transcendentalists in the second quarter of the nineteenth century. The Transcendentalists embodied a loosely held, rather idealistic, system of reflection based on a belief in the essential *unity* of all of natural creation. Ethically, this was accompanied by faith in the *innate* goodness of humankind. Replacing the authority of Scripture or evidence from miracles, individual experience became the primary means for revealing fundamental religious truths. The New England Transcendentalists had multiple influences: Neoplatonism, newly translated Hindu texts, mystics such as Swedenborg and Jakob Böhme.

Ralph Waldo Emerson represents probably the most ethically reasoned view of nature. After his brief ministry, Emerson focused on his direct personal encounter with nature as the form through which any understanding could be expressed of the human relationship with divine power—power now located not in some entity *beyond* creation, but immediately manifest within the human spirit.[10] This was revealed not in the historical evidences of miracles nor in the authority of scripture, but in direct and immediate experience. To appreciate Emerson's understanding of our *ethical* relationship with nature, one can reflect on the following passages from his essay *Nature* of 1849:

10. While in Paris Emerson evidently observed Antoine-Laurent de Jussieu's collection of natural specimens arranged in their developmental order, confirming his belief that the human relationship to nature was a spiritual one.

There are days which occur in this climate, at almost any season
of the year, wherein the world reaches its perfection, when the air,
the heavenly bodies, and the earth, make a harmony, as if nature
would indulge her offspring . . .

[In nature] is a sanctity which shames our religions . . . Here
we find nature to be the circumstance which dwarfs every other
circumstance, and judges like a god all
men that come to her.

The incommunicable trees begin to persuade us to live with
them, and quit our life of solemn trifles. Here no history, or church,
or state, is interpolated on the divine sky and the immortal year.[11]

Nature is always consistent, though she feigns to contravene her
own laws. She keeps her laws, and seems to transcend them.[12]

Emerson's natural world is the Deist's vision of an underlying harmony in the cosmos, including humankind's place in that world. It is a
vision that, in a number of respects, reflects the 'principle of plenitude,'
expressed by Neoplatonists beginning with Plotinus in the *Enneads*,[13]
according to which the universe is an infinite series of forms, a super-
abundance of the maximum types of diverse existences emanating from a
primordial reality, the source of rationality and moral goodness.

Perhaps the most notable twentieth century heir to Emerson's vision
of nature is Arne Naess, Professor Emeritus at the University of Oslo, who,
in the 1970s, became associated with the movement of *deep ecology* and
the belief that nature has intrinsic value, apart from its practical usefulness to human beings.[14] In this view, nature has not derivative but *inherent* value. All forms of life should therefore be allowed to flourish and
fulfill their evolutionary destinies. The spiritual dimension to *deep ecology*
contrasts it with environmental concerns that are based primarily on the

11. Emerson, "Nature," 541.

12. Ibid., 547.

13. With certain elements derived from Plato's 'idea of the good' as seen *The Republic*,
and Aristotle's notion of a continuum of scales of existence.

14. Naess's own term was *ecosophy T* (T standing for Tvergastein, 'crossed stones,' the
mountain hut on the Hallingskarvet range where he did much of his writing). Naess
was evidently greatly influenced by Rachel Carson's *Silent Spring* of 1962, and while his
primary academic interests centered around set theory, as applied to natural language,
extending the work of Euler, from around 1970 onwards Naess devoted most of his energies to environmental activism.

environment's economic utility, its aesthetic appeal—in short, its value for *human* use and needs.[15]

For many in both the secular and religious world, the concept of 'deep ecology' represents a deep emotional and spiritual connection to the earth. One sees it manifested in the beliefs and practices of neo-Pagans, or earth-centered faiths, as well as in more traditional religious groups, such as Unitarian Universalists, whose 'Seventh Principle' is to affirm and honor the "interdependent web of all existence of which we are a part."

Alternatives to the concept of 'stewardship' have their place—both historically and in contemporary secular thought—but they do not alter the fact that the underlying model which frames Western culture's view of the relationship between humankind and nature is that of a *hierarchical* relationship. The Biblical model creates an inescapable logic in the permission given to humankind to have *dominion* over the natural world, even in the context of ethical obligations to be its caretaker. Often this permission is but a step away from the freedom for abuse.

Why do we argue that? Because there are extensions of the underlying *logic* of this relationship that can easily be distorted when the immediate authority governing human behavior is *another human* to whom there are obligations *rather than* (or at least in addition to) those toward God. Stewardship includes human ethical responsibility for the natural order—but as a *created* order, to a universe given as a 'gift' within which we can exist. Our ethical responsibility for nature, therefore, is ultimately governed by our obligations to that which is *superior* to us, to that which gives our existence its opportunity. In addition, in Hebrew Scripture, this means *obedience to the will* of that which is superior to us. That *will* which 'gives us the opportunity to exist' is *personal*—something to which we have a relation *as human*. Religiously, the freedom of our gift of stewardship of nature is derived from a *primary* obligation—our accountability to the *will* of God. But the bare logic itself is simpler—our accountability is to a *power that supersedes our individual power*. And the translation of this logic into the world of economics, and human uses of the natural environment as a resource, is the tendency to always ensure that one has *fully satisfied* those powers and obligations immediately superior to us—those of the captain, the boss, or the owner. How does one know when 'satisfac-

---

15. The American ecologist, Aldo Leopold, also expressed such a deep ecological spirituality in his essay "Land Ethic," published posthumously in *A Sand County Almanac* in 1948.

tion' is achieved? We often don't. In the world of economics and commerce which involves taking resources directly from the natural environment—commercial fishing and shrimping, oil and gas production—it becomes natural to make sure one 'takes enough' to meet the highest possible expectations of those 'powers superior to us'—the stakeholders and owner of the fishing vessel, the shareholders of the oil or gas corporation. The commercial fisherman's goal thus becomes the monstrous, most bounteous catch. The oil prospector keeps looking and digging and erecting rigs until another mother lode is found. It is stewardship's *hierarchy of authority*, in particular, that allows human behavior to slide all too easily into abuse. For those whose living is based on availability of natural resources, how much taken from nature is 'enough' to satisfy those superior powers for whom one works, who underwrite one's labor? Why not just take *more* to ensure the owners' and shareholders' profit? What is sent in motion is a process of continuous escalation: all-season fishing operations, twice as many shrimp trawlers, larger oyster barges, more and more rigs that can serve increasing oil and gas demands.

In contrast with the Biblical concept of stewardship, where recognition of a *creator* power is, at the same time, the recognition of a hierarchical structure of authority, there is a very different logic that existed among the Wampanoag tribes of New England of the late seventeenth century. It is instructive to look at them as a point of comparison. Observed by settlers like Roger Williams, the Indians' creator power that made trees, corn, and other crops grow seems also to have been a force that rewarded those who were good with plenty and the companionship of friends, and punished evil doers to a state of restless wandering and penury. Williams, in 1643, noted a more ritualized expression of gratitude: if an individual received any good in hunting, fishing, or harvest, they acknowledged a particular superior power in it, Cautantowwit or Kiehtan (that Williams identified as 'God').[16] One cannot simply equate the superior power acknowledged by the Wampanoag with the 'God' of Western theology. However, there does appear to have been a way in which the sixteenth and seventeenth century New England Indians conjoined the power that existed in *nature*—which created life and also produced sustenance for the Indians—with a *moral and ethical structure* that provided a basis for judging and guiding their human behavior.

16. Several of the thoughts discussed here emerged through my many conversations with the Rev. Robert Thayer, a historian of New England Indian tribal groups.

It is particularly revealing to see how the logic of this played out for the Wampanoag, in contrast to the logic of the Biblical notion of stewardship. By the seventeenth century, agriculture had largely replaced hunting as the principle source of food for Indians in southern New England. The Wampanoag, nevertheless, still maintained continuity with their pre-agricultural past through beliefs in which they saw themselves as members of a large natural system, their relationship to which was expressed in the idea that the fruits of nature, including the land itself, were entities of value to be used with care and reciprocated for; they were not the exclusive possessions of human beings. The difference of this logic can be seen especially in certain rituals performed in hunting (removing the heart, left rear foot, tongue of a moose before preparing venison). These rituals expressed the belief that the animals had to be respected as sources of spiritual power, and had to be properly addressed and treated even as they were consumed. One effect of this was to discourage the excessive killing of game, and support the awareness that a balanced dependency relationship needed to exist between humans and non-humans. Thus, every act of *taking from nature* was accompanied by an intentional act of *giving back to nature*. Only certain fruits of nature, domesticated grains like corn, were regarded as an essentially infinite source of food.

STEWARDSHIP IN THE REGIONAL ENVIRONMENT

The alluvial plain of the Mississippi delta at its edge with the Gulf of Mexico is a landscape both open and mysterious. Formed by deposits of alluvial soil over centuries from rivers meandering through the Midwest, Coastal Louisiana is a world dominated by sky above and water below—broken up, like a puzzle, into a liquid prairie of *cheniers* and salt marsh hummocks and islets and fields of sea grass. In the sky above is a flyway for five million migratory birds[17] as well as hundreds of indigenous wildfowl. In the waters below are the delicate nutrients that support an entire micro-ecosystem as well as numerous species of fish and shellfish.

Despite efforts to harmonize the model of stewardship in Hebrew Scripture with contemporary environmental awareness,[18] there are nu-

17. Data from Louisiana Department of Wildlife and Fisheries.

18. Or support it, as does Wendell Berry, by merging the Judeo-Christian concept of stewardship with the Buddhist doctrine of "right livelihood." See Wendell Berry, "The Gift

merous examples of how the more negative aspects of that model have been operative in Louisiana's coastal region. The goal here is to describe only a select few that are reflective of the Seven Markers of Complexity described earlier. Major issues are well known: the loss of wetlands as a protective buffer zone and natural habitat, competing interests among oil and gas and fishing and oyster gathering activities, the degradation of water as a supplier of nutrients to marine species. But mere knowledge of issues doesn't entail solutions. Before considering these matters in greater detail, it is revealing to hear voiced two different views of nature in natu- ralistic, rather than theological or scientific, terms.

The first image is a passage from Rachel Carson's *Under the Sea Wind* in which we view nature on its own terms—as if *we* were not present. We see from the eyes of a large, black-winged bird, measuring its progress by shadows across the water. In this vision nature's logic operates by its own mysterious but definitive rhythms.

> The island lay in shadows only a little deeper than those that were swiftly stealing across the sound from the east . . . Here the marsh grasses waded boldly out into dark water . . . With the dusk a strange bird came to the island from its nesting grounds on the outer banks. Its wings were pure black, and from tip to tip their spread was more than the length of a man's arm. It flew steadily and without haste across the sound, its progress measured by shadows that little by little were dulling the bright water path. The bird was called Rynchops, the black skimmer. As he neared the shore of the island the skimmer drifted closer to the water, bringing his dark form into strong silhouette against the gray sheet, like the shadow of a great bird that passed unseen above . . . At the last spring tide, when the thin shell of the new moon brought the water lapping among the sea oats that fringed the dunes of the banks, Rynchops and his kin had arrived on the outer barrier strip of sand between sound and sea. They had journeyed northward from the coast of Yucatan where they had wintered . . . Before the moon had come to the full, Rynchops had remembered the island . . . Through most of the night the skimmers would feed, gliding on slender wings above the water in search of the small fishes that had moved in with the tide to the shelter of the grassy shallows. The skimmers loved nights of darkness and tonight thick clouds lay between the water and the moon's light.[19]

of the Good Land."

19. Carson, "Flood Tide" in *Under the Sea Wind.*

The words of Cajun swamper, Jimmy Bourque, about the Atchafalaya Basin,[20] on the other hand, describe a radically different perception of nature. This is nature already altered by the intervention of human commerce, a vision of the purity of nature lost.

> What [the Corps of Engineers] want to do is cut channels from the river into the swamp to run fresh water in there. But what they gonna do when they run fresh water in there, common sense will tell you, after 2 years of high water it's gonna silt up the whole swamp. Oh, they can't stop the sand. After two years the swamp won't be anymore good. They'll have to think of something else . . . You remember Bayou Eugene, a beautiful bayou. Now the river's got to come to 10 feet before you can travel it. If they want to keep the Basin like it is, they should shut off all the entrances to the swamp and let the water back into the swamp from the south. That way, you'll save what's left of the Basin . . .
>
> I hate to see the Basin get that-a-way. It's dying off. Nobody knows about it dying off unless they're in it. I can see what's happening year after year that cause me to advise my sons not to try to make a living fishing in the Basin. It's sad, but that's the way it is. If the first oil company that ran a pipeline across the Atchafalaya Basin would've plugged it off right at the river, there would be a difference right now that's unbelievable. You wouldn't have that silt in the swamps. You'd still have a beautiful swamp. But it's too far gone now, they done cut so many sections into it, shrunk it up . . . I've seen some beautiful lakes ruined with pipeline canals. Beautiful places. Cochon Bay, for instance. It was the most beautiful swamp you ever seen. Right now that lake is all growed over and choked up with willows and other hardwood trees—it's not good for anything. The levees they built along each side causes a change in the flow of water, and the fish that used to come from the river to spawn in the swamp don't go there anymore . . . What you gonna do without a spawn? If that dies off, we won't have anything.[21]

20. The Atchafalaya Basin is the nation's largest swamp wilderness, a 20 mile wide swath on either side of the river whose name derives from the Choctaw *hach falaia* (= Long River), approximately 150 miles long from north of Krotz Spring to its delta below Morgan City where it meets the Gulf. The basin is a maze of bayous, bald cypress swamps, and marshes, giving way to Spartina grass marshes at the delta, populated by three hundred bird species, crawfish, shrimp, crabs, frogs, snakes, nutrias, beavers, raccoons, foxes, alligators, black bears, and, since the eighteenth century, a small number of Cajun fishermen and trappers. The author has kayaked many, many miles in the Atchafalaya wilderness around Little Bayou Sorrel.

21. Guirard, *Cajun Families of the Atchafalaya*, 8–9.

The eco-regions of southwest Louisiana—both the coastal marshes and the swamplands that feed them—are *not* simply economic resources. For those whose history with the area goes back generations, the natural environment is sacred land, sacred water. This passion is expressed in the words of another Cajun swamper, musician and friend Errol Verret, in his *Ballad of the Atchafalaya.*

> There's a place in the big woods/In the south of Louisiana
> A place where people work hard/To wrest a living from the big
>   cypress swamp
> A life that I love and worship/It is not always good
> But it's a life/That is dear to my heart . . .
> A paddle in my hand, a gun at my side
> I leave to find food/So that the dinner table will not be bare
> I follow the coulees/Along the giant live oaks
> As I drink from my jug/I think of my family far behind
> I think of the future/I think of the past
> And I wonder/What will become of this place
> I hope to see a future/Where the young will comprehend and respect
> What the eyes of the old people/Have seen in the past[22]

The Louisiana coastal wetlands are an ecosystem of enormous national significance, even as an acre of it washes into the sea every half hour, bringing it closer to extinction. In economic terms, billions of dollars in seafood production, oil and gas revenues, commercial shipping, and a wetlands buffer for coastal communities and the City of New Orleans[23] are at risk. But beyond that, an entire culture is threatened. In this sense, all the

22. Lyrics and translation from Cajun French by Errol Verret, reprinted in Guirard, *Cajun Families of the Atchafalaya,* 41. Errol, who lives near Catahoula and whom we have known since 1994, was Michael Doucet and Beausoleil's first accordion player, later playing with Al Berard and the Basin Brothers. Errol is a unique, gentle soul, who exemplifies the necessity of multiple talents life in the swamps of the Basin demands: builder of pirogues and hand-made accordions, tender of catfish nets, preparer of fried alligator, musician and lyrical poet. Errol is one of the few musicians that guardian of Cajun tradition Marc Savoy holds as being worthy of absolute respect (Marc puts it in more colorful, but unprintable, language).

23. An ominous forecast of the consequences of Louisiana's wetlands failure to provide vital hurricane protection for New Orleans was documented less than a year before Hurricane Katrina, October 2004, in Joel Bourne's "The Big Uneasy. Gone With the Water," *National Geographic,* Vol. 206, No. 4, 88–105. It pictured what 18 feet of water on Bourbon Street from a Cat Five storm might look like to suddenly sobered bar denizen onlookers, and noted that "even the Red Cross no longer opens hurricane shelters in New Orleans, claiming the risk to its workers is too great."

complex problems that exist in the stewardship of the regional environment of Gulf coast Louisiana lead to the seventh Marker of Complexity: the Progressive Degradation of Human Values and Quality of Life.

The Coastal Wetlands Planning, Protection and Restoration Act (Public Law 101–646, Title III-CWPPRA) was authorized by Congress and signed into law by President George Bush in 1990, and reauthorized in 2001 until 2009. That Act is perhaps only the most visible attempt to exercise a more ethically grounded stewardship of the coastal wetlands. The Breaux Act lists some 64 projects constructed, with 63 additional projects approved and in the design phase. But CWPPRA also exists among some 403 *other* coastal restoration projects, including 50 State-funded projects, 94 of the Parish coastal Wetlands Restoration Program, 173 Vegetation Planting Program project sites, and 22 other federally assisted projects.[24] CWWPRA was preceded by a 1998 report, "Coast 2050: Toward a Sustainable Coastal Louisiana" that outlined a complex of strategies, informed by ongoing scientific research on wetlands restoration, culminating in costs in the *billions* of dollars. Refining these strategies into something workable, and managing the various federal, state, local agencies, and non-governmental organizations, each with interests in being involved, has seemed to generate an insurmountable task. Anything approaching true and sustained coordination has been elusive. In terms of Markers of Complexity, the history is a classic instance of the *absence* of productive Cross-Domain Interactions, with a considerable flavoring of Problems of Scale.

There is also a financial 'bottom line': current funding levels, as well as those anticipated, by no means support all the necessary restoration projects required to establish a sustainable ecosystem. Stewardship (in its positive sense) may exist in theory—or in the idealizations of various organizations—but, if it is not funded, it simply turns out to be indistinguishable from meaningless gestures or spinning wheels; worse, the absence of funding may reflect despair that a myriad of abuses has left an environment too far gone to be reclaimed.[25]

24. Belhadjali et al., *Coastal Restoration Division Project Annual Project Reviews: December 2002.*

25. The USGS National Wetlands Research Center at the University of Louisiana at Lafayette puts the cost at $14 billion or more (a highly conservative estimate) to restore Louisiana's coast, but the cost of *inaction* at more than $100 billion.

In addition to examining ecosystem problems of Coastal Louisiana in terms of certain 'Markers of Complexity' they appear to represent, they will also be assessed against two additional attributes: *impact* and *magnitude*. 'Impact' refers the proportional contribution that alleviating some destructive environmental condition could have in improving quality of life for both human and natural kind; 'magnitude' refers to the inherent difficulty or complexity of the tasks of alleviating the condition.[26]

While 'impact' and 'magnitude' are independent attributes, they frequently occur as linked conditions. Many of the tasks of coastal restoration are instances of problems of this sort. A good example is the question of the marshland's mixture of salt and fresh water, an essential nursery for many species including oysters, crabs, shrimp, and fish. Such wetlands, known as *ecotones* (transitional areas between deepwater environments and drained uplands), often produce more organic material than either adjacent habitats. They perform multiple functions—serving as 'kidneys' for the upland, removing wastes from both natural and human sources, but also as 'storage facilities' of bio-diversity, providing a habitat and nutrients for a wide variety of plants and animals.[27] In its latter function, ecologists can observe the cycle of a detrital food web. Marsh grasses, as they age, slough off their dead material, which, in turn, is further shredded by small crustaceans and snails, then attacked, colonized, and eaten by microorganisms. This remaining mixture is eaten by shrimp, crabs, and other crustaceans, whose defecations are re-colonized by bacteria and transformed into more potential food, including that which ultimately cycles to larger marine species.

One measure of the high 'impact' of healthy, functioning ecotones in Louisiana's coastal wetlands is that fact that the dockside value of its annual commercial seafood harvest is more than $342 million, and that of recreational fishing is $944 million.[28] However, one of the major difficulties of high 'magnitude' is dealing with just what an ideal mixture of salt and fresh water should be. For example, waters of greater than 50 percent the salinity of the Gulf spell death for oysters, who fall victim to the black

---

26. The concepts of 'impact' and 'magnitude' will be discussed in more detail in chapter 8 as part of a process for prioritizing and selecting solution strategies in post-disaster reconstruction.

27. Watzin et al, *The Fragile Fringe: Coastal Wetlands of the Continental United States.*

28. Louisiana Coastal Wetlands Conservation and Restoration Task Force, "Turning the Tide," 5.

drum (*Pogonias cromi,* a gray or black colored fish with cobblestone-like teeth capable of crushing oysters) and oyster drill (small predatory snails resembling a whelk or conch).[29]

Added to the dilemma of in whose interest is the location, or predominance of one species over another, there is the complex nature of current flow along the coast itself. For example, and in contrast with current flow in the Gulf of Mexico, the Bay of Fundy (between Nova Scotia and New Brunswick) experiences dramatic tidal changes due to the phenomenon of 'resonance'[30] in which water 'sloshes back and forth' with a certain frequency. When the period of oscillation approximates tidal changes, the speed of flow and range of tides can be extreme. This continual turbulence of water in the Bay of Fundy circulates nutrients that would otherwise settle to the bottom, making it one of the most productive natural areas in North America, supporting a food chain that ranges from phytoplankton to humpback whales. The extensive salt marshes around the bay also support this fertility.[31] It can be argued that Coastal Louisiana, by contrast, does not have such an *active* nutrient generator, making its nutrient producing capability more fragile, and, therefore, more vulnerable to the 'unintended consequences' (Marker 1) of runoff from upland farming and cattle raising. The mixture of salt and fresh water is critical. Marshland grasses and vegetation require a minimum level of fresh water, and without the root systems of those plants, there is nothing to hold the land in place and keep it from washing into the sea. But as salt water continually intrudes into freshwater areas, the grasses and vegetation die, and the line of the coast moves steadily inland. Of course, the fact that Louisiana's coastal wetlands *also* support more than 43,000 oil and gas wells and two large petroleum reserve storage sites only contributes further to the degradation of the environment.

Discussion of examples of 'poor stewardship' in Coastal Louisiana will be limited to three areas: (1) oil field waste, including digging op-

---

29. Hallowell, *Holding Back the Sea,* 41; effects also on estuaries providing nutrients for baby shrimp, 58.

30. Or *seiche,* in the sense promoted by Swiss hydrologist François-Alphonse Forel in 1890 observing the oscillations on Lake Geneva; the term derives from a Swiss French dialect expression meaning "to sway back and forth." The term also refers to small standing waves in a partially enclosed body of water.

31. Scott Cunningham, "Tides Without Equal. Paddling the Bay of Fundy," *Sea Kayaker,* August 2007, 33.

erations and the dredging of canals for rigs within the wetlands, (2) the results of levee construction by the Army Corps of Engineers to control the path of the Mississippi River, including the use of jetties, and (3) the interactions and competitions among various agencies and organizations attempting to deal with competing interests in the coastal environment.

Privilege Over Nature: Oil Field Waste

Perhaps the most blatant consequence of poor stewardship that takes the form of assuming human *privilege over* the natural environment has been the problem of oil field waste in the practices of the oil and gas industries—practices that have continued until quite recently. Some practices are documented in Chris Hallowell's *Holding Back the Sea*; others have been recounted to us by our friends, Kirby Verret, tribal elder of the Houma Indians in the Terrebonne Parish coastal village of Dulac, and by Chief Albert Naquin of the Isle de Jean Charles band of Biloxi-Chitimacha, who worked for the Department of the Interior in Mineral Sediment Services for twenty-four years. One of the most striking examples of 'poor stewardship' has involved the Houma Indian community of Grand Bois, near Bourg (south of Houma). This village is adjacent to an 'exploration and production' (E&P) waste disposal facility—one of Louisiana's largest hazardous waste sites. From around 1984, chemicals, including benzene, hydrogen sulfide, lead, and cadmium, were deposited in a facility of eighteen open pits as close as 100 yards to homes. With the site taking in over a million barrels of oil field waste per year, residents complained of respiratory and gastrointestinal problems. The medical records of children showed unusually high levels of lead in blood samples.[32] Public recognition of the severity of the health problems became apparent in 1994 after a combined shipment of E&P waste with other chemical waste. Representatives of the Louisiana Branch of the Sierra Club and the Louisiana Citizens for a Clean Environment contacted the Technical Outreach Services for Communities (TOSC), a program of the Hazardous Substance Research Centers consortia (HSRC),[33] for assistance about concerns in Grand Bois

32. Hallowell, *Holding Back the Sea*, 7.

33. TOSC is a program of the Hazardous Substance Research Centers (HSRC), a national organization that caries out basic and applied research in five regional multiuniversity centers, funded primarily through the Environmental Protection Agency (EPA). The consortium for EPA Regions 4 and 6 consists of LSU, Rice, Georgia Tech, Texas A&M, and the University of Texas (UT) at Austin; one of its founders was Dr.

as well as other Louisiana E&P waste disposal facilities. TOSC provided technical support to the environmental community groups, participated with the Agency for Toxic Substance and Disease Registry (ATSDR) to assess the environmental impact, and advised the Department of Natural Resources on testing protocols. An affiliate of TOSC is the Technical Outreach Services for Native American Communities (TOSNAC); other programs supported by EPA include the Forum on State and Tribal Toxics Action (FOSTTA), a partnership between the EPA's Office of Pollution Prevention and Toxics (OPPT) and state and tribal leaders for the purpose of improving collaboration on toxics and pollution prevention. However. TOSC funding from EPA evidently ended in May of 2007.[34]

The experience with toxicity at Grand Bois raises the question of why this should have happened in the first place. The answer is necessarily complex, but part of it clearly involves the practices of oil companies in meeting their obligation, under Department of Conservation regulations, to clean up the residues after drilling and dredging operations. Oil companies have an obligation to "return the land to its original state." However, what this has meant, even for oil companies like Chevron, which established its own subsidiary to deal with reclamation regulations, has *not* included refilling dredged canals or removing potentially toxic waste,[35] but, in addition to simply cleaning up equipment such as storage tanks and valves, doing "P and A's" on depleted oil wells—simply 'plugging and abandoning' them.[36]

Multiply such practices times the thousands of oil wells *within* the coastal wetlands alone, and one can see where questionable stewardship meets the 'problem of scale' (Marker of Complexity 4). Moreover, what we have considered thus far are only those practices of stewardship that result *directly* from human decision-making. There are also the potential impacts to a fragile environment that come *indirectly* from engineering

---

Danny Reible, formerly of the Department of Civil Engineering at LSU, currently Center Co-Director at UT.

34. Information provided in conversations with Tomeka Prioleau, HSRC Outreach Specialist, Region 6, at LSU, and Dr. Danny Reible.

35. Including naturally occurring radioactive materials (NORMs) that can become concentrated in the materials oil companies were allowed to dump directly next to their drilling derricks. Without levees that included protective linings, these dangerous materials could easily leach out into surrounding waterways.

36. See the discussion in Hallowell, *Holding Back the Sea*, 80.

choices, or which occur by accident. A significant portion of crude oil is piped under high pressure: for example, that to the Cloverly Salt Dome in Lafourche Parish from the Louisiana Offshore Oil Port (the LOOP). This high pressure pipe is but one among at least a half dozen others. Over 20,000 miles of pipelines lie beneath the floor of the coastal marshes, transporting the oil and gas to refineries such as the four Norco-Lake Charles area refineries (Citgo, Conoco, American, Motiva), which have expanded in capacity since 1993 to process an amount approaching a million barrels of oil a day. Apart from the airborne toxic emissions from those facilities themselves, there are dangers in simply getting the oil *to* them. By one estimate, if a high pressure transport pipe should break, the resulting oil spill could amount to 2.5 million gallons per house.[37] Of course, there are more ways to spill oil than by breaks in pipelines going to refineries. On June 19, 2006, a spill from two holding tanks at the Citgo refinery in Lake Charles resulted in pollution from 47,000 barrels of "waste oil," left over *after* the refining process. It also closed the Calcasieu Ship Channel and generally stymied ship traffic along the Gulf.

These examples alone should be an indication of the realities that exist as a direct consequence of a model of stewardship that sees the natural environment in terms of human *privilege*—that is, primarily as a resource for human use. But problems also arise from less obviously 'irresponsible' practices in interacting with the environment. Many are a result of the search for oil and gas locations itself. To reach new sites, numerous canals must be dug and dredged throughout the coastal marshes. Environmental damage occurs, however, as a result of limited, or an absence of, knowledge about the region's drainage patterns. The dredged canals are continually widened from the passage of vessels; this is intensified by wind waves and storm surges. That widening, in turn, allows a further intrusion of salt-water, diminishing the ability of freshwater vegetation to survive. Ultimately, this protective, nutrient-producing vegetation is killed off. From the air, these dredged oil rig canals can easily be identified by their 'keyhole' shape at the end. Once the well is depleted, the canal and its larger dead end circle remain. In this way, environmental damage continues to occur, even after the extraction of oil is finished and the rig removed.

The oil and gas industry, of course, does not operate in a vacuum. It's existence is a consequence of continually increasing demands of the

---

37. Estimate given by Hallowell, *Holding Back the Sea*, 12.

American economy for petroleum products—including the winter heating needs of populations further north. Stewardship—and its inherent problems—must therefore be seen not exclusively as the problem of only those industries who are the suppliers of petroleum based products; it is an issue that involves *all* Americans who *use* those products. In other words, virtually *everyone*. Each of us shares in a responsibility for either the commitment to or an acceptance of a model of human—natural interaction that appears to be, in many ways, self-destructive. Consider the number of Markers of Complexity involved just in this example. At least five out of the seven are involved. Spills, fuel transport line breaks, refinery discharge represent issues of unintended consequences (Marker 2) and lack of backup or redundancy (Marker 5). Thousands of miles of oil and gas pipes beneath the marshes, the sheer number of working rigs and abandoned drilling sites exemplify problems of scale (Marker 4). The inadequate disposal and leaching of drilling waste containing toxins and radioactive material is clearly an issue of the progressive degradation of quality of life (Marker 7). Finally, the interplay of America's demand for oil and gas products and the activities of the oil and gas companies to meet those demands becomes a vicious cycle (Marker 3).

Dominion Over Nature: Levee Construction

Another dimension of stewardship, understood as a warrant to exercise *dominion over* nature—the construction of levees by the Army Corps of Engineers to control the path of the Mississippi River, including the building of jetties at delta outlets—although conducted with better knowledge of the regional environment, has proven equally problematic. The Mississippi River is itself an enormously complex entity—both historically and in the present. Whereas most rivers in North America are ones whose mouths are *embayed*—that is, where the sea regularly enters the river mouth with tidal changes—the Mississippi, with its very large and continually changing delta, is untypical. Over the past 5000 years, there is geologic evidence of multiple old deltas channeling river waters to the Gulf. The oldest and most western is Bayou Teche, a bayou that flows from Opelousas, through Breaux Bridge and St. Martinville on to the Gulf. The next east is Bayou Lafourche. This is the course the river took until its present course was established near Donaldsonville, south of Baton Rouge. To the east of New Orleans, faintly marked, is the St. Bernard delta.

From Cairo, Illinois, the river follows a downward warp in the earth's crust. In addition, the southern end is gradually sinking, most noticeable in the Gulf outlets at the delta where the deposits of silt now pass off the coastal plain into deeper waters and where the delta is met by a continually rising sea. Deposits of river silt have been essential to the creating and maintaining of the delta by forming sandbars and mudbanks which gradually extend the land outward into the Gulf. Pilots who guide ships from the Gulf upriver actually have two independent organizations. 'Bar pilots' guide vessels through the outlet passes, avoiding sandbars and other obstructions; 'river pilots' take over at Pilottown and guide vessels upriver to New Orleans. By 1879 Col. James Eads of the Corps of Engineers had built "Eads Jetties" at South Pass to force the river to scour a reliable, deepwater channel for ships. Keeping a 40 foot deep channel was the responsibility of the Corps.[38]

One of the effects of the levee and jetty construction work by the Army Corps of Engineers is that the Mississippi River now dumps its silt far out into the Gulf off the continental shelf. The result is that the coastal marsh is no longer able to be rebuilt from the silt, mud, and nutrients they carry with them. Thus, in addition to the effects of saltwater intrusion and the loss of nutrients from river silt, the delta marshlands are also simply sinking—in some places by estimates of as much as 18 inches a century. That translates into a land loss described in such popular images as the rate of "two football fields per hour."

What does such land loss translate into for human communities? One example, about which we will speak in greater detail in chapter 10, is Isle de Jean Charles, a long, narrow island that sits off the end of a ridge that follows the small Bayou St. Jean Charles, between Bayou Terrebonne and Bayou Point-au-Chien[39] to the east in Terrebonne Parish. The island

38. For further discussion, see Cowdrey, *Land's End. A History of the New Orleans District, U.S. Army Corps of Engineers, and Its Lifelong Battle with the Lower Mississippi and Other Rivers Wending Their Way to the Sea*, and Lewis, *New Orleans. The Making of an Urban Landscape*.

39. The name Point-au-Chien has been retained by many, although the village of some 500 people (between Bourg and Montegut, at the intersection of Routes 55 and 665) and the wildlife management area to the east were renamed Pointe-aux-Chenes. Around 1994, prompted by Laise Ledet, a local schoolteacher who found the name *Point-au-Chien* unpleasant, State Senator, then Parish Councilman, Reggie P. Dupre, Jr.

is connected across about four miles of open water by a narrow causeway road (Island Road) just above the southern end of Route 665. Even at normal high tides, the causeway road can be covered by four to eight inches of water. The island is home to members of the Isle de Jean Charles Band of the Biloxi-Chitimacha Confederation of Muskogees, lead by Chief Albert Naquin.[40] Until the early 1970s, there was no dependable roadway to connect the community to the rest of Louisiana. The island has gradually been disappearing into the waters of the Gulf, and its population has dwindled by more than one-third.[41]

(serving State Senate District 20 in Lafourche and Terrebonne Parishes) worked to have the name of the town and local school changed. In the 2000–2001 Regular Legislative Session of the Louisiana Legislature, he sponsored a Senate Committee Resolution (SCR No. 25) requesting the Louisiana Wildlife and Fisheries Commission (LWFC) to redesignate the wildlife management area to Pointe-aux-Chenes ("Point of Oaks"). Both names (and multiple spellings) still appear. Information from conversations with Marc Castille, Director of the Pointe-aux-Chenes WMA, Robert Love of LDWF, Lloyd Songe of Houma, and Sen. Dupre. Reggie Dupre added that efforts to change the name of the community and bayou had been going on since before he was born over 50 years ago. In passionately trying to preserve her Cajun heritage, Miss Ledet, a schoolteacher from the days when rural communities like Pointe-aux Chenes had one room schools, discovered the correct spelling through genealogical research, and subsequently wrote a book, *They Came, They Stayed,* which traced many of the original Cajun and Native American families who settled there and Isle de Jean Charles. Miss Ledet first got the Terrebonne School Board to change the name of the elementary school, then the water district to change the name on the water tower, the fire department to change the name on the fire station and trucks, and DODT to change the highway signs. As a State Legislator, Reggie was able to get the Wildlife Management Area's name changed in honor of Miss Ledet.

40. The other members of the Confederation are the Grand Caillou-Dulac Band with Marlene Foret, Chairwoman, and the Bayou Lafourche Band under Chief Randy Verdun. The three Indian communities share a common history, with Biloxi, Chitimacha, Choctaw, Acolapissa, and Atakapa Indian origins. Once under the umbrella of the United Houma Nation, after the Bureau of Indian Affairs (BIA) ruling in 1994 that determined 'Houma' (a Choctaw term meaning "red") ancestors were largely Biloxi, as well as tribal genealogical research that determined who could legitimately be members of tribal rolls, these three groups formed a separate Biloxi-Chitimacha Confederation of Muskogees (BCCM) in 1995. The United Houma Nation, a broadly based group of 16,000 members across five parishes, rather than a tribe, was not recognized by the Bureau of Indian Affairs, only by the State of Louisiana. Although many Houma retain belief in their Indian identity, the BIA determined that at least 16 percent of the 'Houma Nation' had no Indian ancestry whatsoever. Information from conversations with Randy Verdun, Chief of the Bayou Lafourche Band.

41. The current Indian population on Isle de Jean Charles is about 230 persons. The island community lies beyond the U.S. Army Corps of Engineers 72-mile Morganza to the Gulf Hurricane Protection Project levee system. This project consists of approximately

In August 2005, Hurricane Katrina blew the roofs off many houses, ripped apart mobile homes; Hurricane Rita followed, and sent nine feet of seawater over the island, causing even more damage. However, the Biloxi-Chitamacha Confederation of Muskogees (BCCM) and the neighboring Pointe-au-Chien Tribe (PACIT) learned to combine their own initiatives rather than depend on federal assistance to support relief and recovery efforts. After Hurricane Rita, Isle de Jean Charles native Chris Brunet and his uncle, Rev. Roch Naquin, joined with cousin Chief Albert Naquin and others from Catholic Social Services in Houma to run a relief center out of Brunet's home.[42] Tribes also received assistance from a wide variety of sources: the Mennonite Disaster Service, the National Congress of American Indians, France-Louisiane, the Louisiana Coastal Tribes Coalition, and individual churches from places as remote as the Berean Baptist Church of Mansfield, Ohio.[43] The sense of isolation for Louisiana's coastal tribes is more than just the geographical consequence of surviving on fingerlike projections into the Gulf, where waves lap at the edges of homes, and there is a deep reverence for the power of the water and the winds. Chief Albert Naquin points out that Louisiana Indians were prohibited from attending public school with white children until 1966, and that racism played a role in the seizure of Indian lands that were discovered to be rich in oil and gas resources in the 1950s. Struggles for land and other rights of the area's indigenous peoples, who were originally sugar cane farmers until saltwater intrusion made the soil unsuitable for farming,[44] continue at the federal level. A residue of racism from tribal struggles for federal recognition is widely perceived by many enrolled

---

72-miles of earthen levee, nine 56-foot sector gate structures, three 125-foot floodgates, 12 floodgate structures, and a lock complex including one on the Houma Navigational Canal. Information from Bill Maloz, Project Management, New Orleans District, USACE; also from discussions with Carl Anderson, USACE—New Orleans, and Elaine M. Stark, Project Management, Morganza to the Gulf Hurricane Protection Project, USACE.

42. See, for example, Clifford, "Isle de Jean Charles Man Spearheads Relief Efforts," *Houma Today,* January 2, 2006. See also articles in *Indian Country Today* in September and October, 2005.

43. Information from Pointe-au-Chien Tribal Press Release, November 29, 2006, and conversations with Chief Albert Naquin and others.

44. The days of growing white beans and other garden foods, raising hogs, and hunting for land-based animals such as rabbit and deer, are, for the most part, gone; crabs, oysters, shrimp, and fish remain available, and alligator is still hunted.

members to have affected the level of emergency services and government disaster relief made available.[45]

It has not only been Louisiana's Indian tribal groups who have had issues with the federal government, and the Army Corps of Engineers. A perusal of issues of *Louisiana Coastal Law*, a newsletter reviewing bills and resolutions passed in legislative sessions affecting coastal resource use and conservation,[46] reveals numerous instances of conflict with USACE's stewardship of the coastal wetlands by individuals or interest groups, and, at times, the Louisiana Legislature itself. An example of the latter is House Committee Resolution No. 3 (HCR No.3) during the 2000–2001 Regular Legislative Session. The resolution argues that, after construction of the levee along the western edge of the Calcasieu River Ship Channel through Moss Lake in Calcasieu Parish by the United States Army Corps of Engineers, the once sandy, firm bottom of Moss Lake became muddy and covered with silt. Johns et al., authors of the resolution, expressed the "strong belief that the levee is the cause of the siltation problem."[47]

Several 'Markers of Complexity' are identifiable in the stewardship that has attempted to exercise control, or dominion, over the natural environment. The most obvious are those of unintended consequences (Marker 2) and instability (Marker 1), which take the following general form: the construction of a levee along boundary *a* has an unintended effect on some adjacent body of water or causes a secondary problem along boundary *b*. Given the enormous size and length in time of levee projects, there are also issues of scale (Marker 4)—the Mississippi River and its complex delta include massive bodies of water and marsh. Finally, even brief consideration the of circumstances of coastal Indian tribes who inhabit theses slender reaches of land at the edge of the Gulf provides evidence of progressive degradation of quality of life (Marker 7).

---

45. The "Island Road" to Isle de Jean Charles, originally built in 1953, often became impassible when wind shifts and tides flooded the road, preventing emergency vehicles from reaching the island, and forcing children to miss school or be transported to Pointe-aux-Chenes by boat. Through efforts of Reggie Dupre, the road has been elevated several times, but there remains a dire need for a protection levee on the south side of the island.

46. An advisory service of the Louisiana Sea Grant Program (National Oceanic and Atmospheric Administration, U.S. Department of Commerce).

47. *Louisiana Coastal Law*, Number 79, October 2001, 1. It must be noted that in its urging USACE to review and correct the problem, the 'environmental quality' issue was that the silt impeded drainage and restricted recreational use of the lake.

Dark Clouds Over the Gulf

Unproductive Interactions among Agencies

Discussion of *dysfunctional interactions* among various agencies and organizations with competing interests in the coastal environment will be brief, because this particular kind of complexity will also be seen to play a role in many areas of poor stewardship in the urban environment of New Orleans and in its cultural milieu. To get a sense of the sheer *number* of federal and state agencies, acts of Congress or the Louisiana Legislature, national and regional coalitions and programs, and local interest groups involved in developing various policies for the use of Louisiana's coastal environment, we rather quickly assembled a list that was exceeding thirty when we stopped.[48] Each of these agencies and groups has their own history, their own philosophical and scientific presuppositions, their own 'culture.' Prior to the passage of the Coastal Wetlands Planning, Protection and Restoration Act of 1990 (the Breaux Act), the wetlands often were the losers to the infighting among agencies. A flavor of this is captured by Chris Hallowell in *Holding Back the Sea*:

---

48. Major players at the Federal level include the U.S. Army Corps of Engineers (USACE), the U.S. Fish and Wildlife Service (USWFS), the Environmental Protection Agency (EPA), the National Marine Fishers Service (NMFS), the Natural Resources Conservation Service (NRCS) of the Dept. of Commerce, the National Oceanic and Atmospheric Administration (NOAA), Office of Ocean and Coastal Resource Management of the Dept. of Commerce. Major players at the State level include the Louisiana Department of Natural Resources (DNR) which itself has a Coastal Management Division, a Coastal Restoration Division, and a Coastal Engineering Division, the Louisiana Department of Wildlife and Fisheries (LDWF), the Louisiana Wildlife and Fisheries Commission (LWFC), the Wetlands Conservation and Restoration Authority, the Coastal Protection and Restoration Authority of Louisiana (CPRA), restructured in December 2005 from the State Wetlands Conservation and Restoration Authority, the Louisiana Advisory Commission on Coastal and Marine Resources, the Louisiana Wetland Protective Panel, the Governor's Office of Coastal Activities Science Advisory Panel, LaCoast—the State information center on coastal wetlands issues. The major legislative acts and players at from national and regional coalitions and programs and local interest groups include the Coastal Zone Management Act of 1972, the Coastal Zone Protection Act of 1996, the Coastal Wetlands Planning, Protection and Restoration Act of 1990 (CWWPRA, the Breaux Act), Coast 2050—a joint planning initiative at state, federal, and local levels, the Coastal Impact Assistance Program (CIAP), the Louisiana Universities Marine Consortium (LUMCON), the National Estuary Program (NEP), the Barataria-Terrebonne National Estuary Program (BTNEP), Coastal Restoration and Enhancement through Science and Technology (CREST), the Coalition to Restore Coastal Louisiana (CRCL)—a non-profit advocacy organization interested in responsible stewardship of coastal wetlands, the Brown Marsh Data Information Management System, the Association of Levee Boards of Louisiana (ALBL), the Louisiana Landowners Association (LLA), and Parish Police Juries.

> Traditionally, each state and federal agency has its particular con-
> servation, or land use, ethic—its way of being. Each favors man-
> agement techniques that please its constituents. NRCS has always
> like to build earthen levees, for example, around farms in danger
> of sinking into the marsh. The Army Corps of Engineers, along
> with erecting levees on the Mississippi and elsewhere, likes to halt
> erosive forces by erecting rock jetties as protective barriers. The
> Corps has a reputation for concrete, rock, big equipment, and big
> money . . . National Marine Fisheries Service (NMFS) . . . likes to
> plant grasses and build dunes to enhance production of commer-
> cial aquatic life.[49]

But turf wars among agencies ultimately result from more than each agency's internal 'culture.' They arise out of a combination of factors which also include available funding, political influence, favoritism, the power of corporate and local businesses, the efforts of non-governmental interest groups, the perceptions in the popular media of what current issues are 'at stake,' and so forth.

Since numerous examples of dysfunctional cross-domain interac-tions (Marker 7) are discussed at several points throughout the book, it seemed interesting here to try a somewhat different approach. It turns out that very similar issues of complexity obscure attempts to answer what initially seemed a simple question: Who has ownership of various areas of Louisiana coastal wetlands, and, therefore, control over their use?

The Swamp Lands Act of 1849 (with additions to it in 1850) made eligible the title to swampy lands deemed unfit for human habitation or use to pass to the State. Given that oil and gas companies now have rigs and pipelines running all through the coastal marshes, it is natural to wonder how control over these lands passed to the oil and gas enterprises. It turns out that there were many intermediary steps, as well as no clear answer to the original question. The ragged path to this discovery proved interesting and significant.

The path began with a series of very helpful discussions with Bobby Freyou, Records Manager of the Louisiana Department of State Lands in Baton Rouge. According to Freyou, under the Swamp Lands Act, approxi-mately one-third of the land of the State of Louisiana was transferred from the federal government to the State. The State was then able to sell this land to private individuals. Approximately 90 to 95 percent of this land was sold

---

49. Hallowell, *Holding Back the Sea*, 55.

to private individuals during the 1860s–90s, and on into the 1910s. What was left passed to levee districts, who could also sell the land to private individuals to raise revenue. There is some of this land still left in the state, but it represents less than 100,000 acres of vacant State-owned land.

It turns out that every agency with some control over land and land use in Louisiana is largely on its own. There is no State oversight, or super-agency, keeping track of this. Each agency keeps track of its own domain. Therefore, there are no centralized records of what percentage of coastal marshland is owned (or leased by) the oil and gas companies. But at some point, Freyou thought, they would have been purchased or leased from private individuals. Adding to the problem, however, is the fact that each parish has its own way of defining and describing plots of land. There are no general coordinates used. Local GIS[50] data in coastal parishes simply gives a descriptive picture (for example, "a plot of land next to Jean Batiste Fuselier's land bounded by Bayou Mercier Road bounded by . . ."). At best one might hope that the Assessor in the Clerk of the Courts in a given parish keeps records for that parish. The Department of State Lands does have historical records from the Federal Land Office, records which were kept after the Swamp Lands Acts. Both Wildlife and Fisheries (LDWF) and Natural Resources (DNR) are large State landowners in the sense of having management responsibilities for certain areas. But there was no direct path to answer our initial question.

The underlying purpose of this question is to determine who, if anyone, keeps records of which oil and gas companies have control over which areas, and how they obtained that control—including the question of how control over coastal marshes and wetlands passes from one company to another, for example, as when Conoco Phillips bought out Burlington. Bobby Freyou suggested to try the Louisiana Landowners Association, formed in 1965, and its general counsel, Newman Trowbridge in Lafayette. Before doing that, we spoke with Mark Ford, lawyer and Director of the Coalition to Restore Coastal Louisiana (CRCL), since the Coalition's concerns have been not only with the jeopardy of the coastal wetlands, but with the economic dependence of jobs and local economies on the successes and failures of the oil and gas industry. Many workers in that industry—with a two-weeks offshore one-week home, or similar,

50. Geographic Information Systems, a suite of computer hardware, software, and geographic data for capturing, managing, analyzing, and displaying geographically referenced information

schedule—alternate 'careers' between work as pipe fitters and welders on the oil rigs and hunters or trappers or oystermen in the marshes when home. If the Louisiana oil economy slides, as it has since the 1980s, *and* the marshes are disappearing, there will be left nothing as a source of income and the means to support a family. Mark Ford's feeling was that probably 90 percent of the land had been sold to large private companies such as Burlington, rather than still being held by small, individual landowners. We also discussed areas hit by Hurricane Rita—areas of which we were mutually fond. Holly Beach ('Cajun Riviera') flattened, nothing there; Cameron, trying to rebuild from almost nothing, its property owners strongly urged to move further inland. Mark suggested to get in touch with a consultant to some of the major corporations and organizations, Randy Moertle.

In the meantime, through the office their general counsel, Newman Trowbridge, Jr., in Lafayette, we connected with a spokesperson for the Louisiana Landowners Association (LLA). The LLA represents large and small landowners across the state whose interests range from farming, timber, ranches, to oil and gas producers. Joining forces with the Land and Royalty Owners of Louisiana (LAROLA) in 1979, the LLA has lobbied to have legislation passed that blocked efforts to extend State sovereignty over private wetlands (the Phillips Decision), restrict public access to private waterways, and address issues such as leasing, 'levee servitudes,' and hazardous wastes. The LLA has only two paying members from oil companies—Conoco Phillips and BP—and, in fact, a total dues paying membership of just 122. In terms of ownership and the leasing of land in the coastal marshes, the representative with whom we spoke indicated that most private individual owners have 500 acres or less, and that the LLA doesn't have records on who owns what. In many cases, this is because such information is either not gathered or in a state of ambiguity at the parish level. Pointe Coupée Parish was one example of a parish trying to assess who owned what, but there have been many, many disputes.

Randy Moertle, of Randy Moertle and Associates, Inc., is a consultant to corporations and organizations with interests in the usage of Louisiana coastal marshlands. Randy has consulted on the Biloxi Marsh Stabilization and Restoration Plan for the Biloxi Marsh Lands Corporation. The Biloxi Marsh estuary is a 210,000 acre network of coastal wetlands between Chandeleur Sound and Lake Borgne, roughly 30 miles southeast of New Orleans in St. Bernard Parish, and serves as a primary wave and storm surge barrier. To offset the degradation from the unintended effects (Marker 2) of two major engineering projects—the Mississippi River levees and the Mississippi River–Gulf Outlet (MR–GO)—the plan seeks construction of a massive freshwater diversion to restore original hydrology and natural flora that help sustain the area. Randy was both frank and helpful, and aware of the difficulties in answering the seemingly simple question we were asking. He indicated that approximately 80 percent of the land in the coastal marshes is privately owned (vs. owned by the State or by school boards). However, Moertle has necessarily been interested in trying to identify ownership of various areas himself, and always finds it exceedingly difficult. He gave us a pointer to an individual at the successor to Tobin International, an outfit involved with mapping that for 75 years had been one of the most trusted data sources in the Exploration and Production (E&P) industry. We agreed to continue to share information that might help answer the question we both wanted to answer as we came across it.

In 2004, Tobin International was acquired by P2 Energy Solutions, possibly the oil and gas industry's largest provider of exploration, development, management and production solutions through software and data services to improve land and financial production management. P2 Energy Solutions itself was the result of a merger of Paradigm Technologies, Petroleum Financial, Inc., and Novistar in 2003. A delightful and helpful P2 employee, Delicia Phillips in San Antonio, helped us examine a representative map (from Iberia Parish) to see first hand just how complex the answers to an initially simple question such as ours was. Answers (plural) is key here, because to put together a body of information about surface ownership and lessee identity beyond the collection of individual contracts in which that information resides becomes an almost Sisyphean task. Information can exist in descriptive form or through coordinates; more frequently, the former, although there is increasingly a strong movement to use the latter. For the map we examined, on which information was written in miniscule script, we could fairly easily identify landmarks such as drainage canals, parish roads, and old rail branches. In relatively few cases we could see the boundaries of portions of land; in most cases, they were obscure. More serious problems arose, however, in noting that, for example, the name 'H. Partout' (an owner) could appear in many places, not all contiguous, or necessarily even close to one another. Part of the ambiguity could lie in the fact that relatives of H. Partout might be identified by another initial or name (e.g., Eugene Partout) with certain pieces of land in *some* cases but *not* in others. That is, 'H. Partout' could designate land to which H. Partout still held title, or it could not (if title to that land had passed to a relative but the change was not recorded). Or, a piece of land could be designated as belonging to, e.g., Eugene Partout, but whose title was still held by H. Partout. Especially in locations along rivers or bayous, these circumstances might result from law codes regulating the French long-lot (*arpent*) and the division of property from one generation to the next. Additional ambiguities might also lie in the fact that, in French-speaking Louisiana, there are many, many people with the same name simply because many families originally came from the same few areas in Western France, particularly those from Poitou and around La Rochelle. If one picks up a phone book in any village or town in French-speaking, Cajun Louisiana—say, Eunice or Mamou—one will find pages and pages of Fontenots or Manuels (but nary a Richardson or Ross). Finally, difficulty in determining land and title identity may lie in the fact that leasing arrangements (e.g., between H. Partout and Sterling Sugars, Inc.) appear to involve a set of boundaries that are superimposed on a number of tracts of land, and even run across other landowners' property (non-relatives) who may or may not be involved in the leasing arrangement.

The point of this little journey, following what initially struck us as a reasonably simple question, was not to sort out the complexities of Louisiana real estate arrangements, and certainly not to suggest that information about who owns (and leases) which lands in the coastal wetlands simply does not exist. Rather, it is to suggest that such information at the micro-level about ownership, usage, and responsibility in Louisiana's coastal wetlands—and the decisions on which having such information would be based—is highly fragmented, both in itself, and among the various agencies, organizations, corporations, and individuals who have differing interests in it. Moreover, information that exists in highly fragmented states only feeds divisions of individual interests and political agendas that already exist. As *Walking to New Orleans* continues, we will see instances of this problem, this uniquely Louisiana form of the problem of cross-domain interactions (Marker 6) again and again.

Before turning to the question of 'stewardship' in the urban environment, it is necessary to point out that all of the complexities which exist in the coastal wetlands are not human made. Many of them are. Vicious cycles of conflict that *are* human made include attempts to control the

Mississippi River vs. wetlands recession caused by levee and other construction; economic progress and demands for petrochemical products vs. the oil well drilling and pipe transport activities that chop up protective marshes; inland farming and agriculture vs. fertilizer runoff causing the hypoxic 'dead zone'[51] in the waters at the edges of the marshes. But many complexities are *not* human made. There are also endemic complexities that *naturally* exist in this coastal environment. It is an environment *inherently* unstable. The position of coastal marshes relative to the greatest river complex within the geography of North America, the flow of currents along the coast, its location in the path of annual storms of great magnitude, the destructive habits of indigenous and important fauna, such as nutria, land mass that naturally sinks each year in differing amounts—all of these factors, and more, contribute to a fluid and changing environment.

Even apart from the extent to which human 'stewardship' has contributed to the degradation of that environment, to the loss of land (accelerated by the 217 square miles that Hurricanes Katrina and Rita took away), there is an increasing awareness it may be an environment whose instability and vastness is such that not even unending commitment can prevent land loss from saltwater intrusion. From that perspective, attempts to reclaim this environment may very well only produce another version of Marker 7—the sheer exhaustion of effort.

In some cases, it is not altogether clear that what humans perceive as disastrous events such as hurricanes and flooding rains, necessarily end up being destructive of the environment in the long run. There are instances of 'what nature takes away it also gives back.' On August 26, 1992, for example, Hurricane Andrew slammed into the southern coast of Louisiana with wind gusts over 130 mph and a 15-foot storm surge, resulting in millions of fish killed by oxygen depletion, 70 percent

---

51. The Gulf Restoration Network (GRN) estimates this hypoxic zone off the Louisiana shore in the Gulf of Mexico where gill fish and other marine life cannot find sufficient oxygen to sustain life to be as much as 6,000 square miles, or roughly the size of the state of New Jersey, and continuing to grow. At a hearing with the Environmental Protection Agency's Dead Zone Task Force in June, 2007, Jeff Grimes of the GRN attributed the causes not only to pollution from sewage treatment plants and industrial waste, but also to the nitrogen and phosphorous in fertilizers used to grow corn, eventually flushed into the Gulf. Grimes warned the potential for a shift in the entire ecosystem of the Gulf would place its fishery stock at risk. Reported in multiple sources, for example: "Environmentalists say Gulf 'Dead Zone' is growing," *The Louisiana Weekly*, June 25, 2007.

of the oyster reefs in the Barataria-Terrebonne National Estuary damaged, barrier islands and coastal marshes stripped of vegetation. Yet while
such events were clearly destructive, scientists like Karen Westphal of the
Center for Coastal Energy and Environmental Resources argues that, in
the long run, hurricanes can also have positive effects.[52] In fact, marshes
can actually *benefit* from the effects of hurricanes and heavy rains. As a
hurricane's storm surge pushes water inland, while a locally destructive
intrusion of saltwater, it also leaves behind valuable sediment and nutrients as it drains out. Heavy rains also increase sediment runoff from rivers and bayous that is deposited into the estuarial wetlands. According to
Dr. Abby Sallenger of the USGS Center for Coastal Geology, studies show
that hurricanes generally have little long-term effect on marshes. While
foliage may be stripped, the stimulation from new nutrients brought in
quickly returns the beds to their original condition; mangroves and certain species of trees may particularly benefit. The analogy may be that
coastal hurricanes perform a *cleansing* function similar to that of forest
fires in maintaining the overall conditions for healthy forests. The question of ecological trade-offs is, of course, a subject of considerable debate.
But the position of viewing those tradeoffs from the standpoint of the
natural world *on its own terms*—more poetically expressed in the image
of the black skimmer described by Rachel Carson—must be considered
within the totality of data upon which human judgments and decisions
are made.

From the standpoint of nature, these continual forces of change in
Louisiana's coastal environment may need to be regarded, in the longer
time-scale, as simply changes that happen, finite boundaries imposed on
human habitation. From that one could draw the conclusion that it must
be *expected* human life can be sustained in this environment for only a
very limited period of time. It is easy to forget that for 99.99 percent of
the span of Earth's history, there was no human life present at all. The ominous thunderheads that always seem to loom above the horizon of the
Gulf at the edges of where Louisiana meets the sea may not a foreboding
message to humans who stand anxiously on the shore; they may simply

52. Discussed in *Watermarks*, Louisiana Coastal Wetlands Planning, Protection
and Restoration News, published by the Louisiana Coastal Wetlands Conservation
and Restoration Task Force, and the Army Corps of Engineers, New Orleans District,
Summer 1998.

be symbols of one among the many natural processes that occur at this stage of Earth's history.

STEWARDSHIP IN THE URBAN ENVIRONMENT

If one believes that history 'has lessons' to teach, it seems to be in the nature of cities to 'fall.' At least some of them, since modern urbanites are culturally conditioned to believe technology is capable of insulating cities from total annihilation, except for anything short of nuclear warfare, being struck by a wandering asteroid, or the incursion of water from the rise in sea levels. The last, of course, should give many coastal urbanites pause for serious reflection. Many recent maps showing the effect of merely a three foot rise in sea level (a normal tidal range in many areas) predict that Baton Rouge would replace New Orleans as a city near the sea, Lake Pontchartrain would be gone, and the remnants of New Orleans would be stranded on a thin finger far out to sea.[53]

Cities give the illusion of permanence, even as they are changing, building, expanding. This perception has existed from ancient times; expressed in the language of the prophets, Mesopotamia's cities "have become heaps," victims of climate and an inability to rid irrigation of accumulations of salt,[54] but Egypt's monuments still stand, proclaiming a human presence in the natural order. What conclusions might we draw from this perception? Within the processes of an ever-evolving ecology, are cities something desirable or not? Historically, the city has been a locus of human separation from the natural world. Among the things this traditionally entails is the identification of the city as a *sanctuary* for people from the wilderness. In a sense, the existence of the city symbolizes our fear, our distrust of nature, our fundamental inability to come to terms with it. It perpetuates the myth of the human and the natural as two worlds in isolation from one other. The long-term history of New Orleans may compete with that myth, despite historical attempts to uphold it.

53. See, for example, Bourne, "The Perils of New Orleans," *National Geographic*. Vol. 212, No. 2. August, 2007, 61.

54. Heidi Cullen, a researcher at the National Center for Atmospheric Research in Boulder, Colorado, studied droughts and the collapse of the Akkadian civilization of the first Mesopotamian empire. She was able to show that a megadrought at roughly 2200 BCE played a role in its demise, finding the proof by examining the sediment cores of ancient mud. Looking at the mud from the period around the Akkadian collapse, one found a huge spike in the mineral dolomite, an indicator of drought.

Indeed, why should not the city equally be understood as a sanctuary *for* nature *from* people? Or a locus of their mutually beneficial interaction? Why should the city not serve as a symbol of *respect*: nature is something inviolable, and we cannot simply impose human rational and mechanistic structures upon it? Some designers argue the city itself benefits by having organic models from nature incorporated *within* its design. In fact, such a vision for the city can be found in the work of Antonio Gaudi, late nineteenth century architect from Catalonia whose nature-inspired Art Nouveau designs can still be seen in the undulating park walls and biomorphic columns of *La Sagrada Familia* in Barcelona. Such a vision can also be seen in the designs of the Italian-American architect, Paolo Soleri (born in Turin 1919, distinguished lecturer in the College of Architecture at Arizona State University). Influenced by Frank Lloyd Wright and Antonio Gaudi, Soleri has produced designs for vast, self-sufficient communities (called "arcologies") to be built on the top of desert mesas. Leaving the surrounding natural environment intact, Soleri's utopias are proposed alternatives to the problems of over-population, urban decay, and our misuse of the environment. An actual arcology, Arcosanti, the major project of Soleri's foundation, is a prototype town for 7,000 people under construction since 1970. Located at Cordes Junction, in central Arizona, the project is based on Soleri's concept of "Arcology"—architecture coherent with ecology. Arcology advocates cities designed to maximize the interaction and accessibility associated with an urban environment; minimize the use of energy, raw materials and land, reducing waste and environmental pollution; and allow interaction with the surrounding natural environment.

New Orleans is not a city that has historically operated on such a model. Rather, it is a city *wrested* from the natural environment; indeed, constantly at work *staving off* the natural environment. Not that New Orleans doesn't also *reflect* its natural environment; in many ways it does (or perhaps best did during its period of influence under Spanish architectural motifs). But the title of Craig Colten's[55] book *An Unnatural Metropolis: Wresting New Orleans from Nature*, or what Peirce Lewis has called an "impossible but inevitable city," make it clear that New Orleans has from its beginnings represented an enormous gumbo of energy and idiocy, of endless construction and reconstruction, configuration and

55. Carl O. Sauer Professor of Geography at LSU.

reconfiguration of the marshes and bayous within which it was situated. New Orleans grew from a former swamp at a particular bend in the Mississippi River, and not only reflects the evolving, fluid characteristics of that sodden natural environment, but, in a post-Katrina world, may, in any number of respects, be slowly returning to that natural environment. While New Orleans may be the city most dependent on human attempts to transform nature, Colten traces the inability of plans and engineering designs to exclude it.

The complexity of New Orleans' relationship to its natural surroundings in some respects reminds one of the complexity in the relation between human and nature symbolized in Wallace Stevens' round jar, placed upon a hill in Tennessee that "made the slovenly wilderness surround that hill"—a wilderness that "rose up to it,/And sprawled around, no longer wild." The temptingly ambiguous "it" in the last stanza, "It took dominion everywhere,"[56] can be taken to imply that *we* create an imaginative 'fiction' of nature, which, in itself, is 'slovenly', unbound, not organized for humans, so that our only understanding of it appears in attempts to *control* nature, exercise dominion over it through human reason. But "it" could just as easily be nature's ultimate dominion everywhere, including the islands of human culture and civilization. If the jar is a feeble marker or point of orientation placed to make order in the wilderness, there is an underlying conceptual model of a relationship that is compelled to be one of *dominion,* echoing Blake's aphorism, "Where man is not nature is barren." Perhaps relationships of dominion are contests with no winner.

Keeping the city dry, separating it from its watery environment, is a historical record of the need of its inhabitants to attempt to separate themselves from nature. Only much later in its history, with the introduction of parks within the city limits and adjacent wildlife refuges, such as Bayou Sauvage, was consciousness of a relationship to nature by citizens of New Orleans perhaps somewhat modified.

In the earliest days of New Orleans, high ground formed a natural levee for about a mile along a crescent bend in the river. However, moving beyond that high ground towards Lake Pontchartrain lay a mosquito-ridden, sodden, odiferous, tangled swamp—a *miasma* as it would be called by nineteenth century physicians who saw it as a locus of disease and pestilence. While the relationship between New Orleans and its surrounding

56. Stevens, "Anecdote of the Jar," from *Harmonium* in *Wallace Stevens Collected Poetry and Prose*, 60–61.

natural environment was certainly a complex and troublesome one, it is possible to focus on two primary elements that dictated to (and perplexed) those in a position to make decisions for the city: (1) frequent spring flooding from the Mississippi River, and (2) even more frequent standing water from heavy rains that could occur at almost any time of the year.

Levees and River Flooding

The construction of levees became the primary strategy in attempts to control *river flooding*. After initial attempts to depend on barriers erected locally proved quite inadequate, responsibilities were also passed upriver to riparian landholders through their ownership deeds. Reliance on river landholders to build and maintain levees continued into the mid-nineteenth century, but the results were less than satisfactory. Levees were not built to any consistent standard; maintenance was chancy at best. After the flooding of Sauvé's Crevasse in 1849[57] and further flooding in 1850, Congress attempted to have states organize responsibility for levee building and maintenance rather than provide federal action directly. This was unsuccessful. Eventually riparian landholders were able to compel states, through taxation, to pass proportionate economic responsibility for levees onto all residents. The Swamp Lands Act of 1849 and 1850, mentioned earlier, in which Congress granted to states flooded lands within their borders to levee and drain and then sell, was in a sense a 'perpetual cycle' funding scheme designed to use funds from drainage and reclamation to solve flooding problems. This scheme also failed.

By 1856 a complex system emerged in Louisiana based on the concept of the 'levee district.' Levee districts could be a single parish, or several parishes combined. They were run by boards of commissioners who had the power to tax all residents of alluvial land, to issue contracts for constructing new levees, and to repair old levees. They were also empowered to call forced drafts of slaves to combat crevasses.[58] For the first time, regular use was made of civil engineers to plan levee design and establish rules and criteria for levee dimensions. This was an important step in achieving some level of consistency within the levee strategy.

57. At this time Baton Rouge replaced New Orleans as state capitol.

58. Cowdrey, *Land's End*, 9. Four Levee Districts, or Swamp Land Districts, were enacted by the Legislature in 1854 under a Board of Swamp Land Commissioners responsible for construction and upkeep of levees.

As shipping and river traffic increasingly re-entered the picture at the close of the Civil War,[59] engineering practices reflected the belief that the river, confined between levees, would scour its channel deeper[60] and thereby support river traffic of vessels requiring deeper drafts. Faith in these engineering practices, to the exclusion of others (an example of Markers 3 and 7, combined with narrowness of vision), resulted in a federal policy of commitment to flood control by "levees only." While controversial, the "levees only" approach reflected the public policy presuppositions of Congress, the War Dept, and many private interests who wanted it—at least until 1926. It took the mammoth Flood of 1927 to confirm the short-sightedness of such a single-minded approach.

Even a quick tracing of the path that marked the history of responsibility for construction and maintenance of levees reveals a route complex and twisted in which it is difficult to sort out 'who had control and when?'[61] In 1866, a Board of Levee Commissioners was officially recognized by the Louisiana Legislature, Act 20, giving it power over the location, construction, maintenance of levees. In 1867 federal funds voted by Congress authorized the Secretary of War to operate two steam dredges to open navigable channels at the mouth of Mississippi, with responsibility under the Army Corps of Engineers' New Orleans Engineering Office. The following year, in 1868, the Board of Public Works was reestablished under Legislative Act 22 to succeed the Board of Levee Commissioners; the engineers of each levee district were appointed and supervised by this board. In 1871, Legislative Act 7 repealed the Board of Public Works and a Board of State Engineers was created. Particularly severe flooding on the

59. Snag boats had not operated since 1854; dozens of wrecks, including those left by war, clogged the channel. To make the river a main road of commerce and New Orleans a satisfactory port, channels and passes at the river mouth had to be cleared. In March 1867, Congress authorized the Secretary of War to operate two steam dredges to open navigable channels through the bars, and in June the responsibility was passed on to the New Orleans Corps of Engineer Offiice. See Cowdrey, *Land's End*, 17.

60. Colten, *An Unnatural Metropolis*, 12.

61. For further details on the following historical sketch, see John Barry; Craig Colten; Albert Cowdrey; Jed Horne; Peirce Lewis; John Hall of USACE, New Orleans District; Clyde Martin, Director of Hurricane and Flood Control Protection Programs of the Louisiana Department of Transportation and Development, and others from whom historical data (not necessarily its interpretation) is largely drawn. We are also indebted to the Corporate Office of Bucyrus International, Inc. in South Milwaukee for information on Bucyrus steam (supplying 77 of the 102 steam shovels used to dig the Panama Canal in 1904) and electric shovels.

Mississippi in 1874 resulted in Congress creating a Levee Commission. In 1877 the Louisiana Legislature repealed Act 7 that had established the Board of State Engineers, and parish Police Juries were assigned control and management over their own parish levees. The beginnings of more direct federal involvement came in 1879 when Congress created The Mississippi River Commission (MRC), a mixture of U.S. Army Corps of Engineers, representatives from the Coast and Geodetic Survey, and civilians. The MRC represented the first real step towards a national participation in flood protection work. However, even though federal money was made available at times through 1928, the main work of flood control still depended on local efforts. The MRC prompted the State Legislature to formalize Levee Districts as subdivisions of the state government, giving them the power to set up laws for flood control in their respective areas, establish boundaries for the construction of levees and drainage, and give them power of eminent domain and taxation. Between 1879 and 1898, the current Levee Districts were formed, although their boundaries have changed from time to time. 1879 was a busy year in other ways: State Legislative Act 33 re-created a Board of State Engineers in another reorganization, with duties to survey levees and other State public works, and report on their needs to the Governor. More serious flooding on the Mississippi in 1882 overwhelmed many levees, and propelled Congress to allow the Secretary of War to establish four administrative districts below Cairo, each under the responsibility of a USACE officer, and give the MRC direct authorization to build and repair levees as well as improve the harbors of New Orleans and other river cities. The result was a number of improvements in technique for levee building, including the proper selection of levee sites, clearing soil of stumps and decayed debris, and constructing levees to specified height and cross section. Nevertheless, construction itself was still done by wheelbarrow until the twentieth century, then by mules dragging wheeled scrapers until 1910, then by levee machines (A-frame derricks with buckets) that allowed great volumes of earth to be moved. Later, locomotive-type cranes were used—for example, Bucyrus tower excavators, introduced in 1915, close cousins to their crawler mounted dragline used in mining, were specifically designed for construction of levees along the lower Mississippi River. Bucyrus built thirty-three of these excavators through 1931. Work on the levees, however, was always muscle work, with local work gangs consisting of anywhere between 150 and 500 men, black and white. In 1890 a "master laborer" was paid $2.50 a day. Most of the laborers and some supervisors and skilled workers were black; engineers and Army personnel were white.

In 1897 the MRC noted that for the first time a large flood on the Mississippi had been able to pass from the Red River to the Gulf without overflow, appearing to support the federal policy of commitment to flood control by "levees only"—a policy itself rooted in the pressure of residents for immediate and local results rather than comprehensive, long-term planning. The idea that levees could be a complete answer to flooding was always controversial. The belief that levee stabilized banks would allow the river to continually scour a deeper channel for itself was disputed in 1861 by Captain A. A. Humphreys and Lieut. H. L. Abbot's *Report upon the Physics and Hydraulics of the Mississippi River*[62] which declared that the largely clay riverbed would *not* scour. Nevertheless, until the Great Flood of 1927, focus on the river itself, and on levees as the sole means of controlling it, became the public policy of Congress, the War Department, and private interests. One significant problem that resulted from this was that the levees protecting the land against *ordinary* high water levels continually raised the crests of the *great* floods.

A record spring flood in 1903 forced some to begin to reconsider a "levees only" policy, and in the spring of 1926, Congress had requested the Secretary of War make surveys and cost estimates for control spillways between Point Breeze and Fort Jackson, Louisiana. Rather than the MRC, the work was given to a new Spillway Board.

Two years earlier, the highly political Board of Commissioners of the Orleans Levee District was mandated by the State to modernize the Pontchartrain lakefront levee by creating a 5.5 mile stepped concrete wall on the floor of the lake, filling the enclosed area behind with lake bottom material to raise it above sea level, create a public waterfront with a yacht harbor and parks, and make Lake Vista one of the higher points of the city. This work had just begun when a flood of Biblical proportions occurred after exceptionally heavy rains in the middle Mississippi River Valley in the spring of 1927.

The Great Flood of 1927 is worthy of, and has been, the subject of book-length treatment.[63] Further, for the City New Orleans itself, the

62. Humphreys and Abbot, *Report upon the Physics and Hydraulics of the Mississippi River*, 91–95.

63. Notably, John Barry, *Rising Tide: The Great Mississippi Flood of 1927 and How It Changed America*.

flood ultimately became more an issue of its endemic *internal* flooding, which will be discussed subsequently, rather than of the river itself. Nevertheless, a quick sketch of that flood is useful as a transition to further representation of the question of 'who controlled what and when?' that resumes after 1927. On Good Friday, April 15, New Orleans had a deluge of 14.01 inches, more than it had ever seen in such a short period of time. Three days later the river stood at 56.2 feet at Cairo, and the lowlands were flooding rapidly, with over 25,000 people homeless. In New Orleans, armed guards patrolled the levees to override the historic practice of *sauve qui peut* (each for himself) where everyone feared his own levee might by dynamited by neighbors to ease the pressure of water on *their* land. Relatively new giant wooden screw pumps (the Wood Pump)[64] along the city's drainage canals were believed to be able to handle flooding from rain and push it back over the levees. However, lightning knocked out the pumps, and with four feet of water in city streets and a mammoth body of river water bearing down on the city, panic set in. A run on the banks prompted the city's bankers to support the scheme of blowing up a levee thirteen miles downriver from the city at Poydras—an act ultimately resulting in flooding 12,000 people out of St. Bernard and Plaquemines Parishes. Even after federal officials agreed to the plan, it was an act not easily accomplished. On April 20, people in those parishes were evacuated, but when, on April 22, dynamite charges were set off at Poydras, nothing happened. Upriver, all hell was breaking loose—at Mound Landing, Mississippi, the river had become 50 miles wide and 75 miles long; refugee camps were epidemic with mumps, measles, and whooping cough, and at Little Rock a coal train perched on a bridge to help stabilize it caught fire from vibrations, and the train, bridge, and burning coal all toppled into the water. Finally, on April 29, after six successive charges of dynamite, the levee at Poydras was breached. Yet even then, no gigantic torrent was produced, only a trickle, and it took picks and shovels and hours of work to grow the crevasse to its needed size. In the end it required ten days and 39 tons of dynamite to break the levee. Perhaps foreshadowing the aftermath of Katrina, the 12,000 refugees from St. Bernard and Plaquemines

---

64. The pump of engineer Albert Baldwin Wood, who was hired by the Sewerage and Water Board of New Orleans to improve the city's drainage; in 1913 he invented a simple, high volume, wooden screw pump that facilitated development of much of the land now occupied.

Parishes were housed in warehouses, charged for food, and exposed to the underlying levels of true power in city and state and federal politics. For better or worse, the Flood of 1927 demonstrated the insufficiency of a "levees only" approach to the environment.

To complete the brief history of 'who controlled what and when?' by 1928 the Mississippi River Flood Control Act looked to broaden the approaches previously taken. The premise was the use of a "Project Flood" maximum hypothetical flood of 66 feet at the Cairo gage, 74 feet at Arkansas City, and a flow of three million cubic feet per second below the mouth of the Red River.[65] The plan did slightly raise existing levees, but now began to include a system of floodways and spillways to recreate swamp reservoirs and natural outlets to give the river lateral room the levees had taken away. New Orleans would be protected by a spillway at Bonnet Carré, where up to 250,000 cubic feet per second could be channeled across to Lake Pontchartrain. The spillway was completed in 1931, and opened for the first time during the "High Water of 1937," a river flood that in many places exceeded gage readings of 1927.

In 1940, the Louisiana Department of Public Works was established by Act 47 of the State Legislature, with functions of other boards and commissions transferred to it, including the State Planning Commission, the Louisiana Flood Control and Water Conservation Commission, the Board of Control of the New Basin Canal and Shell Road, and the Louisiana Flowage Right Commission. In the same year, the Association of Levee Boards was formed, with the Governor's suggestion to coordinate its lobbying activities with Public Works engineers.

In the post–World War II years, many issues of 'who had control and when?' appeared to shift towards the Port of New Orleans, and its capacity for handling changes in shipping—in particular, the emergence of container ships, some almost a quarter-mile long and a football field and a half wide. The Port was better equipped for the almost equally as large barge carriers such as "LASH" of Central Gulf Steamship Co. or Sea-Bee (Lykes Co.),[66] and the New Orleans Dock Board was unenthusiastic

65. Terms such as "100-year flood" are based on the insurance industry's best guess estimate of the percentage chance of some event happening during the next year. For example, "25-year flood" would mean there are four chances in 100 of such a flood happening during the next year.

66. Having kayaked through locks on the upper Mississippi River, upon opening of the locks, one often finds oneself staring right into the business end of one of these monsters.

about the container ship business.[67] During the 1950s one witnessed a great deal of pulling and tugging among the Army Corps of Engineers, who urged enlarging the Inner Harbor Lock to triple its size to accommodate ocean ships into the port, the Board of Commissioners for the Port of New Orleans (the "Dock Board"), the Public Belt Railroad, created to connect wharf facilities with railroad trunk lines, business interests of various kinds, and State and City agencies with interests as well.

It was not until the 1960s that New Orleans began to overhaul its port for container ships, building a new port at the junction of the Gulf Intracoastal Waterway (GIWW) and the Inner Harbor Navigational Canal (IHNC, also called the Industrial Canal) with two mainline railways, I-10, and the Mississippi River–Gulf Outlet (MR–GO) channel, authorized by a March 29, 1956 Act of Congress (Public Law 84–455).[68] The port and its adjacent waterways became a new field for agencies vying for control. MR–GO, whose construction began in 1958 and was completed with full authorized dimensions and two-way traffic in 1968, connected the Gulf of Mexico with the Industrial Canal.[69] The channel was built to short-cut the route from the Gulf into the Port of New Orleans, bypassing about 80 miles of the old route from the main pass of the Mississippi River via Venice into the Port of New Orleans. The MR–GO channel avoids the twists of the Mississippi in Plaquemines Parish, cuts a straight shot through St. Bernard Parish, and empties into the Inner Harbor Navigational Canal, which then puts ships into the main part of the Port on the southern edge of New Orleans. MR–GO was expected to be an economic boon and eventually replace the Mississippi River waterfront as the city's primary commercial harbor.[70] However, from its early days, it was an environmental

---

67. Lewis, *New Orleans: The Making of an Urban Landscape*, 73.

68. See U.S. Army Corps of Engineers, New Orleans District, "Draft Integrated Final Report to Congress and Legislative Environmental Impact Statement for the Mississippi River—Gulf Outlet Deep-Draft De-authorization Study," June 2007. Public Law 84–455 also authorized replacement of the existing IHNC Lock when economically justified.

69. MR–GO ceased to be used for two-way ship traffic before Katrina. Final completion date from John Hall, USACE, New Orleans District. Dredging of the MR–GO project channel was initiated in 1958, and, except for the restriction at Paris Road, was completed in 1965, including a turning basin at the IHNC terminus. An interim channel (36 x 250 feet) was completed in 1963, at which time the first ship traveled from New Orleans to the Gulf via the channel. The narrow restriction at Paris Road was removed in 1968. See also MR–GO General Design Memorandum 2, supp. 3, p I–1, 1968.

70. In 1968, the River and Harbor Act (Public Law 90–483) authorized the Michoud Canal Project as a modification of the MR–GO Project, it constructed a deep-draft navi-

disaster. It required constant dredging. Its banks were weak and slumped in both calm weather and storms, gradually widening the canal and allowing saltwater intrusions that killed protective marsh grasses and cypress stands, destroying shellfish and fin fish breeding grounds, and, and the same time, increasing the city's risk from storm surge. Moreover, with only a 36 foot draft, it was too shallow for most of the large, new container ships. In recent times, less than one ship a day used the channel.[71] Thus, MR–GO did not live up to its commercial expectations. Moreover, it contributed to the flooding of New Orleans indirectly by degrading and shrinking the city's protective wetlands barrier. And it has been argued as contributing *directly* to the city's flooding when Katrina storm surge up the MR–GO channel acted like a funnel so that it accelerated to eight feet per second as it neared the city and overwhelmed the Industrial Canal Walls.[72]

The original request for an investigation of a Mississippi River–Gulf Outlet was authorized by the River and Harbor Act of 1945. The report was completed in three years but not transmitted to Congress until September, 1951. The USACE plan showed the MR–GO route in the form it would ultimately take: exiting the eastern GIWW. running southeast across the marshes of St. Bernard Parish into the Gulf. An alternative route from the west bank to the Gulf was rejected when the Dock Board proposed a $30 million investment to develop port facilities along the east bank route. The interrelationship of the river, the Industrial Canal, the GIWW, and MR–GO would migrate New Orleans' port trade and industry towards wastelands east of the city. In fairness to USACE, it must be noted that its report found the costs of the MR–GO plan to be high and the benefits of the outlet speculative. In its review, the Bureau of the Budget found that the MR–GO channel could not be justified by itself, but that the channel, together with a new turning basin, could constitute a valuable long-range improvement.[73] In the long run, local supporters of MR–GO politically

---

gation channel in the GIWW and the Michoud Canal by enlargement to a depth of 36 feet over a bottom width of 250 feet from the MR–GO channel to, and including, a turning basin 800 feet square at the north end of the Michoud Canal. The INHC Lock has not yet been replaced.

71. Horne, *Breach of Faith*, 153.

72. Estimate from Ivor van Heerden.

73. Cowdrey, *Land's End*, 71.

overcame USACE's opposition to the project that had held for some twenty-five years before Washington finally decided on it.[74]

It is perhaps ironic that it was in September of 1965—the year of completing the majority of MR–GO—that New Orleans was hit by Hurricane Betsy. Presaging Mayor Ray Nagin's attitude during the hours just prior to the coming of Katrina, Mayor Vic Schiro, prior to Hurricane Betsy's arrival in 1965, to 'prevent panic' told the public, "Don't believe any false rumors, unless you hear them from me." As with flood protection weaknesses revealed by Katrina, Hurricane Betsy forced a breach in the Industrial Canal and produced catastrophic flooding in the Lower Ninth Ward, New Orleans East, and Chalmette in St. Bernard Parish. More than a half million acres in metropolitan New Orleans were inundated.

Levees and Rain Flooding

The second major complexity in 'wresting' New Orleans from its natural environment—one that has existed from the very beginning of the city's emergence from a swamp—is dealing with the problem of *rain and standing water*. It is the problem of drainage. New Orleans typically receives more than 60 inches of rain annually; being situated largely below sea level, this places severe limitations on where the city can put the water.[75] New Orleans currently has twenty-two pumping stations, located in low areas, capable of pumping the equivalent of three inches of rain in five hours. A natural question is: what happens when rainfall exceeds that? Chris Hallowell notes that between 1900–1978, twenty-two storms have delivered *more* than five inches of rain per hour, and in the two decades since 1978, ten storms have dumped that volume of rain or greater.[76] These pumps were designed to handle standing water from rainstorms, not flooding from hurricanes, in which, as occurred with Hurricane

74. Observation by John Hall, USACE, New Orleans District. On the basis of USACE's initial report, not enough "political steam" had gathered to go ahead with MR–GO. The Louisiana Congressional delegation argued in its favor through the Eisenhower years, and the New Orleans Public Service, the Dock Board, and private transportation interests developed an effective spokesman in the Tidewater Development Association. Endorsement was secured from eleven governors in the Mississippi River Valley, resulting in the authorization of MR–GO in 1956. See Cowdrey, *Land's End*, 72.

75. In 1965, Hurricane Betsy had taken a bizarre course of loops and about faces, finally sweeping over Barataria Bay, grazing New Orleans to the east but dropping only four inches of rain.

76. Hallowell, *Holding Back the Sea*, 170.

Katrina, floodwaters become trapped *within* the ring of levees built to protect the city. Nevertheless, people have come from around the world to see these immense marvels of Albert Wood, some pumps enclosed in elaborate mid-nineteenth century brick structures. Drainage Pumping Station No. 1 (Melpomene Street Pumping Station)[77] covers much of New Orleans' uptown area. Drainage Pumping Station No. 6 at Orpheum Street is the largest pumping facility in the world—although when winds come from the north or northeast, as they did with Hurricane Katrina, forcing water into the drainage canals from Lake Pontchartrain, their effectiveness is reduced.

Looking back to New Orleans' early years, as the nineteenth century began, the population of the city began to fill in the original grid laid out by French engineers. In 1794 the Carondelet Canal was dug to connect the back of the city along the river levee with Lake Pontchartrain via Bayou St. John, allowing boats to come into that part of the city and unload, boosting commerce. At the end of the canal, a turning basin was built.[78] As the city grew, the motivation to fill in the backswamp between the old city grid and the lake was not simply for expansion purposes. It was also to rid the city of mosquitoes and what nineteenth century physicians believed was a source of disease.[79] The medical science at the time promoted the idea that inhabitants' health required swamp drainage around the city, as well as the removal of cypress trees which blocked needed cleansing airflow. With the first occurrence of Yellow Fever in 1796, and subsequent epidemics in 1822, 1824, and 1853, when one-third of some 30,000 cases treated died, New Orleans vigorously embarked on a program of drainage canals as the solution. Following the improved Carondelet Canal, the city dug the Melpomene Canal through uptown ridges in 1825, the Poydras Canal, which was replaced by the New Canal in the 1840s, and the Marigny Canal for the lower neighboring suburbs. How much these drainage canals were, in fact, "solutions" is a matter of debate. Even with

---

77. Melpomene, one of the nine Muses, was patroness of tragedy (and the lyre).

78. From which is derived the name Basin Street. While roads such as the 'Old Spanish Trail' (OST), built along Gentilly Ridge, allowed access, the best way in or out of the city was via Bayou St. John, particularly after improvements to what had originally been a drainage canal were ordered by the Governor for whom the improved canal was named. See Peirce Lewis for further discussion.

79. See, for example, Colten, *An Unnatural Metropolis*, 17, 12, 34.

improvements, New Orleans continued to face problems of sewerage, odors, stagnant water, and the septic conditions that resulted.

In 1836, increased antagonism among diversifying cultures of New Orleans (a very white 'Uptown,' the Vieux Carré and Tremé, and new lower class Irish and German immigrants downstream in Faubourg Marigny) resulted in a formal division into three separate communities, each with its own churches, cemeteries, and drainage-navigational canals. Hacking out the New Basin Canal through cypress swamp also altered population distribution, with the Irish hired for this work settling in a rough area upstream from the French Quarter known as the "Irish Channel."[80] Craig Colten concludes that the city's political subdivisions of three separately governed municipalities often put public works projects at odds with one another (an instance of Marker 6, cross-domain interactions), and that the drainage problems especially affected the poor in lower-lying districts, since the urban elite could escape the summer pestilence. As a result, there was little motivation to complete the city's complex drainage plans.[81] Thus, the mixture of failures in regulating and completing plans to handle complex problems such as sewerage, garbage, cemeteries, dangerous industries, and other waste-producing activities not only helped determine the actual configuration of New Orleans' landscape, these failures also resulted in human tragedies, including the city's ineffective delivery of public services during the 1853 Yellow Fever epidemic.[82]

The first vigorous attempt at cleansing New Orleans' sewerage and drainage canals and flushing out gutters and streets was conducted by Union Army General Benjamin F. Butler, 1862–65. Like ancient Rome, however, poor sanitation in garbage and human waste disposal continued to plague New Orleans, and another Yellow Fever epidemic occurred in 1878. It was ultimately not until 1905, when the role of mosquitoes as a cause of spreading Yellow Fever was understood, that the disease was able to be stopped before becoming epidemic. Now there was a clear, rational basis for the city's massive campaign to drain or oil the surface of all standing water. Yet there always seemed to be a tug-of-war between reason and greed (masked as the need for economic expansion). In 1893

80. Lewis, *New Orleans: The Making of an Urban Landscape*, 47.

81. Colten, *An Unnatural Metropolis*, 45.

82. The flooding following Sauvé Crevasse echoed similar issues in which the city's fragmented structure and piecemeal approach to projects did not provide a consistent protective barrier for the entire urban territory. See Ibid., 28–29.

the New Orleans Common Council, concerned that many areas still soggy swamps were an impediment to economic growth and prosperity, appointed an engineering committee to develop a systematic plan for expanding the drainage canals to *eliminate* the swamps.[83] It remained ambiguous how much of the engineers' plan to provide drainage for *every* part of the city was actually based on rational principles. Colten observes that during the 1920s, while the Sewerage and Water Board sought to install a comprehensive system to serve the entire city, many gaps—most apparent in the sewerage system—particularly affected low-lying districts inhabited by blacks.

Over the years, 'stewardship' in New Orleans' urban environment was forced to engage the two major water hazards its physical location faced: frequent spring flooding from the Mississippi River, and even more frequent standing water from heavy rains that could occur at almost any time of the year. These two natural elements continually perplexed those in a position to make decisions for the city. More important, they revealed assumptions city leaders, engineers, businessmen, and others held about the 'proper' relationship between human and natural orders. These assumptions dictated their decisions. But the strategies taken to deal with these problems—levees to control river flooding, drainage canals to fill low-lying swamps and rid the city of standing rainwater—were ultimately inadequate. Not only extreme events, such as hurricanes, but frequent and continual flooding from *normally anticipated rainfall* would to demonstrate their failure. At both critical times and normal times, attempts to *control* nature failed.

In fact, New Orleans' approach to dealing with its natural environment has never been overarching or comprehensive. Neither has that of other American cities. Unlike their European counterparts, most cities in America have grown *organically*—even those planned, as was Washington, DC, by Pierre l'Enfant and, later, Andrew Ellicott. In his essay, "American Cities," Jean-Paul Sartre observes that the American city was, originally, "a camp in the desert," and that even those given the illusion of rationality being laid out in checkerboard-like fashion, nevertheless appear "frail and temporary, formless and unfinished . . . haunted by the presence of im-

---

83. Colten, *An Unnatural Metropolis,* 83, 85. To avoid polluting the Pontchartrain lakefront entertainment district, canals and pumps would carriy drainage east to the Lake Borgne wetlands.

mense geographical space surrounding them."[84] On the plains, American cities were connected across vast spaces by roads that divide a city or town down the middle as a kind of vertebral spinal column. Much of Louisiana is still *platin*, low-lying grasslands, and the towns that lie along its highways often bear this characteristic, although, as in Cajun Country, often with further division of the highway spinal column itself. Traveling west from Baton Rouge along U.S. 190, one sees these separated spines in Opelousas and smaller towns along the way, where the highway divides into an East-West passage, with block or two of homes residing between. With New Orleans, its 'spinal column' lays on its western flank, a very crooked spine indeed—the Mississippi River.

One can surmise that perhaps the very sinewy-ness of the river, and the hyper-fertility of its marshy surroundings contributed to why New Orleans, once expanded beyond its European-style Vieux Carré, grew organically. Once its back swamps were drained and the city began to expand north, and, in mid-twentieth century, further east and west, New Orleans grew 'as if from a mustard seed.' The analogy to the parable of the mustard seed is not simply that sizeable plants grow from tiny seeds, but rather that the mustard plant remains inherently wild, unruly, untamed, unable to be cultivated.[85] One might prefer the model of stewardship as 'dominion' to be replaced by a concept of 'shared interdependence and coordination.'

Markers of Complexity: Who Was in Control and When?

What problems of environmental 'stewardship' manifested themselves as one or more of the Seven Markers of Complexity? Some difficulties were instances of turf wars and ongoing struggles for funding, government support, and inter-agency domination, reflected in our attempts to answer the question 'who was in control and when?' (Marker 6). This extends the idea of 'dominion' over nature to attempts by various interest groups to control *one another*. The frequent results, however, were highly

---

84. Sartre, "American Cities," *Literary and Philosophical Essays*, 124.

85. In the Parable of the Mustard Seed, the analogy with the Kingdom of God is based less on the mustard plant's limited cultivation for medicinal or culinary properties, than on the wild mustard that grew rampantly and was an ever-present danger to destroy gardens and grain fields. Like kudzu, it could take over an entire environment. Thus, if New Orleans saw itself 'taking over' the wilderness, it would also always be in danger of *being taken over* by wilderness. See discussion by John Dominic Crosson, *Jesus: A Revolutionary Biography*, 64–66.

fragmented approaches to building and maintaining levees—not only a lack of standardization of size and construction materials, but also in *where* levees were situated and how levees, locks, and, eventually, spillways interacted with one another. Failures from human struggles for 'dominion' over other humans were also manifest at the level of *implementation*. In current industry jargon, this is called 'stovepiping.' Agencies receiving government favor and funding were inclined to interpret this as resulting from their superior design approach, which would lead to an over-commitment to that one approach. It is the fallacy of 'what gets funded *must* be the correct design approach.' The "levees only" policy is the most glaring historical case.

Fragmented or piecemeal solutions can also result from a *misuse* of funds. For example, just before Hurricane Katrina struck, a $427,000 repair to a crucial floodgate languished in bureaucratic delay while the Orleans Levee District Board went ahead with pursuing building parks, constructing docks, and investing in on-water gambling.[86]

There are a number of historical instances of problems of scale (Marker 4), non-robust solutions (Marker 5), and instability (Marker 1). An example of instability—where an apparent solution to a flooding danger in location *a* precipitates another flooding or water-related problem in location *b*—was the intentional dynamiting of the levee at Poydras Plantation during the Great Flood of 1927. Here, 'instability' within the overall system of levees led directly to a further problem—the degradation of human values and quality of life (Marker 7). When it was decided to destroy the levee fifteen miles south of New Orleans—at the expense of black neighborhoods in St. Bernard Parish—this fundamentally severed the faith of blacks in New Orleans' elite leadership. For many historians, this watershed event stands at the beginning of the migration of blacks to Chicago, Detroit, and New York City, and kindled the first flames of the civil rights movement.[87] It was symbolic of underlying, deep social divisions that many privileged, white families from New Orleans traveled down on special permits to see the spectacle of the explosions at Poydras.

86. Ann Carns, "Long Before Flood, New Orleans' System was Prime for Leaks," *Wall Street Journal*, September 25, 2005, mentioned in Brinkley, *The Great Deluge*, 194.

87. See Barry, *Rising Tide*, 254–58, and Brinkley, *The Great Deluge*, 7 ff.

STEWARDSHIP IN THE CULTURAL MILIEU

Thus far, the Biblically-derived concept of stewardship has been discussed largely as a model for understanding the relationship *between* the human and natural environments. However, stewardship, as a prophetic ideal, is also is applicable *within* the human world and the cultural milieu. Stewardship here elaborates ethical and moral responsibilities within the *human* environment. The consequences of failing to meet those obligations is concern of the later Hebrew prophets. Unlike earlier ecstatic prophets and seers (*roĕ*) from Canaan, whose forms of expression oracles and visions, with the emergence of the classical prophets (*nabî*)—Amos, Hosea, Isaiah—there is a new focus on inequities and social evils that continued to plague the human environment. This social prophecy was expressed through laments, woes, entreaty, intercession, and in in the prophetic role in covenant lawsuits (*rîb*), where the prophet's office became interpreter of history, making the past relevant to present history, and intermediary, an agent of the imperium. Amos, for example, representing a collection of sayings attributed to a Judean peasant farmer living in the early part of the eighth century BCE, denounces the society of the Northern Kingdom, Israel, which had expanded its territory and amassed great prosperity at the expense of the poor, small farmers and landholders. Israel's wealth created a society of vast inequities between the urban elite and rural agricultural folk (echoed at Poydras, during the Flood of 1927). Amos speaks out against these social evils—the luxury of the rich and their oppression of the poor—in which, by manipulating the legal system's process for giving credit, something all farmers needed against the exigencies of weather and uncertain yields, lenders could separate farmers not only from their patrimonial farms and but even their freedom. Amos attacks Israel's decadent opulence and false piety of the elites—those "who lie on beds of ivory, and lounge on their couches, and eat lambs from the flock, and calves from the stall"[88] are the same ones who "trample on the poor and take from them levies of grain."[89] The message of Amos, therefore, is one calling for social equity and justice and "righteousness," where concern for the disadvantaged, rather than oppression of those who have 'fallen

88. Amos 6:4

89. Amos 5:11 Lecture notes from G. Ernest Wright; see also commentary in Oxford Annotated NRSV.

between the cracks' of society, is a significant part of what it means to fulfill human stewardship.[90]

To manage discussion of 'stewardship' in New Orleans' cultural milieu, we focus on three areas: (1) issues of race, class, economics, and political power, including a look at the history of voting power in New Orleans, (2) the relationship of building patterns and *where* one lives in the New Orleans to one's level of peril from storms and flooding, and (3) the significance of demographic changes before Hurricane Katrina as a basis upon which to understand those that occurred afterwards. The section concludes with a consideration of patterns of social inequities that anticipate the tragedies that were experience in Hurricane Katrina and its aftermath.

Race, Class, Economics, and Political Power

Issues of race, class, and access to political power emerge readily from an examination of the history of political struggles and voting in New Orleans. We will examine these issues through several lenses: (1) the role of various social and political organizations in New Orleans, (2) complexities of its creole culture, (3) the matter of race in struggles for political power, and (4) the impact of the Voting Rights Act.

Social Organizations

It is useful to look at race and economics, and changes in power, in the context of the roles played by the variety of voluntary, community-based organizational structures that form part of the fabric of the city's day-to-day life. These social organizations are not only city-wide—churches (Roman Catholic, Protestant, and, more recently, temples of Asian traditions), business and development interest groups, Masonic Lodges, Knights of America, Jewish Community Centers, private clubs like the Pickwick Club; they also include New Orleans' unique, *local* social and beneficent clubs such as the Pigeon Town Steppers, the Zulu Social Aid

---

90. Israel's special relationship with God entails special *ethical* responsibility: God may accept sacrifice for unwitting sins but not hardhearted covenant breaking. Covenant obedience demands social justice—Israel's people were slaves, therefore you must be concerned for the poor and the weak. Israel's attempt to keep rich at the expense of the poor was a violation of their sacred covenant: let justice the roll down like an everlasting stream. Similar messages of concern for social abuses and the oppression of those who have fallen between the cracks of society can be found in Isaiah and Micah; Isaiah adds a dimension of the prophet as watchman, warning Israel of its peril.

and Pleasure Club, and The Big Nine. These local clubs and associations symbolize the special attachment to, the power that resides *within*, each of New Orleans' 73-odd individual neighborhoods. A history of 'attachment to neighborhood' has contributed enormously to New Orleans' special culture: neighborhoods are the locus of much of its music, its color, its art, its festival. But implications of neighborhood attachments have also emerged as among the more solution-resistant *complexities* facing post-Katrina planning and reconstruction, particularly for those neighborhoods that may be forced to change their population make up and character as rebuilding and development goes on.

Some local associations become visible to outsiders during Mardi Gras and other public festival occasions in New Orleans. Less publicly visible are the ways in which they have represented sharp racial and class divisions within the city. For example, the historically white-only Mistick Krewe of Comus, founded in 1856, was connected with membership in the private Pickwick Club until official ties were broken in 1884. Comus, as the first parading organization of Mardi Gras, wore blackface to mock Darwin's theory of evolution and a higher status of blacks in the social order, and carried an effigy of Abraham Lincoln.

Comus' segregation practices was among the reasons for the formation of the predominately black Zulu Social Aid and Pleasure Club in 1916. Zulu traces its immediate origins to a group of laborers who had organized a club named "The Tramps" in 1909, but its social function pre-dates that, and bears a resemblance to various Creole social aid and benevolent societies that could be found in the slave-era Caribbean, such as the *cabildos* or Church-sponsored urban mutual aid societies within Cuban slave society.[91] In New Orleans, these benevolent societies functioned as the earliest forms of insurance in the Black community, where, for a small amount of dues, members received financial help when sick or financial aid when burying deceased members. Such neighborhood-based benevolent societies were spread throughout the city; the city was divided into wards, and each ward had its own benevolent "club." Consistent with

---

91. *The cabildos,* along with the *batey* or slave barracks of sugar plantations, and fortified mountain *palenques* were three institutions of colonial Cuban slave society within which Afro-Cuban religions were born and able to be developed. In *Regla de Ocha (Santeria)*, the *Orisha* tradition in Cuba, this contributed to the syncretization of Catholic saints (*santos*) with Yoruba deities (*orishas*) by worshippers (*santeros*). See, for example, Olmos and Paravisini-Gebert, *Creole Religions of the Caribbean*, 24.

the medieval notion of Mardi Gras as a day of the "rule of misrule," the Zulu group wore raggedy pants, and Jubilee singers in front of King Story, costumed with a lard can crown and a scepter of banana stalk. Later groups began the use of floats decorated with palmetto leaves and moss, with four Dukes accompanying the King; floats became more lavish and outrageous through the years, although until 1968 its route remained on the "back streets" of black neighborhoods. Interestingly, during the civil rights movement of the 1960s, Zulu came under attack from other black organizations who saw dressing in grass skirts and blackface as demeaning, and its membership dwindled. Zulu has grown again, and now sees itself as "the everyman club," with membership composed of men from all walks of life—from laborers, City Mayor, City Councilmen, and State Legislators, to United States Congressman, and educators.

Comus, like many of the carnival krewes, jealously guarded the identities of its membership. This secrecy played very much into the desirability of wanting to participate in the club's activities. One apocryphal story recounts a flying wedge of uninvited ladies attempting to force their way into a Comus ball (many prize its rare invitations and try to steal them to enter the Comus ball). The Mobile, Alabama businessmen who gathered above the old Gem Restaurant to organize this secret society saw their mission as transforming an existing irregular, ragtag carnival into a *flambeaux*-lit procession of pomp and circumstance. A particular Mardi Gras tradition connected with Comus was the ritual of the "Meeting of the Courts," originating in 1892, when the King of Carnival, Rex, and his Queen paid a visit to the throne of Comus. The acting out of such Mardi Gras rituals over time has become more and more elaborate, but also, as will be discussed later, symbolic of certain unfortunate consequences that can attend preoccupation with an *imaginative* sense of reality.

In part to combat the history of racial and class separation that Mardi Gras krewes represented, in 1991 the New Orleans City Council passed an ordinance requiring all social organizations, including Mardi Gras krewes, to publicly certify they did not discriminate on the basis of race, religion, gender or sexual orientation. This was necessary to obtain a parade permit. In principle, this ordinance meant that any private social club would have to abandon its traditional code of secrecy and identify its members to the City's Human Relations Commission. Comus, along with Momus, another krewe with origins in the nineteenth century, withdrew from parading rather than identify its membership. In a constitutional challenge to the city ordinance, the Fifth Circuit held that the New Orleans city ordinance prohibiting discrimination in places of public accommodation could not be applied to the four private clubs, including Comus, Momus, and Proteus, without violating the members' right of intimate association.[92] Indeed, the very restrictive guest and admission policies and the Clubs' isolation constituted grounds by which the Court concluded that these Clubs, on the spectrum of personal attachments, were among the "most intimate," and, therefore, due constitutional protection against unjustified governmental intrusion—even where the City's interest in eradicating discrimination was a "compelling state interest." While Comus still holds its annual Mardi Gras ball, the krewe of Comus, along with Momus and Proteus, no longer parade the streets.

Creole Culture

In discussing the question of social and cultural 'stewardship' in New Orleans, while many issues turn on race, not all of them do. Moreover, issues of race are themselves multi-dimensional. That is, racial attitudes frequently merge with competition for economic power; feelings about what it takes to maintain neighborhood integrity overlap with questions of segregation and racial oppression. The motivations for certain behaviors may start out similar, but because they proceed from quite different places in the social spectrum, eventually become overlaid with attitudes toward race. For example, the neighborhood of an emerging racial or cultural minority in a pre-existing urban environment may attempt to preserve its cultural heritage and identity by 'ghettoizing itself' in various ways. The neighborhood of an old-guard, landed majority may do similar things in order to preserve its own sense of history. Their actions and behavior, however, will be come to be perceived in very different ways as the intention of racial discrimination is attributed to one but not the other. Which perception is correct may ultimately turn on the determination of whether 'ghettoizing' was imposed from within or from without, as a consequence of economic suppression and racial bias. The point is that it is important acknowledge it is not always the case that preservation of the self-identity of cultural group *a* is necessarily at the expense of cultural group *b*.[93]

92. *Louisiana Debating and Literary Association v. City of New Orleans,* 42 F.3d 1483 (5th Cir. 1995).

93. As an example for comparison, while racial divisions were both uncovered and precipitated by forced busing of students into inner-city school from South Boston dur-

In New Orleans, racial identity has historically been something of a crap shoot. For example, while 'quadroon' referred to a person having one-quarter black ancestry,[94] an 'octoroon' to a person whose ancestry was one-eighth black, black identity was, in many cases, self-chosen whenovert discrimination was not an immediate consequence.[95] The question of self-choice will arise in the discussion of *Plessy v. Ferguson*. Racial identity in New Orleans (and elsewhere) was also not simply a question of black *vs.* white. Divisions and subtle discriminations have existed *within* the black community as well.[96] In some of New Orleans's larger black neighborhoods, during the early twentieth century, there were so-called "paper bag parties" in which only blacks whose skin was lighter than a brown paper bag were allowed entry. This arbitrary standard became a way lighter-skinned black Creoles attempted to separate themselves from darker-skinned blacks.

The picture of New Orleans as "a mixture of all the nations," a mingling of all races, a patch-work of peoples is at least as old as Alexis de Tocqueville's 1831 journey to America.[97] But the emergence in New Orleans of the largest concentration of free blacks in the deep South in

ing the days of Louise Day Hicks in the late 1960s and early 1970s, more issues were involved than those of race. South Boston sees itself as the historical legacy of the first Irish immigrants who came to America, and desires to preserve that Irish identity. However, South Boston has functioned in virtually identical ways for Polish, Albanian, Latvian and Lithuanian Americans, and, therefore, must be regarded as a diverse, multi-cultural neighborhood.

Louise Day Hicks was a Catholic Irish-American lawyer and member of the Boston School Committee who opposed court-ordered busing to achieve racial integration, seeing Boston schools as a scapegoat for failure to solve the housing and economic disadvantages of African Americans. Racial discord became particularly public after the 1971 *Swann v. Charlotte-Mecklenburg Board of Education* decision was followed by expanded busing programs. Hicks herself, while conservative and racially bigoted, was a progressive supporter of the National Organization for Women and the ERA. Racial attitudes are rarely the consequence of consistency in beliefs.

94. Modified from the Spanish *cuarterón*, from *cuarto* (quarter).

95. Terms such as *quadroon, octoroon,* and *mulatto* originated with the racial attitudes of the Spanish, then other European colonizers. Since the degree of European blood a person had was an important determiner of civil rights, these classifications were precisely defined and recorded, but in practice such terms were used on the basis of *perceptions* of skin color rather than knowledge of ancestry.

96. As they have regarding different ethnic groups within the white population.

97. Tocqueville's exchange with the lawyer Etienne Mazureau, quoted in Hirsch and Logsdon, eds, *Creole New Orleans: Race and Americanization,* 7.

the nineteenth century—whose relatively light complexions denoted contact with the Spanish, Germans, French, and Indians who made up the population—stood in dramatic contrast with both their status as granted by French and Anglo-Americans and the ruthless institution of black slavery. Toqueville warned that the unwillingness of the French to grant equality to free blacks (*libres*) would ultimately cause them to one day "make themselves your ministers."[98]

One of the factors that may have contributed to cohesiveness within the free black community in New Orleans is the discovery that most slaves brought to Louisiana during the French colonial period were largely confined to a twelve year period between 1719 and 1731, and that they came with an intact Bambana culture from the Senegal River Basin."[99] However, the full emergence of self-conscious identity was as complex as the process by which New World free blacks came into their freedom. For example, one path to free status was the consequence of white French slaveholders taking black women as mistresses, with the offspring, under Napoleonic Code, having certain rights to some proportion of the family inheritance. This path became increasingly frequent in the early nineteenth century. Another path, more rare, was the ability of some New Orleans slaves to purchase their freedom through additional work they performed on holidays and on Sunday. Equally rare were slaves who earned their freedom as a reward for faithful service to their masters. Some, who were able to prove partial Indian ancestry were freed by the Spanish colonial government's ban on Indian slavery. Other slaves might earn their release through military service, for example during the Natchez War (1729–31), or for public service, although this practice became less frequent in the later eighteenth century.[100] Census data for lower Louisiana shows a rapid increase of free blacks from only 82 persons in the New Orleans area in 1763 to 3,350 in 1806 to 18,467 in 1860.[101] Beginning in 1766, some free blacks began into move to the outposts of the Attakapas and Opelousas territories.

98. Toqueville, *Journey to America*, 380.

99. Gwendolyn Midlo Hall, "The Formation of Afro-Creole Culture," in *Creole New Orleans*, 67. Between 1719 and 1731, twenty-two of the twenty-three slave-trading ships came from Africa during French rule: sixteen from the Senegal region, six from a post on the Gulf of Benin near Dahomey, one from Angola.

100. See Brasseaux, et al., *Creoles of Color in the Bayou Country*, 2–5.

101. Ibid.

The term 'creole' has often been used to refer to inhabitants of New Orleans and South Louisiana, black and white. It is a term applied with many meanings. *Créole* is the French-African dialect of Haiti. 'Creolization' describes the syncretistic religious beliefs and cultural practices of Afro-Caribbean peoples, including shared beliefs in a creator complemented by a pantheon of deities (*orishas, loas*), cults of watchful dead ancestors, use of physical objects that organize worship,[102] and community-based rather than central religious authority. 'Creolization' thus refers to the *process* of dynamic encounters, adaptations, and syncretism of the diaspora culture of enslaved African communities that allowed them to overcome devastating loss and preserve group and personal identity. *Créole* also refers to the Afro-French language used in Louisiana, largely created by those slaves brought directly from Africa between 1719 and 1731.[103] *Créole* survives today in older forms of Zydeco music still played in rural Louisiana. An example of even older *Créole* dialect—from by a slave, Pierre, from St. Martinville, before the Civil War is a poem Marie Mouri:

Chère ti zozo. Quoi tapé fè?	Dear little bird. What are you doing?
T'apé sauter. T'apé chanter.	You're jumping. You're singing.
To pas connais n'a pu Marie?	Don't you know Marie is no more?
Marie mouri, Marie mouri.	Marie has died, Marie has died.
Ti z-herbe to vert, ti z-herbe to moux	Little grass you're green . . . so soft.
Faut pu to fais un lit pou nous.	No longer have to make a bed for us.
To pas connais n'a pu Marie?	Don't you know Marie is no more?
Marie mouri, Marie mouri.	Marie has died, Marie has died.
Quand jou vini n'a pu soleil.	When day comes no more sun.
Quand nuit vini n'a pas sommeil.	When night comes there's no sleep.
Quand monde content mo pu ca ri.	When people are happy I can no
Marie mouri, Marie mouri.	longer laugh. Marie has died . . . [104]

102. Such as such as the sacred stones (*otones*) of Regla de Ocha, the *nganga* caldron, the Ekué drum of the Abakuá Secret Society, the *potomitan* of Vodou ritual.

103. Hall argues that linguistic and historical evidence establishes that the creole language of Louisiana was created by the early slaves brought directly from African, and was not imported from the French Caribbean Islands. It is less clear that this remains true after the Haitian Revolution (1791–1804), the most successful of African slave rebellions in the Western Hemisphere.

104. This poem was collected by James Francis Broussard (*Louisiana Creole Dialect*, Kennikat Press, 1972) and sung by David Greeley of Steve Riley and the Mamou Playboys on their Rounder album *Dominos*.

In the Americas, the term *creole* was also redefined for social reasons. Gwendolyn Hall points out that the term appears to derive from the Portuguese word *crioulo*, referring to a slave of African descent born in the New World, but was then extended to include Europeans born there. In Spanish and French colonies, including eighteenth-century Louisiana, *creole* was used to distinguish American-born from African born slaves. During the Latin American struggles for independence in the late eighteenth and early nineteenth centuries, the meaning of the word changed again so that it referred to the Latin American elite, born in the Americas, who, because they were racially mixed, were accused of being incapable of self-rule. To reject that, the creole elite of Latin America redefined *creole* to mean people of exclusively European descent born in the Americas.[105] This was among its uses in New Orleans.

While the conflicts of slave vs. free, black vs. white, form one nexus of issues in the history of New Orleans, Hall notes there was no lack of conflict *among* its European colonizers—French, Spanish, German, Canadian, and pirates of assorted parentage. And part of New Orleans' reputation for violence and debauchery can be seen to stem from Louisiana functioning for France somewhat as did Australia for the British: by 1719 deportation to the new colony of Louisiana was one way to get rid of troublesome vagabonds and incorrigible family members. A special police force in France roamed Paris and the provinces grabbing people, often based on false accusations, for the profit of collecting head taxes for those they apprehended.[106]

The physical surroundings of New Orleans—its cypress swamps and marshes—created an excellent refuge for runaway slaves, who could survive by hunting and fishing. The commonness and relative acceptance of racial mixtures among the population in the early history of the city also contributed to the fluidity of its society in the midst of its struggles against the environment.

New Orleans' early history of disease, flooding, and exploitation combined to make escape desirable for many—not only Indians, the first group enslaved in significant numbers, African slaves, who often escaped with Indians, owned by the same master, but also deportees from France, including women sent against their will, Swiss and French soldiers, and

---

105. Gwendolyn Midlo Hall, "The Formation of Afro-Creole Culture," in *Creole New Orleans*, 60.

106. Ibid., 62, 64.

indentured workers.[107] In addition to the western territories, Havana was a common destination for those who were able to escape by sea.

From its very beginnings, therefore, Spanish and French New Orleans was not a stable society, but a frontier town with a fluid population, and marginal government control. While New Orleans experienced some level of tolerance in race relations, this was overlaid with a heavy atmosphere of suppression, exploitation, and domination of humans against other humans at the same time that the city was engaged in a parallel battle for domination between its marginal existence as a civilized outpost and the natural environment.

If there were a measure of stability in early New Orleans culture, one might point to the African slave population itself. Hall cites a court case that illustrates the solidarity among the Bambana: Biron, a slave who arrived on the ship *Aurore* had run away numerous times, and on one escape attempt, when the master fired shots in the air, then threatened to shoot him, Biron grabbed the gun. Samba Bambana was appointed interpreter for Biron in light of concern about the possibility of rebellion by the increasing number of blacks in the colony. Samba later did lead a conspiracy of slaves to take over Louisiana.[108] During the period of the Company of the Indies' rule of Louisiana, 1720–1731, there is evidence that a sizable number of Bambana cooperated with the Natchez Indians in their revolt against the French settlement, and that subsequently they continued to maintain ties with both Natchez and Choctaws in their opposition to the French.

By 1746, there were already about three thousand blacks in New Orleans against only half as many whites. Sheer numbers, the feebleness of white control, and the reliance on slaves for skilled labor, including performance of certain curative practices, contributed to the degree of self-confidence among blacks in New Orleans. With the increase of communities of *marrons* (maroons)[109] towards the end of the eighteenth century, many became situated in the swamps and marshes surrounding New Orleans, where they learned skills of trapping, fishing, growing squash to

---

107. Ibid, 63.

108. Heloise H. Cruzat, "Trial and Sentence of Biron, Runaway Negro Slave, Before the Superior Council of Louisiana, 1728," RSC LHQ, VIII (1925), 23–27, cited by Hall in *Creole New Orleans*, 71.

109. A corruption of the Spanish *cimarrones*, wild or untamed, used to refer to fugitive or runaway African or Indian slaves.

survive in that environment, retained a strong family structure, and maintained a network of ties with African slaves still on plantations.[110] The first Spanish governor, Antonio de Ulloa, arrived at New Orleans in March of 1766, attempting to rule the colony more severely. In 1768 insurgents who included Creoles and Germans drove him out, but in 1769 General Alejandro O'Reilly restored Spanish control, which lasted for 34 years, despite local administrators remaining French. During the last twenty-five years of the eighteenth century, while the existing slave birthrate remained stable, the total slave population grew as a result of renewed importing of slaves from Africa. This was followed, after the revolution ending in 1804, by massive migrations of Haitians to New Orleans, along with slaves and free blacks from Cuba.

The argument that it was the base culture of Africans from a particular region of Africa—a crossroads of both warfare and cultures, therefore, by necessity, open to the continual amalgamation of outside peoples and belief systems—that eventually formed the core of a coherent black society in New Orleans, also a crossroads, is generally persuasive.[111] Whether or not the Senegal River Basin in fact was such an open and "universalist" culture, one can see its spiritual residue in the cultural life of New Orleans, particularly in possible connections of musical forms,[112] as well as certain practices of Afro-creole folk religion. However, precisely which of these connections can be attributed to input directly from Africa, as opposed to transmission via the syncretistic folk-religious practices that emerged in Cuba, Haiti, and other areas of the Caribbean is difficult to determine.

The nineteenth century experienced a massive influx of white Americans to New Orleans, as well as English speaking slaves from Virginia and elsewhere along the Atlantic coast. In many respects, the history of whites coming into New Orleans was one of seeing the city as a business opportunity—an opportunity for great wealth that entailed wresting the city away not from its natural surroundings but from its creole culture. In the first quarter of the nineteenth century, New Orleans had become an important port, not only for slaves, but also for produce from South America and grain from the Midwest. A classic study of the records of the

110. Competing perceptions have held there was considerable hostility between slaves and free blacks as well as among various 'levels' of mixed-blood blacks.

111. Gwendolyn Hall makes such an argument.

112. For example, music originating from the region of Mali, blues forms, and early Zydeco called 'La La.'

struggle between newcomers and creoles is by Joseph Tregle in the *Journal of Southern History*.[113] Tregle identifies the largest influx of pre-Civil War Americans as originating from the northeastern seaboard—men whose financial resources and business skills soon gave them control over New Orleans' mercantile economy. However, creoles maintained superior voting strength in Louisiana until the 1830s, and were able to keep control of city and state government through constitutional manipulation and legislative gerrymandering until almost mid-century, with the help of politically skilled immigrants who came to Louisiana from France after 1803.[114] According to Tregle, the division of New Orleans into three separate municipalities between 1836 and 1852 (uptown controlled by Anglo-Americans, the other two by French-creoles) was a political arrangement that served to quell more violent conflict between ethnic rivals. Each conducted government business in its own language; each perpetuated its culture in separate school systems. Some of these schools had bilingual programs—a practice that would later come up against prohibitions that prohibited speaking French in the public schools.[115]

Prior to the Civil War, the immigrant influx to New Orleans was dominated by French, German, and Irish; later were added increasing numbers of Italians, Greeks, Latin Americans, Chinese, and Filipinos.[116] New Orleans was eventually becoming the multi-racial, multi-ethnic, polyglot gumbo it likes to proclaim it is. The 'gumbo,' however, often had the taste of conflict, as, during the Reconstruction era, white Anglo-American cultural mores struggled to suppress the historic interconnectedness of white and black creole communities. The stage had been set after New Orleans surrendered to Union forces in 1862, with the State Legislature passing a resolution proclaiming their's was a "Government of white people, made and to be perpetuated for the exclusive benefit of the

113. Tregle, "Early New Orleans Society: A Reappraisal," *Journal of Southern History,* XVIII (February, 1952).

114. Hirsch and Logsdon, eds., *Creole New Orleans: Race and Americanization,* 92.

115. There is a classic photo of a child standing before a blackboard in the process of writing two hundred times "I must not speak french" that is used on the cover of a cassette (Swallow 6088) by Cajun fiddler Hadley Castille; his song, "200 Lines: I must Not Speak French" is an autobiographical account of being punished for speaking French on the school grounds as a child. From conversations with Hadley.

116. See, for example, Joseph Logsdon, "Immigration Through the Port of New Orleans," in *Forgotten Doors: The Other Ports of Entry to the United States,* ed. Mark Stolarik (Philadelphia, 1988).

white race." Perhaps it was the influx of white but non-Anglo immigrants that provided the ethnic space within which New Orleans' free blacks could nevertheless survive.

One factor that provided free and largely Catholic blacks with some power in the city, was the historically large proportion of black property owners in New Orleans as compared to other cities.[117] Leonard Curry points out, for example, that in 1850 the free black population of Baltimore was more than 2.5 times the size of that in New Orleans, but held property ownership worth only 5.5 percent of the $2.5 million in real estate holdings of free blacks in New Orleans.[118]

What begins to emerge in the City of New Orleans is a complex history of *both* racial conflict and racial interconnectedness; of disempowerment and disenfranchisement but also underlying power within New Orleans' black creole community that would assert itself, challenge the restrictions of Jim Crow[119] legislation, and stand at the earliest stages of the civil rights movement. Jim Crow restrictions arose to become a system of subordination that competed with older creole values that repudiated rigid definitions of status based on racial identity. However, the call for racial unity and the appearance in New Orleans of many black community social clubs and political organizations in response to racially-based restrictions may inadvertently have contributed to the polarization, rather than the reuniting, of racial divisions. These issues continued to play a role in city policy-making even after the election of Ernest (Dutch) Morial as the city's first black mayor in 1978. They must still be taken into considerations in sorting out what equitable and faire post-disaster reconstruction strategies should be.

117. Ironically, after disastrous flooding such as in the case of Hurricanes Betsy and Katrina, homeownership created its own dilemmas about returning to flood-prone wards.

118. Curry, *The Free Black in Urban America, 1800–1850: The Shadow of the Dream*, 22–29, 39–44.

119. The laws that enforced racial segregation between the end of the Reconstruction period in 1877 and the beginning of the civil rights movement in the 1950s were named after a minstrel routine, Jump Jim Crow, performed around 1828 by its creator, Thomas Dartmouth "Daddy" Rice. Favors that might have been granted to half-French "free persons of color" were abandoned, as segregation was applied to the suspicion of black ancestry in any degree, and meant separation not only on public transportation and schools, but also theaters, restaurants, parks, and cemeteries.

Struggles for Political Power

Peirce Lewis and others have observed how the city's geography and social history have played into one another. New Orleans' levee boundaries between city and wilderness precipitated closer and more intimate associations among races, but human modifications of its geography it also worked towards the segregation of races. For example, the giant Wood screw pump during the early twentieth century allowed drainage of the city's backswamp and subsequent expansion into that area. However, differentia in what would become desirable residential locations ultimately pushed concentrations of blacks into low-lying, less desirable areas, and, thus, accelerated the process of residential segregation.[120] A second expansion after World War II into newly developed suburbs east and west, and eventually, on the north shore of Lake Pontchartrain, resulted in white flight and further residential segregation. In the twenty years prior to 1980, census data shows New Orleans' white population declining by 155,627 as its non-white population grew by 85,854. Up to 1840 New Orleans was a black majority city; after 1980 it became one again.[121]

Background to the recent history of race, access to political power, and voting patterns in New Orleans can be understood in terms of several key events that, after the Civil War, served to shape levels of cohesion within New Orleans' neighborhoods—particularly its black neighborhoods. The race riots of July, 1866, occurred during a convention on black suffrage, where white citizens, with the compliance of local authorities and police, killed thirty-five black citizens and wounded over one hundred. The protests and violence were outcomes of restrictive "black codes,"

---

120. See Lewis, *New Orleans: The Making of an Urban Landscape*, 67.

121. U.S. Census Bureau, Department of Commerce. The Census Bureau has increasingly used software tools to improve the census-taking process. These include adoption of geographic programs to improve the mail census; for example, the address coding guides (ACGs) of the 1970 Census, and the GBF/DIME-Files of the 1970 and 1980 Censuses. Since the 1990 Census, demographic data has been based on TIGER (Topologically Integrated Geographic Encoding and Referencing system) database files of census blocks. TIGER adapts theories of topology and graph theory to provide a mathematical description for geographic structures of states, counties, cities. The topological structure of the TIGER database defines the location and relationship of streets, rivers, railroads, and other features to each other and to the numerous demographic categories for which the Census Bureau tabulates data. See also Hirsch and Logsdon, eds., *Creole New Orleans: Race and Americanization*, 199. Of the city's 557,482 inhabitants in 1980, whites represented a minority of 42.5 percent, but an increasing majority of over 85 percent in New Orleans' suburbs.

laws enacted in 1865 and 1866 that in many ways replaced the social controls of slavery in which persons were defined as chattel. Black codes not only preserved the 'inferiority' of freed slaves, they also secured a steady stream of cheap labor by forcing apprenticeships to whites, excluding blacks from skilled trades, and limiting the type of property blacks could own. Reconstruction did away with black codes, but many of their restrictions were reenacted in Jim Crow laws, and not eradicated until the Civil Rights Act of 1964. In 1867, Congress initiated a set of laws, referred to by some as the Radical Reconstruction, in which Southern states were divided into five military districts, under the supervision of the U.S. Army. The Freedman's Bureau, established by Congress to help feed and educate emancipated blacks, was a particular source of resentment to racist whites, and it was during this time that secret terrorist organizations such as the Ku Klux Klan and the Knights of the White Camelia were formed. Among them could be included the Crescent City White League, formed by members of the Pickwick Club as a volunteer militia promising to reverse what they regarded as an absurd inversion of the relations of race. The White League engaged in numerous attacks against Republicans and blacks. The bloodiest occurred in April, 1973 in Colfax (near Alexandria) when nearly 100 members of the State's all-black militia were killed, followed in 1974 by a march on the Customs House—the imposing Egyptian Revival Style structure built near the river end of Canal Street in 1848 which had served as a prison for Confederate officers—clashing with the bi-racial police, leaving a dozen dead, and temporarily taking over the city until federal troops restored order.

Two years after the New Orleans race riots, the Fourteenth Amendment granted citizenship to former slaves and placed a federal limitation on states by forbidding them to deny any person life, liberty, or property without due process of law, and guaranteed every person within a state's jurisdiction "equal protection of the laws." Two years later, in 1870, the Fifteenth Amendment prohibited states or the federal government from using race, color, or previous status of servitude as a qualification prohibiting a citizen from voting. But in May of 1896, the U.S. Supreme Court by an eight-to-one majority essentially eviscerated the Fourteenth Amendment by advancing the doctrine of "separate but equal" in assessing the constitutionality of state racial segregation laws. *Plessy v. Ferguson*[122]

---

122. 163 U.S. 537 (1896).

tested a Louisiana law requiring the segregation of passengers on railway cars. The reasoning of the court turned on the idea that as long as
reasonably equal accommodations were provided to each racial group,
there was no violation of "equal protection." One of the ironies of the
case is that Homer Plessy was an octoroon (seven-eights Caucasian, only
one-eighth black), and easily "passed" for white. On June 7, 1892, Homer
Plessy boarded a car of the East Louisiana Railroad designated for use by
whites only; when he refused to leave the white-only car and move to the
colored car, he was forcibly ejected from the train and taken by police to
a New Orleans Parish jail. At the trial (*Plessy v. The State of Louisiana*) for
violating a State Act providing separate intrastate railroad cars for "white
and colored races," the argument that the Act was unconstitutional, violating the Thirteenth and Fourteenth Amendments, was rejected, as it was at
the State Supreme Court. At the U.S. Supreme Court, Mr. Justice Brown,
writing for the majority and citing the Slaughter-House Cases,[123] held that
the object of the Fourteenth Amendment was to secure equality of races
before the law, but that it was not intended to enforce social equality or a
commingling of the two races if the terms were unsatisfactory to either.
By this ruling, the Court gave legitimacy to state laws requiring separation of blacks from whites, including public schools, because the requirement of racial separation did not itself imply the inferiority of either race
to the other. A further irony following the case was that Homer Plessy,
because he easily "passed" for white, often rode in white-only railroad cars
unnoticed. Nevertheless, it is without question that *Plessy* was regarded as
a major setback for civil rights.

In New Orleans, the tendency of some black creoles was to look
inward to perpetuate their distinctive history and culture from within
local neighborhoods; [124] others sought ways by which black voices could
be united across the city. Examples of the former included neighborhood-

123. The Slaughter-House Cases, 83 U.S. 36 (1873), were a block of cases (*The
Butchers' Benevolent Association of New Orleans v. The Crescent City Live-Stock Landing
and Slaughter-House Company* (two cases), and *Esteben et al. and The Live-Stock Dealers'
and Butchers' Association of New Orleans and Cavaroc v. The State of Louisiana*) testing
the new Fourteenth Amendment, in which the Court read the Amendment to protect
only privileges or immunities conferred by national, not state citizenship.

124. Hirsch, "Simply a Matter of Black and White," in *Creole New Orleans: Race and
Americanization,* 265. Arnold sees a three-way tug of war: politics at the local neighborhood level; national concerns about race and segregation; issues involving economic
power within the city somewhere in between.

based social clubs, such as the Autocrat Club and the San Jacintos, which often reflected *intra-black* differences.[125] Examples of the latter were black civic leagues that emerged from the politically important Seventh Ward, raising a more unified voice across a broad range of concerns—education, business, public services, civic pride. A Federation of Civic Leagues from several wards was formed in 1928; the *Civic Leader* was its editorial banner, and it supported the local branch of the NAACP, established in 1915.

As various alliances between black and white political organizations formed and dissolved, the question of whether those living under Jim Crow restrictions should *demand* rather than *hope for* benefits naturally played out along racial lines. As an example of how Jim Crow restrictions could impact *where* one might live, the 1924 Louisiana State Legislature granted cities with populations of more than 25,000 the power to mandate residential segregation; almost immediately New Orleans put an ordinance in place. The prosecution of cases under this restrictive ordinance was met with house bombings by hostile whites and protest from local black leaders. Finally, in 1927, the U.S. Supreme Court declared the legislation unconstitutional.[126]

Equally egregious were Jim Crow restrictions on access to the ballot: poll taxes, literacy qualifications, and the so-called "understanding clause" adopted in 1921 that permitted white registrars to challenge blacks attempting to register to vote. These issues united separate black neighborhood organizations in supporting the NAACP's court challenge[127] to these discriminatory registration procedures. At the same time, there remained concerns about what some black leaders saw as a residue of black dependence on white structures of power.[128]

125. Although they could voice *shared* concerns, such as the quality of black schools.

126. The ordinances were enacted under a State law passed in 1924 preventing white persons from moving into a negro neighborhood without the consent of two-thirds of the negroes resident there, and vice versa. On March 14, 1927, Chief Justice Taft announced that the judgment of the Louisiana court was reversed on the authority of a 1917 case, *Buchanan v. Warley*, 245 U.S. 60 (1917) which involved a Louisville segregation ordinance. In that case, the Court had held that such a city ordinance 'invades the civil right to acquire, enjoy and use property, guaranteed in equal measure.'

127. *Trudeau v. Barnes.*

128. National vs. local structures of power, also at odds, were overcome in 1942 in *McKelpin v. Orleans Parish School Board*, when Thurgood Marshall from the national office of the NAACP worked through local power in the person of Seventh Ward attorney A.P. Tureaud (President of the Autocrat Club) to win equal salaries for black and white teachers. DEBR and Arnold Hirsch.

The hierarchical structure in which blacks remained dependent on white structures of power was not unlike the hierarchy of authority discussed in terms of the concept of stewardship. In the Biblical hierarchy, humankind is given responsibility for and also freedom over nature, but remains dependent on God, who has ultimate power and authority. In 'white populist' Louisiana politics, by analogy, blacks were encouraged to regard their freedoms as 'gifts' from powerful whites, to whom they remained dependent, and who held ultimate power and authority. Visibility of the disjunction and hypocrisy, however, was obscured. White populism, such as that of three times governor Earl Kemp "Uncle Earl" Long, had the ability to mask its underlying conservative paternalism. The result was a kind of *opportunistic* 'racial egalitarianism.' While easing government-induced indignities on blacks and improving access to the vote (from which Long would benefit), "Uncle Earl" did not substantially dismantle the Jim Crow laws of Louisiana. In fact, his first Lieutenant Governor, William J. "Bill" Dodd, in *Peapatch Politics*, argued Long was at heart a conservative and as prejudiced as a Cyclops in the KKK, even as he was giving the state liberal laws. Knowledge of inner truth aside, it was nevertheless the case that while only four hundred blacks were registered to vote in 1940, more than 28,000 had done so by 1952.

To understand the differing levels of access to political power in New Orleans, it is useful to trace various forces—neighborhood-based, city-wide, and national—that operated in the struggles for control of New Orleans politics in its succession of mayors. In April of 1946 DeLessups "Chep" Morrison became mayor of New Orleans. As had Earl Long, Morrison needed to forge connections with the black community, and eventually with the uptown-oriented Orleans Parish Progressive Voters' League (OPPVL), formed in 1949, whose members included A. P. Tureaud, and the Interdenominational Ministers Alliance (IMA), founded under the leadership of the Rev. A.L. Davis of the New Zion Baptist Church.[129] The relationship between Morrison and the black communities[130] also replicated

129. The IMA was an alliance of well over a hundred active black ministers in metropolitan New Orleans. The mutual opportunity Davis and Morrison represented to one another was of considerable irritation to Earl Long, who was reported to complain that Davis was just "a Baptist preacher that didn't preach nothing but Morrison." Quoted in Hirsch, "Simply a Matter of Black and White," in *Creole New Orleans: Race and Americanization*, 275.

130. Which, in the 1950 census, represented about one-third of New Orleans' total population, but who held less than one in 1,000 at the telephone company or in city gov-

features of the 'mask' worn by Long: while many blacks saw Morrison as a friend who improved their position, Morrison would still privately refer to blacks in racially derogatory terms, and continue his paternalistic politics of dispensing favors rather than genuinely sharing power.

On May 17, 1954, the U.S. Supreme Court, under Chief Justice Warren, overturned the so-called "separate but equal" doctrine of racially segregated public school education in *Brown v. Board of Education*.[131] Cases had come to the Court from Kansas, South Carolina, and Delaware, in which, other than Delaware, a three-judge federal district court had denied the plaintiffs on the basis of the 1896 "separate but equal" interpretation of the Fourteenth Amendment in *Plessy*. In holding that the segregation of "white and Negro" children in public schools under state laws permitting segregation violated the Equal Protection Clause, the Court maintained that compulsory school attendance laws and the amount of public funds supporting publication education reinforced the belief that universal education is one of the most important governmental functions in a democracy. The Louisiana State Legislature promptly passed Acts 555 and 556 to protect its segregated public school system from being dismantled, but both were deemed unconstitutional by Judge J. Skelly Wright, federal judge for the U.S. District Court for the Eastern District of Louisiana, in *Bush v. Orleans Parish School Board*[132] on February 15, 1956. The Court disposed of the State's constitutional contention that the laws were enacted in the exercise of the sovereign police power to promote public health, morals, better education and peace in the state, rather than race, by observing that the State failed to positively explain the pupil assignment process on any grounds *other than* race. The Court reinforced the primacy of such ingredients of human rights as education and the necessity to restrain the action of any state ignoring such rights.

During the NAACP and Tureaud's involvement with *Bush*, Chep Morrison's mask slipped away further in his refusal to allow Thurgood Marshall to use the Municipal Auditorium, as well as in his attack on the NAACP, accusing them of sponsoring meetings and speeches "emotion-

---

ernment; there were no black firefighters and only a handful of black police officers. See Ronette King, "Unequal Opportunity: Shifting Landscape," *The Times-Picayune*, March 26, 2001, accessed online at http://www.nola.com/unequalopportunity/index.ssf?/t-p/frontpage/79550842.html.

131. 347 U.S. 483 (1954).

132. 138 F. Supp. 336; 1956 U.S. Dist. LEXIS 3761.

ally arousing members of both races."[133] With the White Citizens' Councils making the NAACP a target, in April, 1956, the Louisiana Supreme Court prohibited NAACP branches from holding meetings or conducting business, and offices of the NAACP were raided by the New Orleans police. Unlike the uptown orientation of the OPPVL, the NAACP very much reflected its downtown creole neighborhoods.

The looseness of the language in *Brown* to desegregate with "all deliberate speed" led to much foot-dragging for a number of years throughout the South in implementing it. One attempted ploy was to try to segregate schools by *gender* (so that no black boys could be with white girls); another was the establishment of all-white private academies. Nevertheless, in New Orleans, on November 14, 1960, six-year old Ruby Bridges, guarded by U.S. Marshals, ran the gamut of screaming, spitting people trying to block her way into the William J. Frantz Elementary School; three other black first-graders entered the McDonough school, following U.S. District Judge J. Skelly Wright's order for desegregation to begin that day.[134] A local citizens' council had called on white parents to boycott the schools; one leader's call for action included the epithet that "burr-heads" were being forced into their schools. Ruby's father was fired from his job, and the white owners of a grocery store refused to allow her family to shop there. By the end of the week, only three white families remained in the Frantz school; all white parents had removed their children from McDonough. As the school year continued, she was joined by a few other black students, as well as some returning white students. But school integration also coincided with the beginnings of an exodus of middle-class white families to the suburbs, where developments were expanding during the

133. Quoted in Hirsch, "Simply a Matter of Black and White," in *Creole New Orleans: Race and Americanization*, 280.

134. Wright was made a pariah by his ruling, received death threats, and ended up appointed to the Circuit Court for the District of Columbia. Judge William Bryant, for whom Deanne clerked in the U.S. District Court for the District of Columbia, became close friends with Judge Wright. One day, on the DC Metro (subway) an older, rather scruffy man came up to Skelly Wright, who greeted him with great warmth and enthusiasm. Judge Bryant asked Wright how he knew this man, and Wright responded by saying this man was one of the few people in New Orleans who stood by him when he made his school desegregation ruling. Wright had attended night school in New Orleans, located opposite a human service agency for the blind. One day Wright watched a Christmas party at the agency, where they led blind white people into one room and blind blacks into another. This event was an emotional awakening about what segregation really meant in actual lives.

1960s. As a result, the proportion of black population in New Orleans rose from 37 percent in 1960 to 45 percent in 1970, and became a majority of 55 percent by 1980. Through a combination of 'white flight' and private, white-only schools, by the early 1970s, more than 70 percent of students in the New Orleans public school system were black.

Metropolitan New Orleans Roman Catholic schools represent an interesting comparison. Archbishop Joseph Rummel had praised *Brown*, and, although, reluctant to desegregate his parochial school system, expressed his intention to do so. This was met by many archdiocesan school boards voting against desegregation. After *Bush*, many white parents began to transfer their children to parochial schools to avoid desegregation; some Catholic parents even petitioned Pope Pius XII, requesting papal support for segregation, but these were emphatically denied. A number of court orders had been issued by Judge Wright to combat attempts by the Orleans Parish School Board to evade desegregation, and in March of 1962 Archbishop Rummel formally announced the end of segregation in parochial schools. Outraged white parents organized 'citizens councils' and threatened to boycott the parochial schools; Rummel responded by pleading for cooperation, threatening excommunication to opponents of desegregation, and, in fact, did excommunicate three protest organizers, including Judge Leander Perez, a seventy-year old St. Bernard Parish judge who called on Catholics to withhold donations and boycott Sunday collections. By September of 1963, some black students began to be admitted to previously all-white Catholic schools.

In July of 1961 Victor Schiro became mayor, initiating a period of political fragmentation, disinterest in black support, and further attacks on the NAACP. Attempts at economic desegregation for a brief time was spearheaded by students from New Orleans' black Catholic Xavier University who had joined the Congress of Racial Equality (CORE). CORE was established by James Farmer in 1942 to end discriminatory policies through direct-action projects. Beginning with a sit-in at a coffee shop in Chicago in 1942, CORE launched the first Freedom Ride as an interracial peaceful protest against states who the U.S. Supreme Court's 1946 decision declaring segregated seating on interstate buses unconstitutional, and in the 1950s supported voter registration drives. In the 1960s, CORE's civil rights activism became more dramatic, after its volunteers were tear gassed and jailed. In New Orleans, student volunteers brought action from the neighborhoods to the business district along Canal Street, seeking especially to desegregate jobs but meeting with only sluggish success. Later to become mayor, Ernest "Dutch" Morial, who was president of the local NAACP chapter from 1963 to 1965, warned Mayor Schiro about black citizens no longer accepting their rights as 'favors' granted by whites. Shiro's non-responsiveness and lack of progress in obtaining racially proportionate representation in city jobs resulted in a black march on City Hall in September of 1963.

Ultimately it would be the Civil Rights Act of 1964, and especially the Voting Rights Act of 1965, that would precipitate substantial changes. At the time of the Voting Rights Act, only 28 percent of eligible blacks were registered to vote; by 1966 that had risen to 42 percent, with blacks constituting more than a quarter of New Orleans' registered voters. To connect the forces behind this growing power of black voters with the particular neighborhoods from which they arose, it is useful to identify a number of the community organizations that were important in this process. Among those that were particularly significant during this period were the Southern Organization for Unified Leadership (SOUL), the Community Organization for Urban Politics (COUP), Total Community Action (TCA), and, somewhat later, the Black Organization for Leadership Development (BOLD).

In 1965, Robert Collins, Nils Collins, and others were among a group who organized SOUL, whose base were the black homeowners and middle-class black citizens in the Lower Ninth Ward. In 1969, Collins started COUP with Seventh Ward professionals. Collins would become the first black federal judge in the South.[135] As an offshoot of CORE, SOUL reflected a grassroots racial consciousness and a heightened level of militancy in pursuing demands of equality. COUP, in which future mayor Sidney Barthelemy was a leader, was less militant and more inclined to cultivate relationships with white political power. It appeared that *both* racial assertiveness *and* accommodation to existing structures of white power remained present in the communities out of which these organizations emerged.

In 1970, Maurice Edwin "Moon" Landrieu[136] began eight years as mayor, having represented New Orleans' Twelfth Ward in the Louisiana House of Representatives from 1960 to 1966, where he was one of the few

135. See, for example, Orissa Arend, "Trio Ignited Controlled Revolution in the '70's," *The Louisiana Weekly,* May 26, 2003.

136. Landrieu eventually had his childhood nickname, "Moon," legally made permanent.

white legislators who voted against bills designed to thwart desegregation of the public schools. A runoff primary against Jimmy Fitzmorris
yielded Landrieu 90 percent of black voters; his defeat of Ben Toledano
in the general election raised that to over 95 percent. Landrieu's tenure
as mayor saw desegregation of both public facilities and city government: in 1970 African Americans made up 19 percent of city employees;
by 1978 that number had risen to 43 percent. Landrieu also appointed
African Americans to high-level positions in City Hall, including his
Chief Administrative Officer, and the Rev. A.L. Davis to fill a vacancy and
become the city's first black member of the City Council. Landrieu had
forged ties with the uptown group, BOLD, as well as to SOUL, TCA, created in 1965 as a vehicle for federal poverty funding, and the Urban League,
whose New Orleans' affiliate was founded in 1938 by the Council of
Social Agencies, and which connected him particularly to the concerns of
black business professionals, economic development, and employment.[137]
Landrieu saw his actions as not simply 'placing' African Americans in city
government positions, but as generally opening opportunities for blacks
to enter the political process, or, as Arnold Hirsch put it, working within
the existing political traditions and racial dichotomy to foster "change
without pain . . . offer new opportunities to blacks without grievously
antagonizing whites."[138] It would be difficult to sort out just how much
Landrieu reflected the traditional practice of creating a patronage network in which larger and larger rewards given to black voters were still
from 'white hands.' However, successes in black leaders gaining positions
of political influence, such as future mayor Sidney Barthelemy's election
as State Senator and Robert Collins' federal judgeship, must be weighed
against whether long-term economic opportunities were achieved for
the black community at large. Scandals such as those associated with
the creation of Superdome Services, Inc. (SSI), and nepotism in the city's
Comprehensive Employment and Training Act (CETA) program, both
undermined Landrieu's legacy of creating a genuine entrance for blacks
into the political process, and failed to contribute to removing fragmentation within black communities.[139]

137. The Urban League maintains a Help Center dedicated to providing long-term
support for residents affected by Hurricane Katrina.
138. Hirsch, "Simply a Matter of Black and White," in Hirsch and Logsdon, eds., *Creole
New Orleans: Race and Americanization*, 297.
139. Hirsch notes, for example, that SOUL's ties to Lendrieu were so close that its

Underlying the question of practical politics is a deeper, ethical concern. This concern can be found in Rodolfe Lucien Desdunes, born in New Orleans in 1849 of Haitian and Cuban parents, among organizers of the *Comité des Citoyens* which launched the *Plessy* case, in pamphlets challenging W.E.B. DuBois' generalizations and in his major work *Nos Hommes et Notre Histoir.* Black racial identity is itself an issue of moral integrity rather than one of practical politics; it is a matter of being respected, not protected. It is certainly not one in which individual political gain would be the measure of the black community's achievement.

In May of 1978, Ernest Nathan "Dutch" Morial was elected mayor of New Orleans, and embodied an ethics of race and politics that sought to transcend divisions of race without ignoring their existence. If organizations like COUP and SOUL symbolized two differing styles of 'cooperative accommodation' vs. 'confrontation' between blacks struggling to enter the political process and whites already in it, Morial's distaste for political patronage put him philosophically at odds with SOUL[140] but also the object of COUP's worries about alienating whites. In a sense, it was Morial's personal philosophy that raised *intra-racial* issues of the competition between solidarity and individual favoritism. Those issues became real in the 1982 election, in which both COUP and SOUL backed a black challenge in the person of State Senator William Jefferson, albeit for different reasons.[141] Morial's attempts to address government waste and his demand for excellence in city workers was a position that, on an ethical level, at least, should have had broad cross-racial appeal. Nevertheless, racial polarization arose. Morial's battles with traditional black political organizations did not substantially reduce his appeal to black voters; however, rigidly enforcing a meritocracy that no longer tolerated old structures of white power through which positions on various commissions such as the Dock Board could be gained ultimately diminished his standing among white voters. Observers of the scene, including Iris Kelso, concluded Dutch Morial was "too white for the blacks, and too black for the whites." A persistent and unanswered question of race in New Orleans' politics is: can a rational, *racially-neutral* policy which supports

members were referred to as "Moons' Coons." Ibid., 302.

140. Arnold Hirsch quotes media critic Iris Kelso as remarking that at least Morial's victory would mean "there won't be any more black political leaders who can mau-mau the Mayor, claim to represent blacks, and walk off with all the rewards." Ibid., 309.

141. COUP also backed Morial's white opponent, Ron Faucheux, in the runoff.

standards of excellence in government overcome the divisiveness of race? Historically, it could be argued that overcoming the divisiveness of race has actually been accomplished more *through* emphasizing racial identity than by suppressing it.

After 1978, when Dutch Morial was elected for a second term, New Orleans continued to elect black mayors, and there was generally little doubt about the racial identity of the eventual winner. Sidney Barthelemy followed Morial in 1986, Marc Morial in 1994, and C. Ray Nagin in 2002.

Impact of the Voting Rights Act

What were some of the more significant aspects of the impact of the Voting Rights Act in Louisiana? In 1976, the Supreme Court in *Beer v. United States* reviewed New Orleans' redistricting proposal under Section 5 of the Voting Rights Act. Section 5 was designed to address voting issues resulting from a retrogression of voting access from the status quo. This might typically include new rules or criteria to make it more difficult for minorities to vote. Section 5 requires certain jurisdictions[142] to submit to the D.C. District Court or the U.S. Department of Justice every voting change for pre-clearance prior to implementation of the proposed voting change. Pre-clearance is a determination by the Department of Justice or the D.C. District Court that a proposed voting change has neither discriminatory purpose nor discriminatory effect, and that the voting change is not retrogressive—i.e., that it does not put minority people in a worse position than they were at the time of the submission.

In 1954, a new City Charter had adopted a redrawn voting district arrangement for the New Orleans City Council. The arrangement consisted of making two City Council seats the result of at-large elections, and five City Council seats elected from single-member districts, which were constructed by combining the seventeen wards of the city into five Council districts. Historically, the five single-member districts had tended to follow a north-south pattern, but by 1970, New Orleans' black population, which tended to reside in an east-west pattern, had risen to about 45 percent of its total population and 35 percent of registered voters. The effect of the north-south orientation of the districting configuration was

---

142. Jurisdictions that meet a formula determined by Congress which identifies states where minorities have not been registered, don't vote, and where there have been impediments to minority voting and registration. These issues are discussed in greater detail in chapter 6.

to disperse black votes *across* districts, diluting their votes, and rendering the black voice politically ineffective. It was the effects of this "five plus two" arrangement that were at issue in *Beer.*[143]

In the 1970s, the redistricting process was controlled by the all-white City Council. Despite the city's growing black electoral strength, no black had ever been elected to council. It is perhaps not surprising that the City Council continued with its north-south districting scheme (although ward boundaries were now being violated in order to comply with the one-person, one-vote rule). The result was two districts with black population majorities, one of less than a half of one percent. More significant is the fact that only one had a clear black majority—64.1 percent of the total population—with 52.6 percent of the voting age population black. The black percentages among registered voters in the other four districts were 43.2, 36.8, 23.3, and 22.6. After the U.S. Attorney General objected because of the fragmentation of black electoral strength, the New Orleans City Council pursued a declaratory judgment alternate in the federal district court in Washington, DC. A unanimous three-judge panel found, as had the Department of Justice, that the plan had a discriminatory effect. The court concluded that the number of seats blacks could expect to win under the plan, given the racially polarized voting patterns in the city, was considerably fewer than the number of seats that both the citywide black population and black registration percentages suggested as their "theoretical entitlement." The districting arrangement, therefore, was found to be an unjustified dilution of the black voting strength.[144] The court also held that the two at-large seats, by themselves, diluted black voting strength. Quite independent of this ruling, as black voters became an increasing majority in New Orleans, some black representatives on City Council would be elected from white-majority districts, and even at-large, suggesting that a voice in the political process accessed through voting patterns ultimately turns on an overall sheer strength of numbers.

Stewardship, Hierarchical Authority, and Authentic Power

With the several preceding historical sketches in mind, we can return to the question of stewardship in New Orleans' cultural milieu. It has been

143. See Richard Engstrom, Stanley Halpin, Jean Hill, and Victoria Caridas-Butterworth, "Louisiana," in Davidson and Grofman, eds., *Quiet Revolution in the South: The Impact of the Voting Rights Act 1965–1990,* 114.

144. Ibid.

put forth that a large part of what goes wrong with the concept of stewardship lies in its hierarchical structure of authority. What, more precisely, is wrong with *that*? There are several things that raise ethical concerns. First, as suggested earlier, the hierarchical structure of authority embedded within stewardship, and also present in its cultural and political analogues, allows an opportunity for the transfer of *inauthentic* freedom. By 'inauthentic' is meant an *appearance* of freedom that masks an underlying relationship of systemic dependency. It means a political system in which minorities are "given" freedom by higher structures of power, rather than being "entitled" to it. Moreover, such 'gifts' of freedom are often only limited or imperfect forms of the freedoms possessed more fully or absolutely by those who hold the greatest power within the political system. In the history of Louisiana politics, we are describing its racially hierarchical structure in which blacks have remained dependent on white structures of power for whatever limited access to political decision-making and power they have been granted. Inauthentic freedom is not freedom at all; it is merely *privilege* bestowed.

A second problem with the hierarchical structure of authority considered here is that it establishes what can be called a 'misinformation pyramid.' The ethical relevance of 'misinformation' is especially raised when decisions involving entire sectors of society are based on information different from that which enters the decision-making process. Misinformation can be data that has been intentionally distorted, because of private political interests. It can be information that has been hidden or suppressed, or overlooked because of incompetence. It can be information that simply degrades as it passes up the pyramid of decision-making. To make this somewhat abstract idea more concrete, consider contemporary information systems whose hierarchy of authority can be represented as a pyramidal structure.

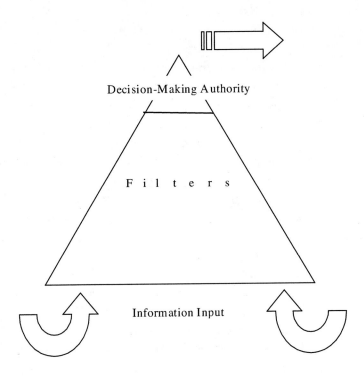

In a pyramidal government decision-making process, information flows into the system from the bottom, via those who interact directly with the outside world (line government workers). Then the information passes through a series of *filters*—by low-level managers or government officials who *accumulate* information, then pass it on to middle-level bureaucrats who *interpret* it, who then pass it on to more senior-level people who *reinterpret* it, and on and on—until it reaches the top level of the pyramid, where there is a concentration of decision-making authority in the form of a small group such as the City Council, or a single individual, such as the mayor. Because of the problems of information transfer in such hierarchical structures, however, the decision-makers frequently make decisions on the basis misinformation—information *different from* that which entered the system. Various internal filters and organizational blocks create inefficiency in information flow, the potential for distortion of information, inaccurate interpretations of information, or even a flat disregard for truth in information. In any of a number of ways, there arises a mismatch between decisions made and information that represents reality. Worse yet, but certainly not uncommon in politics, decisions are made at the top on the basis of belief systems quite independent of *any* data. This is the authority that leadership simply imposes on the organization below it and on the public beyond that.

A third issue with hierarchical structures of authority is that they historically have tended to reinforce political conservativism, and the idea that social inequities are necessarily a part of the human condition, and must be accepted rather than addressed and eliminated. These are the social inequities that result in poverty, the unequal distribution of essential human services such as healthcare, adequate housing, safe streets; they are the social inequities which limit access to political power, to the economic benefits of a city's or region's resources, to full participation in its cultural life. They are the inequities, in short, that perpetuate unfairness in a social system, and ensure that those forced to live and work at the margins of society will always be there to perform the most unwanted tasks, and be objects of abuse by those whose exercise of power is uncontrolled or applied in an ethical vacuum. The conservatism of hierarchical structures of authority results in many ways from the mechanisms for filtering and distorting information, described above. The filtering of information insulates and isolates government leadership from the public, and by default perpetuates the status quo of the bureaucratic system itself, since the interest of mid-level officials in preserving their jobs may compete with what the information input into the process recommends. And if a program to eliminate a certain sector of social problems—crime, for instance—were actually successful, the need for many bureaucratic positions within the hierarchy would go away.

In New Orleans, as in many other urban areas, there appears little chance of either endemic social problems or instances of corruption and incompetence within the government 'going away.' As compared to other large cities, New Orleans, unfortunately, appears to exceed most of them in possessing those factors that are destructive of achieving a coherent, humane society: a continually high crime rate, having among the worst and poorest school systems in the country, its history of political favoritism and corruption. The last of these is probably the most egregious. The levels of corruption in government continually discovered is astounding; each instance feels like another in a series of electric shocks that ultimately render the body comatose. On August 13, 2007, for example, the New Orleans City Council's senior member and former president, Oliver M. Thomas, Jr., pleaded guilty to a federal bribery charge, admitting to taking as much as $19,000 in bribes and kickbacks from Stan "Pampy" Barre, a local businessman and member of former Mayor Marc Morial's inner circle, who was trying to keep a city parking lot contract. Thomas immediately resigned. This unfortunate revelation only added to the pervasive feeling of government corruption that infests public life in the city; it was merely the latest in a string of New Orleans public officials who have been hit with federal corruption charges.[145] Some have suggested New Orleans' history of tolerating social and political corruption is exemplified by the fact that the Mafia first established itself in New Orleans even before it located in metropolitan New York City.

A hierarchy of authority which condones or permits corruption, incompetence, the perpetuation of privilege, and neglect are all instances of failure in 'cultural stewardship.' Corruption and incompetence filters down through the government pyramid just as misinformation filters up. Thus, one finds neglect not merely by those in the highest decision-making positions, but also neglect and simple disregard of one interest group by another. It is the neglect, for example, of a school board in failing meet the needs of the city's students; it is the neglect of the Sewerage and Water Board or the Dock Board in actually keeping a watchful eye the on city's infrastructure and the state of the sub-systems for which it has oversight responsibility. It is neglect that has allowed the city's evolutionary forces replace the early history of blacks and whites commingling with the eventual ghettoization of blacks into certain low-lying and flood-prone neighborhoods as New Orleans' backswamp was drained and habitation progressed towards Lake Pontchartrain. Many of New Orleans' negative

---

145. Thomas had been considered a strong candidate for mayor, but became only the latest in a string of New Orleans public officials who have been hit with federal corruption charges. In June, 2007, the former president of the school board admitted to taking bribes; Representative William J. Jefferson, congressman for the city, was accused by federal authorities of participating in an international bribery scheme; as many as 30 school system employees have been indicted. The U.S. Attorney for the Eastern District of Louisiana, James Letten, indicated that investigations into corruption at New Orleans City Hall from the Marc Morial administration, already yielding 16 convictions, including a nine year federal prison term for a former top aide in a plot to skim $1 million from a city contract. James Bernazzani of the FBI in New Orleans, who indicated that his district ranked second in the nation in public corruption convictions and indictments, despite its relatively small population, said, "In Louisiana they skim the cream, steal the milk, hijack the bottle and look for the cow." See Adam Nossiter, "New Blow to New Orleans in Council Leader's Plea," *The New York Times*, August 14, 2007, accessed at http://www.nytimes.com/2007/08/14/us/14orleans.html?td=&emc=th&pagewanted=print.

social patterns and government incompetence or corruption were the result of narrow economic interests and social privilege at all levels of the food chain in New Orleans' hierarchy of power. Social inequities resulting in the "white flight" of the 1960s and 70s were not exclusively the responsibility of any single group of decision-makers; they also were perpetuated by the interactions among many of New Orleans's racial, ethnic, and cultural groups that have attempted to use one another for political or economic gain.

Local political organizations reflect the cultural identity of the neighborhoods and wards out of which they arise: COUP, SOUL, BOLD, GOLD, LIFE, TIPS, and others over the years.[146] These political organizations that meander around the "near-Byzantine political process"[147] represent a city that through its history has been divided less by party than by political faction, beginning with Creoles opposing Americans, Bourbons facing the Scalawags,[148] evolving into Old Regular Democrats battling the Longites. When African Americans were given the vote, from their neighborhoods emerged cells of political activism, initially working for white candidates such as Moon Landrieu, who were sympathetic to black community needs. But in recent times, the relatively short allegiances of these political organizations, along with deals brokered in back rooms, has done as much to divide, as to unite, the black community and other ethnic communities. It has at least made the political process less visible and public.

Cultural stewardship must ultimately transcend the rule of "reward your friends" and "turn out your vote." Some current election practices appear to compete with that. Election day typically begins looking normal enough. Paid election workers meet at a local church, fan out in teams with cell phones, knock on doors. Runners check vote totals; if they look low, blitz teams bang on doors. But investigators regularly turn up stories

146. BOLD is the Black Organization for Leadership Development; TIPS is Ed Murray's Tremé Improvement Political Society; LIFE was the Louisiana Independent Federation of Electors, Mayor Marc Morial's street organization; it is unclear what GOLD stands for.

147. See Christopher Tidmore, "How to Spell Chaos," *The Louisiana Weekly,* January 28, 2002; also Rich Lowry, "The Big Sleasy," *National Review,* December 23, 1996 and February 10, 1997, and J. Kojo Livingston, "Overcoming Louisiana's Culture of Corruption," *The Louisiana Weekly,* July 2, 2007.

148. Southerners who collaborated with blacks and carpetbaggers from Northern states.

of *abnormalities*. People vote multiple times. Poll commissioners pull the lever for candidates during slack times. People vote on behalf of dead voters. People cast votes for inactive voters on the rolls. Residents are disgruntled because they weren't paid their promised 'gifts'—some as much as $3,000.[149]

Malfeasances, of course, exist independent of hierarchical structures as well as within them. But all of them represent misuses of power. In Louisiana, the crudest misuse of power has been the direct suppression of certain portions of the population by simply eliminating them from the political process entirely—not only the myriad of Jim Crow restrictions after Reconstruction but other practices that persist today and will be discussed in later chapters. An only slightly less obvious misuse of power are systems of privilege, in which those entrenched in political or economic power pass on positions of importance within existing structures of power—nepotism and gift appointments on various commissions and agencies. Below that is the local system of patronage in which leaders within minority communities have surrendered their voting support to those in majority power in return for special favors. Perhaps most distressing is the persistence of racial and ethnic divisions even when a more 'enlightened' leader attempts to move the process of governing away from the doles of privilege and patronage to a meritocracy, in which objective standards of excellence are the measure of where and when resources are directed. This was attempted in the mayoralty of Dutch Morial, but over time proved to be unsuccessful, as New Orleans reverted to its historical tradition of favoritism and political corruption.

The strength of New Orleans' neighborhoods has generally been an asset and an ethical counterweight to corruption and misrule within the city's political systems. Yet even strong neighborhoods—citizens participating in less-political neighborhood associations like the Broadmoor Improvement Association or the Mid-City Neighborhood Organization, primarily interested in rebuilding residential areas and reinvigorating local businesses—have not been able to overcome New Orleans' long and continuing history of dysfunction within its political and social service systems. At a level above neighborhood associations, the networks of both ward-based and city-wide political organizations more clearly continue to reflect exclusionary economic interests, racial divisions, old-guard

---

149. Instances collected from accounts by poll monitors as well as the media.

traditions of white patronage, intra-racial power struggles. How local neighborhoods can function not only as an *implicit* strength within the city but also be *visibly effective* in improving forms of government will be a question *Walking to New Orleans* considers throughout in many forms. Answers to the question will range from use of the concept of Participatory Design and its extended process, Value Analysis, to proposals for legalizing 'councils' of neighborhood associations in a formal Citizen Participation Process, such as urged by Keith Twitchell's Committee for a Better New Orleans/Metropolitan Area Committee (CBNO/MAC).

One might be tempted to argue that the strength of the neighborhoods and the wards from which local political organizations are produced even *compete* with a sense of coherence in the city. In the post-Katrina, world, however, things have changed. The strength of New Orleans' neighborhoods may very well be all there is to go on to accomplish the real work of recovery and reconstruction.

Despite evolutionary forces such as exist within any large urban area, there is in New Orleans the potential to improve social conditions. Any initiatives must also deal with numerous inherently complex problems difficult to bring under rational control; the precariousness of New Orleans' environmental situation only adds to the complexity. At the same time, other countries, such as the Netherlands, are environmentally precarious, and this fact has actually become the occasion for giving focus to and strengthening its society and cultural identity.

The Street Where You Live

In New Orleans, the 'street where you live'—and which one of the its seventy-three (by official counts) neighborhoods frames that street—has been a determiner of many factors over the years, including one's relative peril from storms and flooding. Like many cities, New Orleans has had multiple ways of dividing itself up into geographical, political, and cultural segments. We have noted that in 1836, increased tension among cultural groups of New Orleans resulted in a formal division into three separate communities, each with its own churches, cemeteries, drainage canals: an almost exclusively white 'Uptown,' the Vieux Carré and Tremé, and the downstream 'suburb' of Faubourg Marigny, where newer Irish and German immigrants settled. New Orleans also divides itself into seventeen wards, eleven of which were created in 1852 when the city reformed itself under one centralized government from its three separate communities. As the city continued to expand through the last quarter of the nineteenth century, Wards 12–14 were created by the upriver annexation of Greenville and Jefferson City. Algiers, on the west bank of the river, was annexed and became the Fifteenth Ward, and furthest upriver at the Jefferson Parish line, the city of Carrolton was annexed and formed the Sixteenth and Seventeenth Wards. The first City Council (a mayor, Etienne De Bore, and council of twelve) was created in 1803 by French prefect, Pierre Clément de Laussat, as Louisiana was being handed over to the United States. The 1912 City Charter set up a commission form of government for New Orleans, consisting of a mayor and four councilmen elected at large. The executive and administrative powers of the city government were divided among five departments, each with its own commissioner, designated from among the mayor and councilmen by majority vote of the Council. Thus, from 1912, the city has not had officials elected as representatives of wards, although certain ward designations have continued to be prominent in identifying neighborhood identity. The commission council remained in effect until the passage of the Home Rule Charter in 1954,[150] by which the State gave up much of its arbitrary control over the city. This governmental structure, which has been amended very little since, was intended to protect the city from the whims of the Governor.

Beyond wards and voting precincts, there are numerous other internal divisions. In 1980, for example, the New Orleans City Planning Commission divided the city into thirteen planning districts. These planning districts are currently very much in use with the Unified New Orleans Plan (UNOP), the most recent reconstruction plan initiated by the New Orleans Community Support Foundation in cooperation with the mayor's office, the City Council, and the City Planning Commission. The plan, intended to guide the use of federal funds and the strategic rebuilding of communities throughout Orleans Parish, was presented to the Louisiana Recovery Authority in early 2007 in what is hoped to be a comprehensive, citywide recovery plan.

Orleans Parish also has fourteen districts from which representatives to the Louisiana House of Representatives are chosen, and seven

---

150. New Orleans Dept. of Public Safety Records, City Archives, New Orleans Public Library.

from which State Senators are chosen.[151] There are, of course, many other district divisions as well. Locally, these include the five City Council districts,[152] which are currently those existing on January 1, 1995, excepting for changes in accordance with the Charter. These five districts are subject to redistricting within six months after official publication of the population by precinct from each decennial census, with each council district containing, as nearly as possible, a population whose number equals the total city population divided by five. Divisions also include school districts and those pertaining to the city's infrastructure. Finally, there are the districts created for the election of representation in the United States Congress and Senate.

While many of the cultural traditions associated with particular neighborhoods and districts have been preserved over time, the racial and cultural make up, and geographical distribution of the population of the city, has not been without change. To understand the diversity of problems New Orleans' seventy-three odd neighborhoods have faced *after* Katrina, it will be useful to give a sense of their historic uniqueness *prior* to Katrina. Since New Orleans' thirteen Planning Districts will be the point of reference in discussing the variety of post-Katrina reconstruction plans, such as the Unified New Orleans Plan (UNOP), it also makes sense to sketch the characteristics of some of New Orleans' unique neighborhoods in terms of those Planning Districts, despite the pragmatic rather than historical basis of those planning district designations.

Planning District No. 1

In Planning District No. 1, New Orleans' oldest section, the Vieux Carré, is the neighborhood probably most known to outsiders. By the early twentieth century the area had become rather run down and neglected, attracting artists, writers, and erstwhile bohemians; it has since revitalized and is currently the center of New Orleans' tourism. Jackson Square (formerly Place d'Armes), St. Louis Cathedral, and the elaborate ironwork galleries are among the visual sights of visitors as they wend their way from restaurants (such as Antoine's, Galatoire's, Tujague's, Arnaud's) to Bourbon Street bars and finally to Café du Monde for coffee and *beignets*. Built on

151. These districts must contain at least one precinct within Orleans Parish, but may also include areas well beyond New Orleans (which is co-terminus with Orleans Parish).

152. The City Council continues to have five elected district representatives and two at-large.

a natural levee on higher ground, 'The Quarter' experienced only minor flooding during Katrina—as did many of the areas of in New Orleans developed earlier than the nineteenth century. The traditional dividing line between 'The Quarter' and the old uptown 'American Quarter' (also known as Faubourg S. Mary) is Canal Street, a large boulevard named for a navigational canal never built. The other major area within Planning District No. 1 is New Orleans' Central Business District (CBD), which extends from Canal Street to the downriver side of the Garden District (Howard Avenue). Contributing to the area's early business growth was the American Theater, erected in 1824, gas lighting, construction of the New Basin Canal that encouraged expansion away from the river, the U.S. Customs House and dry goods trade on Canal Street, and the fourth Charity Hospital,[153] built in 1815 on Canal Street between Baronne and University Place. A fire in 1892 destroyed much of the district, but new building and expansion into the backswamp in the 1920s after the invention and utilization of the Wood pump brought prosperity. Post World War II the district went into decline as much commercial industry moved to suburban locales; it then experienced the oil industry's growth and subsequent decline during the 1980s, and more recently has redeveloped an economy based on tourism and convention business. The CBD now contains an old warehouse section along the river, antique and crafts shops along Magazine Street, offices on Poydras, the old and new city halls, courthouses, the Superdome, and the Morial Convention Center, both the sites of evacuees during Katrina.

In 2002 the population of Planning District No. 1 was 6,524, having declined from 8,374 in 1980, a decrease of 22.1 percent; its percentage of black population rose from 11.9 percent to 14.2 percent, an increase of 2.3 percentage points, during the same period.[154] Residential land use, mostly in the Vieux Carré, represents a relatively small percentage in District No. 1 at 92 acres or only 10 percent of the district's total acreage.

153. Charity Hospital was founded in 1736 under a grant from French shipbuilder Jean Louis and originally named l'Hôpital des Pauvres de la Charité. Several locations preceded the one built on Canal Street and two more followed it to its last location on Tulane Avenue as part of the Medical Center of Louisiana at New Orleans (MCLNO).

154. Quantitative data in this section is drawn from the U.S. Census Bureau, the New Orleans City Planning Commission, the Greater New Orleans Community Data Center, the Brookings Institution Katrina Index, and the Unified New Orleans Plan (UNOP) Recovery Assessments, with exceptions to consistency noted where they occur.

Planning District No. 2

Just upriver from The Quarter is Planning District No. 2, which includes the quite diverse neighborhoods of Central City, the Garden District, the Irish Channel, and the former St. Thomas Development, replaced by the mixed-income River Garden. Despite a concentration of one area of the city's private wealth, the district also suffers from blighted buildings, vacant properties, litter, and a high crime rate. The district is additionally challenged by the need to redesign its public housing developments to alleviate their isolation and poor living conditions. Central City, upriver from the CBD and on the back side (away from the river)[155] of St. Charles Avenue, is an old, largely African American neighborhood that developed in the 1830s from a large, mosquito-infested, swampy area with the opening of the New Orleans & Carrollton Railway (which became the St. Charles Avenue Streetcar). Many rural former slaves settled here after the Civil War. The neighborhood has contributed a great deal to New Orleans' jazz and brass band traditions, as well as about 2800 of the city's shotgun houses, raised 2–4 feet on brick piers (still below sea level), set close together with stoops right up against the sidewalk, built as rental property. A concentration of black businesses in the early twentieth century emerged along Dryades Street (on the back side and paralleling St. Charles), but declined sharply by the 1980s. Renamed Oretha Castle Haley Boulevard after the civil rights activist and CORE leader, the neighborhood has received improvement funding. Those areas above the flooding following Katrina expect to get attention for redevelopment. Nevertheless, the Melpomene (Guste Apartments), and especially the Magnolia (C. J. Peete), and Calliope (B. W. Cooper)[156] projects in Central City are areas with a high crime and murder rate. C. J. Peete and B. W. Cooper were closed after Hurricane Katrina, designated for destruction. These and the fate of the other housing projects of New Orleans Housing Authority (HANO) will be discussed in more detail in Chapters 4, 7, and 8. However, it can briefly be noted here that in 1996, the Department of Housing and Urban Development (HUD) took over HANO.[157] In the United States General Accounting Office (GAO) May 1996 Report to the

155. Through the 1950s, Central City was known as "back of town."

156. B. W. Cooper is placed in Planning District No. 4.

157. GAO/RCED-96-67 United States General Accounting Office Report to the honorable Richard H. Baker, House of Representatives, "Public Housing: HUD Takes Over the Housing authority of New Orleans," May, 1996.

House of Representatives, "Public Housing: HUD Takes Over the Housing Authority of New Orleans," Judy A. England-Joseph, Director, Housing and Community Development Issues, noted that while one of the nation's largest housing authorities, operating over 13,000 housing units providing homes to over 24,000 people, for nearly two decades HANO had been one of the country's poorest performing housing authorities and ranked the lowest among large housing authorities in HUD's performance measurement system. With only marginal recent improvement from large federal grants to HANO, hands-on management assistance from professional property managers, the Secretary of HUD's personal involvement with HANO, and much technical assistance, HANO remained among the three percent of housing authorities classified as "troubled." HUD's relationship with HANO, as with all housing authorities, is a contractual one governed by statue and regulation, and to declare a breach of contract would be rare since it could lead to HUD's takeover of a housing authority's assets and propel the authority into receivership.[158] On February 8, 1996, HUD declared HANO in breach of contract, claimed possession of HANO's assets, and dissolved HANO's Board of Commissioners. In place of a contract between HUD and HANO, a "cooperative endeavor agreement" between the Secretary of HUD and the Mayor of New Orleans was put in place.[159] This arrangement more or less continued until 2002 when HANO was put into receivership, and HUD took over running New Orleans' housing development projects directly. Jeffrey Riddel, HUD Deputy Administrator and Executive Director of HANO, in the summer of 2007 indicated that of New Orleans' ten major housing developments,

---

158. Although this has been done to have receivers operate housing authorities in Boston, Kansas City, and Washington, DC; HUD itself has taken control in East St. Louis and Chicago.

159. The report cited to operational problems and continuing obstacles: (1) the failure to provide for routine maintenance, including repairs to plumbing, heating, electrical systems, and upkeep of the grounds, and (2) failure to ensure the viability and safety of the housing assets by carrying out major modernization and rehabilitation work, such as replacing roofs and heating systems or demolishing unsafe buildings. A 1994 audit found that non of 150 units in a random sample met HUD's quality standards, many of which were safety issues. Further, more than 25 percent of the authority's apartments were vacant because of years of neglect. It concluded the Board of Commissioners had not effectively governed the housing authority.

Iberville was able to be reopened after Hurricane Katrina; the remaining nine were in 'redevelopment.'[160]

Close by, but a world away from Central City, the Garden District is a wealthy residential area[161] whose development began just prior to the Civil War and continued to the end of the century. Once an area of plantations whose residential streets were laid out by Barthelemy Lafon, the area preserves numerous large southern Italianate and Greek Revival mansions, often surrounded by late Victorian 'gingerbread' houses. The area is situated on old high ground and escaped most of the flooding during Katrina. The river side of the Garden District is a neighborhood historically known as the Irish Channel because it was originally settled by Irish immigrants fleeing the potato famine in the early nineteenth century. Its exact boundaries have never been precise, but it represents a multi-racial, multi-ethnic, largely working class area, many of whose residents labored in riverfront slaughterhouses, factories, a sugar refinery, and as stevedores in the Port of New Orleans until the era of container ships. A once dangerous housing project located in the Irish Channel neighborhood was St. Thomas Development, originally housing 1,500 families. In 2002, all but a few buildings were demolished under a HUD HOPE VI Grant,[162]

160. This and other information regarding housing projects in New Orleans since 2002 from conversations with Jeffrey Riddel, Deputy Administrator at HUD and Executive Director of HANO. Of the nine major housing projects in redevelopment, three are Hope VI sites; the old Desire Development, for example, will be rebuilt in two phases, first Abundance Square, then Treasure Island.

161. Much of the wealth of the early businessmen who settled there came from their trading in cotton and sugar, which relied on slavery.

162. HOPE VI, which stands for Housing Opportunities for People Everywhere, is a HUD program that began in 1992 to revitalize the worst public housing projects into mixed-income developments. It is predicated on the theoretical model of New Urbanism, which sees apartment buildings as unhealthy for human habitation, and, instead, argues that urban communities must be densely arranged private homes and duplexes, or row houses for public housing. The area must be accessible by public transit or by foot. Typically, houses stand close to the street with small yards or porches, where the belief is that such a design will contribute to revitalizing decayed areas of the city. For this reason, the model also sees private custodianship of public housing a means to instill pride and reduce vandalism. The theoretical model is unproven and not an entirely consistent one and has been criticized especially in its implementation. The National Housing Law Project (along with the Poverty & Race Research Action Council, Sherwood Research Associates, and Everywhere and How Public Housing Residents Organizing Nationally Together (ENPHRONT)) in a June 2002 report entitled False HOPE: A Critical Assessment of the HOPE VI Public Housing Redevelopment Program objected to the lack of standards and hard data on program results, as well as HUD's failure to provide comprehensive and

forcing the relocation of its approximately 3,000 residents. This was soon followed by the construction of 296 of a planned 1,100 apartment 'mixed-income' development called "River Garden." Only 122 of the 296 units were for low-income families, and it remains unlikely that many of those displaced by the demolition will be able to return. It was in the St. Thomas project that Sister Helen Prejean lived in the 1980s when she befriended convicted killer Patrick Sonnier.[163] Magnolia and St. Thomas were the first public housing developments proposed for New Orleans under the United States Housing Act in 1937 (the Wagner Bill). This area is also situated on high ground and escaped flooding. Just upriver from the Irish Channel is East Riverside, a small moderate-income neighborhood that reflects, as much as any, the general racial and ethnic population distribution of the 2000 census with 31 percent white, 64 percent black, and 4 percent Hispanic, Asian, and Native American residents. Its primary landmark is a music venue that began as a neighborhood juke joint in 1977 to provide a place for Professor Longhair to perform in his final years[164]—the famous Tipitina's, co-founded by our friend, Jeanne Dumestre.

In 2002 the population of Planning District No. 2 was 46,022, having declined from 72,412 in 1980, a loss of 36.4 percent; its percentage of black population marginally increased by 2.8 percentage points during the same period, from 73.1 percent to 75.9 percent. Residential land use is 62 percent of the district's 1,692 acres, including (as of 1990) three of the city's high density public housing developments.

Planning District No. 3

Further upriver from the Garden District, Planning District No. 3 follows the river to the Jefferson Parish line and extends back to the lower border of Lakewood. The characteristics of this predominantly residential area are as varied, although differently, than those of District No.2, containing, on the one hand, the cargo-handling facilities of the Port of New Orleans, the Office of the U.S. Army Corps of Engineers, and the new Orleans Water Board Carrollton Water Plant, but also Audubon Park, Tulane and

---

accurate information. Many, including the Urban Institute and the National Low Income Housing Coalition (NLIHC), have criticized new developments for failing to replace old housing units on a "one-for-one" basis, resulting in a net loss of housing for the poor.

163. Subject of the film, *Dead Man Walking*.

164. The venue was named for one of Longhair's (Henry Roeland Byrd) enigmatic recordings, *Tipitina*.

Loyola Universities, and a number of stately mansions and quaint shops along Magazine Street. The 127 acre Audubon Park, encircled by mansions, was the site of the 1884 World Industrial and Cotton Centennial Exposition. Nearby, the first Catholic women's college in America, St. Mary's Dominican College, opened in 1864 but closed in 1984.[165] Tulane University, originally founded as a medical school, was incorporated in 1847 as the University of Louisiana in New Orleans and changed to Tulane after a donation from Paul Tulane in 1883; Loyola University, operated by the Society of Jesus, was founded in 1911. Several major medical services have been located around Audubon Park in addition to Tulane Medical School: Children's Hospital on Leake Avenue; DePaul Hospital on Calhoun Street and Henry Clay Avenue, between Perrier and Camp, currently in transition. The history of DePaul Hospital is fascinating. In 1859, a residence on Nashville St. at Magazine was donated for use as an orphanage to the Sisters of Charity, who named it "The House of the Five Wounds." In 1861 physicians at Hôtel Dieu requested mentally unstable patients be removed from the facility. Five Daughters of St. Vincent de Paul undertook the care of these patients, moving them to a wing of The House of Five Wounds. In 1876 a new hospital, known as the Louisiana Retreat, was built at its present site on Henry Clay Avenue at Camp Street. The remainder of its history, which we'll trace separately, is representative of the intricacies of buying and selling medical care facilities by large, corporate healthcare providers—an arrangement that has both benefited and plagued Louisiana.[166]

165. Sister Helen Prejean graduated from St. Mary's.

166. In 1930, the hospital's name changed to DePaul Sanitarium; a neurological department was added in 1938, and in 1954, the name was changed to DePaul Hospital. In 1969 the DePaul Community Mental Health Center at 1040 Calhoun St. was dedicated, becoming the main building on the hospital campus with the demolition of the 92-year-old building later that year. In 1973, the Daughters of Charity of St. Vincent DePaul sold the facility to American Health Services, Inc., which in turn in 1980 sold it to Hospital Affiliates International, Inc., although the Daughters of Charity continued to own the property from which the hospital operated. In 1981, Hospital Affiliates International, Inc. was bought by Hospital Corporation of America (HCA). In March, 1989, HCA approved a buyout by an investor group, TF Investments Inc., who planned to put HCA's psychiatric hospitals up for sale. In June of that year, employees of DePaul Hospital in New Orleans, Northshore Psychiatric Hospital in Slidell, and three other Louisiana psychiatric hospitals owned by HCA became part owners under an agreement involving 52 psychiatric hospitals being sold by HCA Psychiatric Co., an HCA subsidiary, to an unnamed company for $1.225 billion. In 1994, Hospital Corporation of America and Columbia merged to become ColumbiaHCA. The following year, in 1995,

Characteristic of parts of this planning district that were once water, Broadmoor is a neighborhood that was a twelve-acre lake, popular for fishing and connected to Bayou St. John, in the early nineteenth century. By 1885, drainage canals enabled water to be moved, as did a pumping station built in 1903; the neighborhood's greatest development occurred during the 1920s. As a section of the city that remained low-lying, Broadmoor has always been subject to significant flooding after heavy rain, and was heavily flooded following Katrina;[167] initial Bring New Orleans Back Commission (BNOB)[168] reports suggested turning much of it into park land, something strongly resisted by residents moving back into their mixture of double shotgun, Spanish and mission revival homes; some homes had been elevated when originally built. The Broadmoor Improvement Association, founded in 1969, is a particularly active neighborhood group. The area has had a sizable Jewish population until its decline in the 1990s, in part spurred by synagogue Chevra Thilim, built in 1948; during the 1950s, as many as 30 percent of students at the public grammar school were Jewish.

Neighborhoods in Planning District No. 3 with relatively large African American populations include Hollygrove and portions of Leonidas, both

---

Tulane University Hospital and Clinic sold 80 percent of its facility of ColumbiaHCA, the same corporation that owned DePaul Hospital. In 1997, DePaul merged with Tulane University Hospital and Clinic and became the DePaul-Tulane Behavioral Health Center, featured on PBS NOVA in 2000 as one of the best treatment facilities for eating disorders. In the aftermath of Hurricane Katrina in 2005, the DePaul-Tulane Behavioral Health Center closed. The 13-acre campus, one of the oldest psychiatric facilities in the South, was home to the most complete psychiatric continuum of care in the New Orleans area. It has remained closed since. In February, 2007, to relieve the critical shortage of hospital beds for patients with chronic mental illness, Louisiana State University developed plans to open a psychiatric hospital in Uptown New Orleans by the middle of the summer. LSU had maintained 100 psychiatric beds at Charity Hospital before Hurricane Katrina; the university's health care services division intends to resurrect a smaller unit on the campus of the old DePaul Hospital. The plans have hinged on a pending real estate deal between Children's Hospital and the Daughters of Charity, the order of nuns that started treating mental patients on the campus in 1876. The nuns agreed to sell the property, and Children's plans to lease one of the two main buildings to LSU once the sale goes through. The facility is expected to open under LSU's auspices mid-August. Information for this history was provided by Kate Moran, mental health writer for *The Times-Picayune*.

167. The Claiborne Canal Project, part of a $140 million drainage improvement program authorized by Congress in 1996, involved construction of new underground canals.

168. The second of four post-Katrina recovery planning processes that will be discussed in more detail in chapter 7.

running along the terminus of Orleans with Jefferson Parish; both, particularly Hollygrove, experienced severe flooding after Katrina. Leonidas, originally part of a plantation owned by Le Sieur de Bienville, founder of New Orleans, became a 'suburb' as it was served by the New Orleans and Carrollton Railroad (St. Charles Avenue Streetcar line).[169] During segregation, the streetcar was a focal point of racial tensions. Before the Civil War, whites and blacks rode in separate cars, discontinued during Reconstruction, but in 1902 Jim Crow laws created racially separate streetcars, then modified by becoming white-only and black-only seats, separated by movable "race screens" that said "white only" on one side and "colored only" on the other. Carrollton Cemetery in East Carrollton, the neighborhood just east of Leonidas, was also divided into two sections: colored and white. The Carrollton Transit Station ("Streetcar Barn") at Willow and Dublin Streets and the Maple Leaf Bar are among Leonidas' interesting sites. Three other neighborhoods in Planning District No. 3 include Marlyville, an entirely residential, well-maintained neighborhood convenient to Tulane and Loyola; Black Pearl, the triangular wedge along the river between Audubon and Leonidas, a quiet, flood-free microcosm popular with dogs who take their owners on a path on top of the levee; Freret, named for egalitarian Mayor William Freret (mayor 1842–42; 43–44). Freret Street, the location of small businesses, many lost in the 1970s, is designated a National Trust for Historic Preservation; at 2700 Napoleon Avenue is the site of Ochsner Baptist Medical Center.[170]

In 2002 the population of Planning District No. 3 was 65,485, having declined from 82,942 in 1980, a decline of 21.0 percent; its percentage of black population increased by 5.6 percentage points during the same period, from 45.3 percent to 50.9 percent. Residential land use is 65 percent of the district's 3,121 acres; institutional (458 acres for college and university) uses represent 9.5 percent; parkland accounts for 597.7 acres or 12.5 percent.

169. The new Orleans & Carrollton Railroad was sold to New Orleans Public Service Inc (NOPSI) which consolidated the city's streetcar lines.

170. Formerly Southern Baptist Hospital, founded in 1926, renamed Memorial Medical Center in 1996, changed to its current name in 2006. Memorial is the hospital in which Dr. Anna Pou and two nurses were accused of mercy killings during the horrendous conditions of Katrina, subsequently acquitted.

Planning District No. 4

Planning District No. 4, Mid-City, could be considered *le coeur* of New Orleans, running from Carrollton Avenue to historic Tremé and Esplanade Ridge; appropriately, it contains the Medical Center of Louisiana at New Orleans (MCLNO), teaching hospitals of LSU Medical School, Xavier University, and, until Hurricane Katrina, the Crystal Hot Sauce plant, representing, in a sense, the heart, mind, and soul of the city.[171] Gert Town, also known as *Zion City*, is home to the city's predominantly black Xavier University. Its Johnson and Lincoln parks were the location of jazz band "cutting contests" (informal 'battle of the bands') in the early twentieth century, and its Gold Star Hunters Mardi Gras Indian tribe under Chief Larry Bannock has represented one of the forty or so colorful parading tribes from New Orleans' black neighborhoods that developed in the nineteenth century when segregation produced white-only Mardi Gras krewes.[172] The Mardi Gras Indians, whose elaborate beaded and feathered costumes are painstakingly created new each year, ritually reenact traditions syncretistically combined from African, Creole, Caribbean, and Native American cultures. Tribes are territorial and contain various levels of responsibility in addition to the Chief, and occasional Queen with attendants: Spy Boys, Flag Boys, Wild Men. Spy Boys, for example, referred to in the traditional song "Iko Iko,"[173] spot oncoming tribes and signal danger, convey messages to the Chief who decides to either make way for another tribe or advance with his war lance held up as a signal of mock 'war' to proclaim their singing and dancing greatness. Traditionally, Mardi Gras Indians do not ride floats but parade on secret routes through

---

171. The company's bottling plant on Tulane Avenue in New Orleans was substantially damaged by Hurricane Katrina. As a result, Baumer Foods moved its plant to a new location in Reserve, Louisiana, located just up the river from New Orleans. Crystal was famous for its lighted sign which featured a chef stirring a pot of hot sauce. The sign was a New Orleans landmark, like Boston's CITGO sign. Along with much of the factory, the sign was destroyed by Hurricane Katrina.

172. With names as elaborate as the ritual of hand-sewn orange and turquoise (and every other color of the rainbow) costumes: Fi-Yi-Yi, Golden Eagles, Wild Tchoupitoulas, Seventh Ward Hard Headers, Skull and Bones, Red Hawk Hunters, Creole Osceola, Yellow Pocahontas.

173. *Hey now, Hey now, Iko Iko ah-nay /Joc-a-mo-fee-no-ah-nah-nay, Joc-a-mo-fee-nah-nay / My spy boy to your spy boy, they were sittin' along the bayou, / My spy boy to your spy boy, I'm gonna set your tail on fire . . .*

the backstreets of the city.[174] Hurricane Katrina accelerated the potential for the disappearance of this cultural phenomenon, with only a portion of the city's black population returning.

On the opposite side of the Mid-City neighborhood itself is Tremé, a historic area whose thriving African American businesses along Claiborne Avenue were destroyed in the 1960s to make way for the new I-10. Congo Square,[175] on the edge of the Quarter, where enslaved Africans were allowed to gather to drum and dance and sell produce, is now within Tremé. The site of Forts St. Ferdinand and St. John in 1730, the land was acquired for a plantation by Claude Tremé. and began to be developed after 1794 when a canal was built from the Quarter to Bayou St. John. Many of its early inhabits were free persons of color and Caucasians from Haiti, excelling as artisans, musicians, teachers, and doctors. Its many double shotgun houses and Creole cottages reflect these African and Caribbean cultural roots, as does the architecture of more substantial homes along Esplanade Avenue, the Tremé and Rocheblave farmers markets that flourished until the early twentieth century, and the Social Aid & Pleasure clubs, a social safety net for those at the margins of society in which members could even borrow against their dues in hard times. The Zulu Social Aid & Pleasure Club, discussed earlier, is perhaps the most famous example. Tremé has experienced probably more demolition and construction projects than any other area of the city, creating a continuous stream of disruption to the community. The Tremé Market was demolished in the 1930s for the Municipal Auditorium; in 1941 the Lafitte Development housing project

174. While the relationship between NOPD Captain Anthony Cannatella, commander of the Sixth District, and Mardi Gras Indian tribes had generally been once of tolerance, including their participation in a second annual parade St. Joseph's night, an Italian-American holiday celebrated on March 19th, in 2005 as Cannatella was packing for a long-needed vacation, a disruption took place in which drunken Indians, one carrying a shotgun with feathers, were roughed up and pushed out of the street into A.L. Davis Park at Washington Avenue and LaSalle near Lafayette Cemetery in Central City by police. When Chief Keith "Keke" Gibson tried to explain the tradition to police officers, he was told "I don't want to hear a fucking thing about tradition; get off the street . . . Take the fucking uniform [costume] off or you're going to jail." With community outrage refusing to subside, on June 27 the City Council scheduled a reconciliation session with chiefs of various Mardi Gras Indian tribes. The first to speak was Chief Allison "Tootie" Montana, celebrated craftsman of Indian costumes. As he recounted forty years of NOPD mistreatment of Indians, he coughed, collapsed to the floor, stopped breathing, and died. See Katy Reckdahl, "St. Joseph's Night Gone Blue," *Gambit Weekly*, March 29, 2005, and Dan Baum, "Deluged," *The New Yorker*, January 9, 2006.

175. First referred to in 1729 as the "Place des Négres."

was built. The destruction for I-10 was only the final blow, as it were, resulting not only in the leveling of nine square blocks of historic houses, but also the transformation of many owner-occupied homes to rental units. In 1969, the Tremé Community Improvement Association was formed to encourage renovation of abandoned and blighted properties.

Mid-City, the area between Gert Town and Tremé, is also largely African American, although it once had a large Hispanic population that is still around 10 percent. Its architectural styles vary from shotgun cottages with added gingerbread to Tudor and Mission style homes near City Park, the city's largest green space. Mid-City was another area referred to as "Back of Town" in the nineteenth century, but its development did not become significant until the early twentieth century, even with the existence of the Carondelet and New Basin Canals after the 1830s. Seven cemeteries (Odd Fellows' Rest, Cypress Grove, Masonic Cemetery, St. Patrick One, Two, and Three, Holt Cemetery) and part of an eighth (Greenwood) lie within Mid-City. The custom of burial in elevated vaults is not only because New Orleans is below sea level, but also because it was practiced by both the French and the Spanish. In general, burial in Roman Catholic cemeteries was not segregated as it was for those of other denominations; non-Catholic African Americans were buried in cemeteries of benevolent societies such as Odd Fellows, at the foot of Canal Street. Holt Cemetery, established in 1879, a burial ground for the indigent, was sometimes known as Potter's Field.[176] For the living, one of Mid-City's landmarks is the Rock 'N' Bowl at the Mid-City Bowling Lanes on 4133 S. Carrollton Avenue, started by John Blancher in 1988. Failing to experience a vision of the Virgin Mary at Medjugorje in the former Yugoslavia, Blancher placed a petition on a mountainside altar asking for help in finding something his whole family could be involved in.[177] The Rock 'N' Bowl is the best venue for Zydeco in New Orleans.

It has already seen how the Seventh Ward, downriver from Tremé, has played an important role in New Orleans' black politics, including the work of civil rights activist, A. P. Tureaud, for whom a park and the administrative offices of the Housing Authority of New Orleans (HANO) were named. The portion of the Seventh Ward in Planning District No. 4 stretches between Esplanade Avenue, Broad, and Elysian Fields. A his-

176. The custom in other areas of Louisiana with a high water table. Most of the graves in Holt Cemetery are below ground.

177. Information from Michael Tisserand.

torically quintessential Creole neighborhood, I-10 destroyed much of its business district, along Claiborne Avenue, as it did in Tremé.[178] The live oaks that were cut down to make way for the Interstate are remembered in images of them that were painted on the roadway's concrete pilings. While both German immigrants and French Creole families moved into a subdivision of Bernard Marigny's Faubourg Marigny called Nouveau Marigny, beginning with the connection the Pontchartrain Railroad to Milneburg on the lake in 1830, and especially after mid-century, many free people of color came to reside in the Seventh Ward. New Orleans' only four-year high school for African American students was McDonough #35, opened in 1931, until Booker T. Washington opened in 1942. St. Augustine High School (the 'Purple Knights') is the leading secondary school for black males in Louisiana, and led the way in battling segregation in the city. In the aftermath of Katrina, St. Augustine was closed; in January 2006, St. Mary's Academy, St. Augustine, and Xavier University Preparatory collaborated to establish the MAX School of New Orleans, at 5116 Magazine Street (Uptown), to serve as a continuing resources for the city's African American population.

Four housing projects have been located within Planning District No. 4: St. Bernard, Lafitte, Iberville, and B.W. Cooper (Calliope), although the last is physically contiguous with Central City. With the exception of Iberville, all have remained closed since Hurricane Katrina and are designated to be demolished, despite protests and a year's efforts to re-inhabit them, particularly at St. Bernard. On January 31, 2007, the New Orleans Police Department's SWAT team raided the 'New Day Community Center' located in the St. Bernard Development, kicked in doors and arrested people; a few weeks later, authorities tore down the remaining panels and beams of 'Resurrection City,' an encampment next to St. Bernard that had been a symbol of resistance against the city preventing them from returning. The fate of the HANO's housing projects subsequent to Hurricane Katrina will be discussed in more detail later in the book, but it will be useful here to sketch the background of those in Planning District No. 4.

St. Bernard Development was one of ten projects built between 1940 and 1960, a series of two and three story brick buildings that encircled parking lots and playgrounds. In 1946 a gas explosion in the development resulted in fourteen buildings being demolished; St. Bernard expanded

---

178. I–10 had a similar destructive impact on the neighborhood of St. Roch in the Bywater district.

in the 1950s to become one of city's largest projects. In the late 1960s, the idea of scattering family housing units throughout the city, rather than concentrating them in one location, resulted in the Imperial Scattered Site Housing Development near St. Bernard. In 1980 the St. Bernard Area Community Development Center was built as a recreational resource.

The Calliope Project was completed in 1941 with 690 units and another 860 added in 1954. In 1981 it was renamed the B.W. Cooper Apartments in honor of a man who served HANO for 33 years; sometimes it was referred to as "CP-3" (Calliope Projects, Third Ward). Despite extensive funding from HUD for resident management training in 1988, and the formation of its own B.W. Cooper Resident Management Corporation in 1995, it has been a locus of drug trade, along with Magnolia. As of January, 2007, only a small section had been reopened to residents.

Iberville is located in New Orleans' 4th Ward in the old Storyville jazz district, which was razed after passage of the Housing Act (Wagner Bill) of 1937. With 858 apartment, it was one of the city's smaller developments. The Iberville development neighborhood is also home to the oldest cemetery in New Orleans, St. Louis Cemetery #1, a labyrinth of ornate tombs with cast iron fences dating from Spanish control, and the burial place of Homer Plessy and Dutch Morial.

At the same time as Iberville was completed, in 1941, the Lafitte housing development of 896 units was also completed. Under segregation, Lafitte was to house African American tenants while nearby Iberville development accommodated Caucasian tenants. In August, 2006 MIT's Department of Urban Studies and Planning (DUSP) began working with the Catholic Church sponsored Providence Community Housing and Enterprise, partnered with HUD and HANO, for the "redevelopment" of Lafitte. We will later see debate in the assessment of the need for such redevelopment, but note here that while plans include the demolition of the existing complex, only 50 families from Lafitte had been contacted by the end of 2006, precipitating protest from the 'United Front for Affordable Housing, C3/Hands off Iberville."

In 2002 the population of Planning District No. 4 was 66,893, having declined from 92,799 in 1980, a decline of 27.9 percent; its percentage of black population increased by 8.9 percentage points during the same period, from 75.0 percent to 83.9 percent. As of 2002, residential land use was 51.1 percent or 2,268 of the district's total acres; commercial use was 19.3

percent or 856 acres; industrial use was 11.8 percent or 524 acres; over 10 percent or approximately 464 acres was institutional and hospital use.

Planning District No. 5

Planning District No. 5 is the northwest corner of the city known generally as Lakeview, an area of limited development until 1924 when the Board of Commissioners of the Orleans Levee District was mandated by the State to create a 5.5 mile concrete wall on the floor of the lake, filling the enclosed area behind with lake bottom material to raise it above sea level. The wall was completed in 1927, adding 2,000 of prime lakefront property, half of which went to the Louisiana State University New Orleans, now the University of New Orleans (UNO) and the rest to private developers who created the planned development, Lake Vista in the "city beautiful" tradition of Radburn, NJ. The district contains the New Basin Canal Lighthouse and city marina. The Lakeview neighborhood, which extends south from Lake Vista and is adjacent to City Park, has always been one of the few predominantly white areas of the city. Fairly rural in the early part of the twentieth century, by the late 1920s Lakeview had begun to be a prestigious neighborhood, expanding with largely middle class bungalows after World War II, but some larger homes replacing them towards the end of the twentieth century. Lakeview was severely flooded after Katrina, generally to a depth of 8–10 feet, but in some areas as much as fourteen feet of floodwater. By the spring of 2007, the neighborhood was only partially repopulated, although the most severely damaged homes have been demolished. The West End is the neighborhood that extends along the Jefferson Parish line, and the notorious 17th Street Drainage Canal which crumbled during Hurricane Katrina, causing flooding in that part of the city. Originally called New Lake End, it was a port for craft traveling along the New Basin Canal, but in 1880, when the Southern Yacht Club was established, took the name West End as it served as a resort and yachting area. When the new Basin Canal was closed and filled in 1949, and sewers introduced, housing construction began and continued through the 1970s. South of Lakeview is the neighborhood of Navarre, a white middle and working class residential area that also includes Delgado Community College, Louisiana's oldest community college, founded in 1921 as Delgado Central Trades School, and Greenwood, St. Patrick, and Holt cemeteries.

In 2002 the population of Planning District No. 5 was 24,949, having declined from 27,675 in 1980, a decline of 9.9 percent; its percentage of black population increased by 1.1 percentage points during the same period, from 1.1 percent to 2.2 percent. Land use is largely residential at 2,068 acres; the remaining acreage usage is park and recreational.

Planning District No. 6

To the east of Planning District No. 5 and extending south from the lake, Gentilly is one of New Orleans' newer residential areas and shares many similarities with Lakeview, but also includes four institutions of higher learning and the UNO Research and Technology Park. The Gentilly Terrace neighborhood is one of the relatively few areas of New Orleans that is mostly above sea level, as it sits on a natural ridge created by Bayou Sauvage. This high ground made it a good location for development in the early twentieth century, and the Pontchartrain Railroad provided transportation. Most of the homes are Spanish- and Mediterranean-Revival and California style bungalows. To the east of Gentilly Terrace, the Dillard neighborhood is primarily African American, and includes Dillard University which opened in 1930 and moved to its current location in 1935. Adjacent to Dillard was an area of black professionals called "Sugar Hill," many of whose homes and huge oaks in the southern area were destroyed with the construction of I-610. Dillard University, named for educator James Hardy Dillard, was formed from the merger in 1930 of Straight University, established by the Congregational Church in 1869, and New Orleans University, originally established by the Methodist Episcopal Church as the Union Normal School, also in 1869. In 1889, New Orleans University began the Flint Medical College with an affiliated hospital called the Sarah Goodridge Hospital, which had a nurse training school. The medical college closed in 1911, but the nursing school and hospital continued, renamed the Flint-Goodridge Hospital of Dillard University, located in Central City, which was operated by Dillard until 1983. Hebrew Rest Cemetery is a Jewish burial ground on Pelopidas Street.

North of Gentilly Terrace is the Milneburg neighborhood, named for a Scottish settler who had a brick making business. It has a large percentage of African American home owners. In 1933 the Milne Boys Home was founded as a biracial facility for troubled boys, but with segregation, two of everything, including two identical wings, were built—one for blacks, one for whites; the residential program was discontinued in 1986. One of its development programs was named for Louis Armstrong, who had resided at the Waif's Home for Colored Boys. To the East of Milneburg is St. Anthony, a neighborhood that also has a large percentage of home owners, and includes a Roman Catholic Vietnamese community served by Hoi Nouc Mei Lavang (Our Lady of Lavang Mission) on Vermilion Boulevard. To the east of St. Anthony is Filmore, a former swampland that runs between Bayou St. John and the London Avenue Drainage Canal, which breached and was the cause of much flooding in the aftermath of Katrina. The neighborhood was a mixture of single family homes and apartment dwellings such as the Park Chester Garden Apartment complex, which went into decline and was demolished by HUD in the 1970s. Along the lakefront, Lake Terrace and Lake Oaks was once simply the location of wooden fishing camps built on stilts, then some of the city's first jazz honky-tonks and dance halls, such as Quarelles and the Joy Club. During the 1930s the lakefront was reclaimed by the Levee Board and the WPA; some of the land became part of the New Orleans Naval Air Station and was used also as a test site for the Navy's Higgins boats. In 1958 Louisiana State University in New Orleans opened, changing its name to the University of New Orleans in 1974. Southern University at New Orleans (SUNO) opened near Pontchartrain Park in 1959, becoming a branch of Southern University and Agricultural and Mechanical College in Baton Rouge in 1973.

In 2002 the population of Planning District No. 6 was 40,503, having declined from 48,230 in 1980, a decline of 16.0 percent; its percentage of black population increased substantially by 19.0 percentage points during the same period, from 41.2 percent to 60.2 percent. As of 2002, residential land use was 61.4 percent or 3,112 of the district's total acres; with little commercial or industrial use, a large portion of the remaining acreage is institutional use, especially by Dillard and UNO.

Planning District No. 7

While the last two Planning Districts discussed have been residential and relatively homogeneous, Planning District No. 7 is one of the most diverse in the city, with a mixture of residential, commercial, and industrial uses; there are areas of blight, torn down housing projects, and non-conforming uses such as junk yards, but also areas of renewal and gentrification. Faubourg Marigny, immediately downriver from the Quarter, was the Third Municipality in the nineteenth century, where white Creole men sometimes kept their *placées*,[179] and their offspring, originally laid out by Bernard de Marigny de Mandeville[180] from his family plantation land. In time, many free women of color came to own cottages there; the 'suburb' has always been ethnically and racially diverse, with Spanish, French Creoles, Italians, Germans, Irish as well. Part of Marigny lies in the Seventh Ward, most in the Eighth, and several blocks in the Ninth. Bisecting Marigny, and the first grand boulevard in the city to run from the river to the lake, is Elysian Fields Avenue; the Pontchartrain Railroad ran down its center from 1831 carrying passengers until 1932, freight three more years, when the Milneburg resorts were closed.[181] After a period of decline, Marigny has become a center for the creative arts and live music; its higher areas adjacent to the Quarter escaped major flooding, and lower lying areas received relatively minor damage. Downriver from Marigny lies Bywater, located on the natural levee of the river as is the Quarter, and part of the Ninth Ward to which it was connected until the Inner Harbor Navigational Canal (Industrial Canal) was dredged in 1921. In the early nineteenth century, the Daunois plantation was one of several faubourgs[182] that were collectively called Faubourg Washington. In 1831 the portion of Daunois' plantation near the river was sold to the Levee Steam Cotton Press Company, at once the largest cotton press in the world and a major source of employment. Bywater has a racially and ethnically diverse history, with many immigrants from Haiti settling there, followed by Irish, German, and Italians by the end of the nineteenth century. A Bywater controversy has centered around the lock between the Industrial Canal and the Mississippi River,[183] completed in 1923. The Industrial Canal Lock is narrower than modern locks, has been a bottleneck between the river and the Intracoastal Waterway, and its replacement was

179. Mostly African, Indian, and quadroon (offspring of a European and a mulatto) women kept in extralegal 'common law marriages' by white French and Spanish (and, subsequently, Creole) men. The system of *plaçage*, recognized among free people of color as *marriages de la main gauche*, flourished in the latter third of the eighteenth century in New Orleans, but also in Biloxi, Natchez, St. Augustine, and Haiti.

180. Credited with bringing the game of craps to this country.

181. The line was purchased by the New Orleans, Mobile & Texas Railroad in 1871, then the Louisville & Nashville in 1881.

182. Montegut, DeClouet, Montreuil, Cariby, deLesseps.

183. Located at Lower Mississippi River mile 92.6 AHP (Above the Head of Passes, i.e., from the Gulf), mile 6 EHL (East of Harvey Lock, and mile 63 on the Mississippi River–Gulf Outlet Channel (MR-GO).

authorized by Congress in 1998 when barge tows were waiting as much as ten hours to lock through. Many in the Bywater community have argued against the project on environmental grounds, with worries project construction could re-suspend toxic sediments and contaminate nearby wetlands and drinking water sources. It has also been concerned with the expected impact of eight years of construction on the quality of life in adjacent neighborhoods, as well as the lock's questionable economic value, since deep-draft ship traffic through the existing lock has declined. By February, 2003, demolition of the Galvez Street Wharf was completed; by June, 2005, abandoned industrial sites on the east side of the canal were demolished. The project is currently in a holding pattern until the U.S. Army corps of Engineers completes an environmental impact statement to comply with a court order.[184] On higher ground, Bywater was less affected by flooding than other nearby areas.

Immediately north of Bywater is St. Claude, originally a cypress swamp that did not see substantial development until Franklin Avenue, Florida Avenue, and Alvar Street Canals were covered, between 1919 and 1935, making the drained land suitable for development; the neighborhood was named for a street originally called "Good Children Street," but changed to St. Claude Avenue to honor Claude Tremé. The completion of the Industrial Canal in 1923, and, by 1946, four railroads—the Gulf, Mobile, and Ohio Railroad running alongside the canal, the Louisville & Nashville along Almonaster, the New Orleans and Northeastern Railroad along Peoples, and the Public Belt Railroad along Florida Avenue—encouraged development of light industry.

North of St. Claude is the Florida neighborhood, where Ruby Bridges, the six-year old African American child attended a white only elementary school to enforce integration laws. Also originally a cypress swamp, this residential neighborhood did not really develop until the early twentieth century. From 1920 to 1948, the 'Desire' streetcar ran past the many African American shotgun double houses; in fact, approximately 98 percent of the residents in the Florida neighborhood are African American, almost 60 percent owning their own homes in the 2000 Census. A portion of this

184. See article by Lisa Bacques, "Federal Environmental Study Holding Up New Orleans Industrial Canal Project," *Redorbit News,* 2007/02/19, accessed at http://www.redorbit.com/news/display/?id=845710, and Nicole T. Carter, Charles V. Stern, Congressional Research Service, The Library of Congress, CRS Report for Congress, "Mississippi River Gulf Outlet (MRGO) Issues for Congress," August 4, 2006.

area below Florida Avenue is the Florida Development, the fourth of six low-rent public housing projects built under the Wagner Bill. Initially designated for war workers during World War II who never occupied it, the project salvaged and moved some 20–40 of the dwellings on an isolated parcel of land that had been a squatters paradise along the tracks at the end of Louisa Street.[185] It originally consisted of some 500 units in forty-seven two- and three-story brick apartments built around parking spaces and playgrounds. The apartments were not well-constructed, using generally sub-standard materials. In 1953, 234 additional units were added under the 1949 Housing Act. Hurricane Betsy in September, 1965, inundated the area to as much as six feet, flooding lower apartments and revealing the poor construction. In the 1990s, HANO began a major redevelopment, demolishing 194 plus 500 units in two phases, overhauling 77 units and constructing 62 new ones. By June 2004, 20 of the old buildings remained among those that had been demolished, and there were about 68 residents in 133 newly constructed duplexes. In July, 2007 HANO said it would be repairing and reopening 127 of these units which were occupied before Katrina, including the 77 that were previously rehabilitated.[186]

North of Florida Avenue is the Desire area neighborhood, which includes the old Desire Development project. This section of New Orleans was always focused on infrastructure to support light industry—railroads (the New Orleans, Mobile & Texas, the New Orleans & Northeastern, the Public Belt Railroad), and the Industrial Canal, built in 1923. It is this infrastructure that has also isolated the community from the rest of the city. As was the Florida neighborhood, Desire was a cypress swamp well into the mid-nineteenth century when railroad development began and poor whites settled there in makeshift housing. After World War II, black families bought homes on small 60 x 80 lots, and the neighborhood was given utilities but no public transportation until after 1956, when the Desire Public Housing Development was completed. At that time the Gentilly Industrial District was created; many industries located there were severely damaged by Hurricane Betsy in 1965 as with Hurricane Katrina. Desire Development was the last public housing project built under Title

185. Peirce Lewis points out that racial segregation resulting in New Orleans' ghettos resulted from the fact that the city's poorest blacks historically lived where they could, down by the tracks or along the *battures,* the area on the river side of artificial levees in temporary shacks without flood protection; see Lewis 51 ff.

186. Reported on KLFY News, Lafayette, LA, and elsewhere.

III of the 1949 Housing Program. It was built on a site that included the Hideaway Club where Fats Domino played—a site quite isolated from the rest of the city, surrounded by the Industrial Canal, the Florida Canal, and railroad tracks. This sense of isolation contributed to a reduction of economic opportunity for residents and probably its history of violence and crime. The 262 two-story structures of Desire Development, holding 1860 original units, were both cheaply built[187] and difficult to maintain—wood with a brick veneer without fireproofing. HANO's laxness in making repairs to plumbing and electricity contributed to deterioration. Desire was the only development not constructed of solid masonry on concrete slabs. There were at one time two schools on the 97.2 acre site—Dunn and Moton, but both have since been demolished. With first occupancy in 1956, the population was nearly 10,000 and had grown to 13,540 by 1958; the 1990 Census reported a population of 4164. In 1995, HUD approved a HOPE VI grant to HANO to rehabilitate or redevelop the Desire housing project. In 1996 Tulane University was contracted by HANO to manage much of Desire Development's deteriorating conditions, continued violence, and conflict between residents and NOPD. The majority of the housing development was razed, but almost ten years intervened before ground was broken to begin construction of the new Desire HOPE VI Revitalization Project in November, 2002. The plan called for the 'New Desire' mixed-income community to consist of some 424 units,[188] roughly half rental and half single family homes, the first phase of which was to be called "Abundance Square." With a completion goal of July, 2007 for the entire redevelopment, work was in progress when Hurricane Katrina flooded the area almost to the second floor of the 73 or so buildings that had been constructed.

In 2002 the population of Planning District No. 7 was 43,031, having declined from 61,594 in 1980, a decline of 30.1 percent; its percentage of black population increased by 10.7 percentage points during the same period, from 75.9 percent to 86.6 percent. As of 2002, residential land use was 53.2 percent or 1972 of the district's total acres; industrial use is extensive, the largest being along the Industrial Canal between Claiborne and Almonaster, where Port facilities have expanded with street, rail, and

187. 508 units were built by Pittman Construction Co. and 1352 by R. F. Ball of San Antonio.

188. Michaels Development, Torti Gallas and Partners of Silver Spring, MD, Architects and Master Planners.

water access. The Agriculture Street Landfill and adjacent residences north of Florida Avenue were declared an EPA Superfund toxic waste site.

Planning District No. 8

East of the Inner Harbor Navigational Canal (Industrial Canal) and south of Florida Avenue to the river lies Planning District No. 8, which includes the Lower Ninth Ward, and the neighborhood of Holy Cross, along the river. Further to the east, Jackson Barracks sits on the boundary of Orleans and St. Bernard Parish. Holy Cross, predominately African-American, was once the location of several sugar plantations in the early nineteenth century. Vulnerable to flooding, the area became a home for poorer African Americans, as well as Irish, German, and Italian immigrants. Its homes have been a mixture of shotgun houses, Creole cottages, bungalows, and two octagonal 'steamboat houses' with elevated, wrap around porches reminiscent of the bridge of a paddle wheeler; in 1835 Jackson Barracks were constructed. As did Bywater, Holy Cross, on the opposite side of the Industrial Canal, has resisted the USACE plans to replace its lock at the outlet to the river. In 1965, Hurricane Betsy did considerable damage; the area has declined somewhat since that time. Nevertheless, a strong neighborhood association founded in 1981 and several churches have worked to make the neighborhood safer and cleaner.

The Lower Ninth Ward neighborhood was one of the last New Orleans neighborhoods to be developed. Originally a cypress swamp within plantations that once stretched from the river to the lake, it was not until almost 1920 before the city had installed the Jourdan, Tupelo, and Florida Avenue drainage canals. The area was only partially developed by mid-twentieth century, but industrial and commercial activity grew in the third quarter, especially along the Industrial Canal between Claiborne and St. Claude Avenues. The Ninth Ward's geographic separation from the rest of the city has contributed to its history of activism in response to neglect by city government. It also has a history of civil rights activism: its McDonogh #19 (later called Louis D. Armstrong Elementary) on St. Claude was one of the first to be integrated, precipitating an exit of its white population into adjacent St. Bernard Parish. As it would later with Hurricane Katrina, the Lower Ninth received devastating flooding from Hurricane Betsy in 1965, with more than 80 percent of the area under water, resulting, in part, from the fact that its eight foot high levee was inadequate for Betsy's ten foot storm surge. Many residents did not receive sufficient financial assistance to prevent what became one of the higher rates of population decline in the city. Between 1969 and 1975, the Demonstration Cities and Metropolitan Development Act, passed by 1966, produced a number of attempts by various agencies to improve the general welfare in the neighborhood; only a few remain in operation today. One that had remained was the Lower Ninth Ward Health Clinic—at least until Katrina. Nine months after the storm, there was still no effort to establish a source for preventative and primary healthcare for residents of the Lower Ninth, the Upper Ninth, or the Seventh Ward, despite the fact that some residents were returning and were finding either no access to medical care or 14-hour waits in emergency rooms in other parts of the city. Common Ground's Lower Ninth Ward Project, Leaders Creating Change Through Contribution, and resident health care providers March 1, 2007 were finally able to open a new Lower Ninth Ward Health Clinic at 5228 St. Claude Avenue at Egania Street.[189] The clinic is collaborating with a number of organizations, including Tulane's New Orleans Children's Health Project. Those returning have seen it as an important safety net for residents whose medical needs have gone unaddressed since Katrina. Nowhere in the city was the devastation from the flooding after Hurricane Katrina greater than in the Lower Ninth. There were multiple sources of entry of the flood waters: downriver from St. Bernard Parish, and upriver from the Industrial Canal. The force of the water was strong enough to knock many homes from their foundations, and the floodwater level was high enough that even Holy Cross School, which had been a dry refuge during Hurricane Betsy, was inundated. The area of the Ninth most severely damaged was that north of Claiborne Avenue. Eighteen months after the storm, the area was still sparsely repopulated and uninhabitable, although a few business had returned and some residents were living in FEMA trailers. Among the many competing 'plans' for reconstruction of New Orleans, a report from the 'Bring New Orleans Back' Commission wanted to make the lower elevation portion of the Ninth above Claiborne into park space, an idea violently resisted by residents.

In 2002 the population of Planning District No. 8 was 20,193, having declined from 27,322 in 1980, a decline of 26.1 percent; its percentage of black population increased by 5.0 percentage points during the same period, from 89.3 percent to 94.3 percent. As of 2002, residential land use

189. As reported in *The Louisiana Weekly*, March 5, 2007.

was approximately 70 percent or 1,008 of the district's total acres. The district has experienced not only flooding problems, but also generally poor infrastructure, poor soils, and deterioration of existing homes.

Planning Districts Nos. 9–11

Planning Districts Nos. 9–11 encompass an area of Orleans Parish loosely referred to as "New Orleans East." Planning District No. 9 runs east along the lake from the Industrial Canal, north of Chef Menteur Highway, and includes the neighborhoods of Pines Village, Little Woods, Plum Orchard, West Lake Forest, and Read Boulevard East and West. Planning District No. 10, further east, is the Village de l'Est area; District No. 11 includes Viavant/Venetian Isles. Little Woods, also known as Edgelake, the first lakefront land available in the city, was once teeming with hundreds of fishing camps built on stilts rent free on land owned by the Levee Board, until many were washed away by Hurricane Georges in 1998. A kind of urban analogue of Holly Beach ('Cajun Riviera'), the Edgelake stretch was sometimes referred to as 'The Poor Man's Miami Beach.' Segregation set aside all of a quarter mile stretch of beach in Little Woods in 1939 as a swimming area for African Americans; an amusement park developed there during the 1950s, but after segregation ended after 1964, the area fell into disrepair. New Orleans' Lakefront Airport, completed in 1934, became used only for private aircraft. Read Boulevard, originally wetlands marshes and cypress swamps, was filled and developed as moderate income tract homes in the 1950s and expanded with the final completion of I-10 in 1974[190] as among one of the suburban areas east and west of the city to which whites moved after integration in 1964. Village de l'Est in District No. 10 is a larger area further east of Paris Road. One of its more notable historical owners was Bartholomy Lafon, architect and town planner, but also, according to Jean Lafitte, a privateer and smuggler. Large scale development by the Dallas, Texas corporation, Wynne-Murchison Interest, began in 1961 and drew thousands of Vietnamese immigrants to the area during the 1970s and 1980s; the area is now predominantly African American. As other areas of New Orleans East built on marshland, there

---

190. I-10 was built in bits and pieces over a 25 year period. The first elevated part of I-10 was built near Tulane Avenue in 1959, the Inner Harbor Navigational Canal Bridge in 1965, and the last five mile stretch took five years to construct, from 1970 to 1974, and was officially completed on January 11, 1974. Information from Ronnie Goynes and Robert Tessier, Louisiana Dept of Transportation and Development.

has been serious subsidence and drainage problems. The Viavant/Venetian Isles area, Planning District No. 11, south of Chef Menteur Highway, is the location of a number of manufacturing facilities, most notably the Higgins Aircraft Plant, which produced plywood cargo planes during World War II, tank engines during the Korean War, and then was taken over by NASA's Michoud Facility in 1961 for the assembly of large space vehicles. Coinciding with this was some residential growth. Proctor & Gamble Company's Folgers' brand maintains the world's largest coffee roasting plant in Viavant/Venetian Isles. Damaged during Hurricane Katrina, the plant reopened quite soon on September 20, 2005.[191] The Lake Catherine neighborhood is surrounded by Lake Borgne, Lake St. Catherine, and Lake Pontchartrain, and is the location of the Bayou Sauvage National Wildlife Refuge. In the early 1800s, two forts (Pike and Macomb) were constructed for defense of navigational channels leading into New Orleans. One African American soldier who served at Fort Pike was P. B. S. Pinchback, son of a white planter and a freed slave and a Union officer and lawyer, was the first black governor in the United States, serving as Governor of Louisiana for thirty-five days, from December 9, 1872, to January 13, 1873 after Governor Warmoth was impeached; Pinchback also made Mardi Gras a legal holiday. Opposite Fort Pike, the Rigolets Lighthouse, which looks like a fishing camp on stilts, facilitated passage between Lake Pontchartrain and Lake Borgne.

In 2002 the population of Planning District No. 9 was 71,837 having grown from 62,381 in 1980, an increase of 15.2 percent; its percentage of black population increased by 33.9 percentage points during the same period, from 40.5 percent to 74.4 percent. As of 2002, residential land use consists largely of 18 subdivisions in District No. 9, representing 41.3 percent or 5271 of the district's total of 12,772 acres. Industrial use is 25.1 percent, and Wetlands 12.8 percent.

In 2002 the population of Planning District No. 10 was 16,105, having grown from 12,839 in 1980, an increase of 25.4 percent; its percentage of black population increased by 12.7 percentage points during the same period, from 35.3 percent to 48.0 percent. As of 2002, residential land use consists of two subdivisions, representing 3.5 percent of the district's total of 23,025 acres; industrial use 11.4 percent, and wetlands and parklands combined, 83.9 percent.

191. Information from Emory Zimmer of Folgers.

In 2002 the population of Planning District No. 11 was 1,595, having declined from 1,827 in 1980, a decline of 12.7 percent; its percentage of black population decreased by 37.4 percentage points during the same period, from 37.4 percent to 0.0 percent. As of 2002, residential land use was approximately 3.7 percent, or 1,556 of the district's total acres of 41,577 acres; industrial use 0.9 percent, and wetlands and parklands combined, 94.8 percent.

Planning Districts Nos. 12–13

Planning Districts Nos. 12 and 13 are located on the west bank of the river, and include the Algiers District (No. 12) and New Aurora/English Turn (No. 13). Algiers is at a point of a sharp bend in the Mississippi River, just downriver of what forms the river's crescent past Uptown and the Quarter. USACE refers to the point as mile 94.6 AHP on the Lower Mississippi. Algiers Point Light marks the point. The Algiers side of the river functions as much of the Port of New Orleans' support facility, where ships are built and repaired,[192] moored, and from where towboats run to push barges. Its residential portion is one that has developed a consciousness of its own historical as well as geographical uniqueness. Algiers Point was the home the French colony's slaughterhouse (and sometimes called Slaughterhouse Point) as well as to a 'slave corral' where Africans were sold to colonists. From 1827 a small ferry has transported people between Algiers and Canal Street in the city; the ferry, a railroad yard, and a U.S. Naval Support Station have contributed to the area's economic growth. Residences once consisted of a mixture of shotgun houses, Creole cottages, Victorians with showy trim, but a devastating fire in 1895 destroyed almost 250 of these houses, resulting in their replacement largely by shotgun doubles. Old Aurora is a rather prosperous neighborhood downriver from Algiers. It had been the location of the Jo Ellen Smith Medical Center that once provided full medical services, including a hyperbaric chamber for treatment of offshore divers, but in May, 1999, was closed by Tenet Healthcare Corp. All that remains now is a convalescent center.

On the Jefferson Parish line is the William J. Fischer Development, the last of the conventional public housing projects, opened in 1965. As Desire Development had been, the area was isolated from its surrounding communities by the Southern Pacific Railroad line, an expressway, bridge,

192. Shipbuilding began in 1819 with the first dry dock operated by the New Orleans Floating Dry Dock company.

and the Donner Canal. For this reason, the architects used the scattered site method rather than traditional multiple courtyards. They consolidated open spaces into several large parks and arranged the buildings in lines around them. The complex consisted of one 13 floor high rise building for the elderly and fourteen three-story low-rise buildings, creating a total of 1002 residential units and an elementary school; one additional elementary school was opened in 1967. By 2002, HANO had received a HOPE VI grant for the revitalization of severely distress public housing, and Fischer was among the developments that had experienced high crime rates for a considerable period of time. As of June 2004, the Fischer 13 floor high rise building was demolished, to be replaced by a 100-unit senior village; the fourteen three-floor units remained, with plans to redevelop the area into a mixed-income community of rental and owned units. Many Fischer residents were moved to other housing developments.

Planning District No. 13, New Aurora/English Turn, lies immediately down river from District No. 12. The Intracoastal Waterway on the west bank divides the upriver portion of the district. After Village d l'Est, this area has had the second highest percentage of Asian residents, and a Buddhist Temple that serves them. The Chalmette-Lower Algiers Ferry connects the downriver portion of Orleans Parish with Chalmette, in St. Bernard Parish, between Donald Street and Paris Road, respectively. While New Aurora is largely middle- and low-income families, English Turn is a gated neighborhood of high-income residents. At the southeastern tip of English Turn sits the Audubon Center for Research of Endangered Species and Freeport-McMoRan Audubon Species Survival Center, founded in 1996, on a woodland breeding habitat of 1,123 acres. The Center research team is currently led by Dr. Betsy Dresser, globally recognized for work with *in vitro* fertilization, cryopreservation, and embryo transfer for wildlife conservation. The Planning Districts on the west bank of the Mississippi did not experience severe damage or flooding as did areas across the river.

In 2002 the population of Planning District No. 12 was 52,888, having declined from 58,552 in 1980, a decline of 9.7 percent; its percentage of black population increased by 9.1 percentage points during the same period, from 42.8 percent to 51.9 percent. As of 2002, residential land use was approximately 60.8 percent, or 3,867 of the district's total acres of 6,362 acres.

In 2002 the population of Planning District No. 13 was 567, having grown from 315 in 1980, an increase of 80.0 percent; its percentage of black population increased by 6.9 percentage points during the same period, from 35.6 percent to 42.5 percent. As of 2002, residential land use, all single family, was approximately 49.6 percent, or 2,213 of the district's total acres of 4,461 acres; wetlands and parklands combined, 48.0 percent.

With the sketch of neighborhoods and population data between 1980 and 2002 for New Orleans' thirteen planning districts completed, it is useful to have, as comparison, population for the entire city for that same period. In 2002 the population of Orleans Parish was 456,592, having declined from 557,515 in 1980, a decrease of 18.1 percent; its percentage of black population rose from 55.3 percent to 64.7 percent, an increase of 9.4 percentage points, during the same period.

The Significance of Demographics

To have a basis for understanding the significance and implications of New Orleans' population and demographic changes *after* Hurricanes Katrina and Rita, it is useful to look at some of the changes that were occurring *before* the storms. We have already seen several important shifts in the characteristics of certain neighborhoods during the period of 1980 to 2002. But before we consider them in greater depth, and assess whether any of the Seven Markers of Complexity may have had a presence in the city's cultural milieu before the disastrous flooding of September, 2005, it is worthwhile to examine several other demographic factors over a broader period of time. These include numbers for the overall population of Orleans Parish, and its proportions of racial distribution. It also includes—since *Walking to New Orleans* focuses especially on issues of adequate housing and healthcare facilities in post-disaster planning—information about the adequacy of hospitals and community primary care facilities, and the availability of housing for the poor or under-employed. Finally, we give more limited attention to economics—particularly shifts in opportunities for employment and available jobs—and to the status of public schools as the primary means for preparing young people for employment and adult participation on the life of the city. Then, we pull together some of the themes and patterns that emerge.

For the century prior to 1950, New Orleans' population grew steadily with a steady ratio of approximately 30 percent black to 70 percent white.

Since 1950, when the total population of Orleans Parish was 570,445 New Orleans reached a high of 627,525 in 1960,[193] then began a steady decline until its last census population, in 2000, of 484,674. This represents a decrease of 142,851 people, or 22.76 percent of its population since 1960.[194] Looking at the proportion of racial distribution over the same period, it appears that the mid-1970s—possibly 1974—is the approximate date at which New Orleans became a minority majority (black majority) city.

In 1960, for Orleans Parish total population of 627,525, 62.57 percent (or 392,649) were white; 37.18 percent (or 233,344) were black; Asian and other groups, the balance of 1532, represented 0.24 percent of the total population.[195] In 1970, of Orleans Parish total population of 593,471, 54.49 percent (or 323,420) were white; 45.04 percent (or 267,308) were black; Asian and other groups, the balance of 2,743, represented 0.46 percent of the total population.[196]

By 1980, however, with a total population of 557,515, the white population had *decreased* by 26.7 percent (to 236,987) while the black population had *increased* by 15.3 percent (to 308,206) from 1970. Asian and other groups, the balance of 12,379, represented 2.22 percent of the total population (an increase of 351.29 percent from 1970).[197] The large increase in non-white and non-black population reflects a sizeable influx of Vietnamese during this period. Thus, the 1980 census showed blacks representing a *majority* of 55.25 percent of New Orleans' total population; whites, a minority of 42.52 percent.

193. Bureau of the Census, U.S. Department of Commerce. 1960 Louisiana Census. Table 96. Age by Race, Nativity, and Sex . . . for Standard metropolitan Statistical Areas and Cities of 100,000 or More and Parishes of 250,000 or More. 20–251. Orleans Parish and the City of New Orleans are co-terminus.

194. 1970—593,471; 1980—557,515; 1990—496,938; 2000—484,674. The 2005 American Community Survey lists the estimated population of New Orleans as 437,186; its universe is limited to the household population and excludes the population living in institutions, college dormitories, and other group quarters. This represents a decrease of 30.33 percent.

195. U.S. Census 1960, Louisiana, Table 96. Age by Race, Nativity, and Sex . . . For Standard Metropolitan Statistical Areas and Cities of 1000,000 or More and Parishes of 250,000 or More. 20–251. 'White' includes 'Native White' and 'Foreign-Born White.' Census tables for 1960 and 1970 use the term 'Negro.' Tables for 1980 and later use the term 'black.' See also Table 34, 1970 Census.

196. U.S. Census 1970, Louisiana, Table 23. Race by Sex, for Areas and Places. 20–57.

197. Ibid., Table 15. Persons by Race. 20–15.

By 1990, that shift had increased further. Of New Orleans' total population of 496,938, 34.92 percent (or 173,554) where white; 61.92 percent (or 307,728) were black. Asian and other groups represented 3.15 percent (or 15,656) of the total.[198] These trends only continued to progress at the millennium.

In 2000, of New Orleans' total population of 484,674, 28.05 percent (or 135,956) were white; 67.25 percent (or 325,947) were black. Asian and other groups[199] represented 4.70 percent (or 22,771) of the total population,[200] an increase of 45.45 percent since 1990. One can note that the (rounded to one place) New Orleans' 28.1 percent white population compares to a U.S. average of 75.2 percent; its 67.3 percent black population compares to a U.S. average of 12.3 percent.

In 2005, the American Community Survey (ACS) Data Profile, whose universe is limited to household population, and excludes the population living in institutions, college dormitories, and other group quarters, showed the racial proportionality as approximately the same as the 2000 census: 28.0 percent white; 67.5 percent black or African American.

The conclusions from these data are, of course, harder to draw. One could say that New Orleans, over the last half-century has grown considerably smaller in total population by nearly 25 percent as of 2005. One could say it has radically shifted its racial distribution, becoming a heavily minority majority city of more than two-thirds black, with a growing Asian population. Perhaps this means New Orleans was looking more like the city it was in colonial times. In any case, New Orleans has had the second highest percentage of black population of any city in the nation.[201]

Hospitals and Healthcare

In looking at the state of New Orleans' hospitals and healthcare facilities prior to Katrina, it is less a question of sheer numbers than what kinds of

198. U.S. Census Bureau, American FactFinder P006. Race—Universe: Persons. Data Set: 1990 Summary Tape File 1 (STF 1)—100—Percent data. Also Table 1 Selected Population and Housing Characteristics: 1990 Orleans Parish.

199. Including roughly a third, who self-identified as belong to two or more other races.

200. U.S. Census Bureau, American FactFinder. P7. Race [8]—Universe: Total Population. Data Set: Census 2000 Summary File 1 (SF 1) 100-Percent Data.

201. The 2000 Census puts the percentage of 'Black or African American alone or in combination' of New Orleans at 67.9 percent. Detroit is highest at 82.8 percent, Baltimore third at 65.2 percent.

services were provided, and where were they distributed. That information will become more meaningful when post-Katrina comparisons are considered. Prior to Hurricane Katrina (depending on the cutoff date), Orleans Parish had roughly a dozen hospitals of varying size, a half-dozen mental health facilities, and twenty neighborhood primary care clinics providing a variety of services.

Beginning with a sketch of New Orleans' hospitals, its two largest facilities were part of the Medical Center of Louisiana at New Orleans (MCLNO); both were teaching hospitals of LSU Medical School. Charity Hospital, at 1532 Tulane Avenue, founded May 10, 1736 on grant from French shipbuilder, Jean Louis, was originally named L'Hôpital des Pauvres de la Charité (also called the Hospital of Saint John) and opened at intersection of Chartres and Bienville St in Quarter. It was the second oldest continually operating public hospital in U. S., Bellevue Hospital in New York being one month older. A second hospital building was built in 1743 on Basin St; a third was built nearby in 1785 and renamed San Carlos Hospital in honor of King Charles III of Spain, but was destroyed by fire in 1809. A temporary hospital was established at the Cabildo for a month, then at the Jourdan residence in Faubourg Marigny for six months, then the dilapidated De La Vergne plantation for five years. A fourth hospital was built in 1815 at edge of city on Canal St where Fairmont Hotel currently located; this hospital was criticized as inadequate. A fifth hospital was built within Girod, Gravier, St. Mary, and Common Streets in Faubourg St. Mary in 1832, run by the Sisters of Charity for 100 years and where the hospital developed its reputation. In 1939 a sixth hospital was built on Tulane Avenue, with 2680 beds making it the second largest in the US at the time. The LSU Health Sciences Center was built adjacent to Charity in 1931. In 1970 the Louisiana Department of Health and Human Resources (DHH) took control of Charity, transferred to the Louisiana Health Care Authority (LHCA) in 1991, then the LSU system in 1997. MCLNO's other teaching hospital, the 575-bed University Hospital, at 2921 Perdido Street, adjacent to LSU Medical School, was originally known as Hôtel-Dieu, operated by the Daughters of Charity.

Memorial Medical Center, renamed from Southern Baptist Hospital in 1996, at 2700 Napoleon Avenue, uptown, was founded in 1926 by the Southern Baptist Convention, with specialties in obstetrics, cardiology, and cancer care.[202] In 1969, the religious organization separated itself from the hospital and it became an independent non-profit entity. In the early 1980s the hospital spent over $100,000,000 (Project 2000) to add to and renovate the original building. In 1990 it merged with Mercy Hospital, located near the end of Bayou St. John on Jefferson Davis Parkway, and the two hospitals operated as Mercy-Baptist Medical Center with the old Southern Baptist Hospital called the Uptown Campus and Mercy called the Mid-City campus. The combined hospitals were acquired by Tenet Healthcare and the old Baptist Hospital was renamed Memorial Medical Center in 1996. Lifecare Hospitals of Plano, Texas, leased the seventh floor as a separate, long-term patient facility, operating acute care for complex cases such as infection from complications of rectal cancer.

The Lindy Boggs Medical Center at 301 N. Jefferson Davis Parkway, formerly known as Memorial Medical Center, Mercy Campus, specialized in orthopedics, cardiology, and held the Transplant Institute of New Orleans.

The nonprofit Children's Hospital of New Orleans at 200 Henry Clay Avenue sat on a sliver of old high ground next to the river near Audubon Park and had its own power generating capability.

The Tulane University Hospital and Clinic (TUHC) at 1415 Tulane Avenue, opened in 1964, and specialized in obstetrics and gynecology, treating women and their babies. In July, 2005 it merged with Lakeside Hospital to become a leading teaching facility in the community. Associated with TUHC were the Tulane Abdominal Transplant Institute; the Tulane Primary Care Center—Downtown at 275 LaSalle St; the Tulane Inpatient Rehabilitation Center (TIRC) and the Tulane Metairie Clinic in Metairie; Tulane Hospital for Children at 1415 Tulane Avenue; the Tulane Family Health Center—Uptown Clinic at the Uptown Square Shopping Center, 200 Broadway Avenue; the DePaul-Tulane Behavioral Health Center on Calhoun Street, between Camp and Perrier, also known as DePaul Hospital, founded in 1861 by the Daughters of Charity, as previously noted, originally as an orphanage called the House of the Five Wounds, first used as a mental health facility in 1871 and leased to become part of TUHC in 1997; the Tulane-Xavier National Center of Excellence in Women's Health (TUXCOE).

---

202. Now known as Ochsner Baptist Medical Center.

Touro Infirmary at 1301 Foucher Street near the intersection of Louisiana Avenue and Prytania Street, founded in 1852 as a community-based, faith-based, nonprofit hospital, had cancer, diabetes, heart disease programs, physical therapy, and was affiliated with the LSU Health Science Center and Tulane Health Science Center.

The VA Medical Center of New Orleans of the Southeast Louisiana Veterans Health Care System at 1601 Perdido Street was a 354-bed acute care facility and an outpatient clinic, offering primary care and mental health services on the 9th and 10th floors of the Medical Center's Lindy C. Boggs Transitional Care Unit.

Kindred Hospital at 3601 Coliseum Street (Uptown, bordering the Garden District) was a long-term care facility, specializing in treating medically complex patients (such as complex wound treatment, pre- and post-transplant care, pulmonary rehabilitation, renal failure); the building was originally Coliseum House, a psychiatric hospital, then Vencor, a long-term care facility, then taken over in April 2001 by Kindred Healthcare, based in Kentucky, whose subsidiaries operate long-term acute care hospitals.

Methodist Hospital (Pendleton Memorial Methodist Hospital) at 5620 Read Boulevard was a 300-bed general medical and surgical hospital providing healthcare to Eastern New Orleans.

Flint-Goodridge Hospital in at 2425 Louisiana Avenue in Central City at Freret was operated by Dillard University from 1911–1983. Through the 1950s African American doctors were allowed to practice only at Flint-Goodridge and were barred from membership in the Orleans Parish Medical Society. New Orleans' first three African American mayors were born there. The community role of the hospital grew during the 1950s and 60s, but despite its humanitarian success, financial problems began to multiply. An attempt in the late 1970s and early 80s to sell the hospital to a group of African American physicians failed. In 1981 Dillard university took over daily management of the hospital, but it ceased operation and closed in 1983. The building still stands today now as the Flint-Goodridge Apartments.

Among other medical facilities that have had a place in New Orleans' healthcare services, the 173-bed St. Charles General Hospital at 3700 Saint Charles Avenue opened December, 1972, in uptown New Orleans as part of Tenet Louisiana HealthSystem, then the largest provider of health care delivery in New Orleans. Among its specialties were bariatrics (obesity medicine) with its opening of the Weight Management Center (WMC) in March, 1995. In July, 2004, Stephen Farber, CFO of Tenet resigned, receiving a subpoena from the United States Attorney's Office in New Orleans requesting documents relating to physician relationships and financial arrangements at three New Orleans area hospitals (Memorial Medical Center, Kenner Regional Medical Center, and St. Charles General Hospital). In December, 2004, Tenet Healthcare Corporation of Dallas decided to sell St. Charles General Hospital to Preferred Continuum Care of Birmingham, Alabama.[203]

The 130-bed Bywater Hospital (formerly St. Claude Medical Center) was purchased from United Medical Corporation in June, 2003, as a doctor-owned community infirmary, by physicians who had worked for 20 years for out-of-state investors. Renamed to reflect its community ties, the privately run hospital closed abruptly on March 9, 2005.

The Jo Ellen Smith Medical Center at 4502 General Meyer Avenue in Old Aurora on the west bank had provided full medical services, including a hyperbaric chamber for treatment of offshore divers, but in May, 1999, was closed by Tenet Healthcare Corp.

The 156-bed Lakeland Medical Center, a general and acute care facility at 6000 Bullard Avenue in New Orleans East was closed on January 31, 2004. Healthsouth Specialty Hospital of New Orleans was a rehabilitation facility.

Among New Orleans' mental health facilities not elsewhere discussed were New Orleans Adolescent Hospital and Community Services (NOAH) at 210 State Street, the city's sole inpatient facility providing services for children and adolescents with serious emotional and behavioral problems, Community Care Hospital at 1421 General Taylor Street, in the Uptown area, founded in 1994 as a 40-bed adult and geriatric psychiatric hospital, and the suburban River Oaks Hospital at 1525 River Oaks Road West, a private psychiatric facility treating trauma caused disorders, compulsive behavior, and detox.

The Louisiana Institute of Public Health's examination of neighborhood primary care clinics and health centers has been particularly useful in making comparisons among them before and after Katrina on a service-for-service basis.[204] Of New Orleans' neighborhood primary care clinics,

203. The eleventh of twenty-seven hospitals Tenet promised to divest beginning in January 2004.

204. Information provided in conversations with Susan Bergson of LIPH.

eight were providing both child and adult healthcare services: Algiers-Fischer Health Center in Algiers, Daughters of Charity Health Center in Carrollton-Gert Town, Healthcare for the Homeless on Canal Street serving the CBD and Quarter, Central City Community Health Clinic, Desire-Florida Community Health Center in the Desire-Ninth Ward area, the Lower Ninth Ward Community Health Center, the St. Bernard Family Health Clinic serving Gentilly and Midtown, and EXCELth Family Health Center in New Orleans East. Two more provided adult care: MCL in the CBD-Quarter and St. Thomas Health Center in the Irish Channel; one, the HCH Adolescent Drop-in Center, provided child care. Twelve more provided various lesser services: the Ida Hymel Health Clinic in Algiers, the Mandeville Detiege Health Clinic serving Carrollton-Mid-City, the Orleans Women's Clinic and the Booker T. Washington School Based Clinic in Tulane-Gravier, the Wetmore TB Clinic at Charity Hospital, the Edna Pilsbury Clinic in Central City, The Carver High School Based Clinic and the Helen A. Levy Health Clinic in the Desire-Ninth Ward area, the St. Bernard Parish Clinic, the Katherine Benson Health Clinic in St. Roch-Bywater, and the Mary Buck Health Clinic in the St. Thomas area. Most clinics provided immunization and prenatal/family planning services. Roughly half provided mental health or dental services.

As an example of the vitally important role these neighborhood clinics have played in New Orleans' health care—and in anticipation of the seriousness of the loss of many of them after Katrina—one can recall the crisis precipitated by the closing of Charity Hospital's W-16 walk-in clinic due to budget cuts in the fall of 2003. Many of the city's un- or under-insured counted on 'Big Charity' for their primary care, and it soon became painfully apparent that the city's healthcare infrastructure could not cope with the new flood of healthcare needs. Patients who visited Charity Hospital's walk-in clinic as much as 60,000 times a year spilled onto the other already overtaxed community health centers. For many patients, with chronic aliments such as heart disease and diabetes rampant in the city, this meant getting no treatment at all. The wait time for new patients at Daughters of Charity Health Center on South Carrollton Avenue, for example, jumped from three weeks to three months; subsequently, it was forced to turn away newcomers, directing them to other community health centers where waits might be shorter.[205]

205. Darv Johnson, "Yet another crisis! Walk-in clinic's closing spurs health care emergency," *The Louisiana Weekly,* June 28, 2004.

Housing

Turning to housing in Orleans Parish prior to Katrina, the 2000 census shows a total of 215,091 housing units, of which 87.5 percent were occupied, leaving 12.5 percent (or 28,840 units) vacant. New Orleans' vacancy rate compares with a national rate of 9.0 percent, suggesting a relatively higher number of unused properties. In addition, vacant housing units do not include in the housing inventory those units open to the elements—where the roof, walls, windows, or doors no longer protect the interior—or those units condemned or designated to be demolished.[206] Approximately 40 percent of all houses in New Orleans are duplexes. Most houses are older, with 43.2 percent having been built in 1949 or earlier, as compared to only 22.3 percent nation wide. The length of residency is comparable to that in the United States as a whole: for example, in New Orleans, 35.0 percent had moved in by 1989 or earlier; in the United States, 35.1 percent. The owner occupancy rate of 46.5 percent for Orleans Parish compares with 66.2 percent nation wide.[207] Average rental costs were slightly less than those nationally: in 2000, for example, the average gross rent (contract rent plus utilities) was $518 in Orleans Parish, $657 nation wide; owner costs with mortgage were roughly comparable. The Census Bureau bases housing affordability on whether households pay 30 percent or more of income on housing. In 2000, for Orleans Parish, 31.6 percent of owner occupied households paid 30 percent or more for owner costs (vs. 48.2 percent nationally); 68.4 percent of renter occupied households paid this (vs. 51.8 percent nationally). This perhaps suggests that renter incomes are proportionately lower in New Orleans, which might correlate to its relatively high proportion of hotel and service industry lower-paying jobs.

Many of the problems existing in the pre-Katrina state of New Orleans' public housing 'development projects' have already been discussed in the context of their location within particular neighborhoods and planning districts. The following will look at public housing somewhat more globally. Public housing may not inherently be a racial matter, but it becomes one, and it would be hard to argue that New Orleans' black

---

206. Data from U.S. Census 2000 and Greater New Orleans Community Data Center. A 'housing unit' may be a house, apartment, mobile home or trailer, group of rooms, or single room occupied as separate living quarters.

207. This, however, is not an urban area to urban area comparison.

population has received the equivalent to whites in the quality and location of public housing units. Part of this emerged organically as previously more fragmented black ghettos of economically disadvantaged in New Orleans grew and began to merge into superghettos through the 1980s and 1990s. Poverty was accompanied by an increase in crime. Symbolic of the atmosphere of fear, whites living near the boundaries of poor black neighborhoods often put razor-wire across household walls, padlocked chains around iron gates.[208] Prior to its being taken over by HUD in 1996, the Housing Authority of New Orleans (HANO) operated 11,235 dwelling units, more than 90 percent of them in ten large public housing developments ('the Projects'). Beginning with the concurrent needs to provide extremely low-cost housing for underemployed residents during the Depression and also demolish slum and blighted neighborhoods, New Orleans completed its first major project, Iberville Development, in 1941. Iberville consisted of fairly well-built brick units around grassy courtyards; originally it was all white. But the combination of white flight during the 1960s and 1970s, increased unemployment and poverty levels, including many single mothers with dependent children, and the situation of some poorly built projects, such as Desire Development in totally isolated parts of the city, resulted in the fact that by the late 1970s, New Orleans' public housing projects had become almost totally black—the realization of ghettos of poverty and crime in spite of the attempt to 'demolish' them. The fact that city maps typically failed to show the location of its public housing projects on reflected how easy it was for government leaders to ignore the very problems they had created.

On top of this, New Orleans infrastructure has been increasingly unable to keep up with the city's needs. For example, prior to Katrina, the New Orleans Sewerage and Water Board Board (S&WB) estimated that the city's water supply system would need some $2.8 billion in repairs, and its wastewater system would require evaluation and repairs costing $977 million.

Looking more briefly at the economic characteristics and the status of public education of Orleans Parish, one can see several areas of endemic problems. The 2000 Census shows that while the percentage of New Orleans' population with high school diplomas or bachelor's degrees is on

---

208. See Peirce Lewis and others.

a par with percentages nationally,[209] income is not. Median family income (in 1999 dollars), for example, nationally was $50,046, while in Orleans Parish it was only $32,338. In a sense, the local dollar in New Orleans was worth only 65 cents, assuming basic living costs to be roughly the same as elsewhere. Similarly, the 2000 Census shows that the percentage of families below the poverty level nationally was 9.2 percent, while in New Orleans it was 23.7 percent. The same holds true for individuals, where the percentage of individuals below the poverty level nationally was 12.4 percent, but in New Orleans, 27.9 percent. This means that at least a quarter of the citizens of New Orleans were living under conditions of poverty. In its history, New Orleans has experienced considerable fluctuations of boom or bust in employment opportunities. After a period of relative employment boom from the growth of the port and from the offshore oil and gas industry during the 1950s and 1960s, Louisiana and New Orleans experienced a rapid and rather deep bust in the mid-1980s. During this time unemployment among African Americans increased to almost 11 percent, double that of whites, and as much as 30 percent of the city was living below the poverty level. Towards the end of the twentieth century, New Orleans had begun to rebound, especially in the tourism and service industries; but while this represented some 80,000 jobs in the hospitality sector,[210] these also represented relatively lower-paying jobs. The Port of New Orleans had supported over 160,000 jobs, handling an average of 2000 vessels per year.[211] One area of growth in higher paying jobs has been in the healthcare sector. The Louisiana Department of Labor Monthly Reports, 'Louisiana Workforce at a Glance,' for 2004 and 2005 reports approximately 80,000 jobs in healthcare.

Finally, Orleans Parish public primary and secondary education system has been equally troubled. In the 2003–2004 school year, for example, the Greater New Orleans Community Data Center showed 47 percent of Orleans Parish schools were rated as "academically unacceptable," and

209. Slightly lower for high school graduates, 74.7 percent as compared to 80.4 percent nation wide; slightly higher for bachelor's degrees, 25.8 percent as compared to 24.4 percent nation wide.

210. As reported by the New Orleans Convention and Visitors Bureau, Economic Impacts of Tourism, http://www.neworleanscvb.com/index.cfm/contented/164/sectionD/4/subsectionID/0.

211. But this translates into only an average of five vessels per day. See http://www.portno.com/pno_pages/about_overview.htm.

26.5 percent were rated as under "academic warning." Both the system's high school dropout rate and cost deficits have been excessively high. Efforts by the New Orleans Public Schools (NOPS) to remedy this have generally been too little, too late. In 2001, Louisiana, like a number of other states, began an effort to grade the quality of its schools on the basis of student performance on standardized tests. These tests were given in the 4th, 8th, 10th, and 11th grades. However, in the 2004–2005 school year, as one example, only 44 percent of fourth-graders showe themselves to be proficient in reading; only 26 percent were proficient in math. At the middle school level, things were worse: only 26 percent were proficient in reading, 15 percent in math.[212] The Catholic Diocese of New Orleans opened a number of small elementary schools that poor children could attend tuition-free, but these efforts were on too small a scale to make much difference. One factor that has inadvertently impacted the quality of public education in New Orleans has been the approximately 200 parochial schools in the Greater New Orleans area run by the Roman Catholic Archdiocese of New Orleans. The existence of so many, generally good, parochial schools stands simultaneously as both a consequence of the troubled public schools and also as a cause. The poor quality of public schools in New Orleans has resulted in many white, but also black, middle-class students enrolling in non-public schools. In fact, figures show that public school enrollment in Orleans Parish dropped by 26 percent between 1998 and 2004, from approximately 82,000 to 65,000 students, without a corresponding population change. At the same time, however, the enrollment of so many middle-class students in non-public schools has only contributed to the lack of support and under-funding of the public school system. This kind of complex problem is a classic example of one form of Marker 3—a vicious cycle in which, for an essentially unchanging subject population, the health or growth of one system occurs only at the expense of another.

In October of 2003, with opposition from the Orleans Parish School Board, voters approved a constitutional amendment that allowed the State to assume control of public schools receiving a rating of "academically unacceptable" four years in a row. In the 2004-2005 school year, 15

212. These issues have been widely discussed; see, for example, de Rugy, Veronique, and Newmark, Kathryn G., "Hope After Katrina," *American Enterprise Institute for Public Policy Research*, October 16, 2006, accessed at http://www.aei.org/include/pub_print .asp?pubID=25019.

Orleans Parish schools were made part of a 'Recovery School District,' run by the state by eligible to become charter schools. The first takeover occurred in the summer of 2004, when the State gave control of the P.A. Capdau Middle School to the University of New Orleans; more than 500 students applied for 264 spots.[213] However, despite a reform-minded superintendent imported from Connecticut, Anthony Amato, financial audits followed by indictments in 2005 put the public school system in as great jeopardy as did Katrina itself. Audits estimated the system was running at least a $25 million deficit, the U.S. Department of Education found nearly $70 million in federal money for low-income students improperly accounted for, and federal-state investigations resulted in two dozen indictments for theft, fraud, and kickbacks.[214]

In Anticipation of Tragedy

What are some of the patterns of social inequity in a self-contained (at times self-absorbed) world that can be seen amidst the complexity that constituted New Orleans' cultural milieu in the years before Hurricane Katrina? With a degree of simplification, one can think of New Orleans as in some ways 'symbolized by one of its symbols'—portrayed on websites advertising its tourist lure of festivals: the Mardi Gras mask. Perhaps it would be better to say that New Orleans has an outer face, but also its inner face. Or its *public* face and its *private* face. Not that the two 'faces' do not mutually support and participate in one another. New Orleans' festive public face is shared by the city's inhabitants, many of whom have fully lived and participated in its rituals of Mardi Gras and Jazzfest, its music and dance, over the years. But the private face behind the mask also knows that New Orleans is a city that has experienced great pain. Segregation; poverty; high rates of crime and drug use; decaying housing and infrastructure; a history of corruption and inadequacy among its political leadership; frequent abuse from those given the privilege to uphold the law; hospitals and community primary care health centers unable to meet the medical needs of its citizens, particularly those marginalized by their economic status; public schools that have failed to provide quality

213. de Rugy, Veronique, and Newmark, Kathryn G., "Hope After Katrina," *American Enterprise Institute for Public Policy Research,* October 16, 2006, accessed at http://www.aei.org/include/pub_print.asp?pubID=25019.
214. With 20 guilty pleas by the summer of 2006, ibid.

education for all; and a setting in a natural environment that, through a combination of short-sighted science, poor implementation, neglect, and unfounded faith, has made its very existence precarious. New Orleans is certainly not unique in America as a city that has experienced such pain. But perhaps it is New Orleans' exotic beauty that has only made it all the more painful.

New Orleans in many ways is a city of myths. Beautiful myths, but some, it would have to be said, reality fails to live up to. As one example, despite the common perception of New Orleans as a 'polyglot city'[215] where French is still commonly spoken, in fact, the 2000 Census showed that in New Orleans only 8.3 percent of the population 5-years old and over speak a language other than English at home, as compared to 17.9 percent nationally. The 2005 ACS estimates put the 'other than English' figure at 6.7 percent vs. 19.4 percent nationally. One suspects that shift was due to increasing numbers of Hispanic and Latin speaking people in the population.

The public face of New Orleans over the last quarter century has been seen to grow a robust tourist and hospitality economy, with its convention center, casinos, hotels, and Superdome—the locus of the New England Patriots' losses in Superbowls XX and XXXI but emergence as a football dynasty in Superbowl XXXVI. Yet this occurred in the midst of a decline of nearly a quarter of the population of Orleans Parish. In Peirce Lewis' remarkable book, *New Orleans: The Making of an Urban Landscape*, Figure 49 is a photo looking upriver toward the twin spans of the Greater New Orleans Bridge (The Crescent City Connection) in 1973 from the International Trade Tower on Canal Street. It shows the waterfront as a working-class landscape with wharves, docks, warehouses and the Public Belt Railroad. Figure 50, in recent times and the same view looking upriver, shows a radically changed landscape. The docks and warehouses are gone, replaced by high-rise hotels and tourist attractions, a cruise ship terminal, and a convention center. Thus, not only has New Orleans overall population changed—for the multiple reasons already discussed—the nature of its livelihood and its population make up has shifted considerably. The loss of overall population has been largely by whites moving to suburbs east and west and to the north shore of Lake Pontchartrain, with a cor-

215. In 1861, Louisiana's articles of secession were published in both French and English. See Lewis, 5. Former mayor Marc Morial once remarked that "What made New Orleans is the polyglot, the tapestry, the mosaic, the gumbo."

responding increase of black, and, more recently, Asian people residing within the city. One cultural consequence of changes in the city as a locus of livelihood has been, particularly since the loss of jobs in the oil and gas industries, a widening in the separation of economic classes—between those who have been able to profit from New Orleans suburban development, its tourist industry growth, its *public* culture, as it were—and those who support it, largely with relatively low-paying jobs.

It is *inequities* in the sources and manifestations of New Orleans' pain that are of greatest concern from the standpoint of social ethics. They are also perhaps the largest factor in thinking about how to envisage strategies for its recovery and reconstruction post-Katrina. Inequities in the ability to fully participate in the life of New Orleans go back at least as early in history as the construction of the turning basin at the upper end of the Carondelet Canal, linking New Orleans with Bayou St. John, and Congo Square adjacent to it. From this point on one began to see the conjunction of topographic location and racial segregation, where whites occupied the better-drained sections of the city, blacks the swampy, low-lying 'rear' districts.[216] Thus, New Orleans' image (or myth) of a vibrant city where blacks of varying shades of color, mulattoes, and whites commingled in places of habitation and work, if ever true, has increasingly been replaced by the ghettoization of blacks and poor whites into certain low-lying and flood-prone neighborhoods. These included Gert Town, parts of Central City, B. W. Cooper, the Seventh Ward and St. Roch, the Lower Ninth Ward, Gentilly, Tremé, and New Orleans East. Some of these neighborhoods, as well as others, turned out to be those most affected by flooding into New Orleans 'shallow bowls.' Massive public works programs at the turn of the twentieth century might have been thought to equalize access to the city's infrastructure, but their coincidence with Jim Crow racist policies tended to preclude that. In fact, some historians have pointed out that the new drainage pumps installed after 1917 only became an agent for increased acial segregation, as well as other inequities in benefits from sewerage, water, and desirable land.[217] Progressive Era reforms were meant to improve the lives of whole urban areas, but the exclusion of blacks from areas of better topographic elevation—whether by evolutionary social forces, such as the displacement of blacks by European immigrants, or

216. Noted, for example, by Colten, 77, and Peirce Lewis.
217. See Peirce Lewis; also Colten, 78–79.

by discriminatory intention—resulted in the extension of sewers, water lines, drainage, to the more affluent neighborhoods first. In fact a 1923 assessment of the city's sewer system showed that those neighborhoods without sewer mains were largely in low-lying, African American and industrial districts.[218] Moreover, the fact that, in contrast to its levee system, New Orleans' late nineteenth century internal drainage efforts were piecemeal, disjointed, and largely ineffective[219] only contributed to the risk of flooding and general precariousness of New Orleans' poorer black and multi-racial neighborhoods.

Discrepancies among neighborhoods were likely only exacerbated, rather than ameliorated, by the political struggles we traced through the Jim Crow period and New Orleans' recent mayors. We have seen considerable evidence of its history of political favoritism and corruption, of leaders better at show than leading. This atmosphere has only been intensified by segregation and the resulting white flight to New Orleans' suburbs, east, west, and north; [220] by the city's history of voter discrimination; by voting district battles that as often as not were fought to preserve the interests of particular candidates rather than equalize voting representation across racial lines. One ends up with only a background noise sense of New Orleans as a gumbo harmony of multi-races, multi-languages, multi-colors; one comes to be more impressed by the sense of New Orleans as a city where cultures have learned to use one another selectively. The gumbo does not taste just right; it is unfinished, not ready to be served.

Hurricane Katrina not only has put the 'gumbo' model on indefinite hold, it has raised the serious question as to whether or not it will *ever* be finished. Since the hurricane and subsequent flooding, New Orleans' high crime rate and reputation as having among the worst and poorest public school systems in the country has only become an object of national consciousness, not simply veiled behind New Orleans' seductive atmosphere of sub-tropical foliage, ornate iron balconies, and exotic cultures of music and

218. Colten, 105–6.

219. Ibid., 142.

220. Peirce Lewis' map (Figure 17) shows the black population in metropolitan New Orleans in 1970 is revealing because it stands just at the beginning of massive white flight to the suburbs when blacks were more evenly dispersed across city neighborhoods; the corresponding map (Figure 19) for 2000 shows the emergence of black superghettos occupying most of Mid-City and spreading to the Lake from City Park eastward.

dance, art and literature. The crime rate and public safety, the availability of adequate healthcare services, the quality of the public school system, the question of a home to return to and tentative efforts of various neighborhoods to try to rebuild on their own are now visible as definite decision points in the minds of many still-displaced residents—particularly those from poorer neighborhoods that suffered the greatest flooding and damage—in the ongoing struggle of whether or not they will return at all.

One must ask, with considerable trepidation, that if New Orleans should become a white majority city again—as some, prior to seeing the 2006 American Community Survey (ACS) data have believed[221]—will the old white-black divisions need to be overcome all over again in making meaningful reconstruction plans?

As if high crime rates and a struggling public school system were not enough, New Orleans' capacity to provide adequate, even basic primary care medical services, was in serious trouble even before Katrina. Against the reputation of a great institution like Charity Hospital, we have seen many local hospitals under economic pressure; we have traced the considerable flux in their ownership by corporate 'hospital chain' owners, including serious questions about the effectiveness of their management and the ethical integrity of their managers. 'Big Charity' is no more, and it is a continuing dilemma as to what, if anything, can replace it to meet the city's healthcare needs. There remain enormous holes in New Orleans' primary healthcare facilities, especially east of the Industrial Canal.

Beneath New Orleans' cultural milieu lies its environmental infrastructure. Much of the city was built on land that was itself sinking, in some places sinking rather rapidly. Moreover, although there was ample evidence at the time of their construction, it had remained largely hidden from public consciousness just how weak the foundation soils were that were used to support the city's levees and drainage canal protective walls. The 'bedrock' for foundation support—itself at best compacted clay—lies more than 70 feet below looser muck at the surface.[222] New Orleans' levee walls were situated on organically infused sand and soil that was not stable, that degraded over time, and that could not ultimately support the barriers necessary to protect a city below sea level and river level, even absent the added storm surge from hurricane force winds.

221. But has not as yet proven to be borne out; the city has remained a black majority city, although by a smaller amount.

222. See Lewis and van Heerden discussions of this.

On top of this 'substrate,' only two highways provided egress out of the city—I-10 and US 90. Finally, many residents did not possess the cars or vehicles to use those highways to escape the flooding waters, even if they chose to.

There is also a world beyond the urban environment of New Orleans—South Louisiana, of which the Crescent City is one part. From its coastal wetlands to the levees and spillways of its urban environment, from the tiny communities of American Indians who live on the slender fingers of land protruding into the edge of the Gulf to the inhabitants of New Orleans' historic neighborhoods, ghettos, and housing projects, South Louisiana has proven itself to be far more fragile in the face of nature than its government leaders and protectors ever gave themselves to think. Part of New Orleans' geographic mask may have been created by the belief that if the Mississippi River extends another one hundred miles below the Port of New Orleans, then the city is "not really on the Gulf," but inland from dangerous waters. In fact, New Orleans is as much right at the edge of the Gulf as the other coastal villages of South Louisiana. To the east, there lies only the wetlands and islands of Chandeleur Sound and Lake Borgne. But the barrier islands now are virtually non-existent, at least in any protective sense. And Lake Pontchartrain to the north *just is* the Gulf, connected to it tidally, through passes, and another danger to the city under the conditions that favor the likelihood of strong winds from the northeast as hurricanes pass over the Gulf to landfall.

The recurring question remains: How well was New Orleans prepared to take emergency measures in the reality of hurricanes of Category Three and above and the potential for failure of its protective barriers and levee system? Was New Orleans prepared at all?

Lower Ninth Ward
(December, 2007)

Beyond Recovery
(December, 2007)

3

Katrina's World

An elderly lady stopped one of the rescue workers in her area and said,
"Could you please take me to my house on Mandolin Street
to get my medicine." The rescue worker replied,
"I'm sorry. Your house is not there anymore."

AN APOCALYPSE OF THE QUICK AND THE DEAD

IN THE DAYS FOLLOWING August 29, 2005, devastating details of human tragedy after tragedy unfolded, as citizens of Coastal Louisiana and its largest urban center struggled to survive entrapments in ten thousand watery hells. Many were rescued; more than 1,600 were not. When the watery hells slowly dried into layers of caked mud and putrid muck, they did not vanish, but only transformed themselves into other into other, even more complex hells of despair and degradation of spirit as weeks and months rolled by. The nation's witness to suffering of such magnitude has raised comparisons with other cataclysmic events—September 11, 2001. However, while one could argue that the C.I.A. and government leaders *should have known* about secret actions planned by Al Qaeda operatives to destroy symbols of American power that warm September morning, in the case of Hurricane Katrina, federal, state, and local government leaders *in fact knew* not only the seasonal likelihood of massive ocean storms capable of wreaking havoc on the Gulf Coast, but the actuality of this particular storm. Officials knew, within a relatively small margin of error, the *point* of Katrina's impact on Louisiana's inhabited coastline, the *time* of its impact, and the likely extent of its *effects*—not only damage from hurricane winds and rain, but also damage likely to result from flooding, given the weakened and incomplete state of New Orleans' levee system and drainage canal floodwalls. The fact that some 100,000 or more of New Orleans' citizens would be forced to remain in the city during the storm should only have made the scope of possible tragedy even more visible to those in a position to have put in place plans and actions to avoid or ameliorate that tragedy.

The sufferings witnessed by those without means to be of direct help were captured and documented by many in the media who risked their lives along with the brave men and women of the Coast Guard and other services engaged in search and rescue operations. Local reporters from WWL-TV and *The Times-Picayune*; others from the wire services and national presses. It is not our purpose to recapture the enormous scale of tragic events that occurred, or the records preserved by such excellent pieces of journalism as Jed Horne's *Breach of Faith: Hurricane Katrina and the Near Death of a Great American City*. However, certain events have seared our minds long after the storm passed, and rescue and recovery missions concluded. Certain events have remained in our consciousness because many of their effects continue in reality more than two years later, in the many still-unfinished tasks of rebuilding New Orleans and reclaiming Louisiana's damaged coastal marshes.

In selecting these several events—most of which have been aired or written about in multiple forms—we choose to let them stand on their own, as iconic memories, providing comment and interpretation only where necessary or useful. In subsequent chapters, we will return to the more long-term significance of some of them, as we consider the planning processes, strategies, and dilemmas faced by the region and by New Orleans in raising itself from its watery ashes.

Big Charity

A woman waded through the streets, floating the body of her dead husband on a door that had come off her home.[1] She had seen him die while trying to get him to Charity Hospital. Had they reached Charity, it would have been to no avail: the hospital was without power or essential services. Affectionately known as 'Big Charity,' the hospital has remained closed since the storm. Charity was New Orleans' major public hospital, with a

---

1. Reported by Karen Swenson of WWL-TV, among others, on the Wednesday following the storm.

275-year history of treating patients regardless of their ability to pay—the only local hospital whose explicit mission was to treat all. Charity was where 62 percent of New Orleans residents got their health care. It was the city's only major trauma center. In March, 2006, citizens rallied, demanding President Bush, Governor Kathleen Blanco, and the Louisiana State Legislature repair, re-open, and fund the hospital. But plans have been to raze it, collect millions in federal dollars, replace it with a new hospital that will privatize health care in New Orleans—using federal money to do the job, and abandoning the poor in the process.

The closing of Big Charity was not simply an issue of one hospital, or even of all of New Orleans' hospitals; it symbolized the issue of the adequacy and viability of healthcare throughout the entire Gulf region. Nearly 6,000 doctors along the Gulf Coast were displaced by Hurricane Katrina, the largest unanticipated loss of medical services to occur in United States history. Dr. Thomas Ricketts of the University of North Carolina-Chapel Hill led a study that showed that more than two-thirds (4,486) of the doctors displaced from Louisiana and Mississippi affected by Katrina were from Orleans, Jefferson, and St. Bernard Parishes.[2] How many of those doctors—half of which were specialists, 1292 in primary care, 272 in obstetrics/gynecology—would set up permanently in other cities rather than return to reopen their practices has remained unclear. Many factors complicate the decision of physicians about whether to return: the non-existence of a livable house to return to, sharply reduced patient loads resulting from a 50 percent depopulation of Orleans Parish (considerably more in some neighborhoods), medical needs in the cities to which physicians were forced to move, economic obligations of mortgages and family. Locally, the best that was able to be offered to many citizens—for quite some time—was to be served by a number of mobile clinics set up around the state.[3]

2. In Louisiana. Natalie Gott, AP Writer, "Katrina displaces nearly 6,000 doctors," *The Louisiana Weekly*, September 26, 2006.

3. For example, the five mobile Veterans Affairs clinics set up in LaPlace, Slidell, Hammond, Jennings, and Lake Charles. Such clinics provided only the most basic services: immunizations, prescriptions, and limited primary care. See "VA sets up mobile clinics for Hurricane victims," *The Louisiana Weekly*, October 3, 2005.

Toxic Gumbo

Toxic contamination from flood waters mingled with raw sewage and structures wasting from weeks of submersion. The resulting mold created a breeding ground for insects, disease, more deaths, and the strong likelihood that infested homes would never be inhabitable again. New Orleans City Council President Oliver Thomas, on a reconnaissance boat trip that saw many bodies, looters, and what he called 'a hell of Sodom and Gomorrah', was reported to have remarked, "Maybe God's going to cleanse us."[4]

There were multiple concerns about toxicity in the days and weeks following Katrina: oil contamination from spills at local refineries, dangerous chemicals in the tap water, raw sewerage, flies from accumulated garbage unable to be picked up, uncontained asbestos from demolitions, molds infecting sheetrock and housing materials remaining wet in a high temperature environment, formaldehyde discovered in FEMA trailers. On November 14, 2005, for example, federal agencies warned people of health hazards of living and working in homes still contaminated by oil spills. Unsafe levels of diesel fuel had been found in sediment samples of approximately one million gallons of oil spilled from a Murphy Oil Corp. storage tank at the Meraux refinery. The Agency for Toxic Substances and Disease found oil in some 1,700 homes, yet areas affected were not put off limits.[5] National Guardsmen who did the dirty job of cleaning some of the homes were often presented with nests of snakes. The Environmental Protection Agency's decision to waive certain restrictions on oil refineries following Katrina angered environmentalists such as the Louisiana Bucket Brigade. Samples showed very high levels of benzene, a component of gasoline and a carcinogen, at a Shell Oil Co. refinery near New

---

4. Reported in multiple sources; see, for example, LifeSiteNews.com, September 1, 2005, http://www/lifesite.net/2005/sep/05090111.html. While Gov. Kathleen Blanco called for a state-wide day of prayer, to "turn to God for strength, hope and comfort," New Orleans City Council President Oliver Thomas echoed thoughts of Sodom and Gomorrah and invoked the theme of purification through destruction. Some European papers suggested Katrina was punishment for the United States failing to sign the Kyoto accord. Islamic militants rejoiced that Katrina had joined in the holy war against the U.S. Others saw the hurricane as God's punishment for cooperating in the removal of Jews from the Gaza Strip. See also *Newsweek*, "New Orleans: The Lost City," September 12, 2005.

5. Cain Burdeau, AP Writer, "Oil-contaminated homes pose health risks, feds say," *The Louisiana Weekly*, November 14, 2005.

Orleans—33 parts per billion, ten times the 3.69 parts per billion considered safe by Louisiana.[6]

Hurricane Katrina also dredged up frequent pre-existing concerns about soil contamination in New Orleans. In March, 2006, residents of Mid-City were worried about the Gert Town Family Center, rebuilt among the crumbling houses and piles of debris on its narrow, one-way street. From the mid-1940s to 1988, the Thompson Hayward Chemical Co. had blended pesticides such as DDT at a nearby site, and community leaders believed floodwaters from Katrina carried chemicals and pesticides from the contaminated soil beneath the facility towards the center.[7]

A number of studies downplayed some of the fears about the chemical toxicity of New Orleans' floodwaters. LSU Associate Professor of Civil and Environmental Engineering John Pardue, for example, concluded that flood waters inundating New Orleans after Katrina were, in content, essentially similar to the city's normal storm water, although a year's worth concentrated into a few days. Reporting in the American Chemical Society's online journal, *Environmental Science & Technology,* Pardue agreed that waters containing high levels of toxic metals such as copper and zinc pumped into Lake Pontchartrain could pose a long-term danger to its aquatic life.[8]

Perhaps the greatest toxic unknown following Katrina were the long-term health effects of mold. 'Mold' refers to various fungi found both indoors and outdoors in moist, warm environments. Exposure to molds can cause allergic reactions, asthma attacks, and infections in people with immune system problems. Mold is a particularly dangerous indoor contaminant, where concentrations of spores released from damp surfaces become airborne and are inhaled, causing many respiratory problems. Symptoms from mold following Katrina included headaches, difficulty concentrating, memory loss, skin rashes, diarrhea, pulmonary hemorrhage in infants, and invasive pneumonia in people with weak immune or lung function. However, the long term effects of exposure to mycotoxins

6. See Cain Burdeau, AP Writer, "Environmentalists angry that EPA allowed refineries to pollute following Katrina," *The Louisiana Weekly,* December 5, 2005.

7. See April Capochino, "Gert Town Concern About Contaminated Soil Beneath Abandoned Chemical Co.," *New Orleans CityBusiness,* Dolan Media Newswires, posted on RedOrbit.com, March 13, 2006.

8. "N.O. floodwaters were not as toxic as first thought," *The Louisiana Weekly,* October 17, 2005.

in humans are unknown, and, therefore, continue to remain of high concern. Moreover, there are no U.S. regulatory standards for either indoor or outdoor levels of mold spores in the air. The National Resources Defense Council collected samples for mold spore analysis at two different times in seventeen outdoor and eight indoor locations across the city. Fungal spores were counted and identified by Dr. Mervi Hjelmroos-Koski of the Institute of Arctic and Alpine Research (INSTAAR), University of Colorado. Testing revealed a significant mold problem in the outdoor air of most of the flooded areas of the city, and extremely high levels in not yet remediated indoor locations. Testing the moldy furniture, carpets, and drywall of one home revealed concentrations of 650,000 spores per cubic meter, which would render it dangerously uninhabitable by any definition. Entrance into such a location would require, at a minimum, an N95 dust respirator.[9]

The actions of demolishing and de-roofing damaged homes raised serious issues about airborne asbestos fibers and what was called "Katrina Cough." Between 1948 and 1993, over a quarter million tons of asbestos was shipped into Orleans Parish to plants, some near schoolyards, where it was exfoliated or "popped" to produce vermiculite attic insulation, creating massive amounts of asbestos-contaminated dust. Just days prior to Katrina, twenty-six tons arrived at Camp Street, a site surrounded by residential neighborhoods and restaurants. By January, 2006, it appeared that Senate Bill 852, originally sponsored by Senator Arlen Specter, creating the federal Asbestos Trust Fund to compensate asbestos victims with a trust financed by corporations producing it, would *exclude* home and property owners rushing to demolish, gut, and rehabilitee their hurricane-damaged properties who were exposing themselves to asbestos. Cheron Brylski, Director of the Louisiana Women's Health Access Project, pointed out the inadequacy of EPA warnings and website directives about how to deal with asbestos post-Katrina, and noted a similarity of symptoms with 'trade center cough' after 9/11.[10] The revamped asbestos trust fund legislation, Senate Bill 3274, was challenged as also deeply unfair to seriously ill victims of asbestos-induced diseases by the Alliance for Justice, the Center for Justice & Democracy, Public Citizen, USAction, and U.S. PIRG.

9. See Natural Resources Defense Council, "New Orleans Area Environmental Quality Test Results," accessible at http://www.nrdc.org/health/effects/katrinadata/mold.asp.

10. Christopher Tidmore, "Asbestos Legislation Denies LA Funds, Particles Could Be Cause of 'Katrina Cough,'" *The Louisiana Weekly,* January 23, 2006.

Perhaps the *coup de grace* of Katrina toxicity came in the form of the very replacements provided by FEMA for victims of the storm who had lost use of their homes—the thousands of FEMA trailers trucked into Louisiana and Mississippi to provide shelter. The Sierra Club claimed that 30 out of 32 FEMA trailers it tested had levels of formaldehyde that were unsafe. After people began reporting nosebleeds, constant coughs, and feeling sick, the Sierra Club inserted vapor monitors in FEMA trailers, and reported formaldehyde concentrations up to .34 parts per million in the air.[11] Formaldehyde is a colorless but pungent gas that irritates the eyes, nose, and throat, and causes breathing difficulties and nausea at levels above .1 parts per million. Yet thousands of people were forced to live in FEMA trailers and simply endure the discomforts of the toxic gas because they had no other choice.

Under the Bridge

At 91 years old, Booker Harris ended his days propped on a lawn chair, covered by a yellow quilt, dead and abandoned, in front of the Ernest N. Morial Convention Center. But evacuees able to escape the city found even worse conditions under I-10 overpasses west of the city in Metairie, where they were forced to camp. On the elevated highway above, a group of displaced people pushed a wheelchair carrying a dead woman. She wore pink pajama bottoms, and a white kitchen garbage bag over her head.[12]

The combination of elderly persons, often with diabetes and difficulties walking, intense heat and humidity, and the need to wade through unclean, uncertain waters to reach safety was a recipe for disaster and human degradation. Booker Harris had died in the back of a panel truck when he and his 93-year old wife, Allie, were evacuated from eastern New Orleans. The truck's driver simply had deposited Allie and her husband's body on the neutral ground (center island area) on Convention Center Boulevard. Respectfully collecting the bodies of those who died was not immediately part of anyone's plan or responsibility.

For those who were forced to contend with surviving inhuman conditions, without food or water or shelter or places to discretely meet

11. "Tests show high levels of formaldehyde are being found in FEMA trailers," *The Louisiana Weekly*, May 22, 2006.

12. Events described here documented in multiple sources, including Keith Spera, Staff Writer, "Desperation, death on road to safety," *The Times-Picayune*, August 31, 2005.

one's normal biological needs, feelings of anger quickly migrated into despondency and hopelessness. One 65-year old woman, chased from her home in Central City by rising water, clutched a plastic bag containing something for bedding, a little water, and insulin to treat her diabetes. She was unsure where to find help, thinking she would need to walk the more than 15 blocks to a rumored evacuation pickup beneath the Pontchartrain Expressway. Her feet swollen, she doubted she could walk that far. Another woman pushed a wheelchair in which slumped her brother, wearing only a hospital robe and suffering from diabetes and the after-effects of a stroke. With no bathroom he could use, nobody could even tell them if they were in the right place, heading in the right direction.

Some adults with their children, after being turned away at the Superdome, walked across the Crescent City Connection bridge to the West Bank in hopes of finding transportation to a shelter; others—often groups of African American males—were met by West Bank residents who refused to allow them to cross, fearing their shopping malls or businesses would be looted. All evacuees on the move experienced the frustration of seeing empty buses, vans, and cars pass them by during their long treks. Refugees came from all directions, seemed to be going in all directions. Marjorie Summers of the Paquemines Parish town of Phoenix and her husband of 51 years had fled to the local high school after water flooded their home, then were flooded from the high school as well. The town of Phoenix was completely lost, completely immersed in water, perhaps never to arise again.[13]

For many, it was the rapidity with which the floodwaters rose that proved to be so life-threatening; in some cases, as much as fifteen feet in fifteen minutes. Those who were fortunate enough to float up to their attics were often met by muskrats or nutria before they were able to break through their roofs and wave for rescue.

Hurricane Katrina precipitated a humanitarian crisis of unimaginable proportions. For some, death thankfully came quickly. For others, it was slow and painful, as they ran out of insulin, were severely sunburned, dehydrated from lack of water, contaminated by their own and other's feces. It was a humanitarian crisis that need not have happened. Consider the incongruity of the banner hanging from the roofline of a neighbor-

13. Also documented *The Times-Picayune*, August 31, 2005, in "Scenes from the Wild West Bank." Phoenix is a village half-way between Pointe à La Hache and Belle Chasse at the division of LA 39 and 15.

hood refuge and health-care facility: HELP. THIS IS A HEALTH-CARE FACILITY. NEED MEDICINE. NO FOOD.[14]

Sometimes the willingness of residents to remain in the face of a hurricane seemed a religious act of defiance of nature's dominion. Columnist Lolis Eric Elie of *The Times-Picayune* recalled the proud grandmother and family matriarch of JoNell Kennedy who wrote saying, "After being urged by my aunts, mother and neighbors, who were all packed and ready to move to higher ground, she refused." She told her granddaughter, "JoNell, I'm not running from God. I'm going to sit right here and let King Jesus ride on." What do you do in circumstances like that?

Degradation and death were a plague of the city's poorest, those without the means or opportunity to escape the flooding. But horrors were not confined to those captured within New Orleans' breached levees. For 90-year Pointe-au-Chien tribal members Armantine Marie Verdin and her 72-year old mentally handicapped son, Xavier, surviving Hurricane Katrina meant floating on couches and waiting to be rescued in shrimp boats. After the storm surge at high tide brought in a rush of water, Armantine, Xavier, and others floated on couches, pirogues, and aluminum outboard boats, first seeking refuge in the second story of a neighbor's barn, then staying on a shrimp boat for two days, finally walking the remaining levee until they were herded onto National Guard trucks to a sea of people under a bridge before being loaded onto a bus bound for the Astrodome in Houston.

There were many respects in which Hurricane Katrina brought out the best but also the worst in people. Without even beginning to try to sort things out, it became increasingly clear that the vast majority of the people suffering and dying before the eyes of their fellow Americans were the poorest, the weakest, and the most vulnerable of the Gulf Coast's residents. Did that also make them the most expendable? It seems almost too painful to raise such a question; yet the radical inequities of those who were devastated by Katrina, and those who were able to escape to safety with at least their lives intact, continues to haunt the City of New Orleans and the inundated villages of St. Bernard, Plaquemines, Terrebonne, and Cameron Parishes. Flooding, and the consequences of the flooding, were pervasive, but also concentrated. Loss of life, for example, was concentrated by age—more than 70 percent of deaths were people over the age

14. Doug MacCash and Dante Ramos, "Along Esplanade, pleas for help," *The Times-Picayune,* August 31, 2005.

of 70. Loss of life also correlated to areas of lower elevation and greater depth of flooding, where the poor, elderly, and disabled residents were least likely to be able to evacuate without assistance. Losses of property obviously correlated directly to depth of flooding, but so did recovery. In those areas flooded in the aftermath of Hurricane Katrina, where water depths were relatively small, recovery has been almost complete. However, in areas were water depths were greater, little reinvestment or substantial recovery has taken place.[15]

Some have pointed out that inequities of response and recovery were not simply present in the inchoate process (or the absence of process altogether) of distribution of federal and state aid to certain social groups rather than others. Inequities occurred within institutions that might be thought most likely to have *ensured* the equal treatment of all its members. According to NNPA[16] columnist Rev. Barbara Reynolds, for example, students at Xavier University called their parents in desperation after it appeared University officials had seen to it that school athletes were rescued, but left more than one hundred students unattended.[17]

Ultimately, however, it may have been that the many inequities, exacerbated by the storm but certainly in existence *prior to* the storm, represented less injustice than the ways in which those in highest authority 'hid their eyes' from the realities before them. When President George Bush finally visited the devastated Gulf region, he did not visit or attend to the suffering of people at the Super Dome or the Morial Convention Center, but instead, chose to have his presidential plane gently descend to 2,500 feet where all onboard Air Force One could see desperate people waiting on rooftops, trapped on highway overpasses, wading through floodwaters. "Those in the luxury jet, surrounded by immaculate furnishing, were assured by an aura of order and security. They were 2,500 feet above and a world apart from the victims below."[18] For those whose viewpoint was far

---

15. U.S. Army Corps of Engineers, "Performance Evaluation of the New Orleans and Southeast Louisiana Hurricane Protection System. Final Report of the Interagency Performance Evaluation Task Force," Volume I, Executive Summary and Overview, 26, March 2007, I–3.

16. The National Newspaper Publishers Association (NNPA), also known as the Black Press of America, is a 67-year-old federation of more than 200 Black community newspapers from across the United States.

17. Rev. Barbara Reynolds, NNPA Columnist, "Hurricane Katrina Brought Out the Best and Worst." *The Louisiana Weekly,* September 7, 2005.

18. Brinkley, *The Great Deluge,* 406.

from the heat and the hunger and the horror that was the living environment of hundreds of thousands of people, their eyes were blind.

Searching for Remains

August Blanchard, returning to New Orleans in December after the storm, found his mother still missing and other family members scattered across the country. In February, when he could finally bring himself to enter his pale green house on Reynes Street in the Lower Ninth Ward, his uncle nudged the front door open with his foot and spied Ms. Blanchard's hand. Dressed in her nightgown and robe, she lay under a moldering sofa; with her was a red velvet bedspread that her daughter had given her and a huge teddy bear. Seven months after Katrina, bodies of storm victims were still being discovered. In March alone nine bodies, along with one skull. Skeletonized or half-eaten by animals, with leathery, hardened skin or missing limbs, the bodies were lodged in piles of rubble, dangling from rafters or lying face down, arms outstretched on parlor floors. Many of them, like Ms. Blanchard, were overlooked in initial searches, as was a girl, believed to be about six, wearing a blue backpack. Nearby was part of a man authorities believe had been trying to save her.[19]

In the Lower Ninth Ward the great number of unstable houses made searching difficult and dangerous. A plan by authorities to use cadaver dogs alongside the demolition crews was delayed by lawsuits and protests by homeowners against bulldozing. Throughout the city, it was too often the case that residents died unnoticed because of the absence of neighbors and social networks. By October and November, the Special Operations Team of the New Orleans Fire Department searched the Lower Ninth Ward for remains until they ran out of overtime money. At the time, the NOFD commander reported that FEMA officials rebuffed their requests to pay for continued searches. The official search for bodies in Louisiana was called off October 3rd, but fire departments and people returning to destroyed neighborhoods continued to find human remains. By December, funds were forthcoming from the federal government to help Louisiana

---

19. Shaila Dewan with Happy Blitt, "In Attics and Rubble, More Bodies and Questions," *The New York Times,* April 11, 2006; accessible at http://select.nytimes.com/search/restricted/article?res=FB061EF635540C&28DDDAD084...

authorities identify at least 270 people killed by Hurricane Katrina and the subsequent flooding who had remained as yet unidentified.[20]

Initially, a body's "presumptive identity" was determined by the location in which it was found, or its proximity to a house where someone had been reported missing. In the latter case, relatives were asked to give DNA samples. More frequently, dental records were collected from flooded offices and used to identify people; however, a large number of human remains were ultimately never identified, in part because there were no reliable records of those who may have escaped and moved to another part of the country without giving record of such a move. This group included especially those who were renters, rather than homeowners, or who were extended family members not permanently residing at a given location.

One signal that a former residence might contain human remains was the presence of large numbers of a certain species of phorid flies—also known as the humpback fly or 'the coffin fly.' Able to breed in as little as a few sips left in a soft drink can, according to LSU Agricultural Center entomologist Dale Pollet, decaying organic matter left in the wake of flooding provided the perfect breeding ground. Once an infestation occurred, it was difficult to get rid of. Another signal, for some first responders, was the uncanny ability to distinguish the odor of whether an animal or a human had died inside a house. Some claimed they could tell the difference between a cat and a dog remains.[21]

The common media dark euphemism of 'toxic gumbo' for New Orleans' floodwaters, by all accounts, did not do justice to the overwhelming revulsion and nausea produced by the combination of sewerage, gasoline, dead rats, curdled milk, cheese, and other decaying organic matter. Once the floodwaters became stagnant and were cooked in the intense heat of the days following the storm, the mere act of drawing in a breath was a struggle against all one's normal instincts. Yet beyond even those horrid odors, lay the scents of decomposing flesh, and the knowledge by searchers that some living, human being—someone's mother or sister or grandfather—had lain amongst this fetid mixture in their last minutes on earth.

20. Associated Press story, "270 dead still unidentified," *The Louisiana Weekly*, December 5, 2005.

21 "Flies find home in New Orleans rubble," *The Louisiana Weekly*, November 28, 2005. See also, for example, Brinkley, *The Deluge*, 406.

Morgues on Wheels

All over the city, fluorescent orange Xs sprayed on houses marked searches conducted, bodies found. The fact that many houses were structurally unsound, their contents in heaps, meant that many bodies were overlooked. However, even finding a body brought ambiguity. The reasons for the ambiguity were sometimes hard to stomach. From a report in April, 2006, it appears that of fourteen bodies that had been found since mid-February, none were able to be definitively identified and released for burial because FEMA had closed a $17 million morgue built to handle the dead, but, at the same time, declined to allow the New Orleans coroner, whose own office and morgue were ruined in the storm, continue to use the autopsy site. As a result, newly found bodies were stored in refrigerated trucks in Baton Rouge.[22] Jefferson Parish faced similar problems. After more than one hundred bodies filled its morgue, with more to come, its coroner's office moved in three refrigerated trucks to handle the overflow of corpses. However, they had not yet found generators to keep them cool and avoid body decomposition.[23]

The jurisdictional squabbling that contributed to delays in releasing bodies to their families, to the anguish and anger of relatives who were told they would be unable to bury a loved one, represented perhaps one of the most painful outcomes of the failure of public agencies to work cooperatively together, under previously agreed upon plans of operation and responsibility (Marker 6).

The difficulties faced by searchers, and the length of time necessary to conduct searches was understandable. Much of the landscape was reduced to glue-like muck and quickly growing, chest-high weeds that made movement almost impossible. Partially standing houses were fragile and dangerous: dismembered wall studs with protruding nails, sagging flooring, rafters holding back roof beams that could fall at any moment all made for an 'infiltration course' of opportunities for injury and infection. To search a house could take as long as four to six hours. If the residence was known to be home to a mother and a baby or small child, discovery of the mother but not the baby would propel searchers into spending even

22. Dewan, "In Attics and Rubble, More Bodies and Questions," *The New York Times*, April 11, 2006.

23. See, for example, Jim Varney, Staff Writer, "Scenes from New Orleans," *The Times-Picayune*, September 5, 2005.

more time, until every piece of debris had been lifted and investigated. Not infrequently, some of those searching for others who were missing were themselves counted as missing.

Difficulties resulting from the absence of planning and foresight and the failure of agencies at various levels of government to coordinate work with one another became increasingly apparent and unacceptable. Without mincing words, St. Bernard Parish President, Henry P. Rodriguez, expressed anger at the slow pace of the federal government's relief efforts. "We never had any communication from anybody. Anything that has been done in St. Bernard has been done by local people. We never had any goddamned help."[24]

In July of 2006, ten months after the storm, the Orleans Parish coroner announced that at least forty-nine people found dead in the floodwaters remained unidentified. His expectation was that more bodies would continue to be found as work demolishing heavily damaged homes continued. "The more they go down and do work, the more remains they're finding. I think this is going to go on a good while."[25] Federal officials had shut down their mortuary operation in February.

A Nursing Home in Chalmette

In Chalmette, St. Bernard Parish, twenty miles southeast of New Orleans, elderly residents of St. Rita's Nursing Home nailed a table against one window, and ran a heavy electric wheelchair with a table on top against another. These failed defenses were still visible, along with at least fourteen swollen, unrecognizable bodies when St. Bernard Parish officials determined that thirty-two of the home's sixty residents died on August 29. Weeks after the storm, no one had removed many of the bodies; local officials had no immediate plans to do so. The flood victims still lay where they died—draped over wheelchairs, wrapped in shower curtains, or lying on the floor in several inches of muck. The nursing home was surrounded by three feet of murky water; eight vehicles were still parked in front, covered in debris and mud. Steve Kuiper, Vice President of operations for

24. Quoted by Jan Moller, Capital Bureau in "St. Bernard death toll possibly hundreds," *The Times-Picayune*, September 5, 2005.

25. Quoted in AP story, "49 Katrina Victims Still Unidentified," *The Louisiana Weekly*, July 10, 2006.

Acadian Ambulance, said St. Rita's had an evacuation plan that depended on another nursing home.[26]

The stories of those who tried and failed to make their escape stand in sharp contrast to those able to break out of their attic roofs to reach safety. While the infirmed residents of St. Rita's put up a fight, pounding nails through tables, shoving dressers against windows, signs that the water had risen up to the roof was evidence that these thirty-two souls had eventually run out of time. With military and private helicopters ferrying people out from some areas of St. Bernard Parish, others, including St. Rita's nursing home were obviously missed, despite its being situated in a low area known to be vulnerable to flooding. St. Bernard Parish has five large nursing homes and six smaller ones; almost all but St. Rita's were evacuated before the storm.

On September 13, 2005, Louisiana Attorney General Charles C. Foti, Jr. had Salvador and Mabel Mangano arrested after a public outcry for their inaction which resulted in the drowning death of thirty-five residents of their St. Rita's Nursing Home.[27] A former Orleans Parish Criminal Sheriff, Foti came under public criticism for his aggressive criminal prosecution of Dr. Anna Pou and two nurses for allegedly euthanizing four patients at New Orleans' Memorial Hospital after the city flooded. In July, 2007, the grand jury ultimately declined to indict the women, and Pou sued Foti, accusing him of branding her a murderer to boost his re-election campaign. At the same time, regarding St. Rita's, Foti for many years had been an advocate for the elderly, providing Thanksgiving meals and starting a back to work program for senior citizens. Further complicating judgments about who was responsible, and when, is the fact that in the fall of 2006, Foti himself had filed a $200 billion civil claim in federal court for the State of Louisiana alleging that no one would have drowned if the Army Corps of Engineers had not been negligent. In addition, the Manganos were not exactly absent or passive during the flooding of St. Rita's. The brick building had withstood Katrina's winds without significant damage, and Sal Mangano had just inspected the roof when floodwaters surged toward the building, filling it to the ceiling within twenty minutes, accord-

26. Gardiner Harris, "In Nursing Home, a Fight Lost to Rising Waters," *The New York Times,* September 7, 2005.

27. Laura Parker, "Louisiana nursing home case puts Katrina response on trial," *USA Today,* August 8, 2007; accessible at http://www.usatoday.com/news/nation/2007-08-08-1Acover_N.htm?csp=34. (The original count of thirty-two was modified to thirty-five.)

ing to police. Despite efforts by the Manganos, themselves in their 60s, as well as others in boats, the water rose so fast that only twenty-four of the nursing home's fifty-nine residents were saved. Some were floated out of windows on mattresses, others pulled through holes chopped in the roof.

A large number of nursing homes impacted by Katrina did, in fact, choose to shelter their patients 'in place;' in the case of one—the Lafon Nursing Home in New Orleans—twenty-two people died, but no criminal charges were filed for those deaths.[28] These points have been emphasized by the attorneys for the defense.

On September 7, 2007, Salvador Mangano, 67, and his wife, Mabel, 64, were found not guilty of negligent homicide in the drowning of 35 of their St. Rita's Nursing Home residents. The three-week trial had been moved to St. Francisville, in West Feliciana Parish, north of Baton Rouge, because only a small fraction of St. Bernard Parish's residents have returned. The prosecution depicted the Manganos as greedy and negligent, concerned about the cost of an evacuation, and barely having an evacuation plan, despite the fact that three other nursing homes in the parish evacuated their residents. The defense put the blame on the state and federal governments, arguing that no one would have died if the levees had not failed, if the state had ordered an evacuation, or if officials had a plan to take charge of nursing homes in an emergency; they characterized the Manganos as compassionate and concerned, rescuing two dozen residents when water overtook the building. Gov. Kathleen Blanco was called to defend herself against the charge of failing to order an evacuation; Blanco said she had left evacuations to local officials.[29]

'Who was responsible, and when, and when was a lack of responsibility *criminal*?' are questions that have been asked countless times in the aftermath of Hurricane Katrina. In the many cases where no clear answer seemed forthcoming, it turned out too often be circumstances coinciding with either considerable confusion about far-too-roughly framed disaster response plans in existence or an absence of planning altogether.

28. Ibid.

29. Reported by Adam Nossiter, "Nursing Home Owners Are Acquitted in Deaths," *The New York Times*, September 8, 2007.

Katrina's World

Members of the Family

At the St. Thomas Aquinas Catholic Center on the campus of Nicholls State University in Thibodaux, a woman and her seven-year-old daughter and their pet poodle slept beneath the altar. Fr. Jim Morris gazed down at the family banned from the regular shelter because of the dog, and told a colleague, "Our altar has never been adorned more beautifully than it is with these people seeking the sanctuary of God." Fr. Morris himself had a dog named Blue. When he went to the school shelter Tuesday night, he saw all the people outside, looking dejected and clinging to their animals. "They wouldn't let them inside. So I said, bring them on over to the church." The first night there were 130 people with rottweilers, poodles, Chihuahuas, cats, birds, even a pot-bellied pig. "It was unbelievable . . . people slept on the terrazzo floor and on the pews. We had no electricity. It was like Noah's Ark."

Cora DeRussy, an employee at Dillard's in eastern New Orleans, lived on Vicksburg Street in Lakeview, and watched from her perch in the kitchen sink while one of her dogs swam in the water dumped in her house from the broken canal, and eventually drowned. Wearing a donated blue muumuu, the sixty-five-year-old woman said that when two men in a boat rescued her Tuesday afternoon, she got them to row around the house until she spotted Amber, her collie, its head poking out of a window. Amber swallowed a lot of polluted water and was at Ridgefield Animal Hospital nearby, recovering from her ordeal. Dr. Paul Seemann Jr., the veterinarian, shook his head, saying there would be no bill for any of these refugees' pets. Cora DeRussy observed, "Some people say we're stupid because we wouldn't leave our animals. It's why I'm in the predicament I am now, but I'm glad I'm stupid."

Carole Montet, a recently retired special education teacher, her sister, Patricia, and their eighty-year-old mother, Lillian, were never going to leave their orange tabby cat, McGinty, in the attic of their flooded house on 28th Street in Lakeview, a block from the 17th Street Canal. Her brother in Mississippi had borrowed her car, so they were unable to leave. They punched out the ventilator in the roof of their one-story home to crawl out; two men rescued them in a boat, paddled them to the roof of a nearby house, but when the water rose further, paddled to another rooftop. "Leave McGinty?" Carole Montet asked. "This cat helped my mother get through her hip surgery. McGinty inspired my mother." "She's family," interjected Lillian Montet, from her wheelchair. "Our animals are the only semblance of normalcy we have left," Carole Montet said. "You've lost your home. You've lost your job. You have no possessions ... The animal is the only semblance of your old life."

Jack Weber lived on St. Denis Street near the Fair Grounds in Mid-City. He was able to get out with his family: his wife, Ollie, fifty-six; their daughter, Tamara, thirty; and their Dalmatian-Retriever mix, Spartica. "That's my family," Jack said. Their roof had blown off, the sheetrock fell as the family moved from room to room until there was no more room, then the ceiling fell down. They managed to get into their little boat, avoiding five or six men chasing them and trying to steal it, took on neighbor Leon Gomez, in a wheelchair, and Gomez' Rottweiler, ODB. After getting no help from someone in an official-looking boat, another man paddled by in a child's inflatable plastic wading pool, and told them to get to I-610. There they slept on the concrete until their rescue the next day by helicopter. Weber's wife and daughter were separated, but planned to meet in Laredo, Texas; Weber was on his way to join them there with Spartica.[30]

In some case, the reuniting of 'members of the family' took months or even years. The dispersal of victims from the disastrous winds of Katrina ruptured the bond between many individual animals and the human beings who loved them. Richard Colar, and his Siberian Husky, Princess, survived a harrowing three days in Richard's attic, escaping on a raft. Subsequently, however, they were separated when a neighbor looking after the dog was forced to evacuate and leave Princess with an animal rescue team. Richard was devastated, but never gave up trying to find her. Without a personal computer, he was able to use access to Internet sites amidst the destruction and confusion around him, and contact Cory Smith of the Humane Society of the United States, who helped Richard locate Princess at an Ohio shelter. Cory Smith was able to organize a caravan of volunteers to bring Princess to Charlotte, North Carolina, where the displaced construction worker was living. Richard and Princess have returned to New Orleans, living in a trailer, trying to rebuild their home. Princess knows she is home, wants to visit the neighbors. Richard had raised Princess since she was a puppy, and the two of them are perma-

30. Stories drawn from the excellent piece by Millie Ball, Staff Writer, "Thibodaux church sheltering pets," *The Times-Picayune*, September 5, 2005.

nently bonded. "She knows when I'm coming," Richard said. "She can sense that I'm nearby and she comes to the door."[31]

The Humane Society of the United States, along with other organizations such as the ASPCA and local animal rescue groups, continue their efforts as leading disaster response entities in the post-Katrina era. The loss of an animal companion is no less than a loss of a human 'member of the family.' Perhaps only those who have bonded in that special way with another species can fully understand this; nevertheless, protocols for rescue operations in disaster situations now are beginning to call for the inclusion of family pets and animal companions. The simple fact is that many in Orleans and St. Bernard Parishes, and elsewhere, perished because they would not—*they could not*—leave their beloved animal behind as they were offered the opportunity to be taken to safety.

TOPOGRAPHY, RACE, AND ECONOMICS

Location, Location . . .

Even with massive, but late hour, evacuations from the City of New Orleans, it perhaps should not have been surprising that those tens of thousands who remained, as levee breaches flooded 80 percent of the city, were largely poorer black citizens, only the most fortunate of whom were able to break through the roofs of their modest homes in low-lying neighborhoods and wave for rescue. Perhaps it should not have been surprising that it was the predominately white, higher-elevation, higher-value areas of the French Quarter and the historic Garden District that remained relatively dry and safe; their residents had the opportunity and financial means to escape well before the storm struck. From the varied discussions in the preceding chapter, it should be evident that, while a complex set of factors were at play over the last quarter century or more, the greater New Orleans district had been experiencing a slow economic decline and increasing racial trouble. A reminder of enforced racial segregation was reawakened as the addition of high concentrations of poverty made for a landscape in which the most vulnerable of New Orleans' population were located in the lower segments of Orleans' 'bowls' that were most vul-

31. Reported by Adam Goldfarb, "Reunion Revisited: Richard Colar and Princess Still Happy Together," *PetsforLife*, Humane Society of the United States online newsletter, August 29, 2007. Accessible at http://www.hsus.org/hsus_field_disaster_center/disasters_press_room/Katrina_anniversary . . .

nerable to repeated flooding. The racial distribution of the population of these neighborhoods was heavily black.

Topography, therefore, combined with cultural patterns and population distribution, played a inordinately poisonous role in the unevenness—the *unfairness*—of the destruction wreaked by Hurricane Katrina.[32] We have tracked an overall population decline of 18.1 percent in Orleans Parish between 1980 and 2002, along with an increase in its percentage of black population to 64.7 percent. At the same time we have seen the unevenness of declines and increases from neighborhood to neighborhood, and from one planning district to another. For example, while Planning Districts No. 2 (Central City and the Garden District) and No. 7 (Bywater, St. Claude, St. Roch, Desire) for various reasons[33] showed population declines of 36.4 and 30.1 percent, respectively, Planning Districts No. 9 and No. 10 (New Orleans East), on the other hand, showed increases of 15.2 and 25.4 percent; Planning District No. 13 (New Aurora/English Turn) actually showed an increase of 80.0 percent, although for a very small population. We have also tracked percentages of black, white, and Asian residents in those neighborhoods and planning districts, and seen a similarly uneven distribution. The actual range of the percentage of black population is extraordinary, from a low of 0.0 and 2.2 percent in Planning Districts No. 11 (Viavant/Venetian Isles) and No. 5 (Lakeview and the West End), respectively, to a high of 86.6 and 94.3 percent in Planning Districts No. 7 (Bywater, St. Claude, St. Roch, Desire) and No. 8 (Lower Ninth Ward, Holy Cross).[34]

Hurricane Katrina and its subsequent flooding made it painfully clear that, with the exception of Lakeview and the West End, the neighborhoods with the highest proportion of poorer black residents were also the areas that were lower-lying, continually flood-prone, and economi-

32. The Brookings Institution Metropolitan Policy Program study, "New Orleans After the Storm: Lessons from the Past, a Plan for the Future," October, 2005, for example, noted the uneven impacts of Katrina, based on geographic information system (GIS) technology to analyze residential patterns and socioeconomic profiles in flooded areas, as reflected in the 2000 Census data, in comparison to areas that did not flood.

33. Within Planning District No. 2, the population of the Garden District has remained relatively stable; the closing of the Desire Development project may account for a considerable portion of the loss in Planning District No. 3.

34. The 2000 Census also shows an unevenness in the distribution of racial groups across the metropolitan region: while the City of New Orleans contained 36 percent of the region's population, it held 64 percent of the region's black population.

cally depressed. New Orleans' general economic condition had, over past decades, slowly declined as a whole. One measure of this is that, while nationwide average annual pay grew by 16 percent, in New Orleans it grew by only 7 percent. In addition, the 2000 Census also showed that New Orleans' 18 percent poverty rate and low median household income made it the sixth poorest of 100 large metropolitan areas. Indeed, unskilled jobs in the hotel and service industries, one notable area of some recent economic growth in New Orleans, tend to remain low paying because of their relatively high turnover. However, the segregation of skilled and unskilled jobs, and the division between wealthy and poor, only grew in New Orleans, as it has elsewhere in the United States. Thus, it would not be unreasonable to expect to see the disparity in individual economic growth also unevenly distributed across New Orleans' neighborhoods.

Although New Orleans had developed both large and contiguous (Seventh Ward and Tremé/Lafitte) but also several isolated (e.g., Desire) neighborhoods of black and more economically fragile residents, it was, as Peirce Lewis points out, not always the case.[35] Peirce reminds us that while New Orleans has historically had one of the highest proportions of black populations, it was not *geographically* highly segregated, with blacks living in close proximity to whites throughout much of the city. Not until the second half of the twentieth century, and actually the 1960s and 1970s, did neighborhoods that were almost entirely white vs. others almost entirely black began to emerge. Poverty and economic fragility was similarly distributed more evenly throughout the city until the 1960s and 1970s. By the time of Hurricane Katrina, however, the images of those in need of rescue laid bare the fact that New Orleans had developed very large neighborhoods of those in need—very poor, poorly paid, underinsured residents who turned out to be black. While it can sound almost racist to utter that fact, the parallel occurrence of economic and racial divides has been well documented, not only in Orleans Parish, but in America.[36]

The 2000 Census that showed a city poverty rate of 28 percent also showed a sharp rise in the number of *extreme* poverty tracts—where more than 40 percent live below the poverty line—a rise of two-thirds from 1970.[37] Comparing Planning Districts No. 4 (Gert Town, B.W. Cooper,

35. Lewis, *New Orleans: The Making of an Urban Landscape*, 50ff and passim.

36. See, for example, Massey and Denton, *American Apartheid: Segregation and the Making of the Underclass.*

37. U.S. Census Bureau, Census 1970 and 2000 concentrated poverty statistics; refer-

Iberville, Tremé/Lafitte, Seventh Ward) and 8 (Lower Ninth, Holy Cross), for example, with Planning Districts No. 5 (Lakeview, Lake Vista, the West End) and 13 (New Aurora/English Turn), the 2000 Census found at least half of the population living below the poverty line in the former neighborhoods, while less than 10 percent in the latter.

A Brookings Institution report in 2005 found that a large proportion—84 percent—of New Orleans' poor population was black, and that 43 percent of poor blacks in the city lived in census tracts with extreme poverty levels.[38] Brookings' conclusion was that blacks and whites were living in different worlds before the storm hit. Some of the percentages are impacted by the existence of housing developments within certain neighborhoods, and it is useful to compare neighborhoods with high non-white populations with one another. For example, U.S. Census data for 2000 shows that the neighborhood of B.W. Cooper, mostly a housing development, with a non-white population of 99.8 percent, had an average household income of $13,786, only 3.9 percent owner-occupied housing units, and a poverty rate of 69.2 percent of the total population. The Lower Ninth Ward, on the other hand, also with an almost entirely non-white population of 99.5 percent, had an average household income of $27,522, a high percentage of owner-occupied housing units at 59.0 percent, and a substantially lower poverty rate of 36.4 percent. Of course, both of these neighborhoods together still contrast quite sharply with the Lakeview neighborhood, which has a non-white population of only 6.1 percent, an average household income of $63,178, a 69.5 percent of owner-occupied housing units, and a miniscule poverty rate of 4.9 percent of the total population.[39]

---

ence from The Brookings Institution Metropolitan Policy Program study, "New Orleans After the Storm: Lessons from the Past, a Plan for the Future," October, 2005, 41.

38. Berube and Katz, "Katrina's Window: Confronting Concentrated Poverty Across America," 1–4. The report argued that "New Orleans ranked second among the nation's 50 largest cities on the degree to which its poor families, mostly African American, were clustered in extremely poor neighborhoods like the Lower Ninth Ward. In these places, the average household earned barely more than $20,000 annually, only one in twelve adults held a college degree, four in five children were raised in single-parent families, and four in ten working-age adults—many of them disabled—were not connected to the labor force."

39. The Brookings Institution Metropolitan Policy Program study, "New Orleans After the Storm: Lessons from the Past, a Plan for the Future," census table analysis, October, 7, 2005.

To pull these observations about the coincidence of *location* and *vulnerability* together in the highest relief, we can see a 'winnowing' progression to what could be argued as the 'worst of the worst' of those areas of New Orleans impacted by post-Katrina flooding. Neighborhoods that have had the highest percentages (80 percent or more) of black population include: Hollygrove, Freret, Gert Town, B.W. Cooper, Central City, Tremé/Lafitte, the Seventh Ward, Dillard, St. Bernard Area, St. Roch, St. Claude, Florida and Desire Areas, the Lower Ninth Ward, Pontchartrain Park, and large parts of New Orleans East. Among these neighborhoods, those that also represented areas with high concentrations (40 percent or higher) of poverty include: Gert Town, Freret, B.W. Cooper, Central City, Tremé/Lafitte, parts of the Seventh Ward, St. Roch, parts of the Desire Area and the Lower Ninth Ward.[40] It turns out that all of the neighborhoods in this second list were among those most heavily flooded in the days after Katrina had passed on to the east of New Orleans.[41] While there were other areas with neither high poverty levels nor large concentrations of black citizens that were severely inundated and devastated by post-Katrina flooding as well—Lakeview and the West End, Broadmoor, parts of Mid-City, Filmore, and City Park in Orleans Parish, and large parts of nearby St. Bernard Parish, being the most notable examples—the neighborhoods we have designated in our second list would have to be regarded as those that suffered the most. These were the neighborhoods that received the worst of the flooding that *also* impacted the areas existing under the worst socio-economic conditions within the city as measured by such criteria as poverty levels, average household income, employment rates, educational levels, and percentages of home ownership, used by the U.S. Census Bureau and the Greater New Orleans community Data Center. These were the neighborhoods with the most fragile economies, the least material resources to protect themselves against or to recover from disaster; these were the areas of the city more easily neglected than those visited by tourists or frequented by convention-goers. These were

40. Some other areas with slightly lower percentages of black population were also neighborhoods with high concentrations of poverty. These included: East Riverside and the Irish Channel, parts of Leonidas, Viavant/Venetian Isles, and McDonough on the West Bank. Source: Brookings analysis of U.S. Census data and the Greater New Orleans Community Data Center.

41. Source for Katrina flooding areas as of September 11th, 2005: FEMA flood extent data.

the neighborhoods that suffered the most; and suffered, one might say, most *unfairly*. Yet what these neighborhoods might have lacked in material resources, in the long months after Katrina they have more than made up for by their persistence of heart, their resilience and determination, and through the bonds formed within their communities to engage the struggles to recover together. It is perhaps ironic, but not surprising, that those areas of New Orleans suffering the most were also its very heart and soul—its *people*, not its public mask. For this reason, the recovery of New Orleans will depend not on grandiose schemes for new development, not even on reclaiming its tourist industry; rather, it will depend on a healing of its heart and soul, and on bringing back into the lifeblood of the city those who lived and worked at its very core.

New Orleans Cold Storage

Over the two years since the storm, it has become increasingly apparent that Katrina's most serious impacts resulted from a tragic conjunction of sociological, economic, and geographic factors. Sociologically marginalized neighborhoods—those 'ghettoized' areas of New Orleans that were separated from a fair share of the city's infrastructure, from having a fair voice in the city's political decision-making process—were coextensive with areas of economic marginalization, seen, for example, in census tracts showing extreme poverty, unemployment, and above-normal percentages of people with chronic health issues. These same neighborhoods were geographically situated on top of those parts of the city's topography most exposed to the dangers of frequent flooding, and inadequate drainage, sewerage, and water supply systems. Thus, geographic topography and socio-economic topography merged in such a way that the areas of severest flooding after Hurricane Katrina—the low-lying areas most affected by levee breaches—were also the poorest, and the least economically capable of withstanding or recovering from disaster. Wealthier areas and economic centers of tourism, such as the Garden District and the French Quarter, situated on higher ground, escaped major flood damage. But, with the primary exceptions of Lakeview, a middle-class, white neighborhood in the northwest corner New Orleans that suffered flood inundation of eight feet or more, and St. Bernard Parish to the south, it was the economically most fragile neighborhoods—Gert Town, Tremé/

Lafitte, St. Roch, the Lower Ninth Ward—that were the areas of the city which suffered most severely.

Endemic socio-economic problems often represent instances of Markers of Complexity 7 (progressive degradation of human values), sometimes 3 (unintended consequences), but especially 4 (vicious cycles). The interplay of socio-economic needs with geographic topography that created 'vicious cycle' type problems emerged in other ways. The case of New Orleans Cold Storage illustrates this kind of economic dilemma. To many, it appeared as if the MR–GO shipping channel shortcut, which contributed to sources of employment for thousands of people, had ultimately 'turned against' those who worked in the Port of New Orleans—particularly those laborers who were able to hold themselves above the poverty line. In 2003, the Port of New Orleans ranked fifth in tons of cargo handled among U.S. ports. It was twelfth in total foreign trade.[42] It was a major entry point for foreign manufactured steel, natural rubber, coffee, and, even with containerized cargo, still employed thousands of truck drivers and longshoremen, and other port workers engaged in handling close to 700,000 cruise ship passengers annually. Hurricane Katrina destroyed approximately one-third of the port. With no power for its freezers, New Orleans Cold Storage had 32 million pounds of chicken rot in its waterside warehouse. The reek was detectable from a mile away.[43] The New Orleans Cold Storage (NOCS) plant was constructed in 1980, and provided cold storage space of over one million cubic feet. It was U.S. Customs bonded, a USDA approved import meat inspection facility, and certified for Russian pork and poultry shipments. Its situation in the port also gave it access to Public Belt delivery and other railroads.[44] Before the storm, NOCS had been planning to build a third birth in the port and expand its warehousing capability.

By early 2006, New Orleans Cold Storage had reopened, but its 135 jobs—livelihood for 135 families—as well as an additional 200 union stevedores, were now threatened by the very MR–GO canal to which, like other nearby businesses in the port, it owed its existence and economic

42. Figures from the American Association of Port Authorities.

43. See, for example, John Schwartz, "Debating a Shipping Shortcut That Turned Against New Orleans," *The New York Times,* March 3, 2006, and Alan Sayre, AP, "Entry point is running at half capacity, with a goal of 70 percent by spring," December 28, 2005, printed in *The San Diego Union-Tribune* and *USA Today.*

44. Information from New Orleans Cold Storage and Warehousing, Ltd. home office.

livelihood. For the City of New Orleans, a large part of whose economy was built around shipping and trade, it was not in a position to limit its access to water. At the same time, residents had at last come to acknowledge that the MR–GO channel was an environmental disaster, and that it had contributed directly to the devastation much of St. Bernard Parish, large portions of the Port of New Orleans, and the neighborhoods adjacent to the port during Hurricane Katrina by acting as a funnel for storm surge forced up the shipping channel shortcut to the Inner Harbor Navigational Canal. It was just beyond that funnel and the T-intersection of the two waterways that breaches in the Inner Harbor Navigational Canal resulted in the devastation of the Lower Ninth Ward. Decay and erosion of the MR–GO channel banks had, over the years since its completion in 1965, killed fragile vegetation and destroyed protective wetlands by allowing the intrusion of saltwater from the Gulf. At the same time, the shortcut had never met its expectation of increasing shipping traffic.[45]

For these reasons, many residents, as well as Henry Rodriguez, Jr., President of St. Bernard Parish, came to the position that the MR–GO channel had to be shut down. In February, 2006, the Louisiana State Legislature concurred, and passed a resolution demanding Congress close the canal. Yet if the channel were closed, thousands of jobs would eventually be lost. The dilemma was that the very thing that had become a source of livelihood for many was also something to be afraid of. Rodriguez remarked that "People are really afraid . . . and have a right to be."[46] However, the federal government had made a financial commitment to keep the MR–GO channel clear and deep enough to support ship traffic of the size vessels that would make the canal economically worthwhile for the port. Hurricane Katrina had cut the channel's depth from 36 feet to only 22 feet. The ships of a draft capable of navigating that shallow a depth would be smaller, making a return to the use of the Mississippi River as a shipping route more attractive if not a necessity.[47] An additional problem in this

45. An example of economic disaster elsewhere in the state is the fear of citrus growers in southern Louisiana that they may never be able to plan trees again because of the salt left behind by Katrina's floodwaters. Soil tests in some areas showed salt concentrations at 9,000 parts per million as compared with 2,000 parts per million before the storm. Cain Burdean, AP Writer, "Katrina strangles Louisiana's cherished citrus industry," *The Louisiana Weekly*, December 19, 2005.

46. Quoted by John Schwartz.

47. Even at its normal depth, MR–GO was marginal for large ocean-going container ships capable of carrying 5000 containers. Furthermore, ships now are being built to hold

mix are the limitations of the 80-year old locks between the Inner Harbor Navigational Canal and the Mississippi River. The normal route of most ships would be to reach NOCS from the Gulf via the MR–GO channel, load, continue on by the Inner Harbor Navigational Canal, pass through the Inner Harbor Locks to the river, then return to sea. The locks, already too narrow for many larger ships, were creating ship traffic bottlenecks; but, as we have seen, there was also considerable neighborhood resistance to USACE's plans for enlarging them.

On July 27, 2006, USACE, New Orleans District, announced that Congress had directed the Corps to begin a MR–GO de-authorization study.[48] On May 19, 2007, the New Orleans District office of the U.S. Army corps of Engineers released notice of a plan for the total closure of MR–GO. On the basis of public and stakeholder comments, USACE came to the conclusion that its 'Alternative 1'—construction of a closure structure across MR–GO near Bayou La Loutre—had emerged as the plan most beneficial, both economically and environmentally.[49] On July 2, 2007, USACE made its MR–GO draft final report and legislative environmental impact statement[50] available. The National Environmental Policy Act (NEPA)-required 45-day public comment period began mid-July. On January 29, 2998, by signature of the Chief of Engineers, the U.S. Army Corps of Engineers Chief's Report for the Mississippi River–Gulf Outlet Deep-Draft De-Authorization Study was completed and transmitted to the Assistant Secretary of the Army for Civil Works (ASA(CW)) to review the findings, obtain Office of Management and Budget (OMB) input, and send the report to Congress. In conjunction with the construction of the MR–GO closure, USACE will de-water the Inner Harbor Navigational Canal (IHNC) Lock to perform required repairs to the lock and gate closure.[51]

7000 containers, some as many as 13,000 containers.

48. New release from New Orleans District Public Affairs Office, USACE, July 27, 2006.

49. Ibid., May 19, 2007.

50. "Mississippi River Gulf Outlet Deep-Draft De-Authorization (MRGO) Draft Final Report and Legislative Environmental Impact Statement (LEIS)."

51. USACE and Coastal Protection and Restoration Authority of Louisiana (CPRA) press release, February 11, 2008. Because the IHNC Lock repairs will impact shallow draft traffic, USACE will dredge the Baptiste Collette channel to allow more marine traffic to bypass the lock; the dredged material will be used beneficially to rebuild coastal wetlands. Work on the MR–GO closure will also be coordinated with storm surge protection measures in the IHNC to ultimately provide 100-year risk reduction by 2011.

The dilemma about the MR–GO channel and New Orleans Cold Storage can be seen as a microcosm of the many difficult decisions the city faces. Dilemmas such as these lead directly to issues of post-Katrina reconstruction planning. There are complex intersections of connections between neighborhoods, future flooding risk factors, and sources of employment. Some of these may lead, for example, to the question of whether certain neighborhoods should simply abandoned and not be rebuilt at all. That, however, is not an option one could tell Jarvis Green of the New England Patriots, or Fats Domino, or any of the other thousands of residents of the Lower Ninth Ward for whom the neighborhood—like the neighborhoods of others—has been their family home for generations. Yet the ultimate future of neighborhoods like the Lower Ninth remains in limbo, as the few homes being rebuilt sit almost lost in vast fields of growing brush and grass. Returning to his home ward during the Patriot's 'by-week,' October 15, 2006, Jarvis Green remarked, amidst tears, "After a year, nothing's changed, nothing to smile about. The grass has grown. That's about all." A year later—two years after Hurricane Katrina—progress in the Lower Ninth Ward has been painfully slow; in some places, none visible at all.

The MR–GO channel has *not yet* been closed.[52] The neighborhoods of the Lower Ninth Ward and St. Bernard Parish and many others are *not yet* protected from continued future devastation from flooding and storms. As Henry Rodriguez said, "People are really afraid . . . But people need jobs." And people need neighborhoods to which they wish to return. Thus, there emerges a *cycle* of complexity. One complex problem simply feeds into another problem; the solution x to complex problem a produces complex problem b, whose solution y competes with solution x—an example of instability (Marker of Complexity 1); worse, the union of conjunctions of problems often spawns even further problems not originally anticipated. As many have reflected on the vicious underlying logic, 'You can fix all the houses and make them livable. *But,* if there are no jobs, what good is that going to do? *But,* many jobs depend upon New Orleans' access to the Gulf and to waterways for shipping. *But,* those routes of access to the Gulf and connecting waterways have been the paths of destruction

52. And even when MR–GO is closed, it remains unclear that those areas of the city which had been made more vulnerable to flooding from the construction of MR–GO will be made safe again, due to the open water and loss of marshes still very much present on either side of the channel.

of both homes and jobs. *But . . . but . . . but . . .*' Reconstruction of New Orleans, and the strategies to direct it, therefore, becomes a huge balancing act between people having houses and people having jobs and what else it takes to economically support those houses and those jobs, and, ultimately, between *all of that* and what it will take to ensure a protective environment in which *any of it* can be expected to continue to exist with a reasonable degree of safety.

Soon After Katrina

You Can't Fool Mother Nature
(October, 2005)

4

Katrina's Legacy

Coming to Terms with the Causes and Effects of Disaster

PROXIMATE CAUSES

IN THE AFTERMATH OF Hurricane Katrina, New Orleans suffered numerous failures to its levee system both east and west of the Inner Harbor Navigational Canal (IHNC, also referred to as the Industrial Canal). These included breaches to its drainage canal floodwalls, overtopping along the Mississippi River–Gulf Outlet (MR–GO) channel, and overtopping and breaches along the Gulf Intracoastal Waterway (GIWW) and the Inner Harbor Navigational Canal itself.

It has been a standard assumption that, to the east, the primary cause of flooding resulted from storm surge up the MR–GO channel. This channel, bypassing 80 miles of the old route from the main pass of the Mississippi River, leaves the Gulf at Grace Point, Eloi Bay, joins into the Gulf Intracoastal Waterway at the NASA Michoud facility, just east of I-510/Paris Road. The GIWW, in turn, empties into the Inner Harbor Navigational Canal, and then deposits ships into the main part of the Port of New Orleans on the southern edge of the city. A storm surge higher than predicted for a Category 3 storm preceded Hurricane Katrina through the MR–GO channel. While in the MR–GO and GIWW, the surge overtopped levees along St. Bernard Parish to the south and New Orleans East to the north.

However, the Final Report of the Interagency Performance Evaluation Task Force (IPET) Performance Evaluation of the New Orleans and Southeast Louisiana Hurricane Protection System (the Volume I Interim

Final, 'subject to revisions,' dated 26 March 2007,[1] differed with assumptions about the role of MR–GO. The IPET team was composed of leaders from government agencies, universities, and private industries, as well as the U.S. Army Corps of Engineers (USACE). USACE notes that while the media has often tried to dismiss the report, as successive volumes emerged, as 'the Corps reporting on itself,' IPET was an independent team with independent review panels. For this reason, USACE put the disclaimer "This report is the independent opinion of the IPET and is not necessarily the official position of the U.S. Army Corps of Engineers" on the bottom of each page. The Task Force Project Director was Dr. Lewis E. Link of the University of Maryland; Technical Director was Dr. John Jaeger (USACE); Project Manager was Jeremy Stevenson (USACE).

The IPET report maintained that the southeast trending leg of MR–GO had little influence on the water levels in the IHNC during Katrina. IPET reasoned that the relative size of the channel with respect to the large flow area available when marsh areas were inundated by surge made the amount of water conveyed through the channel a relatively small part

1. See U.S. Army Corps of Engineers, "Performance Evaluation of the New Orleans and Southeast Louisiana Hurricane Protection System. Final Report of the Interagency Performance Evaluation Task Force," Volume I, Executive Summary and Overview, 26 March 2007, I–64. This report appears in multiple volumes, some final, some still under review and revision as late fall, 2007. After an initial full citation, reference to this and other volumes of the report will hereafter be made as follows: IPET Vol. I, IPET Vol. II, IPET Vol. III, etc. The Interagency Performance Evaluation Task Force (IPET) was established by USACE Chief of Engineers, LTG Carl A. Strock "to provide credible and objective scientific and engineering answers to fundamental questions about the performance of the hurricane protection and flood damage reduction system in the New Orleans metropolitan area." It has included more than 150 experts from over 50 federal, state, and local agencies, as well as universities and the private sector. The Task Force conducted in-depth analyses that defined the surge and wave levels resulting from the storm; determined the forces experienced by the hurricane protection system (HPS); determined the most likely causes and mechanisms of observed behavior; characterized the extent and consequences of flooding, including the influence of the pumping stations; and performed a risk and reliability assessment. Analysis also provided input to ongoing efforts to reconstitute the protection system, including repair of areas serious damaged, and the planning and design for achieving 100-year certifiable FEMA flood insurance structures. In the process, IPET sought answers to five major questions: (1) Did the design, construction, and maintenance of the HPS meet pre-Katrina design criteria? (2) What storm surges and waves were used as the basis of the original design, and how did these compare to those generated by Katrina? (3) How did floodwalls, levees, pumping stations, and drainage canals individually and as an integrated system perform in response to Katrina? (4) What were the social consequences of Katrina-related damage? (5) What will be the quantifiable risk to New Orleans and vicinity from future hurricanes?

of the total, findings they said that agreed with those of an independent study conducted for the State of Louisiana. Thus, IPET concluded that "during Katrina, MRGO was far from the 'hurricane highway' moniker with which it has been branded."[2]

Debate about the role of MR–GO in Katrina flooding arose mere weeks after the storm. Environmentalist Mike Tidwell, author of *Bayou Farewell: The Rich Life and Tragic Death of Louisiana's Cajun Coast,* for example, believed that if the MR–GO channel had not been dug, the storm surge would not have been nearly as high; it would have been dissipated by marshes and wetlands that the shipping route had destroyed. Oyster farmers such as Stacy Geraci observed the effects from the way poles were bent. However, Col. Richard Wagenaar, commander of USACE's New Orleans District, disagreed, arguing MR–GO was not to blame, that a twenty-foot storm surge and waves would have come in regardless.[3]

It is not the purpose of *Walking to New Orleans* to decide among differences of technical merit in arguments about the means (and causes) of overtopping and failures to New Orleans' levee system. What we *will* try to do is simply present a general timeline of overtopping, breaches, and flooding events—largely drawn from IPET-Vol. IV—and, afterwards, offer a broad assessment of causation that includes some of the major design and construction features of the levee system, but also goes beyond them to consider some important political and cultural factors as well. It is worth noting, however, that on June 15, 2006, President George W. Bush signed the Emergency Supplemental Appropriations Act for Defense, the Global War on Terror, and Hurricane Recovery (Public Law 109–234) in which the U.S. Congress directed the Secretary of the Army, acting through the Chief of Engineers, to develop a plan for the de-authorization of deep-draft navigation for the Mississippi River–Gulf Outlet from the Gulf of Mexico to the Gulf Intracoastal Waterway (GIWW). Congress also directed that the plan be fully consistent with the Louisiana Coastal Protection and Restoration (LACPR) plan due to Congress in December, 2007.[4] The New Orleans District of USACE released its Draft Integrated

2. IPET Vol I, I–64.

3. Reported by Jake Tapper and Jay LaMonica, "Did Man-Made Canals Channel Katrina's Storm Surge? Scientists, Environmentalists Say Destructive Canal System Served as a 'Trojan Horse' for Floodwaters," ABC news, Sept. 20, 2005. Accessed at http://abcnews.go.com.print?id=114518.

4. See U.S. Army Corps of Engineers, New Orleans District, "Draft Integrated Final

Final Report for the De-authorization of MR–GO in June of 2007, and the completed Chief's Report for De-authorization on January 28, 2008.

In constructing a timeline of overtopping, breaches, and flooding, it is important to caution that there was not a simple flow of events from one area to another; rather, events of failures and consequent flooding were occurring simultaneously. To assess wave heights and periods, the IPET team employed tools such as the COrnell University Long WAVE (COULWAVE) surface modeling package, and the STeady state spectral WAVE (STWAVE) model for near shore wind-wave growth and propagation, modified to simulate the effects of local wind generation inside canals. It is interesting to see that a variety of factors are at work in the assessment of water and wave behavior *inside* New Orleans' various waterways. For example, STWAVE data for maximum wave heights within the MR–GO/GIWW entrance to the IHNC shows that waves entering from relatively open waters decay rapidly from almost 3 feet to about 1.2 feet within one-half mile. However, winds for the 1:00 a.m. to 6:00 a.m. CDT timeframe on August 29, 2005, were aligned with the axis of the MR–GO/GIWW so that local wave generation produced heights of over 4 feet at the intersection with the IHNC during peak periods of 80 knots from the east at about 5:30 a.m. Using a modification of STWAVE suggested that the primary source of wave energy against the floodwalls of the Lower Ninth Ward, one of the earliest areas of breaches, came from waves reflected back to the east side of the IHNC from its west side. These tools were also used to analyze the mechanics of a free-floating barge, such as the Ingram Barge *ING4727* that broke through the floodwall of the IHNC, to generally corroborate the belief that its impact would be capable of inflicting considerable damage to floodwalls.[5]

Some of the first flooding occurred possibly as early as 4:30 a.m., CDT, in the Lower Ninth Ward from overtopping and two breaches along the IHNC, as well as overtopping and numerous breaches along the GIWW and MR–GO. Although only a limited number of interviews were collected, due to few people being back in that area, one eyewitness in the northern part of the Lower Ninth, midway between the IHNC and a local levee that separates the Lower Ninth Ward from St. Bernard Parish, reported that at about 4:30 a.m. water was flowing down Galvez Street

---

Report to Congress and Legislative Environmental Impact Statement for the Mississippi River—Gulf Outlet Deep-Draft De-authorization Study," June 2007.

5. IPET Vol. IV, Figures 161 and 162, and discussion IV–225 to IV–228.

from the west into his home, and that by 5:00 a.m. it was at the top of his first floor. Another eyewitness reported floodwaters 3 or 4 feet above the second story floor at about 5:30 a.m. Also at 5:30 a.m., at Pump Station 5 just off the IHNC near Florida Avenue, the power was turned off for safety due to high water levels; an operator reported first seeing flooding at 4:30 a.m. Two sets of stopped-clock data provided further details on waters entering the Lower Ninth Ward.[6]

Flooding from the west side of the Inner Harbor Navigational Canal (IHNC) constituted one of the more complex areas for investigation. There were three breach locations, including one near I-10 through the railroad line, and a breach in the floodwall (13 feet elevation) and earth levee (11 feet elevation) near Pump Station 19; there were also failures along the floodwall south of the earth levee towards France Road. Consistent eyewitness accounts saw the first signs of rushing water between 6:00 and 7:00 a.m. CDT; some put it as early as 5:45 a.m. Water entering the east-west Florida Canal might explain early flooding times to the east, and water entering the north-south Peoples Canal would conduct it north and south of Gentilly Ridge, with some flowing *across* low areas in the ridge. High-water marks in the area reflected a general passage of water from west to east. Gauge records on the IHNC at I-10 suggest something may have impacted them as early as 4:00 to 5:00 a.m., but mechanical problems or debris could account for that as well as breaching. A gauge at the IHNC Lock, read by the lock operator, showed a high-water of 14.3 feet (mean water level, not reflecting wave activity), which could have overtopped the nearby 11 feet elevation earth levee at 5:45 a.m., and an adjacent 13 feet elevation floodwall at about 7:30 a.m. The exact timing cannot be established with certainty, but it does appear that by midmorning water levels had risen to the point where flow could have crossed Gentilly Ridge into the areas north of it.

Much of the existing floodwall structure has used an 'I' wall (shaped like the letter I) construction. This type of structure generally consists of Z-form steel sheet piling driven through compacted base material to a depth of twenty feet, with an elevation of twelve feet. A concrete wall is formed over the elevated portion of the sheet piling.[7]

---

6. IPET Vol. 4, IV–193 ff. See IPET Vol. IV, IV–164 ff for details on the entire timeline.
7. See IPET Vol. I, Figure 3, I–29.

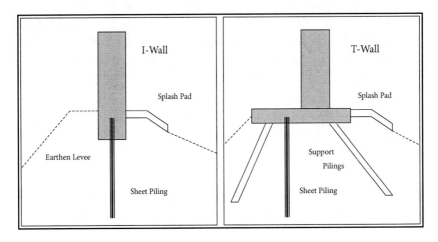

About 4,000 feet of new levee protection is being built, the old structure being replaced with a 'T' wall (shaped like an inverted letter T), to give better base stability and resistance to water scouring. 'T' wall construction generally consists of a reinforced concrete twelve-foot wall, whose base below the level of compacted material is perpendicular (horizontal) to the elevated portion, with a longer horizontal arm being on the flood side. Below the horizontal base of the floodwall, Z-form steel sheet piling is driven to a depth of twenty feet. In addition, from the end portions of the inverted 'T' base, two pre-stressed concrete pilings are angled outwards to a depth of as much as 65 feet. A question that has repeatedly been asked is: why was this latter construction not used in the first place?

Significant levee overtopping and breaches occurred along the GIWW, impacting New Orleans East; overtopping of the floodwall near the Lakefront Airport allowed the New Orleans East area to receive floodwaters from multiple directions. Approximately 25 eyewitness interviews, stopped-clock data, video footage of levee overtopping at the Michoud power plant, and extrapolation from the Paris Road USGS gauge put water influx at a time as early as 6:15 a.m., CDT.

With the 17th Street Drainage Canal, despite limited stage hydrographic information, consistency of eyewitness accounts and supporting time-stamped data strongly suggest that the initial breach occurred as early as 6:30 a.m., CDT. Flooding was exacerbated by the fact that at about 9:00 a.m., the pumps were no longer able to keep up with the rising water, and pumping operations ceased. An account from one man in the Lake Marina Tower high-rise building just north of the seventeenth Street breach reported that just as dawn broke, he saw one section of the wall leaning over; a little later the breach had fully developed, and he noticed a large amount of debris piled against the north side of the Hammond Highway bridge. Interestingly, another person water moving very fast in the seventeenth seventeenth Street Canal—about one foot below the top of the wall—but with no significant waves; however, water was flowing over the top of the wall that had leaned over, and two or three hours later (approximately 9:00 a.m.) he observed many sections all the way down the canal down or completely gone. The catastrophic breaching by 9:00 a.m. could account for some observations that saw water one or two feet below standing walls, since it would likely lower canal water levels.

Initial breaches along the west side of the London Avenue Drainage Canal, placed most reliably somewhere between 7:00 and 7:30 a.m., CDT, were based not on eyewitnesses but on a number of stopped-clocks recorded within a ten-block area of the breach. Here, waters rose more slowly to a peak elevation of 2.8 feet on Tuesday at about 1:00 a.m., CDT. This elevation is equal to high-water marks in the area. Breaches along the east side of the London Avenue Drainage Canal were observed by a large number of people who remained in their homes during the hurricane. In this area, the earliest reported accounts of flooding was between 7:00 and 8:00 a.m. One individual who noticed little water in the street around 7:30 a.m. went back to sleep, but soon after heard gurgling and saw water at the window ledges coming into his house. Going with a friend to look at the floodwall breach, they heard a loud cracking sound, and the wall burst in front of them, gushing water "like twenty fire hydrants." They retreated towards Paris Street, where water was moving in from north to south, and had to swim to reach the Beacon Light Church, where they holed-up for several days.[8]

While some areas of St. Bernard Parish undoubtedly flooded earlier, eyewitness accounts, stopped-clock data, and video indicated that flood-waters first entered areas east of Paris Road, Chalmette, from the northeast at approximately 8:20 a.m., CDT. Video footage from the Corinne Estates subdivision in Chalmette documented large clumps of marsh grass moving from northeast to southwest, representing a flow from the marsh lands surrounding Lake Borgne and MR–GO. By 9:00 a.m., houses in the vicinity of Corinne Estates were inundated to at least 8–10 feet deep.

8. IPET Vol. IV, IV–176.

The flooding from the seventeenth Street Drainage Canal into Lakeview, flooding into the neighborhoods on either side of the London Avenue Drainage Canal, and that which progressed on into the center of the city, occurred as Lake Ponchartrain tried to reach its own level by 'filling the bowl.' This process was further intensified by the fact that the wind-driven water level in Lake Ponchartrain was considerably higher than normal. The walls along the 17th Street Drainage canal that remained intact, and which Deanne and I inspected about four weeks after the storm, surprised us in being made of concrete only two feet wide. The drainage canal walls have been patched but are not now trusted by many. USACE has built closures at the mouth of each canal—what was originally intended—to eliminate these drainage canals from the system in the event of a storm. Each canal has a steel gate that will close and operate with pumps in the event of a storm. By the end of May, 2006, most of this repair work—an effort of $800 million—was completed. Additional repairs have included a better clay base of the MR–GO and other levees for stability, making them higher and wider, with armoring and wave berms to deflect incoming storm surges.

Among the issues that has remained unclear is the question of whether storm surge had, in effect, been 'funneled' by the intersection of the GIWW and the IHNC and further restrictions along the IHNC. By some estimates, incoming waters were accelerated to as much as eight feet per second. Was it perhaps the *speed* of water input into a static, fragile system of defenses, as much as height or sheer volume, that contributed to overtopping of portions of the Industrial Canal walls, scouring beneath the walls producing cave ins, and the shaking loose of Ingram Barge *ING4727* to break through the floodwall? Was it, as some local residents have suggested, levees on the east side of the northern sections of the IHNC, just below the Florida Avenue bridge, that were too low or not built to standard? It was more likely that no *single* factor, but only the multiple factors of wind, water volume, water speed, levee wall and base construction, combined with the pump failure near Florida Avenue, that resulted in the particularly enormous flooding of the Lower Ninth Ward and adjacent neighborhoods.

As Hurricane Katrina approached the Louisiana coast, a National Oceanic and Atmospheric (NOAA) deepwater buoy recorded the highest wave height at 55 feet ever measured in the Gulf of Mexico. Katrina's size and waves combined to also produce the largest storm surges ever observed at 28 feet, surpassing Hurricane Camille's high-water mark of 24.6 feet.[9] The inability to fully predict the effects of hurricanes is reflected by the fact that water levels and waves experienced largely met levee design criteria in some parts of New Orleans' hurricane protection system, but significantly exceeded design specifications in other parts. This, among other things, suggested that such tools as the ADvanced CIRCulation (ADCIRC) model for oceanic, coastal, and estuarine waters, used by USACE and others, had to be modified and supplanted by other models capable of assessing wave behavior and water levels more locally.

The IPET report points out that observed peak water levels at the entrances to the drainage canals on the south shore of Lake Pontchartrain ran from 10.8 to 11.8 feet, less than the designed peak water levels of 12.0 feet. Similarly, with peak water levels at the entrance from Lake Pontchartrain to the northern reach of the IHNC of 11.8 feet, water levels remained at or below design levels north of the intersection with the GIWW. However, with an observed peak water level of 15.0 feet at the intersection of the GIWW with the IHNC, in the southern reach between that intersection and the IHNC Lock, water levels exceeded design specs of 13.5 feet by as much as 2 feet. This was also true along the east-west section of the GIWW/MR–GO passage. Along the MR–GO channel that ran through St. Bernard Parish, peak water levels of 16 to 18 feet exceeded levee height by as much as 5 feet.[10]

IPET also performed an analysis to determine the degree of influence of the MR–GO channel on storm surge and wave propagation into New Orleans. The Inner Harbor Navigational Canal allows Lake Pontchartrain and Lake Borgne to be hydraulically connected. Therefore, storm surge in the IHNC and the GIWW/MR–GO passage is influenced by storm surge conditions in both lakes. However, IPET came to the conclusion that the long southeast reach of the MR–GO channel, subject of much concern and criticism, would generally have little influence on water levels in the IHNC and the GIWW/MR–GO passage during high storm surge events such as Katrina.[11]

9. Interestingly, Camille, a Category 5 storm at landfall, produced a 15.8 foot surge at Biloxi, MS, while Katrina, Category 3 at landfall, generated 24–26 foot surges there. The IPET team suggested that while the Saffir-Simpson scale is a good predictor of wind damage from hurricanes, it is not a good predictor of surge and wave generation potential.

10. ITEP Vol. IV, IV–2.

11. Ibid.

MR–GO clearly brings an influx of higher saline water into the protective marshes and Lake Pontchartrain, and low-amplitude tides propagate through its channels, along with others. The IPET team felt that the southeast reach of MR–GO was not of significance during storm surge conditions, when the wetlands become inundated, and that local wave and water level conditions were of *greater* impact on the flood protection system. Some interested parties, including the authors, have raised the question with scientists of whether the MR–GO channel, and other constricted large water body connectors such as the IHNC and GIWW, although without sufficient fetch to ordinarily generate excessive wave activity, might nevertheless contribute pulses of inflow and outflow of water at increased speeds, if synchronized with tidal change. In that case the behavior of protected but tidal waterways could imitate properties of a tidal 'seiche,'[12] or resonance, in which water sloshes back and forth with a certain frequency. If the period of oscillation of entering and exiting water synchronized with the effects of continually high winds at the right times, the speed of water-flow could become greatly advanced. Interest was stimulated by noting that ITEP simulations with STWAVE, modified to investigate the effects of local wind generation, such as within the seventeenth Street Drainage Canal, suggested that wave heights of over 8 feet incident on canal entrances were quickly dissipated and reduced to less than 1 foot near the breach site. Both COULWAVE and STWAVE showed that wave conditions past the first 500 feet or so inside the London Avenue canal were similarly small, remaining less than 1.5 feet throughout the storm. Thus, if, as the IPET team seems to hold, forces on canal floodwalls were similar to what would be expected if the water level at wave crests were simply taken as the still-water level for force estimation, what *produced* the breaches? Once the breaches occurred, even 1 foot waves could be significant. But that would seem to presume some *prior* failure of the canal floodwalls. If high-water levels remained about one foot below the top of the floodwalls, as observed, with no significant waves, but a rapid passage of water was observed nonetheless, then such water-flow could have aggravated pre-existing construction weaknesses of unstable foundation material, resulting in scouring *beneath* the floodwalls and the ultimate toppling of the floodwalls as water passed quickly into and out of the drainage canal.

12. In the sense, previously discussed, promoted by Swiss hydrologist François-Alphonse Forel in 1890 observing the oscillations on Lake Geneva.

ROOT CAUSES

It is a primary goal of *Walking to New Orleans* to make the case that use of the concept of Participatory Design has both engineering utility and ethical warrant as a process to engage those citizens most severely impacted by the flooding and consequent destruction of their homes and human services in the tasks of their own recovery and reconstruction. It is *beyond* its scope to provide detailed technical assessment of all possible root causes of various failures in its levees, floodwalls, and interior drainage and pumping systems. At the same time, it makes sense to summarize some of the major findings of the IPET team, and others, about the design and performance of those systems, and to put those findings in the context of broader themes which relate to underlying social, economic, and political inequities that have been laid open and discussed through the historical and demographic sections of the book.

While the Army Corps of Engineers has largely achieved its immediate goal of levee repair, most independent engineers regard New Orleans as still very much at risk, even as of the summer of 2007, two years after Hurricane Katrina, comes to a close. In fact, Robert G. Bea, professor of engineering at the University of California, Berkeley, one of the early investigators[13] of the design and construction of New Orleans' levees and author of a National Science Foundation funded report[14] on levee failures in 2006, sees some of the USACE levee repairs as already showing signs of serious flaws. After the storm, USACE made an effort to rapidly reconstruct breaches on 13 miles of levee along the MR–GO channel in St. Bernard Parish. This reconstruction is now showing signs of erosion furrows, or rills, and Bob Bea regards the risks of repeat failure during heavy storms as "still high."[15] On June 20, 2007, USACE released a prototype risk assessment for New Orleans' hurricane protection system,[16] revealing which neighborhoods remained the most vulnerable to flooding as well as those that were better protected. The assessment, and

13. For the Independent Levee Investigation Team.

14. R. B. Seed, R.G. Bea, et al. Investigation of the Performance of the New Orleans Flood Protection Systems in Hurricane Katrina on August 29, 2005, Final Report, July 31, 2006.

15. See John Schwartz, "Critic Says Levee Repairs Show Signs of Flaws," *The New York Times,* May 7, 2007. See also John Schwartz, "New Orleans Still at Risk, Army Data Show," *The New York Times,* June 21, 2007.

16. The risk analysis was developed as part of the IPET mission.

its interactive website,[17] shows the dynamics of risk pre-Katrina and as of June 1, 2007, with the intention to be useful for officials and the public to make informed decisions about the probabilities of different levels of inundation (from minimal to deep flooding), risk to property, and principle sources of risk. The assessment shows that while vulnerable areas within many neighborhoods are smaller than they had been prior to Katrina, a large 100-year (i.e., 1 percent chance each year)[18] storm would still flood neighborhoods like Gentilly and Lakeview to at least eight feet.

Joel K. Bourne, Jr. and photographer Tyrone Turner, a New Orleans native, documented numerous ways in which the city and its surroundings remain still very much at risk from future flooding in the August, 2007 issue of National Geographic.[19] A photograph of the reconstructed MR–GO levee shows obvious erosion: looking towards the expanses of Lake Borgne, a grassy crown is marked with worm-like patterns of rills, carved by the rain; these widen into broad, eroding furrows at the base. Within the city lie even more areas of concern. One photograph shows the Duncan Canal Floodwall, built on soft soil, that is sinking and buckling; adjacent steel pilings, reinforcements, also show signs of movement at the points of buckling. Seemingly unaware of the potential danger, a child on a bike rides by. Another photograph shows one point where water flooded through a gap in the Orleans Avenue floodwall during Katrina; this gap has not yet been closed. Other photographs reveal more gaps and sections still damaged and weakened along the London Avenue Drainage Canal.

USACE has argued that Bob Bea overstates the risks, but continued the process of reinspecting and addressing areas of the levee system he identified as problematic. One area of ongoing contention has been the question of whether the natural growth of vegetation on levee sides can counter areas of erosion vs. the expense of armoring levee bases with concrete and rock to reduce erosion. Richard Varuso, assistant chief of the geotechnical branch of USACE's New Orleans District engineering division, believes that some erosion was to be expected after new reconstruction, but that as vegetation grows in, the levee heals itself.[20]

17. http://nolarisk.usace.army.mil.

18. Hurricane Katrina was considered a 400-year (or 4 percent chance each year) storm.

19. Joel K. Bourne, Jr. and Tyrone Turner, "The Perils of New Orleans," *National Geographic*, Vol. 212, No. 2, August, 2007.

20. Schwartz, "Critic Says Levee Repairs Show Signs of Flaws," *The New York Times*, May 7, 2007.

However, a 'deeper' issue has focused on analyses of the nature of the levee foundation material itself to determine the reasonableness of expectations of future catastrophic failure. This issue has plagued discussion of both original levee construction and post-Katrina reconstruction from the start. In a number of locations it does appear that porous foundation material, dredged from nearby areas and consisting of sand or clay, mixed with organic material that is subject to further decomposition, has proven to be an unstable base for both pilings and floodwalls and for levees. Being porous, the foundation material is naturally subject to erosion, scouring, and general degradation from moving water.

Walter Baumy, Jr., chief of engineering for the New Orleans District of USACE, has maintained that capping the base with a reinforcing layer of clay, ten feet thick, would keep erosion fissures from reaching the porous core. Bob Bea disagrees, citing that recent experience in the Netherlands has shown clay-capped levees with porous cores to be prone to failure.[21] Given such disagreements about what is needed to ensure the stability of the foundation on which levees and floodwalls stand, it is hardly comforting that USACE estimates it will take until at least 2010 to strengthen the existing levee system enough to withstand a Category 3 hurricane, and many decades beyond that to develop a flooding defense system capable of protecting New Orleans from a Category 4 or Category 5 storm.[22]

Disagreements about the most fundamental factors in the design and implementation of New Orleans' levee and floodwall protection system have led geologists such as Robert Giegengack of the University of Pennsylvania to conclude that the United States simply lacks the capacity to protect New Orleans. He recommends selling the French Quarter to Disney and moving the port 150 miles upstream.[23]

Inherent Design Weaknesses

Gilbert Fowler White, Quaker and former President of Haverford College, was a prominent American geographer who worked on natural hazards such as flooding, His emphasis on the importance of water management

---

21. Ibid.

22. Storm Categories are based on the Saffir-Simpson Hurricane Scale of 1–5. Category 4 storms have winds of 131–155 mph with a 13- to 18-foot storm surge; Category 5 storms have winds that exceed 155 mph, with surges above 18 feet.

23. Remarks cited in several sources, including Joel K. Bourne, Jr. and Tyrone Turner, "The Perils of New Orleans," *National Geographic,* Vol. 212, No. 2, August, 2007, 42.

led to his sometimes being referred to as the "father of floodplain management." Moving from the University of Chicago to the University of Colorado in 1970, White was founder and twice Director of the university's Natural Hazards Research and Applications Information Center, and the Gustavson Distinguished Professor Emeritus from 1980 until his death in October, 2006.[24] White's Quaker faith led him to the pervasive recognition that societies must learn "the art of helping others improve their lot even as differences between them grow." In addition to seeing shared water management, and the sciences behind it, as a way to facilitate peace, White also believed that the availability of safe water for all peoples of the world was a fundamental human right.

White's approach to floodplain management was one that championed adaptation to or accommodation of flood hazards, rather than 'structural solutions' such as dams and levees. It was in a University of Chicago Department of Geography Research Paper in 1945 that White made the prescient remark: "Floods are 'acts of God,' but flood losses are largely acts of man."[25] Perhaps even more prescient for New Orleans and its expansion eastward and westward in the 1960s is White's observation that "the broad problem of flood-loss reduction is that the rate at which flood losses are being eliminated by construction of engineering or land-treatment works is of about the same magnitude as the rate at which new property is being subjected to damage."[26] From this standpoint, the construction of levees, dams, and other flood protection structures are likely to actually *increase* flood losses, because they encourage and generate new development in flood-prone areas. The dilemma, sometimes referred to as the "levee effect," is a warning that catastrophic human losses will occur when flood protections fail, as they invariably do over time. Levees extended into undeveloped wetlands are ultimately an *invitation* to danger and risk, masked under the guise of economic progress, political aggrandizement, and the appearance of normalcy and security of U.S.

24. Biographical material from the University of Colorado, accessible at http://www.colorado.edu/hazards/ gfw/bio.html.

25. Gilbert White, *Human Adjustment to Floods,* University of Chicago Department of Geography Research Paper No. 29, Chicago: University of Chicago Department of Geography, 1945.

26. Gilbert White, "Strategic Aspects of Urban Flood Plain Occurrence," *Journal of the Hydraulics Division, Proceedings of the American Society of Civil Engineers,* 86 (HY2): 89–102 (1960).

Government- funded construction in the form of large earthen levees and concrete floodwalls.

Many scientists have come to regard the Lake Pontchartrain and Vicinity Hurricane Protection Project,[27] first authorized by Congress in the Flood Control Act of 1965, and built by USACE to protect New Orleans following the flooding and devastation of Hurricane Betsy, as a classic instance of disregarding Gilbert White's cautions. The project involved a series of control structures, concrete floodwalls, and approximately 125 miles of levees to provide hurricane protection around Lake Pontchartrain in Orleans, Jefferson, St. Bernard, and St. Charles Parishes. The project, when designed, was expected to take 13 years to complete at a cost of $85 million. While federally authorized, the project was a joint federal, state, and local effort.[28] Miles of levees were constructed around thousands of acres of vacant wetlands east and west of New Orleans, paralleling the new I-10 highway that supplanted the old U.S. 90 (OST) and U.S. 61 (Airline Highway). Within a decade, this protective 'invitation' bore fruit in the form of nearly 80,000 new housing units in Jefferson Parish to the west of the city and in New Orleans East.

The original project designs were developed based on a hypothetical fast-moving Category 3 hurricane—the Standard Project Hurricane— whose expectation of striking the Louisiana coast was once in 200–300 years.[29] However, GAO reported in 1976 and again in 1982 that, since the beginning of the project, USACE encountered delays and cost increases as a result of technical design changes, environmental concerns, legal challenges, and local opposition to portions of the project.[30] By 1982, the

27. Congress has authorized USACE to construct five hurricane protection projects for coastal Louisiana. The other project relevant to the New Orleans area is the West Bank and Vicinity Hurricane Protection Project.

28. See testimony of Anu Mittal, Director, Natural Resources and Environment, before the Subcommittee on Energy and Water Development, Committee on Appropriations, House of Representatives, Government Accountability Office report GAO-05-1050T, September 28, 2005.

29. A size hurricane that Wilson Shaffer, storm-surge modeler at the National Weather Service, argued in 1984 was far too small to represent the actual dangers the Louisiana coast faced.

30. GAO, "Cost, Schedule, and Performance Problems of the Lake Pontchartrain and Vicinity, Louisiana, Hurricane Protection Project," GAO/PSAD-76–161, Washington, DC, August 31, 1976, and GAO, "Improved Planning Needed by the Corps of Engineers to Resolve Environmental, Technical, and Financial Issues on the Lake Pontchartrain Hurricane Protection Project," GAO/MASAD-82-39, Washington, DC, August 17, 1982.

project costs had grown to $757 million and the expected completion date had slipped to 2008, ten years beyond the original date planned. As of 2005, estimates of the completion date were being extended to 2015—nearly 50 years after the project was first authorized. The need to protect New Orleans from hurricanes greater than Category 3 was an increasingly serious concern.

Given the nearly 300 years of settlement in New Orleans and the surrounding areas, it is undoubtedly beside the point to suggest that citizens of Louisiana could have simply taken Gilbert White's warnings literally,

---

In defense of USACE's role in how the HPS came to progress 'in fits and starts,' Dr. Lewis E. Link, University of Maryland, IPET Project Director, and Dr. John J. Jaeger, P.E., USACE, IPET Technical Director, point out that the first 17 years of the project focused on a "barrier plan"—a series of levees along the lake front, concrete floodwalls along the IHNC, control structures such as barriers and flood control gates at The Rigolets and Chef Menteur Pass—intended to prevent storm surges from entering Lake Pontchartrain and overflowing the levees along the lake front. Project delays and cost increases occurred as a result of technical issues, environmental concerns, legal challenges, and local opposition to various aspects of the project. A December 1977 court decision enjoined the Corps from constructing the barrier complexes and other parts of the project until a revised environmental impact statement was prepared and accepted. The Corps conducted a "Re-Evaluation Study," published in 1984, in response to the court order, and recommended shifting to the "high level plan" (raising and strengthening levees and floodwalls) originally considered in the early 1960s. Considered (but not built) were butterfly surge gates and pump stations at the lake ends of the drainage canals as well as the use of parallel protection levees and floodwalls along the length of the canals as the sole protection measure. The Energy and Water Development Act of 1992 mandated the use of "parallel protection," which resulted in construction of the levee and I-wall structures in place at the time of Katrina. USACE also points out that the original authorization for protection occurred in 1965, but the final resolution of how to provide protection for a large portion of New Orleans was not determined until 1992, over a quarter of a century later. Thus, construction of the HPS was accomplished only in many separate steps over a long period of time. The first structures were the levees and floodwalls within the IHNC in the late 1960s; construction of floodwalls along the outfall drainage canals occurred from 1993 to 1999; of 10 flood-proof bridges, nine were completed. More important was the fact the protection for Pump Station No. 7 on the Orleans Avenue Canal and Pump Station No. 3 on the London Avenue Canal remained to be done at the time of Katrina. The lack of fronting protection for Pump Station No. 7 left a section of older wall significantly lower than adjacent walls, providing a route for water to enter the city without overtopping. This work had been terminated due to lack of funding, an omission that left a weak link which compromised flood protection. USACE also notes that some components of the HPS (in the West Bank and Vicinity Project) were *not scheduled* to be completed until 2015. Thus, *"at no time has the entire New Orleans and Vicinity area had a reasonably uniform level of protection around its perimeter. At no time has any individual parish or basin had the full authorized protection planned for in 1965 . . . The history of this HPS has been one of continuous incompleteness."*(italics mine) See IPET Vol. I, I–26–28.

and moved elsewhere—perhaps to Arkansas or to Kansas. New Orleans has 300 years of history, 300 years of a unique culture that has flourished, even with all its warts and corruptions. Perhaps it is also beside the point to hold that the *entire concept* of a 'Lake Pontchartrain and Vicinity Hurricane Protection Project' was flawed from the start—a dream of the imagination that could never be executed in reality. Yet, those living their lives, working and raising families in New Orleans, are part of that reality. Perhaps it is beside the point to suggest that development of new suburbs east and west of the city during the 1960s and '70s ought to have been controlled or not allowed to take place. In both New Orleans itself, Jefferson Parish to the west, and the eastern reaches of Orleans Parish, there are no high areas that could be counted on not to flood under extreme storm conditions. Suitable high ground is at least 40 to 60 miles away, with highly limited evacuation routes to get there, even for those who have access to transportation. Yet, in an individualistic, capitalist society, precisely how *would* one be able to stop land acquisition, development, profitability, and greed? How would one have exercised control over the freedom to move by those urban residents who believed a new life in open suburbs would be preferable to existence in a crowded, decaying, sinking city?

The very desire to expand and economically develop new areas east and west of New Orleans was curiously counterbalanced by an argument of frugality. Both the Army Corps of Engineers and the Orleans Parish Levee District Board not only saw massive flooding that might result from a Category 4 or 5 hurricane as an exceedingly rare possibility, they also judged that protection against storms of that magnitude would be prohibitively expensive. Does this reasoning not reveal an inherent underlying contradiction? Moreover, what neither saw was the fact that a well-positioned Category 3 hurricane, combined with design and construction weaknesses in the region's levees and floodwalls could *also* produce massive flooding and destruction and loss of life.

Even if one cannot argue that the *entire concept* of a flood protection system for New Orleans and vicinity was bogus—after all, the Netherlands has successfully protected itself against an equally dangerous North Sea—there are, nevertheless, those who have felt that New Orleans' hurricane and flood protection system was shot full with inherent design weaknesses. For example, Wayne Clough, President of Georgia Institute of Technology and head of the National Academies'[31] National Research Council 16-member Committee on New Orleans Regional Hurricane Protection Projects, requested by the Department of Defense to assess the Katrina disaster, said "Some of these things were poorly designed and were almost pre-ordained to fail." Even after completion, just prior to the 2006 hurricane season, of $800 million in repairs and improvements to the system—tougher concrete floodwalls, installation of drainage canal closure gates that were originally intended in the design of the system—many, including Clough, concluded that New Orleans was still very much at risk. Prof. Clough pointed out that those parts that did not fail in Hurricane Katrina could still have been weakened by stress, and that "just because they've been restored to their condition pre-Katrina doesn't mean they are perfectly safe."[32]

Raymond Seed,[33] Professor of Engineering at the University of California, Berkeley, is one of a number of experts who have studied the accumulation of levees, flood walls, pumps and gates that have been in the process of being built for more than 40 years. While acknowledging that USACE has made the system better and stronger, he doubted it was still 'good enough,' and concluded that the system had *never been adequate* to protect the hundreds of thousands of people who live in an urban setting existing below sea level. The system was *fundamentally flawed*. Even Maj. Gen. Don T. Riley, director of civil works for USACE, said he could not guarantee that the system would not fail again.[34]

Unease that the design of New Orleans' Hurricane Protection System (HPS) has perhaps *always* been fundamentally flawed is compounded by (a) knowledge that Katrina was *not* the worst possible case, and (b) a determination that the amount spent to *rebuild* destroyed and defective levees and flood gates (just under $1 billion) is less than one-tenth the estimates of what it would take to create a thoroughly adequate protection

31. Four organizations comprise the Academies: the National Academy of Sciences, the National Academy of Engineering, the Institute of Medicine, and the National Research Council.

32. John Schwartz, "Levees Rebuilt Just in Time, but Doubts Remain," *The New York Times*, May 25, 2006.

33. Prof. Seed specializes in soil and structure interaction; slope stability and performance of dams and waste fills, and geotechnical earthquake engineering.

34. John Schwartz, "Levees Rebuilt Just in Time, but Doubts Remain," *The New York Times*, May 25, 2006.

system for the city and neighboring parishes. If, by USACE's own admission (and in their defense), the hurricane protection model envisioned is now known as one that was never adequate, how did that come about?

As noted earlier, the Lake Pontchartrain and Vicinity Hurricane Project was intended to protect areas around the lake from flooding caused by storm surge and rainfall associated with a hurricane roughly the same as what is currently classified by the Saffir-Simpson Scale as a fast-moving Category 3 hurricane. The basis for this was the Standard Project Hurricane (SPH) developed by the Weather Bureau (now National Weather Service)—a steady-state storm that does not include consideration of more recently understood storm dynamics, as well as the significance of storm surge and waves generated long before storms reach landfall. Based on data from the period 1900 to 1956, the SPH model represented the most severe storm considered "reasonably characteristic" for the region—a storm with wind speeds assumed to be only 100 miles per hour. After Category 3 Hurricane Betsy flooded New Orleans in 1965, the wind speed criterion was revised upwards, but all other storm characteristics remained the same. When Congress approved New Orleans' Hurricane Protection System, it was based on this 1965 version of the SPH. It was this model that was used in the design of both the Lake Pontchartrain and Vicinity and the New Orleans to Venice Projects. In 1979, when a NOAA report more significantly revised the SPH criteria, these criteria were incorporated into the design of the West Bank and Vicinity Project. However, all design and construction activities for the Lake Pontchartrain and Vicinity Project continued to use the *original* SPH criteria up to the time of Hurricane Katrina.[35]

What begins to emerge is the existence of multiple inherent design problems. From the start, and through implementation of the HPS, the fundamental design criteria were made to a standard that simply fell *considerably short* of the Gulf's most severe storms—Hurricane Camille in 1969, the Labor Day storm of 1935 that impacted the west coast of Florida, or the unnamed storm that devastated Galveston in 1900. There also were no barrier flood gates built at the entrances to the several drainage canals (17th Street, Orleans Avenue, London Avenue) at lakeside to isolate them from the larger bodies of water during a storm. Pumps located at the far ends of the drainage canals, rather than at the lake entrances, had

---

35. See IPET Vol. I, I-26.

been intended for eliminating rainwater from the streets, not keeping the canals themselves from over-flooding during storms. The design and construction of floodwalls themselves (an I-Wall configuration, rather than the stronger T-Wall), as we have seen, was questionable. One is therefore forced to ask: why did this flawed and inadequate model persist with only minor modifications?

Complexity and Unmanageability

The IPET team and others have often noted the enormous complexity of the Louisiana HPS. It is a complexity not only of structural devices, but also of jurisdictions[36] and the processes for managing those devices. In addition to those structures that are *directly* part of various hurricane protection projects, there are components of *other* systems interlinked with the HPS: the levees of the Mississippi River, pump stations, bridges, navigational structures such as locks, spillways, drainage and control structures that all interact in providing the ultimate ability to keep New Orleans from flooding. IPET points out that some of these structures are not part of the HPS and fall under different jurisdictions, which makes their management during storm or flooding conditions more complicated.[37]

Correlated to issues of complexity within the HPS and other systems are issues that relate to the data upon which design specs were formed. As one example, because of the complex and variable rates of subsidence in Southeast Louisiana, it is difficult to establish accurate vertical references for measurements. The IPET team was able to accelerate and use work more recently developed by USACE and NOAA's National Geodetic Survey (NGS) to employ global positioning system (GPS) technology in defining reference points within the region. However, this technology was not available through the design phase and most of the implementation of the HPS.

Subsidence and Erosion

Some of the root causes of failure within New Orleans' HPS could be regarded as natural, and, therefore, unavoidable occurrences. The continual, but irregularly located, subsidence of land masses in Southeast Louisiana,

---

36. Levee boards and USACE, city commissions and parish government, state authorities and federal agencies.

37. IPET Vol I, I–30.

coupled with an additional rising of sea level from global warming and other factors, has resulted in often unpredictable variations of Local Mean Sea Level (LMSL), and. therefore, significant differences of elevation across the HPS. IPET points out that the elevations of many of the current hurricane protection structures are well below their originally authorized heights. A significant contributing factor to this is the natural, unpredicted, and often rapid subsidence of the land.[38]

However, there are other—non-natural—factors as well: basic errors in the elevations of initial constructions *at the time of their construction*; sections where authorized hurricane protection structures were not in place at all. The IPET team provided two maps (Figures 5 and 6, IPET Vol. I) comparing pre-Katrina HPS structure elevations to authorized elevations for the New Orleans metropolitan area and West Bank as part of its risk assessment data. Levees, floodwalls, and other HPS structures at or above authorized levels are shown in green; those 0 to 2 feet below authorized elevations are shown in yellow; those greater than 2 feet below authorized levels are shown in red. It is immediately apparent that the reds and yellows have won out. By themselves, the reds (sections *more than 2 feet below* proper elevation level) comprise a third to nearly one-half the combined total of below-grade yellows and reds.

Particular areas of significant natural subsidence have occurred along the IHNC. But the floodwalls along the several drainage canals that flooded were *constructed* to elevations nearly 2 feet below the original intent because of errors in relating the local geodetic datum (land elevation reference) to the water level datum (mean sea level).[39] That is, some flood control structures were *authorized* and designed relative to mean sea level, but *constructed* relative to the geodetic vertical datum incorrectly assumed to be equivalent to the water level datum, resulting, in the case of those drainage canals, with structures being built 2 feet below the intended elevation. Thus, one root cause of incorrect elevations of some floodwalls was datum misinterpretation, and a misunderstanding of the variability of subsidence in the New Orleans area.[40]

Other natural contributors to failures include erosion and scouring. Erosion is seen on the sides of earthen levees from the effects of rain or

38. Ibid.
39. IPET Vol. I, I–31.
40. Ibid., I–61.

wind-driven rain on soil that is not covered (or fully covered) by vegetation. Rills and parallel shallow, twisting depressions are what remain after soil and other material has been washed away. Scouring refers to the process by which, typically below grade or water level, the action of moving water itself gradually weakens and begins to clear channels through earthen structures or the bases of man-made structures by flushing against them. This can occur during storm conditions, but also from tidal movements.

Of the fifty major breaches in New Orleans' HPS, IPET identifies four as having been caused by foundation-induced failures, and the remainder from a combination of overtopping and scour. Three of the four foundation breaches occurred in the drainage canals, one in the IHNC.[41] I-wall structures were especially vulnerable because of their lack of horizontal base support members. Levees constructed from hydraulic fill, composed of, or invaded by, organic material were also vulnerable, particularly where they ended in transition to other types of flood protection structures. Some weaknesses in levee foundation material were due to natural factors; some were not.

Implementation Limitations

Thus far we have uncovered multiple causes of failure in the Hurricane Protection System for Orleans and surrounding parishes: errors and limitations in the fundamental conceptual model (the level of storm protection); detailed design flaws (type and location and completeness of HPS structures); natural forces of subsidence and erosion; human misinterpretation of data and lack of understanding of natural forces. However, the root causes of other errors occurred because of various kinds of implementation failures. Implementation failures are perhaps most difficult to ferret out—and have been among those most heatedly contested—because it is here that design specifications, USACE implementation, and sub-contracted piece-work have come into conflict.

Two implementation failures were relatively observable: there were sections of the HPS simply never completed, and there were sections of the HPS not built to intended elevation specs—including floodwalls built below intended heights because of data misinterpretation. But there were other implementation failures as well. Some of these involved construc-

41. Ibid., I–41.

tion using I-walls instead of the more stable T-wall or L-wall design because of cost limitations; some were foundation-induced failures due to erroneous assumptions about the soil strength for clay underlayers, or the use of a mixture of clay, sand, and organic materials for foundations; some involved the lack of armoring on the sides of levees to reduce the effects of erosion and scouring; some were simply shoddy construction. In the case of the 17th Street Canal breach, for example, even though water levels were below the designed elevations, a crack on the water side of the floodwall allowed high pressures of water to be introduced directly into the foundation materials of the levee. These materials, being porous beach sand, quickly conveyed the pressure under the levee, resulting in subsurface erosion, and, eventually, a blowout on the protected side through which quantities of sand and water flowed.

Did the *type* of construction of components of the floodwall protection system really matter? Was there any value of cost-saving by using I-walls vs. T-walls? In fact, that there were no T-wall failures with the exception of one small section in southern Plaquemines Parish.[42] Clearly, cost saving was costly. Not only in the present, but in the future, since the vast majority of floodwalls were I-wall structures.

It is not the intention of this work, post-hoc, to assess the existence or degree of missteps in implementation or shoddy sub-contracted work on all the various structures and components of New Orleans' HPS. However, one investigation revealed that, even during the initial construction phase of the seventeenth Street floodwall, the sub-contracted construction company had complained about the quality of the soil. In a lawsuit against USACE dating from 1993, when the floodwalls were upgraded, Pittman Construction Company argued that the Corps had not provided enough information about problems with the soil at the 17th Street Drainage Canal. These soils, which turned out to be weak and shifting and unstable, caused difficulties pouring the concrete for the floodwalls. Pittman also found problems with 12 of 257 sheet steel pilings which had tilted and were out of tolerance. The Corps allowed a variance and accepted the work; Pittman claimed it had incurred cost overruns and was seeking relief. Although the court ruled in favor of the Corps, it was among the implementation issues that gave post-Katrina investigators clues that there were serious problems of instability and seepage with

---

42. See IPET Vol I, I-46–47.

the floodwall foundation soils. In fact, the Corps' original environmental statement from 1982 described soil in the lakefront area as a thin layer of soft clay underlain by silty sands and peat. But peat, as organic matter which decomposes, compresses, and subsides, is an excellent path of least resistance for water erosion and intrusion. Structures built on such soil can tilt, break, slide, float, sink.[43]

IPET acknowledges that all the structures in New Orleans' HPS are constructed on weak and compressible soils, but sees the majority of the structures built as designed. Among the foundation soil issues that account for failures at the 17th Street Drainage Canal, in particular, is IPET's conclusion that the soil strengths were derived from *too widely spaced* borings, at times using average values that did not capture the high variability of soil strengths. Similarly, there were assumptions of uniform shear strengths based on greater densities under the centerline of the levee, applied incorrectly, as an overestimation, to subsurface strength at the levee toe (the outer portions of the base).

Overall, it seems clear that New Orleans' Hurricane Protection System did not perform *as a system*. Hurricane protection was designed and developed in piecemeal fashion, resulting in inconsistent levels of protections.[44] As just one example, the majority of the pumping stations were not part of the HPS—they were put in place to deal with rainwater flooding, and were not designed to provide the pumping capacity that would be needed during large storms.

Finally, the assumption of an altogether inadequate 'Standard Project Hurricane' only made the integrative success of the 'system' under the conditions of a Category 3 hurricane like Katrina doomed. One can only wonder about the devastation that would have occurred had a hurricane with the same track as that of Katrina made landfall as a Category 4 or 5 storm.

Bureaucracy Captured in Its Own Process Web

A further root cause is one not likely to appear within the IPET study, but it is a concern that has been voiced by scientists who have observed the functioning and behavior of USACE, as representative of one federal agency, over the years. When experts and even other federal agencies have urged the Corps to built to higher standards, Corps officials have not

43. van Heerden, *The Storm*, 231–34.
44. See IPET Vol I, I–63.

changed course. The general response from Corps officials has often been that they build what Congress authorizes them to build, and that shifting large projects is difficult once they are under way. Ivor van Heerden, a founder of LSU's Hurricane Center, has said, "the Corps, once it's locked on a track, will not take input from outside groups."[45] What this entails is a dimension to endemic problems in New Orleans' Hurricane Protection System that is not only local but national in scope.

Absent a National Academy of Public Administration or Brookings study, it is not possible to determine the validity of judgments such as those of Ivor van Heerden.[46] However, other media investigators have pointed to USACE organizational behaviors that are in line with the criticisms of van Heerden. For example, much of the Corps' funding appears to originate through 'earmarks,' individual projects requested by members of Congress, although orders, as with the rest of the military, are generally funneled through the Executive branch. Some elements of those 'earmarked' projects may only marginally relate to the intended purpose; one project, as claimed by Michael Grunwald, a *Washington Post* reporter who won the Worth Bingham Prize for investigative coverage of the Corps, involved a "little-used navigation channel that actually amplified Katrina's surge."[47] Grunwald cites five instances as examples of what he calls the "dysfunction of the Corps": (1) its 100-year commitment to a war with the Mississippi River using massive levees; (2) its culture, captured in its motto *essayons* (let us try), of being in love with building projects for their own sake, often to the benefit of influential allies in industry or Congress; (3) building levees that destroy wetlands to hasten urbanization and industrialization, as we have previously discussed; (4) designing Mississippi River levees for an 800-year storm, but hurricane protection (originally) for only a 200-year storm; (5) shoddy engineering such as failing to fight for floodgates to keep Lake Pontchartrain out of the city's drainage canals. The Corps has some awareness of such criticisms of its bureaucratic cul-

45. Remark from communication with van Heerden, and also quoted in Schwartz, "Levees Rebuilt Just in Time, but Doubts Remain," *The New York Times*, May 25, 2006.

46. Whose outspoken book, *The Storm*, made van Heerden a hero to many, but an annoyance to LSU vice chancellors for threatening the university's research funding from the federal government.

47. Michael Grunwald, "Rotten to the Corps. The Army Corps of Engineers is the real culprit behind New Orleans' devastation," August 29, 2006, posted on the environmental news and commentary website, *grist*, www.grist.org/comments/soapbox/2006/08/29/grunwald.

ture. Among its recently adopted "12 Actions for Change" is the directive: "Assess and modify organizational behavior."[48]

USACE has been found to be lacking in other areas of its management functions by the United States Government Accountability Office (GAO). On March 16, 2006, GAO presented a report to Congress, "Agency Management of Contractors Responding to Hurricanes Katrina and Rita."[49] Under the Comptroller General's statutory authority, GAO conducted an assessment of how three agencies—the General Services Administration (GSA), the Federal Emergency Management Agency (FEMA), and the U.S. Army Corps of Engineers (USACE)—planned for and conducted oversight of several key contracts in support of Katrina and Rita response and recovery efforts. The report found failures in three areas: inadequate planning and preparation to anticipate requirements for needed goods and services; lack of clearly communicated responsibilities across agencies and jurisdictions; insufficient numbers and inadequate deployment of personnel to provide for effective contractor oversight. While much of the report focused on FEMA, USACE was called out for poor inter-agency communication and inadequate oversight of contract personnel in its management of Operation Blue Roof for FEMA.[50]

Fatalism

New Orleanians have always had a sense of living on the edge of potential disaster. In the past, this has been perceived as quite distant, or, at least, occurring only at great intervals; now, after Katrina, it is recognized as all too present and real. This attitude is a curious bricolage of fatalism, necessity, and bravado. Recall from Chapter 2, Pat Gomez, manager of Aunt Sally's Original Creole Pralines, who remarked to local media, "You're almost fatalistic, part of the reason New Orleans has that mixture of frivolity and fatalism." Historically, residents of New Orleans have had a certain 'blindness,' a way of looking at the odds and figuring that living at nature's mercy is worth the risk.

However, what is unfortunate is that government leaders, themselves, have often fallen victim, not only to the lure of fatalistic 'blindness,' but to

48. Cited by Grunwald.

49. GAO-060461R Management of Katrina Contractors.

50. Operation Blue Roof provided assistance to storm victims through installation of rolled plastic sheeting on damaged roofs.

a more inexcusable ignoring of basic facts. We have seen, in analyzing some of technical causes for failures in New Orleans' HPS, problems of scale (Marker 4) so vast, so complex no one has successfully been able to envisage how the various components of what are, in fact, multiple systems of flood and hurricane protection (not a single integrated system) can work together in a coherent fashion. Ultimately, there may be simply the *blind faith* that the federal government will take responsibility, bail them out. Unfortunatly, Katrina has shown the folly of that faith, with the debacle of FEMA's utterly *uncoordinated* response.

Pretend Preparedness

In chapter 2, we discussed the July 2004 FEMA and Louisiana Office of Homeland Security and Emergency Preparedness five-day exercise, 'Hurricane Pam.' Pam was based on a scenario of sustained winds of 120 mph, 20 inches of rain, storm surge that topped levees, one million residents evacuated, and 5-600,000 buildings destroyed. Emergency officials from fifty parish, state, federal, and volunteer organizations at the State Emergency Operations Center in Baton Rouge congratulated themselves on a successful exercise. Perhaps those congratulations were somewhat premature.

SOCIAL DIMENSIONS OF DISASTER

Thus far, some of the major effects of Hurricane Katrina have been considered in terms of their geo-physical causes and effects: proximate causes, and some of the more significant root causes of problems in design and implementation. We have also considered issues of organizational structures, particularly involving USACE. All of these continue to manifest themselves along with the legacy of flooding and destruction laid bare by the storm. Perhaps even more important, however, are the broader *social dimensions* of Katrina's legacy. There are two elements to which we will give particular attention.

The first and most obvious consists of the major demographic shifts in Orleans Parish and the surrounding metropolitan area following Hurricane Katrina. These shifts pertain not only to the population as a whole, but also to racial balance, economic consequences, and quality of life *within* the total population. These effects were not distributed evenly across Orleans Parish after Katrina, nor were they in Coastal Louisiana after Hurricane Rita. To the extent they can be known, we will attempt to consider effects of demographic changes on particular neighborhoods within the City of New Orleans. A more selective discussion of the effects of both Katrina and Rita on communities along the Gulf coast occurs in chapter 10.

The second element considered concerns leadership, and early post-disaster planning attempts, particularly in the context of the New Orleans mayoral primary and runoff election in the spring of 2006. This was the first significant election post-Katrina. Did it become an occasion to seriously consider the many problems facing the city and propose possible models for its future, or did it deflect those issue into others, such as race, and become politics as usual?

Throughout the remainder of this chapter, and again in chapters 7 and 8, we will continually return to concerns about housing and healthcare—perhaps the two most significant areas of ambiguity that face those still-displaced citizens who are contemplating return to their former homes and neighborhoods. Is there a *home* to return to? Is there even a *neighborhood* to return to, or merely the *residue* of one—a neighborhood of gaps or still largely empty houses, except for a few scattered attempts at renovation here and there? And what about *healthcare*? Is there an environment of safety to return to: primary care clinics, treatment for chronic illnesses, a semblance of fire or emergency medical services?

The availability of low-income housing became—and remains—a particularly complex human and logistical problem for former residents, and a social and ethical problem for the city, with HUD/HANO's plans not to reopen but to raze almost all of the city's public housing developments. Serious concerns about 'fairness' arose in post-disaster proposals to shift public housing units into 'mixed-income' complexes that would be economically more attractive to developers. Perceptions of the 'fairness' of such plans varied enormously, depending on where on New Orleans' social ladder one stood. In June, 2006, for example, marchers demonstrated in the streets of the French Quarter to protest HUD's plans to privatize public housing, excluding African Americans and working class poor from affordable housing, and preventing them from returning home. After months of fencing off and shuttering public housing, when HUD announced plans for the demolition of the St. Bernard, C. J. Peete, B.W. Cooper, and Lafitte housing developments to be replaced by 'mixed-income' housing—a combination of public housing with rental housing and single-family houses—it was met with outcry. 'Mixed-income' housing would provide too few units for low-income people. "We are tired of seeing our neighborhoods demolished and replaced by housing for wealthier people," said Pamela Mahogany, resident of the St. Bernard housing project who was trying to return home. Cherlynn Gaynor, who grew up in the Lafitte project, argued that "by tearing down developments you're not giving me the choice to come back home to New Orleans, where I was forced to leave."[51] The French Quarter demonstrations were sponsored by the United Front for Affordable Housing and the Citywide Tenant Association.

Housing and healthcare have remained the two most fundamental questions for displaced residents. Beyond any particular economic means of support, there must first be a place to live from which one can *go to* work, and the assurance there are hospitals able to provide care for the high frequency of chronic conditions, such as diabetes, COPD, and those needing kidney dialysis. Health and home are the basics.

Demographics

The Greater New Orleans Community Data Center (GNOCDC)[52] provides extremely useful data and population estimates for Orleans Parish and neighboring parishes, some of which was used in discussion of New Orleans' neighborhood characteristics. There, among other things, we looked at changes in Planning District population figures and racial proportions for the period 1980 to 2002. The following demographic assess-

51. Quotes from "Mixed-income housing demonstrations continue," *The Louisiana Weekly*, June 26, 2006. Subsequently, on June 27, in New Orleans, Baton Rouge, and Houston, further demonstrations led to the filing of a civil rights lawsuit alleging HANO/HUD was preventing low-income families from returning to the city. Sabrina Williams of the Advancement Project said, "the move by federal officials to demolish 5,000 public housing buildings in New Orleans would sabotage the chance for the mostly low-income, Black displaced population to return home . . . For years HUD and HANO have been squeezing Black families out of the city . . ." See Christopher Tidmore, "Public Housing Redevelopment Sparks Multi-City Protest & Lawsuit," *The Louisiana Weekly*, July 3, 2006. The reconstitution of the St. Thomas Housing Project as 'mixed-income' housing has served as a test case for both HUD's and Mayor Nagin's belief that by replacing blighted parts of the city with middle and upper income residents living alongside those with less, a demographic cross section will be created that will bring in investment and economic growth. By design, 60 percent of reconstructed St. Thomas is targeted to middle income or higher renters; 30 percent to middle wage earners, and slightly more than 30 percent to the very poor.

52. A product of the Greater New Orleans Nonprofit Knowledge Works, accessible at http://www.gnocdc.org/census_pop_estimates.html.

ment from GNOCDC, U.S. Census data, American Community Survey (ACS) census data, the Louisiana Public Health Institute, Brookings, and other sources summarizes some of the more significant findings that compares data for 2005 with that of a year later in 2006, and, for certain sectors, into the fall of 2007.

Population

In 2005, the total population of Orleans Parish was estimated to be 452,170 as of July 1. At that same time in 2006, the population had been reduced to 223,388, a loss of 50.6 percent, or 228,782 persons. The figures for St. Bernard Parish were even more striking. On July 1, 2005, the total population of St. Bernard Parish was estimated to be 65,148; a year later in 2006, it was only 15,514, a loss of 76.2 percent, or 49,634 persons. The data for household population (total population excluding students, assisted living facilities, and other transient residents) is comparable, but adds additional time reference points. Household population for Orleans Parish on July 1, 2005, was 453,493. By January, 2006, it had been reduced to 158,353, a loss of 63.4 percent or 276,140 persons; in July of 2006, it had risen to 215,399, a loss of 218,094 persons, or 50.4 percent, a figure comparable to that of the total population. Household population for St. Bernard Parish on July 1, 2005, was estimated to be 64,359. By January, 2006, it had been reduced to 3,361, a loss of 94.8 percent, or 60,988 persons; in July of 2006, it had risen to 15,344, a loss of 49,015 persons, or 76.2 percent, also comparable to that of the total population figures.

Population figures for public school enrollments are equally striking. As of October, 2004, 66,372 students were enrolled in Orleans Parish public schools. In January of 2006, there were only 6,242 students enrolled, a loss of 90.6 percent, or 66,372 students. By February of 2007, public school enrollment stood at 26,165, still a loss of 60.6 percent, or 26,165 students. St. Bernard Parish fared just as poorly. As of October, 2004, 8,872 students were enrolled in St. Bernard Parish public schools. In January of 2006, there were only 955 students enrolled, a loss of 89.2 percent. By February of 2007, public school enrollment stood at 3,764, still a loss of 57.6 percent, or 5,108 students.

The Greater New Orleans Data Center has also tracked the impact of Hurricane Katrina on who had control of New Orleans' public schools. Following Katrina, the State of Louisiana took over a large number of New Orleans public schools, put them under the Recovery School District jurisdiction, and began chartering many schools out to various organizations. By the end of the 2005–2006 school year, there were four different groups of chartering schools. The Orleans Parish School Board also began chartering out many of the schools that were still under its jurisdiction. As of April, 2007, there were 21 schools directly run by the Recovery School District (RSD), plus 11 independent charter schools under the authority of the RSD, and 6 schools of the Algiers Charter School Association, also under the RSD. The Orleans Parish School Board (OPSB) directly ran 4 schools; another 13 independent charter schools operated under the OPSB. Finally, there were two totally independent charter schools: the International School of Louisiana, and the Milestone SABIS Academy of New Orleans.

Initial numbers for the impact of Hurricane Katrina on racial distribution were made available by the 2006 Louisiana Health and Population Survey, conducted by the Louisiana Public Health Institute (LPHI) for the Louisiana Department of Health and Hospitals.[53] Using the American Community Survey (ACS) of census data, in its report of January 17, 2006, LPHI estimates the household population of Orleans Parish in October, 2006 at 191,139, with a 9.6 percent margin of error. It compares the percentage of black residents at 67.9 percent of the total population in 2004 with that of only 47.0 percent in October, 2006.[54] This early data has tended to contribute to the belief by many that New Orleans had become a white majority city again after Katrina.[55] The survey's figures for household population of St. Bernard Parish are comparable to those above. However, in contrast to the considerable racial shift in Orleans Parish, the racial distribution in St. Bernard Parish remained roughly the same before and after Katrina. ACS data showed that whites made up 89.3 percent of the population of St. Bernard Parish in 2004, blacks 7.7 percent, and Asian 1.3 percent. In October, 2006, whites still made up 87.6 percent of the total population, blacks 7.3 percent; Asians dropped to 0.0 percent.[56] Thus, the

53. Louisiana Public Health Institute, "2006 Louisiana Health and Population Survey," January 17, 2007. Survey conducted for the Louisiana Department of Health and Hospitals.

54. With a margin of error of 6.2 percent.

55. Not, in fact, born out. New Orleans has remained a black majority city, although by a reduced margin.

56. With a margin of error of approximately 4.0 percent.

population of St. Bernard Parish, was, and remained, almost exclusively white, despite its radical loss of overall population.

In the two years that have passed since Hurricane Katrina, the numerous efforts to identify just how many people are actually living in Orleans and surrounding parishes—including racial distribution, economic status, repopulation of particular neighborhoods—have been fraught with ambiguity and, often, little solid information. A partnership between the Brookings Institution and the Greater New Orleans Community Data Center (GNOCDC) has worked to provide a more statistically reliable basis for this demographic information, using the 2006 American Community Survey (ACS) of the U.S. Census Bureau in comparison with 2000 ACS measures and IRS data to examine who migrated out and who came back to New Orleans. Its most significant finding was that, one year after the storm. while the black population of Orleans Parish had declined by 57 percent and the white population by only 36 percent, New Orleans remained a minority majority city, with blacks making up 58 percent of its population. In 2005, the white population of New Orleans was 119,620; the black population was 302,580. In July, 2006, the white population was reduced by 43,198 to 76, 422, a 36 percent decline; the black population was reduced by 173,388 to 129,192, a decline of 57 percent. However, while the black proportion of the city's total population decreased from 67 to 58 percent, and the white proportion increased from 26 to 34 percent, in the year after the storm, the city's black population remained in the majority.[57] This data provided evidence contrary to the speculation by many analysts and politicians that the city might shift back to being a white majority city from its both historic and recent tradition as a black majority city.

Also significant are the Brookings-GNOCDC findings that, while New Orleans' post-storm population, as of July 2006, was older, better off economically, had fewer households with children, and was more likely to be white than as recorded in the 2000 Census, those dispersed from greater New Orleans after the storm who remained 'out-migrants' were younger, poorer, represented more households with children, and were more likely to be black. These factors weigh on considerations about how

57. Frey, William H., et. al., "Resettling New Orleans: The First Full Picture from the Census," The Brookings Institution Metropolitan Policy Program, September, 2007, Table 1. New Orleans' Hispanic population increased by 1 percent during the year; other racial-ethnic groups remained the same.

the voices of those who have remained in the post-hurricane *diaspora* can be captured and incorporated into the processes of reconstruction planning and implementation—issues that will be discussed in Chapters 7, 8, and 9. For example, the Brookings-GNOCDC report suggests that those households in the diaspora who have children may be more reluctant to move back into the city, since there is greater representation in the city's post-hurricane population by married couples without children and persons living alone. With the status of public and charter schools for all neighborhoods still very much up in the air; with uncertainties about public safety, fire and emergency medical services, as well as all the other extended services important to school-age children, such reluctance to return is indeed understandable.

The Brookings-GNOCDC report was also able to make some determinations about where those who left New Orleans moved. Lower income, black 'displaced' residents were likely to be living further away from the New Orleans metropolitan area—particularly in cities like Houston, Dallas, and Atlanta. White displaced residents, on the other hand, tended to move elsewhere within the greater New Orleans metropolitan area.[58] This not only has made it easier for those 'nearby displaced' residents to ultimately return to New Orleans, it has also made it easier for them to keep in touch with what has or has not been going on in the process of post-disaster recovery and reconstruction. 'Nearby displaced' residents, for example, would have access to local television and news reports; they would be more easily able to participate in city-wide and neighborhood political processes. Nearly 80 percent of moves back to the city in the 2005—2006 period were from suburbs of greater metropolitan New Orleans or elsewhere in Louisiana; only 7 percent of returnees came from Texas.

Both from the hard data that exists, and also from the authors' conversations with current and former residents of New Orleans and other anecdotal accounts, one begins to build a picture of what those who have been unable to return to the city, and to their extended families, face. In many respects, the reasons fall under the broader canopy of 'lack of in-

58. The greatest out-migration destination, in the 2005-2006 period, was Houston (Harris County) TX, where 19.5 percent of all out-migrants landed. Those migrating to Houston had an average household adjusted gross income (AGI) of $19,602.00. Second highest as a destination was Jefferson Parish, where 13.2 percent of all out-migrants located; their household AGI was $33,304. Dallas, TX (Dallas, Tarrant, and Collin Counties) was the relocation point for 8.7 percent of all out-migrants; Baton Rouge was next at 6.8 percent, then the Atlanta, GA area (Fulton, De Kalb, and Cobb Counties) at 4.0 percent.

formation about future conditions'—perhaps it would be better to say the lack of a 'communication loop.' Such a communication loop is a two-way process: it includes not only valid information *from* New Orleans—about what, in fact, is going on in their home neighborhoods there; it also includes the 'return cycle'—input from the voices of displaced residents *to* the leaders of various processes of recovery and reconstruction.

Many people have not returned because they are uncertain about the public schools—already in trouble before Katrina, with 47 percent rated as academically unacceptable, and 26.5 percent under an 'academic warning' in the 2004–2005 school year.[59] People have also not returned because they are waiting on Road Home funding to be able to repair or rebuild their homes; waiting for endless arguments with insurers to be resolved; waiting to learn what building permits are necessary to allow them to begin to rebuild; waiting for some assurance that nearby levees and floodwalls on which their neighborhoods depend will be able to protect them. People have not returned because they have lost a better paying job than they could secure if they returned. People have not returned because the city lacks adequate medical services for both primary care and more serious or chronic medical conditions; because it lacks sufficient fire protection and EMS services; because it lacks a police force that is capable of dealing with a radical increase in crime, including murder. Because they are afraid. Because they are tired and exhausted. Because the future conditions are so uncertain—the actual wood and brick and concrete progress on reconstruction efforts only slugging along, if, indeed, it is visibly happening at all. Grand plans like the Unified New Orleans Plan (UNOP), individuals given titles such as Recovery Czar like Edward Blakely, have not produced, in the eyes of those with whom we have spoken, any visible or real transformations.

These same uncertainties are reflected in repopulation estimates from one neighborhood to the next, made a little more than a year after Hurricane Katrina. While not at the level of statistical confidence present in the data analyzed by the Brookings report, these estimates by the GNOCDC do provide evidence that those areas most affected by the Katrina flooding—in many cases also those neighborhoods of poorer African Americans least in a position to easily recover from the storm's devastation—are the particular areas of the City of New Orleans that

---

59. Information from GNOCDC.

have least been able to repopulate to their pre-Katrina levels. At the high end of repopulation estimates are Planning Districts 1 (French Quarter, CBC) and 12 (Algiers), both at 96 percent. These were areas of the city that received the least amount of damage. At the other end of repopulation estimates are Planning District 8 (Lower Ninth Ward) at only 6 percent, Planning District 9 (New Orleans East) at 30 percent, and Planning District 6 (Gentilly) at 37 percent. Also near the lower end of the repopulation spectrum is the largely white, middle-class Planning District 5 (Lakeview) at 38 percent. Even a year beyond these estimates, in September, 2007, repopulation in the Lower Ninth Ward has not risen to much more than 7 or 8 percent.

Do those who project New Orleans' populations into the future see reasons for optimism? In providing recovery assessment for the Unified New Orleans Plan (UNOP), GCR & Associates, Inc. (GCR) attempted to ascertain both present and future population projections for New Orleans so that "intelligent planning and investment decisions may be made . . . without any biases and with as dispassionate a perspective as is possible."[60] GCR & Associates, established in 1979, is a planning firm based in New Orleans and Covington that provides services and software for aviation planning, urban and transit planning, resolving issues of real estate and right-of-way, and, most recently, disaster recovery consulting and brownfields data management. In making these projections, GCR evaluated FEMA inspection reports and trailer counts, building permit activity, and various economic analyses. Its generated three projection 'models'—what it called low, moderate, and high scenarios—to create a range of expectations, noting that the outcomes of the Unified New Orleans Plan process would have a considerable effect on the scale and nature of redevelopment efforts. In contrast with the City of New Orleans' Emergency Operations Center (EOC) "rapid population estimating survey" done at the end of January, 2006, GCR began with the premise that the impact of flooding upon the housing stock—in which those neighborhoods that were spared flooding have recovered rapidly, while in those areas that did flood, observable recovery activity is inversely proportional to the depth of flooding—established a ceiling on the pace of recovery and the rate at which neighborhoods could be anticipated to recover. GCR's projected population for New Orleans for January 1, 2008, ranged city-wide from a low of 53

60. The Unified New Orleans Plan (hereafter UNOP), 29 January, 2007, Appendix D, Citywide Baseline Recovery Assessment, 12.

percent of its pre-Katrina population to a high of 59 percent. For January 1, 2009, it ranged from a low of 59 percent to a high of 67 percent (or a maximum population of 323,000). GCR estimated that it would be 10 years out (2017) before New Orleans would even approach its pre-Katrina population level.[61] Thus, even the most optimistic population forecasts do not assume full recovery of severely flood damaged neighborhoods by 2017. One can only conclude that, by that time and one way or another, New Orleans will be a different city.

Housing

The Louisiana Health and Population Survey's data for housing unit damage, revised as of April 7, 2006,[62] is revealing not only of the overall extent of damage, but also in giving some sense of the differentia of housing unit damage that occurred from one neighborhood to the next. In Orleans Parish, of 188,251 occupied units, 71.5 percent, or 134,564, received 'some' damage; 55.9 percent, or 105,323 housing units received 'major or severe' damage. In St. Bernard Parish, of 25,123 occupied units, 80.6 percent, or 20, 247, received some damaged; 78.4 percent, or 19,686 housing units received major or severe damage. For those in Cameron Parish, which experienced the destructive winds of Hurricane Rita, of 3,592 occupied units, 90.2 percent, or 3,241 received some damage; 57.5 percent, or 2,579 housing units received major or severe damage.

Within the New Orleans, housing unit damage was not experienced equally across all areas of the city. This in part results from certain neighborhoods suffering far greater flooding than others, largely by virtue of their lower relative elevation; it is also a consequence of the nature of construction and building materials used in different housing units—resistance to wind damage, for example, and the luck of the draw in being hit by, or avoiding, flying objects. Those neighborhoods suffering the highest percentage of damage to homes, both owner-occupied and renter-occupied, included, in descending order, Village de l'Est (91 percent damage), New Orleans East (90 percent damage), the Lower Ninth Ward (84 percent damage), and Gentilly (81 percent damage). At the other end of the spectrum, those neighborhoods experiencing the least percentage of damage

61. See GCR Tables 2.3 and following, UNOP, Appendix D, 20–23.

62. With data from FEMA individual assistance registrants and Small Business Administration disaster loan applications, and analysis by the U.S. Department of Housing and Urban Development's Office of Policy Development and Research.

to homes were the French Quarter (25 percent damage) and CBD and the Warehouse District (30 percent damage). These neighborhoods were generally those that followed the higher elevation along the river. Roughly in the middle of this range of damage were neighborhoods like Lakeview (72 percent damage) and Bywater (75 percent damage). As GCR's recovery assessment suggests, the level of damage to housing units generally correlates very strongly to rates of returning population. However, largely because of the greater economic means of most residents of Lakeview, despite its high percentage of floodwater damage, Lakeview's rebuilding and repopulation has progressed faster than other neighborhoods with comparable flood damage. One notable exception in the progress of neighborhoods of more modest economic means is Broadmoor. This area also experienced a high percentage of housing damage (77 percent), but in spite of the more constrained economic resources of its residents, Broadmoor has also progressed rather rapidly in rebuilding and repopulating (69 percent repopulation estimate)—due, in part, to the strength of its neighborhood associations and its strong community spirit.

As of November, 2006, there were at least 11,000 FEMA trailers still in the city. Rebuilding has been financed by a combination of private insurance, National Flood Insurance Program claims, SBA loans, and private lenders. The Louisiana Recovery Authority (LRA) has allocated some $4.2 billion to homeowners for repairs, plus an additional $1.8 billion for mixed-income and affordable housing. However, Louisiana's Road Home program disbursement of funds for at least a year after the storms was notoriously slow in gearing up.[63] By the beginning of November, 2006, the Road Home program had received a total of 77,281 applications of which 61,544 had been recorded, but only 16,370 appointments to evalu-

---

63. 'The Road Home' program, operating from Baton Rouge, was created by Gov. Blanco, the Louisiana Recovery Authority, and the Office of Community Development, and approved by the Louisiana Legislature, was intended to help residents of Hurricanes Katrina and Rita get back into their homes as quickly and fairly as possible. The program affords eligible homeowners up to $150,000 in compensation for their losses to get back into their homes. Among the factors complicating and slowing disbursements have been the application process itself, as well as information about the criteria for eligibility. The program has tried to develop a registry of local building professionals to deal with various scams and regulation changes. Also complicating the process has been the fact that homeowners do not receive checks directly; instead, financial awards are placed in a disbursement account and funds are released as related expenses are incurred.

ate those applications were held, and only 675 awards (averaging $57,760) had been calculated.[64]

For those unfortunate enough to have been renters prior to Hurricane Katrina, while New Orleans had not experienced the substantial increases in rental housing prices that occurred in many other cities throughout the United States during the five years preceding 2005, in post-Katrina New Orleans there arose a *severe* crisis of rental housing affordability. Between 2005 and 2006, the range of rental units, from efficiencies to four bedrooms, saw an average increase of 38.9 percent.[65] Moreover, anecdotal accounts suggest that many landlords used the mass forced exodus of the population during Katrina to evict tenants and raise rents. This, in fact, was our own experience in the location of our rented apartment.

Research by *The Times-Picayune* showed the enormous variability of rental increases. In some cases, advertised prices of rental units actually increased by as much as 70 percent after Katrina.[66] Not only did such rental increases limit the ability of thousands of former residents to move back to the city, it also negatively impacted the pace of recovery and re-building, as the ability of skilled construction workers to find affordable housing was also limited.

In terms of public housing, the UNOP recovery assessment report of January 29, 2007, notes that the city had lost almost its entire inventory of affordable housing. Most public housing units were slated to remain closed, and are awaiting demolition and their eventual redevelopment at lower densities.[67] Through early fall of 2007, stable information about the status of specific New Orleans housing development projects has been particularly difficult to secure, not only for us, but also in the minds of many residents of New Orleans with whom we have spoken. Part of this resulted from the fact that the New Orleans' Housing Authority (HANO) has been run directly by the federal agency HUD since 2002. By the end of December, 2007, the picture about which specific housing developments

64. UNOP, Appendix D, 29.

65. Source of data GNOCDC and HUD Fair Market Rents in New Orleans Metro, by Unit Bedrooms, cited in UNOP, Appendix D, 32.

66. From an average of below $800 to $13,357 a month, based on published rents of more than 1,400 properties from nine periods between 2005 and 2006. See J. Meitrodt, "Rising Rent," *The Times-Picayune,* Sunday, October 15, 2006.

67. UNOP, 1.8.

would be demolished was considerably clearer, although distinctly not a happier one for former residents who wished to return.

Chapter 2 pointed to instances in the history of New Orleans in which its public housing failed to meet the needs of residents of limited means, who required some level of subsidization. That should not be surprising, given urban planning of limited vision. The earliest public housing developments, in the process of creating sites for 'urban renewal,' also cleared away neighborhoods of their older, diverse, but still viable working-class housing. In addition, these large housing developments themselves came to contribute to racial segregation, concentrated poverty, high rates of crime, and social disenfranchisement.[68] UNOP's recovery assessment also notes that crime and drugs have plagued HANO's housing developments, with many units dilapidated, run down, and vacant prior to Katrina. Even so, these development units housed more than 12 percent (some 49,000 individuals) of the city's total population. That population did not reflect racial distribution in the city as a whole. According to census data, as well as a Brookings study, between 98 and 100 percent of HANO housing development residents were black.[69]

In several conversations with Jeffrey Riddel, Deputy Administrator (from HUD) of HANO, during August, 2007, we discussed the status of New Orleans' ten major development projects: Between August of 2005 and October of 2006, the number of units in large housing developments had been reduced by over 80 percent (from 7,379 to 1,017). However, HUD/HANO had begun carrying out longer term plans to close and redevelop much of its deteriorating housing projects prior to Katrina. There were at least two HOPE VI programs underway: at the old Desire Development to become a 'New Desire' (Savoy Place), and completion of a reworking of the old St. Thomas Development to become the mixed-income River Garden. Both were close to being finished when Hurricane Katrina struck. In addition, HUD/HANO had begun work on three of its other large housing developments—Fischer, Guste, and Florida—where the plan was to develop some 3,000 mixed-income units that combined traditional public housing with homeownership units and market rate rental units.

68. See, for example, Jed Horne, *Desire Street: A True Story of Death and Deliverance in New Orleans.*

69. See UNOP, Appendix D, 34.

With Jeffrey Riddel, we reviewed the post-storm status, through the summer of 2007, of the large development projects by planning district.[70] In Planning District No. 2, Guste (also known as Melpomene or 'Melph) in Central City, consisted of six three-story buildings of which four were demolished by 2006. One twelve-story high rise for the elderly, renovated in 2002, was mostly open. As of June, 2007, of 82 new affordable mixed-income rental units, 56 were ready for occupancy. HUD/HANO was also in the process of reoccupying 115 of 228 family units in the Guste low-rise complex. C. J. Peete (Magnolia), also in Central City, which housed approximately 2,100 people, was closed and slated for demolition. St. Thomas, in the Irish Channel, was entirely demolished in 2001, except for a few buildings, and had become the mixed-income River Garden. In Planning District No. 4, B. W. Cooper (Calliope), which consisted of 1546 units, for a time had a number of former residents trying to occupy some of

---

70. On October 12, 2007, on the HUD website, http://www.hud.gov/news/editorials/2007-03-19b.cfm, Secretary Alphonso Jackson explained HUD's reasoning. On the premise that every American deserves an opportunity to live in safe communities where children can play and families can thrive and achieve the American dream, New Orleans public housing residents do not deserve the crime-ridden, gang-infested, crumbling buildings that always seem to make their way into the headlines. Hurricane Katrina made a bad situation even worse ... for decades, the properties suffered from neglect and deterioration; many were over 70 years old and had serious maintenance problems. Of the 7379 units in the public housing inventory of the Housing Authority of New Orleans (HANO), only 5146 were occupied. The others had been boarded up and were further deteriorating. HANO had done such a poor job of managing their properties and was unable to account for millions in tax payers dollars, that in 2002 HUD was forced to take over HANO—long before Katrina struck the city. When HUD took it over, it decided to replace the city's public housing with a mixture of traditional public housing, affordable rental housing, and single-family homes, also committing to rent-to-own opportunities. By breaking up concentrations of destitution and crime, HUD felt these mixed-use and mixed-income projects represented the new urban paradigm in many other cities. Since 2002, HUD redeveloped half of New Orleans' largest public housing complexes: St. Thomas, Guste Homes, Abundance Square, (formerly Desire), Fischer and Florida Homes. Residents were either given a new place to live in the redeveloped property or a voucher. When Katrina struck, HUD was making progress toward the redevelopment of B. W. Cooper and C. J. Peete, and had begun the planning process at Lafitte and St. Bernard. Given the massive displacement of residents due to Katrina's destruction of so many homes and the standing water from the broken levees, HUD re-evaluated its redevelopment plans for the remaining projects. Recognizing the urgent need for housing, but after environmental and economic review, HUD decided it made no sense to restore dilapidated buildings that had even more serious problems, including mold, mildew, and severe structural damage. A U.S. district court judge ruled that HUD could move forward with redevelopment.

the units, but was eventually closed and slated for demolition. St. Bernard Development in the Seventh Ward was closed and slated for demolition. Lafitte Development, in Tremé, Sixth Ward, home to over 850 families, was closed and to be demolished, scheduled to be replaced by mixed-income housing. Iberville Development in the Fourth Ward, consisting of 858 units covering ten blocks, reopened. In Planning District No. 7, Desire Development in the Upper Ninth Ward, which had 100 buildings, was completely torn down in 2003, except for two buildings preserved for historical interest. A replacement for the old Desire was undergoing new construction when Katrina hit. Michael's Development Co. of Marlton, NJ, had been chosen by HUD/HANO to build affordable rental housing in the Desire area in phases. As of early 2005, it had built 107 rental units, which were occupied. In February, 2005, Michaels received a $15 million infusion in the $40 million project to build the 318-unit Savoy Place Apartments near the intersection of Alvar Street and Higgins Boulevard. Construction, which had begun in January, was scheduled to end in summer, 2006. Most units would be reserved for residents earning less than 60 percent of the $29,216 median income in Orleans Parish.[71] Katrina destroyed the 107 occupied rental units. In October, 2006, Michael's Development began rebuilding these units. On June 6, 2007, HUD Secretary Jackson and Mayor Ray Nagin opened the first of more than 500 new public housing, mixed-income rental housing and homeownership units to be constructed. The plan for the 'New Desire' included, in addition to the 107 destroyed units being rebuilt, 425 new affordable housing units in three new mixed-income communities—Abundance Square, Treasure Village, and Savoy Place.[72] Florida Development, across from Desire, was closed. In Planning Districts No. 12 and 13, Wm. J. Fischer Development in Algiers consisted of a thirteen-floor high rise, demolished in 2004, and 14 three-floor units that remained.

Thus, four large development projects—B. W. Cooper, C. J. Peete, St. Bernard, and Lafitte—stood in what would become, through the fall and early winter of 2007, a highly contested limbo. In October of 2006, John Fernandez, Associate Professor of Building Technology at MIT's

71. Savoy Place details from "Savoy Place project in New Orleans receives $15M infusion," *New Orleans CityBusiness*, February 28, 2005, http://www.allbusiness.com/personal-finance/real-estate/890548-1.html.

72. See also HUD news release HUD No. 07-081, June 6, 2007, http://www.hud.gov/utilities/print/print2.cfm?page80$^@http%3A%2F%2Fwww%2Ehu.

Department of Architecture, had conducted an assessment of the condition of these four New Orleans' housing projects slated for demolition. Fernandez' particular area of expertise is in the composition and performance of building materials. In his declaration from his inspection and assessment of these housing projects, Fernandez argued that, while he found a range of Katrina-related damage, he did not find any conditions in which the integrity of the structure and exterior envelop of the buildings or the interior conditions of residential units themselves could not be brought to safe and livable conditions. Fernandez also found that a minimum use of cellulose-based (organic) materials in construction significantly aided the very low incidence of moisture retention in the walls and floors of the buildings. Thus, Fernandez concluded that demolition of any of the buildings of these four projects was not supported by the evidence of the survey. Replacement of the buildings with contemporary construction would yield buildings of lower quality and shorter lifetime duration, because the original construction methods and materials of these projects were far superior in their resistance to hurricane conditions than typical new construction. With renovation and regular maintenance, the lifetimes of the buildings in all four projects could provide continued service for decades.[73]

As noted above, there was a period of time in early 2007 when some former residents and activists (such as members of Mayday NOLA) attempted to occupy the community center of the St. Bernard Housing Development. On January 15 (Martin Luther King Day), 2007, the building was taken over by several hundred former residents who broke through the fence surrounding the complex. After HANO/HUD finally closed it, former residents had a difficult time even retrieving their possessions. The perception of many was that the city was simply looking to demolish the complex in order to build up a more profitable housing market.[74]

From post-Katrina developments such as these, one can see that the issues of subsidized public housing are both complex and highly emotional. There have been continuous cycles of acceptance, trust, distrust, attempts to re-establish trust. But it was most of all the bluntness of HUD/

73. Fernandez' declarations available from multiple sources. See, for example, the Gulf Coast Fair Housing Network (http://fairhousingnetwork.org/node/10).

74. See, for example, Anna McRobbie and Logan Price, "St. Bernard residents cleaning up homes despite HANO's hostility," New Orleans Independent Media Center, January 21, 2007, accessible at http://neworleans.indymedia.org/news/2007/01/9522.php.

HANO's decision to abruptly close four public housing developments that, as journalist Nicholai Ouroussoff pointed out, touched a raw nerve.[75] HUD's 'historical amnesia,' in its rush to demolish the complexes and replace them with generic mixed-income suburban-like communities favored by Washington, simply displayed its insensitivity to both displaced tenants and the unique urban fabric of the city. Interestingly, despite their many failures in both construction and upkeep, and even the ill-location of isolated development sites, cut off from the mainstream of the city, there is nevertheless a certain nostalgia that many residents have had for the better among the development projects, such as Lafitte, representing a time in the 1940s of a shared vision of hope for a more humane society.

On February 6, 22, and 23, 2007, the House Committee on Financial Services, chaired by Rep. Barney Frank of Massachusetts, conducted hearings on the federal housing response to Katrina in which HUD had come under fire for its demolition plans. Barney Frank even issued an apology to the residents of Louisiana and Mississippi for what he called "a complete failure of the administration here in Washington to respond to that crisis." Much of the issue turned on the advisability of demolishing these four major complexes with 3,900 housing units, which sustained what many regarded as only minimal damage, at the very time they were needed to be reopened right away. On March 21, 2007, the House passed the Gulf Coast Hurricane Housing Recovery Act of 2007, H.R. 1227, sponsored by Rep. Maxine Waters of California and Barney Frank. If passed by the Senate, and escaping Presidential veto, the bill would end the planned demolition of four public housing projects, guarantee the right of return to public housing residents, and subsidize moving costs for returnees. H.R. 1227 was passed by an overwhelming bipartisan vote of 302 to 125, and, as passed, would order the reopening of 3,000 public housing units by August and mandate one-to-one replacement of all public housing demolished by HUD/HANO, for a total of 7,100 units.

Perhaps most important, underlying the bill was an explicit recognition of the *ethical* basis for citizen participation by guaranteeing involvement of public housing residents in every step of the process. Representative Waters cast the bill as an issue of *fairness*. "Every person

---

75. Nicolai Ouroussoff, "History vs. Homogeneity in New Orleans Housing Fight," *The New York Times*, February 22, 2007.

who desires to live in the Gulf region must be given an opportunity to rebuild and to return home."[76]

On March 23, 2007, H. R. 1227 was received in the Senate and referred to the Committee on Banking, Housing, and Urban Affairs. On June 20, 2007, Senator Christopher Dodd of Connecticut and eight co-sponsors introduced a version of the Gulf Coast housing Recovery Act, S.1668, which was again referred to the Committee on Banking, Housing, and Urban Affairs. Its language was generally consistent with that of H.R. 1227, but more specific about the process for project-based vouchers in requiring HUD/HANO to replace public housing units.[77] S. 1668 would likely undergo modifications as it proceeds through committee. On September 25, 2007, the Senate Committee on Banking, Housing, and Urban Affairs held a general hearing under the title "Two Years After the Storm: Housing Needs in the Gulf Coast" that included testimony from Sen. Mary Landrieu of Louisiana, Orlando Cabrera, Assistant Secretary for Public and Indiana Housing, HUD, James Perry, Executive Director of the Greater New Orleans Fair Housing Action Center, and Ms. Emelda Paul, President of the Lafitte Resident Council.

Even considering demographics alone, one can see that the complexities of both private and public housing issues for returning residents clearly exist on multiple levels—ethical, legal, economic, political, racial, familial, emotional. Therefore, answers and resolution to those issues must equally exist on multiple levels. But the fundamental level is the ethical. Establishing fairness in the decision-making process, and genuine citizen participation in reconstruction design options. It is consistent with this need for fairness, and the call for citizen participation, that the concept of Participatory Design will be proposed as one avenue to link the ethics of a just society and participation in democratic process with the demands of environment and economics and the engineering principles involved in trying to meet those demands.

76. See Jacob Bor, "Victory for Public Housing Residents and Activists: House Passes HR 1227," New Orleans Independent Media Center, March 27, 2007. Accessible at http://neworleans.indymedia.org/news/2007/03/10031.php. See also Library of Congress summary at http://www.thomas.gov/cgi-bin/bdquery/z?d110:HR01227:@@@D&summ2=m&.

77. See Library of Congress summary at http://www.thomas.gov/cgi-bin/bdquery/z?d110:SN01668:@@@D&summ2=m&, and the National Low Income Housing Coalition "Comparison of HR 1227 and S. 1668," accessed at http://www.nlihc.org/doc/s1668_Side-by-Side.pdf.

Healthcare

Relevant demographic information for healthcare is less a matter of sheer numbers than it is of the variety and quality of medical services, trauma centers, and acute and chronic care facilities that a region or an urban environment can provide its citizens. It has been painfully clear that, in New Orleans, healthcare services have been very slow to recover—due most notably to the loss of such major facilities as the Medical Center of Louisiana at New Orleans (MCLNO) Charity Hospital, and the considerable reduction of primary care MDs and nurses. Extensive damage following Katrina forced MCLNO to close. The region's only Level 1 trauma center at Charity Hospital was destroyed. For a period of time, MCLNO attempted to operate twenty-four hour emergency medical services from the first floor of the former Lord & Taylor building in the city, as well as at the Elmwood Medical Center in Jefferson Parish. The few hospitals that remained open were in the southern and western parts of the city.

While numbers alone cannot tell the story, it is useful to get a sense of the magnitude of New Orleans' loss in the area of healthcare capabilities in the quantifiable terms that are available before examining particular medical facilities in more detail. Fourteen months after the storm, as of October, 2006, of the nine acute care hospitals in operation prior to Katrina, only three had reopened—Children's Hospital, Touro Infirmary, and the Tulane University Hospital and Clinic. These facilities were operating with only 515 staffed beds, which represented a loss of over 75 percent of New Orleans' pre-Katrina medical care capacity.[78]

Staffing shortages have been one of the key factors in slowing attempts to rebuild New Orleans' healthcare capabilities. After Katrina, it was estimated that Orleans Parish had lost 77 percent of its primary care doctors, 70 percent of its dentists, and 89 percent of its psychiatrists.[79] Along with these losses have come a shortage of nurses and medical support people.

78. See UNOP, Appendix D, 90 and Table 7.6, 91. Prior to Katrina, there were 2269 staffed beds in Orleans Parish acute care facilities; fourteen months after the storm, in October, 2006, there were only 515 staffed beds, with six of the nine former acute care medical centers (Lindy Boggs Medical Center, Charity and University Hospitals, the former Memorial Medical Center, Methodist Hospital, and the New Orleans VA Medical Center) closed.

79. See John Pope, "N.O. is short on doctors dentists; City becomes eligible for recruitment help," *The Time-Picayune*, April 26, 2006.

With the help of the Louisiana Public Health Institute (LPHI)—in particular Susan Bergson, Program Manager for Urban Health Initiatives, Greg Stone, Program Manager in Health Demographics, and Robert Post, MD—it has been possible to make a summary assessment of New Orleans' healthcare capabilities, two years after the storm, as of the fall of 2007. Of Orleans Parish's nine acute care hospitals, four remained closed, two were operating with very limited services, and three were open.

Closed

Charity Hospital, at 1532 Tulane Avenue, in need of significant renovations prior to Katrina, has remained closed. In June of 2006, LSU announced plans for a $1.2 billion medical complex to be run jointly by the federal Department of Veterans Affairs and LSU; the plans did not include re-use of Charity Hospital. While the federal share of the complex (roughly half) has been appropriated and Gov. Blanco endorsed the project, the Louisiana Recovery Authority criticized the sparseness of the business plan and the Bush administration questioned the need for a new LSU teaching hospital to replace Charity.[80]

Lindy Boggs Medical Center (formerly known as Memorial Medical Center, Mercy Campus) at 301 N. Jefferson Davis Parkway, has remained closed. The hospital will be torn down, replaced by large development plans for Mid-City. In May, 2007, Tenet Healthcare Corp. sold Lindy Boggs MC to Victory Real Estate Investments of Columbus, Georgia.

The VA Medical Center of New Orleans at 1601 Perdido Street is closed as an acute care facility. Very limited behavioral health services (depression, PTSD, anxiety, etc.) have been offered at this location on a Monday to Friday basis only, with behavioral health services and some integrated specialty care services available at locations on 3434 Canal Street and 2237 Poydras Street.

Methodist Hospital (Pendleton Memorial Methodist Hospital) at 5620 Reed Boulevard in New Orleans East, according to LPHI, remains closed.

---

80. See UNOP, Appendix D, 92, Marsha Shuler, "Panel hits LSU on VA venture; Hospital plan late, unclear, officials told," *Capital City Press,* October 6, 2006, and Jan Moller, "LSU hospital plan challenged; Federal, state officials' priorities are at odds," *The Times-Picayune,* October 13, 2006.

Limited Services

University Hospital, at 2921 Perdido Street, adjacent to LSU Medical School, originally known as Hôtel-Dieu operated by the Daughters of Charity, sustained flood damage, but was partially reopened in November of 2006 with approximately 15 percent of its former capacity (85 out of 575 beds).

Ochsner Baptist Medical Center (the former Southern Baptist Hospital, renamed in 1996 to Memorial Medical Center, how it was known during Katrina, and changed to its current name in 2006) at 2700 Napoleon Avenue remained closed after Hurricane Katrina with the complex fenced off at least through January of 2006. In October, 2006, Ochsner purchased the historic campus, and is currently operating the New Orleans Surgery and Heart Institute (NOSHI) at 2626 Napoleon Avenue with 10 inpatient beds, four operating rooms, and a cardiac catheterization lab. Other medical services, including emergency, obstetrics, and cancer care were not yet available; however, renovations are underway and additional medical services are planned.

Open

The nonprofit Children's Hospital at 200 Henry Clay Avenue, which had its own power generator and remained open during Katrina, was fully functional again in October, 2005.

Tulane University Hospital and Clinic at 1415 Tulane Avenue, which in July of 2005 had merged with Lakeside Hospital in Jefferson Parish to become a leading teaching facility in the community, is open, although LPHI indicated that many of its services had been shifted to Lakeside Hospital in Jefferson Parish. Tulane maintains a number of distributed healthcare facilities, including a new primary care center on Rampart Street, the DePaul-Tulane Behavioral Health Center on Calhoun Street (the former DePaul Hospital that it acquired in 1997), and the Tulane-Xavier National Center of Excellence in Women's Health (TUXCOE).

Touro Infirmary at 1301 Foucher Street, affiliated with the LSU Health Science Center and the Tulane Health Science Center, was founded in 1852 as a community-based, nonprofit hospital, guided by the principles and faith of Judaism. It remains open.

Other Facilities

St. Charles Hospital at 3700 St. Charles Avenue is not functioning, but in a state of flux and potential re-use. It was opened in December, 1972 as part of Tenet Louisiana HealthSystem, the largest provider of health-care delivery in New Orleans. However, as previously discussed, in July, 2004, Stephen Farber, CFO of Tenet resigned under subpoena from the U.S. Attorney, and in February, 2005, Tenet agreed to sell the hospital to Preferred Continuum Care of Birmingham, Alabama. In January, 2006, Touro Infirmary bought St. Charles Hospital. Touro president and CEO, Les Hirsch, indicated at that time that plans for use of the hospital build-ing were still being evaluated.

The DePaul-Tulane Behavioral Health Center, mentioned earlier, is one of two areas of progress in renewing mental health services in New Orleans. Founded in 1861 by the Daughters of Charity, originally as an orphanage called the House of the Five Wounds, the facility was first used for mental healthcare in 1871. It was leased as part of Tulane University Hospital and Clinic in 1997, but did not reopen after Katrina. In February of 2007 it was bought by Children's Hospital, and, according to LPHI, LSU opened it as a psychiatric hospital during the summer of 2007.

New Orleans Adolescent Hospital and Community Services (NOAH) at 210 State Street provided the sole city services for children and adoles-cents with serious emotional and behavioral problems. As of 2006, the future of NOAH was uncertain, but, according to LPHI, it has reopened.

Other mental health facilities include the suburban River Oaks Hospital, at 1525 River Oaks Road West, a private psychiatric facility that includes detox, trauma-caused and compulsive behavior disorders, and Community Care Hospital at 3600 Chestnut Street, founded in 1994 as a 40 bed adult and geriatric psychiatric hospital.

Primary Care Community Clinics

The picture of primary care clinics and health centers is more complex, with many being permanently closed, some being closed then partially reopened, and some being closed and replaced by similar clinics nearby. In some cases, the names of clinics and health centers have changed, and in many cases, the services that were provided before Katrina were greatly reduced after the storm. A number of new community healthcare centers were opened after Katrina, some of which have, or will shortly, close. Both

LHPI and Via Link have provided data attempting to track the rapidly changing status of primary care healthcare centers.

As of October, 2007, of twenty-two primary care community clinics in Orleans Parish (plus one in nearby St. Bernard Parish) identified by LPHI as having been open prior to Katrina, eleven (50 percent) were completely lost, three stayed open (often with a loss of some services), and nine closed after Katrina, subsequently reopening but often with very limited services. At various times in the twenty-four months following Katrina, five new clinics were opened. One additional community clinic that was opened will shortly close. While the number of community healthcare centers that are currently open represent approximately 75 percent of New Orleans' pre-Katrina clinics, it would be incorrect to assume that they represent that percentage of pre-Katrina community primary healthcare *capabilities*.

In addition to these community centers, one school-based health center that had closed at one location was reopened at another school location. One new school-based health center opened within a year after the storm, and another school-based health center was planned to open in November, 2007.[81]

It is not surprising that those primary care community healthcare centers which closed were located in the areas that experienced the greatest and most serious flooding. These included the Daughters of Charity Health Center serving Carrollton/Mid-City, those connected with Charity Hospital, and others located in the Desire area of the Ninth Ward, the Lower Ninth Ward, in St. Roch, and in New Orleans East.[82] Of the three

81. The NOC Science and Math High School-Based Health Center—LSUHSC Dept. of Pediatrics had been open at John McDonogh High School before Katrina, and moved to Science and Math on Loyola Avenue after; the McDonogh No. 35 School-Based Health Center on Kelerec St. opened within a year after the storm, and the Eleanor McMain School-Based Health Center—LSUHSC Dept. of Pediatrics on South Claiborne is planning to open in November.

82. The primary care community health clinics that closed after Katrina and did not reopen included: the Daughters of Charity Health Center (Carrollton/Mid-City), the Booker T. Washington School-Based Clinic (Tulane/Gravier), the Wetmore Clinic at Charity Hospital (CBD/French Quarter), the Central City CHC (Central City), the Helen A. Levy Health Clinic (Desire/Ninth Ward), the Carver High School-Based Clinic (Desire/Ninth Ward), the Lower Ninth Ward CHC (Lower Ninth Ward), the St. Bernard Family Health Clinic (Gentilly/St. Bernard), the EXCELth Family Health Center (New Orleans East), the Katherine Benson Health Clinic (St. Roch/Bywater), and the Mary Buck Health Clinic (St. Thomas).

community primary care centers that were open before and remained open after Katrina (with some loss of services), two were in unflooded areas but one was helpfully near severely flooded neighborhoods.[83] Of the nine community primary care centers that closed after Katrina, but subsequently reopened (with often very limited services), most were in the CBD and French Quarter.[84] Somewhat unique to New Orleans is the New Orleans Musicians' Clinic (NOMC), founded in 1998 in collaboration with the LSU Healthcare Network and the Daughters of Charity Services of New Orleans. NOMC provides services to sustain Louisiana's musicians in body, mind, and spirit by providing access to primary care, preventative health services, and social and occupational outreach.

Six new clinics opened after Katrina, including two in the Ninth Ward.[85] The story of the opening of Odyssey House Louisiana (OHL) reflects a particularly poignant response to the fact that Hurricane Katrina effectively dismantled New Orleans' healthcare system for low-income residents in permanently closing Charity's public hospital and disabling most clinics and private practices. A nurse practitioner and professor of nursing at LSU Health Sciences Center School of Nursing, Dr. Jacqueline Rhoads, had been practicing at Healthcare for the Homeless Clinic, which was for some time unable to reopen operations after floodwaters ravaged its building. Dr. Rhoads worked with the Common Ground Collective, a community-initiated volunteer organization that provided short-term relief for Gulf Coast hurricane victims, to open Odyssey House Louisiana

83. The primary care community health clinics that remained open after Katrina included: the Algiers-Fischer Community Health Center (Algiers), the Desire/Florida CHC (Desire/Ninth Ward), and the St. Thomas Health Service (St. Thomas).

84. The primary care community health clinics that closed after Katrina, but subsequently reopened, although often with very limited services, included: the Ida Hymel Health Clinic (Algiers), the Mandeville Detiege Health Clinic (Carrollton/Mid-City), Orleans Women's Clinic (Tulane/Gravier), Delgado STD Clinic—Hutchison Clinic (CBD/French Quarter), Health Care for the Homeless (CBD/French Quarter), HCH Adolescent Drop-in Center (CBD/French Quarter), MCL (CBD/French Quarter), and the Edna Pilsbury Health Clinic (Central City). The New Orleans Musicians/Clinic at 2820 Napoleon Avenue (Uptown/Freret) had been located at 2020 Gravier, was forced to close after the storm, relocated in Lafayette for several months, then returned to New Orleans at a site on Prytania until April, 2007 when it opened at its current location.

85. The primary care community health clinics that opened after Katrina included: the Common Ground Health Clinic (Algiers), the Tulane University community Health Center at Covenant House (CBD/French Quarter), the Daughters of Charity Health Center—St. Cecelia (Desire/Ninth Ward), the Lower Ninth Ward Health Center (Lower Ninth Ward), and the Odyssey House Louisiana Free Outpatient Clinic (Mid-City/City Park).

(OHL) two months after Katrina. OHL was one of the few facilities in New Orleans with running water and power. With equipment and supplies borrowed or donated by Common Ground, the entire community clinic staff worked on a volunteer basis without compensation for over a year. Many patients required treatment from skin infections from exposure to stagnant water or for injuries sustained while trying to gut and repair their homes; many experienced asthma-like symptoms due to mold and dust. Of particular importance, not only for OHL's patients, but for almost all patients in parishes affected by Hurricanes Katrina and Rita, medical records were lost or destroyed. OHL's clinic staff, therefore, had to not only treat patients with only self-reported medical histories, but also recreate medications needs in the uncertain context of patient recollections. In December, 2006, LSU Health Sciences Center School of Nursing signed a contract with OHL to allow other nurse practitioners provide services at the clinic. With generous funding from United Way, and a partnership with St. Vincent DePaul pharmacy, the clinic has been able to expand dramatically, having treated thousands of patients since its opening. One particularly needed post-Katrina service of the clinic has been its providing on-site psychiatric evaluations. Dr. Rhoads has estimated that approximately 70 percent of clinic patients have mental health problems, and that 90 percent of those patients can attribute their mental health problems directly to the trauma of Katrina and its aftermath of flooding and destruction. These are patients who, for most of their lives, had good jobs, insurance, and paid-off homes, but who now have nothing and find themselves on welfare for the first time in their lives.[86]

Unfortunately, the stories regarding all of the new clinics that opened after Katrina are not so encouraging—particularly given certain areas of the city in which such community clinics have been so dearly needed. The Operation Blessing Medical Clinic that opened with promise on Read Boulevard in New Orleans East following the storm would, according to LPHI, soon close.

---

86. Bryan Gros, a psychologist with the Mental Health Association of Louisiana, reported spikes in suicides since the storm, including physicians among them, such as dermatologist Dr. Lisa Osberg-Wilson, whose home and practice building were damaged, whose patients had fled, and whose three little girls were living with relatives in Texas. See Connie Mabin, AP Writer, "Depression plagues Katrina victims," *The Louisiana Weekly*, December 19, 2005.

The need for community healthcare clinics cannot be overestimated, nor can the enormity of the problems in reconstituting patient medical and prescription records, and reestablishing patient transportation capabilities. Both physically and mentally, the wake of Hurricanes Katrina and Rita extended in time far beyond the days or even months that immediately followed their impacts on the Louisiana and Mississippi coasts. Part of this long-term effect was due to the fact that sizable elderly and poor populations were already living with chronic disabilities requiring ongoing medical treatment prior to the storms. Toxic waters and unhealthy, marginal living conditions after the flooding served to precipitate an increase in health complications. Coupled with the sudden unavailability of neighborhood health centers on which people had depended, the healthcare situation in New Orleans and other areas along the Gulf remained dire for over a year after the initial devastation, and still has not reached the levels of healthcare capabilities needed to serve the population.

The Center for Disease Control (CDC) and others have documented how a degradation in health, especially of those patients with chronic diseases that were irregularly or inadequately managed, became increasingly evident after Katrina. This occurred especially in patients with cancer, cardiovascular diseases, human immunodeficiency viral disorders, diabetes, substance abuse, and mental illness.[87] It was reported that as many as 40 percent of displaced survivors who had gone to Houston suffered chronic health conditions, such as heart disease, diabetes, and asthma, and that half lacked any form of health insurance.[88]

Both for those who remained in New Orleans and those who were displaced elsewhere, knowing which hospitals were open and what medical services were available to them was plagued by enormous ambiguity. Information about medical services and healthcare facilities that was both clear and that actually reached those who needed it was sorely lacking, even two years after the storm. The high level of uncertainty about essential medical services only exacerbated a vulnerability to mental disor-

---

87. Nancy G. Kutner, "Health Needs, Health Care, and Katrina," in Brunsma, David L., et al., eds., *The Sociology of Katrina: Perspectives on a Modern Catastrophe*, 205.

88 Mollyann Brodie, et al., "Experiences of Hurricane Katrina Evacuees in Houston Shelters: Implications for Future Planning," *American Journal of Public Health* 96:1402–8, 2006. Many also found that they could not used their Medicaid cards in other states and had to reenroll, because, being a state-based program, Medicaid was not transportable across state lines.

ders endemic among certain segments of the metropolitan New Orleans population. There is evidence, as reported by EMTs, firefighters, and other first responders in the spring of 2006, that there may have been as much as a 25 percent increase in cases of people continuing to experience various post-traumatic stress disorders (PTSD) and depression. The lack of mental health services at that time—when such services as part of the spectrum of community clinic healthcare services were desperately needed—continues to be of grave concern. The Substance Abuse and Mental Health Services Administration (SAMHSA) of the U.S. Department of Health and Human Services funded the Katrina Assistance Project, in which, during the spring of 2006 and ending in June, over 1,200 volunteer mental health and substance abuse conducted counseling sessions and made referrals for treatment. However, the Stafford Act of 1974 allows SAMHSA funding to be used only for crisis management, not *continuing* treatment.

Unfortunately, it has been recognized by practitioners who deal with people suffering from PTSD and PTSD-like symptoms, that there is significant interplay between the 'mental health' elements of those who experience recurrent distressing ideation about disaster-induced stress and an increased risk for chronic 'physical' conditions such as hypertension, diabetes, heart disease, and gastro-intestinal disorders.[89] The potential significant interplay of mental suffering and physical disorders constitutes one of the reasons the authors chose 'housing' and 'hospitals'—especially for those former residents of New Orleans and other Gulf Coast towns who remain displaced—as among the two most important areas in need of solutions in post-disaster reconstruction.

Several studies have reported that mental health problems are more likely to be reported by displaced persons, and that, in fact, the displaced residents of New Orleans reported more stress than non-displaced residents.[90] One obvious antidote for people experiencing such mental and physical stress is the ability to return to the normalizing atmosphere of family and familiar neighborhoods, and to resume their familiar patterns of work and socializing and cultural expression. Yet this capability is precisely what New Orleans and other coastal Gulf towns continued to lack. Displaced children—who have been forced to take on the stress of

---

89. The author (RRNR) is a member of the Bristol-Norfolk County (MA) Critical Incident Stress Management and Debriefing (CISD) Team that works especially with firefighters and police.

90. Kutner, "Health Needs, Health Care, and Katrina," 211.

attending school in other parts of the country for periods of time, some who were forced to live apart from their parent or parents, or even apart from any family altogether—are particularly vulnerable to the migration of acute stress into the various disorders of chronic stress.

The tasks of reassembling the neighborhoods of New Orleans and the towns along the Gulf Coast still in need of reconstruction are incredibly complex. The tasks of reconstituting healthcare systems and schools and other social support mechanisms for returning residents, to replace those that were destroyed and lost, due not only to storms but also government incompetence, are complex and enormous in scope. Population segments were affected by these complexities unequally. And the population *most negatively* affected was a population often without healthcare insurance or adequate property insurance, which did not have the economic means or social safety nets of others who were more easily able to return and resume their lives. It is precisely here that complexity in the abstract transforms itself into issues of fairness, equity, and the distribution of essential services in the concrete. As just one 'concrete' example, poor and uninsured residents in New Orleans had come to depend on subsidized healthcare services at one major centralized medical facility, Charity Hospital. Charity is no more. Literally and figuratively. Non-profit healthcare services are likely to be replaced by for-profit medical businesses. How do these eventualities shift one's understanding of what *fairness* and access to healthcare services should look like? Is access to healthcare services a fundamental human right, regardless of economic circumstances? In post-disaster reconstruction planning, would it be better to try to replicate such a centralized medical facility similar to what was easily recognized and familiar? Would it be better to shift the concept of healthcare for the needy to a decentralized system of safety-net services and partnerships between academic institutions and a mixture of public and private agencies? Would the latter create a bureaucratic nightmare? How would the costs of either conceptual model be borne?

Those contemplating a return to their devastated neighborhoods need, above all else, some assurance of stability and security, some sense that at least fundamental human needs such as housing and medical care are not a constantly shifting, changing scene, requiring them to continually replace misinformation with new information, forcing choices and new decisions every day. There are, moreover, factors beyond housing and hospitals that directly impact considerations of return. Public safety and a dependable criminal justice system; fire and other emergency services; a functioning infrastructure with transportation, electricity, water; levees that work.

Both EMS and fire services suffered a multitude of looses to trucks and equipment. Low and intermittent water pressure impeded fire protection services for months after Katrina; the number of available firefighters was greatly reduced. EMS lost its Moss Street quarters, and, initially, was forced to work from the Convention Center. Crime and homicide rates have sharply risen—and continue to rise—in part due to slow or unpredictable police response times. Vacant buildings have been subject to looting. Even pedestrians or motorists in commercial areas have been subjected to attack and theft. The collapse of the entire criminal justice system, for a time, reduced the perception of there being any accountability for criminal activity. Prisoners were evacuated, courtrooms were shuttered, evidence rooms and their contents destroyed. Police headquarters and the offices of the District Attorney were lost. Trials were put on hold for indefinite periods of time due to a lack of court personnel and the inability to empanel juries of citizens, many of whom were no longer residing in Orleans Parish. Shortages in the Orleans Indigent Defender Program (OIDP) or 'Public Defender' program also limited the scheduling of trials.[91] It was not until June of 2006 that the Orleans Parish Criminal Court building was able to reopen on a limited basis and begin scheduling trials.

In addition to losses of infrastructure and public safety networks, there were devastating losses in the cultural domain. Over 260 non-profit cultural institutions, including museums, arts centers, performance halls, and other venues were severely damaged or destroyed. The Mahalia Jackson Theatre for the Performing Arts was damaged, and work for those employed in the creative arts economy of the city was cut in half. Eight of the twelve branches of the New Orleans Public Library (NOPL) were severely damaged and their contents lost. More than ten of the city's twenty historic districts suffered significant damage, affecting perhaps as many as 25,000 historic properties.[92] All of these losses were not simply of equipment and buildings and material, but losses to the core fabric of a city—losses to the *human* environment often taken for granted, but on

91. All reported in the public television and radio media and *The Times-Picayune*. See also UNOP, 1.12.

92. UNOP, 1.13–14.

which the spiritual dimension of people's lives depends. To feel at home a citizen must have a sense of personal safety, means of defense against unanticipated events such as fire and breaks in water mains or gas lines. In a city below sea level, protection from inundation must be added to the list. But a citizen must also have outlets for human expression that makes urban life not only meaningful but bearable: venues for music, art, theatre, dance, personal learning. All of these are what it takes an individual to truly feel *at home*. So much of this, in the City of New Orleans, was lost.

Leadership and Early Planning

One might have thought that the first public elections for leadership in the City of New Orleans following Hurricane Katrina—in the spring of 2006—would have provided the opportunity for an examination of where the city stood, what were its plans for reconstructing the homes and neighborhood and businesses that still lay in ruins, and who would provide leadership in the planning and rebuilding process. As it turned out, this was not the case.[93]

State and local elections in Louisiana follow an open primary system sometimes called a 'jungle primary' in which candidates of all parties are listed on a single ballot. Voters are not bound by party, and, unless a candidates wins more than 50 percent of the first round vote, a run-off election is held between the top two candidates. The original date of the mayoral primary, February 4, 2006, was postponed, along with other local elections including City Council, until April 22. It was unrealistically hoped that more of the large number of displaced residents would be able to return to participate in the election.

In the jungle primary, more than twenty candidates challenged mayor Ray Nagin for leadership, but only two—president of the Audubon Institute Ron Forman, who had supported Nagin in 2002, and Louisiana Lieutenant Governor Mitch Landrieu, son of the city's last white mayor, Moon Landrieu—were generally considered 'major' threats.[94] With

93. See especially the excellent article by Adam Nossiter, "New Orleans Election Hinges on Race and Not Rebuilding," *The New York Times*, April 4, 2006, many of whose political observations are reflected here.

94. Other candidates included Republican Rob Couhig, former owner of the New Orleans Zephyrs, who campaigned on a platform of a crackdown on crime, selling and privatizing public hospitals, bulldozing blighted property, and shrinking the city's boundaries by restricting rebuilding in the Lower Ninth Ward and New Orleans East (see Bruce

as much as two-thirds of the city's population still displaced, the State Legislature acted to allow absentee voting in satellite polling places set up in ten parishes across the state.[95] Efforts by the Association of Community Organizations for Reform Now (ACORN), the NAACP, and the Grassroots Legal Network to establish polling places in Houston and Atlanta, cities that held large numbers of displaced citizens, were rejected on February 24, 2006 by the federal district court, and again on appeal, March 27. ACORN and the NAACP had argued that a majority of New Orleans residents still living outside the city were poor- to moderate-income blacks and should be given every opportunity to participate in this crucial election. Judge Ivan Lemelle, U.S. District Court, Eastern District of Louisiana, said that Louisiana did not have to provide satellite polling places outside of the state to accommodate displaced voters, and that existing measures met standards laid out in the Voting Rights Act of 1965.[96] The fact that the majority of displaced residents—and most of the poorer, black residents, as indicated above—had been forced to locate outside of Louisiana meant that the voices of large chunks of New Orleans' population might easily go unheard in this most important election. Evidence for this was born out by the fact that fewer than 10,000 registered voters

Nolan, "Rob Couhig: Eager to take a swing at N.O. recovery," *The Times-Picayune,* April 5, 2006.); Rev. Tom Watson, leader of the Greater New Orleans Coalition of Ministers, who focused on the needs of those still displaced and was Nagin's first Black challenger (see Trymaine Lee, "Tom Watson: He's preaching city unity, healing," *The Times-Picayune,* April 10, 2006); Virginia Boulet, who argued for universal health insurance to help displaced residents return; Greta Gladney, director of The Renaissance Project and Lower Ninth Ward activist; and Manny "Chevrolet" Bruno, an out-of-work actor.

95. Caddo, Calcasieu, East Baton Rouge, Jefferson, Ouachita, Rapides, St. Tammany, Lafayette, Tangipahoa, Terrebonne. Of these, only Calcasieu Parish is reasonably close to the large numbers of displaced residents located in Houston. The Association of Community Organizations for Reform Now (ACORN) organized buses to transport out-of-state voters to the satellite polling stations, which were opened from April 10–15; 10,585 votes were cast at the satellite polls (see Jeff Duncan, "More than 10,000 early ballots cast," *The Times-Picayune,* April 17, 2006).

96. Judge Lemelle, nominated by President Clinton in February 1997, and commissioned in April, 1998, is African American. See Sherrel Wheeler Steward, "As New Orleans Mayoral Race Looms, Displaced Residents Urged to Vote Absentee," *New America Media,* BlackAmericaWeb.Com, February 27, 2006. On March 27, 2006, Judge Lemelle also refused a delay in New Orleans' April 22 mayoral election requested by several civil rights groups concerned that many black residents would not be able to participate. Lemelle indicated that voting would help the city rebuild, but warned that the city and civil rights groups would have to find ways to solve any problems that might hinder displaced residents' ability to vote.

had requested absentee ballots, according to Dale Atkins, the civil district court clerk seeking re-election, as well as by numerous complaints about cumbersome absentee ballot procedures, and the frequent movement of precinct locations.[97] On April 1, thousands of civil rights demonstrators marched across the Crescent City Connection, again calling for satellite voting locations to be set up outside the state.[98]

If it were true, as former mayor Marc Morial often liked to quip, that what made New Orleans unique was 'the polyglot, the tapestry, the mosaic, the gumbo,' then it would seem logical, with the city's self-identity secure, that the 2006 mayoral race could properly focus on the issues of rebuilding and reconstruction planning that were so crucial. But what has logic to do with politics? In fact, it was the very issue of New Orleans' racial identity that re-emerged as a diversionary focus in the debates leading up to the mayoral election. It was as if Katrina had thrown New Orleans' identity—its soul—to the winds, and what came down was scattered and shattered. Or perhaps it was not Hurricane Katrina after all, only the politicians themselves who were responsible for the direction (or misdirection) taken in the discussions during the primary debates.

As the first vote since Katrina, the April 22 mayoral primary contestants should have focused on the many critical choices facing their battered city. There were questions to which citizens had a right to hear answers. What specific reconstruction plans did each candidate support? What was the reasoning behind their strategy? Whose interests were being represented? Whose interests were being left out? This did not happen. The three major candidates largely ignored substantive issues of post-disaster

97. See, for example, Cain Burdeau, AP, "Judge Rules Against Civil Rights Groups in New Orleans," March 27, 2006, posted on www.truthout.org.

98. The march was organized by Rev. Jesse Jackson's Rainbow/PUSH Coalition, with participation by Bill Cosby, Al Sharpton, and former mayor Marc Morial. A reminder of the incident three days after the storm when a large group of mostly black New Orleanians trying to escape chaos at the Morial Convention Center by crossing the bridge on foot was turned back by Gretna police, the focus of the demonstration turned to the issue that citizens displaced by the storm might not be able to exercise their vote in the upcoming municipal elections. Henrietta Reed, a widowed mother of three living in Houston, said she would drive in for the April 22 primary election, but that, like other displaced New Orleanians, just did not have the means to return. "I pay taxes, I work, I raised children, I'm not a criminal. I don't know what else I can do to prove I'm an American citizen. I'm working diligently to come back, and I know I'll be back." Quoted in Frank Donze and Gwen Filosa, "Bridge march hails justice, voter rights. Thousands join Jesse Jackson in crossing river," *The Times-Picayune*, April 2, 2006.

reconstruction planning, and instead aligned themselves along racial lines. Each candidate appeared to seek out the correct, although as yet unknown, demographic support. Was this need such a deflective strategy only a measure of how reduced the effectiveness of the Office of Mayor and of the City Council had become in the seven months after the storm?

In January, 2006, Secretary of State Al Ater's plan to reschedule the February elections—the primary to April 22, and the runoff May 20—was signed by Governor Blanco. In addition to Mayor, the election would include seven City Council seats, criminal and civil sheriffs, and potentially City Charter amendments that could empower a yet-to-be-determined hurricane recovery corporation to oversee expenditure of federal money, and the buying, selling, and seizure of homes in flood-ravaged areas.[99] Hundreds of voting machines stored in a warehouse on Chef Menteur Highway were readied, including having their wheels replaced after six inches of water got into the building. Within a week of one another in February, Ron Forman and Mitch Landrieu announced their candidacies. Also in that period, Ray Nagin reconciled with Bishop Paul Morton, a black religious leader and head of the Greater St. Stephen Full Gospel Baptist Church who had once criticized Nagin for not giving black-owned businesses city contracts, and called him "a white man in black skin." In fact, Nagin's election in 2002 as New Orleans' sixtieth mayor had largely been on the strength of support from white businessmen. Nagin himself had been a vice president at Cox Communications, and despite a lack of backing from any of the city's established political organizations, was perceived as a reformer with much appeal to the white business community. In the runoff in March, 2002, Nagin received 85 percent of the white vote, 40 percent of the black vote.

Nagin's first term began with a well-received anti-corruption campaign that saw surprising arrests of city officials, including a cousin of Nagin himself. However, there were also continual clashes with the City Council, and the tendency of Nagin to publicly announce new programs and policies without seeking the Council's support. Politically, while he claimed to be a Democrat, Nagin frequently aligned himself with conservative Republicans, including Bobby Jindal's run against Lieutenant Governor Blanco's bid for governor in 2003.

---

99. Frank Donze, "Election date gets N.O. races moving," *The Times-Picayune*, January 25, 2006.

It was perhaps Nagin's attempt to ensure favor with the empowered business community, and reverse the actions he had taken the previous year, that came back to bite him most of all during Hurricane Katrina. During the threat from Hurricane Ivan in 2004, Nagin ordered evacuation of the city on September 13, telling those who stayed to make sure they 'had an axe in the attic.' Several hundred thousand residents left the city, and were promptly stuck in highway traffic for 12 to 24 hours while the hurricane missed the city. In the hours before Hurricane Katrina struck in 2005, Nagin took the opposite tack, and delayed his orders for mandatory evacuation. Late in the afternoon of Saturday August 27, afraid of incurring the business community's wrath from forcing the closure of hotels and restaurants, Nagin had still issued only a voluntary evacuation.

Nagin's handling of evacuation procedures during Hurricane Katrina was widely criticized in the media, particularly by those who viewed the hundreds of New Orleans City school buses, that might have been used to transport poor and elderly residents, sitting idle in parking lots which were flooded. The unused yellow buses in murky floodwaters became a powerful visual symbol of Nagin's ineptness. Controversies about Nagin's leadership continued after Katrina as well. At a town hall meeting in October, 2005, Nagin's attempt to lend support to having reconstruction labor opportunities go to local, displaced workers offended Hispanic groups, when Nagin uttered words to the effect that people wanted to make sure New Orleans was 'not overrun with Mexican workers.'[100]

During the 2006 mayoral primary, all the candidates made promises of various kinds. However, the real force in rebuilding New Orleans would ultimately be the billions of dollars in pending federal aid. These funds would be portioned out by the State of Louisiana, with the role of mayor only secondary. Any number of analysts of the mayoral election scene have suggested that this underlying fact created a vacuum 'into which rushed the politics of racial identity.' What did become clear was that tough discussions about whether some neighborhoods should not be rebuilt, or whether the city should issue fewer building permits, were largely absent from primary debates. As a diversion from those difficult—

---

100. Hispanic PR Wire, "USHCC [United States Hispanic Chamber of Commerce] Deplores Remarks by New Orleans Mayor Ray Nagin Regarding Mexican Workers and the Rebuilding of New Orleans," referring to Nagin quote published in the October 7, 2005 edition of *The Dallas Morning News*, posted on www.hispanicbusiness.com, October 28, 2005.

and, perhaps, at the time unanswerable questions—arose once again the question of New Orleans' racial identity.

Incumbent Mayor Ray Nagin made the most explicit racial bid. At a Martin Luther King Day celebration on January 16, Nagin gave a speech that only appeared to exacerbate the issues of racial divisions and neighborhood favoritism within the city. Nagin predicted that displaced African American residents would return to the rebuilt city and that it "will be chocolate at the end of the day." Nagin went on to say, "This city will be a majority African American city. It's the way God wants it to be. You can't have it no other way. It wouldn't be New Orleans." Nagin also implied that 2005's devastating hurricanes were signs of God's wrath: "Surely God is mad at America."[101]

Discussion of the surprising number of curious post-Katrina invocations of questions of theodicy will be left to the Postlude of *Walking to New Orleans*. Here, it is enough to sense the irony in Nagin's public proclamation to make New Orleans a black 'chocolate city.' Having been elected through white support, and the target of criticism among blacks for failing to favor black-owned companies, in the political climate post-Katrina Nagin was being abandoned by those same white businessmen who now faulted his lack of leadership. As a result, Nagin appeared to have remade himself into the 'black candidate,' standing against his major white opponents, Mitch Landrieu and Ron Forman. Perhaps this motivation led Nagin to take part in the protest marches over the election organized by Rev. Jesse Jackson and Rev. Al Sharpton, figures to whom he had never previously been strongly attached.

The racially polarized election was in many ways a legacy of the storm's unequal damage, where the greatest suffering and displacement occurred among blacks. In some black neighborhoods, there was worry that whites were about to retake control after nearly three decades of black rule. This worry was reflected in remarks by Bishop Paul Morton who said, "there is anxiety, fear, that this can take us back so many years,"[102] while others saw the election as an opportunity for white voters to take the city back. The fact that the large numbers of displaced black voters

---

101. Quoted in John Pope, "Evoking King, Nagin calls N.O. 'chocolate' city," *The Times-Picayune*, January 17, 2006. Cornel West had used the term 'chocolate cities' in his 1993 book, *Race Matters*.

102. Quoted by Adam Nossiter, who, along with others (including DEBR) has reflected on the irony of Nagin's political relation to race.

living in Texas and other states would have to vote using unfamiliar absentee mechanisms only exacerbated fears that such procedural barriers to a free exercise of all voices in this critical election could easily suppress participation of certain classes of voters.

For many white voters, Ron Forman, rebuilder of the city's once-decrepit zoo, was their chance to take the city back. A local businessman who came from a working-class background, Forman did not explicitly play to such a 'counter-black' racial strategy; nevertheless, his appeal clearly lay with Uptown white professionals, whose children generally attended Newman, Country Day,[103] or Trinity Episcopal School, the city's elite white private schools. Somewhere between Nagin and Forman, Lt. Governor Mitch Landrieu, son of former mayor Moon Landrieu, brother of Senator Mary Landrieu, came from a family tradition that had strong backing from black citizens and political organizations as well as white.

Early polls in February saw Mitch Landrieu leading with 35 percent of the vote, Nagin following with 25 percent, Forman with 9 percent; however, absentee voters were not polled. The first mayoral debate on March 7 at Loyola University saw some discussion of levees, evacuation plans, and neighborhood redevelopment, but a great deal focused on how New Orleans' drastically altered demographics would impact race. A second and more acrimonious debate brought in issues of fiscal management and crime. However, it was in the final days of the primary campaign that a wave of negative ads appeared between Forman and Landrieu, which may have had the effect of improving Nagin's position. The results of the April 22 primary gave Nagin 38 percent of the vote, Landrieu 29 percent, Forman 17 percent. In the runoff on May 20, by four percentage points (52 to 48 percent) voters re-elected Ray Nagin to guide the city through the next four years. About 38 percent (113,591) of the city's 298,512 eligible voters cast ballots. However, something very close to the balance of 184,921 eligible voters were displaced residents, in exile outside New Orleans. Roughly 25 percent of those who cast ballots were either absentee ballots or people who voted in person at one of the ten balloting centers set up around the state for early voting. By some views that appears encouraging, except when realizing that absentee and remote-site votes represented only about 13 percent of the *potential* votes from displaced residents.

---

103. Other Roman Catholic pre-K through twelfth grade schools include Sacred Heart, McGhee, St. Martin's, and Ursuline Academy.

Nagin ended up securing a majority of votes of black residents as well as those of enough conservative white businessmen who did not want to see a very liberal democrat like Mitch Landrieu in power to oversee their coming economic boon arising in reconstruction opportunities. It may also have been that Nagin's leadership 'style' was interpreted as just the bravado many New Orleanseans felt needed in the face of their overwhelming disaster. Nagin won 279 precincts, including Central City, Gentilly, and New Orleans East. While strong in neighborhoods of the city with a black majority, it may have been the white conservative and Republican turnout for Nagin that ultimately put him over 50 percent. Mitch Landrieu won 162 precincts, largely in Uptown, the Quarter, CBD, Lakeview, Faubourg Marigny and Bywater. Both candidates had a respectable percentage black and white crossover votes. However, Nagin's margin of victory of 4 percentage points was possibly the slimmest for an incumbent since Victor Schiro's in 1965 after the disaster of Hurricane Betsy.[104]

For eighteen months after Hurricane Katrina, perceptions of the degree of Nagin's leadership success—and lack of results—would increasingly come to turn on his decreasing ability to influence funding sources, both from in Baton Rouge and from Washington. Surely, the funding tasks were formidable.

At one end of the spectrum in post-Katrina New Orleans arose visions of an extravagant future, awash in federal cash, an arts-infused mecca for youthful risk-takers, a boomtown of entrepreneurs. At the other end of the spectrum were gloomy predictions of a southern Detroit, a sickly urban wasteland abandoned by the middle class, a moldering core surrounded by miles of vacant houses, with wide-open neighborhoods roamed by drug dealers and other criminals.[105]

One year after Katrina, New Orleans was substantially smaller than it had been—reduced from an estimated 452,170 in July, 2005, to an estimated 223,388 as of July, 2006, a loss of 50.6 percent. In that first year, and afterwards, re-population had slowed to a trickle. More recent estimates based on U.S. Postal Service Delivery Statistics have optimistically suggested that New Orleans' population may have risen to as much as 66 percent

104. There were ties in two precincts. For additional discussion, see Michelle Krupa and Matt Scallan, "Broad appeal aided Nagin in the runoff," and Gordon Russell, Frank Donza, and Michelle Krupa, "It's Nagin," *The Times-Picayune,* May 21, 2006.

105. Characterizations sharply expressed by Adam Nossiter, "Outlines Emerge for a Shaken New Orleans," *The New York Times,* August 27, 2006.

of its pre-Katrina level,[106] but even if that turns out to be substantiated, the city was (and still is) well below its pre-storm population. One year after Katrina, the poorest of neighborhoods were still devastated and largely unpopulated. The Lower Ninth Ward, with only about 7 percent returned population, remained a barren wasteland. Much of New Orleans East was empty, unlikely to be rebuilt soon, having recently lost a new community healthcare center set up there. Gentilly's Arts and Crafts stucco houses with wide overhanging eaves, and Tremé's Creole cottages and shotgun houses were only being rebuilt in fits and starts. Public housing projects remained closed, or were slowly being converted to mixed-income housing. As one moved towards Lake Pontchartrain, away from the living zone along the river that was spared flooding, one still saw sagging houses, having regurgitated their interiors, now dead and awaiting being razed; one still saw heaps of rubble and garbage with dogs and rats among them. One still saw, at odd intervals, the occasional householder on a porch, looking out with a 'furrowed brow, trying to make a go of it in the ruins.'[107]

Certainly in the eighteen months following the storm, there was enormous uncertainty. In some cases, many citizens, individually or in groups, attempted to take matters into their own hands. We will later examine some of their successes, as in the case of the neighborhood of Broadmoor. But while speaking with residents of the Lower Ninth Ward, we also became aware that many people, almost in acts of desperation, had bought weed-whackers which they were using to cut the prolific grass and weeds and brush that had grown in front of other houses or in the numerous vacant fields now spreading into the distance, so the 'neighborhood' would look good to prospective returnees. It was a losing battle. Crops of uncut weeds still poked through fractured concrete slabs and grew in the narrow neutral grounds of the wider streets. A sense of measurable progress was difficult to find. For at least eighteen months after the storm, recovery assessors and planners were still squabbling, and city government remained an almost invisible presence.

---

106. Amy Liu and Allison Plyer, "A Review of Key Indicators of Recovery Two Years After Katrina," The New Orleans Index. Second Anniversary Special Edition. The Brookings institution Metropolitan Policy Program and the Greater New Orleans Community Data Center.

107. See also Adam Nossiter, "Outlines Emerge for a Shaken New Orleans," *The New York Times,* August 27, 2006. Many, although not all, of our observations and conversations during the fall and winter of 2007 remained eerily reminiscent of those of 2006.

In August, 2006, Adam Nossiter argued that New Orleans was 'rudderless, filthy, still deeply scarred by the storm, hemorrhaging the people it could least afford to lose.' Nearly half the doctors had left. Tens of thousands of the African-American working-class backbone remained unable to return. Banks were insisting on unusually high collateral in real estate transactions. The homicide rate had doubled its pre-hurricane level. Basic services—water, electricity, garbage pickup—were intermittent. But City Hall, however, had 'settled back into its habitual easygoing rhythms.'

There indeed seemed little sense of urgency among its officials. Mayor Ray Nagin was set to attend an opening at a French Quarter gallery of an exhibit of photographs of himself, taken by his personal photographer. Only a public outcry forced him to cancel plans for a fireworks display and 'comedy show' to commemorate Hurricane Katrina's first anniversary. Something closer to the reality of citizens' views of his leadership was expressed on December 16, 2006, when hundreds of displaced residents rallied outside Mayor Nagin's house to demand the re-opening of New Orleans public housing. Marching to his house from Bynum Drugs Store on St. Bernard Avenue, rally organizer Endesha Juakali of Survivors Village said, "We are going to his home because so many people still aren't being allowed to come home. We will not let rich developers profit from Katrina at the expense of displaced residents. This is corporate welfare in its lowest form, and the Mayor's fingerprints are all over it."[108]

With little concrete direction from the city government, long-term planning for the city's future remained incoherent for a year after Katrina, and at least six months beyond that. Two years after Katrina, definitive planning is *still* unclear in the minds of almost everyone to whom we have spoken—from professors at UNO to personal acquaintances to people in the neighborhoods—this, despite the existence of the fruits of New Orleans' *fourth* planning process: the 'Unified New Orleans Plan' (UNOP). By and large, the UNOP has been regarded as a paper document only, not something being translated into reality. Despite the UNOP containing decent assessments of community needs in a number of areas, and some novel and coherent approaches to reconstruction, planning strategies have still not been put in a form from which actual projects could easily be implemented. The UNOP, and the three other major planning processes that preceded it (or were aborted), will be discussed in

---

108. Quoted on http://www.commongroundrelief.org/node/350, December 16, 2006.

more detail in chapter 7. Here, one can simply acknowledge that for at least eighteen months after the storm, there were no *agreed upon* substantive plans for large-scale infrastructure recovery and repair, or anything like a comprehensive and fair plan for housing and business redevelopment. As evidence of the state of planning *non-agreement,* during August, 2006, one group of official planners took out a full-page advertisement in *The Times-Picayune,* warning citizens to stay away from its rivals. But developers, who wanted to be building houses for displaced residents and renovating destroyed businesses, were forced to wait because no comprehensive plan was forthcoming.

In some neighborhoods, the absence of an overall plan was rather quickly replaced by the necessity for self-determination. There were still piles of fly-covered garbage that citizens were forced to walk past on their way to a community meeting in Broadmoor. But community organizer, Harold Roark, received thunderous applause when he said, "Nobody is going to tell Broadmoor what to do except the people who live and work in Broadmoor!"[109] In other neighborhoods, however, the absence of planning produced only skepticism. Jenel Hazlett of the Northwest Carrollton Civic Association complained, "Why does it seem that every time someone swoops in to help us, it winds up being a mess? They keep moving the players around, and we as citizens keep getting jerked around."[110]

What happened in the months following Katrina appeared to be a fervor of competing and ill-thought-out planning initiatives by competing levels of government. When the confusion these plans raised was increasingly expressed in anger by the public, in the months immediately following his re-election in May of 2006, Mayor Nagin appeared to pull back from comprehensive planning altogether. In its place, Nagin began to espouse an alternative to city-wide planning, and leave it entirely up to neighborhoods to map out their own futures. Eventually, he promised, these individual neighborhood plans would be merged into a single, larger plan. The major problem with this 'alterntive strategy', however, was that only a handful of the city's seventy-three identifiable neighborhoods within its thirteen planning districts were remotely in a position any to do planning. This was true even for those neighborhoods that were fortunate enough to posses strong and active community associations. When citi-

---

109. Recounted by Jeanne Dumestre.

110. Hazlett quoted in Adam Nossiter, "Outlines Emerge for a Shaken New Orleans."

zens complained about the tortoise-like pace of recovery, Nagin generally blamed levels of government beyond the City as being the ones who held the purse strings. They were the reason for slow flow of recovery dollars.

The general sentiment among the several groups of planners, not infrequently voiced, was that the longer the city went without a master plan, the shakier would be the fate of its ruined neighborhoods. One planner from the Urban Land Institute, John McIlwain, suggested that it was "highly probably that there would be many neighborhoods, with block after block of one or two houses restored, surrounded by vacant abandoned houses, no police stations, no services, low water pressure, and unsafe and unhealthy environment."[111] Unfortunately, McIlwain's prophetic vision still accurately described the condition of far too many neighborhoods more than eighteen months year after he made it. Economics, bureaucratic regulations, embedded structures of power and social status, competing levels of government authority, all combined and then festered in their own inabilities to cooperatively interact to become an inedible gumbo of chaos.

Confusion and the absence of standardized or fair rules for rebuilding has existed at the individual, as well as the community levels. In some cases, the standards for rebuilding damaged individual homes have turned out to be artificially lenient. FEMA flood maps and guidelines were interpreted to mean that buildings needed only maintain the previously enforced 100-year flood elevation standards. Thus, many homes, even severely damaged ones, might not have to be raised at all, if they met or exceeded the three-foot requirement. There was natural resistance to requiring that all rebuilt homes meet higher flood elevation standards. The cost factor was significant—to elevate a house by as little as five feet could cost more than $100,000.

The absence of standardized or fair procedures for debris removal was another area that sometimes put one neighborhood in conflict with another. Damaged construction material and general debris from Katrina, for a considerable period of time, was an intractable problem. But the solution for some became a new problem for others. For example, several million tons of debris and remains were simply dumped in man-made pits at the swamp on the eastern side of the city. Yet more than a thousand Vietnamese families were living less than two miles from the edge of these new landfill sites. Quite naturally, they did not want the moldering remains and detritus

---

111. Quoted in Adam Nossiter, "Outlines Emerge for a Shaken New Orleans."

of this horrendous disaster just plunked down nearby—erasing the problem for the well-off, casting it onto the less advantaged.

Beyond urban New Orleans, and still uncertain, is fate of lower Plaquemines Parish, which juts out into the Gulf and contained about 2 percent of the greater New Orleans area population. Here there arises the all-too-familiar problem of scale (Marker of Complexity No. 5). The problem is that Plaquemines Parish—with its relatively low density of population—would require an additional $1.6 billion to raise its levee system to FEMA guidelines. So far, the Bush administration has not promised money to do this. The area is too vast, with too few people, apparently, to warrant such expense.

In the economic sector, and a significant factor in the city's redevelopment, is the importance of recognizing that New Orleans has always been a city lacking a large corporate base. It has been the small businesses—little restaurants, independent stores like the Tabasco Country Store, mom-and-pop groceries, small manufacturers—that *are* its economic base. However, with the reduction in population, the loss of employees, and uncertainties about rebuilding, small business owners have especially feared for New Orleans' future. While tourist areas like Magazine Street and the Quarter have by-and-large recovered, their businesses once again thriving, the opposite has been the case, for example, on St. Claude Avenue which leads into the Lower Ninth Ward. Here, closed businesses still greatly outnumber open ones. It never helped that the Ninth Ward, locally known as 'CTC'—meaning simply 'Cross the Canal'—now had come to designate the reality of crime in 'Cut-throat City.' But the rising incidence of crime was only made more acute by the absence of jobs. An expanding vicious cycle. The New Orleans metropolitan area lost about 184,000 jobs—more than 30 percent of its pre-storm employment, and for at least eighteen months after the storm, has had an unemployment rate of 7.2 percent, the highest of any large city. Its rate of increased crime has kept pace.

Thus, if one simply thinks of the inherent logic of recovery and reconstruction, what was once a single downward cycle, now appears as a *series* of vicious cycles, one nested upon another. To reduce unemployment, jobs must be created. To create jobs, there must be an economic base to pay those who accept them. To accept jobs, people need a place to live. To find a place to live, there must be housing. For there to be housing, there must be people with the skills to construct them. To find people with those skills, there must places to house them, in order that jobs can be created so that people can accept them . . . Are we back to square one yet? It takes money to make money; it takes jobs to create jobs. The difficulty is that, while economies and neighborhoods which support them, ordinarily grow organically, as needs and demands rise, in the case of New Orleans' lowest sectors of its economic strata—the location of those neighborhoods most devastated by flooding—it is as if those neighborhoods and their businesses must be rebuilt *all at once* in order to become viable at all. But that cannot reasonably be expected to happen. It is that this point that the full import of HUD/HANO's decision to demolish most of New Orleans' public housing projects begins to come home. Was it among those decisions that turned at least one version of the reconstruction 'vicious cycle' into a bottomless pit?

In the four planning processes addressing New Orleans' recovery and reconstruction needs, for at least eighteen months there had as yet emerged no 'master plan' that was substantially changing the reality of the city on a city-wide basis. Central tourist and business areas, which received minimal damage from the storms, were able to recover quickly. Some neighborhoods have been able to develop plans on their own and begin a process of recovery. But their successes may only have masked the absence of progress or failures in other areas of the city. Regardless of whether effective recovery and reconstruction plans are generated top-down or neighborhood-up, there at some point must be a *citizen-supported* and *coordinated* plan that eliminates or drastically reduces chaos, bad decisions, and misdirection, and that has secured the funding to allow it to implement genuine city-wide rebuilding.

A truly citizen-supported and coordinated plan cannot be the private vision of one urban planner or developer, or even of a collection of them. It cannot be the private vision of any single sector of government—whether that of the Mayor, City Council, the State, or the federal government. It cannot be a private vision that exists independently of the voices and the input of the citizens of New Orleans. Moreover, citizen input must be continuous and ongoing, through all phases of planning, design, and implementation. Even the slightest acquaintance with the many instances of social and political *unfairness* and *injustice* that have riddled New Orleans in the past, suggests the need for any claimant as 'the coordinated post-Katrina plan for the city's recovery and reconstruction' to position itself to eliminate at least the most blatant forms *unfairness* that have attached to the city's history and politics.

On both engineering and ethical grounds, plans produced by the few, in the silence of their own conceptual or political domains, can be expected to produce only bad decisions, misdirection, and chaos, as implementation unfolds. Such a planning model would only *replicate* historical unfairness—the unfairness of one neighborhood benefiting while another suffers; the unfairness of one economic group benefiting at another's expense; the unfairness of one racial or ethnic group being ignored or degraded while others are able to resume their lives and have opportunities to succeed again.

What would a solution to generate the necessary consensus that can reflect the needs of the community *as a whole* look like? *Walking to New Orleans* will argue, on both engineering and ethical principles, that it must be a process in which *all* citizens—current residents as well as those who have been unable to find a way to *walk back home*—must be in a position to directly participate in post-disaster reconstruction planning, neighborhood redesign, and implementation. Such an ethically-based engineering proposal will be explored through the concept of Participatory Design in Chapter 8; first, it is important to examine the ethical dimensions of the complexities more fully.

Across the Mississippi

Levee, Black Pearl

5

A Fair Voice

Ethical Principles in Reconstruction Planning

SOME PRELIMINARY CONSIDERATIONS

ONE OF THE PRIMARY aims of *Walking to New Orleans* is to examine the concept of Participatory Design—a methodology that may involve not only design of actual objects or structures, but also organizational or social transformations. By its application it is believed citizens of post-disaster South Louisiana can become more directly engaged in the process of planning and implementing their own recovery. To ensure that planning and implementation decisions reflect the actual needs and goals of those affected involves more than general citizen input. It requires that citizens be involved at all stages of the processes leading to some output—whether it is a complex public object (such as a transportation system within urban infrastructure), social change (such as modification of a neighborhood), or broader strategies (such as an environmental program). As an approach to design, its premise is that higher quality products or more suitable results depend on understanding in considerable detail just how they will be used or appropriated, by individuals or affected groups.

However, embedded in the concept of Participatory Design is an ethical premise as well. Design is understood not simply as a creative act, but also as an act involving social responsibility and commitment to values of justice and fairness. One might regard this premise as a matter of *integrity* in design. For example, in a program to facilitate reclamation of coastal wetlands, citizens might insist on program criteria based on the *inherent* value and sustainability of the marine environment, rather than on regarding it simply as a locus of resources serving economic aims. Or, in decisions seeking to reconstruct a neighborhood, citizens would likely insist that any necessary transformations still reflect *human needs and culture* of those who inhabit it, rather than the private interests of developers.

Proposing use of this methodology does not arise in a vacuum. It must be understood against the background of Louisiana's unique environmental circumstances and its often troubled social history. For that reason, considerable attention has been paid the nature of Louisiana's coastal environment and to the social and political dimensions of New Orleans' history. This is fitting, since Participatory Design itself arose from a context in which engineering and ethics were viewed as tightly linked. The methodology commits not only to engineering principles of problem analysis and problem solving, but also to ethical principles that relate to how designs transform a social order. In the case of the latter, it asks the question: how might the structures and institutions of a social order be designed to ensure the creation of a just and fair society? That is the subject of discussion in this chapter.

New Orleans and South Louisiana must be rebuilt from its devastated remains. Of necessity, a new social order will emerge from this process. Will this new social order repeat its preceding history of environmental short-sightedness and social injustice, or can the newly emerging society become more ecologically sensitive and a more just society than it was in the past? In analyses of environmental and social factors that anteceded Hurricanes Katrina and Rita, there have been many reasons to conclude that the destruction of areas of human and natural habitation—urban and coastal—was something that could have, and *should, have,* been anticipated. Even more disturbing, from a social and moral standpoint, is the realization that the many *inequities* in how the destructive effects of Hurricanes Katrina and Rita were distributed—inequities relating to race, class, and economic circumstances that cruelly played into vulnerabilities of geographical location—also should have been anticipated.

It is not the purpose of *Walking to New Orleans* to develop an ethic of a just society *independent* of providing a framework from which to guide decision-making processes and reconstruction activities in a post-disaster setting. A simple framework for that purpose will be discussed shortly. Nevertheless, it is first useful to consider certain underlying meta-ethical concepts that support this framework. This discussion will be drawn from what has been perhaps the most complete recently articulated theory of justice and a just society, John Rawls' *A Theory of Justice*, originally published in 1971, with substantial revisions in its 1999 edition, as well in other later works.[1] Since Rawls' work has been expanded and modified by others, as well as itself the subject of considerable criticism and discussion over the past thirty years, to put reasonable limits on discussion here, the following strategy will be taken. After a very brief review of some of Rawls' major contributions, focus will be directed to three elements in his moral thought: (1) cooperation, coordination, and design in the context of morality understood as rational decision in Rawls' hypothetical 'original position' and its use of the tradition of Kantian liberalism; (2) what Rawls calls the 'difference principle' and the fundamental consideration he believes a theory of justice must give to the least advantaged—those contingently placed by birth into racial, social class, and economic disadvantage; (3) some remarks Rawls makes about concepts of altruism such as benevolence, love, and fraternity, including what he has in mind by the expression 'purity of heart.'

These three elements in Rawls' thought relate generally to three underlying themes in the ethical considerations of *Walking to New Orleans*: (1) the view suggesting that ethics and engineering[2] principles coincide in some important ways that bear on societal considerations for post-disaster reconstruction; (2) the argument that any concept of justice must be based on a context of social diversity—an acknowledgment that contemporary societies (certainly those in the United States) are culturally, racially, ethnically, religiously diverse, with New Orleans and South Louisiana in particular as exemplifications of that; (3) the claim that attention to those unfairly disadvantaged by contingent circumstances of birth, race, social class, or economic status must be redressed in the construction of the institutions of a new society that preserves the best of the old as it also eliminates or reduces its pre-existing inequities. These three themes coalesce in the overarching view that, on both ethical and engineering principles, *toutes les voix de la Louisiane*—all citizens of New Orleans and Louisiana, current residents as well as those who called it home at the time of Hurricanes Katrina and Rita—must be in a position

1. For example, *Political Liberalism, The Law of Peoples*, and *Justice as Fairness: A Restatement.*

2. Use of the term 'engineering' here is meant to include not only engineering of physical objects and environments (such as mechanical engineering, civil engineering, etc.) but also human engineering (the science of human-system and group-system interactions).

to directly participate in post-disaster reconstruction planning, design, and implementation. In short, to argue that *all voices* in Louisiana must be heard.

The task of *A Theory of Justice* is to develop those moral principles upon which the structure of social institutions can be based, and by which they can be guided to ensure a society so created will constitute a just society. By 'social institutions' Rawls is meaning those rules and practices by which relationships among agents are governed. These range from simple performative interactions such as honoring an agreement to the complex relations that occur within economic, legal, and political systems. Rawls approaches this task from the social contract tradition of Locke, Rousseau, and Kant generally, and the moral theory of Kant that understands moral principles as the object of rational choice of free and equal rational beings to govern their conduct in an ethical commonwealth[3] more particularly—intending to avoid what he sees as defects in Utilitarianism at the same time.

Consistent with Kant's view of the absolute autonomy of the moral agent, Rawls begins from position that "each person possesses an inviolability founded on justice that even the welfare of society as a whole cannot override."[4] That is, in a just society the liberties of equal citizenship are fixed, and no pursuit of social goods that would advantage the majority can abridge those basic rights. In particular, Rawls is driven to show that advantageous attributes based on contingencies of race, class, economic status violate our sense of moral fairness even if it could be shown that such inequities might maximize certain social goods.

To develop a conception of justice as *fairness* that can serve as the basis of principles for a stable social order, Rawls moves away from relying on intuitions about what counts as desirable social outcomes, social ends that are often in competition with one another, and proposes a model of what he calls 'procedural justice,'[5] whose design, in its very structure, embodies the moral ideal of justice.[6] The society such a procedure should spawn is one understood as a *cooperative* venture for mutual advantage; this is the public face of justice as fairness. The procedure that embodies

3. Rawls, *A Theory of Justice. Revised Edition,* 221 (hereafter abbreviated as *TJ*).

4. *TJ*, 3.

5. *TJ*, 73–76.

6. See Martha Nussbaum, "The Enduring Significance of John Rawls," *The Chronicle of Higher Education,* July 20, 2001.

fairness is Rawls' postulation of an a-historical, hypothetical 'original position'—a conceptual state in which equally free and rational persons exercise rational judgments in coming to agreement on the basic principles of institutional design and social cooperation. The conditions under which such possible agreement takes place is one of a 'veil of ignorance'—the stipulation that persons engaged in those rational choices among alternative contractual relationships for society are without knowledge of how they are to be placed in the resulting society. Rawls extends the Aristotelian sense of justice as refraining from *pleonexia*—gaining some advantage for oneself by seizing what belongs to another—through a 'veil' in which those deciding the principles of a just society are without any considerations of contingent unearned and unmerited advantages due to social status from family and class origins or natural endowments which permit them to fare better than others in the course of life.[7] Under such conditions, Rawls argues that those in the original position would adopt the heuristic of a maximin[8] strategy that would maximize the position of the least advantaged. The thrust of Rawls' use of this hypothetical original position is to convince us that the principles of justice that we would rationally agree to, if we were in that position, have moral weight. Genuine equality cannot be achieved by worsening the position of the worst-off. It is in that sense that the 'veil' in effect *illuminates* the moral person—it allows a more perspicuous picture of what impartiality demands of us in a state of affairs Rawls calls 'reflective equilibrium' where principles and judgments coincide.

Just what are the principles that come out of the original position? In *A Theory of Justice* they are as follows:

First Principle: Each person is to have an equal right to the most extensive total system[9] of equal basic liberties compatible with a similar system of liberty for all.

---

7. *TJ*, 83.

8. *maximum minimorum*—the rule that tells us to rank alternatives by their worst possible outcomes and adopt the alternative the worst outcome of which is superior to the worst outcomes of the others. *TJ*, 133.

9. Rawls later modifies 'the most extensive total system' to read 'a fully adequate scheme . . . which is compatible with a similar scheme . . .' in *Political Liberalism*, 291. Basic equal liberties include political liberty (right to vote, hold public office); freedom of speech and assembly; liberty of conscience and freedom of thought; freedom of the person (freedom from psychological oppression, physical assault, dismemberment); the right to hold personal property; freedom from arbitrary arrest and seizure. In *Political*

Second Principle: Social and economic inequities are to be arranged so that they are both: (a) to the greatest benefit of the least advantaged, consistent with the just savings principles, and (b) attached to offices and positions open to all under conditions of fair equality of opportunity.[10]

While the two parts of the Second Principle—(a) the difference principle and (b) the opportunity principle—are ordered such that the latter is lexically prior, it is the difference principle that has been the more controversial. It demands that the basic structure of a just society be arranged so that social and economic inequalities are to the greatest benefit of the least advantaged members of society. This adaptation of the maximin strategy essentially eliminates Utilitarianism as a rational choice in the original position, because it would allow a maximum social benefit compatible with benefits and goods below the 'social minimum' of the least advantaged. It is largely the anonymity condition[11] of the veil of ignorance that contributes the 'rationality' of the difference principle: the 'social minimum' is a position that could just as easily be occupied by oneself as someone else.

The key appears to be to strike a balance between those inequalities necessary for generating productiveness in society and moral limits to those inequalities that do not raise the level of the least well-off. Such a balance has been hard to find among Rawls' readers—attacked by conservatives for whom it is offensive to take away from people what they earn by their talents, but also by those extreme liberals who believe tolerating almost any sort of inequality subverts justice.[12]

With this much said about Rawls' views of justice, it should begin to emerge why his proposals are both inviting and problematic as a moral backdrop for the tasks of reconstruction of at least sizable portions of the society that once was New Orleans and South Louisiana. Rawls' reflections about what justice is and how it could, in an ideal state antecedent

---

Liberalism these are extended somewhat to include liberty of conscience and freedom of thought; freedom of association; integrity of person (freedom of movement, occupation, choice of careers; personal property; equal political rights of participation and rights that maintain the rule of law).

10. *TJ*, 266. The principles are governed by two priority rules of lexical order in which basic liberties can be restricted only for the sake of liberty, and in which the second principle of justice is lexically prior to the principle of efficiency and to that of maximizing the sum of advantages, and in which (b) fair opportunity is prior to (a) the difference principle.

11. Suggested also by Thomas Pogge.

12. See also Martha Nussbaum.

to the circumstances of history, be brought about are initially inviting because they might provide a basis for attending to the needs of the least advantaged in a society—something that both historically and recently, post-Katrina and post-Rita, has not occurred in Louisiana. It is not as if the inequities of the society—one should better refer to *societies*—of South Louisiana are without parallels elsewhere in America. It is just that the inequities suffered by those least able to withstand injury from both natural and political causes have been very much brought into the light, and, indeed, magnified by recent natural events. On the other hand, Rawls had himself come to be increasingly concerned with the various elements of pluralism and diversity within society—forces of difference that put the ideal imagined just society under considerable strain. The society Rawls presupposed was one of homogeneity, stability, and relative isolation. Rather than include societies based on kinship or tribal groups or religious affiliation, Rawls' theory addresses something like the modern political state—a large group of people living together in an organized way, in a fixed geographical area, over generations.[13] It is a society that is isolated and self-contained, with a manageable level of scarcity. Certain kinds of diversity within the population are *not* addressed: citizens with severe mental or physical disabilities, families based on varying sexual orientations of its members, the roles of non-human species within society, as examples.

It is perhaps the place of religious pluralism, however, that is the most intriguing area of ambiguity. Rawls did not assume all citizens would accept as true any single faith tradition. This would mean, therefore, that principles of justice would have to allow for a range of diverse beliefs about such things as religious values and whether any entity should be made an object of worship. Where things get testy are those cases in which people put forth a basis in faith for the claim that liberty and equality are *not* more central to the life of the believer than, say, a divine command which supports the authority of one class of person (e.g., by gender or race) over another, or which necessitates, on religious grounds, some other form of social inequality. Rawls' own theory would seem to force a position which holds that freedom of belief and equality *must* coincide—even one in which freedom of belief and equality are themselves an essential core of religious faith. Such a position is quite consistent with the tradi-

13. Pogge, *John Rawls. His Life and Theory of Justice,* 39.

tion of Unitarian Universalism. One might simply note that John Rawls' daughter was married on December 3, 2002, in First Parish (Unitarian Universalist) in Lexington, Massachusetts. Rawls' own memorial service was also held there. Drawing any conclusions from such personal events, of course, would be speculation.

At this point we turn directly to three areas of contact with Rawls' theory of justice, suggested earlier, that bear on proposals for meaningful citizen participation in the physical and social reconstruction of South Louisiana. To put these in the form of questions: (1) How does understanding morality as rational decision support the practical utility of cooperation, coordination, and reciprocity? (2) How should a social order forced into the position of recreating itself respond to the unfairness of citizens contingently born into positions of disadvantage and inequality? (3) Is there a role for altruistic notions of benevolence, caring, and respect? While these are important sub-themes in Rawls, it should be cautioned that extending them for purposes of developing the concept of Participatory Design as a post-disaster reconstruction strategy is not meant to imply that Rawls would have endorsed this.

Cooperation, Coordination, Reciprocity, and Design

Processes supporting fundamental cooperation and the successful coordination of tasks are essential to any design or re-design effort. This is especially the case for highly complex projects such as the construction of components of urban infrastructure—housing, healthcare, transportation, water management systems.[14] Massive projects such as these typically involve not simply multiple individuals, but multiple groups, often multiple organizations, each with their own culture and patterns of behavior.[15] In complex projects with social implications, cooperation and coordination must reach a state where interactions among participants

14. As they are also, from the author's (RRNR) experience, in the development of large, heterogeneous computer networks.

15. 'Culture' applies not only to the recognition of different organizational cultures—for example, those of one agency vs. another, or one level of government vs. another. 'Culture' also applies to different task domains—for example, engineering design vs. manufacturing, planning vs. implementation. Finally, it applies to the increasingly geographically-distributed nature of organizations, in which a certain set of tasks may take place in one location, a second set of tasks in another location quite distant from the first.

exist *as if* they were the result of a process quite similar to that envisioned in Rawls' 'original position.'

The idea that Rawls sees the principles of a just society as a matter of cooperative design is evident from the start. The principles of justice are rules which specify a system of cooperation designed to advance the good of those taking part in it. A society is a cooperative venture for mutual advantage.[16] In addition to a well-ordered society being designed by a public conception of justice that everyone accepts and knows that others accept as well, a prerequisite for a viable human community in particular involves coordination, efficiency, and stability; the plans of individuals must fit together so that their activities are compatible with one another. When Rawls goes on to point out that in the 'original position' we can modify the account of the initial situation or revise existing judgments to eventually produce a state he refers to as 'reflective equilibrium,'[17] he is describing a standard principle of design as an iterative process. In a robust design process, it is a mistake to commit to a final version too soon, before adequate reflection and testing has run its course—to move, say, from prototype to final design without having used the prototype in interactive settings to learn what works and what doesn't. In a certain sense, a design is never fully stable—that is, it can always be improved upon—and Rawls recognizes that the equilibrium in which moral principles and judgments coincide is not necessarily stable: it can be upset by further examination of the conditions that should be imposed on the contractual situation and by particular cases, some of which may lead to a revision of initial judgments. Nevertheless, the justification for the principles of justice Rawls proposes is based not on the claim that they are derivable from necessary truths, but on the design paradigm that the conception of justice is a matter of mutual support of many considerations such that everything fits together into one coherent view.[18]

When Rawls elaborates on the part of his second principle which deals with fair equality of opportunity and pure procedural justice, the goal is to define a procedure that avoids the inequality of opportunity based on contingent social status and talents. Even if those barred from, or unable to participate in, opportunities for offices and positions involv-

16. *TJ*, 4.
17. *TJ*, 18.
18. *TJ*, 19.

ing the exercise of powers should benefit from the efforts of those who *are* allowed to participate in processes of opportunity, those kept out would be unjustly treated.[19] That is, it is not enough that a social system should, in fact, be improved by the efforts of those in power; everyone must have an *equal opportunity to participate* in the processes of social institutions for that society to be truly just. Chapter 8 will argue that universality of the opportunity to participate in processes impacting the structures of the society in which one lives is a cornerstone of the concept of Participatory Design, particularly in proposals for its use in post-disaster reconstruction.

In distinguishing what he calls 'pure procedural justice' from both perfect and imperfect procedural justice, Rawls sets up a contrast that is quite consistent with engineering design principles. Perfect procedural justice is exemplified by the model of dividing a cake into equal portions. One of its characteristics is that there is an independent criterion for what is a fair division—a criterion defined separately from and prior to the procedure which is to be followed. Such a model has an engineering parallel in the circumstance of design commitments made on the basis of top-down, abstract conceptual analysis done 'separately from and prior to' the design and testing procedure itself. An example from automotive engineering might be engineers having decided that since, in general, digital information is more precise than analogue, one should design the speedometers of cars to read out digitally. The fact that digital speedometers turned out to be less usable and analogue speedometers turned out to be far *more* usable, based on discoveries about how people actually drive and engage multiple visual fields (the road, the controls, etc,) is an example of the weakness of committing to designs on the basis of abstract, *a priori* decisions about 'what is best.' Another, more telling, example might be USACE's commitment to a "levees only" policy for controlling the Mississippi River and various waterways in and around the City of New Orleans—a decision made in advance of a complete understanding of the possible causes of and sources of flooding in a city below sea level (i.e., not only the river itself, but also wind-driven water from Lake Pontchartrain, storm surge from the Gulf, heavy rainfall, inherent weaknesses in levee foundations, etc.). In terms of social institutions, as Rawls points out, not only is perfect procedural justice rare, it is generally impossible in practical terms.

19. *TJ*, 73.

Pure procedural justice is also contrasted with imperfect procedural justice, and the example Rawls gives here is of the criminal trial system in which it is impossible to design the legal rules so they always lead to the correct result. Even when the law is carefully followed and the proceedings properly conducted, an innocent man may be found guilty, resulting in a miscarriage of justice. Recent use of DNA testing following recommendations by attorneys like Barry Scheck have shown the frequency of such miscarriages of justice to far exceed what people had previously expected.[20]

Rawls settles on a notion of 'pure procedural justice' in which there is no independent criterion for the right result, only an inherently fair procedure that is necessarily fair, regardless of results, when the procedure is correctly followed. While not especially appealing, the example Rawls gives for such a pure and just procedure is gambling. The point is that the process allows for contingencies of the hands and bets, requires following the betting rules, and honoring the promise to not cheat. Under those conditions, whatever the distribution after the last bet, the process is not unfair. For Rawls, the practical advantage of a 'pure procedure' such as this is simplicity—it is no longer necessary to keep track of the endless variety of circumstances and changing relative positions of the players.[21] It seems safest to say that the emphasis here must be on the fact the procedure is *not unfair*, rather than an exemplification of fairness, given the broader moral view that gambling in general only *redistributes* some finite amount of wealth; it doesn't produce any *new* wealth or goods in society. In latter context, one could indeed argue that the process *creates* inequities; nevertheless, the 'fairness utility' of such a procedure which both allows for contingencies of circumstance and is not *prima facie* unfair is clear.

Moreover, the gain of simplicity has something to be said for it. In thinking about the circumstances, say, in which a government leader would or would not order the evacuation of a city under conditions of an impending hurricane strike, there is—and has been in Louisiana—the sense of its being a gamble. It is a gamble both ways. The risk of *not* ordering the evacuation, of course, is potential loss of life. But the risk of ordering an evacuation, and having the hurricane track one hundred miles east,

---

20. "The post-conviction DNA exoneration cases are telling us that there are more people being convicted for crimes in our criminal justice system who are innocent than any of us wanted to believe. It's really that simple. And there are many causes for this." Quote from Barry Scheck on PBS Frontline.

21. *TJ*, 76.

sparing the city, is also considerable—costing a loss to the city's economy, and, perhaps, itself also resulting in loss of life, since mass evacuations are hardly danger-free. Therefore, if one could assemble the various predictive factors entering an assessment of when, where, and with how much force a hurricane would strike, and create a sliding scale of risk, one could perhaps establish criteria for evacuation decisions on the most rational basis possible—that is, on the basis of the best information available and the best risk assessment based on that information. One would gain the advantages of taking the decision out of the hands of politicians with their own private and political agendas. One could also take the decision out of the hands of those in positions of authority with perhaps the least training and knowledge to make such decisions on their own, or, as has been the case with some mayors of New Orleans, make decisions either ignoring or directly counter to the best scientific and logistical information and advice. The risk assessment and sliding scale of risk would have to allow for changes in decision points over time, as conditions relating to the storm itself change. But there would still have to be a point of GO—NO GO, beyond which no further decision could be either made or recalled. If citizens were equally able to provide input to such a procedure and come to an agreement that the design of the resulting decision tree represented both the most rational and the most fair way of coming to a judgment about whether or when to evacuate their city, it would seem to have some of the characteristics of what Rawls has in mind by the idea of pure procedural justice.

While it also relates to Rawls' discussion of the difference principle, which we will address shortly, it is worth noting that the limits this principle places on various forms of hierarchy is consistent with recent thoughts on how to optimize the management of engineering projects. When Rawls refers to a well-ordered society as a 'social union of social unions,' the limitations on forms of hierarchy and degrees of inequality[22] permitted entails that finite resources must be assessed multi-dimensionally, not solely on the basis of their contribution to a single outcome. For Rawls, this means recognition that resources for education, for example, are not to be allotted solely according to their return of specific capabilities, but also according to their worth in enriching the social and personal life of citizens, including the less favored. Translating that into the context

22. *TJ*, 92.

of engineering management, it would mean ensuring that engineers are trained not only in the specific skills they need to complete a design (e.g., mathematics of structural engineering, or some particular computer language like C++), but also that they have developed a broader awareness of the nature of work environments *unlike* their own (e.g., the tasks and problem-solving strategies of a professional office or a hospital setting). It would also mean recognizing the contribution the *social value* of a design makes to the its perceived quality and utility.

The idea that principles of justice are fundamentally a matter of—part and parcel of—the tasks of *constructing* a society[23] appears again and again in Rawls, including the connection established between cooperative tasks and 'reciprocity' in his rejection of the model of society of classical Utilitarianism. For the latter, the model is one of efficient administration of social resources to maximize satisfaction of the system of desire put forth by an impartial observer from the many given individual systems of desire. For Rawls, the construction of a well-ordered society is a scheme of cooperation for *reciprocal* advantage, as regulated by the principles of fairness chosen in the original position.

The possibility of passage between Rawls' use of the concepts of cooperation and coordination in his model of justice as fairness and contemporary thinking in the domains of engineering and management principles can be seen in a relatively recent development of the discipline of Coordination Science. For example, founded in 1991, the MIT Center for Coordination Science has studied how coordination occurs in a va-

---

23. In the *Nicomachean Ethics* but especially in the *Politics*, Aristotle loosely compares the tasks of the *politicos* to those of a craftsman. The statesman's legislative task is to construct the framework of a society that makes the good life possible. Politics, for Aristotle, is therefore less a struggle among classes for power or even the imposition of order and security than it is the 'crafting' of a *koinônia* of purpose—a community of virtue in aggregations of families for the sake of 'a perfect and self-sufficing life.' The legislator, in a sense, is a craftsman whose material is society and whose aim is the *shared* good life. The construction of an ideal state, while a skill and virtue-based aristocracy, is not, however, absolute, like the rule of a shepherd over his sheep; rather, it is a rule of equals over equals. The insistence that equality is a necessary condition of a state thus not only allows the validity of certain principles of constitutional democracy, but significantly modifies the picture of the legislator as 'craftsman' from being simply a one-way (top-down) process to something that is more a cooperative venture. Those ruled, then, are not mere 'tools' of the legislator—means to some larger end, however virtuous. Individuals have a right to articulate their own ends in life, and the virtuous state that can find a path between human weaknesses and ideal possibilities becomes, as much as possible, the expression of common aspirations and cooperative, coordinated acts.

riety of different systems, including human organizations, markets, and computer networks. The Center's work emphasizes how new information technologies have made it possible to think about organizing businesses and other organizations in new ways. To give greater emphasis on the impact of technology, the Center was reorganized and renamed in July of 2006 as the MIT Center for Collective Intelligence. To support the belief that understanding information technology can help people and social organizations work together more effectively, research has focused on developing a better understanding of the nature of coordination. To that end, the Center has studied coordination from the perspectives of theory, empirical research, and design. In addition to developing and testing theories about how coordination can occur in a variety of human systems, the Center conducts field studies of how people work together now vs. how they might do so differently using new modes of information technology, and then works to design and develop innovative computer systems that help people work together in small or large groups using technologies such as 'groupware,' 'computer-supported cooperative work environments,' and 'electronic markets.' Many of the methods are extensions of Human Engineering and Human-System Interaction technologies into the methods of Total Quality Management, Continuous Process Improvement, and Business Process Reengineering. As one example, the Center has promoted a Process Classification Framework (PCF), developed by the American Productivity and Quality Center (APQC)[24] and member companies as an open standard to facilitate process management and benchmarking, independent of industry, size, or geography. The Center also supports the Supply Chain Operations Reference (SCOR) model.[25] The SCOR model contains standard process definitions, standard terminology, standard metrics, supply-chain best practices, and references to enabling information technology. A third example is the Lean Enterprise Manufacturing model, a structure of 'enabling practices' that promote lean processes, developed by the Lean Aircraft Initiative Consortium led by MIT.

---

24. Founded in 1977, APQC is a member-based nonprofit that provides benchmarking and best-practice research for approximately 500 organizations worldwide in all industries.

25. The Supply Chain Council is a trade association of over 400 companies interested in supply chain management.

The point of exploring this interchange of ethics and engineering is to suggest that, at many points, the moral principles that would be agreed upon to form the basis of the structures and institutions of a just society also coincide with principles of good engineering design and good quality management practices. Both demand a fundamental and pervasive attention to fairness.[26] Both seek to develop practical methodologies for how the concept of fairness can be modeled in ways that are productive of humane social institutions and robust design. Both contribute to the background of understanding the concept of Participatory Design as a technologically and ethically justified approach to the tasks of the reconstruction of human institutions—not only for individuals (e.g., housing and healthcare services), but for NGOs and voluntary community-service organizations and neighborhood associations as well.

Principles of fairness may also stand as a critique of existing political processes in society for decision-making, including how decisions—some beneficial, some harmful—have often been indirectly determined by voting districting schemes and voting patterns, in which certain classes of citizens are ultimately included and others excluded from power and opportunity. The call to universality that principles of fairness demand—argued on both and engineering and ethical grounds—entails that all citizens must be equally in a position to participate directly in post-disaster reconstruction planning, design, and implementation.

In the social contract tradition of Locke, Rousseau, and Kant, Rawls believes every member of society should *mutually* be able to accept the same terms of cooperation because they achieve certain fundamental interests everyone has. It is a contract less in a competitive business sense than it is a contract understood as a mutual commitment—not a bargain of compromise based on a conflict of interests, but based on a mutual, common purpose.[27] Living in New Orleans and South Louisiana, for most who have lived there, is not an arrangement of financial opportunity; it is

26. Even when quality management practices are in support of improved profitability, because they must pay attention to the mutual interconnectedness of supplier, designer, manufacturer, and customer, they promote goals, processes, and behaviors that are very similar to those that would exist in a just social order. Fair practices at one level of a supply chain, for example, spawn children at other levels, because of their interdependence. Contrariwise, with practices that are unfair or operate on the basis of unfair advantage.

27. See, for example, Samuel Freeman, *The Cambridge Companion to Rawls,* 19.

certainly not an arrangement of convenience. It is something far closer to a marriage—for better or worse.

Unfairness and the Difference Principle

Rawls' two principles of justice as fairness are generated from an a-historical, hypothetical original position, but depend on an historical, actual world awareness—namely, that persons born into different positions have different expectations of life, determined not only by the political systems into which they are born, but also by the economic and social circumstances in which they find themselves at birth. It is from these unmerited and unearned contingencies that the institutions of society favor certain starting places over others, and, for Rawls, these are especially deep inequalities.[28] It is from an historical, empirical perspective that Rawls notes such inequities are pervasive. It is a *moral presupposition* to hold such inequities cannot be justified by an appeal to merit or desert.[29] Thus, for Rawls, is these inequities to which the principles of social justice must in the first instance apply.

The need to ameliorate a host of social inequities—especially in the quality of educational resources, economic opportunity, access to reasonably priced housing, adequate healthcare services—was traced over time; they were identified as clearly existing, in varying degrees, prior to Hurricanes Katrina and Rita. These inequities were enormously exacerbated by the effects and aftermath of those storms. The combination of this sudden intensification of inequalities, together Louisiana's unique opportunity to rethink the nature of its society and culture, makes Rawls' theory of justice as fairness particularly inviting in considerations of what principles of social justice need to be operative in post-disaster reconstruction.

Rawls sometimes appears to cast the historical observation of social inequities as if they were attributes endemic to any society—indeed, even inherent in the very concept of society itself—when he remarks that such inequalities are "presumably inevitable in the basic structure of any soci-

---

28. *TJ*, 7.

29. A point on which there has been considerable disagreement with Rawls, for example, from Robert Nozick, who, in *Anarchy, State, and Utopia*, developed an alternative conception of justice based on the legitimacy of historical entitlement as long as it evolves in a morally acceptable way. Nozick was particularly concerned that Rawls' conception of justice would require social engineering by an excessively interventionist government.

ety."[30] This is a particular view one may not be inclined to share. Even if it were the case that societies inevitably formed into states of inequalities over the course of their natural evolution—say, as a consequence of natural selection and adaptation in which contingent advantages increasingly select out—the stronger position initially expressed by Rawls would seem to come far too close to making social inequities a matter of *logical* necessity.[31]

In any case, conjunction of the need, and opportunity, to *intentionally* reconstruct society in a post-disaster setting, places a pause in the processes of existing social, economic, and political evolution. It is a pause of such an extent that the moral principles which define social justice can now come to the fore and make the structures and institutions of society objects of deliberate and conscious decision. The storms of two hurricanes, in effect, have provided an opportunity to *redress* the social, economic, human, and environmental problems that have pervaded the history of New Orleans and South Louisiana.

It is not as if the existing political system itself could not, at some point, have placed a pause on processes of social evolution that were perpetuating social inequalities. One can argue that democratic process, with its representational form of government and elections every two or four years, is designed to do that. Nevertheless, even when injustices have, to some extent, been redressed, as with the Voting Rights Act of 1965, they can all too easily reappear.[32] The economics of political power, along with the residue of old-world social privilege, help ensure that inequities based on unearned privileges of birth, race, family social position, educational opportunities continue largely unabated.

When programs of 'social change' come from above, top-down, instituted by those in political power, they often manifest an inadequate understanding of the needs and circumstances of those on whom change is enacted. Mistaken attempts at urban renewal in which viable businesses

---

30. *TJ*, 7. Rawls subsequently clarifies this by saying he rejects the contention that the ordering of social institutions is always defective because the distribution of natural talents and the contingencies of social circumstances are unjust, so that this injustice inevitably carries over to human arrangements. Rawls holds that the natural distribution of such inequalities as gifts, talents, or perhaps even inherited wealth is neither just nor unjust; what is just or unjust is the way that *institutions* deal with these facts. *TJ*, 87.

31. As certain theologians have done with the notion of original sin—casting it not merely as a inherent propensity to sin, but as a *necessity* to sin (*non possibile non peccare*).

32. For example, Supreme Court decisions regarding voting redistricting, such as *Shaw v. Reno*, that have cut the guts out of certain sections of the Voting Rights Act.

were destroyed, poorly conceived and constructed low-income housing, highways that cut the heart of a neighborhood in two, an academically unacceptable public school system are all examples of failures in New Orleans to understand social needs, because its citizens had not been *ongoing participants* in articulating what their needs were. One alternative to top-down social planning is the model provided by the Industrial Areas Foundation (IAF),[33] originally founded by Saul Alinsky in 1940. The IAF addresses conditions of blight and economic depression in urban environments by *beginning* with an understanding of the actual needs the community itself, letting the voices of citizens and their neighborhood organizations define those needs in such a way that planning for urban renewal is grounded in the very people whose lives will be changed by them. IAF teams work to facilitate a transfer of power—from existing sources of authority and economic means to the least advantaged, who can then be in a position to build their own network to address community improvement goals. The contemporary IAF operates as a grassroots, faith-based, community-organizing group that typically works cooperatively with local interfaith organizations. The Greater Boston Interfaith Organization (GBIO), one of sixty-five members of the IAF, is an example of such an organization. Founded in 1996 by forty-five clergy members seeking to transcend racial and class divisions in the city, the GBIO has worked to coalesce, train, and organize the communities of Greater Boston across all religious, racial, ethnic, class, and neighborhood lines to fight for social justice, and to help initiate actions and programs that communities have defined for themselves to 'redress' their social and economic problems. Among its accomplishments, GBIO has influenced the state to invest an

---

33. The Industrial Areas Foundation (IAF) is a Chicago-based community renewal organization originally established in 1940 by Saul Alinsky with a board of directors that included a Catholic bishop, the daughter of coal miners union leader John L. Lewis, and philanthropist Marshall Field III. The IAF has been less interested in promoting specific political agendas than being a mechanism for transfer of power—from existing sources of authority and economic means to the least advantaged who can then be in a position to build their own network to address community improvement goals. Alinsky's first organizing project was the Back of the Yards Neighborhood Council in Chicago. After World War II, Alinsky worked with Fred Ross in California in Mexican-American communities, resulting in a network of Community Service Organizations (CSOs) where organizers such as Cesar Chavez and Dolores Huerta participated in grassroots organizing 'house-meetings.' The IAF currently has some sixty-five affiliates in the United States, Canada, the UK, and Germany. Alinsky, whose published writings include *Reveille for Radicals* (1946) and *Rules for Radicals* (1971) died in 1972.

additional $100 million toward affordable housing, advocated for better working conditions for Haitian nursing home workers, and campaigned for universal state healthcare.[34] Its methodology develops actions through consensus and deliberation. The IAF model involves one-to-one meetings with members of local congregations, developing trust and cohesion, and teaching members to organize themselves. Thus, the IAF represents an ethical, consensus-driven approach, across a diverse spectrum of social classes, that seeks community-based, bottom-up, social change. This effectively represents the application of principles of user-driven design in order to move communities toward *their own* creation of a moral and just society. As a design principle, it is the belief that social change cannot spring solely from the interests of the 'designer' who holds political power. Ethically, it is the claim that power does not *belong* to those who, politically, hold it; it has only been granted for the purposes of creating a just social order.

The notion of the 'redress' of existing social injustices is particularly important to Rawls' second principle of justice. The 'difference principle' gives a special weight to considerations singled out by the need for redress. "This is the principle that undeserved inequalities call for redress; and since inequalities of birth and natural endowment are undeserved, these inequalities are to be somehow compensated for."[35] While Rawls distinguishes the difference principle from that of redress, the latter characterizes much of the intention of the difference principle—namely, in order to treat all persons equally, to provide genuine equality of opportunity, social institutions must give more attention to those with fewer assets and to those born into less favorable social conditions. The idea is not to even out all handicaps—as if the expectation in a race were to be that everyone one would come out winner (meaning that *no one* would win)—but rather to redress the bias of contingencies in the direction of equality; for example, perhaps to spend greater resources on the education of the less intelligent rather than on the more favored.

In Rawls' original position, the idea of 'redress' informs the conditions of judgments to be made there in such a way that redress is seen *as a matter of rational choice*: social and economic inequalities are just only if they result in compensating benefits for everyone, and in particular for the

---

34. See GBIO website, www.gbio.org.
35. *TJ*, 86.

least advantaged members of society.[36] It is precisely because it is based on *rational judgment* that the 'difference principle' is seen as necessarily part of any concept of justice. It is also what allows Rawls to envision the society that satisfies the principle of justice as fairness as being as close as a society can be to constituting a *voluntary scheme*. It is a voluntary scheme whose members are autonomous and whose obligations they recognize are self-imposed.

As Rawls' difference principle is linked to the idea of redress for inevitable inequalities that exist under political systems and social institutions, the principle is also linked to the concept of 'reciprocity' as a principle of mutual benefit.[37] To answer the criticism that the difference principle is unfairly biased towards the least favored, Rawls proposes a universe consisting of two groups, one more fortunate than the other. Given constraints defined by the priority of equality of liberties of the first principle and the priority of fair equality of opportunity, in this universe it is possible to maximize the expectations of either group but not both. Apart from his argument that, absent the difference principle, maximizing a weighted mean of the two expectations would, in effect, favor those already favored twice over, the main thrust of Rawls' position is the acknowledgment that justice must *mean* a scheme of social cooperation on which a satisfactory life for anyone depends, and in which no one could expect everyone's willing cooperation *unless* the scheme were reasonable. That is, if compensating—even by maximizing a weighted mean—those *already* compensated is *not reasonable* because the advantages are ones to which *no one* could have any prior claim, then the difference principle must *be reasonable*. The well-being of each person depends on a scheme of social cooperation in which the accidents of nature and social circumstance play no role unless a common benefit from them *includes* the least advantaged.

Reciprocity, then, demands every member of a society occupy a position *sub specie aeternitatis* in constructing both the principles for a just society and the design of the social structure and institutions those principles entail. Reciprocity reflects Rawls' original position that he believes keeps every person in society distinct and separate, autonomous in the ability to express and make moral judgments, but impartial—not only among persons at any given time, but across all generations, from

36. *TJ*, 13.
37. *TJ*, 88.

all temporal points of view.[38] Reciprocity is the form in which practical rationality and moral sensibility coincide.

Given the echoes of Kant here, Rawls is at pains to make it clear that the conception of justice on which his principle of equal liberty is derived is based largely on Kant's notion of autonomy, rather the place of the generality and universality of moral principles in Kant's ethics.[39] For Rawls, it is important that, as for Kant, moral principles are the object of *rational choice*. "They define the moral law that men can rationally will to govern their conduct in an ethical commonwealth."[40] The study of that rational decision is the subject of moral philosophy, and entails that moral principles serving as legislation for a kingdom of ends must be agreed to *under conditions in which all persons are free and equal rational beings*. It is here that the idea of persons acting autonomously *as an expression of* their nature as free and equal rational beings—what Rawls also calls "an ethic of mutual respect and self-esteem"—coincides with the difference principle, not on the basis of second-order altruistic notions such as benevolence, but on the assumption that it is *genuine mutual disinterest* which allows for freedom in the choice of a system of final ends.[41] Thus, Rawls concludes that his original position may then be viewed as a 'procedural interpretation' of Kant's conception of autonomy and the categorical imperative.

Purity of Heart and Benevolence

Despite the fact that Rawls at many points wants to push second-order[42] notions of altruism to the background of his formal arguments for principles of justice as fairness, there remains the feeling that concepts of beneficence, benevolence, fraternity, love of mankind, and so forth, nevertheless play important *informal* roles. Rawls distinguishes among beneficence (an act one is at liberty to do or not do and which is intended to advance another's good), benevolence (a good act performed for the sake of another person's good), and a supererogatory act (a benevolent

38. *TJ*, 514.

39. *TJ*, 221–26. Rawls's discussion begins in reference to his first principle of equal liberty but then broadens to include his concept of justice as fairness in general.

40. *TJ*, 221.

41. *TJ*, 223.

42. That is, they depend on a state of affairs that is already given.

act done at considerable risk to the agent).[43] A weakness of second-order altruistic notions is that, if the goods of separate individuals conflict with one another, sentiments such as benevolence are unable to resolve those conflicts, since they do not include principles of right to adjudicate among them.[44] To adjudicate among conflicting goods requires the guidance of what individuals themselves would consent to in a situation in which they have equal representation as moral persons—that is, the 'original position' Rawls establishes as essential to understanding what justice is and how it can come about. Thus, he sees nothing gained by attributing benevolence to the parties in the original position.

At the same time, while benevolence and love of humankind are not the *same* as justice—for example, where benevolence manifests such intensity that it is prepared to go beyond the requirements of natural duties—as long as one assumes the mutual disinterestedness of parties (in the original position), it is not unreasonable to interpret altruistic notions such as benevolence and the love of humankind within the framework of justice as fairness. The mutuality of disinterestedness—the reciprocity of equality of liberties as well as the social necessity of the ability to see oneself in the position of the least advantaged—in effect makes benevolence able to operate within the realm of rational choice. This is what defines an ethic of mutual respect and self-esteem. One might say, benevolence is a matter of pure rational choice rather than the passion of a bleeding heart; rather, it is the *passion* of pure rational choice as genuine fairness.

Rawls makes a similar case for the ideal of fraternity, understood not as unrealistic expectations about ties of sentiment across the wider human society, but as the natural sense of not wanting greater advantages for oneself unless it is to the benefit of others who are less well-off. The family, in its ideal state, is a micro-model of fraternity (or sisterhood, or kinship ties). Again, if fraternity is interpreted as incorporating the requirements of the difference principle, it is a perfectly feasible standard.[45]

The remark with which Rawls ends *A Theory of Justice*—as an explanation, in part, of what it means to speak of the position of *sub specie aeternitatis* as a form of thought and feeling that rational persons can adopt *within* the world—is a claim to the power of shared autonomy. "Purity of

43. *TJ*, 385.
44. *TJ*, 167.
45. *TJ*, 91.

heart, if one could attain it, would be to see clearly and to act with grace and self-command from this point of view."[46]

Purity of heart captures the sense in which the original position is both a model of a deeply held moral norm based on the rationality of genuine reciprocity, and a more distant claim to the possibility of a shared feeling of humanness in the context of an increasing awareness of the pluralism of social values—in particular awareness that the world is the locus of wide-ranging religious and cultural diversity. In his later work and in revisions to *A Theory of Justice*, Rawls more and more turned to try to address questions of religious pluralism in the hope that his theory of justice as fairness could provide principles that not only differing faith traditions but also non-religious and secular approaches to life could accept together as a foundation for justice in a pluralistic society.[47]

Purity of heart, from the hypothetical original position in which rational, self-interested people given the task of choosing principles that will define the structures and institutions of society—people with equal liberties and sufficiently similar capacities so that one cannot overwhelm another—expresses Rawls' belief that individual needs will be better met by cooperative, coordinated modes of social interaction than by alternatives involving competitive supremacy. But purity of heart also derives from the 'veil of ignorance' itself—what in the original position ensures that parties do not know where they will be placed in the resulting society. It is that hypothetical bracketing of race, class, gender, and social position which forms what Martha Nussbaum calls a "morally decent impartiality" towards the projects and life plans of others. It is choice not biased solely by one's own special interests.

Given our contemporary awareness of the issues of competitive life in a pluralistic world—a world of multiple political systems, differing faith traditions, a growing diverse marketplace of secular philosophies and life-improving, longevity-increasing, personal strategies—purity of heart is perhaps best suggested by Rawls' idea of "overlapping consensus."[48] It is a model for how political fairness can be established in the breech of the confrontations of such pluralism, and diverse concepts of what 'the good' is, especially where concepts of the good are informed by

46. *TJ*, 514.

47. A vision not unlike those expressed by the Seven Principles of the Unitarian Universalist Association.

48. *TJ*, 340.

differing religious claims.[49] For Rawls, overlapping consensus allows differing approaches to moral principles—Kantian affirmations of autonomy, Utilitarian promotion of overall utility, Theistic expressions of divine command—to ultimately come together to agree to a more fundamental freedom. That freedom is a matter of rational choice, a freedom based on reciprocity, from which reasonable persons of widely differing views and cultures and sources of moral authority can nevertheless accommodate their views of justice to a public one capable of being sufficiently shared for a just society to exist. New Orleans is a microcosm of a pluralistic world of widely differing approaches to social integrity and values. The question is: can one articulate some process—some procedural interpretation of principles of justice as fairness, as expressed in the moral philosophy of John Rawls and others—that can be of utility in establishing something like an overlapping consensus, and a notion of fairness that in some ways redresses the history of inequalities that have existed in the social milieu of New Orleans for so long? We believe that the concept of Participatory Design can move those involved in the planning for the reconstruction of the infrastructure, neighborhoods, and lives of those in post-Katrina New Orleans and post-Rita Southwest Louisiana in that direction.

To move from the theoretical to the strategic, and, ultimately, to tactical, it will be useful to propose a simple, concrete framework against which to see the possibility of just how more abstract principles of justice as fairness might be enacted at the political, the community, and the individual levels. The following describes one model of such a framework.

A CONCEPTUAL FRAMEWORK

The schema presented here represents an attempt to provide for the integration of meta-ethical considerations—for example, those general moral principles on which a theory of social justice as fairness could be based, as in the preceding discussion of John Rawls—with the more concrete and practical considerations on which strategic and tactical post-disaster reconstruction planning decisions, and implementation processes, will be based. Underlying this schema are three important philosophical view-

---

49. As in Islamic extremists' rejection of Western economic and political values on the basis of religious claims derived from revelation and divine authority, or in Christian missionaries' degradation and suppression of indigenous people's religious practices in South America or the South Pacific.

points that are put forth in support of the ethical considerations both here and in elaboration of the concept of Participatory Design in Chapter 8:

(1) *Walking to New Orleans* argues that ethics and engineering principles (including principles of human-system interaction) must be understood as fundamentally interrelated in any system of justice. Reconstruction planning strategies that result in new infrastructure systems for disaster protection, new models for rebuilding communities, must reasonably be capable of still meeting basic human and community needs. But to understand what 'basic human and community needs' are presupposes having heard and engaged the participation of all citizens in an iterative loop of ongoing communication.

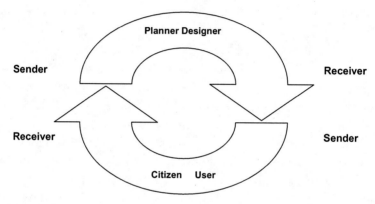

(2) It is also argued that any conception of social justice must be based on recognition of the massive diversity of the racial, ethnic, religious, and cultural environment of New Orleans and South Louisiana. Justice in reconstructing a living and working environment for a population that is so diverse on multiple levels must be based on having heard and engaged the participation of all citizens. There must, in addition, be genuine equality of opportunity in such participation to balance unmerited advantages for some resulting from contingencies of birth, family, social status, and economic position.

(3) Finally, it is argued that particular attention must be given to those segments of the population *most* disadvantaged, not only by social, political, and economic inequalities existing prior to the storms, but also by exacerbation of those inequalities due to the unequal impact of damage and destruction, and especially by losses so severe that *still-displaced* residents have been unable to return at all. 'Most-disadvantaged' is marked by factors that must include

race, quality of public education, adequacy of housing and medical services, fairness in political processes and economic opportunities.

Ethical Modalities

The conceptual framework is a schema that identifies four modalities which must be put in rational relation to one another in order for an ethically coherent and fair reconstruction process to take place. The schema is presented first in its simplest, most general form—consisting of four modalities of process, agencies, facts, and implementation—then as a more detailed model, specific to the requirements of social reconstruction.

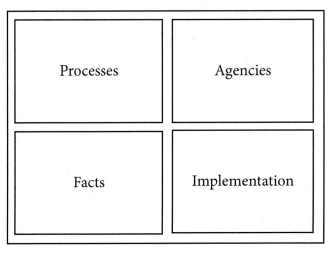

Processes	Agencies
Facts	Implementation

Processes refer to any conceptual or political approach taken, relative to the context, historical setting, and social or organizational entities involved. They also include the meta-structures or principles under which particular processes operate—that is, the underlying model of social dynamics, capable of producing change, and, ideally, that support behavior consistent with a just society. 'Processes,' therefore, incorporate certain meta-ethical considerations about what 'counts' as good, socially desirable, right behavior, and so forth, as well as the implied conceptual or political model on which moral and ethically justified behavior is based. *Agencies* refer to players within the universe of possible processes that, ideally, are consistent with a just society, and include both actors and recipients of actions. This modal element also refers to those indirectly impacted by existing social structures and political organizations. *Facts* refer to the natural, social, and political constraints under which processes must operate. Myriads of things may count as relevant facts, some of which can be modified, some not, but particular attention is given to those facts that are generally accepted as unalterable, such as the climate and geographical setting of the social organizations involved. *Implementation* refers to the actions themselves—the tasks of social construction or reconstruction, as it were—that are proposed by both agencies and recipients. In terms of over-all implementation, both large-scale strategies (e.g., city-wide plans) as well as specific tactics (e.g., at the neighborhood or ward level) are included.

The following expands this schema in more specific terms to include properties relevant to the context of *Walking to New Orleans*:

Principles of Just Democratic Processes

Principles of just democratic processes express the moral basis for achieving fairness in political power, including access to planning and projects for addressing reconstruction needs. Following Hurricane Katrina, it may have been in awareness of the importance of re-establishing a moral basis for democratic process that the New Orleans City Council pushed for an Inspector General and a Board of Ethics in City Hall to combat its historic corruption.

It is common for first principles of democratic process to begin by affirming the importance of human value, to promote the inherent *worth* and the *dignity* of every person.[50] As individuals, we are unique. In participating in democratic process, individual uniqueness is not lost. There is a primacy to one's worth: each individual is important *as* a person; each person is *inherently* of equal rank.

As democratic processes unfold into the political arena, the question of *dignity* arises—what it means for individuals to interact *in community* with others. Dignity is about one's *relation* to others; one's *relative* worth within a society. The value of relative worth is often expressed through principles that speak to the necessity of democratic processes to insure fairness—to insure each individual operates on a level playing field.

At some point, policies, drawn from these general principles, focus on how democratic processes deal with issues of abuse of power. In many instances where this occurs, abuses are sufficiently public to be acted upon through the direct use of democratic processes. However, many instances of abuse of power are *not* public. They are indirect, hidden, unavailable for direct action through democratic processes. Such instances of abuse require the existence of advocacy groups to be made public. Voluntary associations operate somewhat outside normal democratic processes to insure that the interests of those situated beyond, or on the fringes of, existing social structures—handicapped people, the elderly, those economically disadvantaged—are considered and brought into the field of public democratic activity.

Democratic processes must also deal with issues of conflict in their use. Sometimes—when there is wisdom and forethought—policies exist to address how matters of conflict should be handled. Conflict is inevitable—in many respects it is a necessary part of democratic process because of the paramount emphasis given to individual worth and dignity. As a result, it is natural for competition to arise. Even when constrained by broad considerations of justice and fairness, the possibility for conflict emerges precise from the values that assert our uniqueness. If each is unique, every one of us is different. *Every* individual has a different set of skills and capabilities; different ways of thinking, of deciding, of solving problems. Even where there exist shared values or beliefs within a given social structure, we differ about how to achieve common goals, how to function as a body, how to handle financial arrangements, how to operate cooperatively.

50. For example, as in the first of seven principles of the Unitarian Universalist Association.

The root meaning of 'conflict' is *to strike together.* Things in conflict *clash* against one another. The clash may be one of values or ideas; it may be a contest of wills. In either case, 'conflict' connotes *opposition.* Sometimes underlying the opposition may be anxiety about change itself, fear of doing things differently than they have been in the past. Sometimes it is simply the *clash* of personalities.

Democratic processes, and the government entities or voluntary associations which use them, must therefore find ways to manage conflict. Principles of just democratic processes must first *acknowledge* that strong disagreements are natural and exist as part and parcel of their use. But the same principles must also endow each of its processes with the power of making visible a mandatory contract in which, despite inevitable disagreements, persons can and *must* treat one another with respect. That is, democratic processes must give dignity (mutual respect based on an *equivalence* of individual worth) a public face. One would like to believe this is based on an *inner conviction* of each individual's inherent worth. But, assuming it is not possible to know with certainty another's 'inner convictions,' forms of social contract and agreed upon commitments can serve as a proxy to make the value of mutual respect public.[51]

It is often the case that when people have strong disagreements with others—about a particular policy, about a decision, about a future plan—they become antagonistic. They not only degrade the positions of the individuals with whom they differ, they find ways to undermine the plans and decisions themselves that have been agreed upon or voted. The *attack* on those with whom antagonists disagree typically extends to the modes of enacting decisions—on the *processes* for planning or developing strategies for implementation, for example[52]—then moves onto the individuals themselves who proposed or supported those plans or strategies. Often, poorly visible vicious cycles of antagonism are set in motion. Dissention may first be felt on an emotional basis, in which individuals are hurt that their opinion, their view of things, was not supported. For

---

51. Even assuming that mutual respect is a shared value, there may be widely varying interpretations—based on differences of personality and cultural backgrounds—of what behaviors fall within the limits of displaying mutual respect. Rather than leave the determination of what counts as instances of behaviors 'beyond the limits of acceptability' up to the ill-defined court of public opinion, some form of social contract to which people commit is a reasonable alternative.

52. That is, if one disagrees with the outcome, then attack the process that arrived at it.

a certain period, that emotional hurt may be rationalized in arguments against various outcomes—against plans or particular projects. Eventually, however, that emotional hurt may be re-converted into moral judgments against those individuals with whom they disagree. Sometimes, when there are particularly strong disagreements, individuals may *withdraw* from the normal life of the process, and pursue their own agenda from the outside, as it were. They refuse to engage in further debate and discussion, and make judgments—or sometimes even separate plans designed to undercut those that were agreed upon through democratic processes—from the outside.

The reason for this brief consideration of some elements of human dynamics at work in democratic processes is simply to emphasize there are points at which natural behaviors of disagreement can fly in the face of expectations in the use of democratic processes within political structures and voluntary associations. But ultimately, it must be principles of fairness within democratic processes that are used to manage disagreements in a respectful manner; to allow disagreements to be resolved *through* discussion and dialogue; to instantiate, in effect, an *ethic* of interpersonal behavior.

There are three additional characteristics of democratic processes that demand attention as part of any general argument for the universality of participation. First, democratic processes presuppose a social environment that is fluid, capable of modification, and, therefore, that needs continual attention, continuous improvement, including *process* improvement—that is, attention to the effectiveness and quality of the processes themselves. Democratic processes, in short, presuppose an environment that is *dynamic*. While natural cycles of social evolution take place in all but a theoretically absolute totalitarian state, Hurricanes Katrina and Rita brought about a more radical shift in the social and economic conditions in South Louisiana than had been occurring over probably the previous forty years—at least, since Hurricane Betsy in 1965. But apart from calamitous natural events as coastal storms, flooding, yellow fever, civil war, segregation, any democratically structured social environment experiences the dynamic of less violent shifts in natural resources, economic successes and failures, and the entrance or passage of human lives from the scene. To refer to the environment of democratic process as dynamic is similar to the sense implied by Aristotle in treating the 'crafting' of a *koinônia* of purpose—a community of virtue from aggregations of families for the sake of 'a perfect and self-sufficing life.' Insofar as a community, a social structure, is composed of diverse groups, families, and individuals, who have the right to articulate their own ends in life, the communal structure is necessarily a dynamic, living entity. The creation of a virtuous community that can successfully chart a course between shared possibilities and human failings must then be the result of cooperative, coordinated efforts that express common aspirations.

A second element in democratic processes is their normative dimension. Among the obligations the existence of a democratic state entails is the obligation to participate; democracy cannot be sustained by passive involvement. Without active and as universal participation as possible, democratic processes in time wither and the state defaults to other forms of hierarchical or plutocratic control. The obligation to actively participate in political and other social processes, therefore, is not merely ethical; it is a matter of survival. For this reason, the obligation to participate is non-transferable. The rights and responsibilities to act within democratic processes cannot be sold, even for some larger benefit, because the virtue of the state proceeds directly from the equality of opportunity to act and the obligation to fulfill that opportunity. The commitment is not disposable.

A third attribute of just democratic processes is recognition of the rights of diverse groups—the pervasive pluralism that stems directly from the uniqueness of individuals and their inherent worth and dignity. As do individuals, collectives within a society—whether racial, ethnic, religious, cultural or voluntary associations of various sorts—have the right to articulate their own ends in life. From such intrinsic pluralism within a democratically-structured society, it follows that both individuals and collectives may differ not only in their general perceptions of right and wrong, but also in ways to achieve the goals of the community. In terms of post-disaster reconstruction strategies and implementation, then, there can be no imposed orthodoxy—no "one way," unless there has also been a democratic process that has established consensus, or at least sufficient agreement among collectives that have had equal opportunity to participate.

Given the likelihood of a diversity of belief and opinion on the very matters that affect the structure of a post-disaster society—the form of its leadership, the basis of its economy, the character of its neighborhoods— what is the appropriate response to such differences? One possibility is what Aristotle sometimes refers to as 'common aspirations' for a shared good life, where these aspirations constitute the 'soul' of a virtuous community, understood on analogy with the human soul. More specifically, response to the differences that are consequences of the equality of right means accepting that trust and respect for disagreement are themselves crucial *shared* values. Members of a democratic community with 'common aspirations' agree to allow free expression of diverse ideas and opinions, and develop forums for resolving differences without the dominance of personal animosity or retribution. This involves the explicit agreement by participants in democratic processes to resolve differences in a rational and harmonious way in which the authority of one's private opinions and beliefs are bracketed during the process of resolution of conflict.

Accepting *both* the equality of right in which diversity of opinion and belief is an inevitable consequence, *and* a commitment to resolving differences that includes bracketing the authority of one's opinions and beliefs suggests a particular definition of freedom. Freedom now is understood as a 'covenant of cooperation.' Freedom which acts out of selfishness is blind, dangerous, ultimately *self*-destructive. Authentic freedom is the promise to cooperate with fellow members of the community to promote 'common aspirations' for a good life, understanding that such a promise may temporarily restrain individual freedom or limit its exercise as a self-imposed choice. With that promise is also the faith that such commitment to a 'covenant of cooperation' will ultimately allow the rebirth of freedom in forms that can be shared a wider community than before. Such shared freedom is true autonomy—where a community comes to speak as a harmonious chord, despite the different pitches that make up its voice. It is a sentiment echoed by Theodore Parker's remark that "Democracy means not 'I am as good as you are,' but 'you are as good as I am.'" It is the sentiment of a shared belief that cooperation is the best expression of individual freedom.

Agents and Recipients Involved

Discussion of the second modality of the ethical framework can be kept relatively brief because many of its concerns have already been addressed under the first, as well as in the remarks on Rawls. Issues relating to agents and recipients of decisions and actions largely turn on the question of fairness of voice. For democratic processes to meaningfully support equality of right and equality of opportunity, they must include means by which pre-existing inequities and imbalances of living conditions, educational, and economic opportunities—especially those based on race and ethnicity—are redressed to ensure a *proportionately equivalent voice* to the needs of all citizens of the community. 'Voice' refers not only to the needs of individuals, but also to those of racial, ethnic, and cultural groups—there must be *equal access* to the political process.

The primary approach to accomplishing equal access is introduced in the context of discussion of the concept of Participatory Design in chapter 8. There are, however, several practical considerations that can be mentioned here. First, the absence of full participation raises the danger of minority rule by default. Small groups of committed individuals who want to effect change specific to their needs and aims should have timely and reasonable means to assemble and express their views. At the same time, the effectiveness of democratic processes ultimately requires that *all* minority elements of the community are heard and included, so that decisions and actions taken are consistent with the needs and aims of the community as a whole. How does one determine the needs and aims of the community *as a whole*? The traditional approach is to define this by a majority vote of members of the community. However, there are weaknesses in the method. A numerical majority does not by itself establish unanimity or commitment. Often, those *outvoted* may see their tasks as continuing to try to defeat or undermine the decisions supported by the majority vote. Preferable to majority voting is consensus, because, when established, it signifies a degree of unanimity such that, even if there remain disagreements or dissent about what has been discussed and the decisions arrived at, there is nevertheless also the commitment to honor them. Silent vote does not provide the opportunity to achieve that kind of commitment. Processes of consensus are not without their own drawbacks—they can be cumbersome, lengthy, dominated by more powerful individuals; nevertheless, the end result is still preferable to the ambiguity often present after a numeric vote, and discussion of Value Analysis in chapter 8 should provide some ways to avoid the most serious issues in a consensus-driven process of prioritization and decision-making. 'Community as a whole,' when an expression of consensus, means that the needs and aims of the community have been identified and *actually shared among its members* in the process of trying to achieve consensus.

A second practical consideration has to do with those members of a community who are especially likely to lose their full voice in democratic process, or otherwise 'fall through the cracks,' because of such factors such as age, health, geographical location, economic status, work and family commitments, level of education, racial or cultural background.

Individuals who life at the 'margins' of the community must be given every opportunity by the community to exercise their right to participate. This may mean that processes used have to make certain accommodations to ensure the full participation of all its members so they can participate on an equal basis. A visible contemporary example of this is the increasing necessity of cities to provide Spanish or Russian or Vietnamese language versions of publicly disseminated information about city activities, voting rights, procedural requirements of government agencies on the city's website, on the corridors of offices in city hall, in the media, in work places, and at polling places.

One third practical consideration to ensure equality of voice among agents and recipients concerns conditions under which meetings take place. Meetings to discuss topics of common interest must be both public and open. When a group is gathered or convened to discuss matters that pertain to the community as a whole, such discussions should be announced in advance and be open to everyone's participation. The authors have witnessed instances in which the failure to ensure public notice and opportunity to participate in meetings called by groups within a larger association has had disastrous results—even when there was wide agreement about the decisions of those meetings.

Responsibility to Environmental and Demographic Facts

Ethical decisions, and subsequent actions, take place in the context of setting obligation and moral judgments against facts. Rarely can moral judgments be *derived* directly from bare facts, which is not to say that defenses are not given of morally justifiable behavior simply because it was the behavior exhibited. Cases where 'the behavior exhibited' may *rationally* be regarded as identical with 'morally justifiable behavior' occur in circumstances such as in the medical use of *triage* in sorting victims for different levels of treatment or the withholding of treatment in mass casualty incidents (MCIs). But here, such behavior has standing behind it moral judgments *already made,* and it presupposes processes carefully thought through and evaluated in an extensive series of worst-case scenarios.

Decisions involving long-term strategies for rebuilding communities that have experienced massive devastation are especially obligated to develop processes to give ethically justifiable weight to the impact of facts which impact those strategies. For example, one particularly poignant, and complex, issue in post-Katrina New Orleans concerns strategies for neighborhoods that were not only most severely damaged by flooding, but that will likely remain highly vulnerable to flooding in a future that could easily extend for ten years. These are neighborhoods for which levees and floodwalls are either thoroughly inadequate or non-existent. A question that arises is whether it makes sense to rebuild those neighborhoods. Clearly, the interest of former residents of those neighborhoods is that their homes and streets and urban infrastructure be rebuilt. Clearly, it would be wrong for those residents not to be participants in decisions by city and state leadership about whether or not to rebuild. But it might be naïve and equally wrong to simply pour scarce resources into areas that could not be saved, or that could better serve and protect the city as a whole. As in familiar versions of 'lifeboat ethics,' facts alone do not decide issues, especially when some (in this instance, such as the rebuilding of levees) are under human control. However, accuracy in the representation of facts—and their implications—is itself an ethical task.

When decisions based on facts—about the state of the environment or the limitations of human resources—degrade into a two-sided battle between the interests competing groups (e.g., to rebuild or not to rebuild), such disagreements are never resolved happily. On the other hand, when facts can be put on a variable scale of relevance and complexity, there can be room to maneuver in one's thinking, and allow concerned parties to make more refined value judgments through prioritizing what is more important against what is less. Creating scales of value of the roles played by environmental conditions, infrastructure capabilities, population needs, resources available, and so forth, places decision-making processes in a shared, open forum in which residents and government leaders alike can see what is before them and understand *why* the decisions arrived at are the based on the reasons people they were. Citizens of New Orleans, in the first eighteen months after Hurricane Katrina, have experienced decision after decision having been made along with an absence of any ability to articulate the reasoning behind those decisions. In the case of hurricane and flooding protection alone, too many decisions acted on by those who have authorized USACE in the construction of levees, locks, drainage canals, pumps, and floodwalls have been based on incomplete or inadequate information. From the standpoint of responsibility to environmental and demographic facts, the primary responsibility of government leadership is to accurately put before the community what the fact and contingency factors in order that rational deliberation can take place. When accurate factual information fails to be disseminated because of bureaucratic indifference or organizational hierarchies, those agencies have failed in their primary mission: inform the public. Existing technologies exist can create a visual map of an organization's information flow, identify nodes of frequent blockage, design an overlay to restructure communication channels to avoid blockages and points of misinterpretation, so the flow of information can be improved. There is no excuse for such failure.

Planning and Implementation Strategies and Tactics

The fourth modality of the schema concerns the phase at which principles of democratic process, having considered interrelationships among agencies and addressed issues of fact, must now be applied to decision points about actual strategies and actions. It is here, at the point of implementation, that areas of potential conflict or ambiguity arise less from competition among established needs or the global constraints of environmental factors, than from failures in monitoring the ongoing progress of actions taken. How does one ensure that proposed engineering and rebuilding projects go forward in a rational, coordinated, and fair way?

One straightforward model to accomplish this is familiar to those involved with process control and quality management. This is an iterative, four-step implementation monitoring process known as the Shewhart Cycle,[53] sometimes the Deming Cycle,[54] or simply 'Plan-Do-Check-Act' (PDCA).

---

53. After Walter Shewhart (1891–1967),an American physicist, engineer, statistician, often thought of as the father of statistical quality control.

54. After W. Edwards Deming (1900–1993), an American statican, and consultant, most known for improving production and product quality in Japan during the 1950s with the application of statistical methods such as analysis of variance (ANOVA) and hypothesis testing.

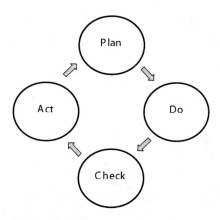

Versions of PDCA are at least as early in descriptions of scientific method as 'hypothesize—experiment—evaluate' in the work of Francis Bacon. In its four-stage form, 'plan' refers to identifying goals and the processes necessary to reach them based on how the goals are specified; 'do' is the initial implementation of these processes; 'check' is evaluation and monitoring of both the results of the implementation, and the processes used to attempt to achieve results; 'act' represents modifications to those processes to improve them, based on analysis of their weaknesses and points of failure.[55] It is most important to understand the cycle as an *iterative* process—that is, while it may be initiated in a planning phase, it is a cycle of continuous improvement that repeats itself endlessly until an ideally perfect output results and an optimally efficient process exists. While that end-state never occurs in the real world, each iteration of the improvement cycle brings greater knowledge of the system of planning and implementation as a whole.

The simplicity of the PDCA cycle makes it appealing to think of its application in a very wide range of settings, and the model has the advantage of at least instilling an attitude that monitoring how well certain processes are actually working is worth the effort. Whether the model is likely to produce small, incremental improvements or large breakthroughs is a matter of debate. A more important question is the suitability of the model for large-scale, long-term projects involving many people and massive resources. The continuous improvement cycle works best when it can be confined to a clearly defined set of outputs, and therefore devotes

55. 'Act,' therefore, connotes a more specific sense of 'do' and is best thought of as 'improve.'

its energy to optimizing the processes used to get there. In the case of the reconstruction of an entire society and the rebuilding and extension of its infrastructure, it is likely that some outputs will only be identified as needed along the way. In those cases, new processes will have to be integrated with older processes, and that adds considerable complexity to the model.

On the other hand, the PDCA cycle is particularly well-suited to the incorporation of multiple levels of participation by personnel who are involved in and working on various aspects of the overall reconstruction objectives. This is because it establishes a simple and easily communicated language about process control and human interaction with processes. The cycle is also well-suited to the evaluation of multiple processes running concurrently, because it is not necessary to fundamentally change the basic cycle to accomplish such evaluation.

Whether this, or some more complex model is chosen to ensure citizen participation throughout all phases of the rebuilding of the social structures and neighborhoods of New Orleans and South Louisiana, it should be part of any overall ethical framework that there be a shared language for talking about the goals, plans, decisions, actions, processes, and degrees of success in achieving all of them. This shared language, as much as anything, enables government leaders, ordinary citizens, planners, developers, federal agencies, contractors to all be on the same page, and to have a basis for communicating with one another. Perhaps the best antidote against perpetuating a history of social injustice, inequities, and abuse of power is the simplest and most wide-open vehicle of communication conceivable. Ethically, speaking about where New Orleans and South Louisiana is (and isn't) at any given stage in its progress of rebuilding should be as easy as reading the progress on the local United Way thermometer showing how close a community is to achieving its donation goals. It is not a question of finding the lowest common denominator of where people are cognitively in their ability to understand the complexities of recovery and rebuilding. It is a question of creating a model that is perspicuous and honest. It is a question of conceptual 'usability'—is the vision for New Orleans and South Louisiana shared, and is it a vision that makes sense? And that is an ethical matter.

Near New Roads

Rural Graveyard

Atchafalaya Basin near Little Bayou Sorrell

Nutria

Courir de Mardi Gras, Church Point

Tout le tour du moyeu

At Marc Savoy's, Eunice

Old Country Home

Man with Dog, New Orleans

Le Vieux, New Orleans

Towards Grand Isle

Crawfish Restaurant, New Orleans

Florida Avenue Bridge

On Florida Avenue

6

Fairness Under the Law

Legal Issues in Reconstruction Planning

CONSIDERATIONS OF THE RIGHT OF ACCESS TO POLITICAL PROCESS

IT SHOULD BE EVIDENT that a sub-theme of *Walking to New Orleans* has been to take the circumstances presented by the necessity for post-disaster reconstruction as an opportunity to move a culture in the direction of a more participatory democracy. This would mean not only a broader participation of citizens in making meaningful contributions to existing decision-making processes, but also a greater involvement in the direction and operation of social systems. Discussion of the concept of Participatory Design and Value Analysis in chapter 8 will elaborate in more detail methodologies by which citizens can become more directly engaged in the processes of planning and implementing their own recovery.

Recognition of weaknesses inherent in representative democracies is not new. A primary concern has been that, in limiting citizen participation to voting, traditional representative democracies default the authority of actual governance to politicians and bureaucrats. Governance through representatives is not genuinely participative; the role of citizens tends to become more one of monitoring the behavior of representatives, rather than fully engaging in dialogue about the issues at hand. When the public media encapsulates the details of complex issues in brief 'sound bites,' discussion of important matters about which there are diverse opinions is truncated even further.

A second criticism—voiced especially by those who advocate the notion of open democracy, or *panocracy*—is that the political processes

338

of representative democracies operate under the false assumption that the mass of people, even within a given locale, can be said to express a single will. One must assume there may be as many 'wills' as there are people to have them; therefore, it is necessary to make a distinction between the results of a majority (or plurality) vote on some proposal and the idea that such a vote represents a 'shared will.'

Walking to New Orleans does not reject the idea that there can be a 'shared will' of a community, or what Aristotle sometimes calls 'common aspirations.' In fact, there is abundant first-hand evidence in New Orleans, particularly at the community level, and through the work of neighborhood associations, that bodies of citizens share not only common concerns that result from living proximate to one another, but also broader goals of social justice and fairness. A community (*koinônia*) in Aristotle's *Politics* is established for the sake of some good; in its function as a collective, its component parts share certain functions and interests in common.[1] In its Christianized usage, *koinônia* adds particular connotations to the meaning of partnership[2] by including notions of fellowship and a shared spiritual purpose. Early Christian communities functioned as mutually beneficial unions with a common purpose, but were also intimately bound together sacramentally.

To advocate a more participatory political process does not demand opting out of representative forms of democracy. A strong argument can be made for the value of keeping participative, community-based initiatives *within* civil society and outside the sphere of government on the grounds that a strong separation between civil society and politics (a) is more efficient, given the volume of information of local issues that must be gathered and prioritized in decision processes, and (b) that it leads governments to become more sensitive to the needs of their constituents, since those needs are strongly and publicly voiced, and, in many cases, acted upon at the community level. Such a separation of the civil and political realms establishes a relationship that is an adversarial one. But with strong participatory processes of cooperation and coordination at the community level, it is one that can exist at a manageable and healthy level.

1. Aristotle adds that a community possesses order only if it has a ruling element or authority.

2. In the sense of holding shares of things in common with others, present in its meaning in classical Greek.

Of course, 'opting out' of representative democracy is *not* an option in America's current political system. Thus, it is useful to consider how various mechanisms for voting and choosing representatives by district can exist through processes that are fair, and that give an equal opportunity of voice, especially to those in society for whom it has historically been denied.

On July 2, the Civil Rights Act of 1964 established landmark legislation that outlawed discrimination based on race, color, religion, sex, or national origin. The Act was originally conceived primarily to protect the rights of black people, but was amended to protect the civil rights of everyone, explicitly including women. Among various protections, the Act sought to enforce the constitutional right to vote by barring unequal application of voter registration requirements. However, it did not abolish literacy tests, that had often been used to prevent African Americans from registering to vote.[3]

3. In order to prevent the registration and participation of African Americans in the political process, Alabama restricted voter assistance (established in 1893 and abolished in 1988, *Harris v. Siegelman*, 695 F. Supp. 517 (M.D. Ala. 1988)); required literacy tests and provided for a voucher system (established in 1901 and abolished in 1965 by the Voting Rights Act); mandated long residency requirements (established in 1901 and abolished in 1972, *Dunn v. Blumstein*, 405 U.S. 330 (1972)); enacted a "petty crime" provision (established in 1901 and abolished in 1985, *Underwood v. Hunter*, 730 F. 2nd 614 (eleventh Cir. 1984) aff'd 471 U.S. 222 (1985)); established white primaries (established in 1902 and abolished in 1944, *Smith v. Allwright*, 321 U.S. 649 (1944)); provided local registrars with unfettered discretion in judging applicants' interpretation of state and federal constitutions (established in 1946 and abolished in 1949, *Davis v. Schnell*, 81 F. Supp. 872 (S.D. Ala. 1949) aff'd 336 U.S. 933 (1949).

In Georgia the payment of taxes was a prerequisite to vote (established in 1868 and abolished in 1931 by Georgia law); laws provided for long durational residency requirements (enacted in 1868, lengthened in 1873 and abolished in 1972 , *Abbot v. Carter*, 356 F. Supp. 280 (N.D. Ga. 1972)); grand jury appointment of the school board (established in 1872 and abolished gradually by local referendums in individual counties—1992 statewide). White primaries were established in Georgia (abolished in 1945, *King v. Chapman*, 62 F. Supp. 639 (M.D. Ga. 1945)) and laws provided for disenfranchising offenses (established in 1877 and upheld in *Kronlund v. Honstein*, 327 F. Supp. 71 (N.D. Ga. 1971)); registration by race (established in 1894 and still required); literacy, good character, and understanding tests (established in 1908 and abolished in 1965 by the Voting Rights Act), including a "grandfather clause" restricting registration (established in 1908 and abolished in 1915 by Georgia law); property ownership as a prerequisite to voter registration (established in 1908 and abolished in 1945 by Georgia law); a county unit system (established by party rules, late in the nineteenth century, by statute in 1917 and abolished in 1963, *Gray v. Sanders*, 372 U.S. 368 (1963)); a "thirty-question" test for voter registration (established in 1949 and abolished by the Voting Rights Act in 1965); and finally, majority vote and numbered vote requirements (established in the late nineteenth century as a local option, replaced by statute, county and statewide, in 1964, operative in municipalities in 1968 and still in use).

On March 7, 1965, some 600 civil rights marchers headed east out of Selma on U.S. Highway 80. They were protesting the refusal of the Registrar in Dallas County and other counties in the State of Alabama to register to vote otherwise qualified black men and women. The marchers made it only as far as the Edmund Pettus Bridge, six blocks away. Alabama State Troopers and the Dallas County Sheriff's Department, some mounted on horseback, awaited them. In the presence of the news media, the troopers and deputy sheriffs attacked the peaceful demonstrators with billy clubs, tear gas, and bull whips, driving them back into Selma. Brutal images of the attack interrupted regularly scheduled television programs. For the first time, large numbers of people throughout the country, now presented with horrifying images of people left bloodied and severely injured, roused their support for the civil rights movement. Amelia Boynton Robinson, whose photo appeared on the front page of papers and news magazines around the world, was beaten and gassed nearly to death. At least seventeen marchers were hospitalized, and this infamous day came to be called "Bloody Sunday." Five months later, President Lyndon Johnson signed into law the Voting Rights Act of 1965.

The Voting Rights Act included a number of features that allowed the federal government to exercise control over the voting process in local jurisdictions. The Act made unlawful the many tests and devices,

---

Mississippi enacted laws that provided for a literacy tests that required an applicant to be able to read and understand any section of the state constitution (1890), which was subsequently amended to require that the applicant read and write any section and give a reasonable interpretation (1955) (established in 1890 and abolished by the Voting Rights Act in 1965); mandated durational residence requirements (two years in the state and one year in the precinct, amended to one year in the state and six months in the precinct (1962) (initially established in 1890 and abolished in 1972 by *Graham v. Waller*, 343 F. Supp. 1 (S.D. Miss. 1972)(three-judge court)); required dual registration in county and with municipal clerk (established in 1892 and abolished in 1987 by *Mississippi State Chapter, Operation PUSH v. Allain*, 674 F. Supp. 1245 (N.D. Miss. 1987), aff'd 932 F. 2nd 400 (fifth Cir. 1991)); provided for white primaries (established in 1907 and abolished in 1947, *Smith v. Allwright*, 321 U.S. 649 (1944)); required party loyalty oaths (established in 1947 and abolished in 1987 by Mississippi legislature); mandated "citizenship understanding tests" (established in 1955 and abolished by the Voting Rights Act in 1965); prohibited satellite registration (established in 1955 and abolished in 1965 by the Mississippi legislature in an effort to avoid coverage under Section 5 of the Voting Rights Act, 42 U.S.C. 1973c ("Section 5")); provided for a "good moral character" test (established in 1960 and abolished in 1965 by the Mississippi legislature in an effort to avoid coverage under Section 5); and required newspaper publication of names of applicants for registration, and procedures for challenging the moral character of an applicant (established in 1962 and abolished in 1965 by the Mississippi legislature in an effort to avoid coverage under Section 5).

such as literacy tests and poll taxes, that had been used by various southern jurisdictions to prevent black citizens from registering to vote. The Voting Rights Act further provided for federal registration of voters (instead of state or local voter registration) in areas in which fewer 50 percent of the eligible minority voters registered. Thus, it authorized federal examiners to go to locations where blacks had not been permitted to register, set up tables on the steps of county courthouses, register black persons, and prevent the purging of any of these federally registered voters without the approval of the federal government (Office of Personnel Management). Finally, but currently most important, the Voting Rights Act of 1965 provides the federal courts and the United States Attorney General authority to certify counties for the assignment of federal observers; it prohibits the adoption and implementation of voting practices and procedures that discriminate on the basis of race, color, or membership in a language minority group; it freezes changes in election practices or procedures in certain states until the new procedures have been determined, either after administrative review by the United States Attorney General, or after a lawsuit before the United States District Court for the District of Columbia, to have neither discriminatory purpose or effect (Section 5 of the Voting Rights Act, 42 U.S.C. 1973c); lastly, it requires certain covered jurisdictions to provide bilingual written materials as well as other voter assistance. On July 27, 2006, President George W. Bush signed a twenty-five year extension of the Voting Rights Act (the Fannie Lou Hamer, Rosa Parks, and Coretta Scott King Voting Rights Act Reauthorization and Amendments Act of 2006).

VOTING RIGHTS AND ACCESS TO POLITICAL POWER

By the 1980s, the language in Section 2 of the Voting Rights Act, 42 U.S.C. 1973 ("Section 2") that prohibited denial or abridgement of the right to vote[4] was used to challenge and change the method by which governing bodies were elected, where election methods made it difficult, if not impossible, for newly registered black citizens to elect 'candidates of choice.' 'Candidates of choice' came to mean candidates who *looked the same* as those who elected them. The social effect of the law, after *Thornburg v.*

---

4. Section 2 of the Voting Rights Act, 42 U.S.C. 1973, provides, in part, that "[n]o voting qualification or prerequisite to voting or standard, practice, or procedure shall be imposed or applied by any State or political subdivision in a manner that results in a denial or abridgement of the right of any citizen of the United States to vote on account of race or color" or membership in a language minority group.

Gingles, was, for example, the notion that black elected officials would better represent black people, that Hispanic elected officials would better represent Hispanics, and so forth. In most cases of early challenges, existing methods of election were at-large elections with majority vote and numbered place requirements, which permitted the voting majority to choose every candidate and subvert differing preferences of a minority that turned out to vote. *Gingles* requires that Section 2 plaintiffs demonstrate that voting is racially polarized; i.e., that white people vote "sufficiently as a bloc to defeat" black candidates, and that black voters cohesively support black candidates (similarly, that other minority groups cohesively support their minority candidates). Since there is no way of knowing which candidates a voter has supported—short of exit polls—statistical analysis, e.g., ecological regression analysis, is used to make estimates of the degree to which one racial or ethnic group has supported a particular candidate (legally significant racial bloc voting).

The most common remedy for a Section 2 violation was the creation of single-member districts[5] that would ensure the election of a minority candidate, which necessitated the use of race as a predominate districting principle—in effect, carving up the jurisdiction to reflect its racial divide.[6] Indeed, district boundaries codified the racial divide in communities. The designation of districts as "black districts" or "white districts" did little to erode racially polarized voting behavior. To some extent, these districts en-

5. A "single-member district" is an election district in which only one candidate is elected. Members of the United States House of Representatives are required by law to be elected from single-member districts. Likewise, most states elect members of state legislative bodies from single-member districts. In a "single-member district" election, a voter is only permitted to vote for one of the several candidates competing in the election district in which he/she is assigned.

6. The Court in *Shaw v. Reno,* 509 U.S. 630 (1993)("Shaw I"), recognized an "analytically distinct" equal protection claim for challenging an election district as a "racial classification." Accordingly, where an election district was created by subordinating traditional districting principles to race, and such racial classification was neither narrowly tailored nor supported by a compelling justification, the Court determined that it violated the Equal Protection Clause and could not stand. As a result, single-member districts created to provide minority electoral opportunities must still be the product of race-neutral, traditional districting principles, including recognition of communities of shared interest, respect for political and other natural boundaries and divisions, and even incumbency protection. These also must be among those considerations that can define the creation of an election district or explain the "shape" of the election district—even where it appears that the district is merely the result of gathering all of the minority persons in an area in order to provide for requisite electoral opportunities.

couraged and supported it. There were "safe" black districts, "safe" white districts, and "swing" districts," in which analysis of voting patterns indicated that minority and non-minority candidates had a roughly equal chance at election. Likewise, it may also not be true that the minority community on whose behalf the remedy was instituted is better represented or more politically empowered. The remedy may ensure that more minority persons serve in local and state elections—that governing bodies look more like the people they represent—but it has not necessarily provided a voice to minority voters to which government must now listen and better respond.

Nevertheless, in a relatively short period of time, these Voting Rights Act challenges dramatically changed the face of local and state government. For example, the challenge to Dallas County's (Selma, Alabama) at-large method of election resulted not only in the election of the first black candidates to the County Commission since Reconstruction, but also—through crafty manipulation of boundary lines by government attorneys—the election of a County Commission the majority of whose membership was black. As a point of history, a majority of the Dallas County Commission are no longer black, as a result of a wave of challenges in the 1990s brought by disgruntled white persons who found themselves in minority-majority single member districts, and who believed that their equal protection rights had been violated. By then, membership on the Supreme Court had changed, and the failure of a jurisdiction to pay heed to the electoral needs of their non-minority citizens was accorded as much—if not more—judicial attention as had been, some twenty-five years previously, to the abject failure of certain jurisdictions to provide minority citizens with any electoral voice.

As a voting rights attorney for the U.S. Department of Justice, I[7] was not among those who believed this interpretation of the Voting Rights Act was the wrong thing to do. It was, however, clearly social engineering. On the other hand, I have also come to realize that such a narrow view of what constituted "equal access to the political process" may very well *not* have provided minority people with the most powerful influence, or resulted in governing bodies that were—as a whole—inclined to be responsive to the particular interests of a minority group. There is considerable evidence that a minority voting population might be *better off* if its votes can influence the election of an *entire slate* of candidates in

7. DEBR.

344

an at-large election, rather than have its influence confined to the election of only one candidate who represents a minority district.

This view of political influence was demonstrated, when, in the 1970s in New Orleans, white persons were the majority and black persons constituted no more than 35 percent of the registered voting age population.[8] That minority voting bloc was nevertheless largely responsible for the election of Moon Landrieu,[9] a white candidate who, among other white candidates,[10] had displayed a responsiveness to the needs of the black community, but who was not supported by conservative white voters. Thirty years later the circumstances were reversed. Now, the irony of the fact that a cohesive minority voting bloc can exercise considerable political power was evident in the 2002 election of Mayor Ray Nagin. In his runoff with black Police Chief Richard Pennington, Nagin received only 40 percent of the black vote, but 85 percent of the white vote, in which a cohesive 35 percent minority of conservative white voters were able to elect the candidate of their choice among the two black candidates.

A 35 percent cohesive minority voting bloc can therefore ensure that candidates most responsive to the needs of the voting bloc are elected. Where elections are at-large—a five-member governing body, for example—a 35 percent cohesive voting bloc can influence, if not dictate, who among *all* of 8–10 candidates running for election will serve on a governing body. An elected official able to gain support of a 35 percent voting bloc need only receive a small percentage of votes of the majority to be successful. But such an elected official would be beholden *more* to that 35 percent bloc who secured his election than the 20+ percent of the majority who also voted for him.

In contrast, where there are single-member districts, and one district of five is a minority-majority district—one in which most of the minority voters are gathered—*one* candidate who is the first choice of persons in that district will be elected. Presumably, this candidate is the same racial or ethnic minority as those who elected him. The gain is that single-member districting ensures there will be *one* minority person serving on the

8. The 1970 Census showed black persons constituting 45 percent of the total population of Orleans Parish; the black percentage of its total voting age population was considerably lower.

9. Moon Landrieu was elected in 1970 and served as mayor until 1978.

10. And his white opponent in the runoff, Jimmy Fitzmorris, who was supported by most of the city's political establishment.

five-member governing body. However, there very likely may remain four non-minority persons serving on the governing body who have *no political reason* to be responsive to the particular needs of the minority community, particularly where there is conflict between the needs and issues of the group who elected the candidate and the minority voters assigned to the minority-majority district. In such circumstances, candidates elected from non-minority districts have every political reason *not* to be responsive. In addition, the minority elected official will be viewed as representing *only* minority persons, and—worse yet—will be *only one* lone voice, *only one* vote of five. Finally, non-minority voters who do not reside in the minority-majority district will not have the opportunity to vote for, and be represented by, a minority candidate, and therefore may not have the experiences which demonstrate that character, integrity, honesty, and intelligence may be better indicators of who should govern than race or ethnicity.

Not surprising, white elected officials and citizens generally opposed the imposition of single-member district remedies, often by arguing that such remedies would create balkanized governing bodies—the members of which would not politically motivated by the best interests of the entire jurisdiction. Yet, twenty years later, in large urban areas that had evolved into minority-majority cities, it has been the single-member district method of election that has *protected* white voters by ensuring a white presence on elected bodies long after white voters had lost the numerical superiority and ability to elect in racially polarized at-large elections.

The short-term goal of using the Voting Rights Act to institute single-member districts was to provide an immediate remedy to give minority groups the best chance of electing minority representatives—after years and years of failure to have done so under the challenged method of election. A longer-term goal was presumably the "waning of racism in American politics,"[11] which would be evidenced by an erosion of racially polarized voting—where electoral choices were based upon a candidate's performance and characteristics *other* than race. Single-member districts created to provide electoral opportunities to minority voters and candidates, however, provide few opportunities to undermine the reliance upon race in making electoral choices, since their creation is largely a product of race-based cartography and a commitment to providing for the election of minority candidates.

11. *Johnson v. DeGrandy*, 512 U.S. 997, 1020 (1994)(Souter, J. writing for the majority).

Some have argued that Section 2 should not have been interpreted to allow for *more* than providing all qualified voters with equal access to the polls. Congressional intent notwithstanding, single-member district remedies to at-large methods of election were necessary in the jurisdictions in which the early cases were brought. In these jurisdictions, racism was intractable, segregation legislated, and methods of election had been adopted for the purpose of preventing the election of minority persons. In these jurisdictions, very few minority candidates had been elected. On the other hand, it is much less clear that such single-member district remedies advantaged minority voters in other more recently challenged jurisdictions with at-large methods of election. In these jurisdictions, the history of voting-related discrimination and racial exclusion had not defined local politics and electoral access; minority persons had never been prevented from registering to vote and otherwise participating in the political process; residential patterns were not strictly defined by race or ethnicity; public education had not been subject to *de jure* segregation; most important, minority candidates had enjoyed success, and support among white voters for minority candidates had been steadily increasing. In these jurisdictions, therefore, at-large elections may have been responsible for the *reduction* of the influence of race in political choices over the last twenty years—particularly in those cities where minority populations grew and became more politically organized and empowered.

COMPARISON WITH A NORTHERN CITY

The City of Springfield, Massachusetts, in which I grew up, may be just such an example. Unlike New Orleans, Springfield is a city dependent upon industry, although the nature its industry has changed over the years. Springfield was founded in 1636 by William Pynchon. The Springfield Armory, which George Washington designated the National Armory, established much of the character of Springfield. Its industries have included production of the M1 or 'Garand Rifle' and the M-14 at the Armory, Smith and Wesson, Indian Motorcycle, Milton Bradley, mills, quarries, and Monsanto Chemical Company. These industries defined the city in the early twentieth century, and supported its significant growth after the War. But like many industrial cities and towns in New England, much of its industrial base has gradually left or been considerably reduced.

Springfield has always had a black population—one that steadily increased during the twentieth century. As early as 1926, black persons were elected to its unwieldy bicameral government, one governing body of which was elected from multi-member wards and the other elected at large. In 1959, young political 'turks'—including my father—campaigned for a "Plan A" form of government that provided for a strong Mayor and a City Council and School Committee elected at large. The chief criticisms of the then-existing governing bodies, and the persons elected in ward-based elections, was that there was little chance of defeating well-established incumbents who became powerful 'ward bosses' controlling the politics of the ward from which they were elected. In addition, there was little accountability due to the size of the bicameral governing body, and the fact that most of the business of the government was conducted by committees comprised of members of the City Council. Misspent funds and municipal projects, mired in cost overruns and other inefficiencies, if not graft, defined the conduct of city government. The Mayor had little or no power. The initiative question passed—even in the black community—although there was a division among African American leaders regarding the election of members of the City Council and the School Committee in at-large elections. Many worried that the powerful, growing Irish population would control city government and politics; others were confident that voters would not fail to elect qualified candidates of different racial and ethnic backgrounds.

"Plan A" provided for the election of the nine-member City Council in at-large, non-partisan elections. Voters were provided the opportunity to vote for as many as nine candidates for City Council and as few as one (or no) candidates; i.e., there was no prohibition against single-shot voting, which has often been used by minority groups to elect candidates of choice and which had been prohibited in many of the southern jurisdictions where the method of election had been found in violation of the Voting Rights Act. The nine candidates receiving the most votes were elected to serve for two-year terms; i.e., there was no majority vote requirement, which had been used in these same southern jurisdictions to prevent the election of minority candidates of choice. School Committee members were elected in at-large elections to four-year staggered terms. Voters were provided the opportunity to vote for as many as three candidates and as few as one (or no) candidates for School Committee. By 1967, a black candidate had been elected to City Council, and by 1972, a black candidate was elected to the School Committee.

Beginning in the 1980s, the Hispanic population—primarily Puerto Rican—began a rapid increase, and, by 1990, numerically outstripped the black population. A Hispanic candidate was elected to the School Committee in 1981, placing first among a field of six candidates. Nevertheless, it was not until 2002 that a Hispanic served on City Council. Hispanic voter turn-out has historically remained low, and the investment of the Hispanic community in the local political process limited. One factor that may account for this is that a large proportion of the Hispanic population divides its time and commitment between family in Puerto Rico and family in Springfield.

A recent Community Service survey indicates that Springfield is no longer a white voting age majority city. This also means that white people will no longer constitute the largest group of those eligible to vote by the 2010 Census. Nevertheless, in 2006, a challenge to the at-large method of election was brought by plaintiffs seeking a single-member district method of election. The limitations of single-member districts, which do not encourage *citywide* campaigning and governing responsibilities, as previously discussed, all but ensure that it will be a long time before a minority candidate has acquired sufficient citywide support to run for and be elected as Mayor of Springfield, the only elected official with any power or authority. The single-member district plan proposed by plaintiffs would limit Hispanic influence to one or at most two out of the nine districts, and it would limit black influence to only one of the nine districts—this despite the fact that two blacks have been elected to City Council under the current method of election.

The remaining six or seven members of City Council (all of whom would be white) would no longer need to campaign in the North End and South End where 40–50 percent of the Hispanic population resides, or need to campaign in the Mason Square or Hill-McKnight area, where a significant proportion of the black population resides. Since once predominately white neighborhoods in Springfield have slowly become more integrated, it has been difficult for the plaintiffs to create a single-member districting plan that provides for the election of more minority candidates than *currently* serve on City Council. In addition, the single-member districting plans would leave many Hispanic voters—but too few to constitute an influential bloc—in white-majority districts. Indeed, more than 50 percent of the Hispanic population and nearly as great a proportion of the African American population would not be able to vote for a minority candidate who was elected to City Council as they are currently able to under the at-large method of election.

Nevertheless, plaintiffs have remained steadfast in their insistence upon single-member districts as a remedy. The insistence is based less on facts or concrete knowledge of the changing demographics of Springfield than on the patronizing belief that "single-member districts provide for the kind of representation *they* (minorities) need" and therefore want. In actuality, much of the commitment to, and interest in, ward-based elections stems more from a desire for neighborhood representation than from an interest in increased minority representation. The fact that such an election scheme would deprive those minority persons who no longer reside in the historical 'centers' of the African American and Hispanic populations in Springfield of the ability to vote for minority candidates of choice has been of little concern to the named plaintiffs, many of whom have had the intention to seek office once a ward-based election scheme is been adopted that would require they do little more than campaign among friends and neighbors and supporters. Likewise, the fact that Hispanic and African American voters would lose their ability to influence the election of all nine members of the City Council, and all six members of the School Committee, has been lost in the clamor for neighborhood representation and the greater accountability that the plaintiffs believe will attend ward-based (single-member district) elections. Finally, the fact that such an election scheme would further isolate the few remaining, relatively affluent, white neighborhoods and absolve its residents of any responsibility for, or interest in, the poorer, crime-ridden minority neighborhoods is not addressed by the plaintiffs. Nor is the notion that the health and continued survival of the City—currently in financial crisis—is dependent upon a strong sense of community and commitment shared by all of the city's citizens of greater importance than the stubbornly held notion that the best representation is neighborhood representation. The plaintiffs have not subscribed to the view that, in order to meet the goal of a fair voice for racial and ethnic minorities in addressing urban needs, the voting system must ensure racial or ethnic majority (historically white) elected officials remain obligated to campaign in neighborhoods where they would otherwise have no need to venture forth. For a voting system to fairly reflect all the voices in a community, it should instill in majority candidates a duty to meet and answer questions from citizens who have significantly different needs than do their immediate neighbors.

This, then, is the dilemma for a voting rights attorney. On the one hand, it is important to support community identity and representation, including instances where it turns out to be defined on racial or ethnic lines. On the other hand, it is equally important to recognize city needs that cross neighborhood (and racial or ethnic) lines. Elected officials must be able to speak to the needs of the *entire* population, not just the needs of those by which election was won.

Both the logic of numbers and the goals of fair representation of all racial and ethnic groups in the political processes of Springfield argue for defending the city's current method of election because it provides for *better* representation for minorities, and will ensure that the face of the City Council and the School Committee changes as the city population changes. It is counter to the goals of fairness of voice in representation to support a voting system in which districts will be created to ensure that a majority of the City Council remains white long after whites have relinquished their numerical superiority.

On the basis of the change in perceptions that make up the ethos of a city's self-awareness, one would like a system in which 'little old Yankee white ladies' are able to use one or two of their nine votes to support a candidate from a *different part of town, who looks different.* Would they vote for the minority candidate if they had *only one* vote? No. Would they even get the chance to *meet* minority candidates at neighborhood 'meet and greet the candidate' nights? No. In fact, the history of minority candidate success in Springfield has shown that, in each subsequent election, minority candidate support among white voters has increased. For example, in the last municipal election (2007), the incumbent Hispanic member of the City Council received the most votes among all of the candidates—incumbent and non-incumbent alike. Presumably, the experience of having voted for and being represented by a minority person contributes to erosion of race or ethnicity as the primary basis of electoral choices.

The history of minority candidates in Springfield suggests it is not always the case that social engineering is as necessary as it was in places such as Selma, where racism was overwhelmingly present and where alternative opportunities to change racial attitudes were so few. On the other hand, social engineering can facilitate the emergence of cooperative, face to face, efforts of social conscience, where people of different races and ethnic backgrounds come together and come to know one another in the context of initiatives that benefit *multiple* groups within a city—working to ensure affordable housing, to build libraries and cultural centers . . . to guide reconstruction after a natural disaster.

The different logic underlying districted versus at-large elections continues to operate after the ballots are counted. It influences how council and school committee members actually govern. Members of a governing body elected in at-large elections cannot safely disregard demands emanating from minority communities, and that need only grows as demographic changes continue. With districted elections, by contrast, members of governing bodies are most responsive to the people who elected them, who are far more racially homogenous than the city's population as a whole, and who are limited to those neighborhoods in the election districts from which members were elected. In addition, districted elections tend to produce candidates who are less moderate, while at-large candidates have an incentive to look for votes everywhere, and tend to moderate their positions accordingly. Under the current at-large system, it makes sense for a white candidate residing in an affluent, non-minority district to campaign in predominately minority communities; minority candidates likewise feel the same pressure to reach out beyond their immediate neighbors. The system encourages racial crossover voting on election day, and produces a governing body with a broader grasp of the public interest and more legitimacy than one elected by a method that rewards insularity and parochialism.

Accordingly, the dilemmas inherent in the application of the Voting Rights Act exemplify the complexity of establishing racially proportionate and fair participation in managing an urban environment. The means of social engineering implemented and advocated by the Department of Justice in enforcing Section 2 of the Voting Rights Act, and administering Section 5 of the Voting Rights Act, while providing for and facilitating the election of more minority persons, has also had the effect of balkanizing, dividing communities even more, thereby making communities less prepared for developing any kind of master plan. During crises such as those in the post-Katrina world of New Orleans, one can see, quite painfully, the potential for loss of city-wide cohesion.

In New Orleans' self-perception as a polyglot, 'gumbo' city, the question of city-wide cohesion becomes even more complex when considering those neighborhoods that have not repopulated to anywhere near their pre-storm numbers. These are neighborhoods that may end up being reconstructed on significantly terms than those that defined them before—areas that will take on different purposes, different uses, different interests from developers. Areas such as Tulane-Gravier or parts of Mid-City or the Lower Ninth or Tremé may now represent spaces for quite different goals and intentions for the city as a whole. How will fairness of voice across racial and ethic divisions be ensured during the transitions?

Residents who pulled together to rebuild in Tulane-Gravier, for instance—meeting on the neutral ground when there were no habitable buildings—now stand to lose both their houses and their newfound sense of solidarity as the city, state, and federal governments have announced their intention to demolish the neighborhood and build two teaching hospitals in its place.[12] The push and pull of benefit and loss in this example captures the seeming irresolvability of the ethical dilemma. For all the benefits of a new hospital campus, there is simultaneously significant 'collateral damage.'

In a different, but ethically related, 'experiment with truth,' which of the following scenarios would best serve the city as a whole? Is it better to rebuild and preserve historically racially homogeneous neighborhoods, or use post-Katrina circumstances to de-ghettoize New Orleans and force various racial and ethnic groups to spread more evenly throughout the city? On the 'gumbo' analogy, the former would retain identifiable 'clumps' of unique and different tastes, while the latter would blend those differences into something that tasted pretty much the same in every spoonful. New Orleans is a city of some *seventy-three* neighborhoods, most with a strong and unique identity, and New Orleanians will tell you in no uncertain terms that their neighborhood identity is perhaps the most important part of what makes New Orleans feel like home. Therefore, the question of which neighborhoods to preserve and which to subsume under the larger needs of the city is one that is likely to arise, again and again.

DIFFERENCES, COOPERATION, AND COORDINATION

A society that is just—one whose political system represents all individuals and groups with fairness and equality—is based on principles that support the freedom to express differences, but an equal importance

12. See Kate Moran, "Land in Limbo. Plans for a new hospital campus hang like a shadow over New Orleans residents largely resigned to their neighborhood's fate," *The Times-Picayune,* February 24, 2008.

of cooperation in decision-making processes, and coordination of tasks in planning and implementing programs of social necessity. Can the inherent right to express differences nevertheless lead to cooperation and coordination? Is belief that from diversity can come a wider unity simply a vague article of faith?

The following personal experience[13] is one that, in microcosm, would appear to allow that a history of diversity and racial differences can nevertheless still produce cooperation, coordination, perhaps even personal bonds. During the period in which the Justice Department was defending against several lawsuits challenging the court-ordered single-member district method of electing members to the County Commission in Dallas County (Selma), Alabama, statistical analysis of election returns continued to demonstrate that voting remained extremely racially polarized. Whites did not vote for blacks, and black voters more often than not supported only black candidates. Nevertheless, after ten years of litigation, from 1978—1988, the establishment of a single-member district method of election resulted in an election scheme that allowed blacks the first opportunity since Reconstruction to elect candidates of their own choosing. In fact, membership of the first County Commission elected from single-member districts was majority African American. In the most recent—and ultimately successful—challenge to this election scheme by white plaintiffs, Judge Hand, who presided over the United States' challenge to the at-large method of election, and who was reversed on appeal and eventually ordered by the Fifth Circuit to order the County to adopt the single-member districting plan created by the United States' expert witness, said he believed the social engineering "experiment"—adoption of a method of election that all but prescribed the number and identity of minority persons elected to the County Commission—had not worked. Based on the evidence, voting was as racially polarized as it had ever been. In reply, it was suggested to Judge Hand that the erosion of racially polarized voting patterns was not a true measure of whether "social engineering" had been successful; rather the better measure was to be found in *personal* and *cooperative* working relationships among members of the County Commission.

A look at the *personal* relationship between two of the witnesses in this case suggests that there can, and, in fact, did emerge a deeper *unity*

13. Of DEBR.

within diversity. Roy Moore was a white, conservative Republican cotton farmer, first elected in 1992, who defeated a white incumbent candidate who had demonstrated too much support for the agenda of the first blacks elected to the County Commission. Perry Varner was a radical, aggressive, out-spoken black man, educated at Boston College Law, who was elected in 1988 to the first black-majority County Commission. As it turned out, over the next eight years it was Perry and Roy who *together* did most of the work of the County Commission. They came to *depend* on one another, to *trust* one another, even to forge something of a friendship. So even though racial equality may have been forced on the local community by federal mandate, a very real consequence of it was the *opportunity* for cooperation and fellowship—the cooperation of individuals on equal terms. Their personal fellowship became a symbol of the possibility of unity of purpose within diversity.

In New Orleans before Katrina there had been numerous instances of cooperative working relationships between black and white officials at the various levels of local government. In the first year after Hurricane Katrina, many believed that New Orleans had become once again a white-majority city. The data now indicates that this did not happen, although the proportion of black residents has been greatly reduced. Perhaps more important than sheer numbers is the potential for a lessening of the voice of black residents in reconstruction planning decisions against the increased political power of the old guard, white business community. From the standpoint of solutions to the complex question of what best serves the city as a whole, New Orleans has not positioned itself very well. For more than eighteen months, the City still had no master plan. Even the Unified New Orleans Plan, finally released in March, 2007, has seemed by many to be regarded at best as an interesting 'paper document.' The reality to which the plan aspires is something else. According to Arnold Hirsch, Professor of History at the University of New Orleans, there have been many draft plans floating around and little going forward in any kind of coordinated way.[14]

Now more than two years after Katrina, there remain too many neighborhoods with too few residents and only marginal economic viability to reasonably expect anything comprehensive that can define the interests of the city as a whole. The Brookings Institution 'Review of Key Indicators of Recovery Two Years After Katrina' notes that while the pace

---

14. Observations made in personal conversations during October, 2007.

of demolitions has increased, residential repairs have slowed as the Road Home program has awarded checks to only one-quarter of applicants. Basic services—including schools, libraries, public transportation, and childcare—remain at less than half the original capacity, and only two-thirds of all licensed hospitals are open in the region.[15] Grassroots initiatives like Common Ground Relief raise their voices against "systematic political and economic neglect as well as the threat of rampant disenfranchisement" against New Orleans' working class and poor communities. Vast delays on insurance policy pay-outs and foot-dragging bureaucracy mires federal disaster fund (Road Home) grants, preventing residents from repairing or rebuilding their homes. More ominous from the standpoint of fairness and social equity against the interests of private developers, "the City has implemented a Health Threat ordinance and a so-called 'Good Neighbor Program' that directs its safety department to condemn properties that have yet to be repaired or rebuilt, demolish the structures, then initiate a process leading to the potential 'expropriation' of such lands by the New Orleans Redevelopment Authority (NORA)."[16] Residents thus face the threat of property loss at an alarming rate. Fighting for one's property rights is made infinitely more difficult for those residents who wish to repair or rebuild their homes, but who are still displaced evacuees scattered in over forty states.

Every post-Katrina urban reconstruction question now seems to spawn sixteen far more complex questions. But they all ultimately come back one: the continual disjunction between the series of at least four planning initiatives, to be discussed in the following chapter, and the identity of anything like 'the shared voice of the people.' In an odd sense, it may have been a luxury that historically New Orleans was never created in any single act or under any single vision, but simply emerged in fits and starts from the swampy wilderness. New Orleans was simply the place *in which one found oneself living.*

Now, however, the tasks of its deliberate and intentional recreation sit before it as if a version of the great temple of Borobudur in Java,

15. Amy Liu and Allison Plyer, "A Review of Key Indicators of Recovery Two Years After Katrina," The New Orleans Index. Second Anniversary Special Edition. The Brookings institution Metropolitan Policy Program and the Greater New Orleans Community Data Center.

16. Conversations and material from Sakura Koné, Special Events and Media Coordinator, Common Ground Relief, New Orleans, November, 2007.

Indonesia—architecture of the infinite under a flaming tropical sky. In the three-dimensional Buddhist vision of the cosmos it symbolizes, the spiritual path one must take—through the World of Desire to the crowning stupa, the World of Formlessness—begins at the foot of steps which rise so steeply that the summit of the monument is lost from view at the start. Construction that was deliberate: the builders wanted to emphasize that one cannot see the end of a spiritual journey from the beginning. One must start out with faith alone.

In many respects, New Orleans is beginning a journey on faith alone. A vision of what it will become is not present at the start or even more than two and one-half years from the start. Quite possibly, citizens are not even in a position to decide what they want the city to become. The most frequent answer one hears from people, on the streets or in their homes, is that they want the city to be *what it was*. But that reality may not be possible. New Orleans will—perhaps must—become something different from what it was. Whether that is for better or worse depends very much on how well fairness and justice and equality of voice can be established and nurtured across all population elements—*all* economic strata, *all* racial and ethnic groups, *all* viable neighborhoods. New Orleans' history of political patronage and its lack of knowledge about how to direct urban reconstruction without creating new, unanticipated problems must be overcome and made into an object of learning. There can be no excuse to repeat decisions such as those that led to the covering of an old city dump, the Agriculture Street Landfill, to turn it into neighborhood low income housing—decisions that produced something drastically unlivable, and ultimately a Superfund toxic cleanup site. New Orleans can no longer afford failures of technology and failures of social morality.

The question 'What racial and ethnic model should the City of New Orleans seek to emulate?' is not, in the end, the right question. The right question is how to imbue its journey of recovery and reconstruction with fairness and justice and some measure of spiritual harmony.

Destroyed Savoy Place Public Housing Development
(December, 2007)

New 17th Street Drainage Canal Pumps

7

Post-Disaster Planning

To set the context for discussion of the concept of Participatory Design and the potential for its use in post-disaster reconstruction in South Louisiana, it is helpful to consider three things. First, to look briefly at the history of planning initiatives in New Orleans and the region prior to Hurricanes Katrina and Rita. Second, to examine more closely the rather disjointed series of four post-hurricane planning processes, giving particular attention to the extent and manner in which citizens were able to provide input to and participate in those processes. Third, to sketch several direct impressions of what life is like, some two years after the storms, both in New Orleans and in the coastal communities along the edge of the Gulf, including economic issues faced by Indian tribal groups there and others who make their living from the Gulf.

PLANNING IN *THE BIG EASY* ISN'T EASY

We have seen that since its earliest days, much 'planning' in New Orleans had concerned itself with protecting the high ground that formed a natural levee for about a mile along a crescent bend in the river. As habitation moved north towards Lake Pontchartrain into the tangled, swampy *miasma,* planning for the relationship between New Orleans and its surrounding natural environment became increasingly complex and troublesome, dictated by frequent spring flooding from the Mississippi River, and more frequent heavy rains that occurred at almost any time of the year. The construction of levees became a primary strategy to control river flooding, and the construction of drainage canals the strategy for filling in the swamp for human use. By mid-nineteenth century, New Orleans began to look at the need for cleansing its sewerage and drainage canals on a more rational basis, confirmed in 1905, when the role of mosquitoes as a cause of spreading Yellow Fever was understood. But during the 1920s, while the Sewerage and Water Board sought to install a comprehensive system to serve the entire city, many gaps affected low-lying districts largely inhabited by working-class blacks. This aspect of urban planning reflected the fact that there was always a tug-of-war between rational planning and the desire for economic expansion. Unfortunately, the consequence of that battle was frequently that those on the margins of the social hierarchy—poorer, working blacks who inhabited less desirable regions of the city, especially—lost out to the economic interests of the privileged few.

In 1918, Louisiana Legislature Act 27 authorized municipalities with over 50,000 residents to regulate the style and manner of construction of buildings as well as permit or prohibit the operation of certain businesses. By the mid-1920s, authorization to zone was established by State law. Prior to 1918, New Orleans had passed several hundred piecemeal zoning ordinances, but the result was a confusing and sometimes contradictory assortment of regulations, inconsistently enforced. In 1923, in response to this confusion, the Commission Council established the City Planning and Zoning Commission (CPZC) to advise the Council on planning and zoning matters. A comprehensive zoning ordinance was adopted June 6, 1929.[1]

How well New Orleans' zoning ordinances constitute fair and socially equitable planning has frequently been a matter of debate. As just one example, in November, 2002, the Regulatory Barriers Clearing House in Washington, DC, argued that New Orleans' zoning codes contained a number of provisions that negatively impacted the ability to create sufficient incentives to provide for affordable housing.[2]

In 1990, the Citizen Advisory Committee held meetings to begin the process of developing a master plan. In 1992, the New Century New Orleans master plan was completed by the Planning Commission.[3] In his report on planning in New Orleans, Daniel Mandelker, Stamper Professor of Law at Washington University in St. Louis, found in 2003 that while

1. City Planning and Zoning Commission: Records relating to the creation of the 1929 Comprehensive Zoning Ordinance, City Archives, New Orleans Public Library, accessed at http://nutrias.org/~nopl/inv/zone1929.htm.

2. Regulatory Barriers Clearinghouse: Solutions that support affordable housing. New Orleans Comprehensive Zoning Ordinance, accessed at http://www.huduser.org/rbc/search/rbcdetails.asp?DocId=683.

3. See planning process timeline prepared by researches at the University of Illinois Urbana-Champaign, available on www.envisioningforplanners.org.

the City had completed a land use plan as part of its effort to complete a master plan, as well as drafting a new zoning ordinance, unfortunately neither would meet the city's needs for guidance in the development and preservation of the city. The draft comprehensive zoning ordinance (CZO) was particularly inadequate and should be shelved. Moreover, Mandelker found the City did not have an adequate legal basis for the planning process. The City Charter requires the Planning Commission to adopt a master plan, but does not require the City Council to adopt the plan and does not require zoning and other land use decisions to be consistent with the master plan.[4] Critical is the historic importance of New Orleans' neighborhoods—with half the city designated as an historic district under the National Historic Preservation Act—but also their fragility, compounded by the fact that prior to Hurricanes Katrina and Rita, New Orleans had as many as 8,000 abandoned housing structures.

The master or comprehensive plan, an accepted element in the design of American cities for eighty years, has not been fully understood in the case of New Orleans. Daniel Mandelker argues strongly that a master plan cannot be handled by zoning; its purpose is to provide a long-range vision for a city that can guide its preservation and development. In 2001, the American Planning Association (APA) published new statutory models for comprehensive planning and land use regulation.[5]

Just prior to the turn of the last century, Louisiana produced a number of 'comprehensive' plans. The ordinance known as the Comprehensive Zoning Law of the City of New Orleans dates from 1995. Its purposes include to encourage and promote the safety, morals, health, order, convenience, prosperity, and general welfare of the citizens; provide for efficiency in the process of development; provide for safe use and occupancy of buildings and provide for development in accord with the Comprehensive Plan.[6] In March of 1996, the Statewide Intermodal Transportation plan

4. Daniel R. Mandelker, Stemper Professor of Law, Washington University in St. Louis, "A Report on Planning in New Orleans: For the Master Plan Coalition," accessed at http://law.wustl.edu/landuselaw/neworl.htm. In our conversation, Daniel gave me the date of 2003 for his report, and indicated that they followed this up with proposed amendments to the city charter. The Bureau of Governmental Research also followed about that time with a report of their own.

5. American Planning Association, *Growing Smart Legislative Guidebook: Model Statutes for Planning and the Management of Change*, 2001.

6. Comprehensive Zoning Law of the City of New Orleans of 1995, accessed at http://ordlink.com/codes/neworleans/_DATA/TITLE01...02, 03ff.

was adopted. In December of 1998, 'Coast 2050: Toward a Sustainable Coastal Louisiana' was completed. Also in 1998, the Louisiana Vision 2020 Economic Development Master Plan was first drafted, and in April of 1999, the Louisiana Land Use Plan was adopted by the New Orleans City Planning Commission as part of the New Century New Orleans Comprehensive Plan.

Mandelker finds New Orleans' 1999 land use plan deficient—failing because it did not include comprehensive planning policies on a scale indicating where future redevelopment could occur, but also by not considering the distinctive quality of the city's historic neighborhoods, deconstructing the city on a block-by-block basis without considering the needs of neighborhoods. We have discussed one example of such failure in the construction of I-10 that destroyed viable business and residential districts of Tremé.

To preserve historic neighborhoods may mean abandoning the idea of arbitrarily applying standardized land use districts and regulations across the city, and designating each historic neighborhood as an independent zoning district, each with its own land use regulations tailored to its character and needs. Most important, and consistent with a primary argument of *Walking to New Orleans,* Mandelker argues that improving the planning and zoning system entails providing an expanded role for citizens, neighborhoods, and community business groups in the planning and zoning process. All citizens and community groups "should have an opportunity to participate fully in the planning process, and to participate as parties in zoning proceedings and to appeal zoning decisions to the courts if they disagree with them." This argument is very much at the basis of the concept of Participatory Design.

Furthermore, to propose that planning must begin at the neighborhood level means that neighborhood associations must be given a legally recognized and formal role in the planning process. To carry this out would involve creation of a formal structure of neighborhood associations able to participate in the planning and zoning process and authorized to comment on proposed plans and zoning changes. We will see precisely such a effort in our discussions about a 'Citizen Participation Program' with Keith Twitchell, President of the Committee for a Better New Orleans/Metropolitan Area Committee (CBNO/MAC) later in this chapter.

The American Planning Association lists ten criteria a city must apply when designating a 'neighborhood' and its area. These criteria include not only patterns of development and physical characteristics, but also resident attitudes that a city council and planning commission should be required to consider. Thus, it comes down to being a question of government truly hearing the voices of the people. In fact, there has often occurred a 'dialogue' *among* residents of various regions of a city in specifying exactly what the boundaries of their neighborhoods should be. For the 73-odd neighborhoods of New Orleans, this has meant that residents have not always agreed on where their local neighborhood begins and ends. Some of the 'dialogue' has been exacerbated by the desire to include certain businesses or historic landmarks, or to exclude New Orleans' public housing development projects, within the boundaries of the neighborhood.

In a personal meeting with former Mayor (1970–78) Maurice Edwin 'Moon' Landrieu in his home neighborhood of South Prieur Street in Broadmoor[7] in December, 2007, Moon said that about thirty years ago, when they first drew up the Planning Districts, they simply sat down with paper and pencil to draw the boundaries of various neighborhoods and give them names. Some neighborhoods were drawn from historical knowledge, some were essentially made up. Moon described it as a rather arbitrary process, and that people hadn't necessarily associated their neighborhood with the names on the Planning District maps showing neighborhood boundaries. However, with only a few notable exceptions, Moon felt that over time people became fairly comfortable with their neighborhood boundaries.

As New Orleans entered the first years of the twenty-first century, there seemed to be a flurry of planning activities of various sorts. Planning encompassed not only the city proper, but the metropolitan region. For example, in 2000, the Army Corps of Engineers began a feasibility study of levees in New Orleans, examining the possibilities of upgrading them to meet a Category 4 or 5 storm, and in July an update of the Statewide Intermodal Transportation plan commenced. A citizen-based initiative to make Southeast Louisiana one of the nation's top ten communities in which to live and work, Project Top 10 by 2010, was started in March of 2001 and released some initial results in June; however the process that was supposed to last eighteen months largely ended at that time.[8]

7. At the home of Jeanne Dumestre, across the street from Moon and Verna's home.

8. A report, 'Regional Indicators of Sustainable Development for Southeast Louisiana,' was eventually released by Top 10 by 2010 in January, 2003.

2002 brought in three elements to the New Orleans Master Plan—Parks, Recreation, and Open Space; Arts and Culture, Tourism Management; Historic Preservation and Economic Development. In April, 2003, the economic development plan, Louisiana Vision 2020, was updated, and the Louisiana Department of Transportation and Development released a Statewide Transportation Plan. The year 2004 was especially busy. In January, Riverfront Charrette, the beginning of the Riverfront Vision 2005 planning process, commenced; the 2004 Transportation Plan for the New Century New Orleans Master Plan was completed in March; in October, the Metropolitan Transportation Plan and Transportation Improvement Program was released by the New Orleans Regional Planning Commission; in November, the main report of the Louisiana Coastal Ecosystem Restoration Study was completed. A first draft and public presentation of Riverfront vision 2005 made its appearance in January of 2005, eight months before Hurricane Katrina.

Amidst this shower of activity at the time, it would have been difficult to determine which of these initiatives were genuinely productive, which were abortive, which were redundant. But in the world of South Louisiana, post-Hurricanes Katrina and Rita, the more meaningful—and perhaps impossible to answer—question would be: which of these planning activities were able to be sustained and provide help to the entirely new set of tasks of post-disaster reconstruction planning that necessarily became the business of urban and regional planners after the storms? Indicative of the view of a broad spectrum of citizens, expressed by one individual very much in a position to be aware of and represent the feelings of other New Orleanians, the answer was essentially: not a great deal. In conversation with Prof. Arnold Hirsch, Ethel and Herman L. Midlo Professor for New Orleans Studies and University Research Professor of Urban History at the University of New Orleans, in October, 2007, I[9] asked what he thought about Edward Blakely, Ray Nagin's 'recovery tsar' and the city's reconstruction planning processes. Arnold's response was understated but nevertheless clear. He saw that there were lots of 'draft' plans being floated about, but nothing really moving forward (except unpredictable increases in property taxes and insurance costs) in any concrete way. As for Blakely, Arnold felt he was perceived primarily as Nagin's personal representative and fundraiser to encourage economic develop-

9. RRNR.

ment. But Arnold's strongest message—one to which we will increasingly turn in the remainder of the book—was that there was a desperate need to genuinely engage citizens and their meaningful participation in all the processes of planning and implementation of New Orleans' reconstruction at both the neighborhood and city-wide levels.

PLANNING PROCESSES ON PARADE

Broadly speaking, post-disaster recovery planning processes in New Orleans can be identified by four distinguishable, somewhat overlapping, efforts: FEMA's Emergency Support Function #14 (ESF-#14), Mayor Nagin's Bring New Orleans Back (BNOB) Commission, the City Council-backed Lambert planning process, and the Unified New Orleans Plan (UNOP),[10] the most current. This does not mean that these four were the *only* planning processes envisioned. For example, less than three weeks after the storm, on September 20, 2005, Lt. Governor Landrieu unveiled his "Louisiana Rebirth: Restoring the Soul of American" plan to restore the state's tourism and culture. A little over a week later, after storm surge from Hurricane Rita on September 22 reopened breaches in the Industrial Canal and re-flooded the Lower Ninth Ward, Mayor Nagin announced the firing of some 3,000 city workers, half of the city's workforce. This would not be the first time things seemed to be going in opposite directions.

ESF-#14[11]

FEMA provides guidance in long-term community recovery planning (LTCR) with the federal interagency Emergency Support Function #14 (ESF-#14) created to facilitate this process. Not long after Hurricane Katrina, FEMA initiated this process that had previously been used on a trial basis in Florida after Hurricane Charley and in Utica, Illinois, after a

10. A most useful unpublished paper, dated October 18, 2006, "An Overview of Post-Katrina Planning in New Orleans," by two researchers from the University of California, Berkeley, Brendan Nee and Jedidiah Horne, who worked both with planning teams involved in the current, officially sanctioned process, but also with individual neighborhood associations in two neighborhoods, De Saix and Tulane/Gravier, provides many first-hand details about the nature of the several processes and the timeline of their transition from one to another; we have freely made use of their excellent work.

11. See FEMA: Long-Term Community Recovery (LTCR) and ESF #14, http://www.fema.gov/rebuild/ltcr/index.shtm and its "Long-Term Community Recovery Planning Process: A Self-Help Guide," December 2005.

tornado in 2004. Under the National Response Plan, Emergency Support Function (ESF #14) Long-Term Community Recovery and Mitigation coordinates the resources of federal departments and agencies to support the long-term recovery of states and communities, and to reduce or eliminate risk from future incidents. ESF #14 efforts are driven by state and local priorities, focusing on permanent restoration of infrastructure, housing, and the local economy. When activated, ESF #14 allows the federal government to, among other things, assess social and economic consequences in the impacted area; advise on long-term community recovery response activities; work with NGOs and private-sector organizations as well as state, local, and tribal governments; avoid duplication of assistance and determine responsibilities for recovery activities; and interact with other federal support agencies including Agriculture, Commerce, Homeland Security, HUD, Treasury, and the SBA.

ESF-#14 employed as many as 325 staff in nineteen hurricane-impacted parishes, including both FEMA staff and local or national experts. On January 21, 2006, FEMA held a nation-wide "Louisiana Planning Day," intended to involve Louisiana residents—both those displaced and those returned—in the planning process. The impact of such citizen involvement remains unclear. Work on the Orleans Parish ESF-#14 recovery plan continued through the end of April, 2006, with the final version of the plan released, as Nee and Horne note, in mid-August, 2006, "without fanfare or publicity." It was with some surprise that the ESF-#14 plan appeared on the State's louisianaspeaks.org website, particularly since the plan has not been incorporated into any other planning processes, nor discussed by major participants in those efforts. Nee and Horne indicate that the impression of one person who worked on the plan was that FEMA thought the results would only confuse the situation where other planning efforts were underway. Thus, for Orleans Parish, at least, the ESF-#14 plan was largely ignored.[12]

Other independent, but planning-related events during the fall of 2005 included, on October 12, the New Orleans City Council's approval of an eleven-person Advisory Committee on Hurricane Recovery; on October 17, Gov. Blanco's creation of the twenty-six-member Louisiana Recovery Authority (LRA);[13] on October 30, Lt. Gov. Landrieu's $550,000 campaign

12. Some other parishes have found the ESF-#14 worthy of adoption.

13. Blanco's chief-of-staff, Andrew Kopplin, became its Executive Director; among the primary functions of the LRA was to encourage parishes and cities about the need for

to promote tourism and show that Louisiana was 'open for business;' on November 10, the Louisiana Recovery and Rebuilding Conference, involving the American Institute of Architects (AIA), the American Planning Association (APA), and the National Trust for Historical Preservation, to begin the LRA planning process. November was particularly busy, with the Louisiana Legislature establishing the Coastal Protection and Restoration Authority (CPRA) for protection of coastal assets, both natural and man-made; the completion of the Louisiana Coastal Area (LCA) Ecosystem Restoration Study; and, on November 17, Gov. Blanco's launch of the Louisiana Family Recovery Corps, an independent, non-profit organization to coordinate the work of government and non-profit agencies.

The Bring New Orleans Back Commission[14]

On September 30, Mayor Nagin announced creation of his seventeen-member Bring New Orleans Back (BNOB) Commission, a group that included attorneys, business people, church leaders, and several academics. Its co-chairs were Maurice L. 'Mel' Lagarde, III, a white health-care executive, President and CEO of the Delta Division of HCA, with responsibility for operations of seventeen hospitals and five surgery centers in the Louisiana, South Mississippi, and Austin, Texas markets, and Barbara Major, a black community activist originally trained in social work, formerly chair of the community driven St. Thomas/Irish Channel Consortium, a nationally acclaimed model for holistic community transformation, and currently Executive Director of the St. Thomas Health Clinic, a non-profit health clinic providing services to the underserved and uninsured. Nagin gave them until the end of the year to develop a rebuilding plan for New Orleans.

As an indication of not uncommon dissention within City Hall, by late October the New Orleans City Planning Commission had begun to feel bypassed by BNOB, but was urged to continue to participate in the process by the American Planning Association. The Planning Commission's ability to function had been severely reduced since its small staff of

---

planning in order to be able to receive Community Development Block Grants.

14. See City of New Orleans, Bring New Orleans Back Commission, Urban Planning Committee: Joseph C. Canizaro, Chairman. "Action Plan for New Orleans: The New American City" (BNOB Plan), January 11, 2006. Wallace Roberts & Todd, LLC—Master Planner.

twenty-four had been cut by two-thirds when Nagin, with little income coming in after the storm, laid off as many as 3,000 city workers.[15]

Among BNOB's subcommittees, its most powerful was the Urban Planning (land-use) Committee, chaired by real estate developer Joseph Canizaro, a friend of George Bush,[16] and founder of the Committee for a Better New Orleans[17] in 2000. His influence is reflected by the fact that BNOB sometimes came to be known as "Canizaro's Committee." Canizaro retained the Urban Land Institute (ULI) to develop a set of recommendations to BNOB that were released in a report by ULI's New Orleans Advisory Services Panel on November 18. None of the recommendations were received with more hatred and vitriol than ULI's devastating suggestion to shrink the footprint of New Orleans. Projections of returning populations indicated it could be many years before the city could expect to recover its pre-Katrina numbers. Since it would become economically impossible to provide city services to all its neighborhoods—not only those most devastated east of the Industrial Canal but those near the center of the city as well, such as Broadmoor—ULI had recommended that lower-lying area be converted back to green space. To make its point, ULI presented a set of maps on which fields and parks were shown as covering neighborhoods where thousands of citizens once lived, and to which many were returning to try to live again. Equally controversial was the proposal to create a public development corporation, the Crescent City Rebuilding Corporation, that would buy and sell property to speed the city's redevelopment, establishing an oversight board with broad powers over the city's finances. One color-coded map showed three 'investment zones,' ranking areas' suitability for rehabilitation. Neighborhoods that had the highest potential for mass buyouts and future green space included New Orleans East, Gentilly, parts of Lakeview, most of the Lower Ninth Ward, Mid-City, Hollygrove, and Broadmoor.[18]

15. Bruce Eggler, "City planners want role in rebuilding," *The Times-Picayune,* October 29, 2005.

16. Canizaro raised about $200,000 for Bush's re-election in 2004.

17. A privately funded group of business and religious leaders seeking to develop a blueprint for the city's future development.

18. See Martha Carr, "Rebuilding should begin on high ground, group says," *The Times-Picayune,* November 19, 2005.

It was in the context of possibly seeing their beloved neighborhood erased from the city's history that the friends with whom I[19] stayed in New Orleans during December, 2007, Jeanne Dumestre and her husband William, decided they had best get themselves back from an upstate farm to their home on South Prieur. Jeanne and Bill's home was directly across the street from Moon Landrieu's residence, and, in fact, was the home in which Moon's wife, Verna Satterlee, had lived as a child. Jeanne and Bill had been staying in the bottom part of Moon and Verna's house while their was being renovated before the storm. When the flooding after Hurricane Katrina left eight feet of water everywhere in Broadmoor, Jeanne and Bill lost most of their furnishings that were in the bottom of Moon's house. With their own home also in disrepair, there was little choice but to exit the city with their many dogs, and stay on a farm between New Orleans and Baton Rouge.

Perhaps it took a test such as the proposal by outsiders that some of New Orleans' historic neighborhoods could simply be 'erased' to arouse the power of self-determination of the people in neighborhoods such as Lakeview and Broadmoor. Perhaps it was the perception that, however beneficial the return of green spaces and wetland protective areas would be, the 'Green Dot'[20] proposal seemed simply a mask for something far too close to some form of economic, or even racial or ethnic, cleansing[21] from less substantial, working-class neighborhoods—the opportunity to rid the city of its poor and claim their properties not simply as green

19. RRNR.

20. January 19, 2006 was the day of the infamous 'Green Dot,' in which Broadmoor, with its 2,900 homes, and other areas, were designated by Mayor Nagin's Bring New Orleans Back Commission as an area to be bulldozed and turned back into parks and green space (dashed green circles on PowerPoint Figure 30.).

21. Robert D. Bullard, Director of the Environmental Justice Resource Center at Clark Atlanta University, cites twenty reasons to support the view that, through a combination systematic lethargy and ineptness, there is the appearance of a plan to destroy black New Orleans. His examples include: selectively handing out FEMA grants, made more difficult for low-income and black survivors; higher rates of denial of SBA loans to poorer blacks than to middle-class whites; lower insurance settlements to black homeowners; discriminatory environmental clean-up standards that fail to clean up black residential areas; sacrifice of low-lying black neighborhoods in the name of environmental restoration; zoning ordinances that push out blacks; no commitment to replace low-income public housing; delay in reconstruction of New Orleans schools; holding elections without appropriate Voting Rights Act safeguards. Robert D. Bullard, "A 20-point Plan To Destroy Black New Orleans," *New American Media*, February 1, 2006, accessible at http://news.newamericanmedia.org /news/view_article.html?article_id=ad54cb41686743eb. Many of these issues have been discussed through this chapter.

space but for economic and industrial development, all in one fell swoop. Neighborhoods just to the east of the Industrial Canal had long been envisioned as suitable for industrial expansion.

Whatever the political and psychological motivation, the neighborhood association to which Jeanne Dumestre and Moon and Verna Landrieu belonged, the Broadmoor Improvement Association—which had not been overly active before Hurricane Katrina—quickly became *very* active. As soon as BNOB showed much of Broadmoor, which experienced flooding of eight feet or more, as an area that would be returned to green and not rebuilt, 'Broadmoor Lives' signs appeared everywhere, and the neighborhood association found itself holding weekly meetings. Jeanne joined those residents who participated in walking patrols, where people gathered and traveled certain routes, walking or by bike, to address the growth of crime in the area, which was becoming considerable.

Mayor Nagin quickly denounced ULI's proposed smaller city, and on November 28, publicly announced his intention to 'rebuild all of New Orleans.' Despite Nagin's own interest in, and popularity with, the city's business people based on policies supporting economic and industrial development, his stated intention would presumably include rebuilding lower-lying neighborhoods as well as those occupying higher ground.

On December 13, 2005, Canizaro proposed a three-year plan in which, for three years, anyone could rebuild anywhere; after that point inadequate neighborhoods would be shrunk.[22] Canizaro did not envision the complete elimination of neighborhoods, but after three years the city would have the power to condemn property in neighborhoods that had failed to sufficiently develop. Some neighborhoods would then be bulldozed for either flood-protection, parks, or new development. On December 15, the City Council passed a resolution that all neighborhoods should get equal treatment and be rebuilt simultaneously. At the same time, Canizaro's 'three-year' window was shortened to a one-year 'free-for-all rebuilding period to discourage residents from delaying. Ultimately, the window was further shortened to four months when the Urban Planning Committee voted on January 11, 2006 to accept its final report calling for a four-month window to allow neighborhoods to prove their viability before being bought out by the powerful proposed Crescent City

22. See Jeffrey Meitrodt and Frank Done, "City commission backs ULI plan," *The Times-Picayune*, December 13, 2005.

Redevelopment Corp.[23] The report recommended a budget for property buyouts and a new light rail system, and that more detailed neighborhood assessment be done beginning in March by local architect Ray Manning and Reed Kroloff, Dean of Tulane University's School of Architecture. At this point, as Nee and Horne note, local residents were afraid that their permit requests would be cut off and swamped the city planning office with petitions. Nagin increasingly appeared to oppose the direction of the BNOB—a commission of his own making, but five days later, on Martin Luther King Day, January 16, sufficiently diverted attention by claiming, first, that 'a vengeful God smote New Orleans' with Hurricane Katrina because of heavenly disapproval of America's involvement in Iraq and rampant violence within urban black communities, then going on to predict divine intervention in the city's future demographics with the prophecy that 'God intended New Orleans to rise again as a chocolate city,'—that is, a black majority city.[24] Nagin later apologized for his remarks, widely perceived as racially divisive as well as theologically inept. On January 22, 2006, at St. Dominic's Church, Mayor Nagin spoke to residents of Lakeview—one of the neighborhoods of which portions were slated to be returned to green space by the BNOB Commission—and promised that he would firmly oppose a moratorium on issuing building permits in flooded neighborhoods and uphold property owners' rights. Residents present seemed beyond the 'chocolate city' debacle; their interest was in facts about their properties and rebuilding.[25]

23. Frank Donze and Gordon Russell, "4 months to decide. Nagin panel says hardest hit areas must prove viability city's, footprint may shrink; full buyouts proposed for those forced to move. New housing to be developed in vast swaths of New Orleans' higher ground," *The Times-Picayune*, January 11, 2006.

The January rollout of the commission's land-use plan set a clock ticking, giving neighborhoods four months to establish their viability. But for independent-minded neighborhoods like Broadmoor, after seeing big green spots covering portions of their neighborhood on a map of a rebuilt New Orleans, the already fired-up Broadmoor Improvement Association now was in full conflagration mode. Seeing those green spots "didn't devastate us; it pissed us off," said Virginia Saussy Bairnsfather, a board member of the association. Within weeks of the map's unveiling by the BNOB Commission, membership in the neighborhood group jumped 400 percent. See Colman Warner, "Locals not waiting to be told what to do. Neighborhoods grab building bull by the horns," *The Times-Picayune*, March 13, 2006.

24. Transcript of Nagin's speech given Monday, January 16, during a program at City Hall commemorating Martin Luther King Jr., published in *The Times-Picayune*, January 17, 2006, and elsewhere.

25. Gwen Filosa, "Nagin says he'll oppose building moratorium. Any homeowner can rebuilt, mayor vows to residents during Lakeview appearance," *The Times-Picayune*,

Over the next two months, community meetings were held to discuss the recommendations of BNOB subcommittees. On March 20, 2006, BNOB issued its final report, but by this time, FEMA had made it apparent that it would not fund the $7.5 million planning process Manning and Kroloff had been asked to direct. One can agree with Nee and Horne's conclusion: "With no funding, BNOB effectively came to a halt, having done significant damage to the public's trust in the planning process and failing to produce a specific list of projects to be funded with CDGB [Community Development Block Grant] money." March 8, 2006, was the last public meeting held by BNOB.

During the period when public perceptions of the BNOB process had not yet grown into complete distrust, it was not as if new planning initiatives weren't arising or older ones sluggishly continuing on their own. For example, on January 20, 2006, Gov. Blanco announced her planning 'dream team' appointment of Peter Calthorpe to lead regional planning for the LRA, Andres Duany to lead neighborhood planning, and Raymond Gindroz of Urban Design Associates to create a pattern book of house designs.[26] Calthorpe, who taught at Berkeley, the University of Oregon, and elsewhere, works particularly in the area of regional design. Under Clinton's administration, he helped direct HUD's Empowerment Zone and Consolidated Planning Programs, as well as the HOPE VI program to re-conceive failing public housing projects. Calthorpe also founded the Congress for New Urbanism, an organization that promotes neo-traditional design and planning theories, one key element of which is the concept of the urban network—a model for automobile travel and public transportation in an urban setting that creates a new hierarchy of arterial roads and boulevards and reinforces walkability.[27]

On January 26, one day before the BNOB was scheduled to release its final report, the New Orleans City Council's Advisory Committee on Hurricane Recovery held its first meeting to advise the Council on ways to facilitate the city's post-hurricane recovery efforts. *The Times-Picayune* notes that this 'first meeting' occurred *150 days after* Hurricane Katrina flooded the city, and *four months after* the Council voted to create the panel. City Council President Oliver Thomas tried to downplay the belief

---

January 22, 2006.

26. Background input also provided through Amy Liu of the Brookings Institution, as well as Calthorpe Associates website, http://www.calthorpe.com.

27. Calthorpe's urban network concept will make an appearance in the UNOP.

that this Advisory Committee was chosen to compete with the BNOB and Gov. Blanco's LRA; however the City Council had been outspoken in its criticism of some of the BNOB's recommendations.[28]

The Lambert Planning Process
(New Orleans Neighborhoods Rebuilding Plan)[29]

Whether to make good on its criticism of BNOB or to assert its independence, on February 16, 2006, the New Orleans City Council approved $2.9 million in Community Development Block Grants to hire the Miami-based Lambert Consulting and Shelia Danzey of New Orleans for its own neighborhood planning project. This new process, officially known as the New Orleans Neighborhoods Rebuilding Plan, was formally announced on April 7, 2006. The Lambert planning process involved teams of architects and planners being assigned to New Orleans' thirteen Planning Districts. Public distrust of the Lambert planning process began early, however, as the public often had only marginal input to hiring decisions of planning teams, and the self-defined neighborhood boundaries used by neighborhood associations at times did not coincide with those defined by the Planning Districts.

As the third major planning process was getting underway, Gov. Blanco, three days after the House of Representatives had killed her housing trust bill, unveiled in Lake Charles on February 20 the framework of the Road Home program—what would eventually become the slow bureaucratic tangle individual homeowners, whose homes were destroyed or damaged by the storms, would have to go through to seek financial assistance. The incentives were geared to encourage people willing to rebuild their homes in Louisiana rather than provide buyout packages for those who didn't rebuild. The entire program of $7.5 billion would depend on the State receiving at least $4 billion of that from Congress. Assistance would help owners of flood-damaged houses with up to $150,000 in direct grants, depending on whether a house was inside or outside the flood plain. For those inside the flood plain who did not have flood insurance, available aid was cut by 30 percent. The cap of $150,000 would be reduced

28. Frank Donze, "Council recovery panel debuts," *The Times-Picayune*, January 27, 2006.

29. See City of New Orleans, Lambert Advisory/SHEDO, Project Management, "City of New Orleans Neighborhoods Rebuilding Plan" (Lambert Planning Process), October, 2006.

by any insurance payments and FEMA aid received.[30] On March 16, the LRA approved Blanco's Road Home program.

Late March and early April, 2006 saw the several planning programs mentioned thus far laid out for view almost simultaneously, as if platters in a delicatessen. On March 20, Mayor Nagin presented the recommendations of the BNOB Commission at a Canal Street hotel ballroom to infrequent applause.[31] On March 28, the ESF-#14 plan was completed, and on April 7, the City Council announced Paul Lambert and Shelia Danzey would be working with neighborhoods devastated by Hurricane Katrina.[32] What is remarkable is that, at this point, at least, these three planning processes appeared to have no direct connection to one another.

Not to be outdone in terms of adding (unintended) complexity to the mix, on April 12, FEMA released guidelines for its Advisory Base Flood Elevation Maps. Already in a purgatory of rebuilding confusion, it was hoped that these elevation standards, along with plans for improving the levee system, would help provide consistent rules for home reconstruction. While the base elevations, last adjusted in 1984, remained unchanged, the requirement of an additional '3 feet above grade' proposed standard meant that thousands of damaged homes would still face the necessity of being raised to remain eligible for federal flood insurance.[33]

Through the spring and summer of 2006, amidst continuing confusion, the Lambert planning process trundled on, assessing the needs of some 46 neighborhoods. Planning teams held as many as 84 meetings, with three in Houston, Atlanta, and Baton Rouge. Nee and Horne report that, according to Lambert, approximately 7,500 residents city-wide were involved.

30. See Laura Maggi, "LRA plan favors those who remain. Leaving state would mean lower buyout," *The Times-Picayune*, February 21, 2006.

31. See Bruce Eggler, "Mayor presents BNOB plan," *The Times-Picayune*, March 20, 2006.

32. Shelia Danzey was New Orleans' housing director in the 1989s under Mayor Sidney Barthelemy. Other architects included Lonnie Hewitt, lead planner on the Pontchartrain Park and Gentilly Woods neighborhood process, planner Stephen Villavaso, Gerald Billes, and M. David Lee, professor of architecture at Harvard's Graduate School of Design. See Bruce Eggler, "N.O. is paying consultants to help neighborhoods plan," *The Times-Picayune*, April 10, 2006.

33. See Brian Thevenot, "Finally, rules for rebuilding. FEMA targets slab home construction; $2.5 billion more slated for levees," *The Times-Picayune*, April 13, 2006. It was of considerable concern to officials in Plaquemines Parish that while funding, when approved by Congress, would finance flood protection for 98 percent of metro New Orleans, it would not include lower Plaquemines Parish.

By September 26, 2006, 46 separate neighborhood plans were drafted and finalized. Yet even with the Lambert planning process just getting under-way in April, on April 20, the Rockefeller Foundation announced it was providing \$3.5 million to fund a fourth planning process—the Unified New Orleans Plan (UNOP), endorsed especially by the LRA.[34]

The BNOB process had not, but the Lambert planning process did attempt to avoid the issue of the 'viability' of neighborhoods. For those cit-izens who participated in the process, the belief that their neighborhoods would eventually be rebuilt was an unshakable assumption. However, as the Lambert plans became complete, citizens increasingly became impa-tient for federal and state funds to materialize so they could begin to see actual concrete progress in the renewal of their neighborhoods. This, of course, had to mean that secure monies would be readily available; but to this day it remains quite unclear just what 'pots of money' really are at hand. As it came later to be seen, the UNOP original proposed budget of some \$14 billion has had to be pared down to only about \$1.1 billion, in terms of representing a figure with which to begin actual work; indeed, not even all of that could be counted on with certainty.

In the opinion of the Berkeley researchers,[35] on the whole, the Lambert planning process was deeply and perhaps fatally flawed.[36] Both City Council and Lambert ignored LRA's publicly voiced requirements that the planning process be a-political, and that the entire city, not just flooded neighborhoods, be included in the plan. Even more important, the Lambert planning process failed to interact with the City Planning Commission during its work; yet the Planning Commission is the gov-ernment body that necessarily will oversee and authorize the implemen-tation of the majority of city recovery and restoration projects.

Perhaps the greatest weakness in the Lambert planning process was that it unnecessarily introduced additional complexity into an already highly complex set of problems by failing to combine its 46 separate neighborhood plans together into a single, coherent city-wide plan. Without *some* model for how neighborhoods and their necessary services fit together and coordinate, across not only adjacent neighborhoods but

34. As well as key stakeholders especially at the state level who were convinced of the existing shortcomings of ESF-#14, the mayor's BNOB, and the Lambert Plan.

35. Jedidiah Horne and Brandon Nee, previously referenced.

36. The local government watchdog group, the Bureau of Government Research, questioned the legality of Lambert's own no-bid contract.

the city as a whole, the planning for elements of infrastructure—electric power, sewerage and water supply, public transportation, police, fire, and emergency medical services—becomes exceedingly difficult, if not impossible. The absence of a process for the funding and coordination of projects impacting more than one geographic area also applied to the manner by which neighborhood projects were given some level of priority or were divided into levels of difficulty by time—that is, whether they were short-term, near-term, or long-term.[37] The upshot is that each neighborhood naturally used its own criteria for defining costs and time involved, and mixed together both public and private-sector projects, with the result that the totality of projects presented across the plan as a whole sat in a kind of stew of confusion. Not only would this ultimately lead to differing expectations about which projects would happen and when, from one neighborhood to the next; it also had the effect of inappropriately lumping together projects of vastly different scale, such as the effort involved in planning for street repairs vs. planning for the introduction of new rail transit capabilities.

Self-defined neighborhood goals that also include city-wide, shared needs likely require not only high levels of funding, but also may involve the engagement of agencies beyond the city and even the state. The most obvious example of such a need is the desire for those neighborhoods that were severely flooded after Hurricane Katrina to have a levee and flood-protection system that could ensure homeowners—after having gone through the enormous cost and effort of gutting, razing, repairing, and rebuilding—that their homes would be protected against future flooding. Every neighborhood that experienced flooding expressed that need as its highest priority. But, as we have seen earlier, not all neighborhoods will be provided such protection—some not for several years, some not for as long as six years or more, some perhaps not ever. The very empowering of neighborhoods to voice widely-shared goals that meet clear and obvious needs has the effect of turning those goals into permanent expectations. This is particularly true of goals for self-preservation and safety—the presuppositions to being able to live in a particular neighborhood at all. However, the voicing of shared goals to meet shared needs does not in any way guarantee that the federal funds necessary to engage federal agencies such as USACE to construct such storm and flood protection systems

---

37. What the process referred to as a 'funding matrix.'

will be forthcoming, or forthcoming to a level that can meet everyone's needs. We have already seen how those living in Plaquemines Parish may very well be out of luck in receiving needed protective levees in the near future, if ever at all.

The Unified New Orleans Plan (UNOP)[38]

On June 5, 2006, the New Orleans Community Support Foundation (NOCSF) issued a Request for Qualifications (RFQ) for city-wide planning teams to provide services for a fourth planning process: the Unified New Orleans Plan (UNOP). While a number of elements of the findings and proposals of the UNOP have earlier been discussed, it will be useful here to briefly trace its origins in the context of the three major planning processes that preceded it. The NOCSF looked for two categories of planning assistance: multiple independent neighborhood planning teams, and one city-wide planning team that would work with the city Planning Commission to develop an overarching plan for city-wide infrastructure. From the start, UNOP appeared to be making an effort to provide a consistent but community-driven format for integrating the city's seventy-three neighborhoods and thirteen planning district plans into a single city-wide plan. The UNOP also presented itself as constituting the 'end stage' of previous 'preliminary' planning efforts, such as that of the BNOB Commission, rather than ignoring them or simply superseding them. Precisely how much and in what ways each of these prior or parallel planning processes contributed to material content in the UNOP is beyond the scope of the focus of *Walking to New Orleans*. However, the UNOP RFQ's Appendix A includes as 'planning precedents': the AIA and APA-run Louisiana Recovery and Rebuilding Conference, held November 10-12, 2005, in which approximately 650 citizens, community leaders, architects, planners, business people, and public officials gathered in New Orleans; the Louisiana Speaks Planning Process initiated in January, 2006, supported through private donations, and led by Peter Calthorpe; the Bring New Orleans Back Commission of Mayor Nagin; the Urban Land Institute Planning initiative; the FEMA ESF-#14 'short term' disaster recovery planning process; and various independent neighborhood planning initiatives. Submissions of qualifications to par-

---

38. See City of New Orleans, Villavaso & Associates/Henry Consulting LLC, "Citywide Strategic Recovery and Rebuilding Plan" (Unified New Orleans Plan), Final Draft: January 29, 2007.

ticipate in the UNOP planning process would be submitted to local school architect and planner Steven Bingler at Concordia, LLC.[39] On June 16, a neighborhood planning guide was distributed, and on July 5, Mayor Nagin, the City Council, and the LRA announced their agreement on the UNOP process. Recommended planning teams were approved by the NOCSF on July 21, 2006.

While it seemed some progress was being made, possibly for the first time at the city-wide level, for individual homeowners requiring funding assistance, the struggle went on in far more haphazard fashion. The vehicle for such assistance for homeowners for whom insurance or their private funds were inadequate was the Road Home program. Publicly voiced complaints about the sluggish bureaucratic process in submitting applications for approval, shifting criteria for receiving compensation, and general confusion about the Road Home program process were rampant. On April 25, 2006, the LRA gave its approval to a final version of the Road Home program; on May 20, it received final legislative approval; on May 30, it was approved by HUD Secretary Alphonso Jackson.[40] Approvals notwithstanding, the following should give just a taste of the kinds of dissatisfaction citizens had with the Road Home program. About a quarter of the 26,000 homeowners who ultimately received final Road Home award letters have challenged the calculations. The state contractor for running Road Home, ICF International, tracked some 7,200 called-in complaints before January 11, 2007, with more than half of those remaining unresolved. The complaints covered things from underestimated pre-storm home values to inadequate storm-loss estimates to the non-resolution of previous complaints. Many lodging complaints were those told they would get no money—in fact, the number of Road Home 'award letters' saying applicants would get nothing to fix their homes was nearly three times greater than the number who had received grant money. Not surprisingly, some of the rejected applicants weren't taking the news well.[41] The

39. See The New Orleans Community Support Foundation "Request for Qualifications for City-Wide Planning Teams," undated.

40. See Laura Maggi, "Recovery authority OKs rebuilding plan," *The Times-Picayune,* April 27, 2006; Laura Maggi, "Housing recovery plan gets final legislative approval," *The Times-Picayune,* May 10, 2005; Gwen Filosa, "HUD chief approves Road Home grants," *The Times-Picayune,* May 31, 2006.

41. See David Hammer, "Road Home grants are often contested," *The Times-Picayune,* January 26, 2007.

point of this consideration of the Road Home as one 'planning process' among the others is to bring attention to the fact that for most citizens of storm-ravaged New Orleans and South Louisiana, planning processes were activities that occurred largely *above* the context of their immediate lives. Individual citizens were very much on their own, and the impact of all of the planning processes to date has remained distinctly in the future, not in the hear-and-now. We will see this far more graphically in the final section of this chapter, when we present a number of observations and conversations with people in New Orleans and South Louisiana that reinforces the sense of just how isolated so many individual homeowners are, even given the strength of community self-identity and neighborhood associations. For renters, the isolation has been far more dire, if they have even been able to return to New Orleans at all, where rental costs in almost all areas of the city have simply skyrocketed and become beyond the means of many.

For those who had formerly been residents of New Orleans' public housing projects—low- or marginal-income, largely African American individuals and families now displaced across the country—June 14, 2006 saw HUD/HANO, the former Housing Authority of New Orleans now being run by HUD, announce that nearly 5,000 public housing units would be razed. Demolition was planned to begin over the next several months. The developments to be demolished were St. Bernard, C. J. Peete, B.W. Cooper, and Lafitte. The many protests against these closing have been previously discussed. Ongoing protests will be addressed again in the context of the most recent time frame[42] at the close of this chapter.

On July 30 and August 1, 2006, the UNOP held its first community meetings to establish criteria for working with planning teams. At these meetings, the idea was that residents would be able to meet and choose among the teams of professionals who would work with various neighborhoods and Planning Districts to craft rebuilding plans. All neighborhoods would then be expected to finish their recovery and rebuilding plans by November, at which point the separate plans would be merged into 13 Planning District plans and then one city-wide plan, to be adopted by the City Council in the spring of 2007.[43] It was two days later, on August 3, in the midst of this push for harmonious interaction between

42. The fall of 2007, through the end of the year.

43. See Bruce Eggler, "Public meetings set on storm recovery plan. Residents can choose among expert teams," *The Times-Picayune*, July 29, 2006.

planners and citizens, that Paul Lambert launched a grenade and took out a full page ad in *The Times-Picayune* denouncing the UNOP. Part of Lambert's criticism was his view that the planning process actually held up federal funds, and that individual neighborhood plans—which would be completed well before an overarching plan for the city—could submit their own, smaller plans to seek government or private grants. However, individual neighborhood plans could not be used to secure federal grants passed through the LRA.[44]

It was on the eve of the one-year anniversary of Hurricane Katrina— 365 days after the storm—that a memorandum of agreement was signed by the mayor, the City Council, and the Greater New Orleans Foundation (GNOF) to go ahead with the UNOP process and designate the assignment of planning teams to neighborhoods. What now offered perhaps the best opportunity for success was the fact that the UNOP process was being financially implemented by the non-governmental entity, the New Orleans Community Support Foundation (NOCSF), a child of the Greater New Orleans Foundation. This arrangement had the potential, at least, to insulate the planning process from the political in-fighting and wrangling that plagued some of the prior planning initiatives. It was the NOCSF that hired Steven Bingler to staff the process and to create the Community Support Organization (CSO) as an advisory board. City Planning Commission Director Yolanda Rodriguez was the one largely responsible for ensuring a planning model in which the various Planning District plans would be combined together into one city-wide plan. After the RFQs were received, the local firm of Villavaso and Associates was chosen as the city-wide planning team. Stephen Villavaso, along with Troy Henry of Henry Consulting LLC, signed the letter that accompanied the presentation of the single, unified plan in January, 2007.

As the UNOP process unfolded, it was not without growing problems of its own. For example, the relationship between neighborhood and Planning District teams remained unclear, and it was not until a month after the UNOP process was announced that it held any city-wide orientation. Some citizens voiced the concern that the very advantages of creating an a-political entity to hire individuals and firms to manage this planning effort effectively *replaced* the responsibility of elected government to do so. In a city with New Orleans' reputation of political infighting,

44. See Coleman Warner, "Recovery planning pact signed. 'Unified plan' is designed to ease conflicts.," *The Times-Picayune*, August 29, 2006.

moreover, it would be unlikely that politics could be kept out of the planning process in the long run.[45] Wherever people's homes and lives were so clearly at stake, planning for change of any kind would almost certainly raise political and personal divisions. Furthermore, the City Planning Commission would ultimately have to step in and make judgments and decisions in the implementation of this UNOP (or any) city-wide plan involving infrastructure. However, that functional role of the Planning Commission, in New Orleans, is in competition with the fact that it is the City Council which has the *legal authority* to authorize infrastructure and development proposals. We have already seen numerous instances of political self-interest and corruption within New Orleans' City Council, and its early hostility to the UNOP process would continue to exhibit itself at various points.

Ultimately, the sense of the predominate mood from our own friends and acquaintances in New Orleans, is that people over time simply became exhausted with the presentation, initiation, and ultimate failure (or non-productiveness) of one planning process after another. There was no longer reason to trust *any* planning process—even those in which citizens had some level of involvement. Indeed, what could be worse than—having *had* the opportunity as a citizen to provide input to some planning process—then see the results of all one's work and input, along with the entire planning process itself, just lie 'lifeless on the floor' and finally get swept away and thrown out the door as so much accumulated dust and debris?

CITIZEN PARTICIPATION

On January 31, 2007, the Unified New Orleans Plan was submitted to the City Planning Commission. During the several preceding months, with funding through the Rockefeller foundation, the Bush-Clinton Katrina Fund, and the Greater New Orleans Foundation (GNOF), various engagements occurred between citizens and the expert planning teams. A citizen liaison board, the Community Support Organization (CSO), held biweekly meetings to monitor progress. There were four rounds of interactive meetings in the city's thirteen Planning Districts.[46] Most visible were

45. A judgment communicated by Arnold Hirsch, Moon Landrieu, and others.

46. The first Planning District meeting was held October 14, 2006; a second round, dealing with recovery scenarios, beginning November 11; a third round, drafting district plans, beginning December 15; the fourth round, finalizing district plans, beginning January 6, 2007.

three Community Congresses that involved as many as 2,500 existing residents as well as some former residents, still dispersed in other cities. UNOP Community Congress I was held on October 28, 2006, addressing the recovery plan framework. The results of surveys from this congress were questioned due to a lack of minority and low-income citizen participation. On November 20, UNOP held a 'student congress' for students from six New Orleans public high schools. UNOP Community Congress II, involving some 2,500 citizens, was held on December 2, simultaneously in New Orleans, Atlanta, Houston, Dallas, and Baton Rouge, reaching sixteen other cities by webcast. Congress II updated citizens on recovery efforts, and addressed prioritized scenarios for city-wide recovery in six areas: flood protection; roads, transit, and utilities; neighborhood stability; rental and affordable housing; education and health services; and other public services. On December 16, UNOP held a second 'student congress' at the Lusher Charter School for thirty high school students from public, parochial, and private schools. Community Congress III, held simultaneously in New Orleans, Atlanta, Dallas, and Houston, involved some 1,300 citizens. Congress III was the public's opportunity to review and give final input to the draft recovery plan.

The UNOP process was not the only game in town, however. During this time, activity from the Lambert planning process proceeded. On September 23, Lambert Advisory presented the results of its planning work to the City Council, and on October 27, the New Orleans City Council, which had remained unenthusiastic about the UNOP process now underway, voted unanimously to endorse the neighborhood plans—the New Orleans Neighborhoods Rebuilding Plans—created by the Lambert Advisory.[47]

Other events with impact on planning occurred during this period as well. On September 30, citizens of New Orleans and Louisiana voted to consolidate and revamp the Levee Districts, reducing the number of Levee Boards in the New Orleans area to two. A report released on November 28 by the University of New Orleans' Survey Research Center, "Keeping People," found that nearly one-third of residents of Orleans and Jefferson Parishes were considering permanently leaving the area in the next two years. Dr. Susan Howell, director of the center, said that to keep people from moving, according to the subjects they interviewed,

47. They were accepted by the LRA on November 6.

local governments had to make people feel safe, slice through red tape, fix levees, prevent flooding, repair streets, and provide more jobs and affordable housing.[48] On November 29, 2007 the preliminary draft of the Comprehensive Coastal Protection Master Plan for Louisiana was released, and starting December 11, several meetings for public comment on the draft plan commenced. On December 4, Mayor Nagin appointed Edward Blakely as the city's 'recovery czar,' and on December 11, the New Orleans Redevelopment Authority (NORA) was put in charge of disposing of adjudicated property, and became the exclusive recipient of all properties bought by the LRA or confiscated due to violations of health codes or debris. One can therefore see this period as a rather busy one.

There is an important 'other side' to the perceptions from post-hurricane residents who were currently living in Orleans and Jefferson Parishes, uncovered in UNO's "Keeping People" survey—that as many as one-third might quite possibly be moving away, permanently. These are the perceptions of those post-hurricane former residents who remained scattered all over the country. The voices of the 'diaspora,' as it came to be called, were not able to be expressed through any single channel of communication, but were themselves scattered and disparate. Nevertheless, one concern that did make it into public consciousness quite clearly was the view of many low-income, African American residents, who had been displaced by the storm—that numerous elements in the several planning efforts were simply masking opportunistic attempts by economic developers and racist whites to prevent them from returning to the city. This arose especially after proposals by the Urban Land Institute to shrink the city's footprint and recast certain historic black neighborhoods. The background atmosphere of racial distrust cannot be underestimated.

In addition to the skepticism and distrust of people not yet able to return to their former homes in New Orleans, there was also the sheer exhaustion of residents who had experienced the continual disappointment of prior planning efforts that ultimately failed or dissolved into nothingness. 'Planning fatigue' was the phenomenon of people who no longer wanted to engage in *any* process that did not materialize into something concrete, into actions they could see. Planning fatigue no doubt had an

---

48. John Pope, "1/3 in Orleans, Jeff consider leaving. Survey examines post-K quality of life," *The Times-Picayune*, November 29, 2006. The poll, one in a series of 'Quality of Life' surveys by UNO's Survey Research Center, questioned 200 persons from Orleans Parish and 200 from Jefferson Parish. See also UNO Survey Research Center website.

impact on the ability to engage people's interest and energies in the city's fourth planning process—the UNOP. People were suspicious that further neighborhood planning under new planners would either simply pick apart work that had already been done, or re-invent it in some slightly different form. Work already done represented an 'investment' not only of people's time and thinking, but, in many cases, their sweat and tears in hammering out compromises beyond their own interests. The fact that the UNOP was truly a city-wide planning effort conducted in large part as a State-run (LRA) initiative did not help matters, and encouraged those inclined to find conspiracies against their own circle of interests to be suspicious. While a city-wide planning effort was indeed needed—certainly to make any meaningful decisions involving major infrastructure—and this was a strength of the UNOP, it was also a weakness insofar as it allowed many marginalized citizens to think that this fourth planning process would end up being of benefit only to wealthy, privileged white citizens who were promoting their own business and economic development interests.

Was the UNOP able to engage the participation of citizens in a more meaningful way than had previous planning efforts? A partial answer to that question is suggested in an unpublished paper by Abigail Williamson, a Ph.D. candidate in Public Policy at Harvard's Kennedy School of Government.[49] Williamson focuses exclusively on the UNOP's second Community Congress, conducted by AmericaSpeaks, an organization specializing in large-scale public engagement. It should also be noted that Williamson primarily assessed the value of citizen input *for government leaders*, rather than simply what citizens thought about the process themselves. Williamson suggests that Community Congress II was able to overcome obstacles to raise the credibility of UNOP in the eyes of public leaders, and that by bringing together a representative group of citizen participants it engendered "buy in" from both the public and their community leaders. However, there was less clarity about the role that public input played in influencing the substance of the plan.

Williamson's evaluation of citizen input to the UNOP process is based on interviews with twenty individuals, fifteen conducted in person in New Orleans from January 17-20, 2007, and five by phone between January 23 and February 11. The interviews ranged in time from 15 to

49. Abigail Williamson, "Citizen Participation in the Unified New Orleans Plan," March 21, 2007.

90 minutes. The informants included ten African Americans, nine whites, and one multiracial; all were connected with the UNOP process in some official capacity or other.[50] Williamson did not speak with any of the most outspoken critics of the plan, and did not interview any members of the general public. Thus, the conclusions Williamson draws are from individuals who, despite some having an initial ambivalence about the UNOP process, were nevertheless strongly connected with the process and its success. This observation is meant not to devalue the sources of information but to put them in their appropriate context.[51]

While Williamson's research methodology does not put her in a position to assess the general public's perception of the level—and the value of—their participation in planning processes, it does, by choice of informants, give a sense of how those public officials and planners thought about the importance of public participation. Rather than an obstacle that consumes their time and resources, undermines their authority, and disrupts implementation of their plans, the planners involved in the UNOP process did appear to insist on public input. Williamson attributes some of this to the fact that developers of the UNOP process were individuals on State-level boards and foundation employees, rather than public officials and city government staff.

In addition, while most planners are aware of checklists of "best practices"[52] that include the need for citizen input, this frequently does *not* include material participation in aspects of *design* and *implementation*. The importance of, and a process for, citizen participation in not only planning, but also design and implementation, will be the subject of the following chapter. Williamson observes—with good justification—that, as

50. Six sat on the Community Support Organization, four were members of the LRA which instigated the UNOP, three were members of the Community Support Foundation Board that had responsibility for the UNOP process, three were City Council members, one a member of a Councilman's staff, one a staff member of the City Planning Commission, two were members of the Mayor's senior staff, one a UNOP planner, one a local media observer, and one on a city-appointed committee.

51. We have discussed the rise in activity by neighborhood associations in the aftermath of the storm. However, when Williamson states that, prior to Hurricane Katrina, "rather than neighborhood associations, community life in New Orleans organized itself around Mardi Gras crews [krewes], social clubs, and churches," this is an inaccurate characterization across all neighborhoods and vastly overstated from one informant's viewpoint.

52. Such as those put forth by the American Planning Association and the American Institute of Architects.

there was widespread agreement that the previous three planning processes had been flawed in numerous ways, the planners and stakeholders involved in the UNOP process concluded their likelihood of success would be far greater if they were able to obtain both official and public 'buy-in.'[53] Nevertheless, despite UNOP's claim to be committed to citizen engagement, community leaders saw the processes of its early events as disasters;[54] in particular, the UNOP failed to engage those New Orleans former residents who were not homeowners, but low-income, largely African American *renters*.

How well, then, did the UNOP process do to justify the view that its citizen participation efforts raised its credibility and engendered 'buy-in' from both the public and their community leaders? On the basis of Community Congress I, not well at all. Congress I failed to meet the expectations of both community leaders and the public. With some 300 citizens attending, it was widely complained that the participants were mostly wealthy, white citizens from non-flooded neighborhoods, many of whom had particular business and economic development interests. Williamson traces the rise in UNOP's credibility with citizens to Community Congress II, conducted by AmericaSpeaks. The planning team of Stephen Villavaso had responsibility for the Community Congresses, but it was the Community Support Foundation that invited AmeriaSpeaks to be involved, which they were in an advisory capacity for Congress I, and actively for Congresses II and III.

Congress II had the atmosphere of a high-tech, global town meeting, with networked laptops that enabled keypad polling. The demographics of participants did succeed in closely matching those of New Orleans' pre-Katrina population, with 64 percent being African American, 27 percent white, 4 percent Asian American, and 2 percent Hispanic; participants also matched well in terms of annual income and distribution among the city's thirteen Planning Districts. Apart from better demographic representation of participants, other factors contributing to the UNOP's

53. Williamson quotes Andy Kopplin of the LRA as saying, "I'm not sure that UNOP would have come out as well if we hadn't learned from [the lack of participation in] BNOB."

54. For example, at an early meeting to help neighborhoods choose their planning teams, the UNOP coordinating staff from Concordia failed to anticipate space needs, provide enough chairs, make themselves audible, or let people break into small groups for discussion.

enhanced credibility, according to Williamson, include primarily the belief by UNOP planners that conversations with a more representative public had given the UNOP legitimacy, some evidence of greater participation by citizens in subsequent meetings, more positive coverage from the media, and increased support from political leaders such as the Mayor.[55] However, Williamson admits that none of her informants spoke of Congress II as a way that the *substance* of UNOP was improved, and it remains quite unclear how planners incorporated citizen views into their final plans. This aspect of the UNOP process was not public or visible. Williamson notes that LRA board members and staff were particularly inclined to avoid examining citizen recommendations. A number of informants questioned whether including 'representative voices' really changed the recommendations of the plan at all, although some UNOP planners claimed they did take citizen recommendations into account.[56] However, given the unavailability of this aspect of the UNOP process—where citizen input of their needs and the 'rubber' of their specific recommendations meet the 'road' of design, as it were—it is hard to truly assess the real impact of gathering input from citizens on the substance of the UNOP at all.

While Community Congress II did achieve something of a balanced representation of citizen voices, this was not a view universally shared. Renters, in particular, appeared to be underrepresented, with only 29 percent of participants being renters (against renters at over 50 percent of New Orleans' pre-Katrina population). But perhaps the biggest concern was skepticism about whether many of the proposals of the UNOP would be able to find adequate funding to bring them into reality. Given the high priority almost all citizens gave to securing flood protection for Category 5 storms, the likelihood that necessary funding would *never* be found, or the endless years of USACE construction work involved in achieving that level of protection even if funding *were* found, left a large residue of 'expectations raised' that would remain 'unable to be met.' For that reason, both leaders and citizens have questioned how realistic the UNOP model is. Thus far, funding secured against that proposed by the UNOP

---

55. Some planners believed, largely without justification, that more former residents in the 'diaspora' were coming home.

56. One of Williamson's informants expressed the view that Congress II was another example of an organization from outside New Orleans (AmericaSpeaks) coming in to 'enhance its resume.' Whether or not that view is justified, it does capture the sense in which New Orleans has traditionally favored clearly home-grown initiatives involving change.

has been only about one-tenth of what is needed. Thus, to the extent that the UNOP process improved the ability of ordinary citizens to 'feel good' about planning in New Orleans, it appears any rise in comfort level would have to be balanced by the sharp fall back to earth when the harsh reality of available sources of funding is considered.

PUBLIC VOICES AND MIXED MESSAGES

Louisianans have never been shy about expressing their opinions and feelings about government leaders, whether at the local, state, or federal level. As Louisiana approached its one-year anniversary of the storms, and on into the second year, many voices of discontent were raised, of which the following are just an unscientific sample. Despite city and state government making visible one planning effort after another, there was a perception of many that there really was no plan. In an editorial, "The Absence of a Recovery Plan,"[57] *The Louisiana Weekly* argued that a month after Nagin took office for a second term as Mayor, there was still no plan for the city's recovery, the city's website was bare, and city employees were baffled. Even as the UNOP was being unveiled, public perceptions focused on the many competing views among developers, some who saw New Orleans as a potential boomtown, others who saw it becoming an urban wasteland. Many neighborhoods, wanting meaningful input and participation of citizens, also wanted a *coherent* planning process that they could count on to *actually act* on their input. For example, some residents in Gert Town remained skeptical about how much their plan for street and drainage repairs, the removal of abandoned homes, and the creation of a building-trades school would be realized. September, 2006 saw 3025 New Orleans buildings cited for violating the gutting requirement, having been given August 29 as the deadline to comply. People who didn't comply after being put on notice would face a range of possible penalties, from liens on their property to the outright seizure or destruction of their homes. Development director Donna Addkison, hired in August as part of Mayor Nagin's 100 Day Implementation plan to reorganize city government, maintained they didn't want this to be an adversarial process.[58] However, some were not convinced. Christopher Tidmore, political columnist, wrote a piece entitled "Nagin Offers Few Specifics on 100 Day Plan, Touts

57. Editorial dated July 17, 2006.
58. Addkison resigned in August, 2007.

Recovery So Far,"[59] saw the patience of citizens having worn thin long ago: how, for example, could a city with every neighborhood open to needed reconstruction avoid a 50 percent electrical rate increase; was it sufficient to *hope* a federal bailout would avert it?

Perhaps wisdom was forthcoming from other lands. Evidently it was with that belief in mind, that on September 23, Donna Addkison, now Nagin's Chief Planning Officer, and City Council President Oliver Thomas, along with a delegation from Jefferson Parish, took a ten day trip to Shanghai to attend a conference sponsored by the Shanghai International Merchandising Center. Addkison announced the trip as a reminder that 'New Orleans was open for business' and on the verge of an economic boom, with over $60 billion in construction activity expected to flow into the region over the next seven years.

When one considers the timing of various planning events against government decisions, the juxtaposition can sometimes seem rather surreal. On December 4, 2006, Edward Blakely was hired as Mayor Nagin's Executive Directory for Recovery Management; on December 7, HUD/HANO gave its final approval to demolish New Orleans' four large housing projects of St. Bernard, B. W. Cooper, C. J. Peete, and Lafitte; on December 8, Blakely, now 'recovery czar,' publicly exuded confidence about his ability to create a better city from the ruins of New Orleans. Was New Orleans only *in ruins,* or also *producing* ruins?

As January rolled on towards the end of the UNOP planning process, some neighborhood plans were nearly complete, but other neighborhoods had not yet even started to plan. On February 5, 2007, UNOP and Stephen Villavaso presented their findings to the City Planning Commission; on February 13, a severe storm struck New Orleans, overturning FEMA trailers, tearing the roofs of many businesses—one 85-year old woman died and many were injured. Mardi Gras on February 20 was unable to hide the widespread devastation in the neighborhoods that lay beyond the French Quarter. Meanwhile, Edward Blakely, Nagin's 'recovery czar,' was on a two week trip to Australia to handle personal business, then go on to China and Hong Kong to do other consulting of his own. March saw adoption of the UNOP by the City Planning Commission, but also release of a scathing critique of the UNOP by the New Orleans government watchdog group, the Bureau of Government Research. The voice of

59. *The Louisiana Weekly,* September 18, 2006.

this watchdog group said the process held promise and good intentions, but was not at all 'ready for prime time' because it had failed to deliver a cohesive, workable roadmap for recovery. In particular, its sweeping list of 91 projects were not placed in a realistic financial context, and the watchdog group concluded that the UNOP was simply a continuation of the divisive and confusing approach that has characterized New Orleans' recovery for a year and one-half.[60]

The UNOP plan focused on 17 'Target Area' Critical Projects in various locations, with New Orleans East and the Lower Ninth Ward designated to receive the largest initial investments, some $145 million. The draft "Target Area Development Plan" was not released by Blakely and the Mayor's Office of Recovery Management until September 27, 2007.[61] The draft plan designated two of the 17 Target Areas as "Re-Build Areas"—the Lower Ninth Ward and New Orleans East Plaza. Six were designated as "Re-Develop Areas"—Broad and Lafitte Greenway/Tremé; Carrollton Avenue at I-10; Gentilly Boulevard at Elysian Fields; Harrison Avenue; S. Claiborne Avenue at Toledano; St. Bernard/AP Tureaud. Nine were designated as "Re-New Areas"—Alcee Fortier Street; Bayou Road/Broad Street Cultural Corridor; Broadmoor; Canal Street; Freret Street; O.C. Haley Corridor; Robert E. Lee at Paris Avenue; St. Roch Market; Tulane Avenue at Jeff Davis. In addition were "Special Areas" (Algiers Nexus/Federal City) and a number of "City Wide Projects." The distinction among the three major categories was roughly that of straight rebuilding of homes and businesses from scratch; economic development; and urban renewal, blight removal, and infrastructure enhancement.

One of the intentions here appeared to be to counter the fear of many citizens that their neighborhoods might be closed altogether. However, Blakely has also wanted residents of those neighborhoods where few had returned to live to agree to a government-subsidized land swap that would allow them to move to more viable areas. The goal was to invoke

---

60. See Bureau of Government Research, "Not Ready for Prime Time. An Analysis of the UNOP Citywide Plan," March, 2007. The Bureau of Government Research is a private, non-profit, independent research organization dedicated to informed public policy making and the effective use of public resources for the improvement of government in the New Orleans metropolitan area. Lynes R. Sloss is Chairman of its Board of Directors; Carolyn W. McLellan is Chairwoman of the BGR Planning Issues Committee. The report is available on BGR's website, www.bgr.org.

61. City of New Orleans "Target Area Development Plan," Mayor's Office of Recovery Management, Draft, September 27, 2007.

the concept of 'cluster housing'—a program of incentives for residents to resettle in 'clusters' on the high ground either in their neighborhood, or in some other neighborhood, and around the 17 zones that the UNOP and the City would target for public spending. As of early 2008, the concept of 'cluster housing' has not appeared to be a workable one. Even for those who see the value of clustering residential dwellings for safety and for greater effectiveness in planning for necessary public services such as schools, fire, police, and emergency medical services, there is little sense of willingness to be a participant, and *no* sense of how such a process could be both workable and fair. The only apparent way to implement 'cluster housing' would be through some form of enforcement. Thus, it would seem at that point to become an instance of 'what one hand gives, the other takes away.' That is, countering the fear of bulldozing entire neighborhoods, on the one hand, with simply forcing the relocation of residents from one neighborhood to a new one, on the other. The non-workability of implementing 'cluster housing' must also be seen in the context of the only *existing* 'incentive' package—the Road Home program buyout, which paid up to $150,000 to homeowners who wanted to dispose of flood-ravaged property. The other form of leverage to invoke 'cluster housing'—hardly an incentive—was the prerogative of the New Orleans Redevelopment Authority (NORA) to dispose of individual properties confiscated due to failure to properly gut and board up homes, violations of health codes, or non-removal of debris.

On May 23, 2007, the City Planning Commission had adopted the UNOP, but with some strong reservations—particularly those based on a lack of secure funding. Nevertheless, on May 30, Nagin publicly patted himself on the back in proclaiming the city's return.[62] Nagin saw his leadership as having accomplished a "tremendous effort," like the "patient who lives and thrives despite a doctor's diagnosis of a disabling illness," and the city's finances as "stable and improving." Yet financial issues and funding problems would not go away. On June 11, Blakely blamed Gov. Blanco and said that construction in redevelopment zones would be limited to the initial $117 million, not the $350 million the Recovery Director said Congress had allocated New Orleans.[63] Thus, right from the start, construction reality

62. Text of Mayor Ray Nagin's State of the City address, posted by *The Times-Picayune*, May 30, 2007.

63. See "Recovery Czar: Construction Starts in September," *The Louisiana Weekly*, June 11, 2007.

was considerably less than previously anticipated. On September 18, 2007, Blakely again acknowledged that rebuilding would have to focus on small-scale projects as long as financing remained sparce.

By fall and early winter of 2007, it had become painfully obvious that an unprecedented scale of autonomous neighborhood-based planning activities were not simply taking place in the *absence* of official planning, but to *counteract* the inept and non-participatory planning processes that had plagued post-Katrina New Orleans. Weeks turned to months, then to years, as New Orleanians waited in vain for leadership and resources from local, state, or federal sources. In the face of that neglect, and with a determination to rebuild their lives and communities, many residents and grassroots organizations had begun planning for their devastated communities on their own.[64] Throughout the remainder of the book, we will be looking at several independent, neighborhood association-based recovery and reconstruction efforts, including those of the Broadmoor Improvement Association and the Mid-City Neighborhood Organization, as well as the work of grassroots organizations such as Common Ground Relief.

PROBLEMS OF PLANNING

We have examined the four most visible post-disaster recovery and planning processes, and some elements of the Road Home program, the default 'recovery process' for individual homeowners whose homes were damaged or destroyed and who were seeking some compensation to enable them to return to the life of the city. We have uncovered many problems in these proposed 'solutions,' and considered both the value but also the weaknesses in attempts to allow citizen input to planning processes. To what extent do some of these planning problems represent more fundamental ambiguities, confusions, and entanglements that fit within our schema of the Seven Markers of Complexity we have discussed earlier in *Walking to New Orleans*?

Marker 1: Instability. Complex problems are rarely stable over time; therefore, a purported 'solution' that exhibits instability over time itself becomes a problem. Louisiana's Road Home program that frustrated and angered so many citizens is just one example of instability. The instability

---

64. Jason Neville and Clara Irazábal, "Grassroots Disaster Recovery Planning: *New Orleans and Beyond*," posted on the Planners Network: The Organization of Progressive Planning, accessed at http://www.plannersnetwork.org/publications/2007_summer/nevilleirazabal.htm.

arose from the fact that the Road Home program was continually changing its bureaucratic procedures, its rules, and its criteria for accepting and
issuing grants. As just one example, Louisiana changed Road Home rules
so that homeowners who owned their damaged homes outright—representing some 1,100 people, or 20 percent of those who had closed on their
grants—could get awards in lump sums. However, these homeowners
soon discovered that there would be an additional unexpected wait, and
a quite complicated involvement with the mortgage bank, Chase Home
Finance, in Columbus, Ohio.[65] The dozens of changes in Road Home rules
have required *twenty-eight upgrades* to the program's computer tracking
software, slowed the process for homeowner applications, and led to errors
in final grant calculations.[66] Instability was also manifest in the uncertainties that plagued storm evacuees who were forced to make use of FEMA
trailers. Wynaen Walker, whose home in Lake Charles had been destroyed
by Hurricane Rita, came home from church to find her FEMA trailer (on
which she always taped handwritten signs with her phone number saying
"I still live here") occupied by someone else. The lock had been changed
and the meager belongings she had accumulated since the hurricane were
gone. "Imagine leaving your house, you're going right up the street . . .
I come back, I ain't got no place." FEMA officials told her to seek out a
homeless shelter.[67]

Marker 2: Unintended Consequences. Some economic losses that
were unexpected occurrences were simply consequences of the storms.
For example, ThyssenKrupp, a German steelmaker, which had sought to
bring a $2.9 billion steel mill to Louisiana, eventually decided to build it
in Alabama.[68] Others, however, were potential consequences of the plans
and schemes of developers themselves. The likelihood of unanticipated
transformations of neighborhoods from post-storm development ideas

---

65. See David Hammer, "Mortgage freedom still means road block. Bank holding
grants of 1,100 applicants," *The Times-Picayune*, April 4, 2007.

66. According to a report by KPMG International (a Swiss cooperative and global
network of professional firms providing audit, tax, and advisory services), delivered
months later than promised, highlighting errors and slowdowns about which frustrated
grant applicants continually complained; see David Hammer, "Changes complicate Road
Home," *The Times-Picayune*, December 12, 2007.

67. Reported by Shaila Dewan, "Storm Evacuees Remain in Grip of Uncertainty," *The
New York Times*, December 6, 2006.

68. See Christopher Tidmore, "Louisiana Loses Steel Plant to Alabama," *The Louisiana
Weekly*, May 4, 2007.

that included 'gentrification' or other forms of reshaping New Orleans' cityscape was undesirable to many residents. Particularly after the Urban Land Institute proposed a smaller footprint for the city, there arose the fear that, in the hands of developers, New Orleans would be transformed into a 'Disneyland' version of itself, focused more exclusively on tourism, with its doors increasingly shut to those low-income residents who still wished to return. Another version of this threat during the UNOP process was expressed in complaints about real estate developers, who appeared to have their eyes on neighborhoods and districts in order to promote their own schemes for large-scale construction such as condo towers, hotels, and new tourist attractions. The fear was that some planning teams were looking on the Katrina catastrophe as an opportunity to fundamentally recast neighborhoods along lines already accomplished by Lafayette architect Steven Oubre, who created a development there, River Branch, as a kind of 300 acre mini-facsimile of New Orleans, with a French Quarter, a Garden District, but with only high-end homes costing in the millions. 'Exclusive' New Orleans.

Marker 3: Vicious Cycles. The dramatic increase in crime rates in New Orleans was one sub-text of vicious cycles of complexity that arose after the storms. While people were anxious to return, they increasingly became aware that they might be entering into areas with intensive criminal activity. It will be seen how this issue impacted even former Mayor Moon Landrieu. New Orleans' suburbs also were not immune from the increase in crime. According to Sheriff Harry Lee, murders in Jefferson Parish were up some 83 percent. As a result, Sheriff Lee ordered videotaping of gatherings of young men in high crime neighborhoods.[69] However, there were more complex vicious cycles of crime. Many crimes in New Orleans were not from gangs, but from contractors caught stealing one another's construction materials. In June, 2006, Mayor Nagin asked National Guard troops to help patrol the streets of New Orleans. A deeper, more insidious vicious cycle centered about HUD/HANO's proposed demolition of four large public housing developments. This marker crosses into Marker 6 as well (Cross-Domain Interactions), with competing philosophical attitudes of various agencies and organizations about how best to provide public housing. At a surface level, the dilemma was the apparently self-imposed paradox that, at the very time when New Orleans needed to be

69. Christopher Tidmore, "Harry Lee orders videotaping gatherings of young men in high crime neighborhoods," *The Louisiana Weekly,* November 7, 2006.

able to provide housing to those former public housing residents displaced by the storms, HUD/HANO was ordering the demolition of four large public housing complexes that could, at least in the opinion of some MIT architects who inspected them, easily be renovated to be suitable for a return of residents. This is an issue that was not fully resolved as the end of 2007 neared, with continued ongoing protests. Turmoil occurred even at the re-opening of the 'New Desire' project (Abundance Square) on June 7, 2007, in which protesters sought support for HR 1227, the Gulf Coast Hurricane Housing Recovery Act, and demanded immediate action for displaced public housing residents. The challenge to Alphonso Jackson and HUD's plans to demolish St. Bernard, B.W. Cooper, C.J Peete, and Lafitte, reflected, as suggested above, deeper philosophical differences. HUD believed black, low-income people would benefit by what they termed 'mixed-income' environments, while those still displaced by the storms pointed out that they needed housing *now* and wanted to go back to what they felt was theirs. The fact that the 'New Desire' development project was located at the same site as the old Desire—a site completely isolated from the rest of the city, surrounded by the Industrial Canal, the smaller Florida Avenue drainage canal, and various railroad tracks—did not help matters.

Marker 4: Problems of Scale. Examples of problems of scale have been quite visible right from the start, due to the severity of damage from flooding in New Orleans, in which 80 percent of the city experienced substantial inundation from two storms, and in which coastal areas were also devastated—both inhabited areas and the precious marshes and wetlands. In terms of planning, problems of scale become evident especially when putting together combined factors: for example, planning that would need to include neighborhoods in which there has been as little as 7 or 8 percent repopulation, others reaching only about 35 percent of their former numbers, on the one hand, and the tasks of planning for the recovery of, or construction of, new infrastructure—water, sewerage, power and light, roads, transit, and so forth—for such a changed population. The very unevenness of New Orleans' post-Katrina population distribution makes the scale of recovery especially complex, because infrastructure needs are generally city-wide, but might be unable to be supported (or needed) in certain still-devastated and un-repopulated districts. The unevenness in distribution of primary healthcare facilities and major hospitals is another example. New Orleans is not now meeting the healthcare needs of its population, and, as with the reconstruction of many elements of its infrastructure and hurricane protection system, is unlikely to be able to meet them over the next five years.

Marker 5: Non-robust Solutions, Lack of Redundancy. One sees the absence of needed redundancy in many areas of necessary citizen services: planning for adequate distribution of fire, police, and emergency medical services.[70] This was not only the case in the immediate aftermath of the storms, but continues to be the case. State and local agencies and the Red Cross were unable to respond to and meet the needs of enormous numbers of citizens. Other entities not primarily in the business of emergency response attempted to fill that void. Bishop C. Garnett Hennings, supervisor of the 284 African Methodist Episcopal churches across Mississippi and Louisiana, who lost his own home in the flood and had thirty-one of his churches damaged, said "the black church was the first responder." As thousands of New Orleans' black population faced the aftermath of the hurricanes, it was often churches and other voluntary associations, not government agencies or the Red Cross, that ultimately provided the quickest and most reliable service.[71] Residents of Broadmoor quickly became familiar with the work of the Rev. Jerry Kramer, rector of the Episcopal Church of the Annunciation at 4505 S. Claiborne Avenue, its sanctuary flooded and ruined by eight feet of murky water, who paddled a rowboat through the neighborhood looking for bodies, hopefully alive, to rescue and bring to safety, who then turned the church into a center of relief—supplying water and food and clothing, medical services, and care giving at every level. We are also familiar with the volunteer medical services still being provided by our friend Jeanne Dumestre at St. Anna's Mobile Clinic at the day refuge for the homeless in the area behind St. Joseph's, just up the street from the dead shell of a building that was once Charity Hospital. These examples represent both voluntary associations and single individuals, barely able to survive themselves, who helped make up for the lack of redundancy of services and resources their city was no longer able to provide. In the planning efforts for New Orleans' recovery, there continues to be a shortfall of resources and secure funds to meet even the barest healthcare and safety needs of its citizens, let along provide the level of redundancy that would make them robust and capable of withstanding another near-term storm or flooding.

70. As of January, 2008 New Orleans had yet to rebuild a single fire station—two and one-half years after Katrina destroyed or damaged 22 of the city's 33 firehouses.

71. Hazel Trice Edney and Zenitha Prince, "Black Churches Filled the Void in New Orleans Left by Agencies and the Red Cross," *The Louisiana Weekly*, March 20, 2006.

The feeling of many citizens is that 'the next storm' only means their permanent exit from the city. New Orleans' back-up systems, where they even exist, are that fragile.

Marker 6: Cross-Doman Interactions. Discussion of the four planning efforts has made it abundantly clear that New Orleans' history of disagreements and non-cooperation among the various functions and agencies of its local and state government, its tradition of political infighting, has remained quite intact. The very fact of the belief in a 'need' for four major, largely unlinked planning initiatives is testimony to the stovepipe isolation of and, in many respects, competition among government levels and agencies: FEMA (ESF-#14, the Mayor (BNOB), the City Council (the Lambert planning process), the LRA and City Planning Commission (UNOP). Further, it is not as if one planning process *followed* another, to make up for and complete, in any coordinated way, limitations or shortcomings discovered in previous plans. In some cases improvements occurred rather inadvertently. Largely, however, the sequence of planning processes was unplanned, unorganized, and the result of competition and disagreement and lack of collaboration. A report released May 9, 2007, by Dr. Susan Howell, Director of the University of New Orleans Survey Research Center, "Keeping People: The 2007 Quality of Life Survey in Orleans and Jefferson Parishes," found that dissatisfaction with New Orleans city government had increased significantly, and that one-third of residents were considering leaving unless their major concerns—crime, a more proactive government, a streamlined Road Home process, improved flood protection—were addressed.[72]

Marker 7: Progressive Degradation of Human Values and Quality of Life. For the most part, such conditions as a shrunken economy, the lack of adequate housing and healthcare services, the numbers of young people not yet back in school, the absence of feelings of safety and security arising from an increase in crime, and threadbare, stretched-thin police, fire, and emergency medical services, constituted the background *against which* planning and recovery initiatives took place—rather than being a direct consequence of them. In some cases, however, one can point to elements of degradation of quality of life as at least the *indirect* residue of 'planning' efforts. As we have seen, none of the planning processes had resolved the issues of public housing, which remains a condition of continued protest

72. 'UNO in the News' press release, "UNO Poll: Lack of Leadership Rivals Crime as Top Concern in New Orleans," May 10, 2007.

and public outcry. Moreover, since HANO is largely under the federal control of HUD, it demonstrates quite clearly the *limits* of Louisiana's planning processes when they are not coordinated with federal programs and funding. Nevertheless, what will eventually be implemented within the UNOP will actually be mostly *dependent upon* federal funding. Another negative planning 'residue' is the unequal treatment of neighborhoods. While the UNOP had made an effort to target the Lower Ninth and New Orleans East among its 17 primary areas designated for concerted recovery work, there remain other neighborhoods equally in need of and worthy of recovery work that have been overlooked. What makes this aspect of the planning process unfair is that the decisions on which areas to target were not made as a result of systematically obtained citizen-based priorities, but solely by the planners themselves in what was essentially a non-public black box. A more deeply buried, but nevertheless insidious, consequence of the planning processes that negatively impacted human values and quality of life were the widespread lowered expectations—or raised expectations subsequently not met—due to the lack of any genuine citizen participation in the *material content* of the planning process. As pointed out, citizen input was primarily of value to government leaders, to bolster *their* confidence, rather than concrete suggestions that would impact day-to-day life of citizens in New Orleans' neighborhoods and local business sectors. The UNO Survey Research Center report, "Keeping People: The 2007 Quality of Life Survey in Orleans and Jefferson Parishes," not only found a significant increase in dissatisfaction with New Orleans' city government, as previously noted, but also quantitatively measured—especially as temporary living arrangements had not improved—a marked worsening of depression and mood levels of citizens.

One further example of the degradation of human values stems from the apparent lack of planning or control of rental property, whose costs skyrocketed after Hurricane Katrina. One of the practices involving rental property was uncovered in a study of five states by the National Fair Housing Alliance in their report "Housing Discrimination Against Hurricane Katrina Survivors." The report showed repeated bias in areas where black displaced persons from Louisiana were seeking rental units. Black displaced persons did not get return phone calls from inquiries about rentals, and were quoted higher rental prices and security deposits.

What this amounted to was 'linguistic profiling,' since assumptions about race were made on the basis of language patterns over the phone.[73]

For all the complex post-Katrina problems that fit within one or more of the Seven Markers of Complexity, some still unresolved problems represent neither 'complexity' nor problems yet to be identified; they simply represent *work that was never completed*. In the aftermath of flooding, New Orleans' most vulnerable neighborhoods were inundated by a hazardous sea of fuel, sewage, and chemicals. Floodwaters containing pathogens from raw sewage and toxic contaminants from oil spills, pesticides, and hazardous waste left behind thick sediment inside homes, in parks, on lawns. In a report two years after the storm, a team of researchers from the National Resources Defense Council (NRDC), working in partnership with local community groups, found hazardous levels of arsenic still present in the soil at schools, playgrounds, and residential areas. People were returning home to communities that still had not been adequately cleaned up. Soil sampling done by NRDC in March, 2007 revealed that nearly 25 percent of the 35 New Orleans playgrounds and schoolyards tested could be classified as arsenic "hot spots." Six schools, two playgrounds, and four residential areas sat on levels of toxic arsenic that exceeded the EPA and Louisiana Department of Environmental Quality (LDEQ) arsenic clean-up guideline of 12 mg/kg.[74] McDonough Elementary (#42) in Mid-City had nearly three times that level at 34.4 mg/kg.[75]

Thus, despite four planning processes, despite the UNOP's three 'Community Congresses,' despite attempts to solicit citizen input through websites or the surveys of the Lambert planning process, citizens and neighborhood association people still felt their voices had not been heard—in precisely those areas where it mattered most for them to have been heard. Citizen input did express the high level, general needs of the city—better flood protection, safer streets, housing, hospitals, employment. But the needs that were heard, therefore, were needs already known and obvious even at the time of the storms. What did *not* happen

73. Reported by Lorinda M. Bullock, "'Linguistic Profiling' of Katrina Survivors," *The Louisiana Weekly*, August 7, 2006.

74. Leslie Fields, et al., "Arsenic-Laced Schools and Playgrounds Put New Orleans Children at Risk," National Resources Defense Council, August, 2007.

75. Other schools that exceeded government clean-up levels for arsenic were: Dibert and Craig Elementary in Mid-City; Drew Elementary in Bywater/St. Claude; Medard H. Nelson Elementary and McMain Magnet Secondary Schools in Uptown/Carrollton.

was a translation of the far more detailed and specific input citizens had provided—about the needs of their local neighborhoods' economies and infrastructure and human services—into actual planning decisions. It did not happen in a way such that a *connection* between citizen input and the material content of planning proposals was evident.

This situation is precisely the kind of disjunctive dynamics that arises in any organizational structure undergoing transformation where senior management or those in power simply force in place a set of 'solutions' to certain problems without having engaged the participation of individuals to determine *why* those particular 'solutions' make sense or are the right ones to deal with the problems. The result is typically little enthusiasm for 'follow-through' other than simply following orders. The underlying principle is simple enough: the form of the problem should determine the form of the solution. That means that people must be able to make the conceptual connection between the *nature* of given problems and the *methods* chosen to address them. Thus, it is not surprising that citizens still feel—even two years after the storms—quite disengaged from the recovery process, because they have not been *direct* participants in decision-making and in the rebuilding of those things most personally close to them—their homes and immediate environments, their health and safety. In the end, 'citizen participation' in New Orleans' post-disaster planning processes continually fell far short of what was needed to fully engage those ordinary citizens ultimately responsible for *and capable of* participating in their own recovery.

TWO YEARS AFTER

What is the look and feel of life in New Orleans and Coastal Louisiana two years after Hurricanes Katrina and Rita? The following personal impressions derive from the fall and winter of 2007.

The Quiet of Empty Spaces

Evenings and times beyond working hours in the neighborhoods—and former neighborhoods—beyond the French Quarter, beyond the tourist areas, can feel vacant and empty. Entering the city from the airport, along Airline Highway or the Interstate, across Broad Street into Broadmoor, it is surprisingly dark and quiet. Even now, street signs are missing, or still bent, turned in wrong directions. The traffic and life during the day, Jeanne

Dumestre says, can be misleading: much of it is just from people coming into the city for work, not living there. Both Jeanne and Moon Landrieu think that estimates of repopulation in Broadmoor and Lakeview are very high, that one shouldn't trust Postal Department mail deliveries for accurate demographics. In some neighborhoods like the Lower Ninth, it is obvious repopulation has not yet reached double-digit; in neighborhoods like Gentilly and Tremé it is harder to tell, but residents there see their repopulation percent as only edging into the mid-thirties.

Even the day itself can feel empty, sparsely populated, compared to recollections of New Orleans before the storms. Just a few people are crossing at the intersection of Canal Street and North Rampart. Some buildings, like the historic Old Mortuary Chapel, are in good shape, but only a homeless woman walks along the sidewalk, carrying a blanket full of her clothing and possessions. Dripping from a *galerie* are the remains of a few strands of icicles, Christmas lights, from three years ago; hanging down, not connected to any others, the windows boarded up. But business at the funeral homes is brisk. Downtown along Canal Street at lunchtime, a large seafood restaurant, near both Bourbon Street and the business district, has only four customers amidst its twenty or thirty tables; not because its crawfish étouffée tastes too mild. The bathroom is clean, but only one of two toilets is working; like the city, half of it is there, half of it isn't. Part of the half that is there now includes enormous new palm trees, planted along Canal Street, costing $10,000 each.

What feels odd is the sense of coming to get *used to* the emptiness, the quiet; seeing houses still in a destroyed state, seeing great areas of non-habitation; seeing people largely working on their own, independently, fixing up their house or leaving it vacant; seeing things that become tucked back into one's consciousness as ordinary expectations. There is a natural human ability to get used to almost any condition, accepting things as they are as part of the fabric of one's life. Those of means can escape to the pleasant, inhabited areas, where functioning businesses thrive; but those in unpopulated, poorer, destroyed neighborhoods are increasingly separated from the mainstream of the city, living in survival zones, emotionally and economically disenfranchised. There is an increasing gap between those well off and the poor or those of modest means.

Crime at Home

Moon and Verna Landrieu live right across the street on South Prieur from Jeanne and William. A large, pleasant, two-story bungalow, one climbs a flight of steps to an elevated porch covered with climbing flowers, wisteria or bougainvillea; there are tended plantings in the front yard, lots flowers, and a little birdbath near the corner. In meeting with Jim Livingston at CityWorks, one of the staff, Karen, said she had proposed a 'Daisy Index'—that is, to use 'those who are planting flowers and gardening' as the best index of people who have returned to a neighborhood and who are committed to recovery. Landscape businesses are capable of supplying plants and sod for homeowners. It's not just a question of neighborhood beautification, she pointed out; rather, it is a way for people in a neighborhood to see that others are committed to staying, if they are putting in plants and flowers.

Moon Landrieu says he won't come out onto his porch any more in the morning with his cigar to read the paper, because diagonally across General Pershing from his house, is a rental property in which there appears to be a great deal of drug activity—comings and goings at all hours, with 'too much cursing and loud, thumping music.' The police have them on watch, and make frequent visits, but the property owner is unresponsive to the situation. William and Jeanne said that a teenage boy was shot to death in their neighborhood only four blocks away from where they live, several weeks before I came.

New Orleans remains on the dubious list of 'most dangerous cities in the U.S.' "There's lots of violent people out in the community, frustrated people, drug addicts, who, if they can't get the money they need to buy their drugs, they try and take it from the drug dealer," Mayor Nagin commented on the news, when it was announced that another double shooting, this time in Algiers, on the 5900 block of Tullis Drive, had taken place on Saturday, December 8. A 17 year-old male, Aaron Williams, was dead, and a 21 year-old female wounded. The shooting brought New Orleans' murder toll for the year to 200. In a separate case, two men were shot and critically wounded and their FEMA trailer set ablaze in eastern New Orleans earlier that morning. In a third unrelated case, the coroner's office released the identity of a man killed Friday in Gert Town.[76] Nagin

76. Reported in the news media, including WDSU-TV, and posted by staff reports, "N.O. murder toll for year reaches 200," *The Times-Picayune*, December 8, 2007. The pat-

attributes the slow progress in rebuilding to the city being hampered by crime. Twenty-eight months after Katrina, trying to cool down a recently heated up crime wave, Nagin observed, "We had gone through a period of a couple of weeks where things were relatively quiet, and we had this explosion."[77] Nearly a dozen people were shot in under 48 hours during one period when I was there in December, 2007.

A Home for the Homeless

Since around the Fourth of July, 2007, homeless people, along with many supporters, occupied the pavilion at Duncan Plaza, directly across the street from City Hall and beneath Mayor Ray Nagin's office windows, which face the encampment. Those who slept over each night, at first on cardboard mats and blankets, later in blue and green tents from Wal-Mart, were mostly black males; dozens more of all races and ethnicities, male and female, ranging in age from teenagers to grandmothers, would gather for the free dinner served every night. By November, the numbers in the encampment had grown to some 250 homeless people in more than 40 tents. But this represented only a tiny fraction of the 12,000 homeless people, up from 6,300 before Katrina, according to UNITY of Greater New Orleans,[78] a group that helps the homeless. UNITY also reported that the hurricanes had reduced the number of beds in homeless shelters from 832 to 232. Days at the encampment typically began with groups such as Homeless Pride leading the chant, "Hey Ray! How about a house today!" Many residents held jobs of some sort, but with rental costs nearly doubling after the storms, finding affordable housing was dire.[79] For some, the presence of National Guard humvees, which began their patrols from a Holiday Inn across the street, provided a measure of safety; however, a

tern of such shootings is eerily repetitive, with almost identical circumstances of shootings reported by the paper on July 23, 2007 and September 27, 2007.

77. Remarks quoted in public media, including WDSU-TV.

78. Noted by John Moreno Gonzales, AP, "Homeless Camp at New Orleans City Hall. Hundreds of Homeless Camp Outside New Orleans City Hall, Urge Mayor to Offer More Housing," November 16, 2007, reported by ABC News, MSNBC.com, CBS News, and elsewhere. Mayor Nagin remarked that while Americans were accustomed to things happening much quicker, with New Orleans' recovery it would take a five to seven year rebuild cycle to be able to handle problems such as housing for the homeless.

79. The nonprofit group, PolicyLink, reported that of the 200,000 homes destroyed by the hurricanes, 41,000 were affordable rental units; after the storms, fair-market monthly rental costs for an efficiency apartment rose from $463 to $764.

39-year old homeless man died in his tent, November 8. City officials grew increasingly concerned with both safety and smell, since many residents of the encampment were forced to use a row of bushes on the grounds.

By December 4, the State was preparing to tear down a shuttered, nine-story State office building bordering Duncan Plaza and an adjacent building that once housed the State Supreme Court. This would require removal of the homeless encampment, now sheltering some 150 people each night.[80] The idea of Duncan Plaza being emptied in less than a week both shocked its residents and generated a considerable confusion. The plan was to erect a fence around the plaza, along Loyola Avenue and Perdido and Gravier Streets. Some said they would need to find other places to sleep—beneath the overpass at Canal Street and Claiborne Avenue or once again in abandoned houses were the immediate thoughts of those with whom I spoke. By December 7, the State had acquiesced and agreed to postpone its plans to totally fence off Duncan Plaza until December 21; the erection of fencing would begin along Loyola, Gravier, Perdido, and LaSalle on December 11, but the plaza would not be completely closed to the public to be cleaned until December 21. By December 12, UNITY of Greater New Orleans had in place its plans to rapidly find housing for as many as 240 homeless people in a combination of traditional emergency shelter beds and temporary hotel rooms, until they could be placed into apartments.[81]

A sense of public compassion was very much in the air in the days before Christmas, when those fortunate enough to be in their houses displayed gaudy colored Christmas lights on their porches and railings, and motor-driven reindeer and elves gyrating on their tiny front lawns. Yet there were many gaps in the efforts to find shelter. By January 2, 2008, cold, dry arctic air drove temperatures overnight into the upper 20s south of Lake Pontchartrain and those remaining homeless and on the street or huddled on the asphalt beneath the overpass at Claiborne and Canal wrapped themselves in donated blankets and tarps from the now emptied Duncan Plaza encampment. On January 4, the freeze killed two homeless people in the city. One Algiers resident had taken a blanket to a woman who had

---

80. See Frank Donze and Katy Reckdahl, "Demolition scheduled to begin next week," *The Times-Picayune*, December 4, 2007. UNITY had been authorized to use $3.9 million from Road Home funds for sheltering the growing homeless population.

81. See Katy Reckdahl, "Plan in place to house occupants of Duncan Plaza," *The Times-Picayune*, December 12, 2007.

been sleeping on benches along a bicycle path beneath the Crescent City Connection, but found her dead of hypothermia the following morning.[82]

Meanwhile, the day shelter for the homeless behind St. Joseph's on Tulane Avenue continued to provide people a place to stay, clean up, brush their teeth, use bathrooms, get medical services and legal advice. The shelter is run by the Sisters of the Presentation of the Blessed Virgin Mary, a Roman Catholic religious congregation of women committed to ministries of service, especially with poor women and children, founded in Ireland in 1775 by Nano Nagle, and now based in New Windsor, New York. There are no sleepover facilities, but a pleasant sheltered area consists of a small cloister made of sturdy wood—a ring of covered benches and sliding panels creating more private areas where people find medical services and other help. Our tireless friend Jeanne Dumestre, who works at Touro Hospital, volunteers at the Musician's Clinic, also volunteers at St. Anna's Mobile Mission, a clinic serving the neighborhoods of New Orleans sponsored by the Episcopal Diocese of Louisiana. People can get a meal at lunch time; musicians come and play sets during the day, so there is often live music going on. People can sit on the benches around the inner courtyard, which has a roof as shelter but through which the sun can come in as well; there they can sit and relax, read, feel comfortable and safe. It is a welcoming environment.

Won't You Be My Neighbor?

There are days when it is 'a beautiful day in the neighborhood,' when the warm Louisiana sun filters through the late fall foliage, through flowers growing relentlessly along trellises, through the palmettos and live oaks, and bathes houses and people beneath in an envelop of comfort. It was an afternoon like that when Moon Landrieu stopped by the house and talked about the varied experiences of neighborhoods in the recovery process. Some neighborhood associations, such as those in Lakewood and Broadmoor became strong forces of unity, but others were at odds with one another and could not give a coherent picture of their needs to planners. The series of planning process New Orleans had undergone had not done much to remove dissension, complexity, and ambiguity at the neighborhood level, and Moon was not inclined to see Nagin's 're-

82. From staff reports, "Freeze kills two homeless people in city," *The Times-Picayune,* January 4, 2008.

covery czar,' Edward Blakely, as much of a positive presence. He found Blakely with only an ephemeral relationship to the city, uncharismatic as a leader; not a voice of the people, not a visionary. Yet neighborhoods had their own strengths among them—not all of them on the surface. We recalled the marvels of the construction of two new drainage canals beneath Napoleon Avenue from Fontainebleau to South Claiborne Avenue beginning back in the fall of 2000 as part of the Southeast Louisiana Urban Flood Control Project (SELA), a cooperative effort between the Sewerage and Water Board and USACE. Each canal was 19 feet wide by 13 feet high—big enough to drive city buses through—paralleling an existing 20 by 12 foot canal, and linking with the South Claiborne Manifold Canal beneath the neutral ground from Nashville Avenue to Jena Street. Neighborhoods linked together, sometimes in spite of themselves.

The fact that different neighborhood associations were in different positions to be useful to their constituents was an observation made by Jim Livingston of CityWorks, a nonprofit organization that tracks the activities of neighborhood associations and provides assistance in helping some of them work more collaboratively. Factors contributing to the unevenness of recovery, from one neighborhood to the next, apart from the obvious differentia in the degree of flooding and damage experienced after the storms, included a great variance in the quality and capacity of different neighborhood lead planning groups, and the fact that neighborhoods were often broken up by racial boundaries, among other things. Jim found that some planning teams like H3 (planning teams had been chosen primarily by the City Planning Commission) had worked well with neighborhoods; others had not. Similarly, neighborhood associations in areas like Broadmoor have worked well together; those in other areas like Gert Town have needed a great deal of help.

A particularly important source of resident dissatisfaction with the Planning District meetings—one we have previously noted—was that taking costs into account, in any systematic way, was not a part of the planning process. Thus, some neighborhood groups were recommending very large-scale infrastructure undertakings that would cost billions, but with no idea how they would be funded. However, in expressing a need for large and costly projects, residents' expectations became set that such projects could actually be realized, intensifying their disappointment when the funding didn't occur. In terms of individual housing, Jim agreed that essentially people were completely on their own. The UNOP operates on two levels: (1) city-wide, in which it addresses the needs of infrastructure across multiple neighborhoods, and (2) needs at the Planning District and neighborhood level. But in the case of the latter, even here the UNOP does not solve problems for the individual homeowner. People will get compensation on an individual basis through the LRA, which Jim saw as becoming, in effect, almost a default BNOB type of recovery strategy. Yet the process for applying and being awarded home damage compensation through the Road Home program, Jim concurred, was fraught with inconsistencies and changing policies.

One of the most visible examples of unevenness of recovery and reconstruction has occurred *within* neighborhoods, as well as from one neighborhood to the next. Driving through the immediate surroundings of many neighborhoods, one sees that one house has been elevated, the one next to it has not. Some residents perceive this as a post-Katrina problem, and complain that their 'neighbors' can now look into their bedroom. However, Jim Livingston observed that this could occur anyway, with a two-story house next to a single-story. Nevertheless, the visual sense is rather odd, if one house in the same floodplain elevation is elevated and the one next to it is not. Some of the unevenness is attributable to differing costs in elevation: to elevate a house built on a slab is about four times as expensive as elevating a house built on pilings.

People strongly express the desire that they want New Orleans to be 'just as it was' before Katrina. Jim agreed that this strong desire to 'return to what was' included even the ramshackle or 'made up' quality that characterized many buildings and homes—houses painted colors that arose from private imaginations; work done by owners possessing varying degrees of carpentry skills; odd additions to homes, like the hump on a camelback shotgun house, to work around tax rates based on street frontage. But it was many of just these 'ad hoc' home-grown characteristics to residences and businesses that formed the basis of resistance to developers who wanted to 'rebuild New Orleans better,' to make it more modern, create high-rise condominiums—to change the 'feel' of the old neighborhoods for economic gain. Mayor Nagin kept talking about building New Orleans better, but that did not seem to resonate with many people.

Unevenness pertained also to who stayed and who left the city after the storms. Was New Orleans' strong neighborhood orientation always a positive choice, or was it due in part to a stable or slightly decreasing population that *wasn't able* to leave? The benefit of longer-term ties to a neighborhood meant that you knew your schools—your old teachers might be teaching your own kids; you developed strong intergenerational family ties when older generations remained in the same neighborhoods as time passed, ties only possible with non-mobile, non-nuclear families. Yet, New Orleans was not thriving economically *before* the storms, so not many newcomers were being drawn to the city. From that standpoint, perhaps New Orleans did need new blood to help it thrive.

The intentional construction of some post-Katrina housing projects, like the Musicians' Village, was something Jim thought was essentially a 'feel good' thing. He found a surprising number of people with negative feelings towards Habitat for Humanity which was responsible for the freshly built houses there in the Upper Ninth Ward just east of Desire Street and north of North Claiborne. On January 9, 2006, eight acres of land on the site of the former Kohn Junior High School were acquired by New Orleans Area Habitat for Humanity (NOAHH) for 72 single-family homes, 5 elder-friendly doubles, and a toddler park; the centerpiece would be the Ellis Marsalis Center for Music, dedicated to the education and development of homeowners and others who would live nearby. Walking by the new homes, one can find oneself having oddly mixed feelings: the two slight variations of rather cookie-cutter houses have pleasing architectures; they're gaily painted different colors, from pale yellow to purple to orange. But they're really all the same. Yet it isn't their *sameness* that gives one an odd feeling. Just what is it? Ownership is subsidized and cheaper than people could rent; housing laws would not permit exclusion of non-musicians. Just what is it, the oddness? Perhaps it is just that it is only one patch of order in a sea of disorder.

CityWorks' core work is helping various neighborhood associations, especially factions that don't get along. For example, the Central City Partnership (CCP), which has existed for fifteen years, and the Central City Renaissance Alliance (CCRA), which has its own board and emerged from the CCP over some long-ago issue, are often at odds with one another. The associations are run by two good women who simply do not like each other. Such neighborhood internecine conflicts, unfortunately, are not uncommon.

In Gert Town, neighborhood associations don't get along. In some neighborhoods, they do, such as the Broadmoor Improvement Association, led by Latoya Cantrell, and the Broadmoor Redevelopment Association. In other areas, like Gentilly, even though an example of fairly well-coordinated efforts among neighborhood associations, Gentilly is still not coming back very quickly. More racially mixed, Gentilly's neighborhood associations seem to engage in theorizing more, but doing less, while Lakeview is an example of neighborhood associations theorizing less but doing more. Because many neighborhood associations started with some instance of NIMBY,[83] they have tended to be cause-oriented, and when the cause went away, the animosities didn't. The fluidity of the existence of neighborhood associations after the storms has also contributed to tensions and ambiguities. While 30 new neighborhood associations, according to CityWorks, have come into existence or become active post-storm, 220 pre-storm neighborhood associations have ended. Finally, Jim pointed out that neighborhood associations have no necessary relationship to either the 13 city Planning Districts or the boundaries of the 73 neighborhoods officially recognized by the city (by some counts, as many as 79 neighborhoods). Neighborhood associations do not base themselves on the official boundaries drawn in part from census tracts; however, the UNOP is using the 13 Planning Districts and standard neighborhood boundaries.

One CityWorks staff person related how some neighborhood associations attempted to "adopt" other neighborhoods, because, as in her case from personal experience, residents north of Claiborne wanted the higher post-flood repopulation numbers of other nearby areas. One begins to see firsthand how complexity that arises initially as a consequence of post-disaster attempts to gain an advantage and survive begins to compete with needed cooperative efforts *across* neighborhoods. At that point, it becomes a more fundamental conceptual complexity planning cannot easily handle, especially in the face of limited resources. The UNOP had settled on 17 major 'Target Areas' projects. Now, however, it was facing the reality of very limited funds—far less than it had assumed would be available. Originally seeking almost $15 billion, the UNOP could now expect only $1 billion, and, of that, it was discovering it could raise only half the amount for sure. Financial reality was no longer matching the expectations of residents that UNOP had set. UNOP had conveyed to people that the things they said they needed would be funded. But now the UNOP process funding *itself* had ended, and New Orleans wasn't awash in lots of outside funds, particularly after the demise of the Baker proposal. The idea of 'cluster housing,' given such a strong voice in earlier UNOP discus-

83. 'Not in my back yard.'

sions, was now clearly relegated to being a concept only even *attempted* within target areas.

Many residents were increasingly finding themselves at the point of 'planning fatigue'—no more planning; what was needed was action. Ultimately, one was forced to the conclusion that neighborhoods would either revitalize on their own or die a natural death. Thousands of tiny lots, with homes boarded up or razed, would then be transformed into thousands of big issues with which to deal. Unclear transfers of title was a major contributing factor, even if the New Orleans Recovery Authority (NORA) took ownership. In principle, ICF was the designee to buy a property, give it to the Road Home Corporation of the LRA, who would then give it to NORA. But then what would happen? Would properties not maintained evolve into larger lots, as in New Orleans East? CityWorks saw the necessity of generating ground rules for homeownership that were stable. And this would mean stable criteria for elevation, lot size, ownership, title, and so forth.

One further look at the question of neighborhoods and the function of neighborhood associations can be seen through the proposals of the Committee for a Better New Orleans/Metropolitan Area Committee (CBNO/MAC). A meeting on another of those warm, sun-filtered afternoons took place at the office and home of Keith Twitchell on Ponce de Leon in a neighborhood exemplifying both geographic indistinctness and competitive interest among neighborhood associations. Ponce de Leon Street is technically in 'Fairgrounds,' a neighborhood which circles the race track. But three different neighborhood associations lay claim to it: Esplanade Ridge Neighborhood Association, Bayou St. John Neighborhood Association, and Bayou Improvement Neighborhood Association.

CBNO/MAC is a racially, culturally diverse group with the mission to provide leadership, and catalyze change towards the achievement of a 'Blueprint for a Better New Orleans.' The Committee provides an advocacy role that encourages partnership and collaboration among citizens and neighborhood associations; its 160 members work on six task forces, addressing city management, finance, economic and workforce development, education, housing, neighborhood development, public safety, and transportation. CBNO/MAC has created a draft model for a Citizen Participation Program (CPP), whose primary purpose is to allow citizens a greater say in city government decision-making and priority-setting, and thereby give government officials a more effective means for communicating with people. However, the CPP is a vehicle for each individual citizen to have greater impact on the policies and actions of city government *through representation*, rather than directly. CPP uses a three-tiered structure: Neighborhood Councils (NCs), Community Councils (CCs) at the Planning District level, using representatives from Neighborhood Councils, and a citywide Citizen's Voice Council (CVC), with representatives from each Community Council. The overarching plan is to formalize the process for channeling citizen input to government leaders. Existing neighborhood associations form the basis of the Neighborhood Council tier. Neighborhood Councils are nonprofit organizations, hold monthly meetings, establish their own bylaws. However, they all must confirm to a set of guidelines that are standardized throughout CPP membership. The plan is for the Citizen Participation Program to eventually become codified in a legal document and formally adopted as part of the New Orleans City Charter. Zoning and land use issues, including all development and redevelopment plans that impact a neighborhood, would be brought to the Neighborhood Councils affected by those issues. The process does not yet make it clear exactly what power Neighborhood Councils would have.

How would this work vis à vis something like the UNOP? According to Keith, while the CPP doesn't ensure that district plans will be accomplished, it does give a basis for holding that if the plans have been legally adopted, then this gives people rights against other development plans that are inconsistent with the UNOP district plan. For example, if 'Victory Development' should turn out to be different from that specified in the Planning District No. 4 UNOP description, citizens would have a strong legal status to prevent it, since the original plan would have been legally adopted by the City Council. The CPP, then, is a way for neighborhood associations to work together, and, by establishing a formal process, give people stronger voices in city government. However, the process would *not* be a way of materially affecting the content of the UNOP or any other redevelopment plans, or of generating aspects of the design of actual projects.

Citizen Participation Programs have operated with varying degrees of success in Portland, Oregon; Birmingham, Alabama; Minneapolis; Dayton, Ohio; and Atlanta. Keith feels the CPP is a better mechanism than currently exists to get information *from* citizens to city government. But it is important to understand that it is essentially a program which operates through representation and the establishment of a shared formal structure among neighborhood associations, rather than by neighborhood associations directly, to present a common voice to City Council and the City Planning Commission. In Keith's mind, New Orleans needs this kind of structured representation of citizens. Far too frequent occurrences in New Orleans have been situations where, when two neighborhoods are competing for different projects, it would be common for the two neighborhood associations to "duke it out" it out in front of the Planning Commission. Now they can settle their issues first.

One of the dilemmas the CPP faces is that of trying to establish standards for being a neighborhood association. Keith believes one standard would have to be outreach and universal participation, not being controlled by a clique. But Keith agreed there is always a propensity for voluntary associations to evolve into being controlled by a small minority or a clique. Rule by the few is a phenomenon hard, if not impossible, to control. Nevertheless, CPP will make the necessity of sharing such basic standards a 'gateway' for their ability to even be 'recognized' as a neighborhood association, and their being able to participate in the CPP at all. If a neighborhood abides by no such standards, it will not be recognized by the CPP.

As the afternoon wore on, we mused about repopulation and mold. Keith put New repopulation of Orleans East, an area to which middle class blacks moved to escape the racism of the 1960s, at no more than 18 to 20 percent. Schools loomed as a big factor in decisions to return. Keith felt families with children in high school would likely not come back until their children were out of school; they might not come back at all. As for mold, Keith pointed out that after Hurricane Rita, there were six months of draught. Had this drought not occurred, the damage from mold would have been far worse.

You Have Been Erased

There are many ways in which former residents of Louisiana and Orleans Parish came to cease to be visible or even to exist at all. On June 15, 2007, Louisiana Secretary of State Jay Dardenne announced the mailing of notices to 53,554 voters, saying they must give up their registrations in other states or risk losing the right to vote in Louisiana.[84] Voters were

84. Reported widely; see, for example, Stephen Maloney, "Voter purge drops 20,000 from Louisiana rolls", *New Orleans CityBusiness,* August 27, 2007, accessible at http://www.neworleanscitybusiness.com/print.cfm?recid=20031 and Alan Sayre, AP, "NAACP Challenges Louisiana Voter Purge," ABC News, August 31, 2007, accessible at http://www.abcnews.go.com/print?id=3544573.

given one month to prove they had canceled out-of-state registrations, then appear in person at their voter registrar's office with documentation. On August 17, more than 21,000 people were in fact dropped from areas hit by the hurricanes, including almost 7,000 in majority black Orleans Parish. On August 30, the NAACP filed a civil rights lawsuit to be heard by a three-judge panel of federal district judges challenging this purge of voters. Potentially even more draconian, on December 4, 2007, as part of the first audit of Louisiana's registered voters since the storms, election officials put on notice more than 100,000 inactive voters in the New Orleans metro area and beyond that they must update their address information or risk being removed from the voting roles.[85] Under State law, voters on published 'inactive lists' could be removed from State registrations after missing two federal election cycles. Moon Landrieu observed the irony of the fact that Mayor Nagin himself hadn't voted in some three elections (other than his own, one would assume). Potentially to be erased from their political enfranchisement in Orleans Parish, where tens of thousands of residents still remain displaced more than two years after Hurricane Katrina, were at least 90,000 inactive voters, a third of the existing 278,307 registered voters on the rolls of Orleans Parish.

The erasure of the artifacts of human identity—not only by the storms, but also by the conventions of government and political society—represented not just a single issue, such as the right and ability to exercise one's vote, but a *nexus* of issues that created a new complexity about just what one's identity, in fact, meant. The erasure of one's identity in their home, their place of residence, was an act of nature. The potential erasure of one's identity in enfranchisement would be a human decision, a *human* act. Other erasures or loss of identity, however, stood somewhere in between, or were based on social patterns lost to history. For example, complexities attached to the ownership of property and determining who might actually hold title to a piece of land if the land were vacant or actually taken over by NORA. We have earlier seen the complexities of identifying title boundaries in regions of coastal Louisiana—recall the search of property boundaries in Terrebonne Parish. In Orleans Parish, the ambiguity of title claims and passage of ownership of property from one member of a family to another, or to some more distant relative, or to some friend not related, manifested itself in areas such as the Lower Ninth

85. Widely discussed; reported by Frank Donze, "State to clear rolls of idle voters. Nearly a third in N.O. inactive," *The Times-Picayune*, December 4, 2007.

Ward, in which large parcels of small plots were now lost in overgrown fields where dry brush and weeds obscured what had once been homes and fences or markers of property. On some streets, where large extended families may have dwelt adjacent or quite near one another, those 'boundaries' might not have meant much anyway. Moon felt there was really a need for knowledgeable lawyers to come in and help people get clear titles to their land—a formidable task, no doubt, but needed if one were to try to make any sense of the process by which NORA seemed to be in a position to simply have a piece of land confiscated on the basis of some nuisance or health code violation. The idea of invoking the concept of 'cluster housing' against the complexities involved in buying and selling property, sorting out deeds, then moving people from a former location to a new one would appear overwhelming.

For those in the 'diaspora' who *did* have a place to return to, once their application for a Road Home grant had been approved, the complex of decisions was still formidable. On December 7, Gov. Blanco announced that the Road Home program was now fully funded, after the federal government chipped in a few billion dollars. Blanco saw Road Home as at the core of getting homeowners back into their houses. However, the deadline for submitting an application to Road Home was December 15, and the perception remained that the Road Home process was still a web of changing requirements and foot dragging. For those in the diaspora, considering whether or not to return, the issues they would face were endless. There was no guarantee of a new job in New Orleans; the cost of rebuilding their home would undoubtedly exceed any Road Home grant or insurance payout. There was also uncertainty about the quality of schools; concerns about safety and crime; increasing insurance rates; home assessments varying all over the place. Thus, there were not just one or two or three factors in decisions that people in the diaspora would have to make to return, there were ten or fifteen—a kind of schizophrenic complexity in which reality fragmented into eight, then sixteen, then thirty-two interlinked, but insurmountable, dilemmas. Finally, there was the appeal and increasing draw of better conditions in the locale to which some former residents had moved. *The Times-Picayune* continues to track families whose lives, schools, income, and quality of life were considerably improved in places other than 'sweet home New Orleans.'

Sweet Home New Orleans

Sweet Home New Orleans (SHNO), with which Jordan Hirsch, son of Arnold Hirsch, Professor of History at UNO, is involved, is a collective of non-profit agencies serving New Orleans' musicians, Mardi Gras Indians, and Social Aid and Pleasure Club members. SHNO is an umbrella organization that integrates these efforts, connecting musicians to an array of services, such as healthcare, grants for building materials, help with school enrollments, and providing direct assistance for relocation and housing. During the fall of 2007, Jordan, along with two score or more other young people, expressed their thoughts on life in New Orleans. These younger residents felt a strong commitment to the city and its traditions, but, in numerous conversations, most expressed the view that current leadership in Louisiana's recovery and reconstruction planning was poor at all levels—from City Hall to the White House. Instead, it was community-based organizations that were providing the most helpful and sustained leadership. Through neighborhood associations, there were opportunities for citizens to provide input. Unfortunately, many recommendations made were ultimately not acted upon—particularly those pertaining to New Orleans' school system. For those who had not yet returned, their greatest needs were for help in securing affordable housing and navigating various relief systems. The most visible shortcoming of the UNOP was seen in its inability to adequately address housing needs, especially for renters. The concept of 'cluster housing' remained largely a mystery, but any proposals in this vein would need to be guided by the city maintaining an adequate affordable housing stock. Available healthcare, particularly for the uninsured, was found to be at a dangerously low level. Increasing the number of beds for the uninsured, and attracting qualified medical personnel back to the area were seen as priorities. For Coastal Louisiana, many young people wanted to see the MR–GO channel closed, far more effort given to restoring wetlands, and the construction of Category 5 levees. It remained unclear just how much there had been a shift in attitudes towards the importance of restoring and maintaining the coastal marshes and wetlands and barrier islands. There was considerable unanimity on the greatest inequities and areas of unfairness occurring for particular groups. The Road Home was viewed as a failure; affordable housing for people of lower economic means was scarce; the reaction of insurance companies in honoring their policies was an abomination. How would younger residents make things better? Among the most often cited suggestions were: an independent review of the Road Home administration, more widely accessible case management services, and monthly progress reports from local and state officials.[86]

Public Housing and Public Health

It has been an intention throughout *Walking to New Orleans* to give particular attention to needs in the areas of housing and public health. As of December 5, 2007, the four public housing projects (B.W. Cooper, St. Bernard, C.J. Peete, and Lafitte) that HUD/HANO had slated for demolition had not been demolished. However, at a City Council meeting, protesters against the looming demolition saw Bill Quigley, civil rights lawyer and law professor at Loyola University New Orleans, part of a team of lawyers representing displaced residents of public housing, manhandled and arrested, as the protests became vigorous.[87] Conservative radio hosts immediately pointed out, repeatedly, 'HUD/HANO owns and controls the projects; it is entirely HUD's decision; protesters must understand the *purview* of City Council, etc.' We have already noted that, in addition to an MIT professor's assessment that the four housing developments were quite suitable for rapid renovation and re-habitation, mere observation of the Lafitte development on Orleans Avenue showed its structures to be very solid and without significant damage. Keith Twitchell of CBNO/MAC agreed Lafitte was in good shape and should be kept; as for St. Bernard, which had seen squatters attempt to reoccupy the project at various times, Keith thought the city should track down every resident, and, if they wanted to come back, provide 1:1 housing for them. Rev. Marshall Truehill, Jr., a board member of CityWorks (along with Stephen Villavaso who led the UNOP planning team), and minister of the First

86. Conversations with younger residents of Louisiana were guided by creation of a template of questions involving both the ability to quantify attitudinal responses on a five-point Likert scale as well as open-ended questions which allowed for any kind of response; in addition, the template prompted for examples of issues and specific recommendations or suggestions for improving the quality of life during Louisiana's period of recovery and reconstruction. The template was not used as a formal research tool, however, but primarily as a guide for conversation to help ensure that each person was being asked about similar topics. The discussion here summarizes themes held by at least 50 percent of persons engaged.

87. Many details beyond what can be covered here can be found on the website, http://www.defendneworleanspublichousing.org.

United Baptist Church, also strongly favored keeping public housing. Jim Livingston of CityWorks emphasized that, contrary to the view that public housing developments were mismanaged, in his dealings with Cynthia Wiggins, who administered one public housing facility, he found that she ran a very tight ship. Thus, there were numerous strong voices throughout the city—from all sectors of leadership—urging that these four public housing developments *not* be demolished, but quickly used to house their displaced low-income former residents who desperately needed a place to live so they could return home.

The final weeks of December, 2007 saw a great deal of activity in both the start of demolition and protests against it. We can only hit the highlights. On December 12, demolition crews arrived at B. W. Cooper and began tearing down fourteen brick buildings.[88] They were met by protesters who tried to block a crane that arrived, chanting "Housing is a human right" and "It's a hate crime against poor people." Bill Quigley, leading the civil rights lawsuit against demolition, said more protests would follow at two other complexes on Saturday, December 15. On Thursday, December 13, angry protesters marched to the HUD offices at the Federal Building, 501 Magazine Street. On Friday, December 14, HUD agreed in court not to demolish the C. J. Peete, St. Bernard, or Lafitte public housing developments until the City Council approved permits for the work; however, it was going ahead with demolition at B.W. Cooper, which had been approved by the City Council in November.[89] On Wednesday, December 19, a woman chained herself to a balcony at B.W. Cooper and sang her protests. However, after a six-hour City Council meeting (which Mayor Ray Nagin did not attend), the Council voted 7-0 to approve demolitions at B.W. Cooper, St. Bernard, C. J. Peete, and Lafitte.[90] Along the way, a local NAACP leader called the Council meeting 'illegal;' others saw it as blatant racism. At one point, proposals for reopening 94 'interim units' at Lafitte and 75 'interim units' at St. Bernard were considered. But in the end, the vote was 'all or nothing,' following the impassioned lead of Council mem-

88. See "T-P on the Scene: Demolition crews arrive at B.W. Cooper," *The Times-Picayune,* December 12, 2007.

89. See, for example, Susan Finch, "HANO halts demolition plans at three public housing sites," *The Times-Picayune,* December 14, 2007.

90. After the meeting, Nagin applauded the Council decision. For a blow-by-blow account of the meeting, see Gwen Filosa, "Live Updates on Demolition Vote from Council Chambers," December 19, 2007, posted on NOLA.com.

ber Shelley Midura who said "Demagogues and terrorists should not be allowed" to lead the debate over public housing ... the choice was either to support redevelopment by approving demolition or to reject redevelopment by denying these permits. Outside the Council chambers, NOPD used chemical spray and stun guns and made fifteen arrests. One woman was sprayed and dragged from the gates; NOPD said there were no serious injuries. The upshot was that on December 19, the City Council—its three black Council members joining four whites—eliminated some 4,500 public housing units.

With the next firm data on existing hospitals and primary care health centers in Orleans Parish (and surrounding areas) not due until February 29, 2008 from the Louisiana Public Health Institute (LPHI) and the Partnership for Access to Healthcare (PATH) with Vialink, it is difficult to accurately assess changes subsequent to our earlier discussion in *Walking to New Orleans*, based on LPHI and PATH data from October, 2007. The situation with community healthcare centers especially has been rather fluid, with new clinics opening, others closing, some returning but with partial services distributed somewhat piecemeal across multiple locations, or open only on certain days. At the time of this writing, there has been talk of a clinic opening once again in New Orleans East, but that has not been confirmed; there are several physicians practicing there independently. Jeanne Dumestre said she believed MCLNO/LSU was taking over Operation Blessing there, and possibly opening other primary care centers in the near future. We also noticed a new Ochsner clinic on St. Charles, and an Urgent Care clinic on Magazine Street.

However, an event that can be confirmed, and which would have a far less positive impact, especially on Mid-City residents concerned about the dearth of healthcare services in their large district, was the outcome of a pact that sealed the demise of the Lindy Boggs Medical Center. When Lindy Boggs MC was sold in May for $9.4 million, Victory Real Estate of Columbus, Georgia said it would use the land for mixed retail development. During the summer, Ochsner Health System announced it was buying three New Orleans area hospitals, and healthcare advocates were excited about the possibility of finally improving the region's medical services. However, the Ochsner deal to buy properties from Tenet Healthcare Corporation hinged on a promise to block the reopening of Lindy Boggs, shuttered since the storm. The pact between Ochsner and Tenet stifled one effort by a group of doctors to buy and revive the facility, and a bill passed by the Legislature that would have allowed the City to operate Lindy Boggs as a public hospital was abandoned. The upshot is that when Tenet sold the hospital to Victory Real Estate, it made sure the hospital would be razed—a consequence in Ochsner's business interest, but, in the view of many, a complete disregard of the public good.[91]

Landscapes

In St. Roch some houses have been elevated, some are still vacant and in disrepair, some are no longer there . . . In the Desire area, along Piety Street, a number of FEMA trailers stand in front of houses in the process of being renovated. In Tremé and St. Roch it struck me that there seemed to be few FEMA trailers until I recalled the obvious reason pointed out by a friend, Ren Green, a lovely, witty, older African American Indian woman, who had lived in Tremé before the storms flooded her out. Homeowners had to have room on their property to bring in a FEMA trailer, so in the city's many neighborhoods where lots were small, such as Tremé, St. Roch, parts of the Lower Ninth, one simply didn't see trailers.

The 'New Desire' development is about as far away from anything in the city as you can imagine. In the haze to the north one sees the elevated structures of I-10; across wide fields of scrub grass and weeds, the blue towers of the Florida Avenue bridge that spans the Industrial Canal; far, far off in the distance to the southwest, the taller buildings of downtown New Orleans. Approaching New Desire (Abundance Square) one comes to a dead end street; then another; then another. A lot of the streets that go into New Desire are blocked off by chain link fence—Oliver White Avenue and Abundance. The painful irony of street names in the area: Abundance Street, Benefit Street, Treasure Street, Humanity Street, Desire . . . New Desire's new homes are nicely built, attractive, but the sense of being truly isolated is overwhelming; 'home' isn't near anything. From inside New Desire, one becomes aware that there is a *lot* of chain link fence blocking one off from the outside. Sakura Koné of Common Ground not only agrees New Desire is remote; he sardonically suggests it was fenced around to *look* like a prison, to get people in the right mindset to be prepared for the big house, Angola or Elayn Hunt. Indeed, all but one street in and out of the whole area is fenced off, and that one street itself has what looks to be a large, closeable

91. See Jen DeGregoria, "Pact seals demise of Mid-City hospital," *The Times-Picayune*, December 23, 2007.

chain link gate. Not a lot of people are around the clean yards, bare of trees or shrubbery. Some unoccupied units have 'No Trespassing' signs. Beyond the chain link of New Desire sits New Orleans Cold Storage on Alvar at Higgins Boulevard; further down Alvar, opposite the France Road Parkway entrance into the Port facility along the Industrial Canal, is Savoy Place, remains of a 318-unit HOPE VI replacement for the old Desire Development, nearly completed in late spring of 2005.[92] The 'abundance' of sunken manhole covers in the streets makes driving hazardous. South of Florida Avenue, behind more chain link fence, are the rows of rusted railings at the site of the former Florida Development.

In New Orleans East, at Read Boulevard, sit many still-boarded up apartment complexes, and a huge shopping center now designated as a 'Household of Faith.' Along the road are large patches of paved areas, now with nothing on them, once the sites of businesses and commercial activity. The local MacDonald's still has most of its golden arches torn off. It is December, and back in town on Fulton Street near the Convention Center, every hour on the hour there is a shower of artificial snow in anticipation of Christmas. Against the expectation that New Orleans East would return to being comfortably nondescript, like Metairie and Kenner, structures here along Morrison Road still show evidence of severe wind damage and remain unrepaired. Repopulation is sparse. Along Hayne Boulevard, which runs beneath the levee, older homes, less sterile than newer ones, seem to have been spared. The unevenness of damage is striking: some homes built on slabs might be in quite good condition, others not. As one pokes through the streets back from the levee, one is met by a surprising mixture of architectural styles: replica New England capes; two-story executive moderns, with upper-level galleries; low-lying structures of little distinctiveness; large Acadian-style houses, with great, overhanging eaves. The Lake Forest Charter School is open. Homes along Bill Street have carports, yards, Christmas decorations. New Orleans East still conveys the image of an atmosphere of relaxed living.

Lakeshore Airport remains seriously damaged, although several private planes sit around. On the grass that runs along Lake Pontchartrain by Lakeshore Drive, near Bayou St. John, I had walked Mandy, years ago; parts of the road are still blocked off, and the palmettos there cling to life, held up by wires. Washed up debris still covers the road behind the sea-

92. Constructed by Michaels Development Co on a 98-acre HOPE VI development site six miles from downtown.

wall. Nagin has continually expressed surprise at the slow pace of recovery when he observes individual homes that still aren't gutted or repaired in Lakeview: "Lakeview is an area I thought would be further along. Not enough people are taking care of their property."

Fats Domino's house and his familiar black and yellow 'FD Publishing' occupies a sizable area on the corner of Caffin Avenue and Marais Street in the Lower Ninth. Most of the purple and yellow trimmed, off-white residence sits on Marais, behind a white wrought iron fence. The media frequently describes the Lower Ninth as a 'wasteland' or an example of 'jack-o-lantern' repopulation. Neither of those characterizations seems right—it is not a total wasteland; individuals are fixing up homes. Some structures remain vacant, in a state of destruction, but even in the quiet isolation, there is visible a state of transition. While talking with a resident, he said people had bought weed whackers to cut back weeds and overgrowth in front of other houses or vacant lots; they wanted the neighborhood to look good to prospective returnees. Perhaps the most lasting impression are the areas overgrown with dry brush and grass. In some places a concrete slab is visible underneath the brush, marking that a house was once there; in other cases two rows of concrete pilings, arranged as supports, lie hidden amongst weeds and dry grass. But everywhere, there is the brush. At the time of its origins as a locale of habitation, the Lower Ninth was a relatively rural area rural, used for farming. One is led to muse 'What if it were simply left to evolve, or devolve, as it currently is, without forcing the area into some overall plan, without letting developers take it over for industrialization?' What if it simply returned to a semi-rural area of brush and grass, with fewer homes, but wider streets so emergency vehicles could more easily travel. The Lower Ninth not that big an area. From Jourdan Street near the Industrial Canal to the St. Bernard Parish line, it is only a little over a mile and one-half. An emergency vehicle could traverse that distance in less than two minutes. The biggest problem is that there is currently no hospital emergency room in eastern New Orleans. Not a few—with interest in the recovery of the Lower Ninth in their hearts—have entertained such musings; they are not, however, feelings that make one comfortable. Out of the past, colors of purple and gold and green porch railings, shouts and laughter of voices, odors of families cooking still seem to linger and make their presence felt, even when nothing is there but dry grass and brush. Further up by the intersection of Florida Avenue and ground-level Almonaster, where railroad bridges curve across drainage canals near the Alabama Division of the Oliver Yard of the Norfolk Southern and the Intermodal at 2900 Florida Avenue, train whistles from the freight yard sound eerie echoes of the past.

Other images contribute to the kaleidoscope of life in South Louisiana some twenty-eight months after Hurricanes Katrina and Rita—the plight of residents displaced by the storms who remain scattered across the country; the innumerable tasks involved to enable their return; the conditions faced by communities on the edges of the Gulf, especially for people of the United Houma Nation or one of the several bands of the Biloxi-Chitimacha Indians; the impact of plans for the Morganza to the Gulf Hurricane Protection Project on those communities; the promise and threat of the federal government's interest in deepwater aquaculture—industrial-scale fish farms in net enclosures in the open Gulf; ongoing struggles for survival waged by neighborhood associations such as the Broadmoor Improvement Association and the Mid-City Neighborhood Organization, and grassroots groups like Common Ground Relief, who fight the takeover of the homes and property of displaced residents by the City. In Chapter 8, we turn to the concept of Participatory Design and its extensions in methods such as Value Analysis, which the authors believe can contribute to deeper and more meaningful interactions between citizens and those who plan and implement their future. In the concluding chapters, however, all the images that constitute the desperate beauty of the kaleidoscope of post-disaster Louisiana, and the complexities associated with them, will come flooding back.

Images of Louisiana as a natural paradise of ruined beauty have become all too familiar in its poetry and art and music: the Mississippi River as 'Cancer Alley;' swamps from which the snowy egret has disappeared. Zachary Richard, Cajun and New Orleans' blues influenced singer, songwriter, and founding member of *Action Cadienne*, a group dedicated to the preservation of the French language, captured such feelings in lines from his 1991 song "Sunset on Louisianne"—*Smokestack burning on the river/From New Orleans to Baton Rouge . . . I take my grandson fishing down at Caminada Pass/I hope some of this beauty will last . . . Sunset on Louisianne/The sun going down on the promised land.*[93]

93. Zachary Richard, Bayou des Mystères (BMI)/Cross Key Publishing/Long Overdue Music (ASCAP). In a letter of November, 1992, Zachary kindly provided me with background to his coming to pen this piece, including his use of the traditional tune "Madame Sosthène" as a concluding tag.

Near New Desire

Gutting in Process Will Rebuild
(December, 2007)

8

Participatory Design

ETHICS, ENVIRONMENT, AND URBAN DESIGN

FOR THOSE DISPLACED BY the storms of 2005 and still scattered across the country, 'walking to New Orleans' is a long and arduous 'road home.' But it is also a long and arduous road for those 'fortunate enough' to remain home in the face of the daily struggle to reclaim the city and the life they once knew. One measure of just *how* long and arduous the road is can be seen in an assessment of perceptions of the recovery nationwide, conducted in December, 2007 by the Survey Research Center at the University of New Orleans.[1] Nearly all respondents (94 percent) indicated a belief that New Orleans was not yet or would never be back to normal. While that perception certainly should not be surprising, what *is* surprising is that almost half (45 percent) of what constituted virtually the entire group of respondents believed that New Orleans would *never* be back to normal, and even of those who believed the city eventually would be back to normal, almost 35 percent still believed this would take more than five years. These views are supported by data from "The New Orleans Index," jointly produced quarterly by the Brookings Institution Metropolitan Policy Program and the Greater New Orleans Community Data Center.[2] The report indicates that while greater New Orleans has

1. Dr. Robert T. Sims, Director, with Alicia N. Jencik and Hung-Chung (Joe) Wang, "The Nation Looks at New Orleans. A Nationwide Online Survey by the UNO Survey Research Center," December 10, 2007. 'Normal' was correlated with factors such as the numbers still living in temporary housing, the number of restaurants reopened, contamination of local water supply, and continued susceptibility to flooding.

2. Amy Liu and Allison Plyer, "The New Orleans Index. State of Policy & Progress. January 2008: 2 Years, 5 Months Since Katrina Made Landfall," *The Brookings Institution Metropolitan Policy Program & Greater New Orleans Community Data Center,* January, 2008.

made economic strides, a notable slowdown in the region's population recovery—the first in nearly two years—has negatively affected the area's ability to attract and retain both skilled and entry level workers, and could seriously jeopardize recovery. These workers are necessary to be able to deliver needed housing, infrastructure, and public services, as well as those hospitality-related occupations that impact tourism. It is encouraging that public school enrollment in the metro area grew to nearly 74 percent of its pre-storm numbers in the fall of 2007. However, the pace of home repairs in New Orleans has slowed significantly, as have the sales of single family homes.

In this chapter we propose use of the concept of Participatory Design as a possible strategy and instrument for post-disaster reconstruction. As a prelude to that discussion, it is worth a brief look at two studies that have addressed some of the core complexities involved in urban design. Both are of interest here because, as does the concept of Participatory Design, there is an attempt to explicitly incorporate ethical and spiritual factors in the consideration of what must be involved in achieving a successful, humane, habitable environment, whose design provides for needed quality of life. In *Ethics and Urban Design: Culture, Form, and Environment,* Gideon Golany[3] challenges design professionals to reexamine their basic assumptions about the urban environment, and offers design strategies based on enduring human values he sees especially as arising in ancient cultures—early urban centers, such as in Mesopotamia, the Indus River Valley, Egyptian cities of the Nile, and the capital cities of ancient China. What Golany finds that contributes to successes of the past are cohesive socio-cultural values that shaped the design of homes, neighborhoods, and cities. These ethical values, he argues, helped maintain equilibrium within the society that permeated its natural, social, and human-made environments. In the present era, conversely, Golany finds major disconnects between human values and the ethics of technology, which has resulted in confusion, imbalance, and dehumanization. Golany makes the assumption that indigenous peoples constructed living environments by "design without designers." Even if indigenous peoples relied primarily on observation skills and instinct to provide habitation products that were recyclable, harmonious, and sensitive to nature, the suggestion of a complete absence of 'designers' is tenuous. Nevertheless, Golany usefully

3. Gideon S. Golany, *Ethics and Urban Design: Culture, Form, and Environment,* 1995.

directs attention to the impact of components of the natural environment on design—climate dynamics, hydrological cycles, soil evolution, solar energy, flora and fauna cycles—as well as the factors of human culture, technological capabilities and growth, economic dynamics, political systems, standards of social behavior, art and spiritual systems. Golany's central argument is that good environmental design is "the art of establishing a synthesis between natural and human-made environments." While this view, in itself, is a commonly expressed criterion of quality in modern urban design, for Golany it is a value that has its roots in, and resonates strongly from, the past. In Western culture, Golany sees that "the need for sensitivity to the natural environment was often mentioned in the Bible, which calls for perfect morality and ethics of conduct in regard to agriculture and nature."[4] But it is to the ancient cultures of Asia that Golany looks to find the earliest and best examples of environmental sensitivity in urban design. "More than any other ancient peoples, the Chinese, followed by the Japanese, have developed strong and distinct environmental ethics of human behavior, conduct constituted in norms and rules towards natural as well as human-made environments."[5] Golany sees these ethical values expressed at multiple levels of design—in landscape architecture (gardens), urban design, and building architecture. However, it is necessary to understand the Sino-Japanese view of the environment in contrast to that of Western culture. In broad generalization, Golany suggests that ancient Chinese philosophers viewed the world as centered around three unified elements: nature, humankind, and heaven. It is a clear and confined pattern of relations between these three elements that provide equilibrium and harmony. Humankind is expected to retain the purity of the earth for its ultimate survival, and ought not change the course of nature; on the other hand, the earth's resources and cycles affect our wellbeing, and heaven, provider of life cycles, is the place where worshipped ancestors reside. Thus, the relationship of nature, humankind, and heaven necessitates unity; the achievement of unity provides harmony. Golany does not present his analysis with reference to *particular* Chinese philosophers, poets, religious figures, nor does he acknowledge the observation that China today hardly represents the view of 'a fundamental harmony with nature,' being a disruptor of nature with the damming of waterways

---

4. Golanyi, *Ethics and Urban Design*, 17.
5. Ibid., 19.

such as the Yangtze river, and a major polluter through the use of coal and the proliferation of automobiles. Nevertheless, Golany believes that "throughout Chinese history, more than in other times and places, architecture, landscape architecture, and urban design have been the art of harmoniously integrating human-made forms with the natural environment." As an example, Golany points to how human-made city objects, such as gates, streets, neighborhoods, and buildings, were identified with names relating to the natural environment and phenomena of the cosmos or the season. The architecture of one's daily life, reinforced and 'educated' Chinese citizens to see themselves as existing in relation to, not separate from, the earth beneath their feet and heaven above them. This meant that design brought together a nexus of values: the natural environment, morality and ethics, human behavior and aesthetics.[6]

In a somewhat similar vein of seeing communities as both physical and cultural entities, but with an emphasis on the 'cultural,' in *Ethics and the Urban Ethos,* Max Stackhouse[7] reinforces the importance of co-operation. If effective urban development must begin with individuals and specific project initiatives, there must also emerge a *collaborative* commitment to establish a new community ethos. Stackhouse describes *ethos* as "the subtle web of values, meanings, purposes, expectations, obligations and legitimations that constitutes the operating norms of a culture in relationship to a social entity."

Thus, at least three themes emerge that are important to our elaboration of the concept of Participatory Design. First, it is important to acknowledge that any area of physical habitation has ethical, spiritual,

---

6. Golany believes that the ability of a society to view human-kind and nature as a unitary system evolved from the earliest stages of agricultural village development. Although Golany's argument, at times, is rather simplistic, it does echo themes discussed earlier in *Walking to New Orleans,* namely, that Western religious and economic practices have tended to reinforce the view that allows for the human dominancy over nature, and, therefore, its detachment from it, with often disastrous results. Golany takes his own argument to a curious conclusion for an urban planner, suggesting that the four ancient urban civilizations he considers (Mesopotamia, the Indus Valley, Egypt, and China) fused social values, norms, and ethics inherited from their tribal and nomadic origins, but were configured into neighborhoods as "architecture without architects" and "urban design without urban designers." It is one thing to say the indigenous design of urban configurations *emerged* from the sense of the environment of the culture; it is quite another to say it emerged *in the absence of design altogether* or "not from the drafting table."

7. Max L. Stackhouse, *Ethics and the Urban Ethos. An Essay in Social Theory and Theological Reconstruction,* 1972.

aesthetic, and socio-cultural dimensions that coexist with the physical. One might argue that a habitat which is successful, that provides for a level of quality of life in which its residents are able to thrive, is one in which these dimensions are bound together into a meaningful whole. They are perceived and understood as interconnected, as mutually supportive. Quite diverse cultural, spiritual, and aesthetic interconnections may support a 'meaningful whole.' It may be the way a church and its steeple at the end of a New England village green is an *expression* of a physical and spiritual unity, a material world in which holiness and divine grace play a living part in its history. Or it may the way, as we previously described, the massive stepped pyramid of Borobudur, cradled by jungle, framed by four smoldering volcanoes, is an *expression* of an 'architecture of the infinite,' a three-dimensional model of the Mahayana Buddhist cosmos and one's spiritual path through it to enlightenment.

A second theme, also raised earlier, and in a sense a corollary to the first, is the importance of seeing any area of human habitation able to exist harmoniously within the biological constraints of its natural environment. This is the scientific interpretation of what the importance of the interrelationship between human-made and natural environments means. Both natural communities (living entities of flora and fauna, as well as geographic collectives of seas, rivers, marshes and wetlands, land masses) and clusters of human habitation (whether cities or farms or villages) are all players in a larger ecological system. Harmony is therefore not only a term of aesthetics, but also refers to how one element in an ecological system interacts with and affects others. We have seen failures of such harmony in our discussion of the impact of the chemical runoff from inland areas of agricultural and animal husbandry activity, down rivers and streams into the Gulf, impacting species fish and oysters and shrimp living in the waters of the Gulf, and, in some cases, creating hypoxic zones devoid of life. This theme will also arise in discussion of the potential effects of deepwater aquaculture on life in the Gulf of Mexico in chapter 10.

The third theme, discussed by Max Stackhouse, will be given particular attention in our presentation of the idea of Participatory Design. This is the notion of *collaboration*. The days of single-designer urban settings, such as that of the nascent New Orleans, or of Pierre-Charles L'Enfant, the French-born engineer, architect, and urban designer who fashioned the basic plan for Washington, DC, have been largely replaced by *teams* of designers working collaboratively, just because of the complexity of the systems in any contemporary urban environment that need to interact: infrastructure with natural features of seas, rivers, and topography; manu-facturing and industrial zones with the locations of residences; businesses and commercial areas with cultural and historical sites. Collaboration and shared tasks must exist on multiple levels. It is not simply a case of several *individuals* combining their efforts to design and implement a *single* complex aspect of an urban environment, such as a light rail system for local and regional transportation. It is rather a need for the integra-tion of *multiple teams* of designers, designing *multiple* complex elements of an overall urban environment, all of which must interact and work together in a way such that their users—citizens—can effectively use them. How a light rail system interacts with surface automobile traffic and bus routes, and with bike paths and walking routes, and with river ferries and industrial truck traffic, for example. The history political pa-tronage that has financed construction of roads that lead 'to nowhere' or bridges that don't join routes on which people travel represents the history of *mis*-design in cities—designs that are ultimately of no use to anyone, apart from their being a waste of the people's resources. Collaboration in design also represents the tasks in which there must be a plan for the *future*—for the evolution of an environment. For example, the old Rigolets Pass Bridge, which opened in 1930 after then-Public Service Commission member Huey Long called for a toll-free bridge there, helping to vault Long into the Governor's Mansion, was recently replaced by a new $50 million high-rise bridge, over a mile long, now allowing marine vessels to pass beneath, rather than requiring motorists to stop when the old bridge's mechanical swing span opened to let boats through.[8] Collaboration can therefore account for future needs, but also lead to better, improved design; improved quality of life.

Ethics and engineering, the interrelationship between human and natural environments, and the importance of collaboration—each of these three themes, and others, will become visible at many points dur-ing our discussion of Participatory Design. A large, urban environment, in many ways, is like a physical representation of a large, heterogeneous computer network. In the architecture of a computer network there are channels of communication, routes for passage of data packets; local area networks within the overall network which reproduce some functions

8. See Christine Harvey, "New Rigolets bridge open to local traffic. Route to N.O. will be clear when Chef Pass span is fixed." *The Times-Picayune,* January 16, 2008.

of the larger network on a smaller scale; there are monitors that gather information about the performance of the network; bridges that allow connections among network entities or functions, such that the behavior of a given network object can change, depending on needs and conditions of the network. But while many, or even most, of the entities of a large, heterogeneous computer network function *behind* the scenes, there is still a point at which the network must become *visible* to individuals—network system managers, who must monitor the behavior of the network and fine-tune its performance; use the data it collects in various ways; identify and solve problems that arise. The network, in other words, must *make sense* to human understanding. The user must have a coherent, conceptual model of the network. In a similar fashion, citizens in a large, complex urban environment must interact with that environment in order to be able to function within it, to use it. They must have some coherent, conceptual model of the urban environment, not only just to survive within it, but to maintain a quality of life that is acceptable to them. Citizens may not need to know, for example, exactly how electrons travel through electrical wires by which electric lights in their homes or on the streets are lit or by which electric-motor trolleys are driven. But they must have a model in their mind so that they know they can depend on certain areas of the city *being lit,* or the range of times when they can expect surface trolleys to be available for their use. They must also have a conceptual model that allows them to act in response to problems that arise in the overall system. For example, since in New Orleans they may live in an area that is below sea level, citizens must understand what they need to do if there should be a failure in the levees or locks or seawalls that keep out the water and protect them from disaster. It was precisely those aspects of a conceptual model of the urban environment that were missing in the aftermath of Hurricanes Katrina and Rita.

CONCEPTUAL MODELS

The idea of building a conceptual model is one that has held an increasingly important place in the design of systems with which human beings must interact. Such systems include not only those involving human-computer interaction, but also interactive systems such as roadways, railways, waterways, buildings, city streets, or the architecture and infrastructure of a town or entire urban environment. In a decade of work as Consulting Engineer and the director of a program that trained software and hardware engineers in various elements of human engineering and user interface design at Digital Equipment Corporation (DEC) of Maynard, Massachusetts, the author[9] was among a growing group of design engineers who came to see the importance of thinking of design in terms of conceptual models.

The need for incorporating an explicit conceptual model into a design in the context of cyber-technology arose as engineers were increasingly being asked to design for use in task environments quite *unlike* their own. When software or hardware engineers had simply been asked to design systems or applications primarily for use by *other engineers*—skilled people who *already* possessed a high level of understanding of the nature of the tasks for which the designs would be employed—little thought needed to be given to incorporating specific features of usability into the design. There already existed a shared knowledge base among engineers about what typical tasks consisted of, the kinds of problem-solving strategies that were employed, how to communicate information about tasks. However, as engineers found themselves being required to design for users in new and unfamiliar task environments—work settings that might include researchers in scientific labs, doctors in hospitals, lawyers or financial advisers in professional offices—the work of design became more complex. No longer was there the ability to assume the existence of any shared knowledge base of tasks or common behaviors. Some engineers continued to design software applications and hardware systems *as if* they were designing for other engineers. In many instances, the applications and systems whose designs were approached in that manner would wind up as failures—not only from a usability standpoint, but ultimately from a profitability standpoint. Alternatively, engineers could begin learn how to build conceptual models by which to bridge the gap between what they, as engineers, knew and understood and what their users knew and understood. Engineers began to see that a well-designed conceptual model would not simply force the user to learn some compressed or abbreviated subset of the engineer's knowledge base. Rather, a powerful conceptual model would be able to express the functionality of the system or application in terms the user could understand, in terms that made sense *within the task environment of the user.*

Historically, some of the early examples of such a design paradigm in computers were those done by the Apple Corporation, in which it

9. In an engineering company, 'Consulting Engineer' designates the highest level of technical leadership requiring the vote of a special committee of senior management.

became an explicit design goal that *anyone*, skilled or novice with computers, could immediately begin to do useful things. The designs and representation of functionality were *transparent*, intuitive, or they used symbols and artifacts that had been adapted from the user's own task environment. The idea of a desktop with files and folders and places to store them became a conceptual translation, in visual images, of abstract software entities such as directories and binary addresses. In the management of complex, heterogeneous networks (such as the old DECnet), it might mean development of a graphical interface to represent various network entities and functions—physical or logical communication paths e.g. a VAX system bus, a LAS Ethernet, for a WAS, DECnet; boundaries to separate but also relate common management and security functions; time synchronization mechanisms; storage facilities; processing facilities; I/O facilities; bridges, and so forth.[10]

As another way to think of conceptual models, consider, by analogy, the difference between two musicians teaching one another new ways of playing or approaching a piece vs. one musician trying to teach the same thing to a non-musician. The two musicians who are already familiar with the language of music theory, notation, genres and styles of playing, the characteristics of different instruments, and so forth, can easily exchange and learn new techniques of playing—new licks—or even share new genres of music. Indeed, they can typically exchange this knowledge simply by *hearing* one another play because an implicit knowledge base against which new information is brought forth is already shared. However, should a musician try to convey the same information to a non-musician, even one sensitive to or interested in the music, the task would be entirely different. With no shared knowledge base, the musician trying to convey information to a non-musician would first have to build some *replica* of a knowledge base—some conceptual model—so that the learner had some way of appropriating the information. The conceptual model would then enable information to be placed within a framework either already understood by the learner, or in some newly developed scheme that was sufficiently grounded in the learner's task environment to be understood by a novice. Some conventions now commonly used within the world of

10. One of the author's patents is as a contributor to the invention of a network management system known as an "Extensible Entity Management System Including a Dispatching Kernel and Modules which Independently Interpret and Execute Commands," a system hopefully more usable than its name.

music have historically developed for just those reasons—'shape notes' in teaching singing, various numbering systems for chords, referring to the notes on a scale by do, ré, mi . . . and so forth.

There are still other ways to think about conceptual models in the context of design that begin to reveal underlying social and ethical dimensions of human interaction with systems of various kinds. Here is one. Recall the 1958 lithograph *Belvedere* by Dutch graphic artist M. C. Escher.[11] What is depicted is three stories of a possibly larger domed structure, with columned, open galleries, connected by ladders and steps and inhabited by a number of people. It is not only an interesting picture, but it also encapsulates an idea that has a lot to do with the way designs are both conceived and *perceived*. This is the idea that one can create something that has consistency locally, but globally makes no sense. The design has a fundamental inconsistency. All the *pieces* make sense, but not the whole. If one looks around in the picture, what person in the picture really knows the extent of the problem? No one, really. The gesture being made by the person on the ladder might raise some suspicions; the youth down below with his puzzle that doesn't make any sense—he may be wondering what sort of world he is in, in which he has a cube that doesn't work right. But none of these people is really aware of the degree to which the entire world doesn't make sense. *Belvedere* illustrates the fact that humans build systems—including environments of human habitation—very much like this. There are lots of people—engineers and designers—who work on their individual pieces of an urban environment. Those pieces come together at various points, and they must work together, interface with adjacent pieces. But the whole system ends up being just like the picture *Belvedere*. The overall system doesn't make sense. There are gross problems that make the system less robust, less usable, even nonsensical. New Orleans' levee and hurricane protection system has been criticized in the IPET reports and elsewhere for not functioning as a coherent system; for failing as a system. Other systems within New Orleans' urban environment have also been accused of similar failings—its system of public housing; its healthcare system; its public school system; and, not the least criticized, its system of city government.[12]

11. The example was first suggested by Richard Rubinstein.

12. For example, in a long-awaited audit of New Orleans' 2006 finances, there was revealed an ineffective, disorganized system of fiscal oversight at City Hall, prone to bookkeeping delays and lacking internal controls, including barriers to prevent corrup-

Therefore, one of the first things necessary to say about the process of design—especially design involving people's place of habitation, people's places of work, people's lives—is that designers must try to build systems in that environment with the citizen's mind in mind. However, the citizen's task environment is forced to become, in many respects, a reflection of the designer's mind, rather than the citizen's mind. From the viewer's perspective, *Belvedere* is a nightmare. The question *Walking to New Orleans* is here concerned with is: whose perspective is reflected in the current design—or absence of design—of New Orleans' urban setting? Or, for Coastal Louisiana, whose perspective is reflected in how human beings and economic interests have made use of—or have enacted abuse upon—that natural environment of Gulf marine life, marshes, and wetlands?

What matters in a system is how the system makes sense to the *user*—and 'user' here must be understood to include not only the *human* citizens of the towns and cities of the land, but also the *natural* flora and fauna of the seas and marshes and waterways; perhaps even the components of the land and sea themselves: the rivers and estuaries as well as those beings that live on and within them.

There is an intentional prescriptive element being stated here; a normative ethic, if you will. It is a position which holds that engineering and ethics must coincide: that engineering carries with it *responsibility* for design, that it entails an *obligation* to users. What matters is ultimately not the designer's point of view, but whether the system—whether cognitive or mechanical or social or cultural—makes sense from the user's point of view. Can the system be used, lived in, appropriated by the user for its intended purposes. To design a system from the user's point of view is to design with a conceptual model in mind that is humane and meaningful to the user.

Another way to think about conceptual models is in terms of language. There are many vehicles of communication that are used by people, including exchanges through design between the designer and the user. The most immediate is natural language. I have an idea in my head, something that makes sense, and I utter a sentence expressing that idea to you. Then you form an idea in your head, and perhaps acknowledge what has

---

tion in the public bidding process. Beyond general criticisms of how the city manages its accounts, auditors identified sloppy procedures for handling cash transactions, gaping holes in the protection of electronically stored information, and deficiencies in recording property, sales, and franchise taxes. See Michelle Krupa, "Broad failings found in audit of N.O. finances," *The Times-Picayune*, January 23, 2008.

been said. Then we go on. That's one idea of how communication takes place. In that model, the sentence is a physical realization of the idea 'in the head.' The sentence isn't the idea itself, but it serves as a way to get an idea that relates to someone else, formed in one's own head, into *another's* head; or, if not 'into their head,' if you're a behaviorist, at least capable of producing the expected behavior in the other person which is *also* the behavior the other person desires. Now, as a designer, I may have an idea about how I want persons to be able to physically move about within an inhabited setting (say, via a transit system), or how to be able to deal with a problem (say, an injury or a disease), or how to interact with other residents (say, in a housing complex, within a neighborhood). I cannot directly create this idea in other persons' heads, but as a designer I can structure the system so that the idea you build in your head is going to be like the one that I was thinking about. That's another way of thinking about the fundamental idea of a conceptual model. I design a system in terms of some model that facilitates communication of the idea in my head to ideas in your head so that expected behaviors on your part can oc-cur—behaviors that are desired and that make sense to you because they reflect your 'task environment' and your goals and constraints. Through a conceptual model, I have translated my original idea into a form that can exist within *your* world so that *you* now become the 'owner' of that idea.

From these examples, it should become clear that it is both possible and necessary to design the way people will think about a system. To ac-complish this through the use of a conceptual model is a natural occur-rence because human beings, quite naturally, are model builders. People develop models for things they use. People use airports, for example, and learn to use airports because they have a certain similar structure.[13] Airports are approachable because they are also terminals for buses or rail or automobiles that allow people to reach them; there are structures and signs that tell people where the airplanes are, where to find luggage, how to move about in the airport. Thus, even if one arrives at an entirely new airport, say, in Frankfort, Germany or Tuscaloosa, Alabama, there is a suf-ficiently common structure among airports that enables prior experience to help people sort out where to go, what they need to do. This does not mean that all airports employ good models, or are good instantiations

13. For a further general discussion of conceptual models, see, for example, Richard Rubinstein and Harry Hersh, *The Human Factor. Designing Computer Systems for People,* 1984.

of some basic model. There may be a variety of reasons for an airport not being a good model: Léopold Sédar Senghor International Airport in Dakar, Senegal because of squalor and danger; Mineralnye Vody Airport in Russia, described by the December 19, 2006 issue of *The Economist* as 'a lower circle of hell'; Fiumicino International Airport in Rome because of the uncontrolled behavior of anxious passengers. These are airports that convey perplexing or ambiguous or frightening messages—either as 'noise' in addition to their intrinsic structure, or as disruptions or failures within their basic structure.

One of the things research learned early on in thinking about creating conceptual models is that they 'tell a story'; in a certain sense, they build a myth. They provide a scenario about how to behave, what the boundaries of expectations and behavior are, how to perform tasks, how to solve problems, and the like. Thus, as with a successful story—one that communicates clearly—a successful conceptual model will build a *consistent* myth. Even if the model does not communicate all the technical details of the system, it develops a consistent myth that enables users of the system to make predictions and to behave in ways that are comfortable. We previously considered one example of a common, fairly consistent and moderately successful myth from the world of software applications—the model of the system being like a desktop, with storage locations like filing cabinets; drawers and folders containing documents, pictures, and other files; devices for moving files and objects around, and so forth. In characterizing the 'myth' that any model creates as consistent, it is important to point out that all models create a set of expectations. When those expectations are met, behavior operates within a zone of comfort. When those expectations are not met, the user's behavior will display anxiousness, confusion, and there will be failures in tasks the user wishes to, or is expected to, perform. Thus, it is important that any conceptual model not raise expectations if they cannot be met within the system. It is important to know the limits of the analogy the myth is attempting to create. In New Orleans, for example, certain expectations had been raised about its levee and hurricane protection system—not only in terms of the completeness of its conceptual design by USACE as a system, but also in assumptions about the robustness of its actual implementation, its ability to withstand attack by natural forces at some planned level. After Hurricanes Katrina and Rita, disagreements that arose about whether the system had been designed to handle a Category 3 force hurricane or higher (or less) only mirrored inherent ambiguities and inconsistencies that lay within the myth that had been created about its overall design as a system. The hurricane protection system failed not only because of unanticipated breaches in various locations; it failed *as a system.*

THE CONCEPT OF PARTICIPATORY DESIGN IN POST-DISASTER RECONSTRUCTION

In many respects, the conditions of post-disaster recovery and reconstruction in New Orleans and South Louisiana will themselves result in some level of social engineering. Population distributions and social structures will be different than what they were before the storms. The economic bases for sustaining the emerging social structure will be different. Perhaps even the culture of New Orleans and South Louisiana will be different. The question that arises is: what *kind* of social engineering? After a series of four planning processes, it is as yet unanswered whether the population makeup, social institutions and structure, and the character of living in those areas of Louisiana impacted by the storms will be different simply as a consequence of some combination of natural evolution, economic greed, political power, and other essentially random factors, or different *by design.* Where does the opportunity for a rational, ethical, and humane restructuring of society exist? It exists where there are opportunities to remove pre-existing social and economic inequities. It exists where it becomes possible to redress historic unfairness in the access by different racial and ethnic groups to have a voice in political processes. It exists in opportunities to restructure and improve inadequate school systems, to reduce poverty, to improve housing conditions for those in marginalized economic strata, to secure public safety for people and recreate a devastated healthcare system. As a rational person and a caring citizen, one would like to think this can be done *by design,* rather than by simply being left up to fate or to the whims of developers or politicians.

However, any ethical, legal, or philosophical justification of the need for rationally re-engineering a dismembered infrastructure and hurricane protection system, still largely vacated neighborhoods, and a broken leadership structure for those especially at the fringes of the society of New Orleans and South Louisiana, recovery, restructuring, and reconstruction, both urban and rural, cannot be accomplished framed by re-engineering or design *in the abstract.* It must involve ongoing, face-to-face interactions

439

that establish genuine, consensus-based, collaborative initiatives from the standpoints of the values of the racially and culturally diverse groups that exist within the society of South Louisiana. How *can* one establish a context of collaboration such that, even grounded in a shared ethic of social justice, social structures can be re-engineered to satisfy the diverse human values that exist? How *can* one ensure that a re-engineered society will be shaped by those ultimately impacted by decisions about which projects receive priority funding, which do not? In short, how can one match engineering decisions with core human values to establish a shared ethos in a culturally, racially, ethically diverse environment?

The concept of Participatory Design puts forth the argument that people *impacted by* the introduction of any new technology that results in social or organizational change—whether innovation for purposes of continuous improvement in work environments, or the wholesale reorganization of social structures, including renewal of urban infrastructures— must be *active participants* in both the processes of problem analysis and decision-making about solutions. The concept of Participatory Design, therefore, is a conceptual model that incorporates an *ethic of technology*. It is a model that advocates for human dignity based on participation, consensus, and coordination of effort to achieve good living and working conditions for everyone in a given environment.

The author's initial introduction to realizing the possibilities of Participatory Design came in Manchester, England in a meeting with Enid Mumford in her office at the University of Manchester.[14] We discussed her approach to collaborative engineering projects, including, especially, the ethical dimensions of design and the importance of responsibility to the user—an interest we shared in common. This meeting was followed, in the early 1980s, by my participation, eventually as a Consulting Engineer, in her work with Digital Equipment Corporation involving the use of her methodology for the collaborative development of new Expert Systems. Enid was, until shortly before her death April 7, 2006, Emeritus Professor of Manchester University; she was a Fellow of the British Computer Society, and the recipient of honorary degrees and numerous awards for her contributions to information science and the human and organizational impact of computer-based systems. Her sociological research was very much face-to-face. Enid spent time working in industry at an aircraft

---

14. Enid uses the term *participative* design in her writings.

factory and as a production manager for an alarm clock manufacturer. After she joined the Faculty of Social Science at Liverpool University, Enid carried out sociological research in industrial relations on the Liverpool docks and in the North West coal industry, where she spent months underground talking with miners at the coal face. Mumford's concept of Participatory Design is based on establishing a workable model for instituting technological and cultural change across task domains and affected social groups. Mumford's basic argument is that people *impacted by* the introduction of new technology resulting in organizational change must be *active participants* in the problem analysis and design decisions that affect them. 'Technology' would include not only new computer-based systems for innovation, but also any of the number of quality or process improvement methodologies, initially used in manufacturing but subsequently applied to organizational structures generally.[15] Thus, Mumford's conceptual model is in many ways an *ethics of technology*. It advocates for human dignity based on participation, consensus, and coordination of effort to achieve good living and working conditions for everyone in a given environment. One of her methods, in fact, went under the acronym ETHICS: Effective Technical and Human Implementation of Computer-based Systems.[16]

Enid Mumford's ground-breaking work coincides with a field now referred to as socio-technical design. Its premise is that managing change of any kind requires effective problem-solving. This is especially critical when change involves designing and implementing new organizational structures, as it certainly does in the case of rebuilding New Orleans' neighborhoods and infrastructure after Hurricanes Katrina and Rita. Effective problem-solving, as earlier discussed in *Walking to New Orleans*, requires the control

15. Including 'technology' in programs that evolved from the Government Performance Results Act of 1993 (GPRA) which sought to provide for establishment of strategic planning and performance measurement in the federal government to address waste and inefficiency in federal programs that undermined confidence in the government, reduced its ability to address vital public needs, and disadvantaged federal managers in their efforts to improve program efficiency and effectiveness because of insufficient articulation of program goals and inadequate information on program performance. Use of Participatory Design and related methodologies was rare, but did occur, on a small scale, in work by the author as Senior Consultant for the National Academy of Public Administration with the Health Resources and Services Administration and the National Security Agency.

16. See Enid Mumford, *Designing Human Systems*, 1983.

of 'entropy'—a concept borrowed from physics to describe energy that exists but is unavailable for productive use. Energy of this kind can lead to chaos. Solving complex problems also requires recognition of the interactions among psychological, economic, technical, cultural, and political factors (Marker of Complexity 6). Questions that must be answered include determining who benefits most from solving the problem, where sources of funding will be found, and which technologies are actually relevant to proposed solutions. Most important is the question of whether solutions will be culturally, socially, and ethically acceptable.[17]

Complex problems are rarely stable over time. Continual changes in a given environment, including its demographic and economic contexts, typically require problems to be rethought and redefined. Solving complex problems is therefore often a balancing act—where there is the risk of problems being partially solved, then returning in new forms, some of which are more difficult to solve than the original dilemmas. Solutions that appear attractive because they are cheap or politically acceptable to the various factions who hold power in government can lead in the wrong direction. We have seen some of the history of this in Louisiana. Thus, designing a robust problem-solving strategy involves not only principles of good engineering; it involves ethics and communication. From the standpoint of ethics, this means identifying and prioritizing a set of *values*, establishing a context of *consensus*, a process for the *sharing of values* and the *responsibilities of commitment* to a given strategy, then implementing a series of practical operations designed to achieve *mutually desired ends*. But clear and unambiguous paths of communication are needed to *support* these ethical requirements; they are critical to maintaining shared values over time. Unambiguous channels of communication function as a 'checks-and-balances' monitoring of actions and behavior so that the ethical grounding of previously agreed upon goals is not lost in the shuffle of implementation. For this reason, it is critical that communication be understood and framed as an iterative loop—a *cycle* of information passage *from* those designing and implementing a problem-solving program to those affected by or benefiting from its results, and then *back from* those affected by the program to those designing and implementing it so

17. See Mumford, *Redesigning Human Systems,* and her other listings in the bibliography for further details on the origin and history of her methodology and various instances of its application.

that its design can be continually improved, modified, and ensured to fit the needs of its users.[18]

It has generally been customary in engineering to think of problem-solving and design as *iterative* processes—iterative cycles of problem identification, preliminary solutions put forth, then tested, then incrementally improved. The design of anything involving relatively high levels of complexity—whether a large computer network or an urban residential and commercial environment—is never something accomplished all at once. It occurs in stages. What the concept of *participatory* design adds to any problem-solving and design process is the recognition that it is not only designs themselves, in their various stages, but *communication about* design in every phase that must be thought of as an iterative process. *Participatory* design is a matter of the creation of a *continuous* communication loop. Why is this so important? Because communication between those affected by design—people who must live with it, whether directly or indirectly—understood as an iterative loop is the best guard against a design solution simply being *imposed* upon people in ignorance of their needs or of potential human and social consequences. Indeed, understanding precisely what the 'needs' of those who must live with a design are is something that itself deepens as people have the opportunity for ongoing reflection about their needs. Often, the determination that significant human or economic needs may *not* have been met is discovered only after an expensive design solution, sometimes with many unanticipated environmental consequences, has been implemented. The MR–GO navigational channel in New Orleans is a prime example. MR–GO ultimately did *not* solve the problem of allowing more efficient vessel passage into the Port of New Orleans, and it created many additional environmental and economic degradations of its own as well. As a result, the channel is now in the process of being closed by USACE. Thus, as any design necessarily emerges through a series of thinking and re-thinking refinements, so does the understanding of users about what their needs and requirements entail.

A planning process—such as any one of the series of four planning processes (ESF-#14, BNOB, Lambert, and the UNOP) that attempted to address how to go about post-disaster recovery and reconstruction in New Orleans—is really *one form* of design process. It is design in its earli-

18. See also discussion in chapter 5.

est stages. The various attempts to gather input from citizens employed by some of those processes—especially in the Community Congresses held by the UNOP—were indeed valuable. However, we have also seen that this was a period of citizen input that had a short-term beginning and end. They were essentially one-shot deals. Moreover, what the planning teams ultimately did with that citizen input remained obscure—certainly to the citizens who had an opportunity to provide input to the planners. Even with the series of neighborhood planning meetings held during the Lambert process, there was the feeling among many who provided input that while the planners listened to it, they then went ahead and proposed what they were going to propose anyway—that the input did not *materially* affect any particular aspects of design or reconstruction solutions. Participatory Design proposes a number of ways in which input from those impacted by a planning process or a design process can be *continually* fed into that process. However, what is most important is that the input is not a one-time event; citizen input must be a continuous, iterative loop that parallels the progress of problem-solving and design. Not only does this help ensure that the output of planning or engineering work actually addresses the needs of its users and meets the intended goals, it also helps secure the ethical paradigm in which planners or engineers remain cognizant of their responsibility to the 'users' of their work. It is really only under such an ethical engineering or design paradigm that users can feel they have taken 'ownership' of the results of planning or design work—what is sometimes called their 'buy-in.' The problem with many planning and engineering processes is that citizen 'buy-in' is something that occurs very early on in the overall process and then is largely forgotten. We believe that to have happened thus far with post-disaster planning in New Orleans. Citizens' expectations about the particulars of infrastructure and neighborhoods and housing being rebuilt were raised both by planners and those in city government. Citizens were eager to give their 'buy-in.' However, that 'buy-in' was left to fallow and wither, rather than grow, as expectations were not met. The absence of meeting citizens' needs for low-cost public housing and adequate healthcare services are perhaps the two most significant areas in which citizens' needs and expectations have most visibly *not* been met. Citizen input and 'buy-in' is not a one-shot deal; it is something that must be engaged and continue through the *entire* planning and implementation process. That, we hold, is an ethical obligation of planning and engineering design. If citizens are not continuously engaged and involved as *participants* throughout the processes of rebuilding their neighborhoods and city, there is no reason to think that they will be inclined to regard of the city as *theirs*. The reconstructed New Orleans will be the city of the developers, or the politicians, or the private visions of the planners, or the speculations by the federal government and its agencies about what New Orleans needs. The momentum in recreating New Orleans will be from the outside, not from within. It will not be a city of its citizens. Ethically, that outcome would be a tragedy.

In applications of Participatory Design, a variety of technical skills derived from cybernetics have come to be useful in recognizing and describing problems. Taking a 'holistic' approach, which differs from traditional scientific methods of dividing large problems into small sections, giving each part to a different group for solution, enables the causes of the problem and their consequences for different situations and groups to be seen as an interlinked whole.

Methods of interpreting problems as interlinked wholes are used in 'pattern recognition,' a research area that classifies data patterns based on a priori knowledge or statistical information extracted from the patterns, and includes such sub-disciplines as discriminant analysis, feature extraction, cluster analysis, grammatical inference and parsing (syntactical pattern recognition), and image analysis. It is related to work in the analysis of artificial neural networks, following the early foundations of Marvin Minsky, co-founder of MIT's Artificial Intelligence Lab,[19] or work in natural language parsing, following early work of Roger Schank, formerly professor of computer science and psychology at Yale, director of the Yale Artificial Intelligence Project, one of the founders of the Center for the Learning Sciences at Carnegie Mellon, whose innovations involved looking at dynamic memory in the form of meaningful 'wholes' or 'stories,' and problem-solving as progressing by using 'cases' (examples) stored in memory as 'schema' based on previous experience.[20] Techniques of 'pattern recognition' have customarily been used by physicians and surgeons to connect signs and symptoms presented with previous encounters to speed diagnosis; within current medical science, pattern recognition is

19. See Marvin L. Minsky and Seymour A. Papert, *Perceptrons. An Introduction to Computational Geometry,* a 1989 MIT Press Expanded Edition of the seminal 1969 work.

20. See, e.g. Roger C. Schank and Robert P. Abelson, *Scripts, Plans, Goals, and Understanding. An Inquiry into Human Knowledge Structures,* 1977; Roger C. Schank, *Dynamic Memory Revisited,* 1999.

the basis for Computer Aided Diagnostic systems that confirm or question a doctor's interpretations and findings.

Skills that aid problem-solving come from a variety of other disciplines as well, including continuous process improvement methods such as TQM (Total Quality Management), Six Sigma (a process for defect reduction using especially in manufacturing), and ISO 9000 (a quality inspection and assessment process). One relatively new approach in particular, known as 'coordination science,' which has been under study at MIT's Sloan School, deals with how designers, users of design, and various groups of implementers can optimize their interactions with one another.

It is fitting and relevant to the post-Katrina environment that socio-technical design historically arose from skills developed to treat war-damaged soldiers regain psychological health and return to civilian life after WWII. The first work was done at the London Tavistock Clinic, now the Tavistock Institute of Human Relations, founded in 1946. These methods, well-known in the United States as Critical-Incident Stress Management (CISM), are now used to deal with post-traumatic stress among firefighters, police, EMTs, as well as soldiers. As this approach began to be applied beyond trauma-induced stress to improve work environments and re-design jobs, one key principle was that *human needs* must not be forgotten when technical systems are introduced. Enid Mumford had always seen the task of problem-solving and design as an ethical one—requiring intensive communication among *all* players, including a recognition of the racial, ethnic, and cultural factors of those involved.

One especially important principle of socio-technical design is the concept of 'redundancy of function.' The need for redundancy applies not only to mechanisms (such as the complex levee system) or infrastructure (such as housing) but to groups and individuals themselves. When *people* have the ability to carry out *different* tasks, even if they do not always use them, greater redundancy, and therefore greater reliability exists within the total system. Firefighters are taught basic EMT skills. EMTs are taught high angle rescue skills or firefighter carry techniques. Incident Command Systems incorporate a chain of responsibility to accommodate the addition of new personnel to deal with a major disaster or event. All of these sorts of redundancy of function give the total system a better capability to cope with *unexpected occurrences*. If one function within the system fails, that function can be replaced through the multiple capabilities of other personnel. The need for such redundancy obviously impacts planning for future Katrina events—a necessary requirement for future hurricane protection and evacuation systems, since, while it may not be known when, hurricanes will assuredly happen again, and there is no reason to have confidence that the systems of protective levees and evacuation plans as they now stand can save lives, protect housing, or provide critical medical services. Redundancy, therefore, provides greater security—multiple evacuation routes, multiple locations for emergency housing, multiple trauma centers, and so forth, coordinated within an overall plan in which communication is *robust*. To speak of communication being 'robust' means that communication is able to occur in multiple concurrent modes. We have previously discussed tragic failures in the ability of police and fire and EMT personnel to communicate with one another during the Katrina event. This was also a tragic failure with the 9/11 destruction of the World Trade Center: the *inability* of various emergency units—fire, police, EMTs—to communicate with one another. The result in that case was over three hundred firefighters and EMTs lost.

The principle of 'redundancy of function' also applies to the tasks of urban reconstruction itself. Consider neighborhoods where rebuilding of residences is allowed in areas that are still vulnerable to recurrent flooding. In such areas, redundancy would consist of constructing emergency 'safe channels' to allow the passage of boats or emergency vehicles when flooding occurs. It would consist of sufficiently decentralized police, fire, and medical units that could not only provide emergency services directly, but also serve as backups during chaotic events when certain services are likely to be lost. It would consist of multiple modes of evacuation, and previously sited emergency shelters into which people could move temporarily, or possibly emergency residences for longer-term use, which had access to living essentials such as food, water, medical units, possibly even structures to serve as substitute school buildings.

Without a significant level of redundancy built into the services and infrastructure of those neighborhoods that remain highly vulnerable to future flooding, other decisions, including *not rebuilding* certain neighborhoods or determining which areas should potentially be targeted for reclamation as buffer zone wetlands become more difficult and complex. What, in that case, happens to the populations displaced? How are decisions to be made about who can and who cannot rebuild? Should neighborhoods try to replicate their character before Katrina? Should they make improvements, perhaps even be built under an entirely new cultural or aesthetic model? What should be built first? Infrastructure? Cultural centers? The priority and importance of New Orleans' as a repository of culture, especially with its history in the area of music—and the corresponding need for cultural centers—has been an approach taken in the Upper Ninth Ward, where Habitat for Humanity has worked with Branford Marsalis building Musician's Village: residences and studios for musicians of modest means as well as other citizens.

What are the basics of Enid Mumford's concept of Participatory Design? It is a *process*—but one in which perhaps the most important thing it contributes is its value system. The world of socio-technical design is democratic and humanistic, but, at the same time, *spiritually* connected to warnings against individual self-aggrandizement and the value of *all* members at *all* levels of society. It is not by accident that one finds in Enid Mumford's accounts of socio-technical design references to religious themes, such as that found in Scripture—for example, in Matt 6:19–29, where one finds the Matthean summary of how to integrate the value of universal human with service to God. Undue focus on possessions can distort one's judgment. "Do not store up for yourselves treasures on earth, where moth and rust consume . . . store up for yourselves treasures in heaven . . . For where your treasure is, there your heart will be also." 'Treasures in heaven,' as treasures of the *heart*, constitute true, egalitarian community—the Kingdom of God. True inward spirituality of the individual determines the outward form of social community. Community development, therefore, is not for the private profit of the few; communities are *shared* enterprises. Similarly, pre-situating emergency shelters and services in anticipation of natural disaster is not hoarding 'treasures for oneself,' but the spiritual act of honoring service to God by extending the notion of a caring community to all levels of humanity in need of protection; that 'caring community' is the earthly Kingdom of God.[21]

Participatory Design also makes use of a notion called 'associative democracy,' which aims to change the relationship between state and citi-

---

21. Enid Mumford, *Redesigning Human Systems,* 29. "The world of socio-technical design is democratic and humanistic and provides both freedom and knowledge to those who are part of it. These concepts are not new . . . Etzioni describes an approach that he calls 'voluntary simplicity.'" Voluntary simplicity is a set of values prepared to limit outward expenditures while emphasizing the importance of inner quality of life, self-expressions and participation; not very different from concepts found in the Sermon on the Mount. But inward quality of life entails the priority of caring for *others* as the form of honoring God.

zen by creating a participative, mutually beneficial society. It does this by giving citizens a more powerful voice in decisions on publicly financed social programs—something we have seen proposed in Keith Twitchell's Committee for a Better New Orleans' Citizen Participation Process—and by making citizens genuine participants in the design and implementation of post-disaster reconstruction of New Orleans and South Louisiana.

Mumford regards two other related concepts as important to socio-technical design. One is 'competence' or what philosopher Gilbert Ryle calls "knowing how." Competence, in terms of socio-technical design, means that the practical is ultimately of more value than the theoretical: knowledge is useful only if it can be applied, if it actually gives to individuals the autonomy to deal with and solve problems on their own. One can regard this as a belief that communities—whether work environments or neighborhoods—are the product of networks of equal, multi-node decision points that address tasks in the dynamic context of everyday living together, rather than the enactment of an independently derived theory through a hierarchical structure of authority. A second, and even more important concept is 'coordination'—the ability of individuals or groups to work democratically with other groups. Coordination plays a significant role in the process of Participatory Design and in implementation of the outputs of that process, where designers and users must work closely together.

It is on a practical, not simply a theoretical level that citizens must be participants in real-world hard choices; some may negatively affect their own homes and neighborhoods. But a fact of reality is that limitations of repopulation and financial resources to rebuild entail that every needed rebuilding project cannot be implemented—not in the near term, perhaps not ever. Thus, choices have to be made about how to incorporate what *cannot* be done within an overall humane, social ethic—choices that involve not only what one wants but what one must decide against. From that position it is similar to the approach to decision-making taken in ancient Greece where decisions 'participatively taken' were ones whose answer to the question 'Who takes it?' was 'more or less everybody.' *All citizens* must have the opportunity to *agree* that it may be in everyone's best to exclude the rebuilding of *one's own* home or neighborhood. It might have felt uplifting to hear Mayor Nagin proclaim 'We will rebuild everything,' but that verbiage quickly fell empty with the realization that it could not and would not be accomplished. What made it unforgivably empty was the absence of citizens having had the opportunity to play an active role, be participants in and therefore share *responsibility* for, the final decisions.

Participatory Design, as a *process,* involves a setting in which designers and those impacted by a design engage in a series of structured meetings where prioritized information is exchanged that enables the designers to come to know and to *internalize* the task environment of those who will use the design. This process has been combined with other forms of obtaining user input, such as prototype user testing, or Wizard of Oz experiments.[22] Prototype user testing, when done properly, involves experimentation with a trial system or application from which certain lessons are learned. Then, after the original prototype has been replaced by a design that has incorporated those learnings in new or modified design features, the testing is repeated in an iterative cycle.[23]

The series of structured user-designer meetings in Participatory Design are *not* simply a free-form exchange of ideas. Their purpose is to allow designers the opportunity to understand in considerable detail just how potential users of a design conduct their work. What are the characteristics of their task environment? With what levels of skill and education do people operate? How do tasks get initiated? How are problems identified and solved? What kinds of error loops typically arise and how are problems eventually solved? What groups need to coordinate and interact with one another? How do people learn from and modify their task environment? And so forth. Ultimately, designers translate this information into a form they can design to—their *design specs.* The difference is that now the design has not come out of their *own* heads, from their *own* conceptual models of how work should be accomplished, but rather from the conceptual models in the heads of the *users* of their design. These are

22. Originally developed in the dissertation work *ca.* 1980 at Johns Hopkins University of John Kelley under Alphonse Chapanis, one of the fathers of human factors and engineering psychology. In Wizard of Oz research experiments, subjects interact with a system designed to be autonomous, such as a computer system or an automated transaction system, but in which some of its features are being operated by an unseen human being. It is a testing and iterative design methodology used especially in human factors analysis and ergonomics. An unseen 'wizard' simulates the behavior of a theoretically intelligent computer application by intercepting communication between the experiment participant and the system. Its purpose is to allow incorporation into the design features of the system capabilities that match the needs and interactive behaviors of humans who will use the system.

23. That is, the prototype is used as a learning opportunity, not itself as the first stage of a final design.

the conceptual models that have evolved quite naturally in the practical context of their day-to-day work, and which represent how humans most typically learn in many environments.

Just how does Participatory Design work in actual practice? To give a sense from a historical case, I will summarize some of my experience as a Consulting Engineer at Digital Equipment Corporation (DEC), where I worked in Artificial Intelligence with Enid Mumford in the creation of two Expert Systems, XSEL and XCON, intended to use the emerging discipline of knowledge engineering to assist in the accurate configuration of complex networks of VAX computers for use in manufacturing plants.[24]

The formal participation structure involved a Knowledge Engineering 'design group' from the technical project team and a 'future users' group. Participation would ultimately involve mechanisms for information transfer from one task domain to another. However, the first step in the process was to capture characteristics of the culture in which both groups worked, as well as characteristics of the nature of the work of each group. For example, in the 1980s, Digital Equipment Corporation both approved of and nurtured its 'insubordinate minority.' These were people who were encouraged by their managers to continually question and challenge what the company was doing, often using and testing DEC products in the process. Sometimes this created an atmosphere resembling anarchy, but it was really DEC founder and President Ken Olsen's[25] vision of an MIT post-doc—with all its freedom of creative thought as well as confusion. As a company, DEC also made prominent a set of values—honesty, profit, quality, responsibility, innovation—that were fostered at every level of the organization. While such values were intended to promote creativity and responsibility, they also produced a considerable degree of chaos and confusion. An abundance of isolated ideas, however good, does not constitute a coherent design. It can just as easily result in 'entropy' or designs that fail in meeting their purpose. Thus, the Knowledge Engineering group's goal was to translate user needs into a working system that would operate in a manner *consistent with the user's* work goals and responsibilities.

24. Again, see Mumford, *Redesigning Human Systems,* for additional discussion and details.

25. Ken Olsen co-founded Digital Equipment Corporation (DEC) in 1957 with colleague Harlan Anderson and venture capital provided by Georges Doriot's American Research and Development Corporation.

The knowledge interchange took place in face-to-face meetings between the user group, who would actually be testing the design, and technical designers, including the development group at Carnegie Mellon and the Digital configuration group. Actual interchanges took place on two levels. (1) Users would articulate *sequenced factual descriptions* of the work they performed, including problem-solving. They would produce utterances of the following general type: "I begin this process by doing X," "The typical steps are A, B, C, D . . . ," "Problems often arise at step C," "When that occurs we do Y." (2) Users would also articulate *value judgments* related to the work they needed to accomplish, such as "X is too complicated to keep up with," "It takes me too long to do Y," "I can't relate to NN when we go on a call together." Statements such as these, after undergoing several processes of categorization and prioritization, were given to the design team who would encode them as a set of rules for the Expert System. These rules would subsequently be presented to the user group who would critique them in conversation with the design team. The design team would then go back and make needed modifications. At various points, modules of the design would be tested, again with feedback, and an indication of what features of the system worked well and which did not. The design process, therefore, was a highly *iterative* one. That is, the project did not strive to have a complete, finished program all at once. It allowed the design to unfold naturally in stages, so it could be adequately tested and validated in actual use *by those who would ultimately be using it.*

This account is probably sufficient to get a basic feel for how the Participatory Design process has worked in a relatively structured environment. In considering how it might be applied in the circumstances of post-disaster reconstruction—as in the case of New Orleans and South Louisiana—it is not as if one has two groups, designers and users, who are members of the same corporate structure, with the same goals, with a common culture, however diverse or loosely organized that culture may be, as it was in the case of Digital Equipment Corporation. On the other hand, presumably, planners, designers, and citizens see themselves as at least virtual citizens of the same city, the same region, with sufficiently shared purposes and needs that could enable them to work towards the same goals. Is the culture of New Orleans and South Louisiana so diverse and fragmented that it *cannot* work? That is a question, finally, for the sociologists or historians to answer. In thinking here about how it *might* work, one goal of *Walking to New Orleans* has been not only to document sometimes overlooked factors in both the pre-Katrina history and the post-Katrina context of New Orleans and South Louisiana that we feel need to be given particular attention; it is also to try to provide at least the basis for a constructive model for how hurricane protection systems, urban infrastructure, public housing, healthcare services, and neighborhood social structure might be rebuilt and reconstructed in a humane and ethical manner—in a manner that will truly meet the needs of all members and groups and strata of society. In a manner in which the voices of *all* citizens will have been heard and applied.

One fairly obvious need, and a possible context for considering the application of Participatory Design, would appear to be in restructuring and better coordinating the emergency services that would have to be deployed in the event of another natural catastrophe such as Hurricane Katrina. Emergency service agencies—including fire, police, and EMTs—historically have had their own independent cultures, and often have been rather territorial towards one another. The culture and self-image of firefighters is one thing; that of law enforcement and the police is another; that of emergency medical services yet another. The process of Participatory Design provides an opportunity for this tradition of territoriality and independence to be overcome. Early stages of the process raise awareness of the need for a common purpose. How this works in more detail will be shown in the discussion of Value Analysis, later in this chapter; here it can simply be pointed out that the earliest stages of Participatory Design are very much concerned with identifying and establishing shared values. This is precisely what was accomplished in the case of its use at Digital Equipment Corporation, in which the first steps in the process were to capture characteristics of the culture in which two very different groups worked, as well as the demands and behavioral attributes of the nature of the work of each group. Similarly, as shared values are identified, it should become possible to facilitate structured interchanges among the various services of fire, police, medics, and other agencies involved with emergency work. As common purposes and consequent values are identified—particularly in responsibility for public safety—there emerges the possibility for acknowledging shared 'cultural' values and establishing an *intentional* basis for working collaboratively. This principle can then be extended to the analysis of both similar and dissimilar tasks, and especially to how each organization responds to and reacts under extreme and hazardous conditions. The discussion of tasks can be a basis for building 'scenarios' of behavior that, effectively, become sharable conceptual models representing how each service operates, and how it might better coordinate with other services. Building up a body of shared scenarios or 'stories' of response-behaviors and problem-solving strategies represents not only the beginning stages of creating a shared knowledge base, but is a technique actually used as part of Critical Incident Stress Debriefings (CISD) with multiple services after incidents such as a mass casualty or natural disaster. In the Second Stage of a typical Seven-Stage group debriefing, each participant describes the traumatic event from their perspective on a cognitive level; in the Third Stage, participants reflect on their reactions and transition to accounts of emotional experiences, which are then prioritized, in the Fourth Stage, by participants identifying the most traumatic aspects of the events and their emotional reactions to them; in the Fifth Stage participants identify personal symptoms of distress they have experienced, and then transition back to the cognitive level where these shared personal scenarios can be followed by more explicit education about normal reactions and adaptive coping or stress management techniques.

In considering any use of a method such as Participatory Design with fire, police, and EMT services, it would be essential that the chiefs and high ranking officers of each service fully commit to working with other services collaboratively, and that they reinforce this commitment throughout the ranks of their organizations. As a methodology, Participatory Design does not especially favor top-down directives—the style by which organizational change typically occurs in fire, police, and EMT services—and it must be acknowledged that, as a philosophical approach, the method is somewhat antithetical to all three of these cultures. Participatory Design institutes collaborative efforts by invoking democratic processes that are generally taken several steps beyond their normal application. Fire, police, EMT, and other emergency services, on the other hand, are typically based on something closer to a military, rather than a democratic, model. Nevertheless, Participatory Design and its related methodology of Value Analysis have been used successfully in a military setting and also within a highly structured federal agency. At Hanscom Air Force Base in Eastern Massachusetts, home to the sixty-sixth Air Base Wing which supports the Electronic Systems Center (ESC)[26] that provides command and control and

26. And units of the ESC, including the 350th Electronic Systems Wing, which develops and sustains communications capabilities for three U.S. services, NORAD, and

information systems for the Air Force, an adaptation of this method was used to improve communication *up* the chain of command from technical field personnel for purposes of instituting many productivity improvements. At the National Security Agency (NSA) at Fort Meade, Maryland, a rather different adaptation of the method was used to better integrate two of NSA's designated functions: Signals Intelligence (SIGINT), involving the collection, decryption and encryption, and analysis of foreign signals, and that of providing information and intelligence for the military and Congress. In both cases, a method that philosophically takes the notion of egalitarian, participative democracy to an extreme, was able to be used with some comfort within organizations that are hierarchical in authority and have often been stovepiped into separate structural units. It did not hurt that this work was done during a period when all federal agencies were under a strong Congressional mandate to improve the quality of their operations in quantifiable terms against clearly defined objectives.

Among the things that fire, police, and EMT services share in common is that the culture of each of these services values practical skills, and recognizes that the individuals who serve at all levels and ranks are repositories of a great deal of knowledge and first-hand experience. This experience and detailed knowledge of how to react to and handle extreme situations and conditions is encouraged by senior officers, and widely shared among individuals rather than suppressed. Participatory Design, then, would provide an opportunity to tap into these resources, and to share this knowledge base for mutually beneficial purposes. Participatory Design would also build on the spirit of cooperative actions that epitomizes firefighters and EMTs on scene, and also police assigned to group details. There is a strong sense of brotherhood (including 'sisterhood,' as women increasingly take their places in these agencies) that underlies those who work in emergency services and share both the dangers and rewards of that work.

The spirit of brotherhood (and sisterhood) is also not unlike the spirit that pervades a neighborhood, where people share not only economics and geography, but also the joys and sorrows of their lives in proximate relation to others who live near them. One would expect, then, that if the concept of Participatory Design were to have a more pervasive value in an urban environment such as New Orleans, or the smaller towns and villages of Coastal Louisiana, that it could be used to implement, for

NATO, and the 551st Electronic Systems Wing, which supports AWACS, Joint STARS with surveillance, mission planning, and weather information.

example, neighborhood-based strategies for making housing repair and rebuilding decisions. Expecting conflicts to arise—where differing views and opinions exist among individuals living in a given neighborhood, not unlike the differing cultures among fire, police, and EMT personnel—the problem-solving elements in the Participatory Design process might very well provide for a way that neighborhoods would agree in advance to some mechanism of mediation. Equally important would also be the possibility to try out and test housing repair and rebuilding design ideas before they are implemented on a vast scale where mistakes or wrong paths would be far more difficult or impossible to correct. This is the aspect of Participatory Design that approximates the familiar idea of prototyping. As previously argued, prototyping, when properly carried out, is the creation of trial designs expressly for the purposes of *learning what works and what does not.* As learnings are accumulated, analyzed, classified, and re-introduced into the recovery and rebuilding process, *new* designs and approaches can be created on the basis of experiential knowledge and provide better assurance that previous faults and errors can be avoided. Later in this chapter we will see aspects of this approach in the Broadmoor Improvement Association's work with Harvard University's Belfer Center for Science and International Affairs at the Kennedy School of Government that used data and experiences gathered by students and residents on repopulation, housing, educational needs, and economic development to create "The Broadmoor Guide for Planning and Implementation. Lessons from Katrina: How a Community Can Spearhead Successful Disaster Recovery."

With destruction on the scale that exists in so many neighborhoods of New Orleans, it would simply be impossible to rebuild everything at once. Thus, Participatory Design becomes a way to take advantage of what might have been thought a weakness—time delay—and turn it into something positive. With a process by which people of different ethnic and racial groups, of different economic means, of different levels of authority and responsibility, can meet together face-to-face and try out ideas that can be corrected more easily than a master plan handed down from above, the neighborhoods that will be built or rebuilt have a greater chance of reflecting the intentions and needs of all their residents.

AN APPLICATION OF PARTICIPATORY DESIGN: THE VALUE ANALYSIS PROCESS

As a Consulting Engineer, one of whose responsibilities was teaching principles of good human engineering to engineers in the United States and Europe, the concept of Participatory Design was adapted to many areas of user-system interaction—physical anthropometrics and workspace design, the graphics of visual fields, cognitive and behavioral aspects of specialized languages, among others. As the needs of private corporations, government agencies, and other large organizations shifted during the 1990s under increasing pressures to improve quality and productivity, there were opportunities to further adapt some elements of Participatory Design for use beyond 'individual-system' interaction to the context of 'organization-system' and 'organization-organization' interaction. This arose especially with organizations that found themselves undergoing radical, and generally unplanned, transitions—downsizing, for economic reasons, or major redefinitions of work and task responsibilities. In some cases the focus was on the interaction of organizations with formal systems, such as their internal technology, but it could also involve changes in policy and management throughout an organization, or the creation of new communication infrastructures, as organizations began to operate more and more in an international context, across diverse cultures and languages. These 'organizations in transition' could also simply be complex organizations that had become dysfunctional as a result of growing internal problems, or because of changes in the market or the political climate.

The adaptation of Participatory Design was generally presented under the title of Value Analysis, highlighting the fact that the process gave particular attention to how cultural and ethical values were identified, shared, and modified in the context of an organization. For some fifteen years the author has been involved, both individually, as Principal of Collaborative Technologies, and as Senior Consultant at the National Academy of Public Administration in Washington (NAPA)[27] in working

27. The National Academy of Public Administration (NAPA) was chartered by Congress (PL 98–257, April 10, 1984) for purposes that include evaluating the structure, administration, operation, and program performance of federal and other government agencies; identifying and analyzing significant problems and suggesting corrective action; foreseeing critical emerging issues in governance and advising on the relationship of federal, state, regional, and local governments to understand and improve the requirements of sound governance. At NAPA from the Value Analysis process, the author developed

with organizations in transition. The organizations have ranged in size from multinational corporations to federal agencies to local communities and voluntary associations within communities—all experiencing substantial change to their purpose and organizational structure that was creating ambiguity and, in some cases, chaos. One project for a large American corporation involved work in western Denmark with a small, old-world company it had acquired that was now experiencing a period of culture clash. Another project involved the interrelationships of units with the U.S. Department of State, as changes in foreign policy forced changes in their roles and responsibilities. Another project dealt with the mission of the Health Resources and Services Administration to ensure medical services in rural areas and for marginalized citizens without healthcare insurance. Another, previously mentioned, dealt with coordinating the multiple functions of the National Security Agency; still another addressing wholesale changes within the National Science Foundation, including its system and criteria for major grant awards.

The time frames for the application of the Value Analysis process also varied enormously—from as long as five years, with a Department of Justice funded project to institute performance-based standards in juvenile correctional and detention facilities across the country, to work in two-year chunks with community voluntary associations dealing with areas of social concern such as establishing shelters for the homeless or local disaster relief, to concentrated, intense twelve-day sessions in Australia beginning at 6:00 in the morning and running straight through to midnight. Specific elements of the methodology were taught in France, Finland, Germany, Israel, Vietnam, the UK, and the Cook Islands in settings as varied as a new technology center to a national prison.

When Value Analysis was focused very much on ferreting out issues and difficulties within an organization, it made considerable use of such problem-solving tools as Contextual Inquiry, Affinity Diagrams, Hoshin Planning, Root Cause Analysis with Ishikawa (Fishbone) Diagrams, Control Charts, Pareto Diagrams, Interrelationship Digraphs, Formal Inspections, Prioritization Matrices, and the like. When it addressed issues

---

a curriculum for "Ethics in the Public Service," work that was presented at the Seventh Annual Conference on Applied Ethics at California State University Long Beach in 1996. The author also served as a consultant with the Center for Quality of Management, a consortium of major corporations addressing new developments in Quality Management Systems associated with MIT and based in Cambridge, Helsinki, and Stuttgart.

of organizational cultures, the impact of, and interaction with, alternative cultures and organizations with different values and priorities, it made use of concepts drawn from ethics and the behavioral sciences.

One of the things that became increasingly apparent was that, as a methodology, Value Analysis was particularly well-suited for circumstances when an organization, a community, or a voluntary association had to take control of changes—transformations or redesign—on its own; when an organization was forced to act, by choice or necessity, independently. Value Analysis allowed an organization to become truly autonomous. Without the luxury of (or, at times, disadvantages of) the presence of a planner or a designer, who would ultimately complete the work of planning or design, even when much of the input to that work was done collaboratively, the organization gained not only a sense of empowerment in being able to control its own future, but also gained a sense of having ultimate responsibility for itself. The story of public housing in New Orleans is very much to the point here. While the need to provide available, low-cost housing for a portion of the city's population is quite manifest, the federal government, under current law, is under no obligation to provide it. It is the responsibility of the city, perhaps even individual neighborhoods, to make this happen. We will see, later in this chapter, how just something like this may be happening in the Gentilly-Pontchartrain Park area for elderly residents as the neighborhood looks to redesign its own future.

Especially when the use of Value Analysis was focused on how people could gain control over the direction their organization or community or voluntary association was headed, it made explicit use of a number of basic ethical concepts that allowed participants to sort out and *prioritize* values and goals that were shared, as well as identify those that were not. Value Analysis was sometimes used in very specific ways—for example, to help service organizations, such as EMTs, sort out decision procedures under the conditions of duress in which ethically ambiguous decisions typically had to be made. Beyond decisions controlled by standing orders and legal directives, dealing with instances such as abuse or neglect, the death of a child, or 'Do Not Resuscitate' (DNR) orders, EMT professionals needed guidance in developing a personal decision process for making appropriate medical ethical judgments. Value Analysis helped determine when it would be appropriate to buy time for deliberation without doing harm, when to use the *impartiality test*, when to use the *universalizability test* and the *justifiability test.*[28] This application of the method, therefore, was highly focused on how the processes of *prioritization* and *making ethical judgments* link together.

Value Analysis typically can operate in two distinct, but often overlapping modes. It can be used in problem-solving applications in some general process of corrective action. It can also be used in a future-oriented mode in which organizations are asked to envision, in concrete terms, what purposes and characteristics they would like in their organization in a relatively long-term future, e.g., five years out. In both cases, it is an underlying principle that the form of the question determines the form of the solution. Only when relevant questions are asked about problems that have been identified or future states that are desired, can they be meaningfully acted upon. That is, people must be able to 'cognitively connect' the choice of any 'solution methodology' with the identified problem or future goal. People need to understand why they are taking the particular corrective they are taking, or why they are choosing some particular program to achieve a desired future state. Far too often, leadership simply decides on some solution strategy independently—often without adequate understanding of problems needing correction, desirable future goals, or even the either 'solution methodology' itself—and *imposes* it on the organization. The result is that people in the organization are being asked to act—to implement a 'solution strategy' not of their own choosing—without any understanding of *why* those methods are the appropriate ones. Not only has there been no opportunity for 'buy-in,' there often are not established criteria to even clearly understand what a successful implementation would look like.[29]

Value Analysis, then, is a process that allows an organization or community control its own transformation. It establishes a clear conceptual connection between goals and methods to achieve them; people understand *why* they adopt the methods they do. The method is adaptable for problem-solving or redefining the future of an organization. It is participatory, interactive, and consensus-based—everyone is involved in decision-making.

28. These 'tests,' in addition to functioning as a mechanism to help reflect and sort out the ethical, medical, personal, and legal issues involved, also helped those making decisions under highly-stressed, non-optimum conditions eliminate personal bias or opinion, consider the range of applicability of one's decision, and invoke rational criteria for judgments rather than momentary 'gut feel.'

29. The worst cases in the author's experience have been implementations of Six Sigma methodologies in non-manufacturing settings quite inappropriate for its use.

It encourages individual expression but also seeks recognition of shared values. It links prioritized values and ethical considerations to eliminate political agendas and power plays. Finally, it creates a visible time-line that connects the identification of values and goals, problem analysis, development of solution strategies, implementation actions, teams responsible for those actions, milestones and completion dates, so that the initial phases of work do not, as they often do, evaporate into nothingness.

The following account sketches in somewhat more concrete terms what an application of the Value Analysis process might look like, taken from work the author has done with community- and neighborhood-level voluntary associations that could be understood as roughly analogous to neighborhoods and neighborhood associations. Specific content, preserving appropriate anonymity, is drawn from actual work in seven different communities over a period of nine years.

In the initial call to participate it is emphasized that the process gives *everyone* the opportunity to shape their future, and to let their thoughts, concerns, and hopes be known. The basic methods and sequence of meeting events is explained, including the enjoyment of everyone getting a chance to know one another better in seeking consensus. Reports on the outcomes of each session are provided to everyone for further reflection.

In the first sessions, large groups of participants[30] develop a profile of their organization and its position in their community. The nature of the profile is determined by the specific work the organization hopes to accomplish, but particular attention is devoted to identifying core values. Input in initial sessions is expressed quite freely—small concerns as well as large issues each 'have their day.' No attempt is made to control input other than to frame it in terms of the overall purpose of the organization, and avoid dead ends. After pervasive organizational values are brought forth, participants then express in concrete terms the things they want present in the organization five years hence. This future oriented has proven to be more constructive than simply voicing complaints and known problems. In addition to getting out a base of shared values and knowledge for future analysis, the first sessions develop an atmosphere of trust.

---

30. Groups as large as forty or fifty can be accommodated in these early sessions, although smaller sizes are preferable. Because this large group will break up into small teams, ideally made up of four but with as many as seven individuals, it may be necessary to run sessions serially or in parallel.

The following are examples of some of the kinds of things that typically have emerged in these sessions:

- Reorganize the association's leadership to make it leaner, more responsive to input from members; make reports on its decisions readily available.

- Improve trust, both within the organization and in the wider community.

- Engage more actively in socially valuable community activities; support community businesses; make the organization's buildings and resources available to the community seven days a week.

- Reconfigure a dangerous intersection; post a guard until this is done.

- Beautify (named) green areas of the community hands-on; refresh paint and repair doors on public buildings; make key buildings handicap accessible.

- Provide a permanent shelter for the increasing numbers of homeless.

- Revitalize and expand music programs; building construction skills programs.

- Agree to follow a democratic process and show respect in association interactions; create a tribunal to resolve differences among people.

One sees the mix of global goals and specific ideas. After these are captured—which may range anywhere from 30 to 70 items—participants submit to process known as 'scrubbing' in which each item is reconsidered to ensure that its *meaning* is the same for everyone. 'Scrubbing' does not require that everyone supports each value or agrees with each suggestion, only that everyone is in agreement with what each item *means*.

In sessions that follow, participants divide into teams of between four and seven individuals to discuss and prioritize these values and specific recommendations. Groups are treated as 'teams' that build consensus; however, each individual is encouraged to freely express judgments and thoughts during the prioritization processes. The evaluation process is highly interactive. A graphical tool allows quite refined judgments to be made. During evaluation and prioritization, individuals on a team compare judgments with one another, move them around incrementally, promoting a sense of being able to 'sculpt' the field under discussion.

Teams are asked to prioritize items in two distinct stages: (1) comparing items with one another on a two-attribute matrix; (2) rank ordering them. Each identified and scrubbed item is assigned a number,[31] written on a post-it to enable it to be moved around by participants on a visual surface.

(1) The first phase prioritization evaluates each item in terms of two attributes: impact and magnitude. *Impact* represents perception of how much realizing a value or achieving a particular goal or recommendation would contribute to the desired future—its importance for the needs of the community or organization.[32] *Magnitude* represents the perception of how difficult or complex it would be to realize that value or implement that goal or recommendation. As the movement of items around this two-attribute grid unfolds, diversity views are freely expressed while striving towards consensus. The graphical device with a sample of numbered items placed in different locations looks as follows:

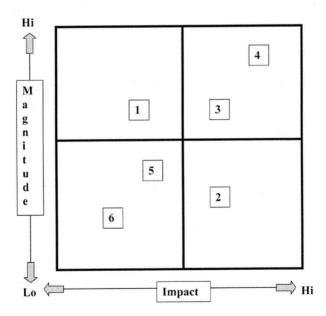

31. Usually the number from the order in which the item was given voice.

32. Participants are free to place numbered post-its individually, then move them around as others express their judgments until everyone on the team is comfortable to commit to its placement even if they do not entirely agree with where it ends up.

In this simplified configuration, item 6 would is judged be relatively low in magnitude (difficulty) but also low in impact (long-term significance). Item 4 is judged as higher in impact but also higher in magnitude—that is, it is important but also difficult to achieve. Item 2 is judged to be high in impact but considerably less difficult to achieve. Individuals on the team move the items being discussed around until all are comfortable enough with the final placement to feel there is sufficient consensus that they can commit to that overall picture judging which values, goals, and recommendations are most important, which are less important, and what the relative degree of achieving any of them is.

(2) Following this, teams proceed to a second phase prioritization in which they are asked to rank order the items. By rank ordering, the team is selecting those areas they feel should be worked on first, second, third, fourth, and so forth. Along with rank ordering, the team gives explanations for its decisions. The reasoning behind this second prioritization is that since all 30—70 items cannot be given attention at the same time, the team now has the opportunity to make an additional, independent evaluation. This second prioritization might be thought of as a *tactical* prioritization, because the team is recommending, on separate criteria, where the organization should put its energies first. For example, while item 4 above was judged to be of greater impact than item 2, a team might decide to begin with item 2 because, like 'low-hanging fruit', it is something easier to achieve and thus able to help convince the organization they can be successful.

At this point, the rank-ordered prioritizations of each of the several teams are compared across all the teams that have participated to see what is shared in common within the organization as a whole. It is often revealing to see just how much commonality *has* occurred among multiple teams working independently. Through the Value Analysis process, the absence of *indirect* ways of capturing the judgments of participants through voting or weighted voting is intentional. All interactions and registered judgments have been *directly* expressed and tabulated, under the belief that conclusions reached by consensus will produce greater levels of commitment than had participants simply voted as individuals. Philosophically, the difference is essentially that between representative and participatory forms of democracy. While capturing votes and making decisions on the basis of a numeric majority or plurality is democratic, it does not by itself establish a commitment to those decisions from individuals whose votes went in different directions. Frequently, experience has shown that organizations, where decisions were made on the basis of a voting process, have found themselves facing the undermining of those decisions by those who voted to do otherwise. This is one negative consequence of the 'silence' of numeric voting. By keeping all phases of evaluation and prioritization public, there is created an atmosphere of trust and commitment because people know *why* the actions being taken are the ones taken. They have been participants in the process all along.

The remaining phases of Value Analysis proceed in a manner more or less common to other processes. Those items judged in common by the several teams to be of high priority—that is, on which the first actions should be taken—are selected for determining exactly *what* actions or methods will best achieve them. Here, it is helpful to use a solutions matrix in which prioritized items are linked to potential solutions or resources to achieve them on the basis of their relevance. A simple example of such a solutions matrix is the following:

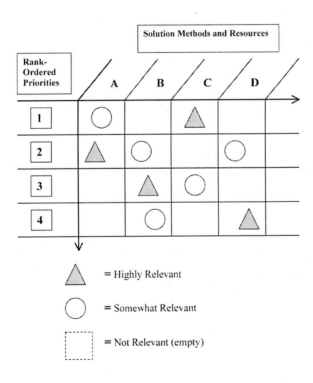

The principle of prioritization is applied once again in the selection of actions to be taken by the organization. Typically, with larger or more global priorities, multiple actions will need to be taken—some requiring 'action teams,' others able to be accomplished by individuals. When all rank-ordered priorities have been assigned to teams or individuals willing to commit to work on them until their completion, a timeline is established, with interim milestones, and periodic reporting of progress back to the organization as a whole. It is critical to the entire Value Analysis process that completion points for all tasks and activities be clearly identified. That is, it is important for the organization to know precisely when it has actually accomplished the things it has set out to do. Far too often, organizations begin work with great enthusiasm, but some efforts peter out and the organization is unable to determine exactly what it has accomplished and what work is yet to be finished. This state generates unhealthy ambiguities. Therefore, publicly visible charts and maps of progress, regularly updated and discussed, are most helpful.

This sketch should be sufficient to suggest how communities and neighborhood associations might work to take control over the forced post-disaster period of transition, and begin to shape their futures in a humane and ethical way. The question now worth examining is: despite the stagnancy of New Orleans' planning processes and the sluggishness of individual rebuilding efforts through the LRA, Road Home,[33] and NORA, are there activities now occurring in New Orleans' neighborhoods and in Coastal Louisiana that are cause for encouragement? We believe there are. We will look at what is happening in several different neighborhoods in the City of New Orleans, all heavily damaged in the storms. One, with a strong neighborhood association and useful help from outside, is increasingly in a position to see itself being reborn into a form very much the way it was before the hurricanes. Two others, forced to direct their efforts to transform their neighborhoods into something different from what they were before the hurricanes, are nevertheless trying to meet the needs of residents in thoughtful ways.

---

33. As of January, 2008, almost two and one-half years after the storms, a full fifth of eligible applicants who applied in 2006 for Road Home grants have not yet received any of the homeowner grant money. See David Hammer, "Many early applicants waiting on Road Home," *The Times-Picayune*, January 23, 2008.

A NEIGHBORHOOD REBORN

Broadmoor, it will be recalled from chapter 2, is a neighborhood that was once a twelve-acre lake, connected to Bayou St. John, and, as a section of the city that remained low-lying, has always been subject to significant flooding. Forming a roughly obelisk-shaped area lakeside of South Claiborne between Toledano Street and Nashville Avenue, with its peak nudging between Gert Town and Marlyville, this residential area consists of a mixture of Spanish and mission revival homes, as well as some double shotgun houses—some homes elevated when originally built, some not.

The Broadmoor Improvement Association (BIA), currently chaired by Latoya Cantrell, has grown into a powerful organizing voice for its community at all levels. On January 19, 2008 the BIA celebrated the anniversary of the infamous Green Dot—the day in January 2006 Broadmoor, with its 2,900 homes, was designated by Mayor Nagin's Bring New Orleans Back Commission as an area to be bulldozed and turned back into parks and green space. Since that day Broadmoor became even more galvanized as a community, determined to return better than before. Even a glance at its most recent activities gives one a sense of its ability to coordinate the diverse voices of the residents of Broadmoor. On December 11, 2007 AT&T announced it had awarded a $50,000 grant to equip the Rosa F. Keller Library and Center with advanced telecommunications services to provide residents with access to wireless Internet. In the fall, with volunteers and help from the Church of the Annunciation, a playground on the corner of South Derbigny and Jena was built in one day. The BIA publicized information about FEMA relocation assistance and its ending sponsorship of debris removal in September; about an investigation by volunteer attorney Doug Levine and law students from Northeastern Law into where the Road Home program failed the people of Broadmoor. It formed a Quality of Life Committee to regularly address the most prevalent concerns of Broadmoor residents—from blighted properties to zoning issues. It supports a weekly Farmer's Market at the Church of the Annunciation, and the renovation of schools such as the Wilson School.

The BIA, one of the oldest neighborhood associations in New Orleans, originally established in 1930 as the Broadmoor Civic Improvement Association, was incorporated as the BIA in 1970 to preserve a multi-racial, multi-ethnic community. Its community outreach was active before the storms—reducing crime, repairing homes of low-income elderly and handicapped, planting trees on the neutral grounds. One of the things the BIA recognized early on was that it would be necessary for communication to occur between it and residents and among residents in multiple modes. In addition to attending meetings, the BIA has also provided information through its website, by email, by phone, through multi-lingual hardcopy literature, and by hosting special public interactive events such as the Neighborhood Evacuation Resource Expo, first held in August, 2007. In planning for this and other events, the BIA has provided many suggestions about how residents could interact with one another in smaller, more local groups.

Latoya Cantrell has expressed BIA's view that not only is the neighborhood committed to coming back, it is committed as a community to making Broadmoor a model for neighborhood revitalization throughout New Orleans and beyond. The post-Hurricane Katrina crisis in New Orleans, as we have documented, provided a great deal of evidence showing the limitations of the city's historical forms of bureaucratic government. Traditionally, government bureaucracies have delivered a mixture of regulations and services—services 'bound by' regulations—in a top down manner. In the case of Broadmoor, its growing successes have occurred *in spite* of that governmental structure. The Broadmoor neighborhood discovered it was not governments that rebuild, but individuals, home-by-home, business-by-business, block-by-block.[34] During the spring and summer of 2006, residents of Broadmoor held over 150 planning meetings to develop a comprehensive 319 page plan for how to rebuild their neighborhood. It was the first plan produced by any neighborhood, released, in July of 2006, six months before any other neighborhood plans. Most significant, it was the only plan produced by the residents themselves.

Providing assistance to Broadmoor's efforts to 'own' its own recovery, as many as eighty students from Harvard University spent spring breaks and summer vacations in New Orleans collecting data on repopulation, housing, educational needs, and economic development. Under the auspices of Harvard's Belfer Center for Science and International Affairs at the Kennedy School of Government, one of the primary objectives of the 'Broadmoor Project' was to track recovery progress and share data with other devastated neighborhoods in the city, as well as with researchers studying large-scale disasters and post-disaster reconstruction. Its June

34. Remark by Doug Ahlers, New Orleans native and research fellow at Harvard's Kennedy School.

2006 housing study, in conjunction with students from Bard College, sur-
veyed the condition of every property in Broadmoor, and continued updates at six month intervals. Data included the percentage of repairs not
started or houses not gutted; repair status by block; correlations with 2000
Census figures for median household income, poverty levels, percentage
of African Americans by block; extent of damage by block; the USACE
flood risk map; and so forth.

Rather than concentrate on one rebuilding issue, such as housing or
education, Harvard's Broadmoor Project was set up for students from the
Kennedy School and other graduate schools at Harvard to work with the
community over a long period of time, and go through all the steps in rebuilding, providing support throughout the entire process. As it had been
in the immediate aftermath of the storm, the Church of the Annunciation
was a major contributor to the neighborhood's rebuilding process, making
available use of their trailers as headquarters for the project. Another key
element in the project was that the development of a Broadmoor plan was
not 'Harvard-driven' but 'neighborhood-driven.' Student volunteers drew
on other plans from around the country to assemble best practices, but it
was the residents themselves, in careful reflection and analysis, supported
by helpful research tools and data from outside volunteers,[35] rather than
urban planners, who developed the remarkable "Redevelopment Plan for
Broadmoor" that the community itself was able to produce. The conceptual
model that guided the development of that plan exemplifies many of the
attributes we have discussed concerning use of the Value Analysis process
and the concept of Participatory Design. It was an effort that exemplified
collaboration—between motivated residents of the Broadmoor neighborhood; their neighborhood association—the BIA; private sector support
from individuals, foundations, and corporations; private developers and
businesses; faith groups, in particular the Church of the Annunciation,
St. Matthias, First Presbyterian, and others; and enlightened academics
who came to see their role as providing not 'answers from above' but
who were willing to work hand-in-hand with communities, sharing the
perspectives their own disciplines could bring to the needs of the community. In this collaboration, it remained clear that the entire process was
community-driven.[36]

35. And funding from the Shell Corporation.

36. See "The Broadmoor Guide for Planning and Implementation. Lessons from Katrina:
How a Community Can Spearhead Successful Disaster Recovery". The Broadmoor Project,

While the Broadmoor experience, and much of the thrust of *Walking to New Orleans*, has appeared to move away from the utility of professional planners, that has been more from the necessity of self-directed work by neighborhoods than from any intention to ignore professional planners. The fact is that in post-disaster New Orleans, the urban planners brought on-scene by various elements of government have done some very good things. The problem is that much of their work has not been realized in actual progress at the level of individual neighborhoods. In the case of Broadmoor, the conclusions of some planners would have *eliminated* the neighborhood altogether. That conclusion, obviously, was unacceptable to its residents, who expect by 2009 to be approaching 90 percent repopulation. Lest professional planners be given an unfair bad rap, however, one can look at the American Institute of Certified Planners (AICP) Code of Ethics and Professional Conduct to see reflected in it at least some of the values that the concepts of Participatory Design and Value Analysis have promoted. While the bulk of the Code of Ethics and Professional Conduct, like the principles of many professional associations, deals with responsibilities to the profession, and to other colleagues, there are also voiced concerns about the profession's responsibility to the public. In particular, among the principles "to which we aspire" are: special concern for the long-range consequences of present actions; special attention to the interrelatedness of decisions; giving people the opportunity to have a meaningful impact on the development of plans and programs that affect them, including participation broad enough to include those who lack formal organization or influence; seeking social justice by working to expand choice and opportunity for all persons, recognizing a special responsibility to plan for the needs of the disadvantaged and to promote racial and economic integration; and the endeavor to conserve and preserve the integrity of the natural and built environment. As "aspirations" these principles fall somewhat short of behavioral guidelines that could actually be enforced. Nevertheless, they speak to an awareness by the profession of the importance of much of what we have discussed that relates especially to the ethical and social dimensions of post-disaster reconstruction.[37]

Belfer Center for Science and International Affairs, John F. Kennedy School of Government, Harvard University, 2007. The report is based on research and interviews conducted in the Broadmoor community in New Orleans from March 2006 through August 2007.

37. See the AICP Code of Ethics and Professional Conduct, adopted March 19, 2005, effective June 1, 2005, accessible at http://www.planning.org/ethics/conduct.html. In an

NEIGHBORHOODS TRANSFORMED

Keith Twitchell, President of the Committee for a Better New Orleans, observed to me that he thought Mid-City was a neighborhood likely to face significant transformation. Its hospital—Lindy Boggs—was not going to be reopening, and much of the commercial sector and light industry was not coming back. The neighborhood association, while very organized, was having to deal with an outside developer (Victory Real Estate Investments) who wanted to locate a major suburban retail development smack in the middle of the area.

Mid-City—*the heart of New Orleans* and birthplace of Louis Armstrong, located midway between the Mississippi River and Lake Pontchartrain—is a large and diverse neighborhood bounded by the Pontchartrain Expressway, South Broad Street, Orleans Avenue, and City Park Avenue. It has always maintained a balance of land uses, with a mixture of restaurants and shops, schools and churches, professional offices, light industry, as well as single-family and owner-occupied homes. Its appeal as a residential area had been improving prior to the storm, with the restoration of the red cars of the Canal Streetcar line in 2004, its proximity to Delgado Community College and Xavier University, its mature vegetation, and being home to one of the largest historic districts in the city, as designated on the National Register.

The 2000 Census showed Mid-City with a population of around 20,000, of which 28 percent of households were homeowners, the remainder renters. Its racial makeup reflected that of the city as a whole, with roughly two-thirds African American, one-third White, but a larger proportion (10 percent) of Hispanic residents than the rest of the city. About a third of residents lived below the poverty line. Despite varied flooding from the storms ranging from inches to up to 8 feet, as of March, 2007, the neighborhood was one of the fastest in repopulating, with something between 55 and 60 percent being estimated from active electrical accounts and door-to-door surveys. About half of its 575 pre-storm businesses had reopened along its commercial corridors. However, despite its relatively

---

article, "The Ethics of Urban Planning: Remembering the Old AICP Code (1978–2005)," Sarah Jo Peterson, Assistant Professor of Regional and City Planning at the University of Oklahoma, chafes somewhat at the switch from the more organized and unified set of responsibilities of the "old" code to the new code's "aspirational" principles, and its distinction between principles and rules in which it appears the AICP "only intends to hold members accountable to the rules section." Article accessible at www.planetizen.com/node/20046.

high level of repopulation and reopened businesses, Mid-City would potentially be facing transformation.

The Mid-City Neighborhood Organization (MCNO) was formed in April, 1990, by the merger of two civic associations: the Mid-City Improvement Association, founded in 1974, and the City Park Mid-City Improvement Association, founded in 1971. Mid-City's need to deal with outside developers was not new; in fact, the two pre-merger associations were formed in the 1970s not only to deal with the decline of the physical appearance of properties and the exodus of long-term residents, but also zoning changes that allowed speculators to change residential properties to industrial and commercial use. While Mid-City, in part through the MCNO, had been rather successful prior to the storm in returning the area to a healthy mixture of residential and business uses, it appears that its old threats may have re-emerged. The MCNO hosts monthly neighborhood meetings, publishes a quarterly newsletter, *Heart of the City*, advocates for projects developed in its Mid-City Plan, and supports community events like the Bayou Boogaloo Festival. The Mid-City Recovery Committees completed their plan by October, 2006. It was especially concerned to deal with its ongoing problem of blighted housing (more than 13 percent unoccupied according to the 2000 Census), a problem made seriously worse by the storms. It took a relatively hard position—supporting the City Council's deadline to secure gutted and boarded properties by August 29, 2006, and adjudicating properties not meeting that deadline. The plan proposed a Mid-City Neighborhood Recovery Corporation (MCNRC) to give neighborhood control over the resale of adjudicated homes and represent Mid-City interests in planning and zoning implementation. A goal of the plan was to achieve 50 percent owner-occupied housing near term, 70 percent long term. Groups of adjacent demolished properties would be converted into park space. It also endorsed development of a Canal Street Overlay (similar to the Carrollton Overlay), and conversion of abandoned structures such as the Dixie and Falstaff breweries, into mixed use buildings.

Of particular importance for Mid-City were the healthcare resources available to it. The post-storm loss of Lindy Boggs Medical Center (formerly known as Memorial Medical Center, Mercy Campus), and the loss of most practicing physicians and specialists, along with two dialysis centers, which constituted a thriving part of the community prior to the storms, was of grave concern. These concerns became fully realized, when, on December 28, 2007, three representatives of MCNO, joined by the President of Faubourg St. John Neighborhood Association and a representative of Friends of Lafitte Corridor (a trail and green space proposal), were informed by lawyers with Johns Walker, representing Victory Real Estate Investments, LLC, a private, closely held, commercial real estate company based in Columbus, Georgia, that Victory *now* had no redevelopment plans for the Lindy Boggs site for the near future—two or three years. This was attributed to the downturn in the housing, retail, and credit markets over the past year. Development sooner than that time would only happen if there were changes in the economy. Nevertheless, demolition of Lindy Boggs would begin in approximately two months (March, 2008) and last about five months, with heavy equipment taking place Monday through Friday from 7:00 a.m. to 5:00 p.m. The MCNO and other neighborhood association representatives were very disappointed with this news, but agreed not to take an adversarial position on the strong assumption that the demolition would be approved anyway by the Housing Conservation District Review Committee (HCDRC).

Conversations with Jennifer Weishaupt, President of the MCNO, and former Treasurer, Doug Joubert and his wife, brought into relief exactly the kind of difficulties such forced transitions brought for New Orleans' neighborhoods. Doug's wife said they had been going to MCNO meetings for almost two years, trying to redevelop the neighborhood in ways that would be beneficial to it. While there were, naturally, disagreements about various things, when MCNO held a neighborhood meeting about Victory Development, the attendance was staggering because no one wanted what Victory had *originally* planned—to put 'big-box' stores right in the middle of their historic neighborhood. There was universal disagreement with that, as well as frustration. MCNO and many citizens had worked to plan everything for their neighborhood—one can see the plan on the MCNO website—and it was frustrating to know that all the work they had put into it was not going to come to any fruition because it wasn't what someone *else* (the developers) wanted.

For Doug Joubert, the problem was in large part because the planners had simply gone off on their own and did what they wanted *without much citizen involvement.* In fact, in Doug's opinion, things had gotten only worse with the city now having a 'Recovery Czar' in the person of Dr. Ed Blakely, who had been given carte blanche to do whatever he wanted to do, no matter what neighborhoods had planned before hand. From

Mid-City's standpoint, it was a matter of outside people having stepped in, and *their* activities taking over. The 17 recovery areas Blakely had targeted were very much funding dependent, and there weren't a lot of funds floating around. And where there was money coming in, Doug felt sure that money wouldn't be going towards the neighborhoods. The neighborhoods *wished* that it would. Doug gave as an example that one of their top priorities had been for a community center. What had happened was that a private organization in California came out and offered to build the community center for free by using private funds and private donations—"what a phenomenal idea." So when MCNO got together, it became Doug's project; they went to the community and asked for input, and they got input from everybody possible before deciding what their plans would be. They then went before the group called V&A,[38] hired the architects, got permission from the City, and started work. But a year later, essentially all that had been done was that part of the lot was cleared and dirt put in. That was it, because the funding had dried up, and because the City had put so many roadblocks up in front of them for permitting—so many roadblocks that the project became almost impossible. Thus, according to Doug, Mid-City had spent millions of dollars just trying to clear those roadblocks, and instead of making it easy for them, the City had made it harder. For two years they have dealing with this, hoping things would get better. "But who knows. After two years of trying, this is getting old."

We talked about Broadmoor, as a point of comparison with the rather different issues Mid-City was facing. Doug agreed Broadmoor was in a position to be reconstituting itself as pretty much the way it was before the storms. But Broadmoor was not as ethnically diverse as Mid-City, and, Doug thought, had deeper pockets. Because of that, Broadmoor was able to draw help from other areas, and get grant money that Mid-City could not get; so much so that Broadmoor could hire their own Executive Director, which Mid-City didn't have the money to do. Mid-City was a very eclectic mix, with some businesses and a mixed-type neighborhood, the majority African American, but whites a close second, and a large proportion of Hispanics. The MCNO has been "very ornery" about making sure their zoning stays as it had been—specifically wanting to ensure that developers do not just buy up a piece of property, and then zone it any way they want. Victory Real Estate originally had one thing in mind—a

38. Vine & Associates, Community Development Financial Consulting, Glendale, California.

big-box development—but it wasn't clear what they had in mind now. Doug said, "I really don't think they knew they were going to get into this kind of fight . . . they were thinking this was going to be easy, and they didn't know that they had a bulldog that was chasing after them." That person was Jennifer Weishaupt, now President of MCNO.

Jennifer explained that the MCNO's planning documents were involved with both the Lambert process and the UNOP. When Mid-City became aware (as had Broadmoor) that as a wet neighborhood it would go through this 'Lambert process,' they started a grassroots effort to brainstorm some general ideas about what were their values, what was important to them as a neighborhood as they recovered. What came out of that was the Mid-City Recovery Plan. That was really a grassroots document. It sits on the MCNO website with the intention to make it clear that MCNO and the neighborhood "owns" the document—which meant they could change it as the landscape changed. MCNO worked its process in parallel to the Lambert process, and Jennifer pointed that if the two documents were read side-by-side, one could clearly see differences between "what Lambert took away" from their sessions with Mid-City residents, and "what the residents themselves took away." Therefore, MCNO created an addendum to the Lambert document in which they said "these are the things we felt strongly about that got left out of the Lambert process." These differences became more serious as things were fed into the UNOP. Jennifer believed Broadmoor probably experienced the same issues they had.

By the time the UNOP process came around, they "really had planning fatigue and were tired of planning." They had already done this, at least two times over. Therefore, MCNO decided to use its own Mid-City Plan and some of the Lambert plan as their guidebook and principles for recovery.

The pivot point of the most significant potential change to the character of Mid-City as a neighborhood was what might happen with the former Lindy Boggs and that medical corridor in particular. Aside from Lindy Boggs, Jennifer explained, they also had a light industrial corridor right in the middle of the neighborhood. In that corridor, the MCNO plans strongly endorsed inclusion of the Lafitte Corridor Greenway. MCNO felt that with the addition of that greenway, rather than abruptly, the businesses in the area would "organically" change over time—change in terms of the types of businesses so that property values would increase. MCNO's hope was that light industrial businesses would not see a great benefit to moving industrial business there; instead, the area would become home to art studios, professional offices, or outdoor-oriented enterprises, so the area would be shifting from light industry to more of a residential neighborhood. In their planning, MCNO called for a mixed-use area, with different commercial uses mixed with residential and professional office space. With respect to the hospital specifically, MCNO called for that to again become a medical facility, although even at the time of the planning they were hearing rumblings to the contrary—even *before* Victory was involved. They were hearing there was some kind of covenant on the land that was still owned by Tenet and was up for sale; so there was the distinct feeling it wouldn't be a hospital again. At the same time, MCNO felt it had some other adaptive re-use, such as senior citizens housing or primary care or things similar to that. When the Victory purchase came in, obviously the intentions for any thing like that had changed. Jennifer believed Lindy Boggs employed approximately 1,000 people; in addition there were people who worked in the surrounding medical infrastructure, so from an economic standpoint, this medical corridor greatly impacted the neighborhood and what its mix was. Now, not only had Lindy Boggs gone, but essentially this entire surrounding medical infrastructure had collapsed. The primary care physicians and doctors that people had gone to for decades—many of them did not return because there was no hospital for them to affiliate with in the area. Therefore, as a result of that change, one of MCNO's major priorities had been how they could encourage and re-introduce some level of primary care back into the neighborhood. MCNO's answer was to replace it with neighborhood-based clinics, but "we can't just snap our fingers and make that happen."

On the other side, the second issue emerging from the demise of Lindy Boggs, was the building-out of heavy retail space. Jennifer felt that this would probably have an even greater impact than what the Victory land purchase had taken away. The idea of developers bringing in plans to plop some big-box retail enterprise where Lindy Boggs had stood would be highly disruptive of the neighborhood's character. Jennifer pointed out that "when you start looking at traffic counts, and you look at the existing infrastructure, this is not an area that supports large businesses." Mid-City did contain some main surface streets, but they were not highways; the neighborhood simply did not have the infrastructure to support 1,000,000 square feet of retail, or anything like what Victory had been proposing. Victory's initial proposal was for something like a big-box Home Depot; now it was unclear what they would do. "All they'll tell us at this point is that the whole project is on hold." Victory owns the land, and the project is on hold. "They've gotten a bit tired of us, so until they have something firm, they don't want to deal with us."

Was it even a business advantage for Victory to put a big-box store in the center of the neighborhood? MCNO's feeling was that it would probably not end up being Home Depot, because there was one going up within three miles; however Lowe's was anxious to get a location on this side of the city. Was the neighborhood totally opposed to this idea? It certainly was on the initially proposed scale. Jennifer had seen examples of urban scale big-box development—over 25,000 square feet, but done in a more urban style design and setting. MCNO thought something like that was a possible fit, but whether it was possible for Victory to do that, they didn't know. Victory did not have that kind of track record, generally being much more involved with large, suburban shopping centers. The preference in the neighborhood might be for "going vertical, rather than using every inch of ground space," but even that created a NIMBY mentality for a neighborhood that had felt "like the sacrificial lamb."

In the end, a primary value for Mid-City was to make sure their historic neighborhood was not sacrificed for the sake of everyone else's shopping ability. This meant commercial development only on a scale appropriate for a neighborhood, not the entire city; it meant considering a mix of business hours and spreading out the traffic so its impact was not all concentrated during one time of day. Having big semi's running through the neighborhood was not going to make residents happy. Yet MCNO had already seen a lot of impact from even a very small Home Depot store that opened in a neighborhood, only a 15,000 square foot store, so if that impact were multiplied up to the 1,000,000 square feet level Victory was proposing, "you can see that would be pretty frightening."

Many people feel New Orleans needs jobs, and that it must keep tax dollars in the city. MCNO agreed with that, but wanted to negotiate the best possible development for the neighborhood, and "not just accept what they have to give us, and say, gee, thank you so much for wanting to develop this, because whatever is developed, we'll be living with the impact of that for decades; and if all we get at the end of the day is a bunch of low-wage, no-benefit jobs, that's not improving anybody's long-term outlook."

Had people in MCNO been able to interact *directly* with Victory, or was the developer free to do whatever they wanted? Jennifer felt they had some input because they were staying in the forefront, and were being very vocal about focusing on their own plan. Their response from City Council members was being told "the neighborhood will be at the table." But other than that, the citizens of Mid-City had no real interaction with Victory. Jennifer could only hope, along with Keith Twitchell, that through a formal Citizen Participation Process, neighborhood associations such as MCNO might be given legal standing with the City Council. At this point, however, things were still in the conceptual stage. MCNO's position is that they've seen all the things that are broken in City Hall, and told them "if you guys can't get the job done, then we feel like we can, so let's introduce this neighborhood council concept." They hope to see it on the 2008 City Council agenda.

The current repopulation percentage of Mid-City is about 65 percent. Mid-City has some of the poorest of the poor and the richest of the rich within neighborhood boundaries. In the past, Mid-City has traditionally had a low homeownership level, below 30 percent; it became primarily a renter-occupied neighborhood in the 1970s. One of MCNO's biggest initiatives, therefore, has been to increase owner occupancy, even in multifamily doubles and larger, because they feel this increases people's stake in the neighborhood. The hope is that the 2010 Census will reflect progress. What they want to see is a historic district that has encouraged a mix of artisans, retail, musicians, and professionals, along with a solid residential base. There are now a number of artists who live in Mid-City and who have studios, and they did create the Mid-City Art Market, which in 2007 was given over to the New Orleans Arts Council because it had become too big the neighborhood to manage without a full-time person. MCNO is a strong organization. It has truly staked its claim in the recovery of the city overall, and has worked hard to be recognized in City Hall. But Mid-City is primarily a working class neighborhood, and, Jennifer says, "we can only do what we can do." Mid-City has not had the funding Broadmoor has. But currently two of the MCNO board members have been dedicated to looking for new funding and for people resources. But Jennifer admits: "We have a typical middle class mentality that you can do it for yourself. But we're so busy 'doing it ourselves' that we're not spending any time for how we're going to do it later. That's our biggest failing point."

That indeed is the dilemma of even highly motivated neighborhood association like the Broadmoor Improvement Association and, under rather different circumstances, the Mid-City Neighborhood Organization. The of effort fighting the barriers of bureaucracy, seeking funding that evaporates, tracking shifting regulations, being bullied by endless planning processes, and playing against the wildcard of commercial developers is both overwhelming and exhausting. Yet with both the BIA and the MCNO, we see a commitment to the human values of neighborhood, the ethics of a fair democratic process, and use of many of the principles of Participatory Design in the high levels of citizen engagement throughout all phases of recovery and rebuilding.

These shared values, goals, and modes of operating notwithstanding, there are quite different circumstances that the BIA and the MCNO each face. While BIA has been able to work towards and begin to realize the rebirth of essentially the same Broadmoor neighborhood that existed before the storms, Mid-City is facing new challenges even beyond those imposed by hurricane damage and flooding, and may well end up being a rather different neighborhood than it was prior to the storms. In some respects Mid-City may be a better neighborhood—and we can certainly see, in talking with Doug Joubert and Jennifer Weishaupt of the MCNO, that the Mid-City neighborhood has expended Herculean measures to manage its change in a fair and humane way by ensuring the participation of its citizens at every step of their rebuilding process. But there are also limits to what citizens can do on their own without full access to the power structures of government and government-supported economic development.

For this reason, it must be acknowledged that while Participatory Design and related methods emphasizing fairness and universal participation like Value Analysis are well suited for organizations that must independently restructure themselves during periods of transition, and well suited for communities that must manage their own recovery after having experienced natural disaster and accompanying social transformations, they are not inherently methods of limitless power. They are, rather, methods of democratic empowerment that operate well in contexts where there is ambiguity or social chaos that needs to be organized and made sense of; where there is a vacuum of power that needs to be filled. Whether these methods of participatory democracy can, by themselves, overcome hierarchical structures of authority in government leadership or in government bureaucracies that seek to retain power rather than distribute it in an egalitarian fashion is an unanswered question.

Before turning to look at difficulties faced by those still-displaced residents of Orleans and other parishes of South Louisiana, many of whom are concentrated in cities like Houston and Dallas, others scattered more widely across the country, it is worth a very brief consideration of one other neighborhood likely to be transformed into something different from what it was prior to the storms. This is in the Gentilly—Pontchartrain Park area people refer to as Pontilly.

Bill Rousselle operates a public relations and advertising company, Bright Moments, that has done a great deal of outreach work to assist in the rebuilding of New Orleans. Bill has also been connected with LA-DAP, the Louisiana Diaspora Advocacy Project, which we will discuss in the following chapter. Bill suggested that in the Gentilly—Pontchartrain Park area, there was an effective and active group of people who have returned to the city, and who are continuing to work toward the redevelopment of that neighborhood. They have maintained good communications with people who have not returned, have a pretty good sense of who is coming back, and what factors have been holding up those who have not returned. There are several neighborhood associations in Gentilly, including the Pontilly Neighborhood Association. In various ways, these neighborhood associations have been making efforts to plan changes in their community in a way that will encourage people to return. According to Bill, the Gentilly Council has representation from the broadest cross-section of the organizations, and all of them are part of it at this point. In addition, the City Councilwoman for that area, Cynthia Hedge-Morell, has been very helpful in trying make sure that everybody had representation, and that everybody came together to planning efforts. Bill felt that at least things were much more well-organized than they had been earlier, when there was more fragmentation among the neighborhood associations there.

Pontilly is a neighborhood that will end up being different than it was before the storms—but not because of forces similar to those faced by Mid-City, with a large outside developer holding title to a big chunk of land in the middle of the neighborhood. Instead, what people in the Pontilly neighborhood have been proposing is essentially to turn it into more of a retirement community. That demographic age profile was actually the profile of many of the residents, particularly in Pontchartrain Park and Gentilly, *before* the storms. But now they have been looking at building senior citizens homes and senior assisted type living facilities in that neighborhood, which would attract the people who had been the residents there. Nevertheless, the neighborhood would still be differently configured, because most of the homes there were single story, stucco type suburban looking homes. Now, Bill said, the neighborhood would have a whole different feel to it, once they got all their plans in place. There would be more high-rise buildings, and developers would certainly find that idea appealing, from a business standpoint. These would not be buildings 15–20 stories high, but 4–5 story structures throughout the community that would allow developers to increase their profitability by constructing multiple salable residences on a single footprint.

It remains unclear whether this plan will turn out to be an instance of a rare harmonious relationship between developers and citizens, who demographically live in someplace other than the uppermost echelons of the economic strata—for these citizens of Pontilly are elderly, of modest income, and often of rather fragile health. One can only hope that it will, if it means the ability to preserve the underlying integrity of the neighborhood. At the very least, it represents one more twist of possibilities in a unique city that already has a thousand possibilities used, and a thousand more yet to be used.

Former Home, Lower Ninth Ward
(December, 2007)

Bayou Petit Caillou

9

Remote Voices

IN THE SEVERAL LANDSCAPES sketched of life in New Orleans, some twenty-eight months after the storms, chapter 7 ended, standing amidst the dry grass and brush of the Lower Ninth Ward, remembering what had once been there—the lingering colors of purple and gold and green porch railings,[1] the shouts and laughter of voices, the odors of cooking of families no longer present. In some ways it felt like a battlefield without corpses—a field of loss in which the circumstances of the passage of people from life there remained incomplete, their meanings still ambiguous. Yet even amidst the emptiness, there were voices—or the hints of voices—in the siren's call of train whistles from the Norfolk Southern freight yard along Florida Avenue. It was as if those hulking train engines themselves were lonely, calling back old residents who had given them the warmth of human life and the complexities of its meanings.

The stories we will share in this chapter—fragments of the loneliness experienced by displaced residents who have been forced to remain living far from home, and accounts of some of the many of efforts by voluntary associations in New Orleans and elsewhere in the country to help to try to bring them home—are necessarily incomplete. They will remain incom-

---

1. In December of 2007, other colors jarred against the brown and olive brush of the Lower Ninth Ward as pink tarp covered structures appeared scattered in the fields just east of the Industrial Canal, from North Derbigny to North Galvez streets. Some were blocks, some tent-shaped, giving the initial impression that these were covering the components of new pre-fab homes for displaced residents. It turned out the pink objects were not themselves homes, but symbolic stand-ins for houses to come and the promise of actor Brad Pitt to help fund some 100 affordable, ecologically sound houses there. "My thinking why it's pink is because it screams the loudest," Pitt explained at a news conference. Details about the design of the housing units can be found on the Archinect website, "The Pink Project," http://archinect.com. Local architects from New Orleans included Billes and Condordia; from Philadelphia Kieran Timberlake; international firms included Adjaye of London, MVRDV of Rotterdam, Shigeru Ban of Tokyo.

plete until every last family, every last person who still longs to return to their families and neighborhoods, villages and cities, has found their way to *walk back home.*

> *Do you know what it means to miss New Orleans*
> *Miss it each night and day . . .*
> *Miss them moss covered vines . . . tall sugar pines*
> *Where mockin' birds used to sing. . .*
> *Moonlight on the bayou . . . Creole tune fills the air*
> *Magnolias in bloom . . . I'm wishin' I was there*

(Fragments of Louis Armstrong song
hummed by displaced resident in Houston)

LA-DAP

The Louisiana Diaspora Advocacy Project (LA-DAP) is a grassroots coalition of several Louisiana organizations, with some national support, that has been pushing for policies to force local and State government to guarantee that all Louisiana residents evacuated in the aftermath of hurricanes Rita and Katrina have the resources they need to return home and rebuild their lives. Policy efforts have focused on voter rights, needed flood protection in damaged neighborhoods, affordable housing, public education, healthcare, public safety, and workforce development. In its push for equity in voter rights, for example, LA-DAP has argued for the restoration of registered voter rosters recently cut by an extension of the automatic mailing of ballots to displaced voters (which ended February 23, 2007) for one year, and perhaps to allow satellite voting. The predominance of black registered voters among the more than 200,000 displaced residents is a critical element in understanding the issue of social equality involved. LA-DAP's concern for flood protection has included not only building stronger levees, but support for programs to reclaim wetlands. In the area of affordable housing, LA-DAP has supported Congressional bills to eliminate subtraction of insurance, SBA, and FEMA payments from Road Home grants; demanded independent monitoring of Road Home programs on race and geographical award satisfaction criteria; and urged a moratorium on demolishing public housing developments until housing was found for all former housing development residents. It has supported an ordinance on inclusionary zoning in which all new market-rate developments over twenty units would be required to include 15–25 percent affordable housing, as well as address the special needs of seniors and disabled citizens. LA-DAP also supports proposals of the People's Hurricane Relief Fund for rent control in New Orleans. For public education, in addition to pushing for renovated school facilities, LA-DAP has argued for pay levels that could recruit and retain qualified teachers and administrators; similarly, it urges recruitment and incentives to bring back primary care doctors.

The remote voices of Louisiana's diaspora represents the most extreme case of a 'distributed group,' bound together by shared neighborhood connections, and portions of New Orleans' diverse culture and history. But other than those groups of displaced residents who are living in close proximity to one another in certain areas of cities like Houston, there is little that bonds this total population together as a collection of 'displaced people.' Many are simply scattered widely across the country, with closer connections to family that has remained in New Orleans than to one another. The fact is that a great deal of information about displaced residents has been largely anecdotal. Some of it has emerged in discussions with the several organizations trying to help former residents deal with the complex processes involved in returning home. Neither of these sources yields especially firm data—at least in trying to get an accurate sense of who, among the total displaced population has returned to New Orleans only to become homeless there vs. those who are still in the process of deciding whether or not to return vs. those who have decided to remain living outside New Orleans.[2] Anecdotally, it did appear that many displaced families with school-age children, who had begun attending schools in their new locale, as well as many elderly or those requiring daily medical assistance they could not count on in New Orleans, but who found it locally, were likely to remain permanent residents in their new locations. At least as long as they were able to receive benefits there.

Bill Rousselle, who runs the public relations and media firm, Bright Moments, is one of the organizers behind the Louisiana Diaspora Advocacy Project (LA-DAP). When I spoke with Bill in December, 2007 he indicated that LA-DAP, as a cooperative effort, had continued to do monthly conference calls to keep various organizations they have worked with informed on activities, but that as a group, a coalition, they had not

2. Or heavily damaged communities in certain coastal parishes.

really initiated any programs since September or October of 2007. Bill's public relations and advertising company has a great deal of outreach work to assist in the rebuilding of New Orleans—enough for him to say, "my wife gets on me because I operate a for-profit business but I'm doing non-profit work." Bill himself, however, doesn't make much of a distinction between work and outreach. The overriding goal of the LA-DAP coalition is to help bring people home.

Bright Moments provided services for the Louisiana Recovery Corps during 2007, but directly conducted special outreach work as well, including providing case management services to get resources to help people come home, and doing outreach in Houston, Dallas, and Atlanta to attract people interested in coming home. Bill also worked to put together a job fair in New Orleans in May of 2007, where busloads of people from Houston were brought in to learn about and access job opportunities in the city. Bright Moments produced a video to give people a realistic understanding of what it would take to make the trip back home, showing them resources they could use in making that effort.

A number of 'remote voices' were collected for a video documenting a LA-DAP organizing meeting in March of 2007. One was of an adolescent girl who talked about how, when she left her immediate family behind elsewhere to return to New Orleans after a year, she had to deal with twelve people living in two bedrooms with only one bathroom. She was constantly being accused of stealing. She worried each night about being accosted by homeless men sleeping on the other side of a thin wall of a homeless shelter. Others who were displaced had difficulty simply keeping voice contact among family members, since most couldn't afford to keep their phones alive. Children were forced to discover new ways to get to school without school bus routes. Adults with children kept asking, again and again—what kind of policies were being put in place for families?

There was confirmation of my perception that mortuaries were one of the few businesses really thriving in the long-term aftermath of the storms. Bill agreed that he had experienced a lot of people dying—people whose participation in LA-DAP was always being interrupted by having funerals to go to. Bill said it was not only a question of the 1,600 people who died in the storm, but the 'tens of thousand who spiritually died after being yanked out of their homes and neighborhoods'—particularly the elderly and the handicapped. The issue of race and social equality was a constant theme. The position of many with LA-DAP was that it was very important to see the impact of race on the whole situation of post-Katrina New Orleans. Many felt that much of American society was constructed with racist institutions built up over the years, and that if we didn't recognize that, 'we would end up with same kind of institutions on the other side of the recovery and rebuilding effort.'

Participatory Design and Value Analysis are processes intended to give voice to those impacted by change and transition, including reconstruction of the environment in which they live. It was therefore fitting in Bill's video that perhaps the strongest theme of all was one expressed by a woman who urged LA-DAP volunteers, "The people have to have a voice. Our responsibility is to help create spaces where people can feel confident about their voices. We who are here helping have to figure out how to talk to each other. It doesn't mean we're always agreeing, but we got to love each other enough to know that we have a responsibility to the people who are scattered."

Bill's video ends with the question: *Did you get tired of looking at empty houses?* The video had attempted to give images of reality and public voice to displaced persons, and what they were facing in trying to return to their homes. But in the background throughout the entire film, was the lonely void of what had been left behind—displayed in the emptiness of the view one would see from a car driving around the streets of the Lower Ninth Ward.

LA-DAP has now moved somewhat away from its direct involvement with displaced persons to trying to organize effective actions to compel local, State, and federal officials to appropriate the necessary resources and employ equity-based policies to rebuild communities and lives. These are the policy efforts we cited above—focused on voter rights, flood protection, emergency preparedness, education, healthcare, public safety, transportation, affordable housing, and workforce development.[3]

In the dry grass and brush of the Lower Ninth Ward, the empty lots of Tremé, the still boarded up homes of New Orleans East, it is not as if the persons to whom those empty places are no longer there at all. They are not *here,* but they are somewhere.

I feel real lonely here in Houston . . . them highways so tall
I think what if I jus' fall off . . . ain't like Tremé and all those

---

3. For more detailed information, see, for example, L. Martin, "Louisiana Diaspora Advocacy Project," accessible at http://www.nola.tv/news/index.php?print/id+250.

little houses all different colors, dogs runnin' all over the street.
Here, all I see is blank walls.

(Displaced former resident)

EDOLA Homecoming Center

Shakoor Aljuwani is a community organizer for the Episcopal Diocese of Louisiana (EDOLA) Homecoming Center as well as for a number of other church organizations. Shakoor initially did work with Common Ground Relief for about seven months, when he came to New Orleans shortly after storm, but then moved to EDOLA because he came to feel that faith-based groups were more productive in providing ongoing work involving New Orleans resident participation.

In speaking with Shakoor, I came to feel, as I had with Bill Rousselle and LA-DAP, that, some two and one-half years after the storms, organizations dealing with the needs of the thousands of displaced New Orleans residents were perhaps less in a position to provide direct assistance through caseworkers, but continued to function as both sources of and vehicles for the dissemination of information about what resources might be available to those still wishing to return home. Shakoor acknowledged that the focus had changed somewhat. EDOLA's Homecoming Center now seeks to partner and collaborate on fighting for the right of displaced residents to return, encouraging participation from current residents. Starting with a database of about 3,000 individuals from AmericaSpeaks' UNOP Community Congresses II and III, the Homecoming Center distributes an email newsletter—"In the N.O."—to some 10,000 recipients who include displaced residents, volunteers, and interested parties from around the country. About 3,000 are former residents, of which about 1,500 live outside the metropolitan New Orleans area or outside the state- Shakoor said the newsletter was emailed out every couple of weeks. The last most current issue was in October, 2007.[4]

4. The lead article in this issue discussed details of the 'Jena Six' incident in which family members of children who were charged with attempted murder organized protests, initiated by an incident in which three nooses had been hung from a schoolyard tree 'reserved' for white students after a black student sat under the tree. Six black students at Jena High School in Central Louisiana had been arrested in December, 2006 after a school fight in which a white student was beaten and suffered a concussion and multiple bruises. The six black students were charged with attempted murder and conspiracy, facing up to 100 years in prison without parole. The second article discussed the resolution of the House of

The Homecoming center has also sent out surveys to find out key issues and concerns among displaced families. The greatest concentration of former residents is still in the Houston and Dallas areas. In Houston, evacuees were put into certain housing developments that accepted survivors. Some displaced residents have been able to travel back and forth to see their extended family, and participate in New Orleans events such as Mardi Gras. But many have also become more and more connected to the places where they have been living, particularly those who have children in school there, or who do not have a place to come back to yet, or who remain unsure about safety in New Orleans. Not a few displaced residents have been signed off the voting register, so they will not be able to vote in New Orleans.

Communicating with people in Houston has been difficult for grassroots, volunteer organizations like EDOLA's Homecoming Center because they do not have much in the way of staff; nor are there mechanisms or funding to locate their staff people in other cities. Shakoor acknowledged this was a serious problem. He also recognized that, even with the Homecoming Center's rather large email distribution, not everyone would have access to computers—especially the elderly or handicapped. On the other hand, Shakoor believes that there has emerged a strong word-of-mouth network. He found, for example, that because displaced residents had been concentrated in certain housing developments in Houston, occupying some 200 to 300 units there, people would meet other displaced individuals in the laundry or on the housing playgrounds and share stories. Nevertheless, Shakoor said it was "very much hit or miss" making contact with displaced residents in Houston and San Antonio and elsewhere.

> We all got FEMA letters telling us we got to get out
> of these houses nobody had been living in, out by
> February 28 [2007]. I work two jobs at crap for pay,
> I never see my daughter . . . I may not pay my bills this month.
> I have to save up some money in case we get turned out.

(Former New Orleanian in San Antonio)[5]

Bishops of the Episcopal Church of the United States to be presented to Congress addressing issues of race and the needs of Gulf Coast victims of the hurricanes.

5. Recounted by caseworker; similar to account reported by Bruce Nolan, "Rent aid ending, FEMA tells some. Notices go to those in HUD homes in Texas," *The Times-Picayune*, January 12, 2007.

Shakoor's own work at public housing developments in Houston and San Antonio has involved conducting surveys—attempting to identify residents who were connected with particular areas in New Orleans in which EDOLA was concentrating its work, such as in Central City. Their general goal was to contact people who still wanted to come back and provide some guidance to them. Shakoor thought there might be something of a wave of returnees, as their public benefits in Texas ran out. New Orleans, therefore, would desperately need to come up with a housing plan for those Texas returnees, just as it needs to have a plan for its growing homeless population, now estimated to be over 12,000 persons. We both shared our experiences on how many people we had seen currently living under elevated sections of I-10, after they had been run out of Duncan Park opposite the mayor's office.

Most recently, EDOLA's Homecoming Center has focused much of its work on Renaissance Village, the largest trailer park of displaced residents, located in Baker, Louisiana, outside of Baton Rouge. There had been as many as 500 trailers; now there were about 350 trailers, housing around 1,000 people. The goal of EDOLA's work has been to find more dignified housing for these citizens, either in Baker or elsewhere, depending on where people wanted to go. In December, 2007, a planning meeting was held in Baker with about 325 participating, including representatives from FEMA, HUD, and Senator Landrieu's office. Time was critical, however, because by May 30, 2008 FEMA would end all trailer parks, eliminating about 3,000 units.

EDOLA has been able to provide a limited number of case managers to assist people in developing a personal recovery plan. The immediate problem they face is that the programs which have funded this work—a grant from Cutter (private), managed through the United Methodist Church, with Catholic Charities and the Salvation Army also involved—would run out on March 31, 2008. Right now, Shakoor observed, there was an insufficient number of case managers, and no plans from the federal government to help people. "But former residents *must* become skilled in managing government bureaucracies, and many people cannot do that easily."

Complicating the ability of caseworkers like Shakoor to find temporary housing for returnees, has been the absence of rent control in New Orleans. Shakoor sees New Orleans' rental laws as "in the dark ages," and, like LA-DAP, wanted rental properties included in any comprehensive housing plan. Returnees were finding that they were now forced to pay as much as $1,000 a month just to get the same kind of apartment for which they had paid $400 before the storms. Various petitions brought to the New Orleans City Council to deal with rental price gouging and tenants' rights have argued that rental rates for private apartments have increased by 80 percent or more. They have urged the City Council, therefore, to establish an anti-price gouging and arbitration authority to standardize rules and regulations for rental rates and criteria for eviction; to hire administrative law judges to conduct hearings for rent adjustments and evictions; and to set the maximum rental rate equal to that collected for the same or comparable property on August 1, 2005, providing for rent increases based on inflation and capitol improvements to not exceed 10 percent of rent. The most immediate way to increase affordable housing was to begin by bringing down rental costs.

As a community activist, Shakoor is convinced that, one way or another, the issues of limited low-cost housing and rental property must be made more visible to the public, because these are the primary factors inhibiting the return of many former residents. Shakoor was among those who participated in the December, 2007 protests at City Hall about public housing. "We were locked outside," Shakoor said, "unable to present our views. We at least wanted a 60-day cooling off period before they went ahead and destroyed any public housing projects." At twenty-eight months after Katrina, it was inexcusable that the City Council still didn't have a comprehensive housing plan for affordable housing. There was therefore no excuse for demolishing buildings that were still in good enough shape to use. Shakoor was planning to participate with a group of volunteers to walk city officials and other people through the old Desire Development replacement project—Savoy Place—which was almost opened before the storms struck. Shakoor feels the site that is still usable. "If you need buildings," Shakoor argued, "what about using *these* buildings. At least we will show them there is abundant land for them on which to build affordable housing." They also needed to put pressure on HUD. "New Orleans is littered with half-finished projects of HUD. So, we're going to try to put a lot of pressure on city leaders."

One other network organization Shakoor talked about was the Neighborhoods Partnership Network (NPN). This network first emerged in a series of meetings among neighborhood groups in the months after Hurricane Katrina, when it became apparent that neighborhood associations were in need of a vehicle to collaborate with one another.

Since the summer of 2006, NPN has hosted monthly forums, conducted workshops to provide training for neighborhood activists, and, starting in January, 2007, published a monthly community newspaper called "The Trumpet." Some of its staff are particularly concerned to facilitate liaisons with government agencies, institutions, and non-profit organizations. Its board members include Latoya Cantrell, President of the Broadmoor Improvement Association; Dorian Hastings, Central City Renaissance Project Manager; Nikki Najiola of the Pontilly Neighborhood Association; Amy Lafont of the Mid-City Neighborhood Association. NPN has also been working with Keith Twitchell of the Committee for a Better New Orleans and supports the idea of a formal Citizen Participation Process. "The Trumpet" is sent to diaspora locations such as community centers and churches in Houston where people from New Orleans hang out. The newsletter contains a lot of news about what is going on in New Orleans, and doesn't shy away from allowing people to voice their anger and emotional frustrations with the process to return. The December 2007 issue (No. 11) of "The Trumpet," for example, contained a 'Letter from the Editors' that encouraged people to 'take time to breathe and find something to celebrate even in the midst of the paleness of successes against the reality of the work of recovery and maintaining everyday life.' A lead piece in the same issue incorporated environmental issues into the difficulties of returning home with a criticism of the November decision by the Louisiana Public Service Commission (LPSC) to allow Entergy Louisiana to convert the "Little Gypsy" power plant in Monte, Louisiana from natural gas to coal and pet coke, one of the dirtiest burning fuel sources available. The Hispanic community found its voice in a piece that discussed the struggles unique to their growing population. It also extolled organizations such as the Hispanic Apostolate, under the umbrella of Catholic Charities, which served as a major advocate for support of the Latino Community. A Ph.D candidate at Howard University talked about her research into how people respond to the emotional effects of disasters like Katrina in different ways, such as fatigue, being stressed, feeling nervous or angry. A group of local crafts artists described their collective, the New Orleans Craft Mafia. What one quickly found, then, in "The Trumpet" was both a vehicle to disseminate information, but perhaps equally important, a vehicle for *individual voices* to express their sorrows and joys, their frustrations and successes, things that did not work and things that did work in the process of recovery—so they could be of help to others. In short, "The Trumpet" had become an opportunity for the displaced people of New Orleans and South Louisiana to connect with one another, one-on-one.

> Not come back? I'm no f***ing refugee; I'm a displaced resident.
> How the hell would you react if somebody told you to simply
> walk away from your entire life?
> And you wanna to tell me the only thing to do is wait.

(Displaced former New Orleans resident)

Common Ground Relief

The Common Ground Collective was established within a week after Hurricane Katrina flooded New Orleans. It was the first organization to open up a medical clinic in Algiers, providing food, water, and supplies to thousands of low-income residents who were unable to evacuate. It's identity is more than a volunteer organization of relief response, however; it is an organization very much concerned with social justice. As we have revealed at various points, the storms and flooding exposed pre-existing and long-standing injustices faced by the residents of lower income, predominantly African American neighborhoods. The City's efforts to repair and make livable the loss of over 275,000 housing units that were destroyed has been painfully slow. As a voluntary association, Common Ground models the importance of *collaborative* efforts of social justice initiatives by encouraging citizens to work *together with* local neighborhood associations and local businesses to build an atmosphere of hope, as well as through networking with other voluntary relief associations.[6]

Common Ground started in New Orleans with only three volunteers and $50 dollars, but has grown to support over 40 fulltime organizers and many additional volunteers who include healthcare workers, community organizers and housing rights advocates, and skilled laborers. Although the organization started with relief work, it very much sees itself involved in the rebuilding of New Orleans for the long haul. In a sense, it has become another of the historical 'mutual aid' societies that have been so

---

6. Another voluntary relief association is ACORN, the Association of Community Organizations for Reform Now, a national volunteer organization serving low- and moderate-income families, doing social justice and community building work. ACORN in New Orleans has gutted over 1,200 homes, helping residents get on track to rebuild. They also helped New Orleans residents outside of Louisiana vote in elections.

much a part of New Orleans' history. For that reason, one of its mottos is "Solidarity Not Charity." The volunteer work is demanding. Common Ground expects its volunteers to work at least six days per week, other than those doing manual labor in the Lower Ninth Ward, who work five days per week, six hours per day.[7]

In numerous conversations with Sakura Koné, a staff volunteer with Common Ground, it became evident there were *multiple* complexities displaced residents faced in simply trying to return to their homes (or what had been their homes). In the Lower Ninth Ward, for example, where a majority of displaced residents were homeowners, there was little disposable income. Therefore, when insurance companies were not forthcoming in honoring their policies, and the Road Home money not forthcoming—Sakura estimated at best 30,000 grants out of 180,000 applicants, with most of those 30,000 on the low end of settlement, and insurance companies only paying for wind, not water damage—many factors caused people who were not back to stay in a state of limbo. They simply did not have the necessary means by which they could repair, if their property were damaged, or reconstruct, if it were totally demolished. One of Common Ground's programs, therefore, has been to try to step in and act as caretaker of properties of displaced residents until they are able to generate sufficient funds to return.

Common Ground likes to say '90 percent of displaced residents still hope to return,' but it is really basing this on a determination that 9 out of every 10 people for whom they are caretaking their property want to come home. Common Ground is actually on site looking after 25 properties. Beyond that, while not on site, it is arranging to keep grass cut and debris removed, and have any structure on the property boarded up per city specifications. That currently amounts to over 100 properties. Most properties are in the Lower Ninth Ward, but also the Upper Ninth, some in Central City, and a few in New Orleans East. But the lion's share is in the Lower Ninth.

7. Common Ground Collaborative in New Orleans has a conceptual but no official relation with another Common Ground organization, founded by MacArthur fellow Rosanne Haggerty in 1990, whose mission is to end homelessness through innovative programs that seek to transform people, buildings, and entire communities through the concept of supportive housing (a three-pronged strategy of affordable housing for the homeless and low-income families, outreach to those been homeless the longest, and addressing causes of homelessness. Common Ground has created more than 2,000 units of permanent and transitional housing in New York City, Connecticut, and upstate New York.

Sakura's thoughts and words reflected the emotional gumbo of what life was like in New Orleans, two and one-half years after the storms—a boiling, shifting mixture of hope and promise and ethical fervor blended with a great deal of frustration and disappointment and cynicism. Sakura enumerated the barriers that existed in front of those contemplating return—the physical tasks of trying to maintain a property from a distance; the economic tasks of securing funds for repairs and rebuilding; the bureaucratic tasks of meeting State and City and Board of Health requirements; legal issues involving establishing clear property deeds. All of these also represented the multitude of conditions under which people would easily end up *losing* their property. 'For example,' Sakura pointed out, 'people whose home was totally demolished but who hadn't paid off their mortgage were still required to continue to pay the mortgage or be in default. That's one way people lose their property. Another way is even when a property has been paid off for multiple generations, the property could be lost from failure to cover un-reassessed property taxes.' Sakura added, "And then, of course, the other way is more draconian, because we're talking about tens of thousands of people, you know. The City has the Health Dept do the condemnation. A property falls into disarray and the City condemns the property, then expropriates it. There is a protocol, but it's ridiculous." A citizen may get a thirty-day notice, but many residents do not even receive those notices because the City doesn't have their current address. A displaced person might be in Utah or Nevada or Maine. The City sends out the notice to the last 'known address,' which often is not the appropriate address; the thirty-day notice is never received. Even for those who do receive it, thirty days is not a realistic amount of time for them to get their property in order. The next step after the thirty days is a hearing. "You get a hearing in front of a hearing officer, and you have to show cause why you have not kept up your property. But again, here we go, they send the hearing notice to the last known address, and some don't even hear about the hearing." Some people come themselves, but most cannot afford the trip. So, people get a family member or a neighbor or a friend who is in New Orleans to go and try to defend their situation at the hearing. Unfortunately, economic hardship is not a defense. "You gotta come up with something else: *I was in an accident in California and I wasn't able to get down here,* or *I was in a hospital.* So even if someone shows up for the hearing in their stead, the deck is stacked against them, and they stand to lose even at the hearing." Whether they lose by actually being at the hearing, or by someone there in their stead, or lose by default by not being there, they lose. The final analysis is that they lose, and the property is turned over to the New Orleans Redevelopment Authority (NORA). The New Orleans Redevelopment Authority supposedly makes a good faith effort to contact the resident and negotiate a price to purchase the property. "If they're successful in reaching the resident, they say *Well we're here to negotiate a cost for your property, we want to purchase your property.* NORA is a strange animal: NORA is a public *and* private entity. On the one hand it's public in that it's contracted by the City; on the other hand it's private in that it's investment for either property purchase or investment for what the property is expropriated for. NORA has the means to develop the property itself, if it's primo property."

> *For people who lived in New Orleans it has unraveled*
> *and we are all spread across the country. I am pretty sad*
> *about the whole thing. I'm at least 5th generation New*
> *Orleanian,*
> *so I want to go back no matter what. I fear for the future,*
> *when everything gets torn down and property speculators*
> *come in and buy it all up. What a f***ing mess.*

(Displaced former resident of New Orleans)

Sakura explained how NORA purchases conveniently end up working to meet the interests of developers. "NORA knows the Rebuild New Orleans Commission appointed by the Mayor is stacked mostly with big economic interests on the board. There are three grassroots representatives on the board, but six representing the big economic interests. So, even if Common Ground had the means, we could not keep up tens of thousands of properties; we're a grassroots organization. If we had the means, the people, the power, the economics, it would still be too enormous a job for us to do by ourselves."

Common Ground's primary work to maintain properties for displaced residents involves grass cutting, keeping debris off the property, and making sure structures are boarded up in the required way. They do this work not just for residential properties, but for small businesses as well. The funding they receive is used mostly for equipment and housing volunteers. But another part of Common Ground is involved with training people in the neighborhoods with critical skills for all aspects of building and reconstruction: electricians, and bringing in journeymen electricians to teach apprentices; journeymen carpenters to teach apprentices; journeymen plumbers to teach apprentices. Sakura indicated they had sixty young people already signed up who wanted to do something towards actual rebuilding. But surprisingly, he said, jobs for local people had not been forthcoming. Even though New Orleans was the biggest boomtown in America right now for reconstruction, they weren't hiring local people. To hire local people, they had to pay them a fair market wage—between $12 and $15 dollars an hour. Instead, contractors were bringing in immigrant workers and paying them $6 an hour. "And they lie to them," Sakura said. "They tell these immigrant workers they're going to get $10 an hour, but when they get here they find out it's only $6 an hour. They tell immigrant workers in Mexico or Salvador or Honduras or the Dominican Republic that room and board is going to be provided, but the workers get here and find out they've got to pay their own room and board out of the $6 an hour." These workers are called 'H-2 workers.'[8] These imported workers had been used primarily in Florida, where Jamaicans and Trinidadians were brought in. But the upshot is that there have been few construction jobs for local people . . . unless they were really skilled professionals they couldn't find among immigrants. "If a skilled professional had the time and energy, he could work 24 hours a day; there's that much work. So Common Ground is launching this skills training program as part of its 'community adoption' program. Providing construction skills training and education so local people are able to get a job." Getting finances for repair and reconstruction to make housing available; pushing for adequate healthcare facilities. These are the two big determining factors for people coming back. "And both of these elements are suffering tremendously."

Sakura expressed the increasing need for Common Ground's transition from simple grassroots concerns about property care and construction skills training to the larger arena of social justice. Common Ground had become especially involved with issues of public housing. Sakura recounted, how, before Common Ground even assessed the damage after the storm, there were meetings about plans for what they wanted to

8. H-2 workers refers generally to temporary alien labor permitted visas to meet temporary needs. U.S. employers may petition for skilled or unskilled alien workers to meet temporary or seasonal positions for which qualified U.S. workers are not available. An H-2A classification applies to seasonal agricultural employment; H-2B applies to non-agricultural employment. There is currently an annual cap of 66,000 visas for H-2B workers; none for H-2A workers.

do about public housing. "The hurricane," he said, "and I use that term loosely, because this was a man-made disaster ... they needed an excuse to eliminate public housing in New Orleans and this situation afforded them an excuse. That's the bottom line." Sakura referred to a commonly quoted remark by one Congressman who said, *We've been trying to do away with public housing for years, and here God has done it for us.*

The solutions to the return of 'remote voices' now became more muddy than the Mississippi. From the post-disaster darkness emerged the interconnections between the bureaucratic complexities standing between displaced families and their return, and all the antecedent, unresolved political issues that extended well beyond matters of individual property. Public housing was just one node of the nexus of problems. "There's equal opportunity disenfranchisement. They'll disenfranchise private property owners; they'll disenfranchise public housing residents, who are mostly African American. Even if Lafitte[9] is kept, they will find a way to turn it into mixed use—which is just a euphemism for only getting a token amount of housing. The bottom line is ethnic cleansing, getting rid of poor black people, turning essentially what was a purple state ... this state was not red or blue ... into a red state. So you can have your cake and eat it too. You can ethnically cleanse, get rid of all these black people, transform the state into a red state, and make a lot of money in the process."

The reasoning *seemed* to fit the politics. You now had a Republican Governor. You now had a mostly white City Council, one that hadn't been white in over thirty years. Probably the next mayor was going to be white as well. So a shift in political power was coming about. But was the picture complete?

Common Ground's function as a liaison between displaced residents living outside New Orleans and their properties in the city has given its volunteers a fairly good read of the factors that determine who will eventually return. In Sakura's thinking, after five years away, living in another state, the likelihood of someone's coming back "diminishes to slim to none." That is one of the reasons he hopes it can be proven there is, effectively, a 'conspiracy connection' between insurance companies and FEMA. Keeping rebuilding funds out of people's hands keeps them in other states, other cities. "So then back at the ranch, the city government

---

9. One of the four major public housing developments HUD plans to raze.

is condemning their property and taking it. Whether you say that's coincidence or conspiracy, it has the same effect."

Sakura feels that, for older displaced residents, as well as for families with young children, after housing, the availability of primary care health centers is the critical factor in the decision to return. Yet there is no major hospital or ER east of the Industrial Canal. Common Ground may have only eight homes they have managed to raise funds for so far. "But what percentage of healthcare facilities have been reopened? At best maybe 35 or 40 percent of the original health facilities. I'm talking private *and* public. But people need health facilities most of all."

In Sakura's thinking, 'cluster housing' proposals are mainly a concept—but a dangerous one, "another way to detach people from their properties." The City's pecking order for reconstruction "was set from Day One." The first priority was the French Quarter, the Garden District, and parts of Uptown. The second were areas for business and more tourism. "And then, guess what, the third priority area is *not* a priority. It's called *yet to be determined.* That's exactly where developers are in house with NORA and the Rebuild New Orleans folk. They know where the concentration is going to be for hotels, casinos, golf courses, industrial parks. They want to industrialize parts of the Lower Ninth Ward. And in the few instances where they *are* going to build houses, they're going to be condominiums. So a modest $150,000 home will be replaced by a $300,000 or $400,000 condominium. But if you build upward, you can put twenty or thirty of them in one building. Now, multiply twenty or thirty times $300,000. That's economic cleansing."

Some of the tone one hears has the feel of cynicism, the belief that the country has been lulled to sleep, that it suffers from 'Katrina fatigue.' But most of it comes from genuine fear—the widespread angst that sees a future city changing on the basis of economic development, high rise condominiums; a city totally different from the one grown up in. The real uniqueness of New Orleans has always lived in its neighborhoods, in the passion of its streets. It surprises many people that the Lower Ninth Ward has one of the highest homeowner rates in the city. Outside of New Orleans, people hear only about how impoverished the Lower Ninth was. But despite the fact it is working class and poor, part of the picture representing this and other neighborhoods of New Orleans has conveniently been left out. Certain political forces want to make sure the American public equates poverty with welfare. In the emptiness of vacant, still struggling neighborhoods, that incomplete picture of reality can take hold just as easily as all the eloquent expressions of hope and optimism.

People are still hurting here. The destruction is all over and the rich white folks across town are going on with their lives as if nothing was happening. But people here are still dying, if not physically, then emotionally. By talking with them, we heal each others' wounds—mine from feeling powerless when I was in Virginia, and theirs, by having someone listen to their stories of what they went through.

(James Madison University student, Spring, 2006)[10]

UUSC Gulf Coast Relief

One example of relief response initiatives from *en dehors*—outside Louisiana—is the Unitarian Universalist Service Committee's (UUSC) Gulf Coast Relief Program, run in collaboration with the Unitarian Universalist Association (UUA), the organization that represents Unitarian Universalist congregations in North America and elsewhere in the world. Two years after the hurricanes, at a special commemorative event in the Lower Ninth Ward, Mary Croom Fontenot, director of All Congregations Together (ACT).[11] The occasion of the second anniversary of Katrina was used to announce the launch of the Resurrection Project, a new initiative designed to speed the delivery of building materials, furniture, food and other necessities by training local residents to serve as a

---

10. Posted on http://www.peoplesorganizing.org/bn_reports.html. The objective of the People's Organizing Committee and Fund is to build a coordinated network of community leaders, organizers, and community based organizations with the organizational infrastructure to meet the needs of people most impacted by Katrina, and facilitate an organizing process that will demand local, grassroots leadership in the relief, return and reconstruction process in New Orleans.

11. All Congregations Together (ACT) is a congregation-based, non-profit organization established in 1991 that is committed to helping families and communities empower themselves to improve the quality of life in Greater New Orleans. The organization is richly diverse, white and black, rich and poor, and includes people of all faiths. The group's priorities are driven neighborhood community's needs, and focus on crime, education, economic development, and housing. Because the majority of neighborhoods it serves are largely African American, with women serving as heads of households, ACT strives to engage female African American pastors where possible. Pre-Katrina, ACT had 15 member congregations; one year later, the number had grown to 32.

clearing house for donated goods. ACT has partnered with the UUSC for the past two years through its JustWorks camps[12] and the UUA-UUSC Gulf Coast Relief Program.

The UUSC's Gulf Coast Response Coordinator, Quo Vadis Breaux, has said that more than 1,000 volunteers organized by the UUSC and Unitarian Universalist churches in New Orleans and Baton Rouge have helped survivors to return to their homes. The UUSC and the UUA has worked with as many as forty community organizations along the entire Gulf Coast. Liberal religious organizations like the UUA and its Moderator, Gina Courter, have not been hesitant to condemn the failure of governmental agencies to respond adequately to the worst natural disaster in U.S. history.

Recent UUA-UUSC volunteers working in New Orleans have included a group of teenagers from inner-city Boston neighborhoods who are part of a youth program of the Unitarian Universalist Urban Ministry, and a group of congregational leaders from Virginia, North Carolina, South Carolina, Tennessee, Georgia, organized by the UUA's Thomas Jefferson District. Their physical labor has included working on rehabilitating homes as well as creating a ball-playing field for youth.

Getting back into a house has been the greatest obstacle for most lower-income Gulf Coast residents. An example of how Project Resurrection has reached out to displaced residents are the Brown family of four, who have resided in the Lower Ninth Ward for fourteen years. Mrs. Brown is a nurse assistant; her husband a self-employed carpenter, currently unable to work because of an injury. In the wake of the failure of the levees, the Brown family exhausted nearly all of their financial resources trying to return and rebuild. The Browns also struggled with finding adequate health care. Project Resurrection volunteers recently helped the family repair, paint, and furnish their living room, bedroom, dining room, and kitchen. Mrs. Brown recently returned to school to become a registered nurse and increase the family's income.[13]

---

12. JustWorks camps are short-term projects that help volunteers understand the causes and damaging effects of injustice. Participants work directly with people in the communities they serve, learning about human rights issues, and are taught advocacy skills to address issues of poverty, discrimination, and racism.

13. See the UUSC website, www.uusc.org, for further accounts of this and other work along the Gulf Coast.

Perhaps the best understanding of the nature of 'hope' in the work voluntary organizations are doing to help displaced residents return to their city, the UUSC acknowledges, is that hope proceeds one step at a time, one person at a time, one family at a time. Volunteers can only paint or put up drywall one room at a time. The sense of progress is glacial. But there is progress. And, for many, there is hope. If a house is to become a home, it needs more than floors and walls and furniture. With the help of volunteer organizations of every ethnic group and faith and strata of society, the houses of New Orleans have a chance to become true homes.

But *does* the sense of hope sounded here by the UUSC, by outsiders who may participate in week-long volunteer efforts balance the previous picture of frustrations and fatigue of those who live the reality every day? This question itself should not diminish the many efforts to help New Orleans and other hurricane ravaged communities by those who are 'outsiders' only as a consequence of geography, not their hearts. Yet the citizens displaced by the hurricanes are 'outsiders' as well, even if *forced* to live in exile. Just how does one sort out the many conflicting pictures of what is true and what is myth in the complex world of recovery and reconstruction of New Orleans and South Louisiana? Perhaps part of the truth—the missing parts of the picture of now vacant neighborhoods—must lie in the 'remote voices' of displaced residents themselves.

These are voices that have been captured in a number of projects, by physicians, by university academics, by individual poets. More than simply creating a legacy of what people experienced, it may ultimately be in the of acts sharing the stories people have to tell that the raw and complex nature of truth may be found. It is to some of those stories we now turn.

Oral Histories

One of more powerful forms of information preservation that arose in the aftermath of Hurricanes Katrina and Rita were a number of Oral Histories projects that captured the stories and experiences of those affected by the storms. While these collected stories might not have had immediate use as a means to help displaced residents return, they have long-term value as personal records, and as a repository of knowledge about how people react to such unprecedented events. In addition, if shared, they might come to have value in helping create networks of communication among displaced persons—while in the 'diaspora' as well as when back home. In hearing the stories of others, there are contained values one might share, decisions one might emulate. The sharing of stories, therefore, can form one basis of shared *community*—in some respects as it had been for veterans returning home from World War II. Those returning to their old New Orleans neighborhoods can say, in effect: *we've all been through hell, we know what living in exile is, so we can damn sure rebuild this place and call it home again.*

The idea of collecting oral histories—especially after traumatic or heartbreaking events—is not new. It is, in fact, part of the core process of Critical Incident Stress Management, discussed earlier in *Walking to New Orleans* as historical background to the concept of Participatory Design. Telling the story of what one has experienced, what one has perceived, during chaotic and painful circumstances in a peer-supported and non-judgmental context has been found to be of great value in helping those in public service and the military return to normal life. Soldiers, police, firefighters, EMTs, who experience the results of violence, trauma, and unanticipated natural disaster on a daily basis have been able to come to terms with their experiences on an emotional level, and learn healthy (vs. unhealthy) ways to guide their responses. The process begins through recounting individual stories—and helps speed the return of needed personnel to their services as functioning individuals.

Early forms of Oral Histories may be found in the oral traditions of Hebrew Scripture as well as in the sacred writings of other faiths. They are central to the belief systems of indigenous peoples; they are found in epic poetry and folklore as well. The recounting of Oral Histories often takes on the role of preserving cultural and historical values to be passed on to inform the way of life of succeeding generations.

I first became struck with the potential healing or 'redemptive' power of 'telling one's story' through developing a course on the Holocaust for mostly Jewish students at Skidmore College. For many of Jewish background of the previous generation, the events of the Holocaust had forced a crisis of faith. It directly called into question the ability to continue speak of Yahweh as the God who *acted* in the history of Israel. Since one's relation to divine reality, as a Jew, was so intensely a *personal* encounter,[14] the failure of God to act in the history of the Jews doomed to extermination during World War II was simultaneously, for many, a loss of the personal

---

14. The *Ich-Du* relationship Martin Buber identified as that which can exist between a human being and God.

core of one's religiousness, of one's spiritual identity. The devastation was so immense that when those in the concentration camps pleaded to have Allied Forces bomb the camps[15] out of existence so at least no more Jews could be sent there, that plea was effectively taking God's action into one's own hands. The Holocaust became a profound spiritual crisis—one many Jews have never overcome—making ambiguous the very intelligibility of the concept of divine transcendence. The spiritual range of stories of Holocaust survivors was enormous. Some stories revealed those who continued to relate to God, but now found anger a legitimate mode of spiritual relationship. Other stories reflected the conclusion that the human and the divine must be on a moral par—some actually saying, on Yom Kippur, "You, O Lord, have committed grievous sins. So have I. Perhaps we should call it even." Some stories removed the teller from the sphere of the divine altogether, finding only the blackness of a spiritual hole. But in all these cases, the sheer act of *telling the story* of one's experience of the Holocaust itself became an act of personal, spiritual *meaning*. It might not bring God back into one's religious life, but it expressed one's religiousness, *where it stood*. Telling the story, again and again, was also the proclamation: *never again.*[16]

I have also experienced the healing power of 'telling one's story' while serving as Chaplain at several Boston hospitals, working especially with elderly patients who were terminally ill, and also as a member of the Bristol-Norfolk County (MA) Critical Incident Stress Management Team, debriefing firefighters and police who have experienced the horrors of their professions. Where there are people with stories that need to be told, and no one to listen, one *must* be there to listen.

Finally, in the course of my current teaching with students at the University of Massachusetts in Boston—students whose unique back-

---

15. Pieces of information regarding Auschwitz, for example, had reached the Allies, beginning with reports in 1941 from Witold Pilecki, who had volunteered to be imprisoned, until his escape in 1943, and more detailed reports from two escaped prisoners, Rudolf Vrba and Alfred Wetzler in 1944. After letters reached both Roosevelt and Churchill from Slovakian Rabbi Michael Ber Weissmandl in May of 1944, there was a growing campaign to persuade the Allies to bomb Auschwitz. The question of why the Allies failed to bomb Auschwitz continues to be explored.

16. An important warning in teaching about the Holocaust—and by extension the use of any stories of deep emotional trauma and spiritual turmoil—is that if you lead someone down into an emotional abyss and spiritual darkness, you must be prepared to lead them out.

grounds and families often represent a most incredible diversity of race, culture, ethnicity, geography, and religious or spiritual beliefs (or their absence)—I had developed a small program to engage them in their own project of capturing Oral Histories. This experimental research project sought to capture oral expressions of what could be referred to as 'lived religion'—that is, beyond compressed theologies uttered in creeds, beyond ritual practices done in the context of institutional bodies, what were those religious and spiritual structures of meaning *as they existed in the actual lives of individuals* and *as they were expressed in the personal stories and shared oral accounts* in which religious and spiritual values were embodied. The idea was for students to discover the symbols, mythic narratives, and personal ritual practices elicited in those stories that constituted how an individual's religious and spiritual meanings were formed, shared, and passed on to others—not only within family structures, but also to the immediate community, and from one generation to the next. With an explanation of methodology and suitable ethical and interpersonal guidelines, students engaged both people they knew and strangers to capture first-hand accounts of these Oral Histories.[17] Relative to their use as an approach to community rebuilding and social healing, it was important that students did not see themselves as 'conducting an interview' in the sense of collecting data for some quantitative study. Rather, they were shown ways to use selected techniques drawn from the fields of Anthropology, Field Ethnography, and other Social Sciences that could be used to 'sound out' perceptions of many things, ranging from social structures to expressions of religious and spiritual meaning directly from

17. One of the secondary goals was to explore the extent to which religious and spiritual meanings were dynamic and individualized. One standard assumption has been that faith traditions that are visible in societies establish varying degrees of stability in religious and spiritual values; however, throughout history and increasingly in our own time, individuals express perceptions of the world that are uniquely their own—different from and even independent of the perceptions and values of the culture in which they live. Even individuals and families who are active participants in a particular faith tradition may nevertheless adapt many beliefs and practices to the circumstances of their own lives. Thus, one hypothesis of the project was that such *adaptive* beliefs and praxis often find expression in the personal anecdotes of experiences occurring at the boundaries of meaning in our lives: birth, growth, marriage, divorce, illness, death. Some adaptive beliefs and praxis may derive from interaction with other faith traditions; some may be uniquely formed within the context of individual or family life. By hearing oral accounts of such *lived* beliefs and praxis, it then becomes possible to consider the extent to which such accounts represent an independent layer of religious and spiritual meaning—one that may differ considerably from common understandings of what it means to be a believer or person of faith.

the individuals or groups involved. The core methodology was anecdotal: letting people "tell it like it is" in their own terms, using their own words and concepts. Thus, the method made use of open-ended questions and interest-based probing in a manner not unlike how a Chaplain might listen to a patient. The purpose was to generate conversation, to elicit and clarify, not to push for immediate conclusions.

A number of Oral Histories projects have tried to capture the stories of the survivors and displaced residents of Hurricanes Katrina and Rita. The following are some of them. The Hurricane Katrina Community Advisory Group at Harvard Medical School's Department of Health Care Policy collected oral histories covering the time between the initial announcement of a coming hurricane to the period when interviews were conducted through March, 2006. The Katrina Video Ethnography Project, based at Louisiana State University's Department of Sociology, is a long-term effort to investigate the causes and effects of the hurricane, and includes over eighty videotaped interviews with displaced persons collected in parking lots and shelters by a team of students and faculty; the project intends to follow individuals, organizations, and legal actions for a ten-year period. The I-10 Witness Project is a community-based story collective administered by the New Orleans production company, Mondo Bizarro, to document narratives of people in the aftermath of the storms in order to create a forum where citizens can voice their concerns about reconstruction. The Library of Congress Oral History Project for Hurricane Survivors works with folklorists at the University of Houston and the University of Texas, Austin, to train academic survivors in tape recording stories to be used for further research. The National Policy & Advocacy Council on Homelessness[18] created a Katrina-Rita Oral History Project that uses audio clips and profiles to better understand the challenges that face those having been forced to abandon their homes. Other similar projects exist at Texas A&M, Middle Tennessee State University, and the Louisiana Folklife Program.[19]

18. The National Policy and Advocacy Council on Homelessness is a grass roots anti-poverty organization whose mission is to ensure that national homelessness policy accurately reflects the needs and experiences of local communities.

19. Descriptions of these and other projects available at the University of Texas Center for Social Work Research Hurricane Recovery Collaborative www.utexas.edu/research/cswr/Katrina/oralhistory.html.

One project was a volunteer effort largely the work of Abe Louise Young, a poet and activist, native of New Orleans' Mid-City neighborhood, and a graduate of Smith College, Northwestern, and the University of Texas at Austin, with help from Kevin Bush, a native of the Lower Ninth Ward, Second Chief in the Flaming Arrows Mardi Gras Indian Tribe. Kevin had been incarcerated in prison, but also served as a mentor to troubled youth. Young's project, "Alive in Truth: The New Orleans Disaster Oral History and Memory Project" records histories of those affected by Hurricane Katrina as a way to help restore community bonds and uphold the voices and rights of those whose voices need an outlet.[20]

Perhaps it is Abe Young's literary ability as a poet; perhaps it was her having heard survivor's stories as an unofficial Red Cross volunteer at the Austin Convention Center; perhaps it was her own background, as coming from a large, extended New Orleans family of 167 cousins, most of whom lived in New Orleans, that gave her the sensitivity to hear and record accounts of those in pain. As a college student, Young had interviewed Holocaust survivors and rescuers as part of a human rights exchange, the Danish-American Dialogue for Human Rights. What is striking in so many of the accounts 'Alive in Truth' has captured is journalism raised to the level of poetry without distortion of the truth. I urge readers to examine these accounts. The following summarizes the flavor of one of them, and suggests that sometimes 'the truth' between hope and despair lies in the unadorned details.

> Eartherine, a 48 year old woman from the Lower Ninth Ward, after having been told hoodlums and gang members from the First Ward were terrorizing people in New Orleans' Convention Center and thinking she should not go there with her husband, recounts: "So we just sit still for a while and I said, 'So what are we gonna do.' And I said, 'Well, the Bible say "If you don't know what do to, stand still"'... So we just sat there on the bridge, thinking and talking to people ...A lady, she didn't have anything but what she had on. So I told her, 'I'm gonna go ahead and get you some clothes.' I asked her what size and she told me. The clothes was really too big for me. So then I understood why God had me to take those clothes. You know, because they were too big for me, but that was her size. So I brought them to her, I told her they was kind of damp. I told

20. Details about the project can be accessed at www.aliveintruth.org.

her, 'So I'm gonna lay them on a chair for you. Maybe they'll dry in time enough for you to change out of your old clothes.'"[21]

This second story is one related directly to me. It is a fragment of a considerably longer account shared by a displaced resident and her two children. They ended up deciding not to return to New Orleans—at least for the time being.

> On my way out of Louisiana I stopped in Texas. There was a parade in which people were dressed up like Eeyore (from Winnie the Pooh). I thought any place that could embrace and celebrate the Eeyore aspects of oneself is the kind of place I'd like to live. I wanted to get married again and raise my two children there, but later I ended up working at Canyonlands. Now, Island in the Sky mesa is my church and the Needles are like the pipes of my organ. It is a place where I feel at-oneness most powerfully. There are time-sculpted rocks there—a particular spot where there are three rocks that resemble turtles. One reminds me of my belief in the earth mother and the two smaller ones look like my children. There is a natural flat stone that I use as a bench to sit on while I meditate. I believe in a very spiritual universe. One dream sums up what I believe. In this dream I was waitressing outside on a porch and I was looking up at the moon. It turned into a ball of electric energy and I was reaching to touch it when I got shot out of earth into space and watched as an asteroid shot down into the ocean. A voice in space was telling me that the reason for the asteroid was because we were destroying the planet. Tidal waves covered the planet and I could see the dolphins swimming and jumping in the water. I heard them squeaking "It's our turn now" over and over again.[22]

In the end, it may be necessary to find some way to balance one-sided pictures of frustrations and fatigue with those of hope and optimism. Stories that represent only one extreme or the other in the spectrum of the experience of tragedy, and attempts to recover, are simplifications of conflicting emotional complexities. They turn reality into a *huis clos* that *precludes* the possibility of authentic future actions. Options that have become polarized—where efforts are either *pointless,* because frustrations justify the cessation of action, or *gratuitous,* because optimistic gestures are self-satisfying but change little—lead to dead ends. In either case, one

21. Archived at the New Zealand Digital Library, the University of Waikato, http://nzdl.sadl.uleth.ca/cgi-bin/library.

22. Several minor details have been altered to preserve anonymity.

winds up with homes that remain unclaimed and neighborhoods largely vacant, devoid of life. It is better to acknowledge that every failure embodies successes, and every success is fraught with frequent failures.

There are an infinite number of ways one could imagine the salvation of a city and its neighborhoods. Perhaps even the bizarre contain seeds of unrealized possibilities. One young woman, a displaced resident of Bayou St. John, said she imagined the stories of displaced persons *themselves* having social force. She envisioned the collective stories of the experiences of former inhabitants gathered in one place within the city, and the voices of their tellers brought to life all at once. They would constitute a community *of voices* capable of sharing their deepest feelings. The events on which the trust of neighbors each had known for years, perhaps generations, had been built would be retold. Heard would be the passion to rebuild what they once had. Frustrations and unrealized hopes would exist as well, but now they would be *in their right place*. They would be home.

In the final chapter we return to where Hurricanes Katrina and Rita first made landfall, and where the first intrusions into the lives of South Louisiana took place—the small coastal communities that exist on the very edges of the Gulf. Surely there were factors disrupting those lives before these storms, as well as those that occurred as a result of them. Among the most vulnerable residents of those communities have been members of the United Houma Nation and the several bands of the Biloxi-Chitimacha Indians. We hear some of their stories, and those of others whose economies and Gulf-dependent lives are undergoing great changes, with even more changes on the horizon in the future. We also hear thoughts from scientists at the research community of LUMCON[23] at Cocodrie. And we will return once more to contemplate the messages of the fragile natural environment to which these human lives cling.

23. The Louisiana Universities Marine Consortium.

Isle de Jean Charles

Dulac

10

Beyond Terrebonne

D AVE ADAMS FLIES HELICOPTERS out of Galveston, Lafayette, and Fourchon to the offshore oil rigs, some as far out as 90 miles. Dave is also a member of the congregation I serve, All Souls, in Braintree, Massachusetts, which means he is away from his family for weeks at a time—exaggerating the typical 14 days on, 14 days off work schedule on rigs. Heli flights are offshore and back, but even more frequently from rig to rig, often involving refueling and overnights on the rig. Piloting is generally done by GPS, but Dave explained how the Gulf area was also divided into 3-mile by 3-mile grids, with rig helipads numbered to correspond with the grid number, e.g., Galveston 255. Coming in under often windy conditions can be tricky, watching out for crane structures, even with elevated helidecks.[1] Tower structures are of several different types. They include Tension Leg Platforms (TLPs), consisting of a floating deck structure anchored to pile heads on the sea floor by long pipes kept under tension, used in water depths greater than 300 meters, and SPARs used in very deep water exploration. But the most common offshore platforms on the Louisiana and Texas coasts are Fixed Tower Structures, with 4-leg, 6-leg, and 8-leg versions, used in water depths typically less than 150 meters. New platforms must be designed to adhere to stricter standards than older platforms. The American Petroleum Institute criteria (API RP-2A 20th edition, Supplement 1) defines three hurricane "Exposure Category Levels" for the Gulf of Mexico. Level L-1 is a "full population hurricanes" design; Level L-2 "sudden hurricanes" design; Level L-3 "winter storms"

---

1. Winds are a mixed blessing. On flights between rigs, high winds can be bothersome; on the other hand, when landing and talking off from a rig with a heavy load, winds exert a force that can actually make landings and takeoffs easier. Still again, if winds cause the rig to sway back and forth, making the markings on the helideck move around, the pilot must fix on the horizon and 'feel' the copter touch down.

design. If a platform does not have significant onboard oil or gas storage facilities, even though it is manned, it is regarded as at the lower Level L-2, since its destruction would be of lower consequence (after evacuation). Everyone, pilots and all passengers, must take a water survival course.

Flying over miles and miles of marshes and wetlands bayous, Dave has a comprehensive view of what we on the ground see only in fragments. The air reveals patterns of keyhole canals where rigs once stood, the myriad of straight cuts for pipelines; the longer reaches of navigational channels and the emaciated remains of barrier islands. Winds constantly carve patterns in the long sea grasses, and out on the horizon of the Gulf, the ever present thunderclouds. Flying above LA 82 that runs east from Sabine Pass at the Texas border one can make out widely separated tiny villages—or what is left of them after Hurricane Rita: Johnsons Bayou, Constance Beach, Holly Beach, Cameron, Creole, Grand Chenier. In a few instances he could see houses on top of quite permanent-looking concrete pilings, the pilings likely worth far more money than the house itself. But most of those elevated houses or trailers were roofless and windowless and as empty as those houses whose empty shells had stood on the sand.

Dave found that the Texans he shuttled had rather negative opinions of people from Louisiana, especially those 'south of I-10.' They did not think these bayou inhabitants were as sophisticated as people from Texas; called them 'Coon-asses'—a pejorative epithet used to refer to Cajuns (though sometimes treated as a badge of ethnic pride by working-class males). The origins of the term remain obscure, including claims by the late Louisiana Congressman James R. "Jimmy" Domengeaux, asked in 1968 by Gov. John McKeithen to serve as president of CODOFIL (Council for the Development of French in Louisiana). His argument that the term was derived from the French slang *connasse* (an offensive word for a woman) has not been widely accepted. Dave heard the word come up amidst derisive laughter about their 'stupid way of life, always getting into fights,' as his passengers peered down on the marshes and bayous and saw tiny ramshackle houses and fishing camps on stilts scattered about, unconnected to solid ground by roads or electricity. Yet the same passengers Dave carried might themselves be bearing the scars—physical or emotional—of having recently been in fights. In fact, a few days before they leave to go offshore, fights will often occur between the men and their women. Something stupid or petty comes up, it degrades into a verbal battle, then more. It becomes a ritual of grieving at forced separations.

Often, the arguments would be picked right up again in the first days after the spouse had returned from offshore. The husband finds himself barking commands at his wife and kids without even thinking, because he was a supervisor offshore, used to telling his crew to get to work over the noise of the machinery.

Coastal Louisiana, however, had far more concerns looming on the horizon than the newly invigorated oil and gas industry that followed the 'diplomacy' of the Iraq War. What loomed from the depths of the Gulf itself was the contemplation of aquaculture.

Aquaculture Take One

On May 30, 2007, the Louisiana Legislature approved a document entitled "Integrated Ecosystem Restoration and Hurricane Protection: Louisiana's Comprehensive Master Plan for a Sustainable Coast." This document represented the Coastal Protection and Restoration Authority of Louisiana's (CPRA) master plan for coastal restoration and hurricane protection, the first document to completely incorporate hurricane protection projects with those aimed at rebuilding the state's rapidly eroding coastal wetlands. Reflecting more than eighteen months of research and input from both stakeholders and the scientific communities, the plan is intended to serve as the guide for all coastal restoration and hurricane protection efforts in Louisiana over the next several decades. In January of 2008, newly elected Governor Bobby Jindal signed an executive order to maximize efficiency in this work. Jindal's order effectively gave the Master Plan even greater authority by requiring all State agencies to comply with the plan, and to adhere to the projects and priorities enumerated in it. CPRA, for the first time in Louisiana's history, became the single state authority responsible for integrating coastal restoration work, including the resources of the Department of Transportation and Development (DOTD) and the Department of Natural Resources (DNR).[2]

While some level of cooperation and shared direction in addressing the needs of Louisiana's coastal region appeared to be emerging at long last with the passage of this Master Plan, other elements of disharmony were arising from further offshore in the Gulf. As the demand for protein in the United States has increased, with nearly 75 percent of seafood con-

2. CPRA was established by Act 8 of the First Extraordinary Session of the Legislature in 2005.

sumed being imported from other countries, commercial wild-capture fishing has been unable to meet the growing demand. Consequently, the National Oceanic and Atmospheric Administration (NOAA) has been promoting offshore aquaculture—growing finfish in semi-submerged nets or cages, with other techniques for shellfish, between three and 200 miles from shore.

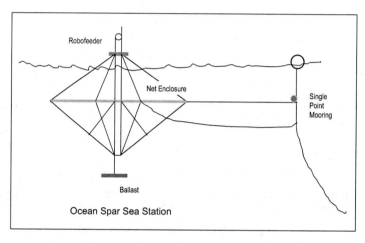

More recently, NOAA has sought to establish large-scale deepwa-ter fish farming in the Gulf of Mexico. Since January, 2007, the Gulf of Mexico Fishery Management Council (GMFMC)[3] has been developing a plan to streamline the permitting and regulation of deepwater aqua-culture. In March, 2007, officials of NOAA announced the news that the Bush administration was launching an effort to transform the way Americans raise and consume fish. In a final report dated December 7, 2007,[4] GMFMC, along with NOAA's National Marine Fisheries Service released for a series of public hearings during the week of December 10[5] a Public Hearing Draft of a proposed generic amendment to the Gulf of Mexico Fishery Management Council's red drum, reef fish, and stone crab

3. One of eight regional councils established by Congress to manage U.S. fisheries in federal waters, including aquaculture.

4. Karen Hoak at the Council's office in Tampa said the earliest versions of the pro-posal were made public in 2004; the amendment itself in April, 2005. No substantive changes were made to the Council's list of actions or alternatives since the November 20, 2007 draft. As of this writing in January, 2008, the Council now expects to hold further hearings in February, with completion and approval of the amendment in April, 2008.

5. They took place in Tampa, New Orleans (Kenner), Biloxi, Mobile, and Houston.

fishery management plans, and the Gulf of Mexico and South Atlantic Fishery Management Council's joint spiny lobster and coastal migratory pelagics fishery management plans.[6] The hearing draft included a programmatic environmental impact statement (PEIS) and a social impact assessment. The ultimate goal of the amendment was to maximize benefits to the nation by establishing a regional permitting process to manage the development of environmentally sound and economically sustainable aquaculture industry—in short, to increase the maximum sustainable yield (MSY) of federal fisheries in the Gulf by supplementing the harvest of wild-caught species with cultured products.

It was complexities hidden in the concept of 'supplementing' that quickly arose to be problematic. Unanticipated mixings of cultured with wild-caught species as a consequence of the release of cultured species from storm-damaged netted enclosures, and the antibiotics and chemicals used in the production of cultured species, were among those key issues that raised fear and distrust among many Louisiana commercial fishermen and shrimpers.

The GMAHD report was equivocal about its ability to assess the social impacts of aquaculture. Social impacts, according to its guidelines, included alterations to the ways in which people live, work, play, relate to one another, organize as members of a society; they also assess changes in values and beliefs that affect the way people identify themselves within their occupation and community.[7] The GMAHD report admitted that in attempting to assess the social impacts of the proposed amendment, there was an overall lack of literature and data available regarding the social impacts of offshore aquaculture in the Gulf of Mexico. There was no baseline data on each Gulf coast fishing community that would allow comparisons

6. Gulf of Mexico Fishery Management Council and National Marine Fisheries Service, National Oceanic & Atmospheric Administration, Public Hearing Draft. Generic Amendment: The Gulf of Mexico Fishery Management Council's Red Drum, Reef Fish, and Stone Crab Fishery Management Plans and the Gulf of Mexico and South Atlantic Fishery Management Council's Joint Spiny Lobster and Coastal Migratory Pelagics Fishery Management Plans. To Provide for Regulation of Offshore Marine Aquaculture (Including a Draft Programmatic Environmental Impact Statement, Initial Regulatory Flexibility Analysis and Regulatory Impact Review), December, 2007 (Hereafter abbreviated as GMAHD, Gulf of Mexico Aquaculture Hearing Draft).

7. Interorganizational Committee on Guidelines and Principles for Social Impact Assessment, National Marine Fisheries Service, National Oceanic and Atmospheric Administration, U.S. Department of Justice, "Guidelines and Principles for Social Impact Assessment," May, 1994.

pre- and post- the introduction of aquaculture, nor specific information on what aquaculture firms might come to exist under the amendment. "Therefore, there is no information to assess whether Gulf coastal communities will benefit or be harmed by their existence."[8]

The eight actions proposed in the report, with alternatives for each action, included what types of aquaculture permits would be required; their duration and conditions; species allowed for aquaculture; and the designation of sites and buffer zones for aquaculture facilities. The preferred alternatives for the latter (Actions 6 and 7) would establish site criteria, reviewed by NOAA and other federal agencies, rather than allow sites anywhere, but they did not establish zones that would restrict access around an aquaculture facility by prohibiting fishing vessels from entering the area.

In considerations of largely economic impact, the report looked at five "fishing-dependent" communities in some detail. The Magnuson-Stevens Fisher Conservation and Management Act (MSFCM), as amended in 1996, defined such a community as one substantially dependent on or engaged in the harvesting or processing of fishery resources, and includes fishing vessel owners, operators, and crews, and U.S. fish processors based in the community.[9] The Generic Essential Fish Habitat Amendment (GMFMC 2004) provided more extensive characterization of fishing-dependent communities: for Louisiana, it lists the towns of Venice, Empire, Grand Isle, Golden Meadow, Cutoff, Chauvin, Dulac, Houma, Delcambre, Morgan City, and Cameron. GMAHD chose one community each from Texas, Louisiana, Alabama, and two from Florida. Port Fourchon was selected for Louisiana because it serves as the main staging area for offshore oil and gas production. If the offshore aquaculture industry utilizes oil and gas structures, the GMAHD report reasoned, Port Fourchon would be a logical location to base the shore industry. However, it is interesting that the report noted there were no fishing-related businesses listed for Port Fourchon in 2003, nor any commercial fishing licenses reported as being held by persons physically living in there in the 2000 Census. Some 483 recreational State saltwater fishing licenses were sold during 2000, and several deep sea charter boats and offshore shrimp trawlers were harbored there.

8. GMAHD, xii.
9. GMAHD, 103.

The idea of deepwater aquaculture has received positive reactions from those contemplating profiting from aquaculture ventures, very negative reactions from environmental groups and many commercial fishermen, and distinctly mixed reactions among those living in Louisiana's coastal communities whose economic well-being is indirectly dependent on the Gulf. The Gulf of Mexico Offshore Aquaculture Consortium, operating from the Gulf Coast Research Laboratory at the University of Southern Mississippi in Ocean Springs is an example of the potential boom aquaculture might bring to university-based interdisciplinary research programs. The Consortium sees past proposals for offshore aquaculture as lacking primary scientific data for site locations, cage and mooring designs, choice of species, and fish culture operations. The Sea Grant Gulf of Mexico Offshore Aquaculture Consortium was formed in February, 2000, to bring the technologies of engineering, fish behavior, environmental studies, and regulatory structures to aquaculture endeavors.[10]

The environmental group, Save Our Wetlands, Inc (SOWL),[11] sees the Gulf Council's draft aquaculture amendment as failing to consider the negative economic consequences of ocean fish farming because it will decrease the off-vessel prices commercial fishers receive for their catch. Thus, rather than accept the claims of proponents of aquaculture that it will lead to more jobs, SOWL points to studies showing its introduction in British Columbia added no new jobs, and in Scotland and Norway actually decreased employment due to mechanization.[12] Other environmental concerns include the consequences of an aquaculture operation being hit by a storm, a certainty in the Gulf, in which hormones and antibiotics used in maintaining fish in offshore net enclosures could be introduced into the natural environment in very large quantities. The plan will have to be approved by the Environmental Protection Agency and

10. Members of the consortium include Auburn University Department of Fisheries and Allied Aquaculture, Brightwaters instruments, Chevron-Texaco, the Louisiana State University Law Center's Sea Grant Legal Program, Land O' Lakes Farmland Feed, MIT Sea Grant Program, National Marine Fisheries Service, Rhode Island Sea Grant College Program, Texas A&M.

11. A coalition of environmental groups, the Gulf Restoration Network, the Sierra Club, Food & Water Watch, wearing buttons saying "I'm with the fish," expressed their opposition to the plan at a GMFMC meeting in Biloxi on October 31. See Chris Kirkham, "Groups oppose aquaculture in Gulf. Environmental coalition airs concerns," *The Times-Picayune*, November 1, 2007.

12. See http://saveourwetlands.org for additional information.

the National Marine Fishers Service division of NOAA before action can be taken. However, the federal government and other proponents of offshore aquaculture see the need to narrow the country's 9.2 billion seafood trade deficit without further depleting wild fish stocks.[13] Thus, NOAA is pushing this Gulf plan as a model. Other environmental concerns involve fish waste, uneaten fish feed, and, in addition to antibiotics and hormones used to maintain cultured fish, the chemicals that would be used to keep unwanted organisms from growing on the nets and cages. Little is known about the capacity of the marine environment to assimilate such pollutants. In addition, parasites and disease can spread from fish farms to wild species. In 2002, the Pacific Fisheries Resource Conservation Council in British Columbia found that an increase in the number of parasitic sea lice from fish farms likely caused the collapse of pink salmon in the Brought Archipelago.[14] Another concern with escaped fish is that farmed fish, coming from a genetically limited breeding stock, could mate with native wild species, spawning genetically inferior wild fish that would be more susceptible to disease or compete with wild species for scarce food resources, leading to fewer fish.

At some of the public hearings held on December 10, 2007—for example, St. Petersburg, Florida[15]—diverse groups including commercial fishermen, recreational fishermen, environmentalists, and ordinary citizens, often adversaries, cheered one another for a mutual cause. A similar union of odd bedfellows, fishermen and environmentalists, occurred at the hearing at the Airport Hilton in Kenner, Louisiana on December 12.[16]

This should give a basic sense of some of the major complexities attached to the contemplation of aquaculture in the Gulf of Mexico. But how have these complexities actually been felt by people living in the small 'fishing-dependent' communities of Houma, Chauvin, and Dulac, where I spent time just prior to the hearings in December, meeting with members of the tribal Indian groups there, and talking with others in several marinas? How did the opinions of people directly involved in the

13. The US exports about 70 percent of its domestic production.

14. See "Offshore Aquaculture: Bad News for the Gulf of Mexico," accessible at http://saveourwetlands.org/badnews4gulf.html.

15. As reported by Stephen Nohlgren, "Unlikely Allies Oppose Gulf Fish Farming," *St. Petersburg Times*, December 11, 2007.

16. See Chris Kirkham, "Fish Farming Proposal Assailed. Foes pack hearing on Gulf aquaculture," *The Times-Picayune*, December 12, 2007.

seafood industries connect with the anxieties of people who were not? What were the competitions between economics and environment that might potentially transform their communities and their entire social structure? The following fragments capture the general sense of many of the voices I heard—in direct conversation, on the radio, in the midst of exchanges among several people. I have grouped them somewhat by topic, and added clarifications of reference where useful.

A woman speaking on the radio, trying to organize the people for whom commercial fishing was a way of life, was dismayed that internal struggles among factions in the seafood and shrimp business were only hurting their cause. 'Blanchard Seafood[17] and LSA (Louisiana Shrimp Association) and I'm going to even give credit to SSA (Southern Shrimp Alliance),' she was saying, 'we are fighting with every ounce of breath we have, with every dollar we can muster. But there's still a lot of contention down here between LSA and SSA, and if every fisherman that gets on their radio and runs their mouth about Dean or Wayne or SSA, if they would put their energy and their money where their mouth is, that we are fighting to preserve their way of life, we would get something accomplished.'

One man pointed out how the economics were even more complicated, ran deeper, than the surface issues in the public discussion.[18] 'The people who are against the fish farming in the Gulf oughta be careful of one thing,' he said. 'If that stuff is produced in the Gulf, don't think it's going to be American vessels or our commercial fisherman who will be doing it. The point is that the cost of producing that pound of fish would be greater than if it was done in Mexico or somewhere else. We saw the same thing happen with catfish farming industry in Louisiana, and with crawfish farming which now everybody relies on. Commercial fisherman are selling king mackerel at, say, three bucks a pound. If a company came in and grew them in the Gulf, it would probably cost this company 3 bucks a pound to *grow* king mackerel. So the price wouldn't compete with the commercial fishermen. But if the company went to Mexico to produce

17. Dean Blanchard Seafood Inc. is a wholesaler and retailer of seafoods in Grand Isle; Blanchard says the 'white-tablecloth' marketplace is the only place the wild shrimp industry can go, but with farmed imports coming in at ever cheaper prices, shrimp became a Wal-Mart item. Wild shrimp can't be produced as inexpensively as imported farmed shrimp, according to Blanchard, because they get $2 a day for labor in Asian countries. See Thyra Porter, "Wild shrimp. Sellers of this crustacean seek upscale markets," *Seafood Business,* October 3, 2007.

18. The father of a charter boat captain.

it, they could probably produce it for one buck a pound there, and sell it for two bucks a pound, and then our commercial fishermen *would* have a problem, being faced with cheaper products. So people trying protect domestic stocks from import, and trying to kill this fish farming in the Gulf, gotta be real careful that the aquaculture industry don't go to some other country that can turn around and dump fish on the market for a cheaper price than we can over here. The companies doing fish farming in the Gulf probably *wouldn't use* our commercial fisherman and American vessels; they would build their own boats and use their own people. They wouldn't go to Grand Isle and say "We need to hire 50 boats." They can tell you that, but that's not gonna happen. They'll use their own boats and people. Don't be mislead by these company that say you're gonna have all these off-season jobs and stuff with these fish net farms, because that's not gonna happen. The plan that's moving forward does not specify *who* can do this fish farming. It very well could be some company from Norway coming in, using their own boats, their own people, their own money, and ship the product somewhere else and leave nothing here but an environmental mess to contend with. I don't want anybody to think I'm for this fish farming deal, because I see it as a threat. I've got a son who's a captain of a 65 foot charter boat, and I'm not for this (aquaculture) industry at all, but we gotta be careful it's not done cheaper in a foreign country.'

Many who had boats in marinas being repaired were particularly concerned about the damage to aquaculture net enclosures from Gulf storms, allowing the escape of cultured fish. 'They're talking about putting these fish farms on oil rigs, and we've all seen what happened in the recent storms where the rigs were carried miles and miles away onto shore,' one said. 'The Gulf is a place that has a lot of *serious* weather incidents, and *a lot* of weather events; it's pretty much inevitable that farmed fish are going to escape.' Another added, 'With these fish it'd be a real concern if they were non-native or genetically modified fish, but luckily that's not something the Gulf Council is leaning towards, and that's a really good thing. We need to make sure they don't allow that.' Still another said, 'But even engineered fish that are native species, if they escape they can cause serious problems for wild fish stocks.[19] These fish could have a different genetic makeup, different appearance, behave differently, and compete with wild fish populations. Especially if they were genetically enhanced.

19. Reflecting commonly held beliefs about the results of genetic engineering.

You'd go fishing and pull up a seven-headed bass or something. That may sound like a joke, but if you start mixing genetically modified fish with other kind of fish, then what do you have?'[20]

Many felt that aquaculture would require the expenditure of a lot of energy producing nothing, particularly when considering what wild fish stocks would feed on. 'We're talking about carnivorous finfish that they want to raise—everything from mahi mahi, cobi, red snapper, the whole range—and these are fish that require other wild fish for feed,' a man with the raspy voice of experience and a relentless logic argued. 'In most cases they eat on average anywhere from 2 to 6 lbs of other wild fish a day—we're talking about forage fish, such as menhaden, that these cultured fish are going to need to eat to be raised. That's a huge undertaking; it's going to require a lot of these forage fish, and that's going to be taking away important food, important prey species, not only for wild fish but for marine mammals and sea birds. These forage fish are a hugely important part of the ecosystem. So you'd *deplete* a certain species of fish just to feed these farmed fish.'

Without passing judgment on the validity of such concerns, they nevertheless represent the perceptions of many citizens in the economically Gulf-dependent coastal communities, south of I-10. South of Houma, they were the topic of conversations in lunch stops like Danny's Fried Chicken in Chauvin, at Bourdeaux's Marina, or Johnny's Propeller Shop, or Gineaux's Seafood; opinions were voiced in the markets, on the internet, even in churches. While many people whose thoughts I asked about aquaculture had not much to say, many did—on any of the seemingly endless proposals for how aquaculture might be done. From even limited observations, the most frequent perception was that aquaculture would end up creating only a non-productive vicious cycle (Marker of Complexity 3). If one starts from the premise that the country needs to farm these fish because wild fish stocks are over-fished, what proponents of aquaculture fail to acknowledge (and, some say, fail to tell the public) is that they also have to *deplete* wild fish stocks to feed their farmed fish.

20. Still another recounted what happened when farmed salmon escaped and bred with wild salmon stock. The wild salmon no longer knew how to breed with each other, or how to go back upstream to spawn. Even if the species farmed were native to the Gulf, it would still not be the same species as wild species. 'If you look at a farmed fish and a wild fish of the same species,' he said, 'they don't even look the same. They are changed just by penning them up.'

Over time, this vicious cycle has the potential for becoming even a net loss of ocean resources. Does it make sense to deplete 2–6 lbs of wild fish for every 1 lb of farmed fish?

Exactly how aquaculture companies would plan to stock these net fish farms, and with what species, remains largely unclear. Would they catch wild fish and farm them, or would companies bring in their own stock? The GMFMC Plan right now leaves it very open ended. But many were anxious that NOAA has been pushing to rush this through without thoroughly investigating all the potential hazards. In addition to economics and the direct effects of genetic tampering, anxieties about the use of antibiotics and chemicals in the fish farming process were also high on the list of worries.

One fellow recounted how he had seen people catch tuna, and put them into net farms to fatten them up. But they had to add antibiotics and chemicals, because when a large number of fish were concentrated in a net, it seemed to make them sick. 'If they were using hatchery-raised stock,' he said, 'the fish would probably have a survival rate of 40–50 percent. But in the wild, many species have a survival rate of sometimes less than 1 percent.[21] This provides for the survival of the fittest. Wild genetic strains are much stronger, and traits are passed from generation to generation. But hatchery-raised fish, with less survival traits, could escape and breed with wild fish, and then pass on poorer survival traits. So escaped hatchery fish would pollute the genetic strain.' The upshot, in his view, was that the use of antibiotics and other chemicals produced weaker fish.

One man had been to China, where shrimp were raised in aquaculture ponds, and food and chemicals put into the water. 'After they drained the water from the pond ten years later, they could not even plant grass there. It would not grow. Everything was contaminated from the medication and antibiotics. So, for ten years of yield in an aquaculture shrimp pond, it ended up causing 100 years of resistance to anything be-

21. This may seem high; however, watchdog groups like Idaho's USConservation.org, in comparing hatchery and wild salmon mortality rates for smolts (young salmon at the stage of first migration to the sea) note a mortality rate of 80–98 percent for wild fish (vs. 80 percent hatchery). See "Steelhead, Salmon and Dams" accessible at http://www.usconservation.org/html/stl_hd.html. By comparison, pelagic marine species such as the Atlantic menhaden, subject to a relatively high mortality rate, have an estimated natural annual mortality rate that ranges from 30–36 percent; Atlantic herring at 18 percent. See Menhaden Resource Council, Arlington, VA, "Biology: Mortality," http://www.menhaden.org/biology_mortality.htm.

ing able to grow because of the acidity it put into the soil and the residue of contaminants."

Finally, one person seemed to sum up the ambiguity underlying all these collective worries, by simply saying, "If you let this aquaculture thing loose in our Gulf, that's just one more thing that we don't know what's going to be going into our water."

Aquaculture Take Two

Are these anxieties about deepwater aquaculture in the Gulf of Mexico warranted? Some of them? None? While it is not a purpose to resolve issues that are still only emerging, it is important to hear a scientist's take on them. Dr. Edward Chesney, Associate Professor at LUMCON—the Louisiana Universities Marine Consortium—graciously shared his thoughts on the realities and myths of aquaculture in an extended conversation in January, 2008, after the flurry of concerns raised in the series of public hearings held during the week of December 10, 2007 had passed.

LUMCON was formed in 1979 to coordinate Louisiana's activities in marine research, and is located in Cocodrie, within the estuarine wetlands complex of the Mississippi River delta plain. LUMCON oversees the Barataria-Terrebonne National Estuary Program (BTNEP) and serves as the administrative agent for the Coastal Restoration and Enhancement through Science and Technology (CREST) program, an alliance of eleven academic institutions in South Louisiana and Mississippi. Ed's research interests include fisheries and fish ecology, especially as they relate to the early life history or larval stages of fish, and the spawning and propagation of marine fishes for aquaculture. Ed received his Ph.D. from the Graduate School of Oceanography at the University of Rhode Island, where I had planned to take my own sabbatical from Skidmore College to investigate philosophical and ethical issues in the relation between human and natural environments.[22]

In terms of the potential economic impact of aquaculture, Ed cautioned that it was a long way from becoming a reality. For locals involved primarily in shrimp and crab fishing, the offshore proposals shouldn't have any impact on them at all economically, because offshore would be targeting a completely different type of fish, primarily those populations overfished in the Gulf of Mexico and facing declining harvest. Ed pointed

---

22. Before unanticipated family matters intervened.

out that there was a lot going on right now with the management of fisheries in the United States that many may not be aware of, as far as changes to the Magnuson-Stevens Act,[23] and some of the lawsuits that have been brought forward to force the federal government to begin to manage fisheries in a sustainable way. Management of fisheries is complicated by politics and the fact that the recommendations of scientists have rarely been followed. As fish stocks have continued to dwindle, the government is being forced to take more drastic measures, cutting down both on catch and the effects of bycatch.[24]

I asked Ed if he agreed that two main concerns with aquaculture were that in storms, fish net enclosures might break apart, allowing intermingling of cultured species with wild species, and the use of antibiotics and chemicals in maintaining the fish. Ed first pointed out that the issue of intermingling of cultured and wild species was overblown. If an outfit was proposing using non-native genetics, non-native species, the laws were going to be tight; moreover, whatever would happen initially would be only a demonstration-type project. When Ed first got out of undergraduate school, he worked at Woods Hole,[25] where his first project was an aquaculture project with John Ryther,[26] who was growing oysters on secondarily treated sewage. At that time aquaculture was going nowhere, but now Ed is convinced that sound, sustainable aquaculture, with best management practices—the types of technologies being developed where one can grow fingerlings indoors in South Dakota just as well as in Coastal Massachusetts or Coastal Louisiana—is worth the investment

23. On January 12, 2007, President Bush signed the Magnuson-Stevens Fishery Conservation and Management Reauthorization Act of 2006. The new law mandates the use of annual catch limits and accountability measures to end overfishing, provides for widespread market-based fishery management through limited access programs, and calls for increased international cooperation.

24. Ed had recently spoken to a recreational fisherman who said the new regulations of the National Marine Fisheries Service required recreational charter fishing boats to carry a venting device so that when they fished for any type of offshore fish, especially snappers, they could vent throw-backs properly.

25. Woods Hole Oceanographic Institution (WHOI) in Massachusetts.

26. John Ryther, who died July 9, 2006 at age 84, in 1941 had enlisted the Army Air Corps, flew P-51 Mustangs in Europe on 83 combat missions, including sorties on D-Day, received his doctorate in Biology from Harvard in 1951 and began his 30 year career at Woods Hole in the fall. John co-authored one of the first comprehensive books on aquaculture and raised the funds to build the Environmental Systems Lab at WHOI to conduct applied aquaculture research.

and using the technology to make it happen in a responsible way. The bottom line, Ed said, is that "the fisheries can't sustain further harvest, and with current management practices, the amount of fish available to the public is going to drop drastically."

It is a economic and environmental fact that the production and consumption of cultured fish has been going up dramatically. The reason is straightforward. There are two forces going in opposite directions: the world human population growth is increasing, but the stock of wild fish, from being overharvested, is decreasing. One way to meet the increased demand and reduced supply is to culture fish. Ed believes "there's no reason that we cannot culture fish in a responsible, sustainable manner." Ed acknowledges people have been irresponsible in the way they have done aquaculture, but thinks we can learn from mistakes and exercise proper controls. "When we first started agricultural farming in this country, we were not very responsible stewards of the land; we had the dust bowl and those kinds of things. But people learn and pass laws and instigate controls. As far as offshore aquaculture, it's going to have a microscope on it."

When Ed attended one of the December public hearing meetings (in Mississippi), he found most of the concerns "strictly hysteria; there were no real facts there." This particularly included concerns about antibiotics and chemicals. First, there was no need for them. As an example, Ed explained that one person in his program had been asked to come to China where they were raising Pompano in offshore nets and having disease problems. When he looked at what was going on, he found the disease problems in the cages *offshore* were because they had poor husbandry practices *onshore* in the tanks. So instead of feeding antibiotics to the fish offshore, they fixed the onshore husbandry problems. The reason why that was the logical thing to do, Ed explained, was because the offshore environment is a very pristine environment. "If you put healthy fish out there, they're going to stay healthy. It's much more healthy than when you are producing fingerlings onshore and you've got them packed in as many as you can. If you reduce those densities and have better bio filters and better controls in the hatchery, and you get happy, healthy fish, and you move them offshore, then they're going to stay happy and healthy. One of the things about the offshore environment is that the water is virtually disease free." While fish will get diseases on their surfaces, they do not get sick; offshore they're not stressed. Where stress occurs more often is typically inshore where there are temperature fluctuations, salinity fluctuations. The low oxygen zone off the coast of Louisiana can stress fish. But offshore, well away from low productivity waters, concerns about nutrients and feed hitting the bottom were non issues. "The public has been fed a lot of misinformation by NGOs that are worried. I'm worried about environmental concerns too, but I can tell you that you should be more worried if somebody wants to put a net in a bay in coastal Massachusetts or Louisiana than if they want to put a net 30 miles offshore in blue water. There really is very little to worry about in that environment." Navigation hazards are legitimate concerns, but there you simply put the enclosures in a place where boats are not going to run over them. The genetics issues, however, were very easily taken care of by simply having well diversified brood stock—lots of males breeding lots of females. "That's just a common good hatchery practice. You use multiple males and rotate your brood stock and you use native genetics; you don't try to blind breed or select or do any of that kind of stuff. That all has to be written into the law."

The proposed aquaculture net farms are for federal waters, which takes them out to the 200 mile limit. There have been a wide variety of design ideas—variations on the very simple device shown above. Ed had just attended a meeting where the Norwegians had been talking about making giant nets, putting motors on them, and riding them around the sea. "I don't know who would want to work on something like that . . . I can see if you're from Norway you might travel south into warmer waters to raise fish in one of these giant moving things, but, golly, what happens if a storm comes?" But there were *many* different types of enclosures, and while only a few offshore net operations were currently coming online in this country, there appeared to be enough globally to support any number of different net enclosure manufacturers. Ed observed it was now known that the type of gravity nets used offshore in some places were not a reliable technology. "But now they have designed nets that can submerge themselves, so you don't have to have anybody out there at all. And if you have a heavy storm, like a tropical storm, because of the dynamics of the wave energy and so forth, the storm just pushes the net and the fish down below the impact from the waves and they just ride it out."

Perhaps the most common attack on aquaculture we heard earlier is that 'you're just harvesting fish to feed fish.' Ed's response was that the species used for fish feeds and animal feeds did not represent all the species out there that could serve as forage fish for other fish. In the Gulf, tons of menhaden are harvested not just for fish feeds; more than half go into chicken and pig feeds, fertilizer, and oils. But there are many, many other species of forage fish available.[27]

In Ed's thinking, "virtually all environmental problems that exist in the world could be resolved by reducing our world's population." He admitted that was not very popular with politicians and religious people, and, coming from a Catholic family of six children himself, Ed was not talking about mandatory birth control, or, like the Chinese, telling people they can only have one child. At the same time, he was troubled by a tax structure that rewards people for having more children. He was also troubled by an unwillingness to even discuss issues of population distribution. Ed had recently attended a science meeting about the effects of coastal eutrophication.[28] When the impact on processes of eutrophication from the tremendous increase in human populations living close to the coast was raised, it was surprising that few scientists wanted to talk about it. But if scientists can't talk about it, how would it ever get into the public arena? Thus, current demographic and economic facts were among the reasons Ed is a strong supporter of sustainable aquaculture—"because at least in the short run it's the only way to save our fisheries from going over the cliff."

Ed has been working with an engineer at LSU developing bio filters that are being used in South Dakota in minus 24 degrees weather. His newest filter has zero discharge, which means you can use saltwater and not lose salt; you only have to add freshwater occasionally for evaporation. A company planning to sell this filter has a new de-nitrification technology that removes nitrogen from the water so that it is not necessary

27. Probably half the fish in the Gulf of Mexico serve as forage species, including herring, little jacks, ground fish and bottom feeders like the croaker (Micropogonias undulatus, also known by the names corcus, hardhead, King Billy, and la corbina), and 'aquarium' fish.

28. The natural aging of a body of water by biological enrichment. As nutrients such as nitrogen and phosphorus, which encourage the growth of aquatic organisms, drain into the body of water, its fertility increases, plant and animal life burgeons, and organic remains begin to be deposited on the lake bottom. Over time, as silt and organic debris pile up, the body of water grows shallower and warmer, with warm-water organisms supplanting those that thrive in a cold environment; marsh plants take root in the shallows and begin to fill in the original basin. For bodies of water that do not drain easily, eventually they give way to become bogs, gradually overgrown with vegetation. However, pollutants from human sources radically accelerate the aging process, and bodies of water in many parts of the earth have been severely eutrophied by sewage and agricultural and industrial wastes. The prime contaminants are nitrates and phosphates that overstimulate growth of algae, and poison whole populations of fish, whose decomposing remains further deplete the water's dissolved oxygen content, creating a 'hypoxic zone.'

to turn the water over. It could be used for almost any type of culture, except perhaps for crawfish and other shellfish which molt and tend to eat each other; a tank wouldn't give them the kind of refuge they get in a pond. But the method works well for fish who are not trying to eat each other—they eat the feeds, the water is recirculated, and the filters remove both solid and liquid waste with efficiency. Ed recounted a story about a farm on which traditional Ag people had wanted to raise chickens and pigs on their property. The local municipality blocked them from doing that, so they looked into fish. When the municipality found out the details involved with fish they said 'have at it.' So they moved out of more traditional type of agriculture into fish.

Ed concluded by saying that what he was trying to do in the latter part of his career was to contribute to ways to see both more sustainable fisheries through better management, and responsible aquaculture that could support fisheries. He feels aquaculture has been harshly treated by environmentalists and NGOs. Questions can be raised about the practices of some environmental groups themselves, such as the Coastal Conservation Association (CCA). CCA strongly supports stock enhancement, rearing fish in captivity, and then releasing them into the environment so they can catch them. As a fisheries scientist, Ed knows that is not a good idea. "Our natural systems would be a lot better off if we reduced overfishing and instead grew those fish and directly marketed them. That would put less pressure on the natural fisheries, because nature can produce fish very efficiently unless we're overharvesting them or damaging the environment to the point where the production capacity of the system is reduced. So there's a synergy there."

Stock enhancement was not *always* a bad idea. With species like sturgeon who live a long time, for example, their habitat has been damaged so badly that they accumulate mercury and other things that make it difficult for them to breed when they get older; so sturgeon need help. But instead of doing stock enhancement with species that have healthy natural populations like red drum and speckled trout in the Gulf, and snook in Florida, just reducing fishing pressure on those species would be enough. Florida especially has way too many fishermen, and the natural ability to sustain fish populations in the face of such tremendous pressure doesn't work out well.

Stock enhancement is going about things the wrong way, Ed thinks. With aquaculture, the chances of escapement are 'slim to none—you harvest that product and then put it back on the land for sale. But with stock enhancement, even using native genetics and diversifying the brood stock, you are still putting out an individual grown on feeds, then throwing it out into nature when it's never seen a predator. Moreover, it's going from feeding on a feed to having to forage for itself. That individual is extremely vulnerable at that stage. Most stock enhancement studies, when they look at effectiveness, show that if stock enhancement contributes to the wild stocks at all, it's on the order of only 3 to 5 percent. You could do so much more for the wild stocks by just cutting down on the fishing pressure.'

Perhaps the strongest evidence for the harm of overfishing came from the hurricanes themselves. "We had Katrina and nobody went fishing for six months. The shrimpers stopped shrimping. The recreational fishermen were too busy dealing with the mess to go fishing. But we had a tremendous crop of speckled trout the following year. The fishing was fantastic. Everybody was saying, 'Why is the fishing so fantastic? Seems like there would have been a lot of damage from Katrina.' Well I can tell you what it was. It was six months without fishing." The fishing pressure on the Louisiana coast is not just from commercial and recreational *fishermen*. In Louisiana each year there are 100,000 metric tons of fish killed in *shrimp nets* going after shrimp. Ed finds it amazing that Louisiana fisheries have been able to sustain that type of pressure and still be highly productive.

A primary theme of *Walking to New Orleans* has been an approach to post-disaster recovery and reconstruction in which principles of good engineering are bound together with principles of ethics. The goal is urban design capable of achieving a just, healthy society with equality of opportunity. In a different, but nevertheless related context, prospects for aquaculture also need to connect science and ethics. One can think of Coastal Louisiana as where two social systems—human and natural—come together; a boundary where one touches the other. It is not enough that each system sustain itself independently. They must coexist in interaction with each other. Environmental organizations and NGOs, for example, whose political positions ignore scientific facts are no more in a position to make correct decisions about aquaculture than technologically-based enterprises that follow the direction of any technology that can be economically profitable. Both strategies are short-sighted, narrow. It is important to see issues more globally—certainly from beyond the perspective of human consumption of fish stocks. The natural and human systems dependent on one another are a *synergy*—a cooperation, from the Greek roots *ergon* (work) and *syn* (together).

The United Houma Nation

The area south of Houma is bayou country. Eight main passages radiate out through the coastal marshes into the Gulf of Mexico and Terrebonne Bay like crow's feet. Six of Louisiana's GMFMC designated 'fishing-dependent' communities are situated on these bayous: Chauvin, Dulac, Houma, Cutoff, Golden Meadow, Grand Isle. Along with the Houma Navigational Canal, these waterways carry fishing and shrimp and oil industry vessels to the Gulf, and support these 'fishing-dependent' and many other smaller Gulf-dependent communities—long, narrow settlements that stretch for miles along the banks of bayous, but are often only one or two blocks deep. By the sides of the several narrow roads leading south from Houma, one sees a few remaining seafood-processing plants but almost no grocery stores; many shrimp boats, but even more yards selling marine equipment and parts; and the endless miles of rozo (Rousseau) cane beneath Gulf skies that always seem mottled with clouds and impending storms. The toll of hurricanes and frequent storms and a changing economy has driven people from these slender communities, made them fragile. From west to east, the bayous and some of their secondary settlements include: Bayou du Large (Theriot), Bayou Grand Caillou which crosses the Houma Navigational Canal (Boudreaux), Bayou Petit Caillou (Chauvin, Cocodrie), Bayou Terrebonne (Montegut, Lapeyrouse), Bayou Isle de Jean Charles, Bayou Pointe-au-Chien (and the renamed Pointe-aux-Chenes), and the long Bayou Lafourche that passes Galliano and Port Fourchon on the way to Grand Isle. Each bayou has come to have its own distinct character, its particular history of families with their unique customs and family loyalties—loyalties that have sometimes resulted in tension and friction across the water from one crow-claw to the next, even as close as one side of a bayou to the other.

Houma Indians and members of the several bands of the Biloxi-Chitimacha Indians live in amongst these bayous and waterways. In some areas, such as the west side of Bayou Grand Caillou that had been settled by Houma Indians, there was no paved road until recently. To the east, the dwindling island community of the Isle de Jean Charles Indians was not connected to the 'mainland' by road across some six miles of marsh and open water at all until the early 1970s. Indian children had to get to school by boat, except when the weather was bad—frequent in the Gulf—in which case they didn't get to school at all. Even today, at high tide, miles of the continually re-elevated stone-base causeway, Island Road, are covered with a half-foot or more of brackish water, and considerably more during storms. On other roads that are similarly flooded, one follows the telephone poles at high tide to know where to drive. During the weekend, local fishermen pull shrimp, crabs, and redfish from the roadsides. The people who inhabit even the most isolated bayous are surprisingly warm and open, even when northern ears have difficulty understanding precisely what may being said, because, throughout the region, one's auditory senses face hearing varieties of Cajun and Creole that intermingle with the several dialects of the Houma and other Indians.

Along U.S. 90 that approaches Houma lie large sugarcane fields. Houma has become a popular place for helicopter pilots who fly out to the oil rigs in the Gulf, and there has been a notable increase in pilots there recently. Many—as many as 100 or more—keep permanent residences in various hotels in the area. On Tunnel Road in Houma on my way down to Dulac, I ride beneath the Intracoastal Waterway. On the radio and on billboards along the road are countless ads seeking to hire able bodied seamen. Along Route 57 that parallels Bayou Grand Caillou, past Bobtown Fire Department and Bobtown Bridge Road, are moored boats with skeletal wings and nets of every variety in shape and size; single story homes rest at ground level sitting next to modular homes that have been elevated high using telephone poles; behind them, older men, work on their boats or rusted vehicles, wearing the ubiquitous blue coveralls so common in Cajun country.

In several meetings and conversations with my friend from Dulac, Kirby Verret, tribal elder of the United Houma Nation who is currently working with Indian education, Kirby would recount pieces of the long history of how the Bureau of Indian Affairs (BIA) had, and continues to, factionalize the Indians into different groups in their quest to seek recognition. There was a period of time when BIA questioned whether there was any identity of the tribal group at all—pointing to a gap between 1820—40, which Kirby sees as period when Indians were removed from the area. Representatives from BIA's Office of Federal Acknowledgment continue to push the view that there is a better chance for recognition with *smaller* tribal groups. Kirby, however, sees this as simply the attempt by BIA to keep Indian tribes fragmented in what he calls a 'divide and conquer' strategy. Even if belief in this 'strategy' were not defensible, BIA's excruciatingly sluggish process for federal recognition has essentially accomplished the same thing, leading to enormous frustration among Indian tribal groups. In a letter to the chairs of the Senate Committee on Indian Affairs, Senator James Webb (D, Virginia) expressed grave concerns about the slow process for recognition through the BIA—some tribes still sitting in a queue awaiting recognition decisions, having initiated their requests in the 1970s—and called for a fix.[29]

When BIA's glacial process and continued regulation changes are matched against the existence of small kinship cliques and general lack of cohesion among some Indians—the view expressed by some tribal members, for example, that the United Houma Nation is more a loose political entity than a cohesive tribal group, with its members spread throughout a wide region of South Louisiana—one can begin to see the multiple, inherent complexities that arise. Bureaucratic regulation changes plus tribal fragmentation (both natural and that promoted by BIA) equals an atmosphere of ambiguity. These quite fluid complexities are made only more difficult to stabilize by questions that arise about self-reported Indian identity, where it is hard to establish genealogical lineage with great clarity, and to which must be added the history of Indians being denied adequate education comparable to the white population. According to Kirby, until 1959, Indian education went only as far as the 8th grade.

29. Bobbie Whitehead, "Senator wants improvements in BIA federal recognition process," *Indian Country Today,* November 19, 2007. The testimony of chairwoman Ann Denson Tucker on behalf of the Muscogee Nation of Florida before the Committee on Indian Affairs of the United States Senate on September 19, 2007 reflects this as well. Ann Tucker noted that her Tribe was the second oldest petitioner in the Office of Federal Acknowledgment, and has been trapped in the BIA recognition system since the mid-1970s. After filing multiple petitions and surviving a number of rule changes over 25 years, they were finally classified as "Ready, Waiting for Active Consideration," and that was four years ago. "All told," she said, "we have been trapped in BIA's bureaucracy for over 30 years and we have nothing but expense and frustration to show for it. My Tribe has exhausted its resources. It can no longer pursue or respond to the BIA's failed process—a process that requires applicants to re-do and re-file papers and studies and to comply with rules, regulations, and interpretations that did not exist when our initial application was made—a process whose pace can be characterized, at best, as glacial or, perhaps, no pace at all. My Tribe has worked, waited, struggled, and sacrificed in this process for over 30 years. At every turn, we have learned that the BIA tribal recognition process is enormously burdensome, confusing and unfair." Testimony accessible at: http://indian.senate.gov/public/_file/AnnTuckertestimony.pdf.

What I increasingly began to discern were a number of curious parallels between the fragmentation that exists among Indian tribal bands and similar disjunctions among many of New Orleans' neighborhood associations, vying for authority or control of a certain district, as Jim Livingston of CityWorks had related to me. Kirby Verret acknowledged there was not any ease of communication among tribal bands across the waters separating each crow-claw of land ridges down into the Gulf. Nor did Kirby point to strong, distinctive, shared pre-Christian Indian religious practices that could serve to bond the diverse tribal groups together. Tribal religiousness is broadly Christian; in fact, Kirby himself wanted to be a priest, and, at one point, took Latin in school for that purpose. Instead of the priesthood, however, Kirby broadcast a radio show on KHOM, a 100,000 watt station, for six years, selling insurance on the side.[30]

Fragmentation of the coastal culture exists within tribal groups, but also surfaces in the form of a certain resentment against the Cajuns living there.[31] In Bayou du Large, for example, Kirby related how Cajuns had taken over businesses and stores, and kept Indians out. Houma Indians who had skills in fishing or shrimping were forced to end up working for Cajun boat owners, rather than be the owners themselves. Many Houma Indians made their living in the seafood industry: packing, maintaining marine equipment as welders or repairmen, as well as being the labor force on boats they did not own. Economically, Indians who worked the shrimp and fishing boats were at the bottom of the ladder. Distribution of pay from a catch would go 60 percent to boat's owner, 40 percent to crew. Then, among the crew, the captain would get his 60 percent, and the crew would have to divide the rest. Even though it was in many instances the Houma Indians who had the skills directly related to a successful catch—the ability to find shrimp or know the feeding grounds of fish—they benefited least from them.

While Houma Indians more recently have been able to serve on public bodies such as Fire or Recreation boards, Houma Indians, who represent

30. In its early years, KHOM served only the Houma area, with varied formats, including a nightly nostalgia program, but in the 1980s it went on a 2000 foot tower (shared with WCKW) in Vacherie, enabling it to put a strong signal into New Orleans and Baton Rouge. Later, the station changed to KUMX, with the KHOM call sign ending up in Salem, Arkansas.

31. Kirby observed that the Verret name could be white Cajun (around Morgan City), black Creole, as well as Houma Indian. Words like choupique, bayou, or pirogue that appear in Cajun songs are Indian words in their origin.

at least 10 percent of the population in Terrebonne Parish, constitute only about 1 percent of its teachers. This residue of the history of racial and economic inequalities begins early in the experience of Indian children.

All of these social inequities are among the circumstances that sociologists like Richard Freeman[32] and others have warned are producing a radical economic bifurcation in America –a two-tiered society in which the more affluent live fundamentally different lives from the working classes and the poor. In bayou country, one has a painfully visible sense of how the biggest barrier between classes is money. Driving down Route 24 south of Houma one comes upon a very, very large Rent-a-Center. It exists on such a grand scale because there are that many people dependent on having to *rent* their furniture; they don't have enough money to buy. For a majority of people in bayou country—Indian, Cajun, Creole—finances are always marginal. Families are simply not free to afford the things many people take for granted—meals other than at fast food places like Checkers or Rallye, or the monthly costs of service in order to get onto the Internet. When government agencies begin to communicate more and more *through* the Internet, they need to be aware of how many people have been *excluded* from receiving those communications—the poor, the elderly, and all who are forced to live at the edges of society. The idea of spending $4.00 or $5.00 for a cup of coffee at a Starbucks is out of the question. A splurge at Mardi Gras for decorations and 'throws' may be one exception, but every day, there is still the constant, gnawing feeling that you don't have enough money to cover your groceries, your rent, your electric bills, gas for the truck. Over the years, the continual fear of running out of money is debilitating.

I was interested if Kirby believed that the attitudes of individuals, or businesses, towards the environment had changed since the hurricanes. Kirby thought ordinary people had become more aware of the environment, especially after water came up more than a foot over the first floor of Terrebonne General Medical Center in Houma. So more people were trying to elevate their homes. Kirby also observed that if a lock had been built on the Houma Navigational Canal in the 1960s, much of the erosion that led to flooding wouldn't have happened. The projects of the Coastal Wetlands Planning, Protection and Restoration Act (CWPPRA) Kirby felt would most impact coastal communities were those working to rebuild

32. Herbert S. Ascherman Professor of Economics at Harvard.

the barrier islands—Timbalier and Raccoon Islands. But Kirby also complained that USACE was not able to use the kinds of dredges that had been used in Dubai to make new palm tree-shaped residential and commercial islands, extending Dubai's coast out into the Persian Gulf, because of political and State Department restrictions. In fact, Kirby pointed out that "USACE had stupidly directed all the sand and silt from dredging out into the Gulf of Mexico, off the continental shelf, rather than use it to build up the barrier islands."

A major environmental and economic concern of Kirby and other tribal leaders was a fear of losing their land, and the need to recapture land that had already been lost. Kirby related how the Harry Bourg Corporation in Dulac had stolen lands from poor Indians. His own experience with the Bourg Corporation was very close to home. During summer drought conditions, the Bourg Corporation had built a canal through nearby land—land that turned out to be owned by the United Methodist Church Clanton Chapel in Dulac—then tried to claim the land in order to put in pilings for buildings and a marina. Over a period of several days, Kirby noticed that Bourg had people clearing out a piece of property right near his church. Kirby went over and thanked them for clearing the land, but the workers told him that the Boug Corporation was having a surveyor come in to survey the land and claim ownership of it. Kirby challenged the surveyor and the Bourg attorneys, arguing the Bourg Corporation didn't have its facts correct about the location of this land, relative to the particular road they assumed, from their plot maps, identified the land and determined its location. Kirby pointed out clearly, and quietly reminded them, that the road in question—Coast Guard Road—did not even exist in the 1940s. In fact, if one were going by the description on their maps, now correctly identified as land south of Grand Caillou Road (Route 3011) along Four Point Road, the road in question (which runs through marsh near the wildlife management area), it might mean the Methodist Church actually owned *more* land—Bourg land—than it had previously thought. Kirby did not pursue this argument, thinking it best to leave well enough alone. However, the episode reveals how fluid land ownership, as well as the land itself, can be down in bayou country. Kirby remembered much of the land that was once farmed is now under water. Kirby's grandmother used to farm land three miles south of where the church is in Dulac. Now that land is under water.

On December 7, 2007, I was invited by Kirby to attend the United Houma Nation banquet at the Municipal Auditorium in Houma. Though hardly needed, the *lagniappe* for me as a musician was an opportunity to play with the tribal Cajun/Zydeco/Swamp Pop band, *Treater (Le Traiteur de Bayou)*.[33] The banquet is an annual event to acknowledge Houma accomplishments over the year, honor the work of its leaders, give out awards, and enjoy a large feed along with live music. I was initially struck by the fact that during the presentations of awards and short speeches that followed, very few paid any attention at all. Eating did not stop, nor did holding forth heated conversations. There seemed an absence of demonstrable expressions from the crowd of being part of a cohesive entity.

But then I remembered Kirby had pointed out that identity was first and foremost family and kinship. The individuals who came to have certain skills—boatbuilding, machine repair, the ability to identify the location of fish or shrimp—all learned those skills through their immediate family, rather than through wider groups. Moreover, the school systems did virtually nothing to encourage awareness of Indian identity, or to reinforce the customs of the area's Indian tribal history. This missing basis for cultural values was, in fact, one reason why Kirby was drawn to Indian education. In the current world, however, Kirby's people live among social institutions that reflect the customs and values of other cultures. These are people very much on their own.

The Grand Caillou-Dulac Band of Biloxi-Chitimacha

The Biloxi-Chitimacha Confederation of Muskogees (BCCM) is an alliance of three Indian communities located in Lafourche and Terrebonne parishes. These three communities—the Grand Caillou-Dulac Band, the Bayou Lafourche Band, and the Isle de Jean Charles Band—share a common ancestral history, and trace their origins to Biloxi, Chitimacha, Choctaw,

33. The band recognizes the healing properties of music, like their *traiteur* (healer) ancestors who treated with the power of faith and prayer. As leader of an *en dehors de la Louisiane* Cajun/Zydeco band, *les cigognes,* the author never passes up an opportunity to play with other groups. Calvin Parfait, band leader who plays Cajun accordion and lead guitar, graciously handed over his handmade Martin 'D' accordion. We both owned instruments made by Junior Martin of Scott, Louisiana, and shared stories about musicians we knew and had played with. Treater has performed throughout the Gulf Coast, the Caribbean, Canada, the Midwest, and South Korea. It's band members include Calvin, Charlie Duthu (vocals, *frottoir*), Alvin Parfait (drums), Esther Billiot (keyboard, vocals), and Richard Rivet (bass).

Acolapissa, and Atakapa Indian tribal groups. Conversations with Randy Verdun, Chief of the Bayou Lafourche Band of Biloxi-Chitimacha over the summer of 2007 revealed pieces of the Confederation's beginnings.[34] Randy recounted how the Confederation was formed in 1995, after the Bureau of Indian Affairs came to the conclusion in 1994 that genealogical research suggested the ancestors of the 'Houma' were *not* Houma but Choctaw, possibly other tribal groups as well, including the great tribal leader, Rosalie Courteau, who died in 1885 and was determined to be Biloxi. While some Houma continue to retain belief in their Indian identity, in Randy's view the United Houma Nation (UHN) is closer to being a broad-based political entity, spread across five parishes, rather than a tribe. Randy said that of its roughly 16,000 members, at least 16 percent have no Indian ancestry whatsoever. This is one source of the fragmentation of Indian groups in Louisiana's coastal communities, discussed earlier.

Marlene Foret, Chairwoman of the Grand Caillou-Dulac band of Biloxi-Chitimacha is a delightful woman with an engaging sense of humor, strong views, and a willingness to express them. While she didn't have any particular thoughts on the potential impact of aquaculture, she did on the ability of CWPPRA projects to help the economy of the region. She felt that if USACE and the other agencies[35] didn't do anything, the buffer zone would be gone, and Houma, which is 17 miles above Dulac and Grand Caillou, 'is gonna be the buffer zone, you know.' The effect on the economy was that the region's key businesses—those needed for day-to-day living—were simply moving out of coastal communities, eventually to be followed by the rest of the population. 'It's sad,' she continued, 'because right now down in Dulac they don't have a grocery store; they have the little stores that just handle bread and cookies and things like that, but no meat, no fresh vegetables. Everyone has to go to Houma, to WalMart or Rouse's (Supermarket), 'cause the Winn Dixie has closed, and some of the Cannata's (Supermarket) stores have closed too. What's sad is that the families are down there and they can't get anything down there, because people don't want to risk rebuilding their businesses if they're

34. Elaborated further by Marlene Foret, Chairwoman of the Grand Caillou-Dulac band.

35. Agencies with CWPPRA projects on the Louisiana Gulf coast include the Army Core of Engineers (USACE), the US Fish and Wildlife Service (USFWS), The Environmental Protection Agency (EPA), NOAA's National Marine Fisheries Service (NMFS), and the Louisiana Department of Natural Resources (LDNR).

gonna be wiped out again. I wish they would. I'm hoping, praying that they do . . . that somebody does something, but it doesn't seem like it's gonna happen. Morganza will protect some but not all of it.'

The Morganza to the Gulf of Mexico Hurricane Protection Project (MGMHPP), as noted in chapter 2, consists of about 72 miles of earthen levee, numerous floodgates and floodgate structures, and the long-awaited 100 x 800 foot lock complex on the Houma Navigational Canal. The system runs from just west of Houma at Bayou Noir (Reach A), crosses the GIWW and heads south along Bayou du Large, then southeast below Dulac to where Bayou Grand Caillou crosses the Houma Navigational Canal—just below which point will be the location of the Houma Navigational Canal Lock, not scheduled to be completed before the year 2014.[36] It then runs further east above Cocodrie where it turns north along the east side of Bayou Terrebonne to just below Montegut; there it turns southeast again, crossing Island Road (Isle de Jean Charles Road) to the end of Highway 665, where it heads north into Terrebonne Parish and ends at the GIWW (Reach L) just before Bayou Lafourche, south of Larose. Two sections of the project (Reach H and Reach J), Work in Kind (WIK) levees, use local sponsors—the Louisiana Department of Transportation and Development (LADOTD), and the Terrebonne Levee and Conservation District (TLCD), who share 35 percent of the project cost. LADOTD was the local sponsor for the feasibility study. Detail about the precise location of MGMHPP levees and floodgates is provided because what the system will include (and not include) will be seen to be of dire importance to the Isle de Jean Charles Indians. This will be discussed further in the next section, but it should be noted here that, while there were studies suggesting slightly different placements for some levees, none of the proposals included Isle de Jean Charles. Carl Anderson of USACE Project Management in New Orleans said that, from a cost-benefit standpoint, it was easier for USACE to build levees along existing bayou ridges. Including Isle de Jean Charles would mean running levees across miles of open water, necessitating that the levees be built from the Gulf floor to their required height. Carl added that the Isle de Jean Charles residents had been offered an opportunity to relocate, but they refused. The matter is still being contested.

Around Houma, eating places were closing because the Gulf shrimping business was closing up. Restaurants couldn't find the help they needed,

36. Information from discussion with Carl E. Anderson, Project Management, USACE New Orleans, who confirmed the expected completion date.

and the shrimpers, discovering there wouldn't be any levee protection for them, were pulling out. What the Morganza to the Gulf Project protected, then, was affecting shrimpers, crabbers, oystermen—everything south of Houma. Marlene remembered that there used to be shrimp factories and ice factories and grocery stores, but they're all gone. Most were gone before the hurricane, but it was still because of the hurricanes that people moved up the road to between Ashland and the Comeau Bridge. Anything below that was just fading away. "That was sad," Marlene added, "because I was raised in Dulac on the Shrimpers Row side. There wasn't much left there." With the closing of the Boudreau's Super Value in Dulac, she and the tribal elders were no longer able to go to that grocery store and shop to give Christmas baskets to the community.

Marlene shared Randy Verdun's view in thinking that the United Houma Nation did not want to have anything to do with the BCCM. This also made her sad. Back in 1994, when the BIA was down, they had told them, 'we know that you are Indians but you do not go back to the historic Houma tribe; redo your genealogy and keep working on your history.' This was in December, and in January, 1995, a group of eight or nine who had faithfully been going to the meetings approached the Houma Council and said 'We were there when the BIA came and said we were not descendents of the Houmas. Are you willing as a Council to work with others and help us find our roots?' The Council's response was, 'No. We were always known as Houmas and no one's gonna tell us we're not.' Marlene countered, saying 'it was not a matter of what you say you are, you have to find your roots, and if you're not willing to go that way, well then, I'm afraid we gotta go. And we each spoke, and then we got up and left. We were gonna try to find someone to do the genealogy to see where our roots were.' Marlene had asked the United Houma Nation's Council many times to see her genealogy, but wasn't shown anything. Following the split, Randy Verdun and Reggie Billiot contacted Audrey Westerman, who did genealogical research and found Biloxi and Chitimacha, Choctaw, Washaw, and Atakapaw origins to the tribes. Marlene and others again went to the Houma Council, told them they had their forms, had done a genealogy, and that they were resigning from the United Houma Nation to pursue what 'Miss Audrey' found. There were close to 1,200 people in Grand Caillou and Dulac who resigned from the United Houma Nation: in all three areas about 2,500 people resigned.

The situation has since been more or less a standoff, with the UHN suggesting BCCM leaders did not know what they were talking about, and vice versa. UHN asked to see 'what they have' but Marlene's view is that it was up to UHN to show their connection to the Houma tribe. Anything they had from Audrey Westerman wouldn't help UHN because 'what they have' only proves they belonged to the Biloxis and Chitimachas and Choctaw. Audrey Westerman told Marlene she was Chitimacha and Biloxi, mostly Chitimacha, and 74 percent Indian. So Marlene concluded, 'why not try to get recognized for who we are and not who we think we are.'

In the meantime, the Grand Caillou-Dulac Band of the Biloxi-Chitimacha has been waiting since they first sent in their petition to BIA in 1996. They were told they would receive findings "in six months." That six months was pushed back. Then it was pushed back another six months, again and again, so that it has now been twelve years without receiving their findings from BIA. The latest news was BIA telling Randy Verdun that they would receive findings in January, 2008. They are still waiting.

What makes Marlene's saga with the BIA so poignant is not simply the familiar story of promises from BIA for findings by a certain date, followed by seemingly unending cycles of more and more waiting. It is the *purpose* Marlene and the BCCM have in mind for seeking federal recognition in the first place. The group has gone before the Terrebonne Parish Council and asked to be recognized us as a tribe. They were. The group received State recognition in 1999 as well. But the reason the BCCM Indians are seeking federal recognition is *not* to pursue land or to set up casinos; casinos have not really done well in Louisiana, anyway. The reason, rather, is because of the schools. Public schools receive a certain amount of money for enrolled Indian children, in part because of a high frequency of AIDS among Indians, but because of other sociological factors as well. Money from the State goes directly to the Terrebonne Parish school system. Every school system gets so much money, according to how many Indian children are registered in the school. *Federal* recognition adds certain entitled moneys to be used for senior citizens, medications, doctors; school children will also benefit from additional dedicated funds through the school systems.[37]

37. BCCM has sought recognition as corporation—Bayou Lafourche, Isle de Jean Charles, and Grand Caillou-Dulac. The Pointe-au-Chien Indian Tribe (PACIT) went for recognition independently, because they were pursuing land, but the BCCM was not. Three communities have gone together and one separately.

Congress has pushed against recognition to the extent that they believe tribal groups want to pursue gambling. For that reason, one of the things Marlene and the BCCM did when they made their by-laws and constitution was to put it in writing that the BCCM would *not* pursue a casino or gambling when they received federal recognition. The Grand Caillou-Dulac Band's interest, and that of the BCCM, is not gambling but education—in addition to funds to benefit Indian children in the public schools, there is a need to expand the tribe's capabilities in businesses and skilled labor. Marlene emphasized there were a lot of talented people who could build boats, build houses, do plumbing, work with electricity. She knew of any number of people who could really do well in business, but just didn't have the education. They were in their 40s and 50s and could do the work. To get hired, the State required them to have a license, but they couldn't afford the education to get a license. Catch 22. However, when the BCCM gets federal recognition, they will be ruling themselves, able to write their own hiring rules also, and then able to give these people work and let them go to work. A lot of people want to go to work and only education holds them back.

Marlene recounted how her first cousin's son told her in October, when his grandpa died, 'You know, when I was in school, all I would think about was getting out of school so I could go shrimping. I did, but you can't make a living with that anymore.' The price of diesel and the price of ice is 'out of the world;' they were now paying more than $3.00 a gallon for diesel. You couldn't come out ahead. 'In today's world the price of shrimp always goes down, but when you go to the store, whether you're a shrimper or you got a job,' the young man told her, 'the price the shrimper pays for that gallon of milk isn't any less than for some guy that's got an office in Houma making big money.'

For Marlene, the biggest challenges her people face are those of being forced to change occupations. As Gulf industries close up, many have had to seek different jobs, but, without education, finding them has been very, very limited. There is clearly a lot of work that needs to be done. The Mennonites, with donations from different churches, came to build a house in each community. Among some members that caused a bit of resentment, who felt the beneficiary was 'better off than he ever was.' Marlene's answer was, 'these people didn't ask for it, they qualified for it; he may be better off, but he's still gonna work the same work he was doing—he's a shrimper, he doesn't know anything else—and that may go away real soon.'

Some tribal Community Centers have tried to start adult education, but also wanted to know where the prospective student was enrolled. Would tribal groups at odds with one another accept non-enrolled students? Those who could afford it might go to Nichols State University in Thibodaux, but the tuition there was high, and most went out of state. "The sad thing about that," Marlene said slowly, "is that most of the time, when they go out of state, they don't return. They come back to visit family, but they make a life elsewhere."

The Isle de Jean Charles Band of Biloxi-Chitimacha

Isle de Jean Charles is a long, narrow island that sits off the end of a ridge that follows the small Bayou St. Jean Charles which runs south of Montegut. It is connected across about four miles of open water by a narrow causeway road (Island Road) just above the end of Route 665 that follows the southward course of Bayou Pointe-au-Chien to the east. On the USGS topographic—bathymetric map of Terrebonne Bay, the island is indistinguishable from the surrounding watery marsh, its existence suggested only by the thinnest, faint blue line. The connecting road has been built up higher twice: it was first raised back in 1953, and again in 1999. However, at high tide it can still run over with water, and with wind, it becomes considerably submerged. The signs along Island Road for those who fish there or launch their boats to pull shrimp and crab from the waters are lengthy and specific.[38] Thirty years ago there were trees and farmland, acres of solid ground where cattle grazed. The men of the Biloxi-Chitimacha trapped game, and women kept gardens of vegetables for the table. Now the slender island is perpetually soggy, skirted by marshes and the wind-driven waters of the Gulf that encroach more and more each year.

Chief Albert Naquin of the Isle de Jean Charles Band of Biloxi-Chitimacha is a man whose warmth and concern for the people of his

38. "Crabbing: cast-netting only (no commercial activity). Deposit entire catch into container (i.e., basket, tub, bucket, etc.). Return "what you do not keep" to the water. Failure to do so may result in $350.00 fine. Limits 25 pounds per boat per day during "Open Season," 10 pounds per boat per day during "Closed Season." Crabbing: Handlines or drop nets only (no commercial activity). Limit 12 dozen per boat per day. No littering. No Loaded Firearms. (Hunting Times—Check Pamphlet). Area open from official sunrise to sunset."

community is immediately evident.[39] Awareness of the depth of his caring has only grown along with our friendship and my small attempts to help the Isle de Jean Charles band achieve federal recognition. Isle de Jean Charles itself has increasingly been in danger of simply vanishing. It is due to a combination of factors—natural subsidence, the gradual elevation of sea level in the Gulf, the parade of storms and hurricanes that erode the barrier islands and hummocks of marsh grasses that serve as fragile protection. But a precious culture and way of life has clung to this slender outpost in quiet defiance of these forces. It is not a heroic effort, although there has been great heroism during hurricanes, some of which was described in chapter 2 of *Walking to New Orleans*. Rather, Isle de Jean Charles symbolizes a culture and an economy so closely born into its environment that, like the island itself, it is barely distinguishable from it.

Most of the island is bisected lengthwise by the meager Bayou St. Charles. Some residences are mobile homes, elevated on telephone pole pilings, a few covered with additional metal roofs; some are the skeletal remains of structures, raised on poles; others sit on the spongy ground itself, their yards strewn with children's plastic toys, faded from the sun, derelict cars or boat hulls of fishing skiffs, odd outbuildings and smoke houses. Other buildings, sheathed in corrugated metal, sit right against the one roadway—some painted red, some rusting to a warmer shade of red. The tan Isle de Jean Charles fire station stands alone and clean. Albert says that before Hurricane Lili in 2002, the island had over 320 people. Now, it's barely 200, counting kids, so they've lost almost 150 people.

We talked about whether the current CWPPRA projects were the right ones for Isle de Jean Charles. The Lake Madison project was not functioning, but there was the attempt to rebuild Timbalier Island.[40] In Albert's mind, the government and USACE were not doing what they needed to do. Instead of building the Morganza to the Gulf Hurricane

39. Albert's education was at the Pointe-au-Chien schools, where some teachers, back then, might have had only a seventh grade education. "At the present they have college degrees, but then it was the bare minimum." Albert went into the Army, worked for a GED, then, on the GI Bill, got an AA degree in life science, and became a petroleum engineer with basic petroleum courses, but not the chemistry and math. Albert worked for the Department of the Interior in the Mineral Sediment Services for 24 years.

40. The barrier islands here, Timbalier and the Isles Dernières, were a first line of protection for the island community as well as other coastal villages. Further east, 30 miles south of Biloxi, six months after the storms almost 90 percent of the barrier islands—the Chandeleur Island chain—was still under water, possibly never to come back .

Protection System, why not fight the problem at its source, at the Gulf of Mexico, and rebuild the barrier islands the way they all used to be? Albert recounted how, as a child, he had lived all the way at the end of the road on Isle de Jean Charles. "When you got to turn around, you go into our driveway. You turn around and look the other way, it's all water." The tidal change was about one foot at that time; now it had grown to 18 inches approaching two feet. The tide can come in fast because of the winds, and if there is a southerly wind, it comes in really fast. All that remains now is the empty shell of a home. Albert's brother, Gustave, died in a tugboat accident; Simon, in Vietnam.

The barrier island that affects Isle de Jean Charles the most is Timbalier Island, where, to the west, there is now a large gap before one reaches the Isles Dernières. Albert believes USACE should re-close that gap. 'That's what I told 'em, there's no traffic there anyway, why don't you just close that off ... well there's boat traffic from Houma that goes by Last Islands [Isles Dernières] down the Navigational Canal, across Terrebonne Bay through Cat Island Pass to get to the oil industry in the Gulf of Mexico. But you could close it all the way to Fourchon, seawall that off, and it will stop the flow of water from coming in. When I was a kid, there was all islands from one end to the other in the area I'm talking about: it was all closed. You had the pass for boats to come in and out of Houma, and then you had Bayou Lafourche for boats to come out of. So if you would seal all that off, that would help us a whole bunch. I told them that already. If you would pump the silt that goes out the mouth of the Mississippi River, instead of pumping it over the shelf into the Gulf, you could pump it up north where we could use it. When I told them that they just laughed at me. But there are pipelines that pump oil from way out in the Gulf of Mexico to God knows how far up into Louisiana ... if they can do that, I know damn well they can pump some sand where it's needed.'

After the Swamp Lands Act of 1849, much of wetlands ownership was passed back to individual citizens.[41] In this part of Coastal Louisiana, private land owners, including tribal members, have leased their land to

41. The sentiment in Congress during the middle of the nineteenth century was that public domain had little value until it became settled, thereby ceasing to be public domain. Wetlands were actually considered a menace and hindrance to land development. As first passed (1849), the Swamp Land Act granted to Louisiana all swamp and overflow lands then unfit for cultivation, the object being to help in controlling floods in the Mississippi River Valley. Of approximately 65 million acres of wetlands given to the States, nearly all are now in private ownership.

oil companies. This is not big business. "We all lease," Albert said. "We don't get much but everybody says, 'Oh, I got my oil check today' and it's thirty-somethin' dollars ... they don't get much but that dog come in and tore us up when they would dredge to bring in a rig, or for a pipeline. It opened up the marsh for the Gulf water to come in even faster." The amount the oil company pays is based on acreage. "The share I get now is not like $30 a month, it's more like $30 every three months. I ain't getting much for my little share."

In addition to the loss of land itself, the biggest problem Isle de Jean Charles faces as a tribal group is the fight to keep the community together. After Lili in 2002 some of the island's 320 people moved off, and after Rita in 2005, more were lost—and this time a lot of them did not want to come back. But Chief Albert's fight—to keep the *community* in tact—is a problem that has become more complex. "I've been trying to convince them, let's let somebody relocate us, and the Corps of Engineers was going to do it, but then we had outside interference from other Indian tribes that said, 'O no, yo'all can't be moving people, its just like a modern-day Trail of Tears.'" When Albert thought about what his *community* needed—a place where everybody could have a little piece of land and a modern home—he decided he was going to change his attitude and pursue relocation. "But then I got interference and so I kinda lost the battle."

Albert had actually just sent an application to someone from Atlanta who was willing to help Indian tribes. Albert and the principal of the local school had also sent a grant form to see if they could get federal money to relocate; but with the federal government, 100 percent of the population would have to relocate. If they received the grant from Atlanta, however, they could start building homes, and as homes were finished, those who wanted to relocate could come on, and the rest could just stay on the island. Albert said, "It's going to be like a mother and her puppies where the mother's gonna move and some puppies come along and the others stay behind. But this is what we're facing now. We have one more hurricane—and for people still living on the island now, if we have the homes already built, well then at least they have some place to go."

What Chief Albert cares about—and that for which he is responsible—is his attachment to his people, his families, his culture, rather than the ground itself on which Isle de Jean Charles sits. Yet it would be false to say there was no attachment to the ground as well, or that there would be no pain from the ambiguity of what was left when the island was gone. The island was the locus of all the memories of Albert's family and his youth. I shared with Albert the story of the loss of the home of my own youth—a rambling old place hidden under giant oaks in another coastal town. Reason would argue the loss of a house shouldn't equal the loss of one's memories; but it *felt* as if they were lost, pulled into a black, empty void.

A lot of homes on Isle de Jean Charles had been elevated. A lot more would like to be elevated, but people didn't have the funds. In many cases, the foundations had been under water seven or eight times, so the wood was rotten and couldn't even be repaired for people to continue living there. Those are the homes Albert wouldn't even try to raise; he would just start from scratch. The fact that mobile homes were the ones mostly raised did not add to an air of permanence. But Albert's thoughts kept returning to his feeling that it was hard to see the loss of the land that was his community, one that had originally been settled back in 1835.

The Isle de Jean Charles Band was among those tribal groups of the BCCM that left the United Houma Nation.[42] Like the experience of Marlene Foret's Grand Caillou-Dulac Band, the BIA knows they exist but has not recognized them yet. Albert had been promised by BIA that they would definitely receive findings in January, 2008. January and February have passed. Albert has heard nothing.

Chief Naquin continually ponders the dilemmas of whether to move or not move his dwindling community on Isle de Jean Charles. "If we relocated, we really don't know where that would be. Not too far, just inside

42. Albert's account of their separation from the United Houma Nation in 1994 parallels that of Marlene's. What happened, Albert recalled, was the BIA sent the Houma Council a proposed finding which said BIA knew they were Indians, but they hadn't proved they were descended from the ancient Houma tribe. The Houma had to prove the existence of a coherent community. But the Houma were scattered all over Terrebonne, Lafourche, St. Mary, and Jefferson Parishes—scattered all over the southern part of Louisiana. So they couldn't prove a community; there wasn't one community they could identify. But the Houma Council refused to change their name from Houma. "At that point a group of us got together to see what the BIA wanted that we needed to give them, and we separated from the Houma Council. The Grand Caillou and Dulac formed a Biloxi-Chitimacha Confederation and we did on the island [Isle de Jean Charles] and Bayou Lafourche, and Pointe-au-Chien. But they [Pointe-au-Chien Indian Tribe (PACIT)] went on their own because they had an interest in fighting for land claims. We didn't want to fight for Indian land claims. We figured if we fought for land claims, the big white landowners were going to fight us tooth and nail to make sure we didn't get federal recognition. So we said we don't want that, the land we'd get would just be water anyway, so why fight for it. We just fight for our recognition and hopefully we can get money to send our kids to college and help them a bit. That's all we're looking for."

the hurricane protection levee, so the kids can attend the same schools, so we wouldn't be moving the kids away from their usual activities." Possibly they would move up towards Pointe-aux-Chenes, where there is land on Hope Farm Road they have; that would be Albert's first option. Instead of traveling north to go to school—sometimes by boat, as in the old times—children would travel south. The fishermen would have to get in their trucks to go down to their boats, because Bayou Pointe-au-Chien is navigable only about to the bridge, after that only by small boats. The work and the culture of people on Isle de Jean Charles has always been shrimping and fishing, but in the last few years that has changed. Isle de Jean Charles is undergoing silent transitions between those staying and those moving away. Some of the young ones living there are fishermen, but the majority are the elders, most of whom have retired. Several who were welders or worked on boats finally moved off after their houses kept flooding. Some who were working in the shipyards or on offshore boats or on tugboats in the river stayed; others moved out. Albert's own house flooded seriously in 1972, and he bought a piece of land in Pointe-aux-Chenes.

The aquaculture proposal was not yet receiving a lot of attention that reached Chief Naquin. There were many different views, and changes of viewpoint—some were against it, then for it, then against it. What is more immediately critical is the position of Isle de Jean Charles within the Morganza to the Gulf Hurricane Protection Project. Albert pointed out that before 1999, Isle de Jean Charles was *included* in the hurricane protection levee, but in 1999 they were *excluded* from the protective levees. He described its route as we detailed earlier—following Bayou Pointe-au-Chien south until it came to about two miles above the road that crossed to the island, and then turning back north to go west toward Montegut, then back south and across towards Chauvin and Dulac. "They kind of put us in a horseshoe." So Albert went to the people at USACE with his ruler and showed the engineers that, with their horseshoe route around the island, the levees would run over 20 miles, while if they went straight across and included the island, the levees would only run 5 or 6 miles. USACE engineers had been putting forth a cost-benefit analysis according to which it was going to cost more to include the island. Now Albert had a counter analysis with the ruler in his hand. Running the levees to include Isle de Jean Charles would save money in the long run, because when you added up the costs of building 20 miles of levees vs. only 5 or 6 miles of levees by keeping Isle de Jean Charles within the levee protection system, the choice should have be clear.

The deeper and still unanswered question is: what of Isle de Jean Charles is of value to Louisiana and to our larger American society? What is the value of a people and its culture?

In 2004, an anthropologist who heads the BIA Branch of Acknowledgment and Recognition, Holly Reckord, came down to Coastal Louisiana and talked with Chief Albert Naquin and other tribal leaders. Holly tried to tell them what more they needed to do to achieve recognition. For Albert it was a generally positive experience, although there still appeared to be great gaps in the federal agency's ability to understand the local tribal culture of Coastal Louisiana. "When Holly was here," Albert recalled, "she was asking where the boundaries were for fisherman and trappers and hunters … she wanted to know where the division was between a Pointe-au-Chien and an Isle de Jean Charles and then a Montegut. I told Holly there was no division. She said, What do you mean? I said, all we had, basically, like for an oyster bed … all you did was put your name on there and that's where you fish at, and they had certain ribbons that they would put on their trap poles and that was their trap. People knew each other and where they hunted or trapped, and they didn't go across hunting areas. We didn't need a division. The guy from Pointe-au-Chien knew where my Dad would fish and trap, and the same thing for Montegut on that side there. They all knew each other so they didn't cross their lines; it's not like today."[43]

"If we don't do this, save Isle de Jean Charles," Albert mused, "the culture's gonna die, it's just going to die. The community is going to die as a whole, because along with the cemetery down there, what we have is the old people, and the old people are gonna die, and the younger ones are just going to pack up and go. As soon as they reach the age to get married, they'll find a job somewhere else and move off, so the island is just gonna die."[44]

---

43. This is similar to Maine and Massachusetts where lobstermen have different colored patterns on their buoys.

44. For Albert Naquin, it continues to be worth trying to get his tribal island included in the hurricane protection levee. Albert has repeatedly gone to his local State Senator, Reggie Dupré—someone who has very publicly pronounced his interest and concern for coastal environmental matters. "I consider him a friend," Albert said, "but he doesn't go to bat for me." When he was running for office, Albert told Dupré about Isle de Jean Charles. Reggie said, "I'm on your side, I'm on your side." Albert Naquin's reply was, "Well, let me give you an example here of what you can do if 'you're on my side." Perhaps it will be best, as Reggie has suggested, to wait until the levee project gets fully approved by Congress,

Le soleil est couché, tu viens loin de la maison
Qu'avez-vous, oui, belle blonde? Qu'avez-vous, oui, belle
brune?
Avec le jogue au plombeau et la ferraille à la poche
Toujours chercher à malfaire, tu reçois la bourouette[45]

As I prepared to leave Isle de Jean Charles one late December afternoon, the orange sun was slowly dripping its fiery liquid into the brown
waters of the Gulf, singeing tips of tan cordgrass (*Spartina alterniflora*)
and saltgrass (*Distichlis spicata*) and black needlerush (*Juncus roemeri-
anus*) with flecks of gold. The reeds and grasses barely swayed in the calm
waters and a vague breeze. But always, on the horizon, loomed the dark,
heavy clouds of impending storms.

Storms not present were always a possibility in the mind here. I thought,
*you could never be sure whether to take the boat out, or pull closed the shutters
in anticipation of winds that could turn a warm breeze from the southwest
into a cold gale from the north. Hell, take the boat out anyway.*[46] There were
always risks in waters that invited to be fished, combed for shrimp.

---

then ask for arealignment of the levee route. Rather than try to start changing the Corps
of Engineers' plans before they gets approved, wait and then go back with amendments.
Too often, however, USACE seems in disarray. Even with the recent authorization for
the closing of the MR–GO navigational channel, it was unclear whether this would fully
solve the problem the channel had created. Traveling in that area, it is quite clear there is
now an enormous amount of open water on either side of channel that can still go into
New Orleans, even if the channel is closed to vessel traffic.

Albert remains confident that the Isle de Jean Charles will achieve recognition; it's
just a question of 'getting in the right stuff' in the right places. "We don't have that many
educated people in our group," Albert observed, "and those that are educated are not
involved, so it kind of leaves the ball to the mediocre people that are interested in getting
recognition but don't have the smarts to do it."

Chief Albert has shared his tribal written history, a folder with pictures, historical
articles from 1940s, a census showing there were Chitimacha and Choctaws separate
from Houmas. In helping Albert in his quest for recognition, it is less a question of the
author having any unique skills, than supporting the goal of seeing tribes benefit from
federal and state money that goes to the schools for Indian education.

45. *The sun is setting, you come far from home / What's the matter, beautiful blonde?
What's the matter, beautiful brunette?/ With a jug on the saddle horn and brass knuckles in
the pocket / Always looking for trouble, you get the wheelbarrow.* Adaptation of *Je m'endors*
(Recorded by John and Alan Lomax, 1934), RRNR Brattydog Music/ASCAP. In old Cajun
songs, "*la bourouette*" (*brouette* in standard French) is used as a prison image because prisoners building the Mississippi River levees used 'wheelbarrows' rolled up and down on six
inch wide planks. Reference from Ann Savoy, *Cajun Music: A Reflection of a People*.

46. Weather patterns affecting mariners along the Gulf are irregular and often squally,

Winds of change were passing over South Louisiana, ambiguities lay in its future. Would the sounds, the tastes, the colors, the smells of its past be transformed into things unanticipated? Would communities at the edge of the Gulf slowly evaporate with the passage of time? The wake of every hurricane leaves things different. But the wake of Hurricane Katrina and Hurricane Rita left the emptiness of a different world altogether. In many respects, the storms detached South Louisiana from the rest of the country. In reality, this unique land has always been detached—but by choice, by the fullness of its life. Now one felt a gnawing emptiness—empty streets of coastal villages no longer inhabited, vacant houses in city neighborhoods no longer lived in. Perhaps it was only the cold winds of winter, perhaps it was the ambiguities of an unknown future. Either way, there was a deadly quiet.

However different the future would come to be, it would be so much easier if one could know now *how* it would be different—*what* would be reborn from watery graves, from the brown sludge that still hung around where no rain or person cared to wash it away. South Louisiana was a world that desperately needed journeymen workers—not just the roustabouts and welders in demand on the rigs, not just the shrimpers and oystermen slowly departing for work elsewhere, but carpenters and plumbers and electricians willing to piece together the fragments of a society. It seemed at times all there was to hear were the politicians, their voices incessantly telling the world what would be and not be. Better the sounds only of musicians, if there were that choice—at least they would reach the soul.

The sadness of South Louisiana, ironically, is a large contributor to its beauty—like the sadness of a love lost, it is still remembered, treasured in one's old age. But when the sadness expresses nothing more than a loss of identity, the heart is no longer a player in its memories. The memories have simply dissipated into the indistinct, brown murkiness of the Gulf, and the grayness of the late winter sky, as the sun completes its journey below the horizon of the waters.

Walking to New Orleans has documented many stories of hard work, perseverance, heroes known and unknown. Let others simply keep their silent prayers for this tragic land to awaken and find itself again.

---

with periods of time in which the prevailing winds are from the southeast, other times with often moist southerlies. The pattern described is more typical of winter months, with fronts crossing from the northwest and causing storm-driven winds from the north or northeast.

Near Dulac

Near Bayou Point-au-Chien

Postlude

Theodicies Reconsidered

FOR PEOPLE OF REASON, the idea that the question of theodicy should even be raised in the context of the flooding that followed Hurricane Katrina might seem offensive. It is common for residents of the city— including those most affected by the flooding—to distinguish between the possibilities of human vs. divine causes of disaster. Most are willing to agree with the observation made by geographer Gilbert White in 1942, noted in Chapter 4, that 'floods are acts of God, but flood losses are largely *acts of man*.' Sakura Koné of Common Ground reflected such a sentiment in his remark about 'what the hurricane caused—I say that loosely because this was a *man-made disaster*.' Patricia Jones, director of the Neighborhood Empowerment Network Association (NENA), a grassroots organization in the Lower Ninth Ward and a UUSC program partner, also described Katrina as a "man-made disaster." Kit Senter, another community activist, echoed Patricia when he characterized the seventeen breaches in levees around New Orleans as a 'massive failure of the system.' The IPET report has documented in considerable detail exactly what 'massive failure of the system' means, in scientific and engineering terms. Beyond these immediate observations, *Walking to New Orleans* has taken pains to identify many of the large number of *pre-existing* conditions of social injustice and political-economic inequities, as well as geographical and topographical vulnerability in New Orleans and Coastal Louisiana, that intensified the 'evil' consequences of disaster on a human level.

Nevertheless, neither reasoning nor data have prevented some from raising questions of theodicy in a variety of ways. In its sparest form, one can think of the matter of theodicy as a dilemma inherent in the notion of a transcendent God itself. The conjunction of two attributes, divine omnipotence and benevolence, intrinsic to the concept of God as understood in Western religious traditions, would seem to be inconsistent in the presence of evil in the world. Formulations of the problem arise as early as ancient Mesopotamia, where the chaotic, disruptive nature of the world was interpreted to be a consequence of many deities battling for control. Epicurus treats the problem as a riddle; it appears in Lucretius' *De Rerum Natura*. But the term 'theodicy,' derived from the Greek roots *theos* (God) and *dike* (justice), was employed in Leibniz' 1710 *Essais de Théodicée sur la bonté de Dieu, la liberté de l'homme et l'origine du mal* and discussion with skeptic Pierre Bayle about divine governance of the world in relation to the nature of humankind.[1]

Theodicies take the general form of attempts, on the premise of divine omnipotence, to justify God's benevolence and justice in the face of the reality of evil in the world. Some follow a neo-Platonic and Augustinian[2] path that seeks to eliminate the reality of evil by characterizing it as a *privatio boni*—a 'privation' of being in the way that darkness is an *absence* of light. Others focus on a domain that encapsulates evil *within* human sinfulness, leaving the matter of natural evil—the consequences of natural disaster and pestilence, for example—in a state of some theological ambiguity. Hume formulates Epicurus' "old question" in *Dialogues Concerning Natural Religion* in its strongest, and analytic form. If a perfectly benevolent God would prevent evil but is unable to do so, then God cannot be omnipotent. If God is capable of preventing evil, but unwilling to do so, then God cannot be perfectly benevolent. But if it is analytically true that God must be perfectly benevolent and omnipotent, then why is there evil in the world? Put this way, the existence of evil calls

1. Leibniz' conclusion was that the best of all possible worlds, created by a perfect being (God), did not entail a perfect world—rather, the best of all possible worlds contains the most fortunate combination of possibilities, including moral and natural evil, that allows the largest number of 'possibles' to be actualized together (principle of plenitude). The Lisbon earthquake of 1755 that destroyed a third of the city's population put such ideas under considerable pressure. Voltaire's *Poème sur le désastre de Lisbonne* and *Candide* expressed a "cure" to Leibniz' theodicy; Rousseau pointed out the dangers of too many people living too close together in cities.

2. Representative especially of Augustine's earlier period, in which Augustine is attacking the mythology of the Manicheans, among whom he had spent nine years and who proposed the idea of a perpetual struggle between co-eternal principles of good and evil (Light and Darkness), with the human soul as a particle of Light entrapped in the Darkness of the physical world.

into question the logical possibility of any case for orthodox theism. One may be forced to acknowledge the outcome in which, if the problem of evil is irresolvable, it is because the concept of God itself is *fundamentally* inconsistent, and, therefore, unintelligible.[3] At the very least, when Hume asks why God does not act to prevent specific disasters (e.g., hurricanes that endanger ships at sea and cities on land), while there may be reasons "why providence interposes not in this manner," those reasons are unknown to us, and *that* may constitute good reason to doubt the existence of such a God.

For purposes of discussion here, it is helpful to distinguish two forms the problem of evil may take in human experience. The more radical form, prompted by Hume, comes to the conclusion that the presence of evil in the world—whether human sin or natural events—ultimately renders the concept of a divine reality, a singular existing being to which one would attribute both absolute power and absolute benevolence, incoherent. It would be incoherent in the way a 'round square' is incoherent. However, to actually come to hold such a position would likely be dependent on other personal experience that convinced one that the idea of God was incoherent.

A second form that leads to a rejection of the idea of God may be closer to what many people actually do experience, given the circumstances of their life. This is the form expressed by Dr. Rieux in Camus' *La Peste* (The Plague, 1947). This is a view that might allow the concept of God as intelligible, but, at the same time, finds the idea of God *morally* repugnant and unacceptable. In attempting to treat those suffering from the ravages of plague in Algeria's city of Oran, especially its children, Dr. Rieux attacks the theological and metaphysical framework of his friend, Father Paneloux, arguing that a God who allows innocent children to die is a God he cannot accept, a God he must morally reject. Interestingly, Paneloux is subsequently inspired to deliver a sermon addressing not the death of innocents, but an understanding of death as an expression of divine will, such that the death of a child becomes a 'test' for Christians who must choose, in a Kierkegaardian sense, between following God totally and absolutely or not at all. At several points, Paneloux implies those who die from the plague are 'sinful,' although this suggestion might be

3. In the *Enquiry Concerning Human Understanding*, rather than argue that the reality of evil itself proves God cannot exist (evil renders perfect goodness and omnipotence inconsistent), Hume says we are not in a position to *know* how God's actions might justify some (re)distribution of evil in the world.

mitigated by interpreting his view in light of the many theologies (e.g., Augustine, Calvin) that emphasize the *universality* and inescapable nature of human sin. Eventually, Paneloux is stricken ill with plague, and dies with a crucifix in his hands.

In some instances during the aftermath of Katrina, it is hard to know exactly what was in the mind of those who raised issues of theodicy, in one form or another. For example, Mayor Ray Nagin himself had at one point implied the devastating hurricanes were signs of God's wrath: "Surely God is mad at America."[4] Apart from leaving it quite open exactly *what* God might be 'mad about,' it is a remark that takes the notion of a 'personal God' to an anthropomorphized absurdity. Was it meant to be taken in some sense in which God suddenly became 'pissed off' at America and just couldn't hold it in any longer?

The most offensive theodicies are *punitive* theodicies expressed by religious conservatives and fundamentalists, who frequently interpret natural disasters as occasions for divine vengeance—punishment of various forms of 'human sinfulness' that turn out to be identical with issues about social values or lifestyle choices that are high on the list of the political agenda religious conservatives ordain themselves to be set against. Conservative ministers have seen Hurricane Katrina as a justifiable attack on New Orleans' history of flaunting its immorality and open sexuality, its disregard of Christian values, its abortion clinics, its annual gay pride parades, the dependence of its citizens on welfare, its high crime rate, and pretty much anything else on the political agenda worthy of vengeance and in need of 'purification.' For the most conservative believers who are also Biblical literalists, attacks on human sinfulness are combined with a Millenarian timetable. Natural disasters are the vehicles that usher in the onset of a new apocalyptic age[5] in which *only* divine vengeance can cleanse the earth of its evil.

Interestingly, the idea of natural disaster as divine punishment can fit a variety of political agendas. Michael Eric Dyson quotes a *Toronto Sun* piece in which Louis Farrakhan interprets Katrina as God's way of punishing America for its racist caste system—something which has to

4. Quoted in John Pope, "Evoking King, Nagin calls N.O. 'chocolate' city," *The Times-Picayune*, January 17, 2006.

5. A religious view not unique to Christians; Hindus have a concept of the Kali Yuga (age of vice), the fourth cycle of Yugas, the age most corrupt and dark, in which human civilization has spiritually degenerated and become the furthest possible from God.

be destroyed and replaced.[6] Conservative black Baptist pastor Dwight McKissic warned against the practice of voodoo and devil worship in New Orleans, saying "You can't shake your fist in God's face 364 days a year and then ask, 'Where was God when Katrina struck?'"[7] Especially where issues of race became intermingled with economics, punitive theodicies arose through a variety of involuted reasonings. Did the suffering of poor, less educated African American victims of the flooding who didn't evacuate, for example, only symbolize the evils of a welfare state mentality, because the white population, also potential victims of flooding, *had the sense to get out*? Closer to home, recall Sakura Koné's observation that Katrina became an excuse to eliminate public housing in New Orleans—expressed by the Congressman who suggested "We've been trying to do away with public housing for years, and here God has done it for us."

Those who find themselves, religiously, in the prophetic tradition of Martin Luther King and the black church, might be hard pressed to simply ignore the Scriptural bases for punitive theodicies. On the other hand, someone like Dyson, who honors black prophetic religion, finds the suggestion that God chose the storm to speak as "anachronistic," and suggests instead that if God really were going to invoke vengeful destruction, he "usually warns the righteous to scram before disaster descends."[8] Whether or not one agrees, the conclusion that "only a revival of black prophetic religion will aid the largely black survivors to stand on solid ground after swimming in the toxic waters of Katrina" has considerable resonance. But that seems to me to be more a question of finding a basis for social equality rather than divine vengeance.

Suppose one steps back from asking how God could allow the brimming, turbulent Lake Pontchartrain to break the levees, and instead ask how God could allow self-interested, shortsighted politicians put off reinforcing the levees or allow the negligence, racism, and social indifference that long gnawed at the social fabric of New Orleans.[9] If American society

6. Dyson, *Come Hell or High Water,* 180.

7. Selwyn Crawford, "Storms as Wrath of God?" *Dallas Morning News,"* October 5, 2005, quoted in Dyson and elsewhere.

8. Dyson, 183. "The rule of divine anger usually operates like this: If God gets ready to strike, God usually offers up ample chariots, or a whale—it was good enough for Jonah—or plenty of Fords or Chevys, to let folk scamper out of town."

9. As does Peter Steinfels, "Beliefs; The scarcely heard question is how God could have allowed the catastrophe to occur," in the *New York Times,* September 10, 2005.

has made independence and individual human freedom a secular, ersatz God, does this amount to the avoidance of deeper social self-examination of the sources of evil; a moral universe bound only by what is *effective*? Worse, is it reducible to justifying the attitude that what cannot be fixed cannot be thought about—so fundamental problems of poverty, crime, and homelessness must be accepted as inherently part of the human condition? Avoiding the paradoxes of self-examination that prophetic religion brings—however impossible it may be to resolve them—may simply remove them from the table of genuine scrutiny. Thus, Steinfels suggests delving into such mysteries might very well lead to a more profound understanding of the human condition.

Whether the concept of God is 'on or off the table' may be less important than the large numbers of people who remain wedded to the need to find *some* basis in the structure of reality that makes moral action intelligible, that serves as a context for thinking of human life as purposeful. Even the traditional concept of a transcendent God is not *simply* awesome, mysterious power,[10] the source of inexplicable events that may result in human suffering; the same God is also an agency of human empowerment,[11] that which is infinitely inviting, drawing human nature to it as a source of meaning and a basis of moral truth.

Were there expressions of non-punitive, positive theodicies in the post-Katrina environment in which a human relationship to the reason-resistant mysteries of divine power could become a source of human empowerment in the very face of disaster and destruction? There were, and their formulations ranged from restatements of ancient (and still unsatisfying) pastoral theodicies to youthful discoveries of evidence of God's work in acts of restoration to the call to renew the social value of prophetic traditions to the emergence of a new understanding of nature itself.

A Divine Test

An example of the attempt to come up with a positive theodicy could be seen in religious interpretation of disasters such as hurricanes and floods by clergy who were comfortable within the scholastic tradition of actually providing arguments in support of their beliefs (as opposed to funda-

---

10. In Rudolf Otto's sense of *mysterium tremendum* in *Das Heilige—Über das Irrationale in der Idee des Göttlichen und sein Verhältnis zum Rationalen Heilege,* 1917.

11. What Otto calls *fascinans*.

mentalist clergy who either discerned God's word directly or regarded themselves as the sole interpreter of the 'true' meaning of Scripture). The idea of religious belief as a matter available for discussion is admirable; unfortunately, the arguments themselves were often less than robust. Father Thomas Rosica, a Roman Catholic priest, reflected on the meaning of Hurricane Katrina and suggested that "God doesn't intervene to prevent such things, because God loves us too much. If we had a God who simply swooped down to halt natural catastrophes, prevent human tragedy and sinfulness, then religion and faith would simply be reduced to some form of magic or fate, and we would be helpless pawns on some divine chess board."[12] Rosica's argument is a form of free will defense, and turns on the implicit assumption that a limited existence of some evil is necessary to avoid the human race being reduced to automata. Other versions emphasize that certain unequal natural differences among people have value, for example, by generating the competition among humans that produces art and science. Still others proclaim how the need to struggle against the forces of nature itself can elicit human greatness and compassion. The latter is especially emphasized by Fr. Jerome LeDoux in a piece entitled "Even chaos and tragedy are God's tools."[13] Fr. LeDoux recounts the story of a storm evacuee, lying helpless and homeless, "thanks to evil twins Katrina and Rita," with her days numbered, suffering a large wound on her back, until she was discovered to be a nun, Sister Annunciata, after which she was 'rescued' and showered with love and attention by family and Church until she regained health. Fr. LeDoux sees this as the work of Divine Providence, quoting St. Paul, "We know that in all things God works for good with those who love him, those whom he has called according to his purpose" (Romans 8:28). While the LeDoux account is uplifting, in a pastoral sense, and provides encouragement, one still has to ask: what about all those who suffered and were *not* rescued by family or Church, who succumbed to the toxic waters or died from infection or sheer exhaustion alone and uncomforted? What about "the

12. Fr. Thomas Rosica, "Where Was God in This Crisis," in the *Toronto Sun*, September 11, 2005.

13. Fr. Jerome LeDoux, "Even Chaos and Tragedy are God's Tools," *The Louisiana Weekly*, January 22, 2007. The philosopher John Hick in *Evil and the God of Love* has defended the belief that evil in the world can be justified if it contributes to spiritual growth, an accumulation of 'right choices,' and the development of a positive and responsible character from "mastering temptation"—as well as, presumably, acting bravely in the face of natural disaster.

heart-rending moans, groans, screams and shrieks of the helpless residents," as Fr. LeDoux describes, that *did* fall on deaf ears? Ultimately, this theodicy—and its variants—makes the value of human differences that may result in artistic achievement and scientific discovery pay the price for the annihilation of the innocent. The attempt to support a suitably tempered Divine Providence by the suggestion that "God is caught in the same dilemma we are"[14] does not help, unless we are truly to accept *all* the consequences of God's 'not being able to derail the machinery and circumstance' of disasters and floods.

God is Here Among Us

An example of a positive and charmingly innocent theodicy is expressed in a January 25, 2008 report of the Mennonite Disaster Service (MDS)—a volunteer network through which various constituencies of the Anabaptist Church respond to those affected by disasters in Canada and the United States. The MDS has been probably one of the strongest and most consistent exemplars of a religious body that makes outreach and help and hard work for others in disaster situations a hallmark of its religious self-identity, even as it partners cooperatively with other ecumenical faith organizations. While its main focus in Louisiana has been on clean up, repair and the rebuilding of homes, MDS understands this activity as a means of touching lives and helping people regain faith and wholeness. Cameron Parish, in the southwest corner of Louisiana, was a beach and fishing destination before it was devastated by Hurricane Rita. The coastal town of Cameron was virtually flattened. Two and one-half years after the storm, the community is very much in the recovery process, with many still living in FEMA trailers. MDS has been repairing and rebuilding homes in partnership with Faith Share, an ecumenical group. The work crews were challenged to look for God during their week of work and fellowship, based on Psalm 127 which says that if the Lord does not build the house, the labor is in vain.

> So we thought it would be a good idea to check and see if God was involved in the work in Cameron Parish. Well, the reports on Wednesday evening and the experiences during the week indicated

14. As does Michael Eric Dyson in what appears as a nod to some form of process theology (185–86). "[God] shares a frustration born of love and respect for human freedom..."

that God is indeed deeply involved in the process of getting these new houses built. God's encouragement for the workers during a wet and uncomfortable week came in several forms. One of the most notable was a special delivery of cookies to the jobsite by a pair of neighborhood children. A deputy sheriff encountered in a hardware store also provided affirmation of the work . . . saying that these selected clients were just the right people to be building a house for. . . . The kitchen was also a place of Godly encounters. In near miraculous circumstances, needed ingredients appeared on RV shelves, so we could have some delicious rolls that evening. And all of those dining with us would confirm that the lemon and chocolate pies were heavenly.[15]

While it may be hard, even from a religious standpoint, to know exactly how to interpret these youthful utterances, it would be equally wrong to dismiss them as naively proclaiming nothing more than the absence of any need for theodicy—that *anything* good is something God does, and nothing God does is not also good. Overriding both of those positions must be a deeper sense of the thankfulness of the workers for having their labor appreciated, and in those human thanks, hearing at the same time the word of God. At that point the 'benignly optimistic' is transformed into the powerfully spiritual.

Prophetic Religion Renewed

Theodicies that emphasize the positive and renewing function of prophetic religion, that call for a reawakening of social values as did the prophets, can perhaps be understood as less about finding evidence for or against God's role in natural events (God's action in history is always presumed) than they are about examining the place of the house of humanity in the cosmos—its moral health, and how well its societies serve the needs of all citizens at all levels of social structures, especially those forced to live at the margins of economic and social well being. To the extent that prophetic theodicy is located specifically within the black church, it does not seem appropriate for a non-black to speak to how it *could* be meaningful. Michael Eric Dyson occupies that position, and suggests black prophetic faith offers believers three resources in the face of natural disasters such as Hurricane Katrina. First, it provides moral and theological insight into

15. "Report to January 25, 2008," Mennonite Disaster Service, accessible at http://mds .mennonite.net/Projects/Cameron_LA.

'natural disaster,' not as a punitive theodicy, but by focusing on the evil that is wrought by human beings, understanding God's will to be that human beings flourish and live in harmony with each other and nature. Second, it offers a prophetic critique of the persistent racial, class, and economic inequalities brought to the surface by Katrina and its aftermath. Finally, it challenges black churches to recapture their prophetic anger and transform that passion into social action.

Are there aspects of the prophetic tradition that can be argued apply universally, independent of race and class? I believe so. Whether driven from *within* the particularity of a race that has experienced a history of inequity of opportunity and exploitation at the hands of others, or from a moral awareness *outside* the experience of what certain races or classes have suffered, many prophetic visions can lead to an awareness of corporate and systemic, as well as individual, forms of evil.[16] Many routes lead to activism in the eradication of the sources of evil in human social structures. One, strongly suggested in *Walking to New Orleans,* is a route that comes through the sciences and engineering as well as through political criticism.

The Deuteronomic transformation of prophecy—viewing the prophet as the spokesperson of Torah, and Moses as the paradigmatic prophet—is perhaps less about the claim that God alone appoints the prophet, than about giving the prophet enough independence from human institutions to be able to challenge them. That may be a clue to why prophecy is important to us today. Texts from Mari (Tall al-Hariri, eighteenth century BCE) in northwest Mesopotamia show striking parallels to Hebrew prophecy, including oracles that dealt with the king's duty to protect the poor and needy, and ethical admonitions, threats, accusations, as well as predictions of disaster or fortune. Ultimately, prophecy was not about divination, but about society and what is wrong with it. Even among ecstatic seer prophets such as Zoroaster, the ca tenth century BCE founder of Persian religion, one can find a concern with social evil.

The Hebrew term for prophet is *navi*, and there were a great many of them; the Talmud (Megillah 14a) says there had been twice as many prophets as the number of people who left Egypt. In the southern king-

16. In the sense of Walter Rauschenbusch's *Theology for the Social Gospel,* 1917. Rauschenbusch was a Baptist Minister in New York's Hell's Kitchen minister, whose theology demonstrated that evil exists in corporate entities, including the combination of graft and political power, militarism, and the institutional corruption of justice.

dom of eighth century BCE Judah, Isaiah prophesied in Jerusalem, initially focusing on the corruption of Judah's society before coming to see the advance of Assyria as divine chastisement, "the rod of God's wrath," in turn to be broken on the mountains of Judah, with Israel renewed to prosper under the reign of an ideal Davidic king. Micah, contemporary with Isaiah, touched on a similar vision of universal peace, but more strongly announced that the wickedness of rulers would cause Zion to become a plowed field and Jerusalem a heap of ruins; social morality took precedence over the cult itself. The prophets were not simply predictors of the future, but *harbingers* of reform—an office concerned with social reform and ethics, and therefore, about doing something concrete in the present.[17]

From this sketch, one sees how the prophetic tradition can be appropriated as a means of empowerment in the face of disaster whose pre-existing conditions of social inequities and government corruption is well known. The prophetic tradition arouses both people and governments to observe what is really going on in society—ethically, morally, and in terms of basic principles of social justice. Modern prophets are social critics, as were Walter Raushenbusch or Upton Sinclair,[18] Martin Luther King and Malcolm X. Lest one think social criticism is not without risk, one can be reminded that Jeremiah was killed for his preaching. The prophetic tradition empowers not only a *priesthood of all believers*, but *the prophecy of all believers*. All are called to respond to the reality of social and moral evils; all are called to create a more just society. Clara Barton, founder of the American Red Cross, once said, "It irritates me to be told how things always have been done ... I go for anything new that might *improve* the past." The prophetic tradition is a faith of deeds, rather than creeds; a spirituality of action.

A New Understanding of Nature

The final example of a positive theodicy—the necessity to recognize the natural and human worlds as a cooperative system in whose understanding is acknowledgment of a sacred universe—is one that contrasts very strongly with the Biblical concept of stewardship and its hierarchical

17. Background drawn from lectures given in the period 1965–68 by G. Ernest Wright, Parkman Professor of Divinity and Curator of the Semitic Museum, Harvard University until his death in 1974.

18. Muckraker and socialist novelist who wrote *The Jungle*, 1906, an exposé of the meatpacking industry in Chicago.

model of the human control of nature. In chapter 2 we had looked at the appearance of that hierarchy in the prophetic tradition—the role of prophet as an intermediary and messenger between the heavenly court, scene of the covenant lawsuit, and the human community of Israel. This overall structure within which the office of the prophet operated was consistent with a hierarchy of authority from the divine to the human. Prophecy was not, however, primarily concerned with nature—at least as an entity separate from divine power. Its focus was on the social structures in which evil was embedded, and on the call for a renewal of society to establish the right relationship between humankind, society, and God.

It is perhaps pushing the limits of traditional theology to call the view of nature and humankind as a cooperative system a 'theodicy' because its focus is nature—not *instead of* God, but nature *inclusive of* God. At the same time, what is proposed equally pushes the limits of anthropology (i.e., its theory of human nature), because a truly eco-centric perspective rejects all exclusively anthropocentric ways of understanding the relation between humankind and nature. It rejects the view, for example, that the value of nature is its utility for human consumption. Focus is given to non human-centered value systems, or values that are not defined only in terms of human need.

A cooperative system of nature and humankind appears to eliminate the necessity of divine power as the sole, creative, singular existing being, responsible for the world—and the ultimate source of human purpose. In such a system, where is there room for anything like a theodicy, insofar as it constitutes justification for the 'actions' of some infinitely powerful individual, causally responsible for natural events such as hurricanes and floods? On the other hand, it may *function* as a theodicy to the extent that it reveals a new way to understand natural events and the human role in them. The recognition of nature and humankind as being ontologically linked within a cooperative system may reveal the universe as *sacred*. Moreover, it is not to say the system itself is without spiritual significance, or even a position from which expressions of prayer are a priori meaningless. But it is not an anthropomorphized version of sacred divine power understood on the model of a supremely powerful *person*—one who is sometimes benevolent but also angry and vengeful.

To the extent that the idea of God is retained at all, it may end up resembling Paul Tillich's concept of God as being-itself, or inviting comparison with Spinoza's "eternal and infinite Being, which we call God or

Nature (*Deus sive Natura*)."[19] While the concept of God of Spinoza's *Ethics* is hardly the idea of a providential God as creator, divine lawgiver, agent in human history, and judge, is there another sense in which it helps connect understanding nature and humankind as a cooperative system with principles of a just and moral society? Does the non-teleological nature of a deterministic universe in which "all things proceed by a certain eternal necessity of nature" eliminate responsibility and justice altogether?

After concluding that "Whatever is, is in God, and nothing can be or be conceived without God" (Part I, Prop XV), Spinoza is at pains to establish that talk implying God's existence precludes anthropomorphizing divine reality. To avoid the oddness from Prop. XV that talk about God implies physical objects like people and houses, oceans and mountains (and their states) are *properties* of God,[20] in Prop. XVI Spinoza shifts to talk of God as the underlying and sustaining cause of all things.[21] But the God here is quite distinct from the God of Western theology, a transcendent being who creates a universe separate from himself *ex nihilo*. Spinoza's God is the infinite power from which "all things have necessarily flowed forth in an infinite number of ways, or always follow from the same necessity; in the same way as from the nature of a triangle it follows, from eternity and for eternity, that its three interior angles are equal to two right angles" (Part I, Prop. XVII, scholium). The universe thereby becomes logically necessary, such that it is impossible that God should exist *without* the universe. What is especially interesting, however, is that among the reasons such anthropomorphizing is destructive is that it leads to a view of the relationship between humankind and nature (one Spinoza appears to find offensive) that echoes the argument that the hierarchical structure of authority which emerges from the Biblical notion of stewardship perpetuates the ethically repugnant idea that nature is divinely ordained for human use. In the Appendix to Part I, Spinoza speaks of how humans

19. Spinoza, *Ethics*, Part IV, Preface.

20. From which it could follow that if *N.N.* is in pain, and *N.N.* is "in God," then God feels pain.

21. The notion of cause, which arises from how substances interact and change, in accordance with the laws of their own nature, as Stuart Hampshire points out, must be divested of its contemporary associations with the causal laws of modern experimental science. A *cause* is simply that which *explains* how one true proposition is the logically necessary consequence of some other; the ideal of scientific explanation in rationalist philosophies generally is deductive, with Euclid's geometry as the standard of genuine explanation. See Hampshire, *Spinoza*, 35.

find, both in themselves and outside themselves, many means that assist them in seeking their own advantage—eyes for seeing, plants and animals for food, the sea for supporting fish. Hence, humans come to "consider all natural things as means to their own advantage." After having considered natural things as means for human use and consumption, and with the awareness that humans had "found these means, not provided them for themselves," it is a short step to teleology—the idea that there must have been "someone else who had prepared those means for their use." That step is one Spinoza wishes us not to take. Not simply because it leads to the wrong picture of God, but also, I would argue, because it leads to the wrong picture of human morality and social justice. It leads to "blind cupidity and insatiable avarice" and the self-centered assumption that the whole course of nature has been constructed for human satisfaction. To find purpose in nature in *this* way is to misconstrue nature, within which humanity, in the end, must be included. It also leads to the wrong picture of what worship of God should look like, because each human person "has thought up from his own temperament different ways of worshipping God, so that God might love them above all the rest, and direct the whole of Nature according to the needs of their blind desire and insatiable greed." This *prejudice* (which Spinoza regards as superstition) has struck deep roots in the human mind.

As it is wrong to find divinely ordained helps or benefits in nature for human utility, it is equally wrong to regard its hindrances—storms, earthquakes, and so forth—as enactments of a God who is "angry at some wrong . . . done by men." Day by day experience shows by "infinite examples that good and evil fortunes fall to the lot of the pious and impious alike."[22] To perpetuate this hierarchy of authority and a nature divinely ordained for human use is an "inveterate prejudice."

In the Preface to Part IV of the *Ethics*, Spinoza's metaphysic is summarily expressed in the statement "For the eternal and infinite Being, which we call God or Nature (*Deus sive Natura*), acts by the same necessity as that whereby it exists." This strict identity means that to talk about nature *just is* to talk about God. Nature, the infinite universe seen as a totality, is understood in two ways: as active (*natura naturans*) and productive and expressing God insofar as he is considered a free cause, and passive (*na-*

22. *Ethics*, Part I, Appendix.

tura naturata),[23] all that follows from the necessity of the nature of God, without which God cannot be conceived. The concept of nature that is established, therefore, is that of an uncaused, deterministic whole, outside of which nothing can exist. Because nature operates through necessity, it acts for no purpose or ends; there is no teleology. In this regard, it is not entirely unlike the Buddhist notion of *dharma*, in which reality is understood as being composed of a play of *impersonal* forces (*dharma events*), continually in flux, subject to the law of dependent origination (causality), but also constituting the impersonal moral order of the universe.

If nature is not the product of a singular existing creator who has designed the universe, has a plan for its purpose, and will finally judge how well human agents have exercised their free will, does this mean that any notion of benevolence must be absent from nature? Surely it could not be *benevolence granted*. Nature is without interests or desires or purposes. There is no divine candidate (God or gods) against which goodness in nature could be measured. But from that must it follow that the natural order is without goodness? If one can perceive beauty in nature, then why not its goodness? That may depend on what one wants out of 'goodness.' One speaks of nature's *bounty* at harvest time, or *success* on return from a fishing voyage. Those events are a goodness, but they are also simply *facts* of nature. They need no longer be thought of as directly the result of divine providence, despite the fact that thanks *are* offered to God at the time of the harvest or safe return from the catch. To force into spiritual reality the notion that every goodness must have a *giver*—a source based on the assumption of human attributes—is to have become captured by the picture of 'goodness' as requiring a giver independent from nature itself.

When the reference to 'God' is dissociated from all objective descriptions and images, especially those that picture the deity as a person, logic leads one to the recognition that God and nature cannot be distinguished. However, while Spinoza's identification of God with nature may have inspired poets of the Romantic Movement, for Spinoza this identification was not a matter of the imagination but the outcome of strict logic.[24] Imagining God as the singular Creator, on the basis of analogy with a human giver, renders theological and metaphysical dilemmas such as the problem of evil, and the issue of God's 'freedom of choice,' contradictions in terms, if the

23. *Ethics,* Part I, Prop. XXIX, scholium, 'Nature natur*ing*' and 'Nature natur*ed*,' respectively.
24. See Hampshire, 40–41.

only self-dependent substance, whose attributes are explicable in terms of its own infinite nature, is *nature itself*, conceived as a whole.

The "new understanding of nature" envisioned, then, has an eco-centric focus that rejects the anthropocentrism, grounded in Western religion and philosophy, which values nature exclusively in terms of its usefulness to humans. Its prophetic message is that the hierarchy of authority embedded in the model of 'stewardship' must be radically transformed because it perpetuates an ontological inequity between the human and the natural orders. The analogous model of authority that perpetuates unmerited differentia of class and economic position in society, which result in injustice, must also be rejected. In a sense a new understanding of nature calls for a *new humanity*—stimulated by our increased awareness that humans must learn to live sustainably on the earth; that we must interact with the many bio-systems of the earth in an ethically justifiable way. Not simply to serve the practical necessity of ensuring there will be natural resources left for the use and consumption of future generations, but because natural systems have certain 'rights'[25] analogous to the rights of freedom and equality of opportunity held by humans, regardless of unearned positions at some level of society, resulting from birth contingencies of economic status, race or ethnicity, intellectual capacities, health, or natural attractiveness.[26]

The American ecologist Aldo Leopold expressed something like this transcending, universal ecological worldview in his essay "Land Ethic," published posthumously in *A Sand County Almanac* in 1948. In it, Leopold argued that an ecologically just human society must be constructed and maintained in ways that protect the long-term flourishing of *all* ecosystems and each of their constituent parts. The emergence of such a new understanding of nature itself seems to move towards a sacralizing of the natural world. There is nothing wrong with that, although I might prefer to think of it as simply *honoring* our interconnectedness with other living

---

25. In the sense of their 'inherent value,' rather than *legal* rights.

26. It could (and has) been argued that some contingencies of birth may be rights—for example, being a citizen of Country Y—because they result from the meritorious actions of forebears; however, that right is only *in addition* to 'inherent values,' shared equally, by citizens of any country. The analogue in nature might be seen in the Taoist notion of *absolute relativism* as the order of nature. In nature there is no intrinsic value to a thing's being *long* vs. another being *short*. Tao not any more one thing than another. Tao is everywhere; it is in all things, and in all things *equally*. See R. R. N. Ross, "Non-Being and Being in Taoist and Western Philosophy," *Religious Traditions*, Vol. I, No. 2.

and non-living systems—and basing that interconnected relationship on scientific knowledge in which entire ecosystems are understood as existing on a par with human interests as a matter of empirical necessity. It is a scientific understanding that is connected with an ethic of nature seen in its broadest dimensions, and which recognizes that human interests are always more restrictive than those of nature as a whole.

To avert planetary ecological catastrophe, humankind and the social environments that have been created, must be able to exist harmoniously within the natural world. While 'sacralizing nature' or 'honoring nature' have come to involve forms of ritual behavior whose level of appeal varies considerably—earth-centered rites of neo-pagans who search for a deeper source of meaning for *their* spiritual lives, reinterpretations of Asian traditions such as Taoism or Buddhism, even the usurping of religious practices of indigenous cultures—I see seeking harmony as essentially something far more simple, although requiring a body of validated empirical knowledge on a vast scale. It means learning the ability to *think* on a scale that includes not only the interrelationships among all living species, but also the various geological and oceanographic and atmospheric systems that support life. It is thinking on a scale that ultimately transcends any particular, culturally bound set of religious beliefs and practices; that transcends the minute time-span human habitation has existed on earth.

It may mean, for example, to think of responsibilities for species of fish we do *not* eat. It may mean that, while it might be nonsense to think of entities such as trees and mountains as having 'rights,' it is important to understand why is it so obviously *wrong* to clear cut forests or to strip away sides of mountains for coal like butchers carving up pieces of meat.

The Biblical notion of stewardship, with its embedded hierarchical world view and structure of authority, raises serious questions about how humankind effectively acquires divine agency[27] in its privilege to make use of the natural order. Understanding the *entire* natural world as a sacred system that includes *both* the human and the natural presents a new model for moral agency. We stand not *above* the natural world—either as its user or as its steward—but instead exist as *part* of it. We are part of a world that has value in and of itself; we do not have *more* value than that world. We are, as the old cyber people used to say, co-routines that have to communicate.

27. That is, the *functional* equivalent of divine agency, at some level, regarded as morally justified.

Postlude

If God is nature, is not honoring the natural world also honoring God? If there is a need for salvation, must salvation be not *from* the world but *to* the world? Is that natural world now one which can be seen in a radically new and ethically responsible way? In the Christian tradition, salvation through resurrection expresses the need for a God who heals absolutely, makes all things new, but also preserves what makes life interesting and worthwhile.[28] How will such a life eternal be attractive and satisfying? One such vision comes from the fourteenth century French nun and mystic, Marguerite of Oingt, who wrote that "the saints will be completely within their Creator as the fish within the sea: They will drink to satiety, without getting tired and without in any way diminishing the water. They will drink and eat the great sweetness of God. And the more they eat, the more their hunger will grow. And this sweetness cannot decrease any more or less than can the water of the sea."[29] Such a vision may be a mixed blessing. We are still eternally dependent on the benevolence of our Creator. On the other hand, *all* of nature appears to be preserved and to exist in some form of harmony.

Through our technological skills and scientific understanding, we have made of this world a system of interconnections. We see our relation to the natural environment more clearly than in the past. We have ways to measure climatic changes, the progress of great ocean storms, the rising of the seas; we have the ability to not just pursue and catch fish but to farm them. Yet we have not yet had the ethical commitment to make of this natural system a community of caring. In some way we must be able to do this in the same way that we must find a way share the bounty of our own harvest with those who innocently suffer the consequences of drought or civil war. Humankind and nature are tied together into what Martin Luther King, Jr. once called a 'single garment of destiny, caught in an inescapable network of mutuality.'[30] Whatever affects one directly affects all indirectly. This is the way nature is made; this is the way it is structured.

---

28. It preserves the spiritual value of *embodied beings* as a unity of soul and body, rather than the sterility of souls as eternally *disembodied* beings.

29. Reference from David Callahan's Ingersoll Lecture for 2003.

30. In *Remaining Awake Through a Great Revolution*.

On Island Road

Near Isle de Jean Charles

Bibliography

American Planning Association. *American Institute of Certified Planners Code of Ethics and Professional Conduct.* Effective June 1, 2005. Online: http://www.planning.org/ethics/conduct.html.

Ancelet, Barry Jean, et al. *Cajun Country.* Folklife in the South Series. Jackson, MS and London, UK: University Press of Mississippi, 1991.

Aristotle. *The Basic Works of Aristotle.* Edited by Richard McKeon. New York, NY: Random House, 1941.

Attfield, Robin. *Environmental Ethics: An Overview for the Twenty-First Century.* Cambridge, UK: Polity Press, and Malden, MA: Blackwell Publishing, Inc., 2003.

———. *The Ethics of Environmental Concern.* New York, NY: Columbia University Press, 1983.

———. "Social and Economic Impacts of Outer Continental Shelf Activity on Individuals and Families. Volume I: Final Report" Minerals Management Service, Gulf of Mexico OCS Region, U.S. Department of the Interior, New Orleans, July 2004. Prepared under MMS Contract 1435-01-98-CT-30897 by Bureau of Applied Research in Anthropology, University of Arizona, Tucson, AZ.

Austin, Diane, et. al. "History of the Offshore Oil and Gas Industry in Southern Louisiana. Interim Report. Volume I: Papers on the Evolving Offshore Industry." Minerals Management Service, Gulf of Mexico OCS Region, U.S. Department of the Interior, New Orleans, July 2004. Prepared under MMS Contract 1435-01-02-CA-85169 by Center for Energy Studies, Louisiana State University, Baton Rouge, LA.

Barras, John A. "Land Area Changes in Coastal Louisiana After the 2005 Hurricanes." U.S. Geological Survey Open-File Report 066-1274.

Barrett, Carol D. *Everyday Ethics for Practicing Planners.* Washington, DC: American Planning Association, 2001.

Barry, John M. *Rising Tide: The Great Mississippi Flood of 1927 and How It Changed America.* New York, NY: Touchstone, Simon & Schuster, 1998.

Baum, Dan. "Deluged. When Katrina hit, where were the police?" *The New Yorker,* January 9, 2006.

Belhadjali, K.C., et al. "Coastal Restoration Division Annual Project Reviews: 2002. Louisiana Department of Natural Resources, Baton Rouge, LA, 2002.

Bell, Caryn Cossé. *Revolution, Romanticism, and the Afro-Creole Protest Tradition in Louisiana, 1718–1868.* Baton Rouge, LA and London, UK: Louisiana State University Press, 1997.

Berry, Wendell. *The Gift of Good Land. Further Essays Cultural and Agricultural. North Point Press.* New York, NY: Farrar, Straus and Giroux, 1981.

Bibliography

Berube, Alan, and Katz, Bruce. "Katrina's Window: Confronting Concentrated Poverty Across America." The Brookings Institution Metropolitan Policy Program, The Brookings Institution. Washingnton, DC. October, 2005.

Bourne, Jr., Joel K. "The Big Uneasy. Gone With the Water." *National Geographic.* Vol. 206, No. 4, October, 2004, 88–105.

———, and Turner, Tyrone. "The Perils of New Orleans." *National Geographic,* Vol. 212, No. 2, August, 2007, 32–65.

Brasseaux, Carl A., et al. *Creoles of Color in the Bayou Country.* Jackson, MS: University Press of Mississippi, 1994.

Brinkley, Douglas. *The Great Deluge: Hurricane Katrina, New Orleans, and the Mississippi Gulf Coast.* New York, NY: William Morrow, Harper Collins, 2006.

Broadmoor Project, The. "The Broadmoor Guide for Planning and Implementation. Lessons from Katrina: How a Community Can Spearhead Successful Disaster Recovery." Belfer Center for Science and International Affairs, John F. Kennedy School of Government, Harvard University, 2007, President and Fellows of Harvard College. The report is based on research and interviews conducted in the Broadmoor community in New Orleans from March 2006 through August 2007.

Brookings Institution, The. Metropolitan Policy Program. "New Orleans After the Storm: Lessons from the Past, a Plan for the Future." Washington, DC: The Brookings Institution, 2005.

———. The. Metropolitan Policy Program and the Greater New Orleans Community Data Center: A Product of Nonprofit Knowledge Works (GNODC). "The Katrina Index. Tracking Recovery of New Orleans & The Metro Area. Updated monthly. Renamed "The New Orleans Index" and also listed under Amy Liu (Brookings) and Allison Plyer (GNODC). Online: http://www.gnocdc.org and http://www3.brookings.edu/metro/pubs/20070517_katrinaES.pdf (June 14, 2007); summaries from January 2006 at http://www3.brookings.edu/metro/pubs/200601_KatrinaIndexes.pdf; January, 2008 report: http://www.gnocdc.org/NOLAIndex/ESNOLAIndex.pdf.

Broussard, James Francis. *Louisiana Creole Dialect.* Port Washington, NY: Kennikat Press, 1972.

Brunsma, David L., et al., eds. *The Sociology of Katrina: Perspectives on a Modern Catastrophe.* Lanham, MD: Rowman & Littlefield Publishers, Inc., 2007.Carson, Rachel. *Under Sea Wind.* New York, NY: Oxford University Press, 1941, renewed 1968 by Roger Christie-Child.

Chesney, Edward J., et al., "Louisiana Estuarine and Coastal Fisheries and Habitats: Perspectives from a Fish's Eye View," *Ecological Applications,* Vol. 10, No. 2, 2000, 350–66.

Childs, John Brown, ed. *Hurricane Katrina: Response and Responsibilities.* Santa Cruz, CA: New Pacific Press, 2005. CityWorks. "Directory of Neighborhood Organizations. Orleans Parish." 8.02.06, Updated 4.08.07.

Clifford, Jan. "Isle de Jean Charles Man Spearheads Relief Efforts," *Houma Today,* January 2, 2006. Online: www.houmatoday.com/apps/pbcs.dll/article?Date=2006102.

Coastal Protection and Restoration Authority of Louisiana. "Integrated Ecosystem Restoration and Hurricane Protection: Louisiana's Comprehensive Master Plan for a Sustainable Coast." Baton Rouge, LA 2007.

Colten, Craig E. *An Unnatural Metropolis: Wresting New Orleans from Nature.* Baton Rouge, LA: Louisiana State University Press, 2005; Louisiana Paperback Edition, 2006.

Bibliography

——. *Transforming New Orleans and Its Environs: Centuries of Change.* Pittsburgh, PA: University of Pittsburgh Press, 2000.

Cooper, Christopher, and Robert Block. *Disaster: Hurricane Katrina and the Failure of Homeland Security.* New York, NY: Henry Holt and Company, 2006.

Cowdrey, Albert E. *Land's End: A History of the New Orleans District, U.S. Army Corps of Engineers, and Its Lifelong Battle with the Lower Mississippi and Other Rivers Wending Their Way to the Sea.* U.S. Army Corps of Engineers, 1977. Downloaded in its entirety from the U.S. Army Corps of Engineers website:http://www.mvn.usace.army.mil/pao/history/LandsEnd/LandsEnd.htm.

Crosson, John Dominic. *Jesus: A Revolutionary Biography.* New York, NY: HarperSanFrancisco, HarperCollins Publishers, Inc., 1995.

Curry, Leonard P. *The Free Black in Urban America, 1800–1850: The Shadow of the Dream.* Chicago, IL: University of Chicago Press, 1986.

Cunningham, Scott. "Tides Without Equal. Paddling the Bay of Fundy," *Sea Kayaker,* August, 2007.

Dalley, Stephanie, ed. and transl. *Myths from Mesopotamia: Creation, the Flood, Gilgamesh, and Others.* Revised ed. Oxford, UK: Oxford University Press, 2000.

Davidson, Chandler, and Bernard Grofman, eds. *Quiet Revolution in the South: The Impact of the Voting Rights Act, 1965–1990.* Princeton, NJ: Princeton University Press, 1994.

Donagan, Alan. *Spinoza.* Chicago: University of Chicago Press, 1988.

Dunne, Mike, and Bevil Knapp. *America's Wetland: Louisiana's Vanishing Coast.* Baton Rouge, LA: Louisiana State University Press, 2005.

Dyson, Michael Eric. *Come Hell or High Water: Hurricane Katrina and the Color of Disaster.* New York, NY: Basic Civitas, 2006.

Elliot, Robert, ed. *Environmental Ethics: Oxford Readings in Philosophy.* Oxford, UK and New York, NY: Oxford University Press, 1995; Reprinted 2004.

Emerson, Ralph Waldo. *Essays and Lectures. Nature; Addresses, and Lectures. Essays: First and Second Series. Representative Men. English Traits. The Conduct of Life.* New York, NY: The Library of America. Literary Classics of the United States, Inc., 1983.

ESRI (Redlands, CA). "ESRI Gulf Coast Updates. Methodology: 2006/2011." An ESRI White Paper. August, 2006.

ESRI (Redlands, CA) "ESRI Demographic Update. Methodology: 2007/2012." An ESRI White Paper. June, 2007.

——. "Emergency Support Function #14—Long-Term Community Recovery and Mitigation Annex." National Response Plan. Washington, DC: December, 2004.

——. "Long-Term Community Recovery Planning Process: A Self-Help Guide." Washington, DC: December, 2005. On March 1, 2003, the Federal Emergency Management Agency (FEMA) became part of the U.S. Department of Homeland Security (DHS).

Fields, Leslie, et al. "Arsenic-Laced Schools and Playgrounds Put New Orleans Children at Risk," New York, NY: National Resources Defense Council, August, 2007.

Frey, William H., et al. "Resettling New Orleans: The First Full Picture from the Census," Washington, DC: The Brookings Institution Metropolitan Policy Program, September, 2007.

Golanyi, Gideon S. *Ethics and Urban Design: Culture, Form, and Environment.* New York, NY: John Wiley & Sons, Inc., 1995.

Gore, Al. *Earth in the Balance: Ecology and the Human Spirit.* New York, NY: Rodale, Inc., 1992; Forward, 2006.

Bibliography

Guirard, Greg. *Cajun Families of the Atchafalaya: Their Ways & Words.* St. Martinville, LA: Greg Guirard, 1990.

Hall, Gwendolyn Midlo. *Africans in Colonial Louisiana: The Development of Afro-Creole Culture in the Eighteenth Century.* Baton Rouge, LA: Louisiana State University Press, 1992.

Hallowell, Christopher. *Holding Back the Sea: The Struggle for America's Natural Legacy on the Gulf Coast.* New York, NY: HarperCollins, 2001.

———. *People of the Bayou: Cajun Life in Lost America.* Gretna, LA: Pelican Publishing Company, 2003.

Hampshire, Stuart. *Spinoza.* Baltimore, MD: Penguin Books, 1951; with revisions, 1962.

Hanger, Kimberly S. *Bounded Lives, Bounded Places: Free Black Society in Colonial New Orleans, 1769–1803.* Durham, NC: Duke University Press, 1997.

Hartman, Chester, and Gregory D. Squires. *There is No Thing as a Natural Disaster: Race, Class, and Hurricane Katrina.* New York, NY: Routledge, Taylor & Francis Group, 2006.

Hirsch, Arnold. R., and Joseph Logsdon, eds. *Creole New Orleans. Race and Americanization.* Baton Rouge, LA: Louisiana State University Press, 1992.

Horne, Jed. *Breach of Faith: Hurricane Katrina and the Near Death of a Great American City.* New York, NY: Random House, 2006.

———. *Desire Street: A True Story of Death and Deliverance in New Orleans.* New York, NY: Farrar, Straus, and Giroux, 2005.

Horne, Jedediah, and Brendan Nee. "An Overview of Post-Katrina Planning in New Orleans." Department of City and Regional Planning, University of California, Berkeley, CA. Unpublished manuscript, October 18, 2006. Online: http://www .nolaplans.com/research.

Horst, Jerald, and Mike Lane. *Angler's Guide to Fishes of the Gulf of Mexico.* Illustrated by Duane Raver. Gretna, LA: Pelican Publishing Company, 2007.

Howell, Dr. Susan E. "Keeping People: The 2007 Quality of Life Survey in Orleans and Jefferson Parishes." Survey Research Center, University of New Orleans, May 9, 2007. Online:http://poli.uno.edu website.

Humphreys, Andrew Atkinson. *Report upon the physics and hydraulics of the Mississippi River; upon the protection of the alluvial region against overflow; and upon the deepening of the mouths.* Philadelphia, PA: J. B. Lippincott & Co., 1861. Submitted to the Bureau of Topographical Engineers, War Department, 1861. Prepared by Captain A. A. Humphreys and Lieut. H. L. Abbot (Half-title: Professional papers of the Corps of Topographical Engineers, United States Army . . . no. 4).

Jacobsen, Linda, et al. "New Data Sources and Applications for Population and Household Estimates." Claritas Inc. Presented at the Annual Meeting of the Population Association of America, Atlanta Georgia, May 9–11, 2002.

Junger, Sebastian. "The Pumps of New Orleans." *Invention and Technology.* (Vol. 8, Issue 2). Fall, 1992, 42–48.

Kein, Sybil, ed. *Creole: The History and Legacy of Louisiana's Free People of Color.* Baton Rouge, LA: Louisiana State University Press, 2000.

Kelman, Ari. *A River and Its City: The Nature of Landscape in New Orleans.* Berkeley, CA: University of California Press, 2006.

Koerber, Kim. "Migration Patterns and Mover Characteristics from the 2005 ACS Gulf Coast Special Products." Housing and Economic Household Statistics Division, U.S.

Bibliography

Census Bureau. Presented at the Southern Demographic Association Conference. Durham, NC. November 2–4, 2006.

Lee, Douglas. Photographs by C. C. Lockwood. "Mississippi Delta. The Land of the River." *National Geographic.* Vol. 164, No. 2. August, 1983, 226–53.

Leopold, Aldo. *A Sand County Almanac. And Sketches Here and There.* New York, NY: Oxford University Press, 1949. Introduction by Robert Finch, 1987. Special Commemorative Edition.

Levy, Walter, and Christopher Hallowell, eds. *Green Perspectives: Thinking and Writing About Nature and the Environment.* New York, NY: Harper Collins, 1994

Lewis, Peirce F. *New Orleans: The Making of an Urban Landscape.* Second Edition. Santa Fe, NM and Harrisonburg, VA: The Center for American Places in association with the University of Virginia Press, 2003. Lilienthal, David E. *Tennessee Valley Authority: Democracy on the March.* London, UK: Penguin Books, 1944.

Lockwood, C. C., and Rhea Gary. *Marsh Mission: Capturing the Vanishing Wetlands.* Baton Rouge, LA: Louisiana State University Press, 2005.

Logan, John R., Director, American Communities Project, Brown University. "Population Displacement and Post-Katrina Politics: The New Orleans Mayoral Race, 2006," Revised June 1, 2006. Online: http://www.s4.brown.edu/Katrina/report2.pdf.

Louisiana, State of. Governor's Office of Homeland Security and Emergency Preparedness (GOHSEP). "Hurricane Pam Exercise Concludes," July 28, 2004 press release of FEMA press release, July 23, 2004. Online: http://www.ohsep.louisiana.gov/newsrelated/ hurricanepamends.htm; www://www.fema.gov/news/newsrelease.fema?id=13051.

Louisiana, State of. Louisiana Coastal Wetlands Conservation and Restoration Task Force. "Turning the Tide." Information packet from the Coastal Wetlands Planning, Protection and Restoration Act (CWPPRA), USGS National Wetlands Research Center, University of Louisiana at Lafayette, 2007.

Louisiana, State of. Louisiana Coastal Wetlands Conservation and Restoration Task Force and the U.S. Army Corps of Engineers, New Orleans District. *Watermarks.* Louisiana Coastal Wetlands Planning, Protection and Restoration News. Issues: Summer 1998; Fall 1998; Winter 1999; Summer 1999; Winter 2000; Number 16, June 2000; Number 17, November 2000; Number 18, May 2001; Number 19, October 2001; Number 20, June 2002; Number 21, September 2002; Number 22, February 2003; Number 23, August 2003; Number 24, January 2004; Number 26, September 2004; Number 25, April 2004; Number 27, February 2005; Number 28, April 2005; Number 29, August 2005; Number 30, March 2006; Number 31, June 2006; Number 32, November 2006; Number 33, February 2007.

Louisiana, State of. Louisiana Coastal Wetlands Conservation and Restoration Task Force and the Wetlands Conservation and Restoration Authority. "Coast 2050: Toward a Sustainable Coastal Louisiana." Louisiana Department of Natural Resources. Baton Rouge, LA 1998.

Louisiana, State of. Louisiana Coastal Wetlands Conservation and Restoration Task Force. "Coastal Wetlands Planning, Protection and Restoration Act (CWPPRA): A Response To Louisiana's Land Loss," 2006.

Louisiana, State of. Louisiana Coastal Wetlands Conservation and Restoration Task Force. "The 2006 Evaluation Report to the U.S. Congress on the Effectiveness of Coastal Wetlands Planning, Protection and Restoration Act Projects." Submitted by the Chairman of the Louisiana Coastal Wetlands Conservation and Restoration Task Force, U.S. Army Corps of Engineers—New Orleans District. 2006.

Bibliography

Louisiana, State of. Louisiana Department of Wildlife and Fisheries. Map of the Atchafalaya Basin. Compiled from NASA Infrared Aerial Photographs and U.S. Geological Survey Quadrangles.

Louisiana Public Health Institute. "2006 Louisiana Health and Population Survey." January 17, 2007. Survey conducted for the Louisiana Department of Health and Hospitals.

————, Greater New Orleans Planning Group. "Framework for a Healthier Greater New Orleans." November 10, 2005. Online: http://www.lphi.org/LPHIadmin/uploads/Framework%20fi.

Margavio, Anthony V., and Craig J. Forsyth. *Caught in the Net: The Conflict Between Shrimpers and Conservationists.* College Station, TX: Texas A & M University Press, 1996.

Marsh, George Perkins. *Man and Nature.* Edited, with a new introduction by David Lowenthal. Seattle, WA and London, UK: University of Washington Press, 2003. Originally published in 1864; the edition edited by David Lowenthal was published by Harvard University Press in 1965; reprinted with new Introduction by David Lowenthall, 2003.

Massey, Douglas, and Nancy Denton. *American Apartheid: Segregation and the Making of the Underclass.* Cambridge, MA: Harvard University Press, 1998.

Maygarden, Benjamin D., et al. "National Register Evaluation of New Orleans Drainage System, Orleans Parish, Louisiana." Final Report: 1996 through 1999. Conducted by Earth Search, Inc., P.O. Box 850219, New Orleans, LA 70185-0319 for the U.S. Army Corps of Engineers, New Orleans District.

Mumford, Enid, and Don Henshall. *A participative approach to computer systems design. A case study of the introduction of a new computer system.* New York, NY: Halsted Press, John Wiley & Sons, 1979.

————. *Designing Participatively: A Participative Approach to Computer Systems Design.* Manchester, UK: Manchester Business School, 1983.

Mumford, Enid, and Mary Weir. *Computer systems in work design—the ETHICS method. Effective Technical and Human Implementation of Computer Systems.* New York, NY: Halsted Press, John Wiley & Sons, 1979.

Mumford, Enid. *Designing Human Systems for New Technology: The ETHICS Method.* Manchester, UK: Manchester Business School, 1983.

————. *Redesigning Human Systems.* Hershey, PA: IRM Press, 2003.

Nagel, Thomas. "What Is It Like to Be a Bat?" *The Philosophical Review* 83 (1974) 435–50.

Naquin, Chief Albert P. "Isle de Jean Charles Indian Community." Draft history prepared to meet criteria for federal recognition that an American Indian group exists as an Indian Tribe. ca. 1996.

Nash, J. Madeleine. "Chronicling the Ice." *Smithsonian.* July, 2007, 67–74.

National Housing Law Project, et al. "False HOPE: A Critical Assessment of the HOPE VI Public Housing Redevelopment Program." June, 2002.

Neff, Thomas. *Holding Out and Hanging On: Surviving Hurricane Katrina.* Columbia, MO and London, UK: University of Missouri Press, 2007.

New Orleans, City of. Bring New Orleans Back Commission. Urban Planning Committee: Joseph C. Canizaro, Chairman. "Action Plan for New Orleans: The New American City." (BNOB Plan). January 11, 2006. Wallace Roberts & Todd, LLC—Master Planner.

————. Lambert Advisory/SHEDO, Project Management. "City of New Orleans Neighborhoods Rebuilding Plan." (Lambert Planning Process). October, 2006.

Bibliography

——. Villavaso & Associates/Henry Consulting LLC. "Citywide Strategic Recovery and Rebuilding Plan." (Unified New Orleans Plan). Final Draft: January 29, 2007.

——. Mayor's Office of Recovery Management. "City of New Orleans Target Area Development Plan." Draft, September 27, 2007. Proposed 17 Target Area Critical Projects from Unified New Orleans Plan.

——. *Specifications for the Construction of a System of Drainage for the City of New Orleans*. New Orleans, LA: L. Graham & Son, Ltd., 1896.

Norman, Donald A., and Stephen W. Draper, eds. *User Centered System Design: New Perspectives of Human-Computer Interaction*. Hillsdale, NJ: Lawrence Erlbaum Associates, Publishers, 1986.

Nozick, Robert. *Anarchy, State. and Utopia*. New York, NY: Basic Books, Inc., Publishers, 1974.

Nussbaum, Martha C. *Frontiers of Justice: Disability, Nationality, Species Membership*. The Tanner Lectures on Human Values. Cambridge, MA: The Belknap Press of Harvard University Press, 2006.

Olmos, Margarite Fernandez, and Lizabeth Paravisini-Gebert. *Creole Religions of the Caribbean. An Introduction: From Vodou and Santeria to Obeah and Espiritismo*. New York, NY: New York University Press, 2003.

Patterson, Curtis G., Secretary-Treasurer of the Association of Levee Boards of Louisiana. "A Short History of Levee Boards of Louisiana and Association of Levee Boards of Louisiana." Presented to Second Annual Workshop, August 14, 1987. FAX from Clyde P. Martin, Jr., Director, Hurricane & Flood Protection

Programs, State of Louisiana Department of Transportation and Development.

Penrose, Roger. *The Road to Reality: A Complete Guide to the Laws of the Universe*. New York, NY: Alfred A. Knopf, 2006.

Peyronnin, Chester, and Vincent Greco. *The Pumps that Built a City: New Orleans Drainage and the Pumps*, New York, NY: The American Society of Mechanical Engineers, 1977.

Plyer, Allison, with Joy Bonaguro. "Using U.S. Postal Service Delivery Statistics To Track the Repopulation of New Orleans & the Metropolitan Area." Greater New Orleans Community Data Center. May, 2007.

Popkin, Susan J., et al. "A Decade of HOPE VI: Research Findings and Policy Challenges." The Urban Institute and the Brookings Institution. May, 2004. Online: http://www.urban.org/url.cfm?ID=411002.

Politz, Henry. Circuit Judge. Memorandum Opinion. *Major v. Treen*. 574 F Supp. 325 (1983) Civil Action no. 82–1192, Section C. United States District Court, Eastern District of Louisiana.

Post, Lauren C. *Cajun Sketches: From the Prairies of Southwest Louisiana*. Baton Rouge, LA: Louisiana State University Press, 1962.

Preus, J. Samuel. *Spinoza and the Irrelevance of Biblical Authority*. Cambridge, UK: Cambridge University Press, 2001.

Pritchard, James B., ed. *The Ancient Near East: An Anthology of Texts and Pictures*. Princeton, NJ: Princeton University Press and London, UK: Oxford University Press, 1958.

Rabelais, Nancy N., et al. "Characterization of Hypoxia: Topic 1, Report for the Integrated Assessment on Hypoxia in the Gulf of Mexico." U.S. Department of Commerce. National Oceanic and Atmospheric Coastal Ocean Program. Decision Analysis Series No. 15. May, 1999.

Rawls, John. *A Theory of Justice*. Cambridge, MA: The Belknap Press of Harvard University Press, 1971.

————. *A Theory of Justice. Revised Edition.* Cambridge, MA: The Belknap Press of Harvard University Press, 1999.

————. *Justice as Fairness. A Restatement.* Edited by Erin Kelly. Cambridge, MA: The Belknap Press of Harvard University Press, 2001.

————. *Political Liberalism. Expanded Edition.* New York, NY: Columbia University Press, 2005.

————. *The Law of Peoples. With "The Idea of Public Reason Revisited."* Cambridge, MA: Harvard University Press, 1999.

Regan, Tom, and Peter Singer, eds. *Animal Rights and Human Obligations.* Englewood Cliffs, NJ: Prentice-Hall, Inc., 1976.

Reuss, Martin. *Designing the Bayous: The control of Water in the Atchafalaya Basin, 1800–1995.* College Station, TX: Texas A&M University Press, 2004. Originally published by the U.S. Army Corps of Engineers, Alexandria, VA.

Rose, Chris. *1 Dead in Attic: After Katrina.* New York, NY: Simon & Schuster, 2007.

Ross, R. R. N. "Non-Being and Being in Taoist and Western Philosophy," *Religious Traditions.* Vol. I, No. 2, 24–38.

Rubinstein, Richard, and Harry Hersh. *The Human Factor: Designing Computer Systems for People.* Burlington, MA: Digital Press, Digital Equipment Corporation, 1984.

Santmire, H. Paul. *The Travail of Nature: The Ambiguous Ecological Promise of Christian Theology.* Minneapolis, MN: Augsburg Fortress Publishers, 1985.

Sartre, Jean-Paul. "American Cities." In *Literary and Philosophical Essays.* New York, NY: Collier Books, 1965.

Savoy, Ann Allen. *Cajun Music: A Reflection of a People.* Eunice, LA: Bluebird Press, Inc., 1984.

Seed, R. B., et al. "Investigation of the Performance of the New Orleans Flood Protection Systems in Hurricane Katrina on August 29, 2005. Final Report." July 31, 2006. Supported by National Science Foundation Grants No. CMS-0413327 and CMS-0611632.

Singer, Peter. *Animal Liberation: A New Ethic for Our Treatment of Animals.* New York: HarperCollins Publishers, 2002. (Originally published 1975).

Sothern, Billy. *Down in New Orleans: Reflections From a Drowned City.* Berkeley, CA: University of California Press, 2007.

Spinoza, Benedictus de. *The Chief Works of Benedict de Spinoza.* Vols. I and II. Translated by R. H. M. Elwes. New York, NY: Dover Publications, Inc., 1955. Unabridged and unaltered republication of the Bohn Library edition originally published by George Bell and Sons in 1883.

Spinoza, Benedictus de. *The Collected Works of Spinoza.* Volume I. Edited and Translated by Edwin Curley. Princeton: Princeton University Press, 1985.

Stackhouse, Max L. *Ethics and the Urban Ethos: An Essay in Social Theory and Theological Reconstruction.* Boston, MA: Beacon Press, 1972.

Stevens, Wallace. *Collected Poetry and Prose.* New York, NY: The Library of America. Literary Classics of the United States, 1997.

Stolarik, M. Mark, ed. *Forgotten Doors: The Other Ports of Entry to the United States.* The Balch Institute for Ethnic Studies of The Historical Society of Pennsylvania. Philadelphia, PA: Balch Institute Press, 1988.

Sunstein, Cass. R. *The Second Bill of Rights: FDR's Unfinished Revolution and Why We Need It More Than Ever.* New York, NY: Basic Books, 2004.

————. *Worst-Case Scenarios.* Cambridge, MA: Harvard University Press, 2007.

Bibliography

Thompson, Ray. M. "Albert Baldwin Wood: The Man Who Made Water Run Uphill," *New Orleans Magazine,* August, 1973.

Tidwell, Mike. *Bayou Farewell: The Rich Life and Tragic Death of Louisiana'sCajun Coast.* New York, NY: Pantheon Books, 2003.

Tocqueville, Alexis de. *Journey to America.* Edited by J.P Mayer. New Haven, CT: Yale University Press, 1959.

Tregle, Jr., Joseph G. "Early New Orleans Society: A Reappraisal," *Journal of Southern History,* XVIII, February, 1952.

Troutt, David Dante, ed. *After the Storm: Black Intellectuals Explore the Meaning of Katrina.* New York: The New Press, 2006, with Afterword, 2007. *United States v. State of Louisiana.* 225 F. Supp. 353 (1963).

U.S. Army Corps of Engineers. "Performance Evaluation of the New Orleans and Southeast Louisiana Hurricane Protection System. Draft Final Report of the Interagency Performance Evaluation Task Force." Volume I—Executive Summary and Overview. June 1, 2006.

——. "Performance Evaluation of the New Orleans and Southeast Louisiana Hurricane Protection System. Final Report of the Interagency Performance Evaluation Task Force." Volume I, Executive Summary and Overview, 26 March 2007 (IPET Vol. I).

——. "Performance Evaluation of the New Orleans and Southeast Louisiana Hurricane Protection System. Final Report of the Interagency Performance Evaluation Task Force." Volume II—Geodetic Vertical and Water Level Datums. 26 March 2007 (IPET Vol. II).

——. "Performance Evaluation of the New Orleans and Southeast Louisiana Hurricane Protection System. Final Report of the Interagency Performance Evaluation Task Force." Volume III—The Hurricane Protection System. 22 August 2007 (IPET Vol. III).

——. Performance Evaluation of the New Orleans and Southeast Louisiana Hurricane Protection System. Final Report of the Interagency Performance Evaluation Task Force. Volume IV—The Storm. 26 March 2007 (IPET Vol. IV).

——. "Performance Evaluation of the New Orleans and Southeast Louisiana Hurricane Protection System. Final Report of the Interagency Performance Evaluation Task Force." Volume V—The Performance—Levees and Floodwalls. June 2007 (IPET Vol. V).

——. "Performance Evaluation of the New Orleans and Southeast Louisiana Hurricane Protection System. Final Report of the Interagency Performance Evaluation Task Force." Volume VI—The Performance—Interior Drainage and Pumping. 26 March 2007 (IPET Vol. VI).

——. "Performance Evaluation of the New Orleans and Southeast Louisiana Hurricane Protection System. Final Report of the Interagency Performance Evaluation Task Force." Volume VII—The Consequences. 26 March 2007 (IPET Vol. VII).

U.S. Army Corps of Engineers, New Orleans District. Hurricane Levee Maps for Orleans, Jefferson, Lafourche, Plaquemines, St. Bernard, and St. Charles Parishes. Online: http://www.mvn.usace.army.mil/pao/response/amaps.asp.

——. New Orleans District. "Draft Integrated Final Report to Congress and Legislative Environmental Impact Statement for the Mississippi River—Gulf Outlet Deep-Draft De-Authorization Study," June, 2007.

U.S. Congress. Senate. U.S. Senate S. Rept 109–322. *Hurricane Katrina: A Nation Still Unprepared. Special Report of the Committee on Homeland Security and Government Affairs.* Washington, DC: United States Senate, 2006. van Heerden, Ivor, and Mike

Bibliography

Bryan. *The Storm: What Went Wrong and Why During Hurricane Katrina—the Inside Story from One Louisiana Scientist.* New York, NY: Viking Press, 2006.

Watzin, M. C., and J.G. Gosselink. "The Fragile Fringe: Coastal Wetlands of the Continental United States." Louisiana Sea Grant College Program, Louisiana State University, Baton Rouge, LA; U.S. Fish and Wildlife Service, Washington, DC; and National Oceanic and Atmospheric Administration, Rockville, MD. Received 2007.

Welch, Holmes. *Taoism: The Parting of the Way.* Revised Edition. Boston, MA: Beacon Press, 1965.

Wenz, Peter S. *Environmental Ethics Today.* New York, NY: Oxford University Press, 2001.

Williams, Scott B. "Life After Katrina. The Mississippi Gulf coast in the Wake of a Major Hurricane." *Sea Kayaker.* June, 2006, 51–58.

Williamson, Abigail. "Citizen Participation in the Unified New Orleans Plan," March 21, 2007. Unpublished paper by Ph.D. candidate in Public Policy at Harvard's Kennedy School of Government.

Wing-Tsit Chan, transl. *A Source Book in Chinese Philosophy.* Princeton, NJ: Princeton University Press, 1963 and 1972.

Winograd, Terry, and Fernando Flores. *Understanding Computers and Cognition: A New Foundation for Design.* Norwood, NJ: Ablex Publishing Corporation, 1986.

World Socialist Web Site. "Hurricane Katrina: Social Consequences & Political Lessons." Statements from the World Socialist Web Site, 2005. Online: http://www.wsws.org.